"In addressing so many different aspects of the New Testament in light of the church's mission to spread the gospel, this collection of essays by I. Howard Marshall's friends, colleagues, and former students instantiates, and resolves, the problem of unity and diversity that stands at the heart of NT theology. It is therefore a most fitting tribute, both to the man and his work."

—**Kevin J. Vanhoozer**
Blanchard Professor of Theology, Wheaton College Graduate School, Illinois

"I can't think of a more fitting tribute to Howard Marshall—the man and the scholar—than this book. It's spot on in picking up his twin commitments to New Testament scholarship and mission. It is written by a galaxy of NT scholars, many of who are his former research students, which is testimony enough to his achievements. The book sets before us not a fast food meal but a scintillating smorgasbord of delights to savor in an unhurried fashion. Then we must remember, as the one the book honors would want, that the energy derived from the food we enjoy must be turned into active mission."

—**Derek Tidball**
Former Principal of London School of Theology; currently Vice-President of the Evangelical Alliance UK and Visiting Scholar at Spurgeon's College, London

"The quality of the essays in this volume make it a worthy tribute to one of the finest exegetical scholars of our time. The essays cover a fascinating range of issues related to mission in the New Testament, approaching them with both scholarly rigour and a concern for their relevance to the mission of the church today. All readers who appreciate both will find much here to learn and to savor."

—**Richard Bauckham**
Professor Emeritus, University of St Andrews, Scotland; Senior Scholar at Ridley Hall, Cambridge

New Testament Theology in Light of the Church's Mission

New Testament Theology in Light of the Church's Mission

Essays in Honor of I. Howard Marshall

Edited by

Jon C. Laansma, Grant R. Osborne,
and Ray F. Van Neste

CASCADE *Books* • Eugene, Oregon

NEW TESTAMENT THEOLOGY IN LIGHT OF THE CHURCH'S MISSION
Essays in Honor of I. Howard Marshall

Copyright © 2011 Jon C. Laansma, Grant R. Osborne, Ray F. Van Neste, and the contributers 2011. All rights reserved. Except for brief quotations in critical publications or reviews, no part of this book may be reproduced in any manner without prior written permission from the publisher. Write: Permissions, Wipf and Stock Publishers, 199 W. 8th Ave., Suite 3, Eugene, OR 97401.

First published in Great Britain in the Paternoster Biblical Monographs series by Paternoster, 2011. First U.S. edition published by Cascade Books under license from Paternoster. Typeset by Ray F. Van Neste

Cascade Books
A Division of Wipf and Stock Publishers
199 W. 8th Ave., Suite 3
Eugene, OR 97401

www.wipfandstock.com

ISBN 13: 978-1-61097-530-8

Cataloging-in-Publication data:

New Testament theology in light of the church's mission : essays in honor of I. Howard Marshall / Jon C. Laansma. Grant R. Osborn. Ray F. Van Neste.

xxii + 398 p. ; 23 cm. Includes bibliographical references and index.

ISBN 13: 978-1-61097-530-8

1. Bible. N.T.—Criticism, interpretation, etc. 2. Bible. N.T.—Theology. 3. Missions—Biblical teaching. 4. Missions—History—Early church, ca. 30-600. I. Laansma, Jon. II. Osborne, Grant R. III. Van Neste, Ray. IV. Marshall, I. Howard. V. Title.

BS2397 L33 2011

Manufactured in the U.S.A.

Professor I. Howard Marshall

Contents

Contributors	xiii
Acknowledgements	xv
Abbreviations	xvii

I. Howard Marshall: An Appreciation
Ray F. Van Neste — 1

A Bibliography of I. Howard Marshall — 11

The Gospel for All Peoples: Method, Integrity, Translation

1. Methodology of Evangelism in the New Testament: Some Preliminary Reflections
James D. G. Dunn — 25

2. Freedom from the Law Only for Gentiles? A Non-Supersessionist Alternative to Mark Kinzer's "Postmissionary Messianic Judaism"
Craig L. Blomberg — 41

3. Hearing Voices: The Foreign Voice of Paul under the Stress of Contemporary English Localization
Philip H. Towner — 57

4. The Son of Man in Hebrews 2:6: A Dilemma for Bible Translators
Richard T. France   81

Gospels and Acts

5. The Gospel before the Gospels: The Preached Core Narrative
Darrell L. Bock   97

6. Matthew 5:17–20 and "A Tale of Two Missions"?
Esther Yue L. Ng   105

7. Revisiting the Johannine Water Motif: Jesus, Ritual Cleansing and Two Purification Pools in Jerusalem
Gary M. Burge   123

8. The Purpose of Luke-Acts: Reaching a Consensus
Mark L. Strauss   135

9. Neglecting Widows and Serving the Word? Acts 6:1–7 as a Test Case for a Missional Hermeneutic
Joel B. Green   151

10. Luke: Historian, Rhetor, and Theologian. Historiography and the Theology of the Speeches in Acts
Gene L. Green   161

Paul

11. The Missionary Character of 1 Corinthians
Brian S. Rosner   181

12. Church Membership and the ἰδιώτης in the Early Corinthian Community
Andrew D. Clarke   197

13. Old Testament Paradoxes in Galatians: Rethinking the

Theology of Galatians
Maureen W. Yeung   213

14. *Missio Dei* and *Imitatio Dei* in Ephesians
Roy E. Ciampa   229

15. An Ideal Missionary Prayer Letter: Reflections on Paul's Mission Theology as Expressed in Philippians
Alistair I. Wilson   245

16. Paul's Missionary Preaching in 1 Thessalonians 2:1–16, with an Apocalyptic Addition from 2 Thessalonians
Anthony C. Thiselton   265

17. "Prayer" and the Public Square: 1 Timothy 2:1–7 and Christian Political Engagement
Greg A. Couser   277

18. Schlatter on the Pastorals: Mission in the Academy
Robert W. Yarbrough   295

19. "Nobody knows de trouble I seen": Hardship Lists in Paul and Elsewhere
Paul Ellingworth   317

Hebrews and Revelation

20. Hebrews and the Mission of the Earliest Church
Jon C. Laansma   327

21. The Mission to the Nations in the Book of Revelation
Grant R. Osborne   347

22. Early Christian Mission and Christian Identity in the Context of the Ethnic, Social, and Political Affiliations in Revelation
Eckhard J. Schnabel   369

Index of Modern Authors 387

Index of Ancient Sources 394

Contributors

CRAIG L. BLOMBERG (PhD, University of Aberdeen), Distinguished Professor of New Testament, Denver Seminary

DARRELL L. BOCK (PhD, University of Aberdeen), Research Professor of New Testament Studies, Dallas Theological Seminary

GARY M. BURGE (PhD, University of Aberdeen), Professor of New Testament, Wheaton College and Graduate School

ROY E. CIAMPA (PhD, University of Aberdeen), Professor of New Testament and Chair of the Division of Biblical Studies, Gordon-Conwell Theological Seminary

ANDREW D. CLARKE (PhD, University of Cambridge), Senior Lecturer in New Testament, University of Aberdeen

GREG A. COUSER (PhD, University of Aberdeen), Professor of Bible and Greek, Cedarville University

JAMES D. G. DUNN (PhD, DD, University of Cambridge; FBA), Emeritus Lightfoot Professor of Divinity, Durham University

PAUL ELLINGWORTH (PhD, University of Aberdeen), former translation consultant, United Bible Societies; former Honorary Professor of New Testament, University of Aberdeen

RICHARD T. FRANCE (PhD, University of Bristol), retired, formerly Principal of Wycliffe Hall, Oxford; Honorary Research Fellow of Bangor University, North Wales

GENE L. GREEN (PhD, University of Aberdeen), Professor of New Testament, Wheaton College and Graduate School

JOEL B. GREEN (PhD, University of Aberdeen), Professor of New Testament Interpretation and Associate Dean for the Center for Advanced Theological Studies, Fuller Theological Seminary

JON C. LAANSMA (PhD, University of Aberdeen), Associate Professor of Ancient Languages and New Testament, Wheaton College and Graduate School

ESTHER YUE L. NG (PhD, University of Aberdeen), Associate Professor of New Testament and Academic Dean, Christian Witness Theological Seminary

GRANT R. OSBORNE (PhD, University of Aberdeen) Professor of New Testament, Trinity Evangelical Divinity School

BRIAN S. ROSNER (PhD, University of Cambridge), Senior Lecturer in New Testament and Ethics, Moore Theological College; Honorary Senior Research Fellow in Ancient History, Macquarie University

ECKHARD J. SCHNABEL (PhD, University of Aberdeen), Professor of New Testament, Trinity Evangelical Divinity School

MARK L. STRAUSS (PhD, University of Aberdeen), Professor of New Testament, Bethel Seminary, San Diego

ANTHONY C. THISELTON (PhD, University of Sheffield; DD, University of Durham; FBA; FKC), Professor of Christian Theology, University of Nottingham

PHILIP H. TOWNER (PhD, University of Aberdeen), Dean, The Eugene A. Nida Institute for Biblical Scholarship of the American Bible Society

RAY F. VAN NESTE (PhD, University of Aberdeen), Associate Professor of Biblical Studies, Union University

ALISTAIR I. WILSON (PhD, University of Aberdeen), Principal, Dumisani Theological Institute and Extraordinary Associate Professor of New Testament, North-West University, South Africa

ROBERT W. YARBROUGH (PhD, University of Aberdeen), Professor of New Testament, Covenant Theological Seminary

MAUREEN W. YEUNG (PhD, University of Aberdeen), President and Associate Professor of New Testament, Evangel Seminary, Hong Kong

Acknowledgements

The editors are grateful to Robin Parry, Mike Parsons, and the people at Paternoster and Wipf and Stock for partnering with us to make this volume possible. We are also grateful to Wheaton College for the granting of a semester's sabbatical as well as an Aldeen Grant, both of which aided the preparation of this volume. Thanks are also due to Andrew Burlingame and Brian Denker for the countless hours spent editing the essays and for their contribution, along with Todd Heckman, toward compiling the bibliography of Howard's publications. Thanks are due also to Patrick Brown for his work on the index for this volume. Of course our wives and families are always involved in all our work and were glad to be a part of honoring Howard.

Abbreviations

AB	Anchor Bible
Ag. Ap.	*Against Apion* (Josephus)
AGJU	Arbeiten zur Geschichte des antiken Judentums und des Urchristentums
Alleg. Interp.	*Allegorical Interpretation* (Philo)
ANF	*The Ante-Nicene Fathers*. Edited by Alexander Roberts and James Donaldson. 1885–1887. 10 vols. Repr. Peabody, Mass.: Hendrickson, 1994
ANQ	*Andover Newton Quarterly*
Ant.	*Jewish Antiquities* (Josephus)
Ant. rom.	*Antiquitates romanae* (Dionysius of Halicarnassus)
1 Apol.	*First Apology* (Justin)
Ascen. Isa.	*Martyrdom and Ascension of Isaiah* 6–11
Ath. pol.	*Athēnaiōn politeia* (Aristotle)
Att.	*Epistulae ad Atticum* (Cicero)
BAR	*Biblical Archaeology Review*
BBR	*Bulletin for Biblical Research*
BECNT	Baker Exegetical Commentary on the New Testament
BDAG	Danker, F. W., W. Bauer, W. F. Arndt, and F. W. Gingrich. *Greek-English Lexicon of the New Testament and Other Early Christian Literature*. 3d ed. Chicago, 2000
Bib	*Biblica*
BibB	Biblische Beiträge
BJRL	*Bulletin of the John Rylands University Library of Manchester*
BNTC	Black's New Testament Commentary
BNP	*Brill's New Pauly: Encyclopedia of the Ancient World*. Edited by Hubert Cancik, Helmuth Schneider, and Manfred Landfester. 20 vols. Leiden: Brill, 2002–2012
BR	*Biblical Research*
BRev	*Bible Review*
b. Šabb	*Babylonian Talmud Šabbat*
CBET	Contributions to Biblical Exegesis and Theology

CBQ	*Catholic Biblical Quarterly*
1–2 Clem.	*1–2 Clement*
CTM	*Concordia Theological Monthly*
Decalogue	*On the Decalogue* (Philo)
DLNT	*Dictionary of the Later New Testament and Its Developments.* Edited by R. P. Martin and P. H. Davids. Downers Grove: InterVarsity, 1997
DPL	*Dictionary of Paul and His Letters.* Edited by G. F. Hawthorne and R. P. Martin. Downers Grove: InterVarsity, 1993
EDNT	*Exegetical Dictionary of the New Testament.* Edited by H. Balz, G. Schneider. ET. Grand Rapids, 1990–1993
EKKNT	Evangelisch-katholischer Kommentar zum Neuen Testament
1–3 En.	*1–3 Enoch*
EPRO	Etudes preliminaries aux religions orientales dans l'empire romain
1–2 Esd	*1–2 Esdras*
EuroJTh	*European Journal of Theology*
EvQ	*Evangelical Quarterly*
EvT	*Evangelische Theologie*
ExpTim	*Expository Times*
FC	Fathers of the Church. Washington, D.C.: Catholic University of America, 1947–
FRLANT	Forschungen zur Religion und Literatur des Alten und Neuen Testaments
Geogr.	*Geography* (Strabo)
GNS	Good News Studies
HB	Hebrew Bible
Hist.	*Histories* (Polybius)
Hist. eccl.	*Historia Ecclesiastica* (Eusebius)
Hom. Eph.	*Homiliae in epistulam ad Ephesios* (John Chrysostom)
Hom. 1 Thess.	*Homiliae in epistulam i ad Thessalonicenses* (John Chrysostom)
HTKNT	Herders theologischer Kommentar zume Neuen Testament
HTS	Harvard Theological Studies
HUT	Hermeneutische Untersuchungen zur Theologie
ICC	International Critical Commentary
IDBSup	*Interpreter's Dictionary of the Bible: Supplementary Volume.* Edited by K. Crim. Nashville, 1976
IDidyma	Rehm, R., ed. *Didyma.* II. *Die Inschriften.* Berlin, 1958.
IEph	Wankel, H. et al., eds. *Die Inschriften von Ephesos.* 7 vols. and index vol. 1974–1984.
IG	*Inscriptiones Graecae.* Berlin, 1873—
Ign. *Eph.*	Ignatius, *To the Ephesians*
Ign. *Magn.*	Ignatius, *To the Magnesians*
Ign. *Phld.*	Ignatius, *To the Philadelphians*

Ign. Rom.	Ignatius, *To the Romans*
Ign. Smyrn.	Ignatius, *To the Smyrnaeans*
IIlion	Frisch, P., ed. *Die Inschriften von Ilion*. Bonn: Habelt, 1975.
Il.	*Iliad* (Homer)
ILaodikeia	Corsten, T. *Die Inschriften von Laodikeia am Lykos*. Bonn, 1997.
Inst.	*Institutio oratoria* (Quintilian)
Int	*Interpretation*
IPergamon	Fränkel, Max, ed. *Die Inschriften von Pergamon*. Altertümer von Pergamon. VIII,1–2. Berlin: Spemann, 1890.
Is.	*De Isaeo* (Dionysius of Halicarnassus)
ISardBR	Buckler, W. H., and D. M. Robinson, eds. *Sardis VII, 1: Greek and Latin Inscriptions*. Leiden: Brill, 1932.
JBL	*Journal of Biblical Literature*
Jdt	*Judith*
JESHO	*Journal of the Economic and Social History of the Orient*
JHC	*Journal of Higher Criticism*
JJS	*Journal of Jewish Studies*
JOTT	*Journal of Translation and Textlinguistics*
JSNT	*Journal for the Study of the New Testament*
JSNTSup	Journal for the Study of the New Testament: Supplement Series
JTSA	*Journal of Theology for Southern Africa*
J.W.	*Jewish War* (Josephus)
KEK	Kritisch-exegetischer Kommentar über das Neue Testament (Meyer-Kommentar)
L&N	*Greek-English Lexicon of the New Testament: Based on Semantic Domains*. Edited by J. P. Louw and E. A. Nida. 2d ed. New York, 1989
LCL	Loeb Classical Library
Life	*The Life* (Josephus)
LNTS	Library of New Testament Studies
LSJ	Liddell, H. G., R. Scott, H. S. Jones, *A Greek-English Lexicon*. 9th ed. with revised supplement. Oxford, 1996
LXX	Septuagint
m. Kelim	*Mishnah Kelim*
MM	Moulton, J. H., and G. Milligan. *The Vocabulary of the Greek Testament*. London, 1930. Reprint, Peabody, Mass., 1997
m. Miqw.	*Mishnah Miqwa'ot*
MNTC	Moffatt New Testament Commentary
MNTS	McMaster New Testament Studies
m. Šabb.	*Mishnah Šabbat*
m. Yad.	*Mishnah Yadayim*
NCBC	New Century Bible Commentary
NDBT	*New Dictionary of Biblical Theology: Exploring the Unity*

	and Diversity of Scripture
Neot	*Neotestamentica*
NIBC	New International Biblical Commentary
NICNT	New International Commentary on the New Testament
NIDOTTE	*New International Dictionary of Old Testament Theology and Exegesis*. Edited by W. A. VanGemeren. 5 vols. Grand Rapids, 1997
NIGTC	New International Greek Testament Commentary
NIVAC	NIV Application Commentary
NovT	*Novum Testamentum*
NovTSup	Supplements to Novum Testamentum
NPNF[1]	*The Nicene and Post-Nicene Fathers*, Series 1. Edited by Philip Schaff. 1886–1889. 14 vols. Repr. Peabody, Mass.: Hendrickson, 1994
NSBT	New Studies in Biblical Theology
NT	New Testament
NTS	*New Testament Studies*
NTT	New Testament Theology (Cambridge)
Od.	*Odyssey* (Homer)
Odes Sol.	*Odes of Solomon*
OGIS	Dittenberger, W., ed. *Orientis graeci inscriptiones selectae*, 2 vols. Leipzig, 1903–1905
OT	Old Testament
Pesiq. Rab Kah.	*Pesiqta de Rab Kahana*
PGL	*Patristic Greek Lexicon*. Edited by G. W. H. Lampe. Oxford, 1968
PHI#7	CD (version 7) of the Packard Humanities Institute.
P.Köln	*Kölner Papyri*
Pol.	*Politics* (Aristotle)
Pomp.	*Epistula ad Pompeium Geminum* (Dionysius of Halicarnassus)
P.Oxy.	*The Oxyrynchus Papyri*
P.Petr.	*The Flinders Petrie Papyri*
P.Rev.	Grenfell, B. P., ed. *Revenue Laws of Ptolemy Philadelphus*. Oxford, 1896.
Pr. Man.	*Prayer of Manasseh*
PRSt	*Perspectives in Religious Studies*
PSI	*Papiri greci e latini*. Pubblicazioni della Società Italiana per la ricerca dei papiri greci e latini in Egitto. Florence, 1912—.
P.Stras.	Preisigke, F., ed. *Griechische Papyrus der kaiserlichen Universitäts-und Landesbibliothek zu Strassburg*. Leipzig, 1912-1986.
P.Tebt.	*The Tebtunis Papyri*. 5 vols. London, 1902-2005.
RB	*Revue biblique*
RBL	*Review of Biblical Literature*
RNT	Regensburger Neues Testament

Rom.	*Romulus* (Plutarch)
SB	*Sammelbuch griechischer Urkunden aus Aegypten,* ed. F. Preisigke. Berlin, de Gruyter; Wiesbaden: Harrassowitz, 1913-2006.
SBJT	*Southern Baptist Journal of Theology*
SBL	Society of Biblical Literature
SBLBSNA	Society of Biblical Literature Biblical Scholarship in North America
SBLDS	Society of Biblical Literature Dissertation Series
SBLSymS	Society of Biblical Literature Symposium Series
SBT	Studies in Biblical Theology
Schol	*Scholastik*
Sib. Or.	*Sibylline Oracles*
SIG	Dittenberger, W., ed. *Sylloge inscriptionum graecarum.* 4 vols. 3d ed. Leipzig, 1915–1924.
SNT	Studien zum Neuen Testament
SNTSMS	Society for New Testament Studies Monograph Series
SNTSU	Studien zum Neuen Testament und seiner Umwelt
SNTW	Studies of the New Testament and Its World
SP	Sacra pagina
SPCK	Society for Promoting Christian Knowledge
Spec.	*De specialibus legibus* (Philo)
TDNT	*Theological Dictionary of the New Testament.* Edited by G. Kittel and G. Friedrich. Translated by G.W. Bromiley. 10 vols. Grand Rapids, 1964-1976
Tg Isa	*Targum Isaiah*
Them	*Themelios*
THNTC	Two Horizons New Testament Commentary
TLNT	*Theological Lexicon of the New Testament.* C. Spicq. Translated and edited by J. D. Ernest. 3 vols. Peabody, Mass., 1994
TLZ	*Theologische Literaturzeitung*
TRu	*Theologische Rundschau*
t. Šabb.	*Tosefta Šabbat*
TSAJ	Texte und Studien zum antiken Judentum
TVG	Theologische Verlagsgemeinschaft
TynBul	*Tyndale Bulletin*
UPZ	*Urkunden der Ptolemäerzeit,* ed. U. Wilckens. Berlin: de Gruyter, 1927/1957.
Vit. soph.	*Vitae sophistarum* (Philostratus)
WBC	Word Biblical Commentary
WTJ	*Westminster Theological Journal*
WUNT	Wissenschaftliche Untersuchungen zum Neuen Testament
ZNW	*Zeitschrift für die neutestamentliche Wissenschaft und die Kunde der älteren Kirche*
ZPE	*Zeitschrift für Papyrologie und Epigraph*

I. HOWARD MARSHALL: AN APPRECIATION

Ray F. Van Neste

It is fitting both that Howard Marshall be honored with a second festschrift and that its theme be "mission."[1] The idea of another festschrift for Howard Marshall first came to my mind when, during my doctoral work in Scotland, I came across the second festschrift for F. F. Bruce. Many have seen Howard[2] as the heir of Bruce, and he has been the worthy heir of a worthy tradition.[3] With his prodigious writing—thirty-eight books (authored and edited) and over 120 essays and articles—Howard Marshall has had a significant impact both on biblical scholarship and the church. In addition to his writing he has served widely in fellowships and societies fostering evangelical scholarship. He has served as Chair of the Tyndale Fellowship for Biblical and Theological Research (Chair of the New Testament Study Group prior to that), President of the British New Testament Society, and Chair of the Fellowship of European Evangelical Theologians. He continues to serve as President of the Scottish Evangelical Theological Society, Chair of the board of theological advisors for Paternoster, and as Editor (for nearly thirty years) of the *Evangelical Quarterly*, being the successor of Bruce in this task. He has taught New Testament at the University of Aberdeen since 1964. Because of Howard Aberdeen was for decades a primary destination for postgraduate study for evangelical students from around the world. Howard's words concerning F. F. Bruce can be aptly used of him as well, as we can say that Howard Marshall

> will obviously be remembered first of all for his highly distinguished academic

---

[1] The first festschrift was Joel B. Green and Max Turner, *Jesus of Nazareth, Lord and Christ: Essays on the Historical Jesus and New Testament Christology* (Grand Rapids: Eerdmans; Carlisle: Paternoster, 1994).

2 In deference to Howard's clearly and regularly stated preference I will refer to him by his first name in this essay. I was particularly slow to accommodate this request when I arrived in Aberdeen because it is contrary to my common practice and upbringing. Early on we had a conversation something like this: "Please simply call me Howard." "Yes sir, Professor Marshall." Eventually, after about a year, when he began to refer to me as "Mr. Van Neste" I conceded. Since it took him some time to secure this practice, I will continue it here.

[3] Howard wrote of Bruce that he "has derived more scholarly inspiration from him than from anybody else" ("F. F. Bruce as a Biblical Scholar," *Christian Brethren Research Fellowship Journal* 22 [Nov. 1971]: 5-12 [5]).

career as a university teacher and a prolific writer who did more than anybody else in this century to develop and encourage conservative evangelical scholarship. Possessed of outstanding intellectual ability, a phenomenal memory, and encyclopaedic knowledge, a colossal capacity for work, and a limpid style, he produced a remarkable output of books and essays which will continue to be read for years to come, and he trained directly or indirectly many younger scholars now working in all parts of the world.[4]

"Mission" then is an apt theme for this volume because it is also an appropriate way to summarize the goal and effect of Howard's work. In an interview in 2000, Howard, when asked about the key challenges ahead, stated "mission and evangelism remain the challenge that we have to face as we go into the new millennium."[5] This concern for the spread of the gospel is a unifying theme in the work of Howard Marshall.

WRITINGS ON EVANGELICAL FAITH

A significant aspect of Howard's writing has dealt with defense of evangelical tenets of the faith. It is difficult for some younger scholars to comprehend the state of evangelical academic work forty or fifty years ago. Many of us have grown up accustomed to conservative evangelical seminaries and publishing houses as well as a steady stream of evangelical publications and well-established, prominent evangelical scholars. This, of course, though, is a relatively recent phenomenon, a benefit bequeathed to us by those who have gone before us including Howard. Howard has been a key leader in demonstrating how faith and scholarship coincide by both defending biblical truths from critical attack and demonstrating the value of academic rigor to conservative believers. R. T. France, a long time friend of Howard's, has written, "Many of us have had cause to be grateful for his calm but assured defence in print of orthodox Christian positions which have been rejected by others."[6] In articles and books Howard has helped believers articulate the biblical grounds for their faith, looking for unity but being clear about where dividing lines occur. His convictions are clear in this excerpt from an article supporting young Christians who encounter liberal pastors:

> ... where criticism takes place on the basis of anti-supernaturalist presuppositions and the teaching of scripture is assessed in terms of what modern, unbelieving western man is prepared to accept, again the evangelical will have no truck with it. The kind of ecumenism which tries to assure us that really we all believe the

---

[4] I. Howard Marshall, "Editorial: Professor F. F. Bruce," *EvQ* 62, no. 4 (Oct. 1990): 291.
[5] Carl Trueman, "Interview With Professor Howard Marshall," *Them* 26, no. 1 (Autumn 2000): 48-53 [52].
[6] R. T. France, "Profile: Howard Marshall," *Epworth Review* 29, no. 4 (Oct. 2002): 15-21 [16].

same things will not cut much ice here with evangelicals, for they know that without a clear acceptance of the supreme authority of scripture the gospel which they treasure is liable to be tossed to and fro and carried about by every wind of human teaching.[7]

To say that Howard defended is not to say he was defensive. Howard's approach has always been gracious and winsome, exemplifying the goal not so much of defeating an opponent as winning him to truth.

Mission, however, involves not only defense but the active propagation of the faith. A number of Howard's articles and books deal with Christian life and practice, whether it is discussion of the Lord's Supper, preaching, virtues and vices or one of many other categories. Howard's work has embodied the highest academic quality and integrity, which more critical scholars, even if they have not agreed, have still respected. Here one also sees Howard's commitment to both technical and popular-level writing. On the technical side, Howard helped launch a new commentary series focused on the Greek text,[8] contributed an early volume to the series,[9] has edited a new edition of a standard Greek language tool[10] and has written many more technical pieces. On the popular level Howard has written often for Scripture Union,[11] producing Bible study materials for laypeople, several more popular commentaries as well as numerous articles. Howard is not among those who disparage popular writing as something beneath a true scholar. Rather, he has stated, ". . . it seems to me that those of us who are Christians studying the Bible have a very strong responsibility towards the church to produce what will be helpful particularly to preachers, and also to the church generally."[12] Again he followed Bruce here. Writing in commendation of Bruce, Howard stated:

> Far too often the accusation is heard that the pulpit is fifty years behind the teacher's rostrum, and the pew even further out-of-date. Some of the blame for this situation undoubtedly rests on a scholarship which does not trouble to communicate with both pulpit and pew in a way that both can understand. . . . to write at a popular level is not inconsistent with a truly scholarly approach, and it may be argued that one test of a person's scholarship is the ability to express arguments and conclusions in a manner that is generally intelligible.[13]

---

[7] I. Howard Marshall. "The Young Christian and the 'Liberal' Pastor," *ExpTim* 95 (1984): 364-67 [367].

[8] I. Howard Marshall and Donald A. Hagner, *New International Greek Testament Commentary* (Grand Rapids: Eerdmans, 1978–2005).

[9] I. Howard Marshall, *The Gospel of Luke* (NIGTC; Grand Rapids: Eerdmans, 1978).

[10] I. Howard Marshall, *Moulton & Geden: A Concordance to the Greek Testament* (London: T&T Clark, 2002).

[11] See the list in the bibliography.

[12] Trueman, "Interview With Professor Howard Marshall," 49.

[13] I. Howard Marshall, "Frederick Fyvie Bruce, 1910–1990," *Proceedings of the British Academy* 80 (1991): 245-60 [249].

Howard has been true to this vision, and is one who has well succeeded in communicating scholarship in an intelligible way to the broader public. He once cited the words of David Hubbard as stating his own convictions: "We are not scholars who happen to be disciples, we are disciples who happen to be scholars."[14]

MENTORING

Writing is only one facet of Howard's career, though it may be the most well-known facet. Another key aspect has been mentoring and facilitating the work of others, particularly younger scholars. For example he has invested untold hours in his work with the Tyndale Fellowship, the British New Testament Society, and the Fellowship of European Evangelical Theologians, each of which he has led at one time. R. T. France has commented on Howard's continued commitment to attendance at these fellowships even when others pulled back due to other commitments.[15] Many can attest to the encouragement gained from presenting papers in the presence of Howard and receiving helpful critique and advice. Tyndale Fellowship particularly has been a key catalyst to the growth of evangelical scholarship, and Howard's efforts and involvement have played a key role.

Howard has also helped greatly to further the dissemination of evangelical scholarship, not least in his work with Paternoster, where he has been involved for forty years or more. He has served as Chair of the board of theological advisors for Paternoster for at least ten years and remains in that position. He has been deeply involved in several of the monograph series of Paternoster, helping to make decisions on publications. Howard has given significant time and effort in promoting and defending Paternoster, helping to secure its integrity and success within the wider company of which Paternoster was a part. Robin Parry, formerly of Paternoster, commented on Howard's involvement saying:

> It was a lot of work and he was doing Paternoster work most weeks over the (almost) nine years that I was around. . . . For Howard supporting and working for Paternoster was never simply "something to do" or "an obligation." It has always been something he passionately believes in. That unwavering support has been personally very encouraging for me over the years. And Paternoster owes him a debt that it could never repay.[16]

I remember well talking with a Paternoster representative at a conference

---

[14] Trueman, "Interview With Professor Howard Marshall," 48.
[15] France, "Profile: Howard Marshall," 17.
[16] Robin Parry, personal email correspondence, received July 22, 2010.

booth and mentioning that I was about to move to Aberdeen to study with Howard Marshall. The man's face lit up as he spoke of the crucial role Howard had already by that time played in the life of Paternoster. He also gave me a free book! Many pastors and scholars have enhanced their libraries not only with books written by Howard Marshall but also with books that he helped bring to print and to make affordable.

Howard has also maintained an amazing schedule of lecturing around the world. Though this list may not be comprehensive, he has lectured in Australia, Austria, Canada, Croatia, the Czech Republic, Denmark, Finland, Germany, Ghana, Hong Kong, Kenya, the Netherlands, Norway, the Philippines, Singapore, South Africa, Sweden, Taiwan, and numerous places in the USA.[17] This travel is another aspect of mission as Howard continues to take the fruits of his scholarship to "the ends of the earth," encouraging pastors and educators, supporting educational institutions and helping to advance the kingdom.

One key aspect of Howard's work has been the supervising of postgraduate students. Evangelical students from around the world have been drawn to study with this man who embodied the combination of academic rigor with deep, evangelical faith. Aberdeen has now for decades been a prime destination for evangelical students due in large part to the work of Howard Marshall, with many postgraduate students coming to Aberdeen because of Howard Marshall even when they did not end up having him as their supervisor.[18] And the work which drew these students involved not only his published work but a lot of lesser recognized work including official administrative and informal recruiting work. It is significant that in many circles "Aberdeen" has come to mean "conservative, evangelical biblical scholarship."

Howard has obviously seen his work with postgraduates as an important aspect of his labors. Students have commonly reported on his gracious and willing investment in their work. In spite of his many other commitments, one always received prompt, thorough attention to work that was handed in. Howard has a legendary eye for detail, breadth of knowledge and grasp of issues. He provided insightful critique and suggestions of broader literature as well as suggestions for style and clarity in writing, typically with wit. I remember him once noting a certain phrase of mine as a "dodgy Americanism." He would regularly note to students (those he was supervising as well as others) something he had seen or read which he thought might be useful for their work. This care for others helped engender a sense of community.

Howard's investment in his students has in turn produced benefit to the broader scholarly world, as many of those students have been productive in publishing. Many of Howard's interests have been furthered by his students.

---

[17] France, "Profile: Howard Marshall," 16, is the source for most, but not all, of these locations.

[18] We used to joke that only the oil companies rivaled Howard for the distinction of bringing the most internationals to Aberdeen.

Hermeneutics has been a long standing concern of Howard's and one of the major textbooks on hermeneutics was written by Howard's student, Grant Osborne.[19] Howard has worked for some time on Luke–Acts, and now among the key major commentaries on these books are those by his students, Darrell Bock[20] and Joel Green.[21] More recently, of course, Howard focused on the Pastoral Epistles, and now two of the major commentaries, in addition to Howard's own, are those by William Mounce[22] and Phil Towner.[23] This does not even account for the innumerable monographs, essays and articles which have come from those who studied with Howard.[24]

Visits in the Marshall home and his visits in our homes were a particular delight. He is a gracious host and warm guest. My wife was anxious about preparations for dinner on Howard's first visit to our place, but in the end she had a long after-dinner conversation with Howard about Christmas pudding recipes. We met Howard after the death of his dear wife, Joyce, and on our visits he would typically apologize for his cooking. However we were amazed to find that he seemed to have mastered this skill as well.

Student life with Howard was animated by his humor, an aspect that those who know him only by his scholarly writings may not know. Howard has a ready wit, and a favorite memory of mine is often seeing him in a gathering slightly hunched over with his wide grin and slightly shaking shoulders as he chuckled over a comment. During my time as a student he met with several of us as we worked on our German. This was not a class and thus involved no remuneration or lessening of responsibilities, but Howard willingly gave his time to help us. One day as we wrestled with a specific text, one of us noted a footnote referring to "U. Fries" and asked who that referred to. Howard without missing a beat said, "Must be a German chip shop." His breadth of knowledge and quickness of wit sometimes meant you had to keep up or miss the point. I once went to ask Howard a question only to find a note on his door saying he was out. This was not terribly uncommon, but the note this time was different. It read, "Gon out. Back son." I went back to my study room puzzled by this obvious slip in spelling. I mentioned it to a couple of other students as we wondered and worried. When I went back later and found Howard in his office I said nothing of the note not wanting to embarrass him. However, Howard asked, "Did you see my sign?" Tentatively, and more puzzled, I said I did. He

---

[19] Grant Osborne, *The Hermeneutical Spiral: A Comprehensive Introduction to Biblical Interpretation* (rev. and exp. ed.; Downers Grove: InterVarsity, 2006).

[20] Darrell Bock, *Luke* (2 vols.; BECNT; Grand Rapids: Baker, 1994–1996) and *Acts* (BECNT; Grand Rapids: Baker, 2007).

[21] Joel B. Green, *The Gospel of Luke* (NICNT; Grand Rapids: Eerdmans, 1997).

[22] William Mounce, *Pastoral Epistles* (WBC; Nashville: Thomas Nelson, 2000).

[23] Philip H. Towner, *The Letters to Timothy and Titus* (NICNT; Grand Rapids: Eerdmans, 2006).

[24] I remember Howard making a particular point of the preposition used in such a statement. He made it clear that people did not study "under" him but "with" him.

asked if I "got" it and I had to confess I did not. That day was the anniversary of something associated with A. A. Milne's Winnie-the-Pooh, so Howard had intentionally used the language of Pooh's door sign in *The House at Pooh Corner*.[25] Instead of a spelling slip, we Ph.D. students had been stumped by our supervisor's astute allusion to classic children's literature.

CHURCH LIFE

At the root of this teaching and writing is Howard's own Christian faith and life in his church. Howard has served as a pastor in the Methodist Church and has been a faithful, active member of Crown Terrace Methodist Church for many years. He has recently served as Circuit Steward and then as local Church Steward, as well as serving with young people and in various other capacities over the years. Howard's Christmas letters, sent faithfully each year, always contain updates on the church, typically with requests for prayer that they have vision for reaching others or for strength to fulfill this vision. The concern at root is always to be effective evangelistically.

For Howard, such church involvement is nothing special but is simply part of Christian living. As France has commented of Howard: "The son of a local preacher, and now also the father of one, it has never occurred to him that academic eminence and advanced critical skills could be in any conflict with loyal and active church membership."[26] Howard has encouraged by example and word this integration of church life and academic work. In an interview directed particularly at religious and theological students, Howard stated: "I think it is important to be in a good Christian fellowship to have support from it and to be occupied in Christian work of one kind or another, and if possible to try and relate your studies to your practical Christian work."[27]

Joel Green spoke for many of us when in answer to the question, "Why Scotland for post-graduate work?" he answered, "To study with a major New Testament scholar who remained committed to and involved in the local church."[28]

Additionally, Howard's church involvement extends beyond his own local church. He has been a frequent preacher in churches of various denominations in the area. This exemplifies his concern for the health of the church. Academic study is not meant to be confined to lecture halls but is to enrich the church, building disciples and gaining converts. Howard has encouraged others in this area suggesting that preaching on passages one is studying academically is "a

---

[25] A. A. Milne, *The House at Pooh Corner* (London: Methuen & Co., Ltd., 1928).
[26] France, "Profile: Howard Marshall," 15.
[27] Trueman, "Interview With Professor Howard Marshall," 49.
[28] Joel B. Green and Max Turner, eds., *Jesus of Nazareth: Lord and Christ: Essays on the Historical Jesus and New Testament Christology* (Grand Rapids: Eerdmans, 1994), ix.

good discipline for people engaged in academic study to keep them firmly rooted in the real world."[29] At least part of the fruitfulness and appeal of Howard's labors has come from this connection with the everyday life of the church. It was a joy, for example, to have a meeting with Howard during the week in which I received back a chapter with Greek accents in my footnotes corrected and then on Sunday hear him proclaim the gospel as a guest preacher in the Baptist church I attended.

While in Aberdeen, I did a fair bit of preaching in the area and in each church the name of Howard Marshall was held in high regard. Throughout the history of the church the collective witness of the people of God has been regarded as significant. In northeast Scotland I found the people of God grateful for this man who uses his gifts to help them better understand the treasure of God's word. And the church is held in high regard by Howard. Today, each time we have the opportunity of conversation, the topic eventually turns to the health of the churches in the Aberdeen area.

Lastly, Howard's personal example of humble, faithful living has been an inspiration to many. Those who have worked with Howard commonly refer to the deep humility of the man. More than once in conversation I found myself amazed at his genuine lack of awareness of who he "is" in the eyes of others. To hear him express admiration of the abilities of others you would think he had none himself. Once in a conversation in our home in Bridge of Don, Howard lamented, "I have never been that good with languages." This was no coy, back-handed pursuit of a compliment. It was uttered in complete sincerity and even for a moment took me in. I believed him! Then, I recovered myself and began to ask him about his listening to lectures in German, how he read French items I could not understand, and his well known acquaintance with Greek and Latin. All this was true. He just did not consider that as being very good with languages.

This was exemplified at Howard's retirement when he was asked to preach in the university chapel on the day of the retirement activities. Howard has continued to serve at the university but the rules required retirement from his regular post at age sixty-five, and thus he had already moved from his office to a smaller one. As he ascended the pulpit in the chapel at Old King's College, where years before John Wesley had preached on his visit to Aberdeen, I wondered what his text would be. Without fanfare, he declared his text and read John 3:25-30 which concludes with these words: "He must increase, but I must decrease."

Proverbs declares, "with the humble is wisdom" (11:2; NASB), and Howard Marshall has demonstrated that. Proverbs also states, "a humble spirit will obtain honor" (29:23; NASB), and thus it is fitting that we honor Howard Marshall with this volume. May the Lord give him many more years of faithful

---

[29] I. Howard Marshall, "Preaching from the New Testament," *Scottish Bulletin of Evangelical Theology* 9 (1991): 104-17 [108].

service.

BIBLIOGRAPHY OF I. HOWARD MARSHALL[1]

BOOKS

1963
Christian Beliefs: A Brief Introduction. Leicester, UK: InterVarsity, 1963.
    1969—republished as *Christian Beliefs: An Introductory Study Guide.*
    1972—2d ed. London: InterVarsity.
    1978—3d ed. *A Pocket Guide to Christian Beliefs.* Leicester, UK and Downers Grove: InterVarsity.

Eschatology and the Parables. London: Tyndale, 1963.
    1973—Corrected reprint, London: Theological Students Fellowship.

"Perseverance, Falling Away and Apostasy." PhD diss., Aberdeen, 1963.

1967
The Books of Kings and Chronicles. London: Scripture Union, 1967; Grand Rapids: Eerdmans, 1968.
    1977 - republished in *Daily Bible Commentary Volume 1*, I. H. Marshall and J. Stafford Wright. London: Scripture Union.
    1978 – republished as *Understanding the Old Testament.* London: Scripture Union.

St. Mark. London: Scripture Union, 1967; Grand Rapids: Eerdmans, 1968.

1969
Kept by the Power of God: A Study of Perseverance and Falling Away. London: Epworth, 1969.
    1974—2d ed. Minneapolis: Bethany Fellowship.
    2008 - Reprint. Eugene, OR: Wipf & Stock.

The Work of Christ. Exeter: Paternoster, 1969; Grand Rapids: Zondervan, 1970.

1970
Luke: Historian and Theologian. Exeter: Paternoster, 1970; Grand Rapids: Zondervan, 1971.
    1979—2d ed. Exeter: Paternoster; Grand Rapids: Zondervan.
    1988—3d ed. Exeter: Paternoster; Grand Rapids: Zondervan.

---

[1] We have sought to make this bibliography as comprehensive as possible and have sought to indicate where a certain book has been re-published under a new title. Almost certainly, however, we will have missed a few items.

2006 – Reprint. Eugene, OR: Wipf & Stock.

1976
The Origins of New Testament Christology. Downers Grove: InterVarsity, 1976.
1990—Updated ed. Leicester, UK: Apollos; Downers Grove: InterVarsity.

1977
I Believe in the Historical Jesus. London: Hodder & Stoughton; Grand Rapids: Eerdmans, 1977.
2004—Rev. ed. Vancouver, BC: Regent.

Marshall, I. H., ed. *New Testament Interpretation: Essays on Principles and Methods.* Exeter: Paternoster; Grand Rapids: Eerdmans, 1977.
1985—Rev. ed. Exeter: Paternoster.
2006 – Reprint. Eugene, OR: Wipf & Stock.

1978
The Epistles of John. Grand Rapids: Eerdmans, 1978.

The Gospel of Luke: A Commentary on the Greek Text. Exeter: Paternoster; Grand Rapids: Eerdmans, 1978.

1980
The Acts of the Apostles: An Introduction and Commentary. Leicester, UK: InterVarsity; Grand Rapids: Eerdmans, 1980.

Last Supper and Lord's Supper. Exeter: Paternoster, 1980; Grand Rapids: Eerdmans, 1981.

1982
Biblical Inspiration. London: Hodder & Stoughton; Grand Rapids: Eerdmans, 1982.
1995—2d ed. Carlisle, UK: Paternoster, 1995.

God's Word in Man's Words. London: Hodder & Stoughton, 1982.

1983
First and Second Thessalonians. London: Marshall, Morgan & Scott; Grand Rapids: Eerdmans, 1983.

1988
Marshall, I. H., editor. *Christian Experience in Theology and Life: Papers Read at the 1984 Conference of the Fellowship of European Evangelical Theologians.* Exeter: Paternoster; Edinburgh: Rutherford House, 1988.

1990
Jesus the Saviour: Studies in New Testament Theology. London: SPCK; Downers Grove: InterVarsity, 1990.

1991
First Peter. Downers Grove: InterVarsity, 1991.

1992
Green, Joel B., Scot McKnight, and I. H. Marshall, eds. *Dictionary of Jesus and the Gospels*. Downers Grove: InterVarsity, 1992.

Epistle to the Philippians. London: Epworth, 1992.

A Fresh Look at the Acts of the Apostles. Homebush West, New South Wales: Lancer/Anzea, 1992.

1993
Donfried, Karl P. and I. H. Marshall. *The Theology of the Shorter Pauline Letters*. Cambridge: Cambridge University Press, 1993.

1996
Marshall, I. H. and D. R. W. Wood, eds. *New Bible Dictionary*. Downers Grove: InterVarsity, 1996.

1998
Marshall, I. H. and David Peterson, eds. *Witness to the Gospel: The Theology of Acts*. Grand Rapids: Eerdmans, 1998.

1999
A Critical and Exegetical Commentary on the Pastoral Epistles. Edinburgh: T&T Clark, 1999.

Jesus at AD 2000. Cambridge: Grove, 1999.

The Bible and Its Authority. Ilkeston, UK: Moorleys, 1999.

2002
Marshall, I. H., Stephen H. Travis, and Ian Paul. *A Guide to the Letters and Revelation*. Vol. 2 of *Exploring the New Testament*. London: SPCK; Downers Grove: InterVarsity, 2002.

Marshall, I. H, ed. *Moulton & Geden: A Concordance to the Greek Testament*. 6th rev. ed. London: T&T Clark, 2002.

2004
New Testament Theology: Many Witnesses, One Gospel. Nottingham, UK; Downers Grove: InterVarsity, 2004.

Beyond the Bible: Moving from Scripture to Theology: With Essays by Kevin J. Vanhoozer and Stanley E. Porter. Milton Keynes: Paternoster; Grand Rapids: Baker, 2004.

2007
Aspects of the Atonement: Cross and Resurrection in the Reconciling of God and Humanity. London: Paternoster, 2007.

2008
Marshall, I. H., Rollin Grams, Peter Penner, and Robin Routledge, eds. *Bible and Mission: A Conversation Between Biblical Studies and Missiology.* Schwarzenfeld: Neufeld Verlag, 2008.

A Concise New Testament Theology. Nottingham, UK; Downers Grove: InterVarsity, 2008.

ARTICLES/ESSAYS

1962
"Sanctification in the Teaching of John Wesley and John Calvin." *Evangelical Quarterly* 34 (1962): 75-82.

1964
"Hard Sayings." *Theology* 67 (1964): 65-67.

1966
"Synoptic Son of Man Sayings in Recent Discussion." *New Testament Studies* 12 (1966): 327-51.

1967
"Worship: The Christian Year." Pages 409-413 in *Baker's Dictionary of Practical Theology.* Edited by Ralph G. Turnbull. Grand Rapids: Baker, 1967.

"Divine Sonship of Jesus." *Interpretation* 21 (1967): 87-103.

"Professor Ferdinand Hahn's Christologische Hoheitstitel." *Expository Times* 78 (1967): 212-15.

"The Development of Christology in the Early Church." *Tyndale Bulletin* 18 (1967): 77-93.

1968

"Luke 16:8: Who Commended the Unjust Steward?" *Journal of Theological Studies* (1968): 617-19.

"Recent Study of the Gospel According to St. Luke." *Expository Times* 80 (1968): 4-8.

"The Christ-Hymn in Philippians." *Tyndale Bulletin* 19 (1968): 104-27.

1969

"Recent Study of the Acts of the Apostles." *Expository Times* 80 (1969): 292-96.

"Son of God or Servant of Yahweh: A Reconsideration of Mark 1:11." *New Testament Studies* 15 (1969): 326-36.

"Tradition and Theology in Luke (Luke 8:5-15)." *Tyndale Bulletin* 20 (1969): 56-75.

1970

"Fear Him Who can Destroy both Soul and Body in Hell: Mt 10:28; Lk 12:4f." *Expository Times* 81 (1970): 276-80.

"The Resurrection in the Acts of the Apostles." Pages 92-107 in *Apostolic History and the Gospel: Biblical and Historical Essays Presented to F. F. Bruce on His 60th Birthday*. Edited by W. W. Gasque and R. P. Martin. Exeter, UK: Paternoster; Grand Rapids: Eerdmans, 1970.

"Son of Man in Contemporary Debate." *Evangelical Quarterly* 42 (1970): 67-87.

1971

"F.F. Bruce as a Biblical Scholar," *Christian Brethren Research Fellowship Journal* 22 (Nov. 1971): 5-12.

1973

"Meaning of the Verb 'to Baptize.'" *Evangelical Quarterly* 45 (1973): 130-40.

"New Wine in Old Wineskins." *Expository Times* 84 (1973): 359-64.

"Palestinian and Hellenistic Christianity: Some Critical Comments." *New Testament Studies* 19 (1973): 271-87.

"The Resurrection of Jesus in Luke." *Tyndale Bulletin* 24 (1973): 55-98.

1974

"The Development of the Concept of Redemption in the New Testament."
Pages 153-69 in *Reconciliation and Hope: New Testament Essays on Atonement and Eschatology; Presented to L. L. Morris on His 60th Birthday*. Edited by R. Banks. Grand Rapids: Eerdmans, 1974.

"'Early Catholicism' in the New Testament." Pages 217-31 in *New Dimensions in New Testament Study*. Edited by R. N. Longenecker and M. C. Tenney. Grand Rapids: Zondervan, 1974.

"Problem of New Testament Exegesis." *Journal of the Evangelical Theological Society* 17 (1974): 67-73.

1975

"Predestination in the New Testament." Pages 127-43 in *Grace Unlimited*. Edited by C. H. Pinnock. Minneapolis: Bethany Fellowship, 1975.

1977

"Historical Criticism." Pages 126-38 in *New Testament Interpretation: Essays on Principles and Methods*. Edited by I. H. Marshall. Exeter, UK: Paternoster, 1977.

"Preaching the Kingdom of God." *Expository Times* 89 (1977): 13-16.

"Significance of Pentecost." *Scottish Journal of Theology* 30 (1977): 347-69.

1978

"The Meaning of 'Reconciliation.'" Pages 117-32 in *Unity and Diversity in New Testament Theology: Essays in Honor of George E. Ladd*. Edited by R. A. Guelich. Grand Rapids: Eerdmans, 1978.

"Slippery Words, 1: Eschatology." *Expository Times* 89 (1978): 264-69.

"Using the Bible in Ethics." Pages 39-55 in *Essays in Evangelical Social Ethics*. Edited by D. F. Wright. Exeter: Paternoster, 1978.

1980

"Culture and the New Testament." Pages 17-31 in *Down to Earth: Studies in Christianity and Culture*. Edited by R. T. Coote and J. R. W. Stott. Grand Rapids: Eerdmans, 1980.

"How do We Interpret the Bible Today?" *Themelios* 5, no. 2 (January 1980): 4-12.

1982

"Incarnational Christology in the New Testament." Pages 1-16 in *Christ the Lord: Studies in Christology Presented to Donald Guthrie*. Edited by H. R. Rowdon. Leicester, UK: InterVarsity, 1982.

"Pauline Theology in the Thessalonian Correspondence." Pages 173-83 in *Paul and Paulinism: Essays in Honour of C. K. Barrett*. Edited by M. D. Hooker and S. G. Wilson. London: SPCK, 1982.

1983

"Luke and His 'Gospel.'" Pages 289-308 in *Evangelium Und Die Evangelien: Vortrage vom Tübinger Symposium*. Edited by P. Stuhlmacher. Tübingen, Germany: Mohr (Siebeck), 1983.

"The Death of Jesus in Recent New Testament Study." *Word & World* 3 (1983): 12-21.

"Some Considerations Regarding the Lord's Supper Today." *Searching Together* 12 (1983): 9-10.

1984

"How to Solve the Synoptic Problem: Luke 11:43 and Parallels." Pages 313-25 in *New Testament Age: Essays in Honor of Bo Reicke*. Edited by W. C. Weinrich. Macon, Ga.: Mercer University Press, 1984.

"The Role of Women in the Church." Pages 177-97 in *The Role of Women*. Edited by S. Lees. Leicester, UK: InterVarsity, 1984.

"The Young Christian and the 'Liberal' Pastor." *Expository Times* 95 (1984): 364-67.

1985

"How Far Did the Early Christians Worship God." *Churchman* 99 (1985): 216-29.

"New Testament Perspectives on War." *Evangelical Quarterly* 57 (1985): 115-32.

"The Hope of a New Age: The Kingdom of God in the New Testament." *Themelios* 11, no. 1 (1985): 5-15.

1986

"New Testament Worship," Pages 389-91 in *The New Westminster Dictionary of Liturgy and Worship*. Edited by J. G. Davies. Philadelphia: Westminster, 1986.

"The Ministry." Pages 13-25 in *Ministry in the Local Church*. Edited by H. Belben. London: Epworth, 1986.

1987

"Apg 12—Ein Schlüssel Zum Verständnis Der Apostelgeschichte." Pages 192-220 in *Petrusbild in Der Neueren Forschung*. Edited by C. P. Thiede. Wuppertal, Germany: R Brockhaus, 1987.

"Is Apocalyptic the Mother of Christian Theology?" Pages 33-42 in *Tradition and Interpretation in the New Testament: Essays in Honor of E. Earle Ellis for His 60th Birthday*. Edited by G. F. Hawthorne with O. Betz. Grand Rapids: Eerdmans, 1987.

"The Christian Life in 1 Timothy." *Taiwan Journal of Theology* (1987): 151-64.

"The Problem of Apostasy in New Testament Theology." *Perspectives in Religious Studies* 14 (1987): 65-80.

1988

"An Assessment of Recent Developments." Pages 1-21 in *It is Written—Scripture Citing Scripture: Essays in Honour of Barnabas Lindars, SSF*. Edited by D. A. Carson and H. G. M. Williamson. Cambridge, UK: Cambridge University Press, 1988.

"An Evangelical Approach to 'Theological Criticism.'" *Themelios* 13 (1988): 79-85.

"Jesus as Lord: The Development of the Concept." Pages 129-45 in *Eschatology and the New Testament: Essays in Honor of George Raymond Beasley-Murray*. Edited by W. Hulitt Gloer. Peabody, Mass.: Hendrickson, 1988.

"They Set Us in New Paths, Pt 1: The New Testament: Paths Without Destinations." *Expository Times* 100 (1988): 9-13.

1989

"Church and Temple in the New Testament." *Tyndale Bulletin* 40 (1989): 203-22.

"Does the New Testament Teach Universal Salvation?" Pages 313-28 in *Christ in our Place: The Humanity of God in Christ for the Reconciliation of the World: Essays Presented to Professor James Torrance*. Allison Park, Penn.: Pickwick, 1989.

"Inter-Faith Dialogue in the New Testament." *Evangelical Review of Theology* 13 (1989): 196-215.

"The Present State of Lucan Studies." *Themelios* 14 (1989): 52-56.

"Universal Grace and Atonement in the Pastoral Epistles." Pages 51-69 in *The Grace of God, the Will of Man: A Case for Arminianism*. Edited by C. H. Pinnock. Grand Rapids: Zondervan, 1989.

1990

"Editorial: Professor F. F. Bruce." *Evangelical Quarterly* 62 (1990): 291.

"The Christian Life in 1 Timothy." *Reformed Theological Review* 49 (1990): 81-90.

"Election and Calling to Salvation in 1 and 2 Thessalonians." Pages 259-76 in *The Thessalonian Correspondence*. Edited by R. F. Collins. Louvain: Leuven University Press, 1990.

"Luke's View of Paul." *Southwestern Journal of Theology* 33 (1990): 41-51.

1991

"Preaching from the New Testament." *Scottish Bulletin of Evangelical Theology* 9 (1991): 104-17.

"The Son of Man and the Incarnation." *Ex Auditu* 7 (1991): 29-43.

"Which is the Best Commentary? Philippians." *Expository Times* 103 (1991): 39-42.

"Frederick Fyvie Bruce, 1910–1990," *Proceedings of the British Academy* 80 (1991): 245-60.

1992

"Are Evangelicals Fundamentalists?" *Vox Evangelica* 22 (1992): 7-24.

"Dialogue with Non-Christians in the New Testament." *Evangelical Review of Theology* 16 (1992): 28-47.

"The Parousia in the New Testament—and Today." Pages 194-211 in *Worship, Theology and Ministry in the Early Church: Essays in Honor of Ralph P. Martin*. Edited by M. J. Wilkins and T. Paige. Sheffield, UK: JSOT Press, 1992.

1993

"Acts and the 'Former Treatise.'" Pages 163-82 in *The Book of Acts in Its Ancient Literary Setting*. Vol. 1 of *The Book of Acts in its First*

Century Setting. Edited by B. W. Winter and A. D. Clarke. Grand Rapids: Eerdmans; Carlisle, UK: Paternoster, 1993.

"Faith and Scholarship." *Themelios* 19 (1993): 35.

"The Messiah in the First Century: A Review Article." *Criswell Theological Review* 7 (1993): 67-83.

"Response." *Epworth Review* 20 (1993): 55-56.

"'Sometimes Only Orthodox'—Is there More to the Pastoral Epistles?" *Epworth Review* 20 (1993): 12-24.

1994

"The Christology of Luke–Acts and the Pastoral Epistles." Pages 167-82 in *Crossing the Boundaries: Essays in Biblical Interpretation in Honour of Michael D. Goulder.* Edited by S. E. Porter, P. Joyce, and D. E. Orton. Leiden: Brill, 1994.

"Climbing Ropes, Ellipses and Symphonies: The Relation between Biblical and Systematic Theology." Pages 199-219 in *A Pathway into the Holy Scripture.* Edited by P. E. Satterthwaite and D. F. Wright. Grand Rapids: Eerdmans, 1994.

"Commentaries on the Synoptic Gospels: Mark and Luke." *Bible Translator* 45 (1994): 139-50.

"New Occasions Teach New Duties? 2. The use of the New Testament in Christian Ethics." *Expository Times* 105 (1994): 131-36.

"The Synoptic 'Son of Man' Sayings in the Light of Linguistic Study." Pages 72-94 in *To Tell the Mystery: Essays on New Testament Eschatology in Honor of Robert H. Gundry.* Edited by T. E. Schmidt and M. Silva. Sheffield, UK: JSOT Press, 1994.

1996

"Prospects for the Pastoral Epistles." Pages 137-55 in *Doing Theology for the People of God: Studies in Honor of J. I. Packer.* Edited by D. Lewis and A. McGrath. Downers Grove: InterVarsity, 1996.

"Salvation, Grace and Works in the Later Writings in the Pauline Corpus." *New Testament Studies* 42 (1996): 339-58.

"Salvation in the Pastoral Epistles." Pages 449-69 in vol. 3 of *Geschichte— Tradition—Reflexion: Festschriften Für Martin Hengel Zum 70.*

Geburtstag. Edited by H. Cancik, H. Lichtenberger, and P. Schäfer. Tübingen: Mohr (Siebeck), 1996.

1997

"'To Find Out what God is Saying': Reflections on the Authorizing of Scripture." Pages 49-55 in *Disciplining Hermeneutics: Interpretation in Christian Perspective.* Edited by R. Lundin. Grand Rapids: Eerdmans; Leicester, UK: Apollos, 1997.

"Luke–Acts." *Expository Times* 108 (1997): 196-200.

"A New Understanding of the Present and the Future: Paul and Eschatology." Pages 43-61 in *The Road from Damascus: The Impact of Paul's Conversion on His Life, Thought, and Ministry.* Edited by R. N. Longenecker. Grand Rapids: Eerdmans, 1997.

"Recent Study of the Pastoral Epistles." *Themelios* 23 (1997): 3-29.

1998

"How does One Write on the Theology of Acts?" Pages 3-16 in *Witness to the Gospel: The Theology of Acts.* Edited by I. H. Marshall and D. Peterson. Grand Rapids: Eerdmans, 1998.

1999

"'Israel' and the Story of Salvation: One Theme in Two Parts." Pages 340-57 in *Jesus and the Heritage of Israel: Luke's Narrative Claim upon Israel's Legacy.* Edited by D. P. Moessner. Harrisburg, Pa.: Trinity, 1999.

"Romans 16:25-27: An Apt Conclusion." Pages 170-84 in *Romans and the People of God: Essays in Honor of Gordon D. Fee on the Occasion of His 65th Birthday.* Edited by S. K. Soderlund and N. T. Wright. Grand Rapids: Eerdmans, 1999.

2000

"The Christian Millennium." *Evangelical Quarterly* 72 (2000): 217-35.

"'In Honesty of Preaching' 8. An Assessment." *Expository Times* 112 (2000): 41-43.

Marshall, I. H., and Carl R. Trueman. "Interview with Professor Howard Marshall." *Themelios* 26 (2000): 48-53.

"Luke's Portrait of the Pauline Mission." Pages 99-113 in *The Gospel to the Nations: Perspectives on Paul's Mission: In Honour of Peter T. O'Brien.* Downers Grove: InterVarsity; Leicester, UK: Apollos, 2000.

"Who were the Evangelists?" Pages 251-63 in *Mission of the Early Church to Jews and Gentiles*. Edited by J. Ådna and H. Kvalbein. Tübingen: Mohr (Siebeck), 2000.

2001

"Being Human: Made in the Image of God." *Stone-Campbell Journal* 4 (2001): 47-67.

"Jesus—Example and Teacher of Prayer in the Synoptic Gospels." Pages 113-31 in *Into God's Presence: Prayer in the New Testament*. Edited by R. N. Longenecker. Grand Rapids: Eerdmans, 2001.

2002

"Congregation and Ministry in the Pastoral Epistles." Pages 105-25 in *Community Formation in the Early Church and in the Church Today*. Edited by R. N. Longenecker. Peabody, Mass.: Hendrickson, 2002.

"Living in the 'Flesh.'" *Bibliotheca Sacra* 159 (2002): 387-403.

"The Meaning of the Word 'Baptize.'" Pages 8-24 in *Dimensions of Baptism: Biblical and Theological Studies*. Edited by S. E. Porter and A. R. Cross. London: Sheffield Academic, 2002.

"Should Christians Boast?" *Bibliotheca Sacra* 159 (2002): 259-76.

"'Sins' and 'Sin.'" *Bibliotheca Sacra* 159 (2002): 3-20.

"Who is a Hypocrite?" *Bibliotheca Sacra* 159 (2002): 131-50.

"Worshipping Biblically." *Scottish Bulletin of Evangelical Theology* 20 (2002): 146-61.

2003

"Acts in Current Study." *Expository Times* 115 (2003): 49-52.

"Evangelicalism and Biblical Interpretation." Pages 100-23 in *The Futures of Evangelicalism: Issues and Prospects*. Edited by C. Bartholomew, R. Parry, and A. West. Leicester, UK: InterVarsity, 2003; Grand Rapids: Kregel, 2004.

"The New Testament Does *Not* Teach Universal Salvation." Pages 55-76 in *Universal Salvation? The Current Debate*. Edited by R. A. Parry and C. H. Partridge. Grand Rapids: Eerdmans, 2003.

2004

"Bernard Lord Manning—The Voice of 'Orthodox Dissent.'" *Evangel* 22 (2004): 43-47.

"Brothers Embracing Sisters?" *Bible Translator* 55 (2004): 303-10.

"The Holy Spirit in the Pastoral Epistles and the Apostolic Fathers." Pages 257-69 in *The Holy Spirit and Christian Origins: Essays in Honor of James D. G. Dunn*. Edited by G. N. Stanton, B. W. Longenecker, and S. Barton. Grand Rapids: Eerdmans, 2004.

"Mutual Love and Submission in Marriage: Colossians 3:18-19 and Ephesians 5:21-33." Pages 186-204 in *Discovering Biblical Equality: Complementarity without Hierarchy*. Edited by R. W. Pierce, R. M. Groothuis, and G. D. Fee. Leicester, UK: InterVarsity, 2004. 2005—2d ed. Downers Grove: InterVarsity; Leicester, UK: Apollos.

"The Religious Enemy: The Response of the Church to Religious Pressure in Acts." *Anvil* 21 (2004): 179-87.

2005

"Biblical Patterns for Public Theology." *European Journal of Theology* 14 (2005): 73-86.

2006

"Gospels." Pages 185-205 in *IVP Introduction to the Bible*. Edited by P. S. Johnston. Downers Grove: IVP Academic, 2006.

"Some Recent Commentaries on the Pastoral Epistles." *Expository Times* 117 (2006): 140-43.

"Testimony and Interpretation: Early Christology in its Judeo-Hellenistic Milieu." *The Journal of Theological Studies* 57 (2006): 215-16.

2007

"Fracture: The Cross as Irreconcilable in the Language and Thought of the Biblical Writers." *The Journal of Theological Studies* 58 (2007): 645-47.

"Holiness in the Book of Acts." Pages 114-28 in *Holiness and Ecclesiology in the New Testament*. Edited by K. E. Brower and A. Johnson. Grand Rapids: Eerdmans, 2007.

"Jesus as Messiah in Mark and Matthew." Pages 117-43 in *The Messiah in the Old and New Testaments*. Edited by S. E. Porter. Grand Rapids: Eerdmans, 2007.

2008

"1 Timothy." Pages 162-68 in *Theological Interpretation of the New Testament: A Book by Book Survey.* Edited by Daniel J. Treier and N. T. Wright. Grand Rapids: Baker Academic, 2008.

"2 Timothy." Pages 169-74 in *Theological Interpretation of the New Testament: A Book by Book Survey.* Edited by Daniel J. Treier and N. T. Wright. Grand Rapids: Baker Academic, 2008.

"A Fresh Look at the Lord's Supper: Ben Witherington III, *Making a Meal of It: Rethinking the Theology of the Lord's Supper.*" *The Expository Times* 120 (2008): 80.

"Johannine Epistles." Pages 222-28 in *Theological Interpretation of the New Testament: A Book by Book Survey.* Edited by Daniel J. Treier and N. T. Wright. Grand Rapids: Baker Academic, 2008.

"Paul's Mission According to Romans." Pages 96-131 in *Bible and Mission: A Conversation Between Biblical Studies and Missiology.* Edited by Rollin Grams, Howard Marshall, Peter Penner, and Robin Routledge. Schwarzenfeld: Neufeld Verlag, 2008.

"Paul's Use of the Old Testament in Romans 9:1-9: An Intertextual and Theological Exegesis." *The Journal of Theological Studies* 59 (2008): 285-87.

"The Theology of the Atonement." Pages 49-68 in *The Atonement Debate: Papers from the London Symposium on the Theology of Atonement.* Edited by D. Tidball, D. Hilborn, and J. Thacker. Grand Rapids: Zondervan, 2008.

2009

"The Last Supper." Pages 481-588 in *Key Events in the Life of the Historical Jesus: A Collaborative Exploration of Context and Coherence.* Edited by D. L. Bock and R. L. Webb. Tübingen: Mohr (Siebeck), 2009.

2010

"The Pastoral Epistles in Recent Study." Pages 268-312 in *Entrusted with the Gospel: Paul's Theology in the Pastoral Epistles.* Edited by Andreas J. Kostenberger and Terry L. Wilder. Nashville: B&H Academic, 2010.

1

METHODOLOGY OF EVANGELISM IN THE NEW TESTAMENT: SOME PRELIMINARY REFLECTIONS

James D. G. Dunn

INTRODUCTION

I hesitate slightly in offering this paper on "New Testament Methodology in Evangelism." Not because the topic needs justifying or defending in a Festschrift for Howard Marshall. For the subject is close to the heart of one who, after all, is truly the doyen of evangelical UK and European NT scholarship.[1] What provokes my hesitations, first of all, is that the topic is really too big to deal with adequately in a single essay. In fact, most of what follows has arisen for me as corollaries to some of the more detailed research carried out over many years (though not as many as Howard's). So I am fully aware that in what follows I will be making claims and mounting arguments without the detailed substantiation that they require. The only solution I found to this dilemma is to refer in the notes to these earlier writings in which I hope I have been able to argue points with some care and persuasiveness. At the same time, however, the word limit has meant that I had less space for footnotes than I usually find necessary. The unfortunate result is that the notes are dominated to an embarrassing extent by references to my own publications. I apologize for this, with the small self-justification that these references in the notes will usually contain a fuller biography relevant to the point being made.

I am also hesitant because the title of the paper carries the implication that there is such a subject. So before we pose the question, "What is the NT methodology of evangelism?" we should ask ourselves what sort of answer we can expect. In other words, this topic may be an example of the danger of treating the NT as a textbook on all matters pertaining to Christian faith and life, an example of the danger of distorting the purpose and intent of individual NT documents in order to provide answers to *our* questions, questions which were never actually addressed by the NT writers themselves.

The fact is that no NT document sets out to serve as a guide on methods of evangelism. So any answers provided will come to us at best incidentally. In some cases because the document provides relevant material, even though

---

[1] I need refer only to Howard's *magnum opus—New Testament Theology* (Downers Grove: InterVarsity, 2004)—where he emphasizes the mission focus of the NT writings, "the documents of a mission" (34).

presented for another purpose. In others because the NT text provides narrative and teaching from which we may make certain deductions.

Even these very preliminary observations at once indicate the degree of caution which will be necessary. For one thing, whatever we derive will almost certainly be incomplete. Because no NT writer has set himself to address our topic, methodology in evangelism, there are bound to be gaps. We cannot assume that the writer has said all he would have wanted to say on the subject, or that he would have ordered any fuller treatment with the same emphases which we now find. And for another, we can never be wholly certain as to how much any action or method recorded in the text has been determined by the particular circumstances of the occasion recorded or addressed. That is to say, we will have to be very cautious about assuming that any method is of wider application (to our own day, for example) simply because it has been documented in sacred scripture.

To cite a few examples. (1) The Mission charge in Mark 6 and parallels. Characteristics include particularly the strong eschatological note—"Preach as you go, saying, 'The kingdom of God is at hand'" (Matt 10:7); also the complete unconcern for material provision (Mark 6:8-9 pars.). How widely applicable may we take these instructions to be? Already within the first generation of Christianity we may compare Paul who was quite familiar with the dominical word about gaining a living from the gospel (1 Cor 9:14), but who insisted on earning his own living (9:15-18).

(2) Correlated with this is the comparison between Jesus' mission and that of Paul. Jesus' mission seems to have been very largely among the villages in and around Galilee. This was very different in kind and method from Paul's missionary activity in the major Mediterranean cities of Asia Minor and Europe. Once again the question of relevance outside the particular circumstances of these missions arises, with the corollary danger of absolutizing a method (or methodology) which was very largely contingent in content and character.

(3) A further issue is the extent to which we should think and speak of all the first Christians as evangelistic. Even with careful discussion,[2] there remains a danger of perpetuating the myth which idealizes the first Christian generation as the perfect church or golden age of the church by assuming that all Christians of that period were enthusiastic and compelling evangelists. No doubt there were many such, and proportionally many more than today. And

---

[2] I have in mind the continuing debate as to the involvement of Paul's congregations in active evangelism, stimulated by P. T. O'Brien, *Gospel and Mission in the Writings of Paul* (Grand Rapids: Baker, 1995) chs. 4–5, a debate to which Howard has made his typically judicious contribution—"Who Were the Evangelists?," in *The Mission of the Early Church to Jews and Gentiles* (ed. J. Ådna and H. Kvalbein; WUNT 127; Tübingen: Mohr [Siebeck], 2000), 251-63. See also my *Beginning from Jerusalem* (Grand Rapids: Eerdmans, 2009), 566-72 and n. 229.

the impact of such passages as Matt 28:19-20 and Acts 1:8, and evidence of such as Acts 11:19 should not be lightly discounted. On the other hand, the commission of Mark 6:7-13 was given to a select band; there were many who stayed at home, like Mary and Martha, as well as those who literally followed Jesus. And the fact that "evangelist" is a specific function given to and exercised by only a few in Eph 4:11 should not be discounted either. In other words, the NT writings do not warrant any guilt-inducing generalization that only those Christians who are active in explicit evangelism are true to the spirit of the NT.

(4) As a final cautionary example we might cite the "signs and wonders" issue. What conclusions may justly be drawn from the fact that miracles are recorded as part of much at least of the early missions (e.g., Gal 3:5; Heb 2:4)? What weight are we to give to Jesus' rebuke of sign-seeking (Mark 8:11-12 pars.), and to the fact that the promise of "signs accompanying" comes only in the longer ending to Mark's Gospel (16:17), added probably a century or so after the original composition? What are we to make of the fact that while on one occasion Paul speaks positively of his ministry of "signs and wonders" (Rom 15:19), on another he speaks more dismissively of the same criterion of apostleship (2 Cor 12:12)? Or of the fact that outside Acts, it is regularly understood that "signs and wonders" need to be treated with the greatest caution if not suspicion (Mark 13:22 par.; John 4:48; 2 Cor 12:12; 2 Thess 2:9)?[3]

On the other hand, so long as we do not build our hopes too high or try to force all the data into a pattern derived from elsewhere, we can hope for at least some illumination on the subject of our inquiry. If we set our material as firmly and as fully as possible into the different first-century contexts from which it derived, then we can expect to see something at least of how evangelism was undertaken in the beginning of Christianity. Not only so, but by seeing it in context we may well be able to observe whether there are distinctive features which stand out and which may (like the texts themselves) be of more than merely local significance.

We proceed by asking a few basic questions—Where? How? and What?

WHERE? WHERE WAS EVANGELISM CARRIED OUT?

If we look first to Jesus himself, the clear answer from the Gospels is that Jesus began his preaching ministry in the *synagogues* of Galilee. We should not treat Mark, almost certainly the earliest connected account of Jesus' ministry, as a straight chronological account. Nevertheless the broad sequence of Mark's accounts of individual episodes strongly suggests that Jesus made the synagogue the focus of his teaching and preaching in the early stages of his

---

[3] See further K. J. Hacking, *Signs and Wonders Then and Now: Miracle-working, Commissioning and Discipleship* (Nottingham: Apollos, 2006), with full bibliography.

ministry (Mark 1:21, 39; 3:1; 6:2); and that it was only when his popularity began to draw larger crowds that he took more to *the open air*. This is not entirely unexpected, since the synagogue would be the natural community center in most villages.[4]

When we look next at the Jewish and Gentile mission, a similar picture emerges. Both seem to have made their main evangelistic thrust in the *synagogue* (or in Jerusalem, in the temple). Again this is what we would expect in the case of the Jewish mission. For Jews speaking to Jews the synagogue was the natural common ground for preaching and discussion (Acts 6:9; 9:20; 11:19).

But the same seems to have been true of the Gentile mission.[5] According to Acts, Paul almost always made the synagogue the focus of his initial attempts at evangelism (Acts 13:5, 14; 14:1; 17:1-2, 10, 17; etc.). The claim is sometimes disputed, in view of Paul's own self-designation as "apostle to the Gentiles" (Rom 11:13). But the fact is that many Gentiles at this period found Judaism attractive and associated themselves in varying degrees with the Jewish synagogue; the testimony of Josephus and Greco-Roman writers is sufficiently clear and consistent on the point. A number of these of course became proselytes, but most it would appear, attracted, for example, by Judaism's austere monotheism and practice of one regular day in seven as a day of rest, maintained a looser association. They are usually called "God-fearers" or "God-worshippers." The point is that Paul would usually find a number of God-fearing, Judaism-sympathizing Gentiles in the synagogues of the larger Mediterranean cities.[6] And since he saw the promise to the Gentiles as part of God's original covenant with Abraham (Gal 3; Rom 4), it was natural that he should look to such Gentiles as those most likely to respond to his message. Natural too that he should see the synagogue as the obvious point of contact for such already sympathetic Gentiles. An interesting confirmation of all this is given by the fact that Paul can assume that his Gentile readers were familiar with the Septuagint (LXX = the Greek version of the Jewish scriptures). Since the LXX was not well known outside Jewish circles, it must be that Paul was able to assume that many or most of his initial Gentile audiences/readers had gained some familiarity with the LXX during their association with the synagogue.

We can draw an interesting preliminary conclusion at once. That the earliest Christian mission, including Jesus and Paul, shows *a readiness to stay within the established religious structures*—that is, the religious structures of Judaism.

---

[4] The term translated "synagogue" would perhaps be better translated as "assembly"; see my *Jesus Remembered* (Grand Rapids: Eerdmans, 2003), 302-306.

[5] This is a surprisingly controversial claim; see, e.g., those who believe the Acts references which follow to be unhistorical (Dunn, *Beginning*, 420 n.17) and further Dunn, *Beginning*, 557-60.

[6] See further Dunn, *Beginning*, 560-63.

The question needs a much wider discussion, of course, but here we can say that at least so far as means of outreach were concerned, there seems to have been no thought, on the part of the first Christian missionaries, of the new movement as a new religion, separate or distinct from Judaism. This is not to dispute that use of the synagogue as a location for outreach to Gentiles often became impracticable or impossible after a time (e.g., Acts18:6-7; 19:8-9). But law-observant Jewish Christians were able to function as loyal Jews for some time yet, and in Palestine and Syria it was probably only towards the end of the first century that the new movement was forced to become officially separate from Judaism as the latter in turn came more and more completely under the control of the rabbis and successors to the Pharisees. Only then, it would appear, did it become impossible for Jewish believers to remain within the synagogue—a situation probably reflected in the Fourth Gospel (John 9:22; 12:42). Even so, there is good evidence that the frequenters of both church and synagogue continued to overlap for some centuries, despite exhortations for Christians to stop attending the synagogue on Saturday and observing the Jewish feasts from such as Ignatius, Origen and Chrysostom.[7]

In any case the point remains, that as far as we can tell, initial evangelistic outreach attempted to operate within the given structures of Judaism. However soon or late the breach between emerging Christianity and emerging rabbinic Judaism came about, and whatever other methods of evangelism were used, the first Christian evangelists did not begin by presupposing or working for such a breach.

HOW? HOW WAS EVANGELISM CARRIED OUT?—JESUS

With Jesus the most obvious answer would be—by *preaching and teaching*. It is unnecessary to cite strings of references to demonstrate the claim that the single most characteristic means of evangelism used by Jesus was the spoken word.[8] All four Gospels bear consistent testimony in their own way to this point—e.g., Mark with his characteristic emphasis on Jesus "teaching," Matthew by his grouping of Jesus' teaching into five great blocks, Luke by the prominence he gives to Jesus' parables, and John by his elaborate sequence of discourses. That preaching and teaching cannot be neatly separated and only the former linked to evangelism may be significant. Jesus' proclamation of good news was as much an interpretation of the old word to Israel as an announcement of the new word of the kingdom.

Since mode and location are interrelated in this case we can further

---

[7] The "When?" and "How soon?" of the separation between Judaism and Christianity is much debated. See my *The Partings of the Way between Christianity and Judaism and their Significance for the Character of Christianity* (London: SCM, 1991), and especially the second edition (2006), xi-xxx.

[8] On Jesus as teacher see, e.g., my *Jesus Remembered*, 177, 697-98.

elaborate the "Where?" by clarifying the "How?" In our sources it is often the case that nothing is said about the location of a particular episode or utterance. It is simply recalled that an encounter took place or that Jesus said something; the teaching is remembered without a context. Even so, however, enough has been preserved for us to build up a picture.

In the *synagogues* Jesus would speak by invitation. But beyond that, when the synagogue venue became impracticable, for one reason or another, we become aware of at least two other contexts. One was the open air. Whether this was by design or something which just happened as reports of Jesus' ministry drew larger crowds than could be contained in synagogues remains unclear. A passage like Mark 3:7-8 suggests the latter, resulting in a pattern which Jesus willingly adopted (e.g., Mark 4:1). On other occasions he seems to have been trying to escape from the pressures of his popularity, only to find himself confronted by eager crowds whom he could not deny (e.g., Mark 6:31-34). At all events we can say that much of Jesus' preaching was not the outcome of careful planning and campaigning, but was his response to the demands and needs which confronted him.

The other most typical context appears to have been the *home*, at *the meal table*. Here too the style would not be so strange. The family meal was (and is) characteristically the most sacred event of the Jewish household, and it would not be unusual for the participants to spend long over the meal and to use the occasion for discussing important issues. In the case of Jesus it is not clear whether he had a "home base" himself (as could be implied by Mark 2:1 and 15 when these stories were told separately—"his home" = Jesus' home?), or whether his "table talk" took place chiefly at meals to which he had been invited as guest (as in Luke 7:36 and 14:1). What would be more striking and unusual about this context of his teaching would be those who attended—the "sinners and tax collectors" who brought such criticism upon his head (Mark 2:16; Matt 11:19; Luke 15:2). This is a different subject into which we had better not become sidetracked, but it is of considerable importance for our subject (e.g., Mark 2:17; Luke 15:1-32).[9]

The other context in which Jesus is remembered as preaching is, of course, the *temple* in Jerusalem. In terms of Synoptic chronology that means only during the last week of his ministry (Mark 11:17, 27; 12:35; etc.); but John agrees in specifying the temple as the location of much of Jesus' "set-piece" preaching (John 8:20; 10:23). This too is only to be expected, the temple courts easily providing the largest open area of concourse, and the obvious location for Pharisees and any other would-be teachers to offer their insights and claims to pupils and passers by. Here too, in other words, Jesus uses the "normal" means and location for conveying his message. What caused most comment was not the mode of communication but the *authority* with which he spoke, as one who had not been trained as lawyer/scribe, or priest, and who was not

---

[9] See Dunn, *Jesus Remembered*, 526-34.

known as the pupil of any Pharisaic teacher (Mark 11:28; as earlier, 1:27, etc). But here too we touch on a subject which would require more discussion than we can devote to it now.[10]

In all this we should also take care lest we be misled by the degree of structure we find in Jesus' preaching/teaching as recorded in the Gospels. Much at least of that structure is a structure given to the tradition by those who used that tradition for catechetical instruction etc. in the earliest churches, or by the Evangelists themselves (as is evident, e.g., when we compare "the Sermon on the Mount" in Matt 5–7 with the scatter of the same material in a range of disparate contexts in Luke). The extent to which we have a connected sequence of Jesus' teaching as delivered by Jesus himself remains unclear. According to the evidence of the Synoptics, Jesus' preaching/teaching was frequently if not chiefly remembered as a series of short epigrammatic sayings and parables, usually without any necessary connection the one to another. In other words, although Jesus is often remembered as teaching for lengthy periods (as in Mark 6:34-5), we do not actually have any clear examples of a single structured message of any length. We must return to the evidence of the Fourth Gospel later.

What emerges here then is nothing of great originality in method. What was most striking was the *openness* of his message to a wide circle—wider than polite or religious society could approve of—and the surprisingly *authoritative* character of his teaching.[11] But communication by means of preaching and teaching in contexts particularly of synagogue, temple and home was hardly an innovation in evangelistic method.

Although preaching/teaching was clearly Jesus' chief "method of evangelism," there is an important corollary to be remembered. I refer to the fact that *the rest of Jesus' ministry and life-style cohered with his preaching*, and to some extent at least served as a vehicle for his message as well.

This includes his healing ministry. The point is not that his healings were designed as a means of evangelism. Rather that wholeness of body and person were part of the good news—the sort of thing which could be expected under God's kingly rule, alongside the proclamation of the good news to the poor (Matt 11:5; 12:28). At the same time we need to recall that according to Jesus' teaching, miracles are no proof in and of themselves of divine action or approval (Mark 13:22). The "sign" value of miracles may encourage the wrong kind of faith (John 2:23-25; 4:48; 6:26-30). Even the greatest miracle (resurrection) will convince no one if the word has been ignored (Luke 16:31).

More important than his healing ministry as bearing testimony to his message was Jesus' whole lifestyle. His consorting with "sinners and tax collectors" was itself an expression of God's good news for the poor. His table fellowship open to those devalued by law-abiding society was indicative of the

---

[10] I must again simply refer to the discussion of *Jesus Remembered*, 698-704.

[11] On both points see Dunn, *Jesus Remembered*, 599-607 and 698-702.

character of life under God's kingly rule as imaged by the banquet (particularly Luke 14:12-24). Jesus lived in the light of the coming kingdom as well as proclaiming it.[12]

This coherence of word, action and lifestyle meant that Jesus' whole life was evangelistic in a proper sense. All that he sought to convey to his hearers and to win from them in terms of response was the focused and specifically directed challenge of a "whole-life" message. In other words, if Jesus' "evangelistic method" was anchored in the institutions of his own day (synagogue and meal table), it was also wholly expressive of himself.

HOW? HOW WAS EVANGELISM CARRIED OUT?—THE FIRST CHRISTIANS

When we turn our attention to the wider mission of the first Christians, first within Palestine and then in steadily widening circles beyond, what do we find? Here again we need to recall the fragmentary nature of the evidence. Luke does not set himself the task in Acts of outlining evangelistic method. And our other best source, the letters of Paul, only provides evidence by allusion or implication. Moreover the evidence refers primarily to a very few named missionaries, particularly Paul. It tells us very little indeed, and nothing in detail, about evangelism insofar as it was carried on by others not engaged in actual mission as such. The simplest procedure is to itemize briefly the main foci of evangelism, drawing together the information from a fairly wide scatter of evidence.

Once they were deprived of the synagogue as the natural initial locus for communicating the message of Jesus, what did the first Christians do? On at least one occasion we read of Paul using *a lecture hall*, rather like a visiting professor (Acts 19:9)—the hall presumably hired for him or lent to him through the good offices of wealthy or influential sympathizers.

But probably he would more often have followed the normal pattern of the wandering philosopher and purveyor of new ideas by going into *the market place* to engage in discussion (but only explicitly attested in Acts 17:17). At this point we should perhaps remind ourselves that open-air preaching was in no way distinctive of the first Christians and hardly invented by them. On the contrary they might often have been confused, at least in terms of method and style, with other religious philosophers and peddlers of saving knowledge. By way of some confirmation, we might simply note that the commissioning of the twelve in Mark 6:8-11 has been shaped, presumably for the more widely ranging mission beyond Palestine, in a way which suggests that (many of) the first Christian missionaries went about in a style very similar to that of Cynic philosophers of the time (with the most minimal resources).

A third way in which Paul probably often made initial contact was through *the work place*. The point is often missed that Paul often or usually went out of

---

[12] Again, see further Dunn, *Jesus Remembered*, ch. 14, here particularly 607-11.

his way to earn his own living (e.g., 1 Thess 2:9). Consequently he must have spent a substantial part of each day or of most days working at his tent-making trade. We can probably assume that he would have engaged in evangelism through conversing with customers and casual visitors while sewing away.[13] Unfortunately we have no evidence whatsoever on the point, and any further speculation as to how he conducted himself or as to how successful such evangelism was would be entirely guesswork.

Once a group had been gathered outside the synagogue the regular meeting place was clearly *the home* of one of those involved (Acts 17:5-7; 18:7; Rom 16:5, 23; 1 Cor 16:19; Col 4:15; Phlm 2). We should not assume that this was unusual either: we know from archaeological evidence of a number of private houses containing cult meeting rooms.[14] We should also avoid thinking of such churches in terms of the larger enterprises to which history has accustomed us: the larger of typical houses of the time, even well-to-do houses, would be hard-pushed to take more than about thirty-five. When we talk about the home churches of the NT, therefore, we are almost certainly talking of small gatherings, often quite intimate in size, and no doubt often round the meal table.[15] And if we include the tenement flats in which most of the urban poor lived,[16] the meeting space was even more restricted. I do not want to be sidetracked into a discussion of the role of the home church in earliest Christianity.[17] All we need note here is that such gatherings in larger houses seem to have been very or relatively open—so that the unbeliever or uninstructed was able to enter while they were engaged in worship (1 Cor 14:23-25). We may perhaps envisage the sort of house we know of from Ostia Antica or Pompeii in Italy, with the outer street door left open to allow the sounds of worship to attract the curious or interested in from the street. But probably the more frequent case was of members of the group bringing friends, visitors, etc. to one of the gatherings. That in turn, of course, implies a degree of involvement of individual believers in wider social activity and relationships,

---

[13] This was the important suggestion of R. F. Hock, *The Social Context of Paul's Ministry: Tentmaking and Apostleship* (Philadelphia: Fortress, 1980). See further Dunn, *Beginning from Jerusalem*, 563-66.

[14] See also S. K. Stowers, "Social Status, Public Speaking and Private Teaching: The Circumstances of Paul's Preaching Activity," *NovT* 26 (1984): 59-82 (particularly 64-73).

[15] See further Dunn, *Beginning from Jerusalem*, 601-608.

[16] For some years R. Jewett has urged us to recognize that the more realistic term for early Christian gatherings is "tenement churches" rather than "house churches"; see his "Tenement Churches and Communal Meals in the Early Church," *BR* 38 (1993): 23-43; also *Romans* (Hermeneia; Minneapolis: Fortress, 2007), 53-55, 64-66.

[17] The contribution of R. J. Banks, *Paul's Idea of Community* (Exeter: Paternoster, 1980) retains its importance. See also D. G. Horrell, "Domestic Space and Christian Meetings in Corinth: Imagining New Contexts and the Buildings East of the Theatre," *NTS* 50 (2004): 349-69.

so that they would have friends and contacts in trade, etc. Which raises in turn questions about social involvement such as those posed in 1 Cor 10:14-30. The more enduring point so far as method in evangelism is concerned is presumably the effectiveness of the small group in a private home or tenement flat into which others can venture or be brought to find both acceptance and a life-changing message.

Nor should we forget the importance of *relationships within families*, particularly in split families, where only one member of the family had been converted. Through faithful commitment, and not necessarily by spoken word, both Paul and 1 Peter hold out the hope that the unbelieving partner will yet be converted (1 Cor 7:16; 1 Pet 3:1). Such relationships (only one partner converted, almost always the wife—conversion of the *pater familias* would typically carry the rest of the household with him) were evidently characteristic of Christianity from the first.

Finally we may draw an inference from such counsel as Paul gives in Rom 12:14–13:10—namely, that Paul would not be unmindful of the missionary effect of *good neighborliness, good citizenship*, and readiness to return good for evil, in short, of the evangelistic effect of a good life.[18] Similarly with the advice to one of the largest social groups who formed part of the earliest Christian congregations—slaves (slavery not yet being thought of as immoral, simply as the lowest social status of the time). The counsel is simply that they should do the best job they could, not just to please their masters, but as serving Christ and as following his example (Eph 6:5-6; Col 3:22; 1 Pet 2:18-21). In 1 Peter in particular, it should be noted, such counsel is tied into readiness to give defense of one's hope when challenged (1 Pet 3:15-16). In all this, as with Jesus, the message spoken could not be separated from the character of the whole life. May we not assume that the unusualness of returning blessing for persecution (Rom 12:14; 1 Pet 3:9), of maintaining good behavior under stress and unjust abuse (1 Pet 3:16-17), of uncomplaining acceptance of harsh taxation (Rom 13:1-7—Rome was no democracy!), of loving the neighbor as oneself (Rom 13:8-10; Jas 2:8), drew the attention of many to these Christians, winning first respect and admiration, and then faith in their Christ?

To sum up. The picture which emerges is surprisingly straightforward. We see the missionaries using the normal means of the time to spread their message—in synagogue and lecture hall, when available, in market place and at work bench, and most of all at home and round the meal table. We see ordinary Christians in the everyday encounters of business, market place and friendship, slaves in large households, wives with their unbelieving husbands, not necessarily going out of their way to bear testimony to their faith, but by the quality of their lives occasioning comment, and ready to invite the inquirer to come with them to the next meeting in the home of hosts like Priscilla and

---

[18] See further my *The Theology of Paul the Apostle* (Grand Rapids: Eerdmans; Edinburgh: T&T Clark, 1998), 674-80.

Aquila. By such means Christianity evidently spread and established itself in many urban centers with surprising rapidity.

WHAT? WHAT WAS THE CONTENT OF EVANGELISM?

Here we will have to narrow the question right down. There is space to deal only with the spoken word of evangelism. What the content of evangelism by means of lived relationships would have been has been hinted at in earlier reference to lifestyle and daily life. But to deal with it adequately would involve a larger discussion of several large topics which have traditionally fallen under such heads as justification, sanctification, and personal and social ethics. Nor do I intend here to go into the question of the subject matter of the gospel. Discussion of whether there was a regular kerygmatic outline within the first churches, evidenced still in Acts and Paul, has been around since the topic was opened up so effectively by C. H. Dodd over sixty years ago.[19] I will not rehash the debate and simply assume that the content of the gospel is another topic for another day.[20]

What seems more appropriate for a discussion of method is content in the sense of the *forms* in which the gospel was presented. Or perhaps to prevent confusion we should avoid the word "content" and speak rather of the "packaging," of the *medium* rather than the message itself. Since we are dealing only with the spoken and written word let me focus my attention simply on the adaptability and diversity of the gospel in its different forms in the NT.

In the case of Jesus himself, it is clear that the most distinctive form of his teaching was that of the parable. Much of the rest of his preaching as remembered in the Synoptic Gospels is in the more familiar style of prophet or wisdom teacher. And parables as such are not unique to Jesus. But the number of parables attributed to Jesus marks him out. Parables were remembered as particularly characteristic of his preaching and teaching.[21]

All I want to note here are two of the important features of these parables. First, the way in which they were designed to gain attention and assent by telling a story with familiar figures and features with which an audience could easily identify. And second, the way the stories so often have an unexpected twist, a surprising turn which invites if not requires a response from the audience. Having been drawn into the story, the listener finds that the

---

[19] C. H. Dodd, *The Apostolic Preaching and its Developments* (London: Hodder & Stoughton, 1936, 1944).

[20] I attempt a sketch of the typical emphases of Paul's evangelistic preaching, so far as they can be deduced from his letters—*Beginning from Jerusalem*, 572-87, with further bibliography.

[21] For up-to-date discussion and full bibliography I need only refer to K. R. Snodgrass, *Stories with Intent: A Comprehensive Guide to the Parables of Jesus* (Grand Rapids: Eerdmans, 2008).

surprising turn of events forces him or her to look at familiar ideas about God and about human responsibility in a new light. This power of the parable to engage the listener made them probably one of the most powerful means of communication that the world has known. To put it another way, the parable does not communicate information directly, since it is a story which requires some interpretation. It communicates because it engages the listener. The story has a message, but what the message is depends on the hearer's response.[22]

If there is anything in all this it would suggest that fuller thought needs to be given to the parable as a model of effective communication. Here we may simply note the degree to which Jesus' mode of teaching was geared to his audience and used the data of their own everyday experience to communicate a message with radical challenge.

I turn next to the Gospels themselves. We should never forget that these documents are called "gospels" because each was understood from the first to contain the gospel, or more precisely, to be a form of the gospel of Jesus Christ (Mark 1:1). Whatever else they are, and whatever other function they were intended to serve, they were also tools of evangelism, means of spreading further the good news of Jesus. Here all I want to do is to draw attention to the different ways in which they present Christ. One can see the point clearly enough even with the Synoptics. With regard to the main bulk of Matthew, Mark and Luke, their accounts of the ministry of Jesus, the substance is very much the same. But the slant is significantly different.

Effective examples here really need the assistance of a synopsis, setting out the canonical Gospels in parallel. But the most obvious case in point is the different presentations of Jesus in his relation to the law by Mark and Matthew. Mark depicts Jesus as significantly free-er with regard to such a fundamental law as the laws of clean and unclean. "Nothing from outside a man by entering into him is able to render him impure . . . thus pronouncing all foods clean" (Mark 7:15, 18-19). According to Mark Jesus annulled the whole sequence of laws on clean and unclean foods, so important in determining the possibilities and limits of social intercourse. In Matthew, however, the equivalent teaching is significantly more restrained: Jesus posing a contrast which need mean little more than pointing out with prophetic emphasis that inner purity is more important than ritual purity, with no suggestion whatsoever that the laws on clean and unclean foods have been abrogated (Matt 15:11, 17-20). The emphasis clearly ties in with the distinctive Matthean record of Jesus declaring that the law continues in force even for those belonging to the kingdom of heaven (Matt 5:17-20)—an emphasis, in turn, quite lacking in Mark.

The most obvious explanation for such variation in the presentation of Jesus is that each Evangelist had in view different audiences. Matthew was probably

---

[22] Parables are the best illustration of the overstated postmodern hermeneutical principle that meaning is created by the act of hearing/reading and not (just) by the speaker/author.

writing for Christian congregations in areas where Jewish numbers and influence were still strong; so he emphasizes the continuity between Jesus' message and the law. Mark was writing more with the churches of the Gentile mission in view; so he emphasizes the degree of *dis*continuity between Jesus' teaching and the law. Here, in other words, is a clear example of the way in which the situation addressed helped shape the gospel being presented. There was sufficient flexibility among the Christian churches on a rather contentious subject for the *same* gospel to be presented with such *different* emphases. Perhaps we should add that it is only when these different contexts are ignored that such differences begin to appear as contradictions. Futile disputes on that issue (possible contradictions between the Gospels) can be prevented, or resolved, only by a proper appreciation of the flexibility within the sacred tradition itself and of its consequent adaptability to different situations.[23]

More challenging is the contrast between the Synoptic Gospels and John's gospel in their respective portrayals of Jesus' teaching. It is impossible to ignore these differences, even though many do in fact simply interweave Synoptic and Johannine tradition in their presentations of Jesus' message, without apparently recognizing their different character. This is all the more important for our subject, since of all four Gospels John is the most explicit in his evangelistic intent (20:31). But who is this Jesus whom he presents? A Jesus who speaks of himself as the Son of Man who has descended from heaven (3:13; 6:62). A Jesus who constantly speaks of himself as the one sent by the Father (4:34; 5:23, 37; 6:44; etc). A Jesus who uses the divine "I am" formula to make a series of stunning claims for himself (6:35, 48; 8:12, 23-24, 58; etc). At none of these points do we find a matching tradition in the Synoptic tradition. Frankly I find it impossible to see in these consistent Johannine emphases anything like a strictly historical portrayal of Jesus (please note I am not talking about the historical value of John's Gospel as a whole, which is substantial, only of the characteristic features of his portrayal of Jesus' teaching just noted). It seems to me to put far too great a strain on credulity to argue that such emphases were part of the common memory of the first Christians, widely remembered as running through the whole gamut of his teaching, to Galilean crowd, to Jerusalem intelligentsia, as well as to his disciples, but that all three of the other Evangelists ignored them completely, and only John thought fit to

---

[23] This emphasis on the inherent variability of even key gospel truth or Jesus tradition has been a repeated theme of my writing, starting with *Unity and Diversity in the New Testament* (London: SCM, 1977; 3d ed. 2006), and more recently with *Jesus Remembered*; also "Altering the Default Setting: Re-envisaging the Early Transmission of the Jesus Tradition," *NTS* 49 (2003): 139-75; also *The Living Word* (2d ed.; Minneapolis: Fortress, 2009), ch. 10. In so arguing I do not dispute with Howard that despite the diversity of the NT documents "a synthetic New Testament theology is a real possibility" (*New Testament Theology*, 726), though I do want to emphasize the "theologizing" dimension of NT theology; I refer to my *New Testament Theology: An Introduction* (Nashville: Abingdon, 2009).

pick them up.

In fact it is probably a mistake to let the issue come down to a question about the historical value of these peculiarly Johannine traditions. For that is most likely to mistake John's own intention. The evidence strongly suggests that John's own intention was to portray Jesus in the light of the fuller reflection which John himself or those with him also had devoted to the common memory of Jesus, so that his portrayal amounts in effect to an extended meditation on typical miracles and sayings of Jesus, designed to bring out the full significance of Jesus as they now saw it to be. If the Synoptic Gospels can be likened to traditional portraits, John's Gospel is more like an impressionistic portrait. John, in other words, probably did not intend to provide a straightforward historical picture of Jesus, but to provide a dramatic presentation of the challenge of the truth of Jesus, quite different in character from the portrayals of his predecessors.

The reason for the differences is probably, once again, in part at least, that John was addressing a different audience.[24] An audience whose concern was to gain insight to the mysteries of heaven, the true knowledge of God, who were looking for some prophetic figure who had been taken into the heavenly counsels or who had even been taken to heaven itself, like several heroic figures in contemporary Jewish speculation (hence the emphases of passages like 3:13, 6:46 and 14:9). John's claim boils down to the assertion that Jesus is not one such, who starts from below and is then taken to heaven. His starting point is heaven itself, as incarnating the Word of God, as embodying the self-revelation of God himself. To proclaim such a gospel, traditions such as we find in the Synoptics are largely inadequate. It requires a fuller portrayal, which draws out the more profound truth of Jesus in terms which speak to these concerns. In fact there evidently was some risk attached to John's presentation, since it seems to have resulted in a split in the congregations for which he wrote (1 John 2:19), and subsequently John was almost taken over by the Gnostics! But in the event and in the end his Gospel was received as an acceptable and canonically important expression of the gospel.

The point then is to note a further example of the *diversity* in presenting the gospel within the NT itself. The point is important.[25] For if I am right, then simply to mesh Synoptic Jesus and Johannine Jesus into a composite and uniform historical whole is not to respect the Gospels, but to do them and the gospel a disservice. To homogenize the gospel into a single undifferentiated form is to lose the very adaptability which enabled the first Christians to speak the gospel to a widely diverse range of concerns and people, the very

---

[24] I may refer again simply to Dunn, *The Partings of the Ways*, 287-300, with further bibliography.

[25] See also my "John and the Synoptics as a Theological Question," in *Exploring the Gospel of John in Honor of D. Moody Smith* (ed. R. A. Culpepper and C. C. Black; Louisville: Westminster/John Knox, 1996), 301-13.

adaptability which led the Church of the earliest centuries to recognize *four* Gospels and not just one Gospel as canonical. To recognize the extent to which the situation addressed determined the shape of the gospel within the NT underlines the importance of framing the gospel today to take account of contemporary concerns and situations. To recognize that John was not attempting a straightforwardly historical portrayal of Jesus underlines the value, and dangers, of allowing a fair degree of artistic license in the portrayal of Jesus today.

A final example of the different forms of the gospel within earliest Christianity is the basic disagreement which we find on some fundamental points between the Jewish and the Gentile mission. There was certainly formal agreement on the basic outline of the gospel (1 Cor 15:1-11; Gal 2:1-10). But beyond that we find some very vigorous disagreement. Paul speaks of "a different gospel," "another Jesus," "a different Spirit" (2 Cor 11:4; Gal 1:6). But those being criticized were Christian missionaries; in Corinth certainly they regarded themselves as "apostles of Christ" and were accepted as such, probably commissioned from Palestine. And they in turn probably believed strongly that Paul's gospel was wrong, that he was going too far in opening the gospel to the Gentiles.[26]

In other words, there was every bit as vigorous disagreement about evangelism and the acceptability of different ways of preaching the gospel as we find today. The question of circumcision was bound up with the issue of scriptural authority, since Gen 17:9-14 is so clear that circumcision is an everlasting obligation on the people of God. The questions of food laws and holy days (Rom 14) were no small issues. They involved the whole self-understanding of the Christian community: was the covenant law still binding on those who counted themselves members of the covenant people? And they involved the whole issue of lifestyle: to what extent could believers mix socially with unbelievers? It is not surprising then to find Paul and James at some odds on the issue of faith and works—James indeed seeming to go out of his way to counter a typically Pauline argument, that belief in God as one leads to the inevitable corollary that faith alone is the sole means of justification, as attested by Gen 15:6 (cf. Rom 3:28–4:3 with James 2:18-24).[27]

All this is again simply to make and extend the same points. There was no single or uniform means of presenting the gospel in the earliest days of Christianity.[28] There were disputes on how the gospel should be presented and on the lifestyle necessarily consequent upon the gospel; different opinions were evidently held in good faith on both sides. The form and emphases with which the gospel message was proclaimed inevitably reflected something of the different contexts within which and to which they were proclaimed. As others

---

[26] See also Phil 1:15-18.

[27] See further Dunn, *Beginning from Jerusalem*, 1141-45.

[28] See again Dunn, *Unity and Diversity in the New Testament*, ch. 2.

wiser than I have long ago noted: for the gospel to remain the same it must change. Even where human need is basically the same, different languages and cultures will require that the same gospel speaks with different accents and tones. And where human need takes diverse forms the gospel would not be the gospel presented to us in the NT if it did not speak with different force and emphases to these different needs.

Of course there is a danger in saying that the gospel must change, a risk of changing the gospel itself. But that is a risk which must be taken. To insist on an unchanging gospel, in form and emphasis as well as content, may help increase one's own sense of security; but it will also ensure that the gospel cannot be heard by others and that it is all too easily dismissed as a fossilized relic of an older age. Nor do I pretend that the distinction between form, emphasis and content is always easy to draw; it is not. Here we must look to the body of Christ to sustain both the unity and the proper diversity of the gospel. But that is to open up further dimensions of the subject, which can hardly be gone into now.

CONCLUSION

This paper has not provided a complete picture of earliest Christian evangelistic method by any means, but it does highlight a number of important themes worth underlining.

  a. Christianity began as a renewal movement within Judaism and within the structures of Judaism. That formative period of Christianity remains formative for Christianity's self-understanding and its understanding of mission.

  b. The gospel was not merely about "soul-salvation," far less about escape from bodily life in this world. It had in view the whole person and the wholeness of life.

  c. So too evangelism was an every day affair: its context was consistently the home, the meal table, a matter of hospitality; also the work place and the market place.

  d. The gospel was never fixed; it was always adaptable. It was not monolithic, uniform or requiring the same emphasis and words in all situations; it was diverse and adaptable to many different situations.

In all these cases there is considerable food for thought about the where, how, and what of modern evangelism.

2

FREEDOM FROM THE LAW ONLY FOR GENTILES? A NON-SUPERSESSIONIST ALTERNATIVE TO MARK KINZER'S "POSTMISSIONARY MESSIANIC JUDAISM"

Craig L. Blomberg

It was during my initial visit to Israel in 1986 with a British Christian tour group while my wife and I were living in Cambridge that I first encountered two self-identified evangelical Christians promoting what I came to learn was sometimes called the two-covenants theory. On one occasion at one of the tourist sites, the conversation turned to the spiritual condition of contemporary Jews who did not follow Jesus. The two English pastors leading our group, one charismatic and one Anglican, explained that they believed Jewish individuals could be "saved" even while rejecting Christ. Their logic proceeded as follows: If Jews under the Mosaic covenant were right with God before Jesus' ministry, did the cross put them out? It was a way of posing the question I had never heard before. After giving it some thought, I chimed in and pointed out that the Bible never claims that all Jews of *any* era were right with God; indeed, sadly, the Hebrew Scriptures point out that more often than not there was only a righteous remnant. Presumably, therefore, whichever Jews truly were in a faithful covenant relationship with God at the time of Jesus were those who became his followers. Those who rejected him showed that they had not truly understood God's way or his word. The pastors had no reply to this response and changed the topic.

In 2005, Rabbi Mark S. Kinzer, president of the messianic Jewish Theological Institute, the leadership-training center for the Union of Messianic Jewish Congregations, chair of its theology department, and an adjunct professor of Jewish studies at Fuller Seminary, wrote a three-hundred page book entitled *Postmissionary Messianic Judaism: Redefining Christian Engagement with the Jewish People*.[1] In his commendatory blurb on the back cover, Richard Mouw, president of Fuller Seminary, declares,

> This is a breakthrough study for all who care about Jewish-Christian relationships. Mark Kinzer makes a convincing case for seeing those relationships in a state of schism that desperately needs to be healed. He also offers refreshing clarity for those of us who have not been able to decide until now how to approach the supersessionist issue.

---

[1] Mark S. Kinzer, *Postmissionary Messianic Judaism: Redefining Christian Engagement with the Jewish People* (Grand Rapids: Brazos, 2005).

Until the last decade or so, the two-covenants perspective has hovered around the fringes of the organizations of Messianic congregations throughout the world, but today it is common enough that it is dividing the Jewish-Christian movement down the middle. Is it a viable approach for twenty-first century mission to Jewish people?

I strongly agree with Mouw about the relationships between both non-Christian and Christian Jews and between Jewish and Gentile Christians being in states of schism that desperately need healing. I strongly disagree with him that Kinzer offers refreshing clarity in approaching the supersessionist issue. In fact, I find Kinzer's actual exegesis of NT texts consistently quite unconvincing. Although Kinzer never refers to his view as a form of the two-covenant theory, it is precisely that—very sophisticated, intricate and subtle, and it deserves serious engagement by the world of NT scholarship. In the rest of this paper, I would like to take a few initial steps toward that engagement.

KINZER'S THESIS

Kinzer's thesis, which he repeats verbatim in italics eight times in his book, is that the church must adopt "a bilateral ecclesiology in solidarity with Israel that affirms Israel's covenant, Torah, and religious tradition."[2] Kinzer strongly believes that the Mosaic covenant, at least as reflected in the distinctive ritual laws of Judaism that do not require a functioning temple in Jerusalem, and interpreted by means of post-Christian rabbinic Judaism, remains obligatory for Jewish believers in Jesus. This means not merely an individual Jewish believer being circumcised (if male), keeping a kosher table, worshipping on the Sabbath according to ancestral traditions, observing the annual festivals and the like, but doing so in the context of an ordered community that represents Judaism in its fullest, most complete form to the world. Because this cannot be done in a mixed gathering of Jews and Gentiles worshipping in one of the many contemporary forms adopted by the primarily Gentile Christian churches of the world, Messianic congregations must be formed to preserve the traditional covenantal obligations of Jews, even as every aspect of corporate Jewish life is (re-)interpreted in light of what Jesus has done. Gentile-Christian congregations must then be in solidarity with Jewish-Christian ones, presumably through some combination of Gentiles who actually attach themselves to Messianic congregations and churches that cooperate closely with, learn from, and support those congregations, although Kinzer never actually spells out what his desired solidarity would look like in any detail.

Thus far, the only major difference between Kinzer's thesis and what seems to have been the majority viewpoint of Messianic Judaism, at least during the twentieth century, is his emphasis that Mosaic-covenant keeping for Jewish

---

[2] Kinzer, *Postmissionary Messianic Judaism*, 24, 264, 265, 299, 300, 302, 307, 309-10.

believers is "obligatory."³ Again, Kinzer never defines this term. He acknowledges that there may be times and places where Jews come to believe in Jesus but without any Messianic congregations anywhere nearby to whom they can attach themselves, and so they must worship in Gentile churches as a less than ideal scenario. So presumably he cannot think that law-keeping is a requirement for their salvation. But it does appear that he thinks that the Jew who wants to obey God as much as possible will recognize such law-keeping, as Kinzer has defined it, as mandatory and not optional. Most Messianic Jews, on the other hand, have seen Torah-obedience as an evangelistic strategy to make their form of Christianity more palatable to unsaved Jews and therefore, like Paul in 1 Corinthians 9:19-23, to be all things to all people, so as by all possible means to win some to faith in Jesus.⁴ Many individual Jewish believers have gone one step further by adding that it feels very appropriate and natural for them to engage in Torah-observance beyond whatever missions-enhancing effect it may have. Some have sensed a personal calling from the Lord to remain Torah-observant.⁵ Both of these steps seem fully in sync with the NT. But to maintain that *all* Jewish believers *must* keep these laws and do so in the specific forms mediated to the contemporary world through post-Christian rabbinic tradition appears to fly in the face of the fundamental and pervasive NT teaching about freedom from the law.⁶ How then does Kinzer attempt to bolster his claims exegetically?

To begin with, Kinzer is fully aware of the iconoclastic nature of his proposals. Early in his introduction, he refers to his position as "a previously unrecognized New Testament mandate."⁷ Without suggesting that God's Spirit can *never* lead one of his people into new truth that the entire history of the church has previously missed, I would insist that this admission should raise some very reddish-orange flags, if not quite the full-fledged red flag that would alert people to stop in their tracks altogether. The primary reason Kinzer believes he must pursue this line of reasoning is because he thinks it is the only way to maintain two other demonstrably central NT teachings without contradiction: (1) "the mediation of Jesus in all of God's creative, revelatory,

---

³ Kinzer, *Postmissionary Messianic Judaism*, 95.
⁴ E.g., David H. Stern, *Messianic Judaism: A Modern Movement with an Ancient Past* (rev. ed.; Clarksville, Md.: Messianic Jewish Publishers, 2007), 242.
⁵ Jeffrey S. Wasserman (*Messianic Jewish Congregations: Who Sold This Business to the Gentiles?* [Lanham, Md.: University Press of America, 2000], 61) lists as representatives of this view Joseph "Rabinowitz, the former Hebrew Christian Alliance, Jews for Jesus, Arnold Fruchtenbaum, and the majority of Messianic congregations in Israel."
⁶ Wasserman (*Messianic Jewish Congregations*, 61-62) includes Michael Schiffman, Dan Juster and John Fischer among those who at least come close to saying that Jewish believers must keep the written Torah wherever possible, except for the sacrifices, while placing the rabbinic halakah into a much more non-binding category.
⁷ Kinzer, *Postmissionary Messianic Judaism*, 25.

reconciling, and redemptive activity, and (2) the church's participation through Jesus in Israel's covenantal privileges."[8] What Kinzer fails to grapple with adequately, however, are those numerous NT teachings that demonstrate the extent of change in God's economy with his people precisely due to Jesus' mediation in history, so that participating in Israel's covenantal privileges does not *require* even *Jewish* believers to obey the ritual law, even though they certainly may *choose* to do so.[9]

Kinzer likewise realizes that my response will be that of many readers based on the most common and straightforward exegesis of many NT passages. So before he offers his alternative exegeses, he discusses important preliminary presuppositional issues. Specifically, he calls for a "hermeneutics of ethical accountability," which he describes as follows: "The *theoretical* truths that the Bible conveys about . . . God are thus inextricably bound to the *practical* precepts whose purpose is to form the character of God in the people of God."[10] What this apparently means for Kinzer, in light of the tragic history of professing Gentile Christians' behavior toward Jews throughout church history, is that the ethical interpretation of any text of Scripture is that which not only avoids anti-Semitism but promotes views of Judaism, including non-Christian and post-Christian rabbinic forms of Judaism, that are as positive as possible. If there is even the slightest chance that a certain exegesis of a given text is correct and it simultaneously fosters good will among all observant Jews, Christian or not, then it is to be preferred to alternative interpretations.

One can certainly sympathize with Kinzer's well-motivated desire to avoid causing any further unnecessary heartache in relationships between followers of Jesus, Jew or Gentile, and the larger, parent body of Judaism. While Kinzer does not advocate his approach for the sake of missions (hence the "postmissionary" label for his approach), by the end of the volume he does concede there is the need for a far more chastened, courteous, and dialogical form of witness, particularly by Jewish believers, to the rest of the Jewish world, but apparently not before adopting the viewpoints that the rest of the book develops. He also appears to affirm that faithful, practicing, orthodox Jews throughout history may well be saved even apart from such witness, though he never comes out and says so in so many words. His logic here is that if Paul argues in Rom 11 that Jewish disbelief in Jesus was and is a prerequisite for the gospel go to the Gentiles, which in turn would stimulate jealousy and faith on the part of Jews, then Jewish rejection of Jesus was actually God's sovereign means for accomplishing the salvation of his people and therefore he

---

[8] Kinzer, *Postmissionary Messianic Judaism*, 12.
[9] See the excellent, detailed survey of "The Law and Salvation History," in Thomas R. Schreiner, *New Testament Theology: Magnifying God in Christ* (Grand Rapids: Baker, 2008), 617-72.
[10] Kinzer, *Postmissionary Messianic Judaism*, 33.

must be intending to save those who so fit into his plan.[11] This reasoning, unfortunately, misses the major swath of teaching, even in the Hebrew Scriptures, that God works through the disobedience of his people and even through the actions of unbelieving Gentiles to accomplish his sovereign purposes without ever failing to hold those who are faithless or disobedient accountable for their actions.[12]

As for Kinzer's hermeneutic of ethical accountability, certainly any viable interpretation of a NT text that avoids the impression of anti-Semitism should be preferred, because Jesus the Jew by definition could not have been anti-Semitic, and nothing in the NT is as pejorative or sweeping in its criticism of *certain* Israelites as the prophets in the Hebrew Scriptures are.[13] But that very phenomenon—the frequent prophetic indictment of *some* Israelites and, on occasion, a substantial majority of the nation—makes it invalid to assume that we should automatically look for the interpretation of a given NT passage that is the most positive toward Judaism in the first century. Indeed, given Jesus' consistent conflicts with various Jewish leaders, not over written Torah, but over Pharisaic halakah (the oral law or "traditions of the ancestors"), it seems inherently unlikely that we can diminish Jesus' concerns to merely combating one interpretive tradition within the halakah, as Kinzer affirms.[14] Furthermore, what may appear to be the most "ethical" in the sense of supportive of Jewish people today is not necessarily the most "ethical" in the sense of supporting other nationalities of Christians. Surely the whole vexed question of how to relate to Palestinian Christians in Israel will not be solved "ethically" by adjudicating in favor of Jews against the Palestinians on every issue without exception.[15]

The other presuppositional move that Kinzer makes early on in his work is to explain that he is not going to start with NT teachings about Torah in general, as most people do. Instead, following in good Jewish tradition that values praxis at least as much as theory, he will begin with those passages that

---

[11] See Kinzer, *Postmissionary Messianic Judaism*, esp. 223-26.

[12] Cf., e.g., D. A. Carson, *Divine Sovereignty and Human Responsibility: Biblical Perspectives in Tension* (London: Marshall, Morgan & Scott; Atlanta: John Knox, 1981; repr., Eugene, Oreg.: Wipf & Stock, 2002), 9-38.

[13] Contra the charges of anti-Semitism in the NT in general, see esp. Craig A. Evans and Donald A. Hagner, eds., *Anti-Semitism and Early Christianity: Issues of Polemic and Faith* (Minneapolis: Fortress, 1993).

[14] Sometimes Jesus appears to side more with one of the leadership parties in Israel, sometimes more with another. Sometimes he appears more Hillelite, sometimes more Shammaite, and sometimes he goes a third way altogether. See esp. Samuel T. Lachs, *A Rabbinic Commentary on the New Testament: The Gospels of Matthew, Mark and Luke* (Hoboken, N.J.: KTAV, 1987).

[15] Very helpful and balanced in this task are the writings of Gary M. Burge on the subject. Most recently, see his *Jesus and the Land: The New Testament Challenge to "Holy Land" Theology* (Grand Rapids: Baker, 2010).

actually describe Jesus or the apostles and their behavior in the first century. Fair enough. But what actually happens is that Kinzer never gets around to dealing with some of the NT texts that most clearly introduce a major change in salvation history via the death, resurrection and ascension of Jesus—not a word about Rom 10:4 on Christ as the end of the law, or about 2 Cor 3:11 on the Mosaic covenant as transitory, or about Gal 4:21-31 on who are the true spiritual descendants of Abraham by Sarah, or about Heb 8:13 on the new covenant making the first one "obsolete" and about to disappear. Nor does he ever address the most explicit text in the NT on the status of the ritual law after the coming of Jesus—Col 2:16-17: "Do not let anyone judge you by what you eat or drink, or with regard to a religious festival, a New Moon celebration or a Sabbath day. These are a shadow of the things that were to come; the reality, however, is found in Christ."[16]

The second major problem with focusing predominantly on what Jesus and his followers did rather than what they taught in the first generation of Christianity is that Kinzer bypasses altogether the key hermeneutical question of what is descriptive versus what is prescriptive. Of course, there was no town herald who arrived in the temple precincts the day after Pentecost announcing, "Ritual Law Fulfilled in Jesus: Torah Observance Now Optional"! The first believers, all Jewish, would naturally have continued to follow the ritual laws. It would have dawned on different individuals and groups at different times in different places what the full significance of the fulfillment of the Tanak meant for their new loyalties. So Kinzer's detailed rehearsal of all the places in the Gospels and Acts where Jesus and his followers kept the law really proves irrelevant to his thesis unless there are narrative clues in those contexts to help us understand why they did so.[17]

KINZER'S EXEGESIS

Kinzer does, nevertheless, engage in detailed exegesis of at least some prescriptive texts as well—texts that have usually been understood as doing away with the ritual law, at least in terms of its need to be literally implemented in the same fashion as under the Mosaic covenant, whether by Gentiles or by Jews. It is these texts to which we must now turn.

The first main text Kinzer addresses is Mark 7:19b, Mark's parenthetical aside after Jesus' teaching about how it was not what went into a person but what came out of one that was defiling. All major, current English translations render this as, "In saying this, he declared all foods clean," or some semantic

---

[16] All English quotations of the Bible are taken from Today's New International Version.
[17] See further Craig L. Blomberg, "The Christian and the Law of Moses," in *Witness to the Gospel: The Theology of Acts* (ed. I. Howard Marshall and David Peterson; Grand Rapids: Eerdmans, 1998), 397-416.

equivalent to that sentence. A woodenly literal translation would be "cleansing all foods." Kinzer argues that if this were Jesus' intention then there is no explanation for the continued observance of the dietary laws by Jewish followers of Jesus or for Peter needing to have the heavenly revelation and command to eat unclean food in Acts 10. But Kinzer never entertains the standard resolution of this tension, namely, that v. 19b reflects Mark's understanding at the time he wrote his Gospel, no earlier than the 60s, more than thirty years after Jesus' death. Mark is not claiming that anyone present when Jesus spoke these words understood their full significance, nor that Jesus could have meant, while the Mosaic covenant was still in effect, before his death and resurrection and sending of the Spirit, that Jews could stop observing the kosher laws.[18] All this would indeed come later, but it *would come* during the first Christian generation.[19]

Kinzer's second move, though, is to argue that even by Mark's time, Mark understood this freedom to eat ritually impure food as applying only to Gentiles.[20] His only support for this assertion, however, is that the explanations of various Aramaic terms in Mark's Gospel demonstrate that Mark was writing for Gentiles. In fact, all these explanations demonstrate is that *some* in Mark's audience were Gentiles. If we actually consult what the early Church Fathers taught, then there is strong evidence that Mark was writing to *Roman* Christians, and we know from the book of Romans and the letter to the Hebrews that there were plenty of Jews in the church in Rome.[21]

Finally, Kinzer argues that even if Mark were writing to a mixed audience, declaring all foods clean doesn't necessarily mean that Jews were now permitted to eat them. Kinzer cites an anecdote in *Pesiq. Rab Kah.* 4:7 in which a Gentile is debating with Yohanan ben Zakkai about the ritual Torah. After the Gentile leaves, ben Zakkai's followers press him further on the topic, leading him to declare that an object or entity itself does not impart uncleanness but the decree of God that it is unclean imparts uncleanness. Thus Kinzer argues that

---

[18] For a plausible explanation of one way many in Jesus' audience might have understood his teaching at that time, see Yair Furstenberg, "Defilement Penetrating the Body: A New Understanding of Contamination in Mark 7.15," *NTS* 54 (2008): 176-200. John Fischer ("Messianic Congregations Should Exist and Should Be Very Jewish," in *How Jewish Is Christianity? 2 Views on the Messianic Movement* [ed. Louis Goldberg; Grand Rapids: Zondervan, 2003], 133) asserts that the AV "makes abundantly clear" that what Mark 7:19b actually means is that what one eats "goeth out into the draught, purging all meats." But the "draught" or toilet (ἀφεδρῶνα) cannot be the subject of the participle καθαρίζων, because the former is accusative and the latter is nominative.

[19] Cf., e.g., Adela Y. Collins, *Mark* (Hermeneia; Minneapolis: Fortress, 2007), 356; Robert H. Stein, *Mark* (BECNT; Grand Rapids: Baker, 2008), 345-46.

[20] Cf. also David J. Rudolph, "Jesus and the Food Laws: A Reassessment of Mark 7:19b," *EvQ* 74 (2002): 291-311.

[21] See esp. B. J. Incigneri, *The Gospel to the Romans: The Setting and Rhetoric of Mark's Gospel* (Leiden: Brill, 2003).

Jesus could have declared the food clean even without revoking God's decree that Jews should not eat it. In a different context, this makes fine sense, but not in Mark. Mark inserts the explanatory aside to comment on Jesus' teaching that it is not what goes into but what comes out of a person that is defiling. The contrast is not between an entity and God but between two kinds of entities. If saying that something does not defile does not imply permission to have contact with it, then to be consistent Kinzer would have to say that saying that something *does* defile does not imply a prohibition against *having* contact with it. Then it would still be permissible, even if defiling, to have "evil thoughts, sexual immorality, theft, murder, adultery, greed, malice, deceit, lewdness, envy, slander, arrogance and folly" (vv. 21-22), which of course is patent nonsense.

What then of Acts 10 and Peter's vision of a sheet descending from heaven with both clean and unclean animals and the thrice-repeated heavenly voice commanding him to rise, kill and eat? Here Kinzer correctly observes that Peter does not explicitly deduce from his experience that God has purified all food but rather purified all people, thus making it appropriate for him to meet with Cornelius, the Gentile centurion (v. 28). This leads to his entering their house, preaching the gospel, seeing them respond positively to it, and staying with Cornelius and his household "for a few days" (v. 48). Such hospitality would, of course, have required Cornelius' family to provide meals for Peter. But, instead of taking the typical tack of arguing that it was precisely because Peter understood God to be cleansing all foods that made him willing to associate with Cornelius in this fashion,[22] Kinzer argues that the clean and unclean animals in Peter's vision symbolize Jews and Gentiles, respectively. Thus Peter could have deduced, as it were, that all people were clean *without* coming to the conclusion that all food was clean. But, in context, is this interpretation at all plausible? If the animals directly represent people, is God then telling Peter, to rise, kill and eat people? Surely not! Why, moreover, would Paul later in Galatians oppose Peter when he stopped *eating* with Gentile Christians in Syrian Antioch because he was afraid of "the circumcision group" (Gal 2:11-12)? Why would Paul berate Peter's hypocrisy in backpedaling on his now customary lifestyle of living like a *Gentile* and not like a Jew (v. 14)? This brings us to our next major passage.

Kinzer correctly points out that "the text nowhere speaks of *what* Peter eats. Instead, it focuses on those with *whom* he eats."[23] Thus Kinzer concludes that Peter could easily have still been keeping a kosher diet even while being willing to eat with those who didn't. What Paul criticizes is Peter's

---

[22] Richard I. Pervo (*Acts* [Minneapolis: Fortress, 2009], 278) sums it up nicely: "Verses 34-35 show that Luke was interested not in *kashrut* but in barriers based on ethnocentricity." Cf. Clinton Wahlen, "Peter's Vision and Conflicting Definitions of Purity," *NTS* 51 (2005): 505-18 [515].

[23] Kinzer, *Postmissionary Messianic Judaism*, 83.

withdrawing from table fellowship altogether. This much is plausible enough. But when Kinzer tries to explain why Paul then refers to Peter having previously lived "like a Gentile" (v. 14), he has to resort to the assumption that Paul is speaking ironically, using a label that others, doubtless including the circumcision group, had applied to Peter. For them, even *some* deviation from their version of halakah could be considered living like a Gentile. This interpretation allows Kinzer to interpret Gal 2 consistently and meaningfully, but it must be said that there is nothing in the context of Peter's and Paul's exchange to suggest such irony. After all, living "like a Gentile" is in antithetical parallelism to living "like a Jew" in this verse, and there is no meaningful way to take living "like a Jew" ironically, referring to only partial obedience to Torah.[24]

What about the rest of Paul's writings? Again, one has to read Kinzer carefully, because what a superficial consideration might deem plausible falls apart on closer scrutiny. With respect to Gal 5:3, in which Paul testifies to everyone that any man who lets himself be circumcised becomes obligated to obey the entire law, Kinzer writes, "All who are circumcised are obligated to observe the Torah."[25] But that is precisely *not* what the text says! Those who *let themselves be circumcised* in Gal 5 are not Jewish babies, who have no say in the matter, but adult *Gentiles*, convinced by the circumcision group that they must be circumcised to be saved. Kinzer could actually have bolstered his argument, at least at first glance, by pointing out that the Greek perfect passive participle could yield the more woodenly literal translation, "to every man *having been circumcised* [περιτεμνομένῳ] that he is obligated to obey all the Law." But in context, Paul is arguing for Christian freedom from the law. His point is that those who become circumcised for the express purpose of agreeing with the Judaizers in Galatia that one must be circumcised to be saved are, however unwittingly, committing themselves to perfect obedience to the entire law of Moses as the means to salvation (cf. Gal 3:10), which, of course dooms them to failure and damnation. As Gordon Fee explains,

> One can add nothing to grace and still experience grace. It is like doing a special favor for someone (on the basis of "grace" alone) and then watch them try to "pay you back," which has the effect of negating the gift of grace. Grace is grace; and adding law-keeping to grace as a means of righteousness is to insult grace and thus to nullify it altogether.[26]

---

[24] Indeed, while he does not have contemporary Messianic congregations explicitly in view, the explanation of the importance of Jews and Gentiles worshiping and eating together without the past strictures of either Jew or pagan practice, by Bengt Holmberg ("Jewish *versus* Christian Identity in the Early Church?" *RB* 105 [1998]: 397-425), directly addresses several of Kinzer's points.

[25] Kinzer, *Postmissionary Messianic Judaism*, 73.

[26] Gordon D. Fee, *Galatians: Pentecostal Commentary* (Blandford Forum, Dorset: Deo, 2007), 189.

A reading alert to the larger context is similarly absent from Kinzer's conclusions concerning 1 Cor 7:18. Here Paul tells those who are circumcised followers of Jesus not to think they have to erase the marks of circumcision. Some Hellenized Jews, embarrassed by their distinctive anatomy yet eager to mingle with Gentile men in the gymnasium or bathhouses, underwent a form of surgery known as *epispasm*, involving a small skin graft to try to reconstruct an appearance of foreskin.[27] In 7:17-24, Paul is illustrating with a variety of examples that becoming a believer does not require one to make drastic changes in one's life situation, whether with respect to one's marital status or concerning one's role as slave or free, or, in this instance, whether one is circumcised or uncircumcised. Nothing in the context suggests, as Kinzer alleges, that Paul is absolutely *forbidding* Jewish believers to engage in epispasm, much less that they must commit themselves to maintain Torah-obedience in other areas of the ritual law and halakah.[28]

Most of the rest of Kinzer's treatments of specific NT texts address passages where he shows that the reigning theories of interpretation are not as watertight as they might at first seem. In some instances, he does succeed in showing plausible alternative interpretations, even if they may not be the most probable. But we do not need to discuss the rest of these, because none of them positively *advances* Kinzer's case that Messianic Jews *must* obey the entire ritual law as interpreted through rabbinic halakah. In several places, Kinzer aligns himself with mainstream biblical scholarship to show that texts often viewed as inherently anti-Semitic are nothing of the kind, and we may only applaud his emphases at these junctions. But again that is a separate matter. Before turning to a non-supersessionist alternative to Kinzer, however, we do need to look briefly at his treatment of three other key texts that help explain his passion for his perspective, despite the fragile exegetical limbs on which he ventures out in order to defend them.

The first is the Apostolic Council in Acts 15. Here Kinzer actually follows an established branch of biblical scholarship, pioneered especially by Jacob Jervell, in arguing that James' decisive voice in the council demonstrates two separate "people" within the new covenant community of the redeemed—Gentile believers, who form a "people for [God's] name" (v. 14) and the Jewish believers ("David's fallen tent"—v. 16), to whom they are linked.[29] Classic dispensationalism has similarly used this episode to stress how distinct Israel

---

[27] See esp. Robert G. Hall, "Epispasm: Circumcision in Reverse," *BRev* 8 (1992): 52-57.

[28] Despite stressing that people need not rush to change their status, Paul's overall view to each of the conditions of life itemized in 1 Cor 7:17-24, except for slavery, is rightly termed by Gregory W. Dawes ("'But If You Can Gain Your Freedom' [1 Corinthians 7:17-24]," *CBQ* 52 [1990]: 681-97 [696]) as matters of "indifference."

[29] Jacob Jervell, *Luke and the People of God: A New Look at Luke-Acts* (Minneapolis: Augsburg, 1979; repr., Eugene, Oreg.: Wipf & Stock, 2002), 41-74.

and the church are.³⁰ But Greek has no indefinite article, so λαός in v. 14 could just as easily be translated "people" as "a people." Again context proves decisive. Peter has already made it clear that *salvation* is by grace rather than law (vv. 6-11). Paul and Barnabas have then narrated the miraculous experiences that led them to take unanticipated theological liberties (v. 12). Finally, James appeals to Amos 9:11-12 for prophetic support for the perspectives just enunciated (vv. 13-18). Rebuilding "David's fallen tent," to use the words of Amos, is defined precisely as including the action of God taking people for himself from among the Gentiles (vv. 16-17). In other words, the Gentiles must form at least *part of* David's tent rather than being separate from it. David's tent must refer to Jewish and Gentile believers together. There is no support for two completely distinct peoples in this passage, as the movement begun in the late 1980s known as progressive dispensationalism is now widely acknowledging. Darrell Bock, a key spokesman for the movement, phrases it this way: "The passage declares the rebuilding of the dynasty of David, fulfilled here in Jesus' messianic arrival, along with the current inclusion of Gentiles." Again, "James argues that this Gentile inclusion is part of the plan of Davidic restoration that God through the prophets said he would do . . . So both divine events and Scripture sustain the church's inclusion of Gentiles."³¹

The second text still to be considered is Rom 9–11. Kinzer correctly observes that right at the beginning of this three-chapter unit, Paul affirms that to the Israelites belong the adoption, the glory, the covenants, the giving of the law, the worship, the promise, and so on (9:4). More literally, the Greek reads, "who are Israelites, from whom the adoption and the glory and the covenants . . ." A verb has to be supplied after "whom." A form of "to be" is the most common verb to be supplied in NT ellipses, which would yield, "Israelites of whom *are* the adoption and the glory and the covenants . . ." This could then potentially imply that these privileges remain in force for Torah-observant Jews.³² But the genitive relative pronoun could just as easily denote source or origin rather than actual possession and mean that these various spiritual privileges *come from* the Israelites. Whether or not they still possess and enjoy any or all of them then remains an open question.³³ Kinzer will have to

---

³⁰ See the discussion in Robert L. Saucy (*The Case for Progressive Dispensationalism* [Chicago: Moody, 1993], 76-80), who rejects this classic approach.
³¹ Darrell L. Bock, *Acts* (BECNT; Grand Rapids: Baker, 2007), 504.
³² As, e.g., for Robert Jewett, *Romans* (Hermeneia; Minneapolis: Fortress, 2007), 561-62.
³³ Thomas R. Schreiner (*Romans* [BECNT; Grand Rapids: Baker, 1998], 482) summarizes the contribution of vv. 4-5 to Paul's argument as follows: "Given that Israel *was* God's elect people, they *were* recipients of his special affection and care in the *past*, and they *were granted* promises of his saving righteousness for the *future*. Thus their failure to realize these saving promises [in the present] is all the more agonizing, particularly because it calls into question the faithfulness of God (v. 6a)" (italics mine).

demonstrate which of these fits Paul better from other texts in his letters and, as we have seen thus far, he has not succeeded in doing that.

Indeed, Paul has just declared in Rom 9:3 possibly the most astonishing statement by a mere mortal anywhere in Scripture: "For I could wish that I myself were cursed and cut off from Christ for the sake of my people, the people of my own race, the people of Israel." Nothing short of his horror at the prospect of the present and eternal separation of a huge number of those countrymen from God and all things good could have sparked such a self-damning desire. This one verse by itself destroys the credibility of the standard two-covenants hypothesis that sees Jews in great numbers able to be saved by faithfulness to the law even while rejecting the gospel.[34] But it also calls Kinzer's views into serious question. Given the unfortunate fact, as Paul explains in 9:31-32, that the majority of Israel failed to attain God's righteousness because they treated the law as if it were a meritorious system by which they could earn God's favor when indeed it was meant to be a way of living out a relationship with God established by faith, would he risk encouraging *Jewish* Christians (and only them) to continue to follow that same law, *as a mandatory obligation*, but expect them to excise all hints of works-righteousness in so doing? Surely the dangers would be too great that they would fall victim to the same error as their countrymen who did not follow Jesus, as indeed *many* professing Christians of every nationality have fallen victim at one time or another in church history.[35]

What then of 11:29 that speaks of God's gifts and calling as irrevocable, explicitly with reference to Israel? These clearly cannot include the gift of salvation, because v. 28 has just said that according to the gospel they are enemies. But it also adds that according to election they are beloved. Election to what? Again, context must prove decisive. Verses 25-27 have just explained that in some undescribed fashion, the general response of Jewish people at the end of this age, when the full number of Gentiles whom God knows will come to faith have done so, will be to welcome their Messiah and receive forgiveness of sins. With respect to these three verses, Kinzer's exegesis is impeccable. But this, then, must be the election Paul is describing in v. 28.[36] The gifts and calling of v. 29 would match well with the privileges described in 9:4. But none of this adds up to the notion that the Mosaic covenant is still in force for

---

[34] Kinzer's only reference to Rom 9:3 (*Postmissionary Messianic Judaism*, 123) leads him to write that in this verse, "Paul wishes that he were in a position to put his life on the line for Israel, just as Moses did." However, this fails to deal with the reality stated in this verse that Jews who do not trust Christ stand condemned.

[35] This observation holds no matter where one comes down on the various debates associated with the so-called new perspective on Paul.

[36] Cf. Douglas J. Moo, *The Epistle to the Romans* (NICNT; Grand Rapids: Eerdmans, 1996), 729-32. A corporate election for temporal blessings may well be in view also (731).

anyone, including Jewish believers.

Finally, we need to comment on Kinzer's treatment of Ephesians and particularly Eph 3. Once again, Kinzer recognizes that he is taking a minority view, though one supported by no less than Karl Barth and his son, Markus, who wrote the two-volume Anchor Bible commentary on Ephesians. Despite the recurring theme in Ephesians of reconciliation between Jew and Gentile in Jesus the Messiah and despite the dominant theme of unity between the two categories of believers, Kinzer, like the two Barths before him, accurately observes that nothing in the concepts of reconciliation or unity per se necessarily precludes separate congregations, different forms of worship, or different approaches to Torah. After all, evangelicals have regularly insisted that unity among Christians and Christian churches scarcely requires denominational mergers or institutional homogeneity. But the one verse Kinzer says nothing about, which dooms his position, is Eph 3:10. Whatever that unity looks like, in which Jew and Gentile are together members of one body, a doctrine which Paul has called the mystery not previously revealed as it now has been in Jesus (v. 6), it must be some sort of *visible* unity so that even the rulers and authorities in heavenly realms—angels and demons—will take notice.[37] This is the same concept articulated even more clearly in Jesus' so-called high-priestly prayer in John 17, that his followers' unity—not just the unity of the Twelve who were all Jewish but of all those who would come to believe because of their testimony, thus Jew and Gentile alike (v. 20)—would be seen by the world so that they would know that God sent Jesus and loved them even as he loved him (v. 23).[38] Strikingly, despite 125 references to John's Gospel in Kinzer's volume from eighteen of its twenty-one chapters, not even a passing mention to anything in John 17 appears anywhere.

Markus Barth does, however, capture the significance of the kind of unity called for here and in Eph 3. He would not have supported everything for which Kinzer argues. For in his extended comment on Eph 3:10, Barth writes, "Following this verse the church would unduly limit her task if she cared only for the souls of men or for an increase in membership. Rather she has to be a sign and proof of a change that affects the institutions and structures, patterns and spans of the bodily and spiritual, social and individual existence of all men."[39] This is a far more sweeping agenda than that which two largely

---

[37] Cf. Andrew T. Lincoln, *Paradise Now and Not Yet: Studies in the Role of the Heavenly Dimension in Paul's Thought with Special Reference to His Eschatology* (Cambridge: Cambridge University Press, 1981; repr., Grand Rapids: Baker, 1991), 154-55.

[38] Cf. Andreas Köstenberger, *John* (BECNT; Grand Rapids: Baker, 2004), 499; J. E. Staton, "A Vision of Unity—Christian Unity in the Fourth Gospel," *EvQ* 69 (1997): 291-305.

[39] Markus Barth, *Ephesians* (2 vols.; AB 34-34A; Garden City: Doubleday, 1974), 1:365. Cf. also Timothy Gombis ("Ephesians 3:2-13: Pointless Digression or Epitome of the Triumph of God in Christ?" *WTJ* 66 [2004]: 313-23), who adds that, paradoxically,

separate "peoples" (Jewish and Gentile believers), even if united invisibly in one spiritual entity called the church, can accomplish, especially if it is precisely their visible unity that is to have such profound, structural, international, and even cosmic dimensions and effects.

AN ALTERNATIVE APPROACH

What then is our way forward together? Despite my repeated sense that at key places Kinzer has profoundly misunderstood the NT, I applaud his desires to be true to his Jewish identity and roots, his outrage at the even more egregious abuses of the text committed by Gentile Christians down through the centuries in acts of violent anti-Semitism, his appreciation of numerous faith-filled features of Pharisaic and Rabbinic Judaism, his recognition that God may well save some people who trust in him as best as they understand him who have not heard the gospel or who have heard only something proclaimed as the gospel which in fact is a vicious misrepresentation of it, his understanding of divine sovereignty as working through people and forces that at one level are pitted against him, and his non-supersessionist interpretation of Rom 11:25-26 and various other NT texts.[40]

Kinzer may also be correct that at this point in history, with all that has preceded it, the best form of witness to non-Christian Jews may well be the quiet, restrained approaches and models of predominantly or exclusively Jewish followers of Jesus worshiping in traditional fashion and keeping key elements of the ritual law as mediated through rabbinic Judaism. He may also be right that for some Messianic Jews, these forms of worship and Torah-observance will prove the most meaningful. But we dare not claim that ritual and oral Torah is *mandatory* for Jewish believers based on the claim that the Mosaic covenant is still in effect. Although he insists that Jews need Jesus just as Gentiles do, and need him to complete their Jewishness, Kinzer's approach, however unwittingly, amounts to saying that Jesus died only for the sins of Gentiles and that Jews who obey Torah, not out of a desire for works-righteousness but by faith, can reject a clear, accurate, and loving presentation of the gospel and still be right with God. Yet 1 John 2:23 declares in as straightforward language as possible that "no one who denies the Son has the

---

this kind of church's very existence in the context of the suffering unleashed on it vindicates the power of God's purposes and promises.

[40] I. Howard Marshall (*New Testament Theology: Many Witnesses, One Gospel* [Leicester: InterVarsity, 2004], 454-55) explains: ". . . *supersessionism* is not the right term. God's promise to the descendants of Jacob that they would be his people has not been revoked." But, contra the two-covenants theory, "it is now made clear that it is not a matter simply of physical descent but rather of faith that recognizes that God has sent the promised Messiah, and the promise is enlarged to include non-Jews." In n. 51, Marshall suggests the label "spiritual inclusivism" for this position (455).

Father," while "whoever acknowledges the Son has the Father also." For an outstanding non-supersessionist anthology of state-of-the-art essays on the need for Jewish evangelism, with appropriate contextualized sensitivity, see now the book edited by Darrell L. Bock and Mitch Glaser, *To the Jew First: The Case for Jewish Evangelism in Scripture and History*.[41]

Is the only alternative, then, to admit that in a fallen world the best we can do is to create homogeneous congregations, not just Messianic Jewish ones but Chinese and Korean, white and black, rich and poor, suburban and urban, Baptist and Presbyterian, and so on? The church growth movement of the 1970s and 1980s positively promoted such a program. It correctly recognized that people are more likely going to feel comfortable sharing Christ with others with whom they have a lot in common and that, more often than not, new believers are birthed from such comfortable conversations rather than from someone more awkwardly trying to build bridges with a person with whom he or she has very little in common. To use just one of many possible illustrations, a middle-aged male Japanese banker who becomes a Christian will more likely succeed, with the Spirit's empowerment, in winning fellow middle-aged male Japanese bankers to the Lord than elderly impoverished Namibian seamstresses.

Unfortunately, too many churches or congregations have perpetuated the idea that Christian fellowship and nurture *subsequent* to conversion should likewise preserve such homogeneous groupings, when in fact texts like John 17, Eph 3, and many others that could be cited, remind us that people grow best by being pushed, with appropriate support mechanisms, outside of their comfort zones, that they learn the most when they associate with people quite different from themselves, and that the church as a collective or corporate organism or body offers the world its best witness when it is as heterogeneous as possible. It is little wonder that some of the most effective witness in Israel has emerged when Jewish and Palestinian believers have made the effort to work and worship together, or when Protestants and Catholics have done so in Northern Ireland, or Hutus and Tutsis in various African countries, and so on.

Let us move past our "worship wars" and create congregations where a rich variety of forms of worship and instruction, prayer and fellowship alternate or rotate so that everyone can have their preferred forms from time to time, and when they are not experiencing them they know that the reason is so that others can be experiencing *their* most meaningful forms. There are a handful of such churches around the world. I have been in some of them, more often outside rather than inside the United States. Bruce Milne supplies many of the details for this model in his *Dynamic Diversity: The New Humanity Church for Today and Tomorrow*.[42]

Milne does not discuss the Jew-Gentile divide, and one could easily imagine

---

[41] (Grand Rapids: Kregel, 2008).
[42] (Downers Grove: InterVarsity, 2007).

some Christians adopting his model and taking it in a supersessionist direction. But there is nothing about it that requires this move. One can still recognize the salvation-historical priority of ministering "to the Jew first." One can still appreciate the unique and perhaps even uniquely important cultural and religious legacy of Judaism. One can still hold out a lively hope for the salvation of "all Israel," interpreted as literal, ethnic Jews, at some time in the future in conjunction with the events that herald the end of this age (Rom 11:25-27).[43] But we dare not avoid the implications of the gospel for heterogenous grouping in the meanwhile. The best small groups I have ever been in have been those with people from several countries or ethnicities and of many different ages.[44] After all, we will not be segregated in the new heavens and the new earth, but believers from every tribe, nation, tongue and race will be thrown in together, not to be assimilated to some dominant culture, nor to be blended into some new and unidentifiable hybrid, but with each culture and tradition sanctified and perfected. The kings of the earth and their glory (Rev 21:24) will not be the only carry-over from this world, but the nations—the peoples—will walk by the light of the Lamb, and their glory and honor will be brought into God's marvelous, eternal new cosmos for *everyone* to enjoy (vv. 23-24).[45] Surely this multicultural vision for God's new covenant people should be the ideal for which we strive in the present as well, however imperfectly it is implemented.[46]

---

[43] See esp. C. E. B. Cranfield, *A Critical and Exegetical Commentary on the Epistle to the Romans* (2 vols.; Edinburgh: T&T Clark, 1979), 2:574-77. Also helpful in avoiding both supersessionism and the two-covenants approach to these verses is Terence L. Donaldson, "Jewish Christianity, Israel's Stumbling and the *Sonderweg* Reading of Paul," *JSNT* 29 (2006): 27-54. Donaldson concludes that "while Paul does not envision a *Sonderweg* for Israel, he nevertheless assigns his own people to a *Sonderplatz* within God's single program of salvation" (52).

[44] Not least while my wife and I lived in Aberdeen, when I was studying for my PhD under Howard Marshall, and when we were part of Gilcomston Park Baptist Church (today Gerrard Street Baptist Church) in the city.

[45] Cf. Grant R. Osborne, *Revelation* (BECNT; Grand Rapids: Baker, 2002), 767: "This culminates the mission theme in Scripture . . . . Thus, the nations have been evangelized . . . and those who responded to the gospel's proclamation now enter the eternal city. This is an incredible moment, one the evangelizing church constantly awaits with all its heart." See also Dave Mathewson, "The Destiny of the Nations in Revelation 21:1–22:5," *TynBul* 53 (2002): 121-42.

[46] An earlier draft of this paper was delivered at the Denver Seminary Institute of Contextualized Biblical Studies annual conference in February 2009, that year on the theme of Messianic Judaism. I dedicate it to Howard Marshall with gratitude for his emphasis on mission as a unifying theme of NT theology.

3

HEARING VOICES:
THE FOREIGN VOICE OF PAUL UNDER THE STRESS OF CONTEMPORARY ENGLISH LOCALIZATION

Philip H. Towner

PART 1—TRANSLATION STUDIES AS THE APPROPRIATE CONTEXT FOR SACRED TEXT TRANSLATION

This paper applies insights coming from Translation Studies to evaluate the effects of translation on a New Testament letter (2 Corinthians). This application is both necessary and possible to do. On the one hand, the New Testament is of course an eminently translated corpus of writings (known to most of its readers only through translation). On the other hand, its translations are as susceptible as any other literary translations to the discourses and critiques belonging to Translation Studies. These discourses and critiques seek to explore how translations function as transporters of culture, how translations treat the stakeholders (author and authorial culture; readers of the translation and their culture), how translations assume certain cognitive maps for the original texts and readers and are able to impose cognitive maps on modern readers and their received text; and how sponsoring institutions constrain the translation of the works they commission. This approach to a biblical text assumes, however, that the biblical text (or sacred texts in general) can be treated as a literary text, a common assumption in academic circles where the Bible as Literature is a frequently taught course and a legitimate object of research. In ecclesial circles, this assumption has a less familiar ring to it.

My assumption states that translation of the biblical text is not only subject to the scrutiny and rules of Translation Studies but also stands to benefit from exposure to its operations. Against this is a perspective held by a good many literary translators—and seconded at least implicitly by an equal, if not greater, number of translators of the Bible—that the two activities can (should?) be distinguished. Some literary translators argue that their distinctive focus is on the author's social location and cultural context as chief determinants in a successful translation—a view brought to the fore in connection with postcolonial interests in literary translation. These literary translators also argue that those who translate texts from a linguistic perspective (sacred text translators, but the application is to a wider group of texts) focus on the text as a linguistic artifact, the translation of which is reduced, then, mainly to operations on the structure(s) of the text.

This distinction is somewhat overstated, for the development of social-history and social-science approaches in biblical studies in the past decades reveals the cultural turn taken (or at least being contemplated) by biblical scholars and translators and the growing conviction that human meaning-making and textual message owe as much, if not more, to the social and cultural forces as the linguistic features of a text. Nevertheless, substantiating the distinction to some degree is the lingering influence in many Bible translation projects of certain presuppositions or perceptions of the text that determine its treatment. At the heart are the beliefs that biblical texts are uniquely authoritative, authored by people inspired by God, imbued with the very voice of God, so that at the end of the day it is God, and not the human writers, who determines the meaning and essence of the text.

In popular culture and in not a few sermons this view takes the form of assumptions that the ancient biblical languages are somehow different from all other languages, that is, they are "Holy Ghost languages." As this superordinate quality of the Scriptures filters through theological and ecclesial hierarchies, it may work to diminish the significance of authorial social and cultural context for translation. The distance in time between the translator/translation audience and the original writing might seem to compound this effect. Yet the church(es) as authenticator and custodian of the Bible in each generation mitigates the authorial distance as it speaks for the author(s)—they therefore also typically exert force on translation shape and specific decisions (e.g., the "virgin" of Isa 7:14). It should of course be immediately stated that the academy is just as insistent and assertive in the standards and rules of operation it insists define "scholarship," to the extent that the decisions and claims of ecclesiastical tradition in the reading and reception of sacred texts are regarded as secondary, if not irrelevant, in matters of scientific textual and theological inquiry. Nevertheless, we notice here the cluster of special conditions often applied to the biblical texts that qualify their literary character and can restrict and determine their assessment and translation.

Without taking a position on ecclesial assumptions, the following translation analysis seeks to disturb the literary-linguistic distinction. I will need first to develop some frames of reference.

1. TRANSLATION, CULTURE AND POWER

The discipline of Translation Studies is a network of discourses whose scholarly conversation and definition have been evolving from the mid-twentieth century. As it has evolved, several features of the inter-cultural activity of translation have emerged with clarity. Translation may be generally thought of as cultural transfer, the movement of inescapably value-laden information across cultural boundaries by the application of forces of "localization"; more recently translation is also being thought of as a form of human cognitive activity. Translation occurs in all spaces of human life and communication. As especially identified by the postcolonial and feminist critiques, translation is equally and unavoidably a means of exerting power—social power, cultural power, religious power, and cognitive power. Many acknowledge that the positive use of such power in translation has been and can be one of the keys to achieving authentic and conciliatory understanding across the cultures. Yet all too often translation has abetted subjugation (colonial, political, commercial, patriarchal); translators and sponsoring institutions have the power, if not the right, to tilt the language of discourse in particular directions, accentuating certain voices while intentionally diminishing, obscuring or erasing "Other" foreign voices.

A growing number of Translation Studies scholars have identified this abuse of power and the consequent silencing of the foreign "Other" voice(s) with domesticating translation strategies designed to render foreign texts (written and oral) into a form that receiving audiences regard as fluently familiar. An extreme example, typical in the localization of foreign films, is dubbing by which original dialogue in a film soundtrack is replaced by a local language equivalent. Fluency itself is not the problem; rather to be lamented is the erasure of all traces of foreignness in the text or dialogue, and along with them the voice of the foreign Other, with its potential to communicate something new, even if jarringly strange, to a receiving cultural discourse. But what if the comprehensive translation act that seeks authentic cultural transfer (of literature, poetry, sacred texts, etc.) succeeds in bringing home the truly Other? Now this voice rendered understandable as "different and equal"[1] can take its place in the receiving culture's discourse. One school of Translation Studies describes this receiving discourse as a "polysystem," made up of a mother tongue and translated expressions of (once foreign) literary, cultural goods.[2] The exciting hazard to be faced in this process of transfer in the case of literature is that the Other voice, upon entering the polysystem, would alter the systemic chemistry, dislocating and relocating preexisting voices in the new discursive environment as it claims its space.

George Steiner described this stage of the translational process of cultural intake as that of "incorporation" and "assimilation" and "ingestion" of the foreign text: varying degrees of force and motive yield a range of results from "complete domestication," that feeling of a translated text's "naturalization" and "at-homeness," to utter foreignness, strangeness and marginality.[3] As the

---

[1] The concept is adapted from H. K. Bhabha's engagement with E. Balibar (*Masses, Classes, Ideas* [trans J. Swenson; London: Routledge, 1994], 56) in *The Location of Culture* (London: Routledge, 1994), xvii, xxv.

[2] See I. Even-Zohar, "The Position of Translated Literature within the Literary Polysystem," *Poetics Today* 11 (1990): 45-51.

[3] G. Steiner, *After Babel: Aspects of Language and Translation* (3rd ed.; Oxford: Oxford University Press, 1998), 367, 314-16, 312-435.

postcolonial critique might suggest, it is somewhere in this stage of the process that translations may achieve a brutal, obliterating level of domestication (a new colonization of the Other). But there is the capacity in and through the art of translation to render the Other, inscribed in the original foreign text, in such a way that its authentic voice sounds clearly, articulating its "difference," in its new conversational context.

What has any of this to do with the sacred text or religious discourse we know as Christian Scriptures? Actually, quite a lot! No corpus, sacred or otherwise, has been translated as often and into as many languages as the Bible, in part or in whole. Translation of the Bible, as it has been done through history and is done throughout the churches of the world today (often under the control of commercial publishers and their sense of market and profit margin) is a culture-shaping and identity-creating activity and equally a means of exerting power with a range of effects. Thus those in positions of authority will determine what is translated for their churches and church communities. They will determine which source texts are authoritative and so should be the basis of a translation; which existing translations may serve as relay or model translations and so perpetuate a translational "shape"; which level of language should be used and so control the target audience's reception. They will also control which approach to translation will be applied, formal equivalence or functional equivalence, form-based or meaning-based, which could deliver extreme results that are either foreignizing or domesticating.[4] This binarism is deceptive, for the extremes are insufficient for the description of translation as that activity of cultural exchange. And the duality does not account for translation that is truly mediatory, seeking a translational outcome that succeeds at bringing together audience and author at some new intercultural place, located neither within the source culture, nor the target culture, but in a new third space that is both cultural and cognitive. Yet the extremes can indeed be achieved, more or less, and the foreignizing-domesticating duality may sometimes apply to translation approaches over-determined by only a part of the stakeholders, investors (supported by endorsers and those who determine price-points). And sometimes translations so assimilate the foreignness of a text that its authorial voice, its "difference," can no longer be detected.

Translations of the Bible have in recent times served as a laboratory for observing the colonizing exertions of power.[5] My own aims in this paper are far less ambitious, and I would join the person whom this essay seeks to honor in wishing for Bible translation the very best of culture-shaping outcomes.

---

[4] Such control and outcomes may be even more pronounced in the case of personal initiatives (*The Cotton Patch Gospel*; *The Message*).

[5] See V. L. Rafael, *Contracting Colonialism: Translation and Christian Conversion in Tagalog Society under Early Spanish Rule* (Durham, NC: Duke University Press, 1993); M. Dube, "Consuming the Colonial Cultural Bomb: Translating *Badimo* into Demons in the Setswana Bible (Matt. 8:28-34; 15:22; 10:8)," *JSNT* 73 (1999): 33-59.

Nevertheless, the legitimate existence, however distant, of the foreign Other in biblical literature (a voice imagined earlier and configured differently in the works and disciplines of Fanon, Lacan, Bakhtin, Kristeva and Barthes), and its suppression or expression in translation, does concern me. In synchronic translational situations—the import of contemporary foreign literature—expression of the Other voice in translation might benefit both the receiving culture (challenge, critique, movement, growth, enlightenment by the Other) and the Other him/herself (authentication of the Other as a "different and equal" individual and expression of human culture). But in the case of Bible/sacred text translation, where diachronicity stretches two millennia and more and the Other exists only in textuality (and in traditionally and institutionally "shaped" memories), has the Other ceased to exist?

2. CONTEMPORARY ENGLISH, READER-ORIENTED, FAMILIARIZING TRANSLATIONS:
FLUENCY, RESISTANCE AND RESONANCE

"Contemporary English translations" of the Bible, I would argue, can be located within the framework of translation studies, its discourses and concerns for the expression of foreign "difference" and the political nature of the translation act. Occupying the freer end of the cline (delineating translation types in this linear way is overly simplisitic), the *CEV* and *The Message*[6] may be viewed in terms of fluency, resistance and resonance. It is these elements and their effect upon textual voices, as distinguished from matters of fidelity, that is of chief interest.

First, our main contemporizing translations seek to address readers in an easy level of language that is colloquial and fluent. Each translation achieves fluency in its own ways, and each must measure the benefits gained against costs expended.

Fluency in translation might be a measurement of the naturalness of language style and flow in the translated text. Functional equivalence methodology (meaning for meaning) combined with a goal of rendering the foreign into accessible levels of modern (American) English entails easily imaginable risks. Consider the claim of one contemporary translation: "The *CEV* has created a text that transcends traditional readability measurements and appeals to readers of all grade levels, because the language is natural and the style is lucid and lyrical."[7] This means the apostle Paul, for instance, has been

---

[6] The term "paraphrase" is still applied as a non-technical description of *The Message* (as it was years ago of the *Good News for Modern Man*). However, the term is misunderstood in this application if it is thought by its use to describe something other than translational activity. Similar English translations, which exhibit a variety of translational decisions, are the *Good News Translation* (*TEV* 2nd ed.), ABS, 1992 and the *New Living Translation*, Tyndale, 2004.

[7] Unpublished *CEV* Booklet, Feb 1996.

made to speak in "a vocabulary and sentence structure that communicates effectively to [American] youth."[8] To accomplish this, all manner of "difficulty" (for modern readers) must be addressed, and foreign "difference" removed, to yield a sufficiently fluent, lively, modern American English text. The commitment is to utter clarity. The risk: will there remain in the translated text traces of that foreign Other voice and the "difference" it enunciated, or will this have been swept away, effectively censored in the contemporization process?

Then, there is the risk associated with disambiguation. In common language translations, ambiguity is treated as a dysfunction of a text, not a function, and dysfunctionality must be resolved. But when this agenda clashes with the patterns of the foreign voice, in which ambiguity *is* meaning, readerly paths may not arrive at foreign "difference." When fluency entails simplicity and the translation must "work" for readers of limited language facility, the "difference" of the foreign text may be considered expendable or its erasure defined as collateral damage.

Second is the practice in translation of resistance. Within certain twentieth-century literary discourses, and taken up by Translation Studies, "resistance" defines a method of reading or translating that goes against the grain: for example, readings of texts from the ancient or modern canons against the patriarchal or male-oriented or colonial or Western grain to create space for the disenfranchised or subaltern voices to speak. I would argue that contemporary English language Bible translations are no strangers to resistance in this sense. Whether their translators thought in these terms or not, they were themselves applying resistance in their translation activity at every turn. In a language such as English, there is already a history of Bible translation against which a new translation will be measured. The KJV was the dominant voice for nearly four centuries. It determined English "biblical parlance" and in some ways still does. Its offspring, the ASV, RSV and NRSV, colloquialized the KJV, staying within the formal equivalence sector, and these revisions, along with the NAB, NIV, NASB and others, established a dominant voice in the USA. The contemporary language approaches, inclining to dynamic or functional equivalence, resisted the foreignness of the KJV language, and then also the formality of the more "literal" renderings of twentieth-century translations and revisions. They also, obviously, resisted the syntactical formalities of the Greek and Hebrew. And this combination of resistant forces was exerted to achieve a contemporizing of the ancient texts and their formal equivalent translations—on behalf of work-a-day folk or youth who could not or would not penetrate the formalities and foreignness of formal equivalent translations, let alone the ancient languages. This perceived audience has as much right to a text in "its language" as any other audience, and resistance was exercised in its behalf.

Third is the matter of resonance. Perhaps the better term here is

---

[8] Unpublished promotional material for the *Contemporary English Version*.

intertextuality. In poststructuralist literary studies, texts do not enjoy the status of originality, priority, seminality—certainly not modern texts or translations. We leave aside the phenomenon of oral discourse. All texts are derivative in some sense, whether this is determinate or random derivation, and whether precursor discourses are textual or social in content. To the degree that this holds, the boundaries of texts—viewed from their function and meaning—become permeable and their messages unbound. It was partly out of this crucible of literary derivativeness and polyvalence that the descriptor "intertextuality" came into being.[9] It is simply a character of texts that they have their existence in resonance with the larger literary and social discourses (poetic, historical, classical, contemporary, religious, technical, popular, specialized, etc.), diachronically and synchronically, and whatever they convey, they do so in relation to other texts. Even without consuming the entire poststructuralist meal, the prospect of the openness of textuality represents a challenge to translation.

Intertextuality may be thought of as a multi-directional feature of texts, by which their resonance with precursor and contemporary texts and discourses, as well as those ongoing among intended audiences, is established and their relevance and meaning determined. The contemporary English language translations in view are first of all, by virtue of being translations, in connection with prior texts (Greek and Hebrew, but also the whole tradition of English translation that has gone before them). They are also projections of future texts and textual effects upon future generations of readers. Translation *is* intertextuality of the first order. Then, they achieve their fluency, and create their resistant forces, by forging those intertextual resonances with the discourses in which their intended audiences live and breathe. The translation language is *their*, the audience's, language. In the case of *The Message*, one might go so far as to say the translator's main intertextual connection is with his own voice, his pulpit, folksy, "this is where we really live" voice. His readers know that voice, and now they hear/read the Scriptures in that voice. Intertextuality, resonance.

What remains to be seen, and we will explore below, is how the forces exerted to create these audience-orientated resonances, to articulate these voices of familiarity, involve decisions that erase or obscure foreign resonances inherent to the foreign text. Priorities collide; negotiation is unavoidable.

The *CEV* and *The Message* seek to leave their readerships feeling as if the biblical text belongs to their culture. The emphasis is on naturalness, "at-homeness." And this indeed involves a kind of fluency. But it is a narrow fluency, in that what it delivers is channeled through an interpretive grid that anticipates and then resolves all readerly difficulties, articulated in strict accordance with the receiving culture's rules for creating easily read, accessible texts. In theory there is no reason why such translational features could not be

---

[9] See G. Allen, *Intertextuality* (New York: Routledge, 2000).

employed to turn a reader back to the foreign Other to draw attention to "difference" and allow the difference to interact with the familiar. But for some reason—absorption of the authorial presence into the translating institution, mislocation of the modern reader in the textual conversation—in the process of creating relevance for translation readers, the "difference" of the foreign Other is identified as an obstacle to reception and it is naturalized, co-opted, or annexed and relieved of its "difference," or altogether erased.

In what follows I will show how this happens and assess the cost. I will also illustrate what might result from attending to the voice of the foreign Other, its own unique patterns and resonances, as space is created in the conversation for foreign difference to have its say.

3. Parameters for Reading 2 Corinthians

Although there is much that remains unsettled about the background of the Corinthian church and the circumstances that gave rise to the writing(s) of 2 Corinthians, a general framework for reading the letter can be constructed. In various ways Paul's letters were associated with his mission and his activities in and with the communities of believers he established or wished to visit. They were linked to specific occasions and circumstances. His letters generally assume an already existing conversation, and this is sometimes thought to be a fairly straightforward element of background (because mentioned), as in the case of the Thessalonian letters, and sometimes rather convoluted, as in the case of 2 Corinthians within the Corinthian correspondence. These points are not disputed, though a given epistolary occasion may be complex, leaving its scholarly reconstruction in the provisional category

In the original communication situation, as far as we can reconstruct it, the "voices" that can be discerned include Paul's "audible" voice (perhaps including in some sense those who belong to his mission team) and several others that are, we might say, silent or indistinct though they are detectable from what Paul says and from what we can imagine of the situation in which the letter(s) would have been performed or read. We would include "the church of God in Corinth with all the saints of Achaia" (2 Cor 1:1). This description alone means there will have been multiple readings or performances. But Corinth was the chief destination, and embedded in that corporate Corinthian voice are several other voices: the leaders, whoever they might be (probably associated with the house churches, maybe even with local Jewish meeting places); those skeptical of Paul's authority (not everyone but some and not all of them leaders); the opponents, who are palpably real and undoubtedly present but frustratingly difficult to pin down; the "sinner" of 2:6; and the majority that punished him. The voices commingle, but they were a part of the larger conversation and present, even if inaudible, in the reception situation.

Paul may have imagined the further copying of the letter for didactic use among other churches in his orbit, but his imagination in this respect almost certainly did not exceed his basic historical, linguistic and cultural horizon. These are surely observations that help to establish certain exegetical parameters. But they are also crucial in determining the goals of translation for later readers who seek access to the biblical narrative through such occasional, far-removed literary windows as Paul's letters. Eugene Peterson, mastermind of *The Message*, suggests to his reading audience: "As we read . . . we soon realize that we are included in the conversation. . . . The Bible is not only written about us but to us."[10] While I can imagine such a statement intended only good, it defines a "Christian" ideology of reading that, perhaps unintentionally, encourages impatience with the foreign Other and with the enunciation of foreign "difference."

2 Corinthians is the authentic Pauline letter with the most complicated literary, historical, social and ecclesiastical background. The canonical form of the letter probably represents several literary parts or stages of writing (at least two, perhaps more). From the text(s), there emerge a complex textual/ intertextual conversation and a confusing web of human relationships.

One of the major issues engaged by Paul in 2 Corinthians is the disruptive presence of a distinct opposition. The identity of this group is uncertain. But from the outset Paul seeks to answer apparent charges leveled against him, in his absence, by an opposition that is present and whose sentiments are beginning to spread. Criticism includes skepticism about his apostolic authority; ambiguity in his relation to Jerusalem and lack of credentials (3:1-3); his heavy-handed style (1:24; 10:8); flippancy or insincerity (1:17-19; 10:2); and above all the suspicion that his sufferings and weakness invalidate his claims to apostleship,[11] calling for reconsideration of any commitment to his collection for Jerusalem (chs. 8–9).

As Steven Kraftchick has argued, Paul could not avoid addressing the charges. He attempted less of an apologia and more of a cognitive reorientation or subversion of the current opinion. Kraftchick's reconstruction unifies Paul's discourse.[12] However, two notable features of Paul's argument need examination for the fundamental theological framework and the strategy of his engagement to be understood. First, a fresh listening to Paul's voice will reveal how he accesses a prophetic paradigm to interpret his ministry. Second, this interpretive perspective will itself reveal a rhetorical tactic, seen in a number of statements in which he implicates or emplots the Corinthians in the narrative he accesses intertextually. This exegesis is important in its own right; but in this

---

[10] Eugene H. Peterson, *The Message: The Bible in Contemporary Language* (Colorado Springs: NavPress, 2002), 9.

[11] See S. J. Kraftchick, "Death in Us, Life in You: The Apostolic Medium," in *Pauline Theology, Volume Two: 1 and 2 Corinthians* (ed. David. M. Hay; SBLSymS 22. Atlanta: SBL, 2002), 175; V. P. Furnish, *II Corinthians* (AB 32A; Garden City: Doubleday, 1984), 277.

[12] Kraftchick, "Death in Us, Life in You," 156-81.

case it is the necessary groundwork that allows us to observe the effects of overfamiliarization (*CEV*, *The Message*) on the foreign voice of the text.

Samples will be examined from two of the most colloquializing translations available today. These seek to render the speech and thought of the ancient Mediterranean foreigner into those of an acceptably Western, familiar and conversational figure. It is precisely at this place in the translation cline, whose one end is total foreignization and whose other end is perfect domestication, where the most accessible evidence of stress and censorship lies. But these samples are chosen mainly for convenience, suited to the text and the scope of this essay. For I readily admit: there is no neutrality in translation. Even the ostensible impartiality or ambivalence of the more formal equivalent translations and their revisions can in some instances only thinly disguise their own exercise in ideological colonization, as all who are familiar with the backstory of the ESV will know.

Beginning from 1:3-7, my goals are as follows. First, I will consider briefly how the text "works." Second, we will observe how the text reaches back to other texts to create the theological paradigm of the Pauline mission. Third, we will evaluate ways in which two contemporary English translations force the foreign text into uttering familiar things, placing Paul's foreign voice, and the "difference" it enunciates, under duress. Finally, under the influence of my rehearing of the Other, another voice will be audible: it will define the parameters of the Pauline mission narrative and the emplotment of the Corinthians within it.

PART 2—READING 2 CORINTHIANS 1:3-7: THE TEXT

3 Εὐλογητὸς ὁ θεὸς καὶ πατὴρ τοῦ κυρίου ἡμῶν Ἰησοῦ Χριστοῦ, ὁ πατὴρ τῶν οἰκτιρμῶν καὶ θεὸς πάσης παρακλήσεως,
4 ὁ παρακαλῶν ἡμᾶς ἐπὶ πάσῃ τῇ θλίψει ἡμῶν εἰς τὸ δύνασθαι ἡμᾶς παρακαλεῖν τοὺς ἐν πάσῃ θλίψει διὰ τῆς παρακλήσεως ἧς παρακαλούμεθα αὐτοὶ ὑπὸ τοῦ θεοῦ.
5 ὅτι καθὼς περισσεύει τὰ παθήματα τοῦ Χριστοῦ εἰς ἡμᾶς, οὕτως διὰ τοῦ Χριστοῦ περισσεύει καὶ ἡ παράκλησις ἡμῶν.
6 εἴτε δὲ θλιβόμεθα, ὑπὲρ τῆς ὑμῶν παρακλήσεως καὶ σωτηρίας· εἴτε παρακαλούμεθα, ὑπὲρ τῆς ὑμῶν παρακλήσεως τῆς ἐνεργουμένης ἐν ὑπομονῇ τῶν αὐτῶν παθημάτων ὧν καὶ ἡμεῖς πάσχομεν.
7 καὶ ἡ ἐλπὶς ἡμῶν βεβαία ὑπὲρ ὑμῶν εἰδότες ὅτι ὡς κοινωνοί ἐστε τῶν παθημάτων, οὕτως καὶ τῆς παρακλήσεως.

The opening section of 2 Corinthians is somewhat unusual among the other Pauline letters. First, 1:3-4 takes the form of a Jewish blessing (see Eph 1:3) and omits or greatly mutes any statement of thanksgiving (like Galatians; the formal statement of thanksgiving in Ephesians is delayed until 1:16).

Second, further distinguishing this Pauline letter is the presence in the opening lines (1:3-7) of a striking verbal scheme, produced by ten occurrences of the παρακαλέω word group that create the theme of divine comfort.[13] The theme provides a major interpretive cue (see below). It has been played in a particular way by the contemporary language translations to be observed below, and by some commentators, and we will need to return to this matter shortly.

Third, in 1:5-6 we encounter the first evidence of a curious rhetorical strategy. It will recur at various points in the first several chapters of the letter, and it is a crucial piece of Paul's discursive methodology designed to engage his audience in a particular way. Although this device requires thorough follow-up, I am only able to introduce it here and examine it briefly below. Following the opening statement about divine comfort (vv. 3-4), v. 5 is a straightforward enough expression of Paul's insistence that suffering is not a sign of his distance from Christ, that Christ is in some way present in the process Paul is undergoing. Paul's next comment, however, introduces some turbulence and surprise: he implicates the Corinthians in this experience of his suffering, two times. The question is why? But in any case it cannot be shrugged off as a pastoral overstatement.

The foreign voice articulates with care. In the opening sentence, Paul immediately juxtaposes two concepts: divine comfort (5x) and Paul's suffering (1x and another in broader relation to others).

1:3-4
Εὐλογητὸς ὁ θεὸς καὶ πατὴρ τοῦ κυρίου ἡμῶν Ἰησοῦ Χριστοῦ, ὁ πατὴρ τῶν οἰκτιρμῶν καὶ θεὸς πάσης παρακλήσεως, ὁ παρακαλῶν ἡμᾶς ἐπὶ πάσῃ τῇ θλίψει ἡμῶν εἰς τὸ δύνασθαι ἡμᾶς παρακαλεῖν τοὺς ἐν πάσῃ θλίψει διὰ τῆς παρακλήσεως ἧς παρακαλούμεθα αὐτοὶ ὑπὸ τοῦ θεοῦ.

However surprising and enigmatic vv. 5-7 might be as a follow-on to vv. 3-4, the Greek of 1:5 is a neatly balanced "just as, so also" sentence (καθὼς . . . οὕτως . . .):

ὅτι καθὼς περισσεύει τὰ παθήματα τοῦ Χριστοῦ εἰς ἡμᾶς,
οὕτως διὰ τοῦ Χριστοῦ περισσεύει καὶ ἡ παράκλησις ἡμῶν.

Equally balanced are the two poetically resonant, inanimate, contrasting noun-subjects, τὰ παθήματα and ἡ παράκλησις. By repeating the main verb, "to abound" (περισσεύειν), Paul has foregrounded the abundance both of (1) "the sufferings of Christ" and, in balance, (2) "the comfort which is through Christ." Reference to the recipients of these things is made by use of the first person plural accusative pronoun "us" (ἡμᾶς; referring to Paul or Paul and his team), related to the verb by preposition in the first case, and by the genitive case in

---

[13] Different, but notable, is the clustering of 5 occurrences of εὐαγγέλιον (κτλ) in Gal 1:6-9.

the second (ἡμῶν).
1:6 was written with an equal attention to balance as is readily apparent:

εἴτε δὲ θλιβόμεθα, ὑπὲρ τῆς ὑμῶν παρακλήσεως καὶ σωτηρίας·
εἴτε παρακαλούμεθα, ὑπὲρ τῆς ὑμῶν παρακλήσεως
τῆς ἐνεργουμένης ἐν ὑπομονῇ τῶν
αὐτῶν παθημάτων ὧν καὶ ἡμεῖς
πάσχομεν.

But through the balanced statements, Paul opens the discourse, which had been about himself (and his "us"), to involve the Corinthians. Here Paul initiates his rhetorical dance with the addressees (what I am calling "emplotment," see below), and different language features produce the effect. There is a shift from inanimate to animate subjects, through which Paul creates relevance. But in what sense? The twofold use of εἴτε . . . ὑπέρ enfolds the Corinthians in Paul's discourse about suffering in some way, while the continuation of the present tense, the threefold use of παράκλησις and the reference to the explanatory σωτηρία together begin to define the audience's new frame of reference.

1:7 is a very positive summation, a confident claim that the addressees are indeed invested, whether they acknowledge this or not, in the experiential and theological formula that Paul has just articulated:

καὶ ἡ ἐλπὶς ἡμῶν βεβαία ὑπὲρ ὑμῶν εἰδότες ὅτι ὡς κοινωνοί ἐστε τῶν παθημάτων, οὕτως καὶ τῆς παρακλήσεως.

My reading of this potentially ambiguous reference to "hope" (see the alternative readings of the contemporary English translations below and the commentaries) understands Paul to be looking forward to an (eschatological) reference point, expressing a confident hope for the addressees, and grounding it in the present claim about their participation in the extremes of suffering and comfort that characterize his apostolic mission. This theological and eschatological reading coheres with the precursor narrative drawn forward by Paul's voice.

PART 3—2 CORINTHIANS AND THE PROMISE OF DIVINE COMFORT: SEEKING THE VOICE OF THE OTHER

Ten occurrences of the παρακαλέω word group in such a short span of text is unusual. It attracts attention, but to what? The theme of divine comfort is surely what Paul pulls into the orbit of this discussion. But it is precisely Paul's (and his team's) involvement in this activity that he wishes to define. In the LXX of Isaiah, from the important turning point of 40:1 (παρακαλεῖτε παρακαλεῖτε τὸν λαόν μου λέγει ὁ θεός) onwards, the παρακαλέω word group occurs twenty-two times, all but one of which (57:5) refer to divine comfort in one way or another.[14] Such references were not simply to the divine disposition of compassion towards human beings, but in fact to the dawning of salvation, the forgiveness of sin, marked by the fulfillment of YHWH's promise to restore the people from their exile to their proper place of blessing as the beloved and redeemed.[15] While Barrett's observation of the term's use in 2 Cor 1:3-7—that "no single translation will suffice"—must surely be granted as a caution against thinking that the English language could ever plumb the depths of the divine παράκλησις, the point Paul is making by his repeated use of the term is theological and eschatological not semantic. Paul, by evoking the redemptive narrative of Isa 40–66, defines his experience of divine comfort, folded into which is his experience of "the sufferings of Christ," as emblematic of the arrival of the salvation promised in the prophetic precursor text. Moreover, he interprets his apostolic activity, as one emplotted in this salvific narrative, as the divine outworking of promise. The divine "comfort" he has experienced, and the divine comfort he extends to the Corinthians, is precisely the fulfillment of eschatological salvation in and through his apostolic ministry.

The echo of the prophetic precursor reverberates as Paul's voice sets up its own harmonic in the unfolding discourse. In this way, the theological intention of the intertextual resonance at this opening of the letter is substantiated when later we read in 5:20, with its use of παρακαλέω: Ὑπὲρ Χριστοῦ οὖν πρεσβεύομεν ὡς τοῦ θεοῦ παρακαλοῦντος δι᾽ ἡμῶν· δεόμεθα ὑπὲρ Χριστοῦ, καταλλάγητε τῷ θεῷ. Essentially, at this point, Paul concludes his interpretation of the Pauline mission: the agency of the fulfillment of God's promise—to "comfort" his people. And with increasing clarity, the enfolding of the Corinthians in this redemptive process, begun in 1:3-7, here becomes inescapable: the Pauline ministry of comfort is directed again to (is still directed to) the Corinthians. Whatever nuance translators might try to squeeze from παρακαλοῦντος in this case ("as though God were *making his appeal*"; NRSV, NIV), the missiological linkage with Isaiah interprets the activity in eschatological terms.[16]

In the next breath, Paul deepens (and verifies) the intentional reflection on the salvation promise of Isaiah. First, in 6:1 he reiterates his "partnership" with God in the gospel (just set out in 5:16-21), now making explicit this

---

[14] Isa 40:1[2x], 2, 11; 41:27; 49:10, 13; 51:3[2x], 12, 18, 19; 54:11; 57:5, 18[2x]; 61:2; 66:11, 12, 13[3x]; see also Jer 38:9; Ps 134:14.
[15] See O. Schmitz and G. Staehlin, "παρακαλέω, παράκλησις," *TDNT* 5:773-99 [789-90]; C. K. Barrett, *The Second Epistle to the Corinthians* (New York: Harper and Row, 1973), 60; R. P. Martin, *2 Corinthians* (WBC 40; Waco: Word Books, 1986), 9; M. Thrall, *A Critical and Exegetical Commentary on the Second Epistle to the Corinthians 1-7* (ICC; Edinburgh: T&T Clark, 1994), 103.
[16] So also resonance of the καινὴ κτίσις image of 5:17, drawing on Isa 51:9-10; 54:9 (42:9; 43:18-19); Martin, *2 Corinthians*, 152.

proclamation of God's comfort to the Corinthians: Συνεργοῦντες δὲ καὶ παρακαλοῦμεν μὴ εἰς κενὸν τὴν χάριν τοῦ θεοῦ δέξασθαι ὑμᾶς. Of course the key verb, παρακαλοῦμεν, could be rendered weakly as "we urge" (NRSV, NIV), but the theological sense of the term, coming as it does immediately following 5:20, and in light of 1:3-7, requires a translation with a kerygmatic edge. In this (Corinthian) context, Paul's "urging" has been and continues to be kerygmatic. The intertextual resonance of the Greek verb creates far more connections (to Isaiah, to 1:3-7, to 5:20, as well as forward to 7:6-7) than can be adequately expressed in a direct English translation. The statement is not only a warning about squandering the grace already experienced, but also at the same time a re-preaching of the gospel to the Corinthians. And it is done in a way that is designed to remind the Corinthians (1) of their location in the eschatological redemptive drama and (2) their indebtedness to the Pauline gospel.

The proof follows immediately in 6:1-2 by explicit citation of Isaiah 49:8 and Paul's twofold "now" that interprets and defines Corinth as the precise site of salvation's eschatological fulfillment:

καιρῷ δεκτῷ ἐπήκουσά σου
καὶ ἐν ἡμέρᾳ σωτηρίας ἐβοήθησά σοι.
ἰδοὺ νῦν καιρὸς εὐπρόσδεκτος, ἰδοὺ νῦν ἡμέρα σωτηρίας.

The importance of this pivotal, grounding statement for 1:3-7 and the theological and eschatological frame of Paul's thinking should be obvious. But there is possibly still more evidence to assess. In 7:6-7, the LXX of Isa 49:13 is detectable in Paul's voice:

ὅτι ἠλέησεν ὁ θεὸς τὸν λαὸν αὐτοῦ καὶ τοὺς ταπεινοὺς τοῦ λαοῦ αὐτοῦ παρεκάλεσεν.

It inspires and shapes his description of God and his current experience of divine comfort in the arrival of Titus:

ἀλλ ὁ παρακαλῶν τοὺς ταπεινοὺς παρεκάλεσεν ἡμᾶς ὁ θεὸς ἐν τῇ παρουσίᾳ Τίτου, οὐ μόνον δὲ ἐν τῇ παρουσίᾳ αὐτοῦ ἀλλὰ καὶ ἐν τῇ παρακλήσει ᾗ παρεκλήθη ἐφ ὑμῖν, ἀναγγέλλων ἡμῖν τὴν ὑμῶν ἐπιπόθησιν, τὸν ὑμῶν ὀδυρμόν, τὸν ὑμῶν ζῆλον ὑπὲρ ἐμοῦ ὥστε με μᾶλλον χαρῆναι.

Into this current "salvation/comfort" experience, the apostle also weaves the Corinthians, whose longing, sorrow and zeal for Paul were communicated by Titus. Although it may be stretching translation to render these feelings for Paul and Titus's arrival in keygmatic terms, there is every reason to regard Paul's reflection here as an extension of the outworking of God's salvific comfort where salvation is understood in its widest theological sense as a blessing that defines the very environment of Christian existence.

It is tempting to extend this description of Paul's intertextual strategy still further, by pointing specifically to the fivefold use of the παρακαλέω word group in Isa 66 (11, 12, 13[3x]) in such close proximity to an OT promise concerning a mission to the Gentiles (66:18-20).[17] But Paul seems to have refrained from doing so, and he has as much as drawn this conclusion, in any case, in the span of text running from 5:20 to 6:2 (see also Luke 2:25-32).

In light of the intertextual movement, diachronic and synchronic, of the divine comfort theme, the opening section of the letter can be read to begin the process of "locating" the Corinthians (and their experience of grace, salvation, the Spirit) eschatologically within the Pauline gospel mission. It may be helpful to point out that the statement of 1:19 (ὁ τοῦ θεοῦ γὰρ υἱὸς Ἰησοῦς Χριστὸς ὁ ἐν ὑμῖν δι' ἡμῶν κηρυχθείς), written as an aside in the developing argument, makes much the same point. Paul's strategy for Corinthian reeducation—his way of addressing particularly the growing skepticism about his apostolic claim and authority—involved constructing a specific salvation historical frame and convincing his audience of its location within the frame.

With the text of 1:3-7 primarily in focus, what I have just done illustrates at least partially what might happen, in interpretation in preparation for a subsequent translation (though completing the latter task remains), if the goal is to open up for a reader the resonances and ambitions of the foreign (authorial) voice of Paul. The translation that would emerge as the result would creatively and clearly shade the translation of παρακαλέω/παράκλησις in ways that invite a hearing of the primary precursor text and, in the light of that prophetic frame, that make sense in the authorial literary context. The desire is not slavish adherence to the author or his form. Rather, this fresh hearing seeks to achieve a resistant or "abusive fidelity"[18] that reveals aspects of the foreign text (intertextualities, plurivocities, syntactical structures, etc.), often treated as obstacles to receptor audience understanding (and so in need of familiarizing), that become windows open to the angular (because foreign, Other) voice of the author. Heard in this way, the voice of "the resistant-because-foreign" may challenge the receiving culture.

PART 4—SEEKING CONTEMPORARY ENGLISH SPEAKERS

But through translation strategies of the Contemporary Language Bibles to be considered next, "Paul's" voice assumes a different pitch. The *Contemporary English Version*, is described as "user-friendly" and "mission-driven." The

---

[17] See R. Riesner, *Paul's Early Period* (trans. D. Stott; Grand Rapids: Eerdmans, 1998), 245-56; but see the discussion in T. L. Donaldson, *Paul and the Gentiles* (Minneapolis: Fortress, 1997), 362 n. 38.

[18] The concept is Philip E. Lewis's; see L. Venuti, *The Translator's Invisibility: A History of Translation* (2d ed.; London: Routledge, 2008), 18.

essence of the first term was explored above, but a similar promotional description bears quoting here: "[it] can be read aloud without stumbling, heard without misunderstanding, and listened to with enjoyment and appreciation, because the language is contemporary and the style is lucid and lyrical."[19] This claim calls to mind George Steiner's description of the excessive (or incomplete) translation activity that produces a text "better" than the original, diminishing the source![20] But the essence is a familiarizing translation strategy that prioritizes readerly understanding. This is of course a noble set of goals, and not without significant merit. However, in a project so designed, there will be little patience for the jarring and cognitively disruptive elements of "difference" that make the foreign voice an Other voice and provide glimpses of the foreign culture (and its values). Such textual phenomena must be brought under domestic control. The utterly foreign must be naturalized. Underlying this commitment to "lucidity" and "understanding" is a presupposition about the biblical text (linked to the "mission-driven" agenda) that its own cultural beginnings and values are in some sense neutral and that the authorial voices, belonging to people long since dead, no longer have claims on the message and the ways it might be rendered.

What are we to make of the translational strategy of the *CEV*?

> 3 Praise God, the Father of our Lord Jesus Christ! The Father is a merciful God, who always gives us comfort.
> 4 He comforts us when we are in trouble, so that we can share that same comfort with others in trouble.
> 5 We share in the terrible sufferings of Christ, but also in the wonderful comfort he gives.
> 6 We suffer in the hope that you will be comforted and saved. And because we are comforted, you will also be comforted, as you patiently endure suffering like ours.
> 7 You never disappoint us. You suffered as much as we did, and we know that you will be comforted as we were.

In 1:3-7, the multiplication of sentences is immediately apparent. While NA[27] punctutes the text to produce four sentences, the *CEV* doubles this to eight sentences. This shortening and multiplying of sentences carries with it a necessary addition of pronouns (explicitation) and the repositioning of pronouns from object to subject or relocation of pronouns to the heads of sentences. Eight of the ten occurrences of παρακαλέω /παράκλησις are retained, translated consistently as "comfort." While this translational activity reflects current English strategies for clarity and simplicity of communication, it also has certain domesticating results.

Taking vv. 3-4 first, I note some decisions that seem minor and innocuous,

---

[19] Foreword to the *Contemporary English Version* in *The Essential Study Bible* (New York: Putnam, 2008).

[20] Steiner, *After Babel*, 423-28.

but which actually set the text in a particular tone at the outset.

3 Εὐλογητὸς ὁ θεὸς καὶ πατὴρ τοῦ κυρίου ἡμῶν Ἰησοῦ Χριστοῦ, ὁ πατὴρ τῶν οἰκτιρμῶν καὶ θεὸς πάσης παρακλήσεως,

3 Praise God, the Father of our Lord Jesus Christ! The Father is a merciful God, who always gives us comfort.

The opening vocative "Praise God," conforming only minimally to a Pauline liturgical register and much more to an English-speaking Evangelical register, diminishes the solemnity of the blessing/doxology moment, designed to focus concentration on God's characteristics, and, more in keeping with the Pauline thanksgiving (e.g., 1 Cor 1:5-7), invites reflection on the people themselves.[21] The decision to "personalize" θεὸς πάσης παρακλήσεως, originally a part of the blessing, with "who always gives us comfort," confirms and strengthens the tilt of the text in the direction of the readers. While readerly interest and a sense of immediate relevance may be thought to be established in this way, the shift of emphasis away from the God of comfort to "us" as the recipients is noticeable (see also below).

4 ὁ παρακαλῶν ἡμᾶς ἐπὶ πάσῃ τῇ θλίψει ἡμῶν εἰς τὸ δύνασθαι ἡμᾶς παρακαλεῖν τοὺς ἐν πάσῃ θλίψει διὰ τῆς παρακλήσεως ἧς παρακαλούμεθα αὐτοὶ ὑπὸ τοῦ θεοῦ.

4 He comforts us when we are in trouble, so that we can share that same comfort with others in trouble.

While it should be acknowledged that v. 4, with its repetition of παρακαλέω /παράκλησις (4x) and the tortuous διά phrase, pose a challenge for English translation, the decision made by the *CEV* assists the humanward slide of emphasis by subtly replacing the entire διά phrase (including the pronounced, if awkward for English, παρακαλούμεθα αὐτοὶ ὑπὸ τοῦ θεοῦ) with "same." Translating θλῖψις as "trouble" not only colloquializes the more formal "afflictions" (NRSV), but more significantly renders Paul's references to his missional suffering into rather ordinary terms that pave the way for a pastoral reading of the text. However, Paul has marked his text very heavily for divine emphasis (four occurrences of παρακαλέω /παράκλησις and the extra effort

---

[21] See Furnish, *II Corinthians*, 116-17. The *GNB* at 1:3 ("Let us give thanks to the God and Father") may overcome the antiquated and liturgical feel of "blessed be" (though oddly the same form in Luke 1:68 is translated more appropriately "Let us praise the Lord"; and at 2 Cor 11:31 it has of God the Father "blessed be his name"; cf. Rom 1:25; 9:5), but it has mistakenly converted the Jewish blessing form (and inappropriately pluralized it in the rendering; "Let us") into Paul's more typical Thanksgiving form (as with his use of εὐχαριστῶ in Rom 1:8; 1 Cor 1:4; Phil 1:3; 1 Thess 1:1; etc.).

of the διά phrase), and this has been reshaped into a text deemed to be more readily accessible and interesting to modern English readers. While that may be, the domestic voice that has staged the actors and the action for this effect is not the voice of the Other.

The *CEV's* approach to the structure and language of vv. 5-6 is interesting.

> 5 ὅτι καθὼς περισσεύει τὰ παθήματα τοῦ Χριστοῦ εἰς ἡμᾶς,
> οὕτως διὰ τοῦ Χριστοῦ περισσεύει καὶ ἡ παράκλησις ἡμῶν.

> 5 We *share* in the *terrible* sufferings of Christ;
> but also *share* in the *wonderful* comfort he gives (my italics)

Notice the divergence from the Greek. First, original subjects ("the sufferings of Christ"; "our comfort") become objects, in keeping with the shift of emphasis away from the divine. Correspondingly, by moving the original pronoun ("us"; object of the preposition) to the subject position, "we," the *CEV* continues its redirection of focus on people. The thought of the "abundance" of these things expressed through the repeated verb (περισσεύει), which is a measure of "amount," is altered to a *shared* experience of things described by their quality ("terrible"; "wonderful").

The *CEV's* translational decisions in v. 6 are also notable.

> 6 εἴτε δὲ θλιβόμεθα, ὑπὲρ τῆς ὑμῶν παρακλήσεως καὶ σωτηρίας·
> εἴτε παρακαλούμεθα, ὑπὲρ τῆς ὑμῶν παρακλήσεως
>   τῆς ἐνεργουμένης ἐν ὑπομονῇ
>   τῶν αὐτῶν παθημάτων ὧν
>   καὶ ἡμεῖς πάσχομεν.

> 6 We suffer in the hope that you will be comforted and saved. And because we are comforted, you will also be comforted, as you patiently endure suffering like ours.

First, the original conditional tone of the statements (εἴτε . . . ὑπέρ 2x), and the formulaic certitude it lends to the discourse, is removed. Second, the note of uncertainty or futurity of "hope" is inserted, with the future "you will be comforted," in v. 6a, while any original causality latent in this statement's interpretation of suffering/comfort and that of the Corinthian's is removed. Third, ignoring (or improving upon) the neat balance created by the repetition of εἴτε . . . ὑπέρ at the head of each statement, which suggests the same rhetorical dynamic controlling the whole, a note of causality is added here ("because") with, again, a future horizon ("you will also be comforted").

Finally, the *CEV* treatment of v. 7 is not surprising.

> 7 καὶ ἡ ἐλπὶς ἡμῶν βεβαία ὑπὲρ ὑμῶν εἰδότες ὅτι ὡς κοινωνοί ἐστε τῶν παθημάτων, οὕτως καὶ τῆς παρακλήσεως.

7 You never disappoint us. You suffered as much as we did, and we know that you will be comforted as we were.

In translation the text has become a study in interpersonal dynamics. "You never disappoint us" is not only an extremely banal translation of what may well be a note of Paul's confident hope in the Corinthians' eschatological outcome, but it retrieves less than the text offers. Morever, it excludes the possibility that Paul's comment was actually far more grave. Within the theological frame observed above, the "hope" expressed is eschatological, though grounded in present experience, and the "partnership" (κοινωνοί) attributed to the Corinthians, rather subdued by the "as much as we did," is in Pauline parlance nothing short of a badge of full membership in the faith linked to Paul's gospel and collaboration in the mission (8:23; 1 Cor 1:9; Phil 1:5; 2:1; 4:14-15).[22] Furthermore, if the ambiguity of Paul's voice left space for the exhortative, implying that the anticipated outcome will require demonstration of their partnership (as 1:13-14 suggests),[23] the *CEV* closes this space. Conceptually, the text develops so:

v.3 God is the God of (eschatological) comfort/salvation;
v.4 God's comfort/salvation has made Paul the channel of salvation (to the Gentiles);
v.5 The present sufferings ("of Christ"), experienced by Paul, are part and parcel of God's salvation;
v.6 Paul's gospel sufferings mean salvation for the Corinthians;
Paul's salvation means salvation for the Corinthians and it produces perseverance as they undergo gospel sufferings;
v.7 The end result of this history is Paul's confident hope in the Corinthians, based on the knowledge (a restatement of what has been said) that they are/will prove themselves to be κοινωνοί of the same sufferings and hence also of the same salvation.

What emerges from the *CEV* rendering of 1:3-7 is a determined relandscaping of the foreign text—different foreground, different emphasis—and "refinement" of Paul's description (of circumstances that he experienced personally). The *CEV* has lightened the mood considerably, presumably to lend to Paul's rather twisting syntax and the sudden inclusion of the addressees in v. 6[24] an acceptable pastoral ambience and a sense of immediate relevance for

---

[22] See J. Hainz, "κοινωνία," *EDNT* 2:303-305 [305]; Furnish, *II Corinthians*, 112.
[23] See Furnish, *II Corinthians*, 121.
[24] *The Net Bible*'s translation of 1:5 ("For just as the sufferings of Christ overflow toward us, so also our comfort through Christ overflows *to you*"; my emphasis) errs in adding "to you" at the end. The justification ("The words 'to you' are not in the Greek text, but are implied by the statements in the following verse.") seems to assume that the Corinthians would normally have read the letter (or heard it read) from end to beginning.

modern readers. The reorientation of the text produced by the choice of "terrible" and "wonderful," as replacements for the language of abundance and overflow, is truly puzzling, but the decision to foreground the human element ("we share") necessitated a semantic shift. On the whole, the *CEV* translation transposes the text into a message about people, and the rest, after that prominence is settled, is either "terrible" or "wonderful"; yet another listening discovers a voice speaking about "divine comfort" and "the sufferings of Christ" and and how Paul first and then the addressees relate to these things.

The *CEV* has heard a much different voice from the one I described above. Its familiarizing result gives the illusion of close proximity and a sense of accessibility and relevance to the modern reader: the impression created is that the reader in the twenty-first century is among the "we" of the original reminiscence in this text. Despite the consistent translation of παρακαλέω/παράκλησις as "comfort," the humanward tilt and resultant pastoral-counseling flavor of the text provide little incentive to detect a primal resonance and trace it to its source. And the choice to eschew the eschatological comfort theme makes Paul's reflection on God's comfort into an "everything happens to us for a reason" homily designed to somehow appease the agitated Corinthians as it speaks to the modern reader.

Eugene Peterson's *The Message* is self-described as "the Bible in contemporary language."

- All praise to the God and Father of our Master, Jesus the Messiah! Father of all mercy! God of all healing counsel!
- He comes alongside us when we go through hard times, and before you know it, he brings us alongside someone else who is going through hard times so that we can be there for that person just as God was there for us.
- We have plenty of hard times that come from following the Messiah, but no more so than the good times of his healing comfort—we get a full measure of that, too.
- When we suffer for Jesus, it works out for your healing and salvation. If we are treated well, given a helping hand and encouraging word, that also works to your benefit, spurring you on, face forward, unflinching. Your hard times are also our hard times.
- When we see that you're just as willing to endure the hard times as to enjoy the good times, we know you're going to make it, no doubt about it.

This depth of commitment to a style and register of speech, for the sake of delivering clarity and that sense of relevance to the intended audience, requires an equally wholehearted commitment to a particular intepretation of the text. As Peterson renders the text, he engages in an exercise of contextualization. Having decided what the text means, he asks, "How would Paul have said this in Baltimore, Maryland, or Helena, Montana, or Vancouver, British Columbia, at the close of the twentieth century?" And having determined that this text is about experiencing God's comfort, healing counsel, ameliorative presence, and even more so about the possibility of a human, Christian embodiment of this ministry, the epochal actions of God that I have detected in Paul's multiple uses of παρακαλέω/παράκλησις are transposed into work-a-day life.

Several translational choices, comparable to those of the *CEV*, reveal less dramatically an equal humanward tilt of the text that obscures the possible resonances of a precursor text. While the opening "All praise" initiates the blessing/doxology in a way that more closely approximates the liturgical register, the choice in v. 4 to translate θλῖψις as ordinary "hard times" and then (apparently) to principle-ize the whole statement within the developing argument reveals the dominance of the pastoral interpretive grid: "He comes alongside us when we go through hard times, and before you know it, he brings us alongside someone else who is going through hard times so that we can be there for that person just as God was there for us."

More distinctive is the variation in the translation of παρακαλέω/παράκλησις. The range runs from "healing counsel" to "healing comfort" to "benefit" and "good times." He retains all ten occurrences, and the general statement of v. 4 seems to equate the concept with the presence of God. In addition to a desire to create interesting prose, this variety may echo Barrett's concern for the absence in English of a suitable term to translate παρακαλέω. The fact, however, is that in Greek the same term is used ten times and the tenfold use will have had its semiotic and auditory force. While current English usage might require avoidance of such repetition, this strategy runs the risk of failing to recreate a resonance associated with an original voice. Interestingly, for all Peterson's helpful contextualizing and colloquializing of a fulsome biblical concept in 2 Corinthians, when he renders Isa 40:1, he cannot resist the call of the Authorized Version: "Comfort, oh comfort my people." If Paul was also answering that call and inviting his audience to make a significant connection to the Isaianic tradition, the invitation is not given in *The Message*.

So, again, it is a choice between voices. The ordinariness of Peterson's description of Paul's experience of divine comfort in 1:3-7 ("and before you know it, he brings us alongside someone else who is going through hard times") raises the possibility of relevance, heightens the awareness of God's presence among his people, and even urges that the modern reader too can be involved in God's redemptive ministry. *The Message*'s translation sends this signal clearly. But in sending the signal it does, it severs all but the most random and general connections with the salvation drama unveiled in LXX Isa 40–66. And therein lies the foreign "difference."

PART 5—THE VOICE OF THE OTHER

Once the resonance has been traced and the eschatological frame plotted, the subtlety with which the voice of Paul involves his audience in this narrative can be observed. The technique of emplotment, a series of reciprocating statements of varying length and complexity that "involve" the Corinthians with Paul and relate Paul's activities to them, begins in 1:6. But it is in listening to 1:3-7 that something other than a plea for understanding emerges. The first person plural pronoun in its various cases in vv. 3-5 signals an openness. But curiosity and courtesy make me a spectator. I am not a part of the original conversation; there are original, foreign voices to be heard. But at v. 6 a determined shift occurs with the first occurrence in this section of the plural "you." Here, the author engages the Corinthians in his discourse. More to the point, he enfolds them into his narrative of suffering. He lays a trap of emplotment over the next several chapters, and this statement is the enticement to enter. Its startling appearance in the discourse is perhaps best seen by considering again the impact of familiarizing translations on the text.

> 6 εἴτε δὲ θλιβόμεθα, ὑπὲρ τῆς ὑμῶν παρακλήσεως καὶ σωτηρίας·
> εἴτε παρακαλούμεθα, ὑπὲρ τῆς ὑμῶν παρακλήσεως
> τῆς ἐνεργουμένης ἐν ὑπομονῇ
> τῶν αὐτῶν παθημάτων ὧν
> καὶ ἡμεῖς πάσχομεν.

The Greek is finely balanced, making the opening to the Corinthians decisive. The shift from inanimate to animate subjects creates relevance. The twofold use of εἴτε . . . ὑπέρ draws the Corinthians into Paul's suffering, as the present tense, repetition of παρακαλέω/παράκλησις and the explanatory σωτηρία define a new frame of reference.

Compare the *CEV*:

> 6 We suffer in the hope that you will be comforted and saved. And because we are comforted, you will also be comforted, as you patiently endure suffering like ours.

This translation lessens the shock of the discourse's original "if . . . then it was for you" that could well have left the Corinthians (skeptical and critical of Paul's suffering) surprised (shocked) at the abrupt discursive turn. But the *CEV's* "in the hope that" articulates a softer voice of transition in which foreign abruptness and turbulence have been moderated into a plea to be understood, but the "difference" has been familiarized.

The Message, however, provokes another response.

> When we suffer for Jesus, it works out for your healing and salvation. If we are treated well, given a helping hand and encouraging word, that also works to your benefit, spurring you on, face forward, unflinching. Your hard times are also our hard times.

There is impatience here with the abrupt foreign voice. Sermonic loquacity cloaks an unease with silence and concision. The foreign text's carefully structured economy of words is judged to be too puzzling, too allusive to deliver the impact chosen by the translator, demanded by the domestic audience; yet the foreign argument is cumulative in design and its rate of information delivery carefully measured.

A resistant reading allows the muffled foreign voice to come again to expression. This will disturb the pastoral intimacy imagined by the translations, the volubility of *The Message*.

> If *I* am afflicted, it is for the sake of the comfort and salvation of *you Corinthians*;
> if *I* am comforted, it is for the sake of *your* comfort which will enable *you* to endure the same sufferings *I* suffer.

First, the rhetorical "we" is sharpened to "I" (cf. 4:5). In opposition to the pronoun "I" stands the plural "you," and some distance can be restored (from both Paul and the modern reader) by translating "you, Corinthians." Only a first explicit reference to "Corinthians" is needed to create this sharpness. This stroke distinguishes original voices and discourages inappropriate fantasizing on the part of modern readers, delaying entrance until the original conversation has been understood. This treatment of pronouns also sharpens the contrast between Paul and the Corinthians and makes space for the adversarial atmosphere to be considered, as it also heightens the surprise that comes in the "emplotment" statement here, as well as in those to come.

The dramatic goal of the foreign Other in 2 Corinthians, entirely missed by these colloquializing strategies, is to define for the Corinthians, theologically and eschatologically, their location in the story of God's comfort/salvation. In near context and remote, 1:6 takes its cue from the eschatological "divine comfort" theme with which Paul defines mission. Given the adversarial atmosphere and the urgency of reshaping Corinthian understanding, Paul does not "sweet talk" this dubious church; he instead creates a theological landscape, defines the prophetic source of his apostolic mission, and here entices the audience to admit and accept their place in what is coming to pass—in the end (5:20–6:2) enticement becomes urgent exhortation (also with παρακαλέω!).

After 1:6, a string of similar statements unfold the emplotment strategy. We can only trace the path here: 1:13-14; 1:15-22; 1:23-24; 2:1-5; 2:10; 3:2-3; 4:12, 14; 5:11-13. Each statement in its own way weaves together the fates of Paul the Apostle and his skeptical converts. From boasting at the Eschaton, to pain, distress and forgiveness in the present, to living letters of recommendation and present experiences of the Spirit, Paul has written the Corinthians indisputably into his mission narrative. To refuse to be emplotted is to deny the Spirit whose presence they themselves cherish.

The foreign voice emits a discernible "difference" that colloquialization and domestication can suppress or censor altogether. I have measured this "difference" in various ways. While the foreign text observed may be more resistant to the pastoral reading extracted by contemporary English translations, it does reveal more readily a primal intertextual resonance that locates the apostle's mission decisively in the redemptive narrative of Isa 40–66, not as a reliving of the past, but as the continuation of a precursor narrative. It reveals equally the shared identity of the apostle and his churches, emplotted within the unfolding redemptive drama. Identity itself—apostolic, Christian—is redefined as missional identity: as the apostle interprets his identity and being in terms of the proclamation of fulfilled promise, the Corinthians are invited to find their place in the narrative, both as beneficiaries and κοινωνοί of the mission of divine comfort.

4

THE SON OF MAN IN HEBREWS 2:6:
A DILEMMA FOR BIBLE TRANSLATORS

Dick France

One of the lesser-known aspects of Howard Marshall's contribution to biblical scholarship is his involvement over several years as a consultant to the Committee on Bible Translation, which has had responsibility for the text of the *New International Version*. In this capacity Howard participated in several of the Committee's annual workshops, during the period when the revised version of the NIV, known as *Today's New International Version* (2005), was being prepared. As one of the British members of the Committee, I have happy memories of Howard's contributions to our exegetical decisions, and to the search for the appropriate English (or occasionally Scottish) idiom to express the agreed meaning. This article relates to that collaboration, though I hope it may also convey my profound gratitude to Howard over a wider field, not only for many important exegetical and theological insights across a wide range of NT scholarship, but also for his personal example as both a rigorously honest scholar and a committed evangelical who has never lost his concern for the life and mission of the church outside the lecture hall.[1]

One of the important issues facing all biblical translators at that period was the question of "gender-accurate language" (or, as we called it then, "inclusive language"). No Bible translation since the last two decades of the twentieth century can afford to ignore the fact that for many (but not all) readers of English it had by then become unacceptable to use masculine terms such as "man," "men" or "brother(s)," with the associated masculine pronouns "he," "him" and "his" to refer to people in general rather than specifically to those of the male gender. Yet the biblical languages were full of such "generic masculines," and traditional Bible translations had been content to preserve these idioms. As long as the "generic masculine" remained acceptable in modern English, this was the obvious course to follow. But once linguistic sensitivity had begun to change, and some women readers had come to regard such language as excluding them, translators could no longer hide behind the idioms of the biblical languages if they were to convey the thought of the biblical writers appropriately for a changed linguistic situation. If biblical

---

[1] Nearly a decade ago I was privileged to contribute a biographical assessment of Howard's contribution in R. T. France, "Profile: Howard Marshall," *Epworth Review* 29, no. 4 (October 2002): 14-21. The article contains a bibliography of books (not articles) published by Howard up to that date.

references to "men" or "brothers" were intended to be understood as inclusive of both genders, but contemporary English usage no longer allowed that option, to use such masculine-specific terms where the text was not intended to speak only of males was simply mistranslation. And it was a mistranslation which was likely to have increasingly serious consequences for the reception of the Bible's message. If women, particularly younger women, and those who were sensitive to their concerns, were being alienated by old-fashioned insistence on reproducing the Hebrew and Greek idioms literally into English, this was not a matter merely of scholarly preference but of mission. A Bible translation which could be read as excluding half the human race from God's saving concern would be a serious impediment to the church's mission. As this volume is focused especially on Howard Marshall's concern for mission, it seems appropriate to explore here this issue of gender-accurate language, especially as it relates to one controversial passage in the NT.

TRANSLATION AND GENDER

The problems confronting the biblical translator in this area are many. There is, first of all, the basic task of deciding exegetically whether a given passage which uses masculine language is or is not intended to be universal in its scope. This can be decided only on a case-by-case basis, taking the wider literary and cultural context into account, and many such decisions will inevitably leave room for disagreement. But even when all are agreed that the reference is to people of both genders, the translator is constantly frustrated by the poverty of the English language when it comes to means of expressing this universal reference without recourse to the outdated use of "generic masculine" language—especially in a Bible version which is intended to be easily read by ordinary people, not only by scholars who may be more attuned to the gender issue. It might be correct to make frequent use of "man or woman" or "he or she," but few of us feel that such tedious repetition is in the best interests of a readable translation.

One regularly used method of evading the problem is to move to the plural, where English pronouns make no gender distinction, so that for instance "The man who ... his ..." becomes "Those who ... their ... " Where the passage is clearly talking about people in general this is often the best method, but in some passages it can reasonably be argued that it is the situation of a specific person that is in view, and that the use of the plural may "de-individualize" the impression on the reader and thus weaken the impact of the passage.

Another option has been to move, where the context allows, from the third person to the second, since the English "you" is not gender-specific. What is expressed with regard to people in general may sometimes be clearly intended to apply in the immediate context to those being addressed in the text. But here there is the opposite danger, that the reader, seeing the second person address, may conclude that the challenge applies *only* to those originally addressed and so may evade its wider and contemporary application.

Such problems do not apply only to biblical language. Most contemporary writers of English take care to avoid the generic masculine, and when you are composing from scratch rather than translating a preexisting text that is much easier to achieve without the cumbersome and repetitive use of "he or she" etc. The pedantic formula "s/he" is not a serious option for a literary text, but some authors alternate between using "he" and "she" for a non-specific person. Others use "she" consistently simply in order to redress the gender balance over against traditional usage. Some have suggested, I hope not seriously, the adoption of a specially invented gender-neutral third person pronoun ("ha," "ho," "hum," etc.). But by far the most striking change in English usage in the last few decades has been the increasing acceptance of the so-called "singular they/their," as in "Everyone must make up their own mind" or "A good child will wash their hands before they eat." Most of us who are of a certain age still prickle when we see such formulations, but they have a long pedigree,[2] and now they appear increasingly boldly in the media and even in "serious" literature. When the Committee on Bible Translation first began to discuss the issue of gender-accurate language, most of us instinctively shied away from the singular "their," even in its least offensive form when it follows a "whoever" or "anyone who," but as years have gone by it becomes increasingly clear that this is the way the English language is moving, and the only question for the translator is whether it is our role to lead or to follow in the process of change.[3]

There are many such fascinating questions which arise for the Bible translator who embraces the need for gender-accurate language, and the goalposts seem to keep moving as English usage evolves. A suitable strategy for today is likely to be outdated in ten or twenty years' time. In this, as in so many respects, the work of translation is never done, only fulfilled to the best of one's ability for the present time. But the problems go beyond the vagaries of English usage, and I want in this article to illustrate something of the challenge (and indeed ultimately the impossibility) of the translation process by focusing on one particular NT text which has been the subject of extended debate within the Committee. I do not now remember how Howard's vote went on this issue, but I doubt whether any of the Committee have felt that any of the translation options offers a perfect solution to the problem of putting this masculine-

---

[2] Examples are quoted from as early as Chaucer, and in such respected writers as Shakespeare, Jane Austen and Charles Dickens. Even the KJV could use a singular "their" (Matt 18:35).

[3] The latest edition of *Fowler's Modern English Usage* (ed. R. W. Burchfield; 3d ed.; Oxford: Oxford University Press, 1998) concludes with regard to the use of "they," "their" and "them" with a singular reference: "The process now seems irreversible" (779). Contrast the second edition, 1965, which rejected the use of "their" after "one" as "horrible" (417), on 404 declared of the use of "themselves" after "anybody" that "It sets the literary man's teeth on edge." (Notice "literary *man*"; no consideration was given to the literary woman!)

formulated text into gender-appropriate language.

HEBREWS 2:6—THE EXEGESIS

A fairly literal translation of Heb 2:5-9 might run as follows:

> [5] For it was not to angels that he subjected the coming world, about which we are speaking. [6] But someone has testified somewhere, saying,
> "What is a man that you should remember him,
> or a son of a man that you should take care of him?
> [7] You made him a little (*or* for a little time) lower than angels;
> you crowned him with glory and honor;
> [8] you subjected everything beneath his feet."
> For in subjecting everything to him, he left nothing not subject to him. But as it is we do not yet see everything subjected to him. [9] But we see the one who was made a little (*or* for a little time) lower than angels, Jesus, crowned with glory and honor through the suffering of death, so that by God's grace he might taste death on behalf of everyone.

The letter focuses from 1:4 to 2:18 on a comparison between "the Son" and angels, showing the superiority of the former to the latter. But whereas in ch. 1 that argument takes the relatively straightforward course of demonstrating by a series of (often surprising) biblical quotations that the Son is superior in honor and authority to angels, in 2:5-18 that same point is made paradoxically by celebrating the Son's (temporary) humiliation, made for a little time "lower than the angels" by his incarnation, because only so could he achieve salvation for humanity—something angels could never do. In that argument Ps 8 plays a key role, as the "text" on which this mini-sermon is based.[4]

Psalm 8 celebrates the glory of God the creator, in comparison with whose created world humanity seems so insignificant, and yet paradoxically God has placed humanity in a position of authority second only to that of God himself, giving them the responsibility of ruling over the rest of his animal creation. That summary might seem to offer little scope for demonstrating the superiority of the Son to angels, since it mentions neither, but the writer of Hebrews is nothing if not ingenious. In this case he[5] gains help from three linguistic

---

[4] I have discussed the significance of such "expository sermons" in Hebrews in R. T. France, "The Writer of Hebrews as a Biblical Expositor," *TynBul* 47 (1996): 245-76. This particular exposition is briefly discussed ibid., 261-63.

[5] In relation to the author of Hebrews I am spared the necessity of making repeated use of "he or she" by the fact that the author uses the unambiguously masculine participle διηγούμενον when referring to himself in 11:32. If, as a few have suggested, the unknown author was a woman, she appears to have deliberately presented herself as a man, and I am content to follow her lead!

features of the text.

(a) the LXX phrase βραχύ τι (and *possibly* the Hebrew מְעַט, "a little," which it represents) can be taken to mean "for a short time," even though in the psalm context the meaning seems clearly to be "to a small degree";

(b) the LXX translates the Hebrew אֱלֹהִים in v. 5 not in its normal sense "God," which is probably the sense intended here in the psalm, but as "angels";[6]

(c) in the parallelism of v. 4 the second term used for humanity is the well-known Semitic idiom "a son of man," which LXX translates literally as υἱὸς ἀνθρώπου; in Hebrew the phrase is a natural idiom, but that idiom does not exist in Greek, so that the literal Greek rendering draws attention to itself as "translation Greek."

The first two of these features enable Hebrews to find in Ps 8:5 a description of the incarnation—"made for a little while lower than angels"—which would have been very hard to discern in the Hebrew text. In the psalm the two successive clauses of v.5, "made them a little lower than God" and "crowned them with glory and honor," are *parallel* statements of the extraordinary dignity of humanity, whereas Hebrews has made them serve as *contrasting* statements of, first, a temporary humiliation ("made for a little while lower than angels") followed by a return to glory and honor. On this basis the author has been able to "see Jesus" (v. 9) in the psalm, and moreover to find him placed in explicit comparison with angels. The fact that he is presented as *lower than* the angels thus prompts the writer's paradoxical argument that it was precisely because he accepted that temporary loss of status ("for a little while") before resuming his inherently superior status in the divine economy that he was able to achieve the salvation of humanity, and thus provide a service superior to anything that angels could offer.

So far so good, if a little "creative" in the light of what we understand to be proper biblical exegesis. But what has that conclusion to do with the psalm's celebration of the high status of humanity? Indeed, why should he have thought that the psalm had anything to do with Jesus in the first place? This is where the third linguistic feature comes into play, for surely any Christian writing in the latter part of the first century could hardly read the "translation Greek" phrase υἱὸς ἀνθρώπου without thinking of Jesus, whose chosen public title, ὁ υἱὸς τοῦ ἀνθρώπου, had by now been widely disseminated in the gospel

---

[6] That this is not simply an idiosyncratic LXX rendering, but a recognized exegetical option, is shown by its appearance also in Targum, Syriac and Vulgate, and in later Jewish commentaries on the psalm. It is adopted not only in the KJV but also in NIV/TNIV "heavenly beings" (followed by ESV). NEB/REB and NJB render it "a god." On the other hand, it is surely significant that the later Jewish Greek versions, Aquila, Symmachus and Theodotion, did not follow the lead of the LXX, but rendered it as "God."

traditions.⁷ And so it is no surprise that our author, as he reads this psalm in the LXX version, is able to "see Jesus" there as the one who was made for a little while lower than the angels but is now crowned with glory and honor.

So many have concluded, and they have gone on to charge the author with having completely misunderstood, or at least misappropriated, the text of the psalm. For surely anyone with even a smattering of Semitic culture (and the author of Hebrews had a lot more than a smattering) must have known that the phrase "a son of a man" in such a context is not talking about an individual, but is, just like the "man" with which it stands in parallel, an idiomatic generic term for humanity understood corporately.

But what this charge fails to take into account is that in fact our author has clearly understood the psalm perfectly well in its natural Hebrew sense, and indeed has based his whole argument on that sense. It is precisely the subjection of the animal creation to humanity as a whole that he is thinking of when he makes his exegetical comment that "we do not yet see everything subjected to him." Human beings were supposed to be able to control the rest of the animal creation, but it does not take much observation (and still less in the less ecologically diminished world of the first-century Middle East) to make one aware that a great deal of the animal creation shows no subservience to its supposed human overlords. The divine purpose expressed in the psalm still remains to be fully implemented.

So the introduction of Jesus into the author's "sermon" is not an arbitrary departure from what the psalm was actually talking about, but rather is the means by which the psalmist's ecological vision is now at last to reach its fulfillment. We do not yet see humanity as a whole in the intended position of supreme authority, but instead that corporate role of humanity has been assumed by the individual Jesus, so that in his being "crowned with glory and honor" humankind has been vicariously elevated to the authoritative status for which the creator had designed it. This sovereign role for Jesus is also suggested by the phrase "subjected everything beneath his feet" quoted from Ps 8:6, which recalls the messianic authority of the "Lord" in Ps 110:1, a text which our author has already applied to Jesus in Heb 1:13 (cf. 10:13).

But how is it possible for Jesus, now named for the first time in this letter as the divine "Son" whom the author wishes to elevate above the angels, to represent humanity as a whole? It is because he, who as Paul once put it "was in the form of God" (Phil 2:6),⁸ was prepared to step down "for a little while"

---

⁷ *Pace* H. W. Attridge, *The Epistle to the Hebrews* (Hermeneia; Philadelphia: Fortress, 1989), 73-74, who attributes the use of "the Son of Man" as a title for Jesus to "the early church" and therefore argues that the author of Hebrews "simply did not know the Son of Man tradition".

⁸ L. D. Hurst, *The Epistle to the Hebrews: Its Background of Thought* (SNTSMS 65; Cambridge: Cambridge University Press, 1990) 114-19, explores the parallels between the thought of Phil 2:6-11 and this passage.

to a position "lower than the angels" and so by incarnation to be identified with humanity, "so that by God's grace he might taste death on behalf of everyone." The rest of ch. 2 will be devoted to exploring this essential element in the Christian gospel of salvation, that Jesus had to "become like his brothers and sisters in every respect" (v. 17) in order to be able to "taste death on their behalf." Here in Heb 2 is one of the NT's most penetrating answers to Anselm's famous question *Cur Deus Homo?* ("Why [did] God [become] Man?"). The incarnation (being made "lower than the angels") is the clinching argument for the Son's superiority to angels—only he, through becoming truly human, can bring salvation to humanity.

So Jesus, the incarnate Son, sums up humanity in himself. And that is why he is able also to fulfill the vision of Ps 8 on behalf of humanity. When the author "sees Jesus" he sees humanity as it was meant to be (cf. Paul's imagery of Christ as the "second Adam"). And so he sees him as "the Son of Man," a term which conveniently *both* denotes the human race corporately, *and*, being singular in form, allows itself to be adopted as a designation for a single human being—which is of course precisely what the historical Jesus has so memorably done when he adopted "the Son of Man" as his public title. While I believe that the primary OT influence in Jesus' choice of this title was Dan 7:13, where the term denotes an individual human figure who represents the corporate destiny of Israel, there have been some NT scholars who have insisted that even in Jesus' most individual uses of the title there remains an element of corporate identity.[9] Certainly anyone conversant with Hebrew idiom would always be open to that nuance, and the author of Hebrews was more than merely "conversant" with Hebrew idiom. So the appearance of the term "son of man" in the text of Ps 8:4 provided a perfect lead in to the argument for Jesus as the representative Man that our author wished to develop in ch. 2. It is perhaps conceivable that he could have developed this argument simply from the corporate understanding of Ps 8 together with the linguistic convenience of "a little while" and the LXX "angels." But in view of his full quotation of the psalm with its "unGreek" but suggestive phrase υἱὸς ἀνθρώπου and his following declaration that in this psalm he can "see Jesus," it seems to me much more probable that the ambiguity of the phrase appealed to his subtle mind, and that he is deliberately exploiting "son of man" in both its senses, as a natural Hebrew corporate idiom and at the same time as the chosen title of Jesus, the representative Man.

The exegetical approach I have outlined above is to be clearly distinguished from the "messianic psalm" exegesis,[10] which supposes that the author of

---

[9] This was famously argued by T. W. Manson, *The Teaching of Jesus* (2d ed.; Cambridge: Cambridge University Press, 1935) 211-34; idem, "The Son of Man in Daniel, Enoch and the Gospels," *BJRL* 32 (1949–1950): 171-95.

[10] See e.g., F. J. Moloney, "The Re-interpretation of Psalm VIII and the Son of Man Debate," *NTS* 27 (1981): 656-72.

Hebrews belonged to a tradition which saw this psalm, like Ps 110, as in itself a messianic prediction, so that the "son of man" (and presumably also the parallel "man") was in fact intended by the psalm's author to denote the Messiah. The nature of our author's exposition makes it clear, however, that he understood the psalm to be talking about humanity in general; indeed it *demands* that understanding. It is only if the psalm is about humanity's so far unfulfilled destiny that it provides the basis for the argument that in fact a new representative Man has come on the scene to carry forward God's original purpose. The relevance of the phrase "a son of man" in the psalm is not that our author thought it originally *meant* the Messiah, but that in the light of Jesus' chosen title its occurrence in this psalm formed a suggestive bridge which enabled him to "see Jesus," and so to develop his theology of Jesus as the representative Man. It was the familiarity of the phrase in Christian usage that provided the trigger that enabled our author to link Jesus, the Son, with the corporate destiny of humanity which the psalm had celebrated. It was, we might say, a serendipitous linguistic accident that the psalmist had, all unknowing, used a natural Hebrew idiom which in its Greek form would allow this Christian reader to make a connection which his theology of Jesus as the "proper man"[11] already required. The discovery of an individual person in the psalmist's phrase "a son of man" is thus an original development by our author, in full awareness of the psalmist's corporate intention, not an already current exegetical tradition to which he subscribed.[12]

There are many more exegetical debates around Heb 2 which I have not touched on here, and much of what I have written would be disputed by one commentator or another, but I hope the above is enough to indicate how I understand the argument to be constructed, and the significant role which the actual phrase υἱὸς ἀνθρώπου played in its construction.

HEBREWS 2:6 AND PSALM 8:4—THE TRANSLATOR'S DILEMMA

The argument of Heb 2:5-9 poses several distinct problems for the translator. Some of them have not even been hinted at in my selective exegetical comments above, but even within the issues I have focused on there are the obvious questions raised by the author's creative exegesis of βραχύ τι ("a little" or "a little while") and of ἀγγέλους where his understanding of the LXX text parts company with the accepted exegesis of Ps 8. If the Hebrews passage

---

[11] This phrase from the English version of Luther's hymn *Ein feste Burg* has suggested itself to some commentators as a summary of the theology of Heb 2:5-9; so e.g., F. F. Bruce, R. P. Gordon.

[12] "Hebrews fully understands that 'man' and 'son of man' in the psalm are collective terms, even though he interprets them individually of Jesus in the first instance" (B. Lindars, *The Theology of the Letter to the Hebrews* [Cambridge: Cambridge University Press, 1991], 39).

could be taken in isolation, it would be relatively simple to translate these phrases by "a little while" and "angels," since that is clearly what the author's argument requires. But the translator must also be alert to intertextual connections, and if Ps 8 is translated in its normally accepted sense ("only a little lower than God") the English reader would then be left with a puzzling mismatch between the original text and its quotation. Such problems arise quite often in translating the NT where the LXX text quoted by the NT author differs from the natural sense of the Hebrew, and most translators would agree that it is our responsibility to translate the Greek as it stands, and leave the resultant problems of "harmonization" to the commentator and the preacher.

In this case it seems clear that ἀγγέλους must be rendered as "angels," since not to do so would obscure the relevance of the author's psalm-quotation to the whole surrounding argument about the Son's relation to angels that this quotation is designed to forward.

Βραχύ τι is less straightforward: the author's exposition in Heb 2:9 is surely made clearer by translating the phrase "for a little while" there, but should the translator also anticipate this argument by using the same phrase in the psalm quotation in v. 7 even though it is most unlikely that that was what the psalmist or his LXX translator intended? The RSV/NRSV took the latter course, putting "for a little while" in both verses, while the NIV had simply "a little" in both verses. The TNIV has cut between the two, rendering by "a little" in the psalm quotation in v. 7, but "for a little while" in the exposition in v. 9. It is an interesting question which of these options most helps the reader to grasp how the author's argument is derived from his reading of the psalm.

My purpose here, however, is not to pursue these other translation issues, but to focus on the one which results from the desire to use gender-accurate language. This too arises especially from the question of how far it is appropriate for the "correct" translation of Ps 8 to determine how we should render its quotation in Heb 2. Before the issue of gender sensitivity arose, there was no problem. The masculine singulars "man" and "son of man" and the resultant masculine singular pronouns in the following verses worked equally well in both OT and NT contexts, and the presence of the phrase "son of man" in the text of Heb 2:6 left the field open for commentators to discuss what role this "title" might have played in the author's subsequent argument. But once "man" is perceived as an unacceptable way of referring to humanity, the translator faces a challenging problem.

If Ps 8 is translated on its own, without reference to its intertextual link with Heb 2, there is of course no problem in principle, however much we may disagree about the best English terms to use to denote humanity corporately. Unless you believe that the psalmist was thinking of an individual messianic figure when he spoke of "a son of man"—and I am not aware that that option is seriously canvassed in contemporary scholarship—the whole of vv. 4-6 of the psalm should be rendered as referring to humanity as a whole, and in modern gender-accurate language that is most naturally done by using plural nouns followed by the plural pronouns "them" and "their."[13] Linguistic tastes vary as to whether humanity is best referred to in contemporary English as, e.g., "human beings," "mortals," "mere mortals," "humans" or "people." Few of these terms sit easily in this poetic context, and the choice is further restricted in this case by the need to find two terms for the parallel lines of poetry. So translators have had to make their subjective choices among the available plural terms in English. But some such plural terminology seems essential if the passage as a whole is to be read as referring to the whole of humanity, not only to its male half.

But of course the translator cannot afford to consider Ps 8 in isolation. How then is the quotation of the LXX version of the psalm in Heb 2:6-8 to be rendered?

The apparently straight-forward approach is to use the same plural terms in Hebrews as in the psalm. After all, the terms "man" and "son of man" mean exactly the same in Hebrews as they do in the psalm, and we have seen in our exegesis above that the author of Hebrews so understood them: this is a psalm about the status and destiny of the human race as a whole. The English reader will then be able to see the same words in both passages, and the issue of harmonization will be limited to the difference between "angels" and "God," and possibly the issue of "a little" against "for a little while."

This is the approach followed, e.g., by NRSV and TNIV. But it raises two significant problems. First, whereas the Hebrew בן־אדם is a natural and recognized idiom for humanity, the Greek υἱὸς ἀνθρώπου is not; it is "translation Greek." Should the translator then make it possible for the English reader to recognize this by using the English phrase "a son of man" which is equally unidiomatic? But secondly, and more importantly for the exegesis of the passage, I have argued above that the actual phrase "son of man" played a significant role in the author's development of his argument, so that if it no longer appears in his quotation from the psalm the English reader is deprived of the means of discerning how he managed to "see Jesus" in this psalm in the first place.

For clarity, let me repeat that I do not believe either that the psalmist intended "the son of man" to denote a singular (messianic) figure, or that the author of Hebrews thought that that was the psalmist's intention. If that were the case it would of course be misleading for the translator to use plural,

---

[13] Some versions, however, while avoiding the blatantly masculine terms "man" and "son of man," have nevertheless chosen to use a singular generic term followed by the masculine pronouns "him" and "his." Thus REB renders "What is a frail mortal, that you should be mindful of him, a human being that you should take notice of him?" while NJB mixes plural and singular: "What are human beings that you spare a thought for them, or the child of Adam that you care for him." Such apparently mediating versions in fact leave the essential problem unsolved, since the pronouns remain inescapably masculine.

inclusive language in either Ps 8 or Heb 2.[14] Our author understood the corporate reference of the psalm clearly enough, and based his argument on it. But in doing so he found in the unidiomatic LXX phrase "a son of man" a suggestive trigger for his observation that the corporate destiny of humanity has in fact found its fulfillment in an individual representative Man, the one who historically described himself as "the Son of Man."

What then are the options before the English translator? There seem to be essentially three:[15]

(1) to translate both the psalm and the Hebrews quotation using plural, inclusive language throughout, and thus, by not allowing the phrase "son of man" to appear in the text, to deprive the English reader of the chance of seeing how (on my view) the author of Hebrews constructed his argument;

(2) to retain the traditional singular language (including the phrase "son of man") in both the psalm and Hebrews, and thus to perpetuate the masculine language for what was clearly meant to be an inclusive statement, and at the same time to run the risk of obscuring the corporate intention of the psalm, which is also essential to the argument in Hebrews 2;

(3) to translate the psalm in the natural plural sense of the Hebrew idioms, but to translate the LXX quotation in Heb 2 in a way which retains the stylistic peculiarity of the translation Greek phrase υἱὸς ἀνθρώπου.

Clearly none of these options is entirely satisfactory. Surely the least attractive for anyone who takes seriously the need for gender-accurate language is option 2, which is that followed by ESV. This option is likely to appeal only to those who really believe that the psalmist was intending to speak of an individual messianic figure (or at least that the author of Hebrews thought he was). Option 1 has the merit of simplicity and of consistency, but leaves to the commentator or the preacher the task of explaining how the author of Hebrews

---

[14] Cf. R. P. Gordon, *Hebrews* (Sheffield: Sheffield Academic Press, 2000), 50: "The 'direct reference' approach is, of course, difficult to sustain on the basis of inclusive renderings such as NRSV's 'human beings' and 'mortals'. (NRSV excludes it in any case by translating v. 8b, 'we do not yet see everything in subjection *to them*'.)"

[15] After I had written this article my attention was drawn to a recent article on the same subject by my colleague on the Committee for Bible Translation, Craig Blomberg (C. L. Blomberg, "'But We See Jesus': The Relationship between the Son of Man in Hebrews 2:6 and Verse 9, and the Implications for English Translation," in *A Cloud of Witnesses: The Theology of Hebrews in Its Ancient Contexts*, [LNTS; ed. R. Bauckham et al.; London: T&T Clark, 2008], 88-99). Blomberg discusses only two translation approaches, corresponding respectively to what he terms the "anthropological" and the "Christological" understandings of the argument of Heb 2:5-9. These are my options 1 and 2. He does not consider the possibility of a mediating approach which retains the term "son of man" in the text while still recognizing the author's "anthropological" understanding of the psalm, since he queries whether the author of Hebrews, especially if writing in the early 60s, would have been familiar with "the Son of Man" as a title of Jesus.

was able to "see Jesus" in the phrase "son of man" when that phrase no longer appears in the English text.

Option 3 is a compromise, and, like most compromises, leaves the purist unsatisfied. By trying to have its cake and eat it, it leaves the reader with two significantly different renderings of the same psalm text. This is not necessarily unacceptable, since the LXX text quoted by a NT author is often different from the Hebrew translated in our OT, and the English versions frequently display these differences. In this case the LXX use of ἀγγέλους for אלהים means that the two renderings will in any case differ in at least one point, and I have argued above that the translator may be justified also in alerting the English reader to the awkwardness of the Greek idiom υἱὸς ἀνθρώπου, if by so doing he or she can enable the reader to follow how the argument is developed. But that argument depends as much on the agreed corporate sense of the psalm as it does on the singular form of the phrase "a son of man," so that it seems impossible for a single English rendering to do full justice to the author's creative exegesis.

A further dilemma is introduced if option 3 is followed. Should (a) "a son of man" in Heb 2:6 be allowed to stand as a solitary singular (with its resumptive "him"), surrounded by the plural "human beings" (or the like) and the plural pronouns "them" and "their," or should (b) the whole of the Hebrews quotation retain the singulars of the original, thus reintroducing in the NT the masculine language which has been removed from the psalm? Option (a) would do the least damage to the properly corporate understanding of the psalm both in itself and in our author's interpretation of it, but at the cost of some stylistic awkwardness: the resumptive pronouns "them" and "their" in v. 7 would follow uneasily after "a son of man" and "him" in v. 6c—though of course this might in itself help the reader to recognize more easily the corporate meaning of the Hebrew phrase "a son of man." Option (b) with its singular pronouns in vv. 6-8 would ease the reader's transition to the individual figure of Jesus as the one in whom the psalm's vision is fulfilled, but at the cost of obscuring the psalm's corporate vision, and leaving the reader puzzled as to why the translator has treated the same psalm so differently in its OT and NT contexts.

My preference would be for option 3a, which, using the TNIV as base, would read as follows for vv. 6-9:

> [6] But there is a place where someone has testified:
> "What are mere mortals that you are mindful of them,
> a son of man that you care for him?
> [7] You made them a little (*or* for a little while) lower than the angels;
> you crowned them with glory and honor
> [8] and put everything under their feet."

In putting everything under them, God left nothing that is not subject to them. Yet at present we do not see everything subject to them. [9] But we do see Jesus, . . .

DOES ANYONE READ FOOTNOTES?

The dilemmas outlined above all arise from the fact that the translator, as translator, does not have the luxury of adding explanatory comments or presenting alternative renderings side by side. A single form of words must be selected which will on its own enable the reader to get as close as possible to what the original text would have conveyed. And there the chosen rendering must stand, naked and alone, exposed to all the distortions and misunderstandings which readers from a wide variety of cultures and educational experiences may bring to it.

But surely there is help at hand, in the form of footnotes? Here the translator has the opportunity to introduce the reader to the ambiguities and sometimes deliberate word-plays of the text, and perhaps to salve his or her conscience, and to deflect criticism, for having been obliged to set aside a widely supported alternative understanding of the text. The temptation is strong to fill the bottom of the page with such notes, wherever a difficult exegetical or linguistic decision has had to be made. But who wants their Bible page to be cluttered with footnotes like an academic textbook? And will this not give the uninitiated reader the impression that everything is up for grabs, and that no one really knows what the text means? So most translators are instinctively wary of adding footnotes except where they are absolutely necessary.

Here, however, is surely a case where footnotes really are needed, whichever of the translation options may be followed. Perhaps this is not essential in Ps 8, unless one wants to leave the option open that the author did in fact intend his singular terms to denote an individual messianic figure. But in Heb 2, whichever of the above options is followed, footnotes seem to be essential. On option 1 footnotes informing the reader that in the original the term "son of man" appears and the following pronouns are singular will provide the reader with the necessary clue to follow the author's argument. On option 2 a footnote acknowledging the corporate sense of the psalmist's singular terms may help the reader to see that it is as the representative of all humanity that Jesus now fulfils the psalm's vision. And on option 3 a footnote giving the corporate sense of "son of man" will help to relieve the reader's unease when they observe the difference between the OT and NT forms of the same text.

Or at least that is the theory, and any translator will gratefully accept this convenient means of escape from the dilemma. But how real an escape is it? Can we really take it for granted that most Bible readers take any notice of footnotes? When the Bible is read aloud in church, of course, no footnote is heard; it is up to the preacher expounding the text to introduce the congregation to the exegetical options and debates, if they are so inclined. But is the private reader any better served by footnotes? I do not know whether any research has been done to ascertain the average reader's awareness of the footnotes, but I suspect that it is easy to overestimate their effect. They may serve well to alleviate the translator's conscience, but can we assume that because we have put an alternative rendering or an explanatory phrase in a footnote the average reader will consult it? And even if they do, can we assume that the few bare words at the bottom of the page will be enough to enable them to follow us through the exegetical pilgrimage which led us to adopt the printed text?

So in a tricky passage such as Heb 2:6-8 I believe there is no avoiding the need to make a choice between renderings, in the likely expectation that those words, and only those words, will be the ones that most readers encounter. Our responsibility is to choose the wording which will best enable the reader unaided to follow the sense of the passage. In the end, that may mean judging which is the least misleading of a number of not totally satisfactory alternatives.

Conclusion

This article has not attempted to prescribe which of the translation options for Heb 2:6-8 is the "right" option, even though I have indicated a preference for my option 3a. My aim was rather to set out what sort of options are available to the translator, and to indicate the problems with which each is confronted. My object in doing so was to illustrate the complexity of the task of Bible translation, especially with regard to the search for a gender-accurate rendering for today's world of a text which used masculine terms with a generic sense. In the end, I have suggested, there is no perfect solution. The wording we eventually choose may be, in our view, the best available, but none is likely to leave us, or our readers, fully satisfied.

The principal problems in translating Heb 2:6-8 arise from the demand for what I have called gender accuracy. In view of the complications which have arisen, would it not after all be simpler to revert to a supposedly "literal" translation, which simply reproduces the masculine language of the Hebrew and Greek texts? If such a rendering has served the church well for nearly two thousand years, why make things difficult for ourselves by trying to evade the masculinity of the text? Is this not after all an unnecessary capitulation to political correctness, kowtowing to what may in the end turn out to be a passing trend?

But the aim of a translation is to communicate, and if a "literal" rendering no longer communicates what the scriptural authors intended, it is not a translation for today. There will no doubt continue for some time to be many speakers of English, particularly those of an older generation, who find no fault with the traditional use of the generic masculine. But the issue of linguistic exclusion will not go away, and current evidence suggests that the number of readers who feel that the generic masculine excludes or devalues women is increasing substantially, so that those of the younger generation, both women and men, who are comfortable with the continued use of generic masculine language are probably already in a minority. If it is the mission of the church to communicate the good news in language which will not alienate those who hear it, and which will enable them to enter sympathetically into the Christian heritage, then it is the duty of translators to wrestle with the issue of inclusive language, whatever the dilemmas it may pose in a passage like Heb 2:5-9. To do so is to be engaged at a fundamental level in the *missio Dei*.

5

THE GOSPEL BEFORE THE GOSPELS: THE PREACHED CORE NARRATIVE

Darrell L. Bock

Today it is common to present the gospel in very Pauline terms. This means it is about death for sin accomplished through atonement (see Rom 1–4 or 1 Cor 15:1-5).[1] One of the oddities of this presentation is that this emphasis is almost entirely lacking in the speeches in Acts where evangelism is being done, and the gospel is seemingly being presented. This dissonance has always bothered me. So in this study I want to simply draw some lines of emphasis emerging out of the preached speeches in Acts where drawing people to appreciate what God did through Jesus is the emphasis. I focus on Acts because it is here we see samples of what the early church of the first century actually preached.[2] What is interesting is that when we are done, I think we will be able to see the points of contact with Paul and other NT writings, so that we have a better appreciation for the hope and depth of the gospel, not to mention why it is called good news.

I present this study not as a technical scholarly piece, but as a piece of reflection for those in the church. I can think of no better person to dedicate such a study to than I. Howard Marshall, whose commitment to care and quality in biblical study was a value he passed on to his grateful students with a gentleness and rigor that helped one move toward the goal. Yet here was a scholar who cared about the church and God's people. His commitment to excellence was a commitment to serve the church faithfully. He exemplified that to his students as well. So this study is submitted with gratitude for the work of this fine Christian gentleman.

---

[1] This tract is admirably summarized by Greg Gilbert, *What is the Gospel?* (Wheaton: Crossway, 2010).

[2] The following point is important however one views these speeches. These texts represent the best examples we have of efforts at evangelism in the first century. As such they are the gospel before the gospels were written to summarize how we are to see Jesus. Since Luke is written somewhere between the sixties and eighties (I prefer the sixties), this is our earliest evidence for how the gospel was presented. Of course, if the speeches reflect the gist of earlier apostolic preaching, as C. H. Dodd contended in his work on the kerygma, then we are in the thirties; *Apostolic Preaching and Its Developments: Three Lectures With an Appendix on Eschatology and History* (Grand Rapids; Baker Books, 1982 repr.).

ACTS 2: THE SPIRIT AS SIGN OF THE ARRIVAL OF MESSIAH AND PROMISE

The first speech Luke presents in Acts is Peter's Pentecost address. The central thesis of the preaching is found in v. 36. Israel can know that Jesus is both Lord and Christ because God had vindicated Jesus enabling him to mediate the Spirit he had received from the Father. To make the point, Peter highlights three passages from the sacred Scripture of the Hebrews. Joel 2 promised the coming of the Spirit in the last days and the promise that those who call on the name of the Lord will be saved. Psalm 16 promised the hope of resurrection. Psalm 110 promised the seating of the one addressed at the right hand of God. Peter reads Joel 2 as explaining the distribution of the Spirit. Luke had already set up the significance of this by things he had said earlier in his gospel. In Luke 3:16 John the Baptist explains that the way to know the Messiah had come (and that the Messiah was not him) would be when one stronger than him baptizes with the Spirit and fire. In Luke 24:49 this is described as the promise of the Father. The disciples will be clothed by God with power from on high. Acts 1:4-5 echoes the remarks of John the Baptist as something Jesus also taught. In other words, the sign and proof of the arrival of the new promised era and one to come is shown by the exaltation of Jesus which permits the distribution of the long awaited Spirit of God. This in vv. 38-39 is described as the offer of forgiveness and the gift of the Spirit, a promise God had made to those God called Acts 2:38-39 summarizes the gospel of this early speech. It involves God reclaiming his own by offering forgiveness of sins and life in the Spirit of God. This act is performed in the name of the exalted Jesus, who acts through the direction and initiation of the God of Israel. What is significant here is that the gospel is seen in more than forgiveness of sins. It extends to what forgiveness provides for, life energized by the Spirit of God, enablement that points to the arrival of the long-awaited, promised new era from God.

In the church today we often present the gospel as if it were about forgiveness of sins alone. Jesus died for our sins, so believe and be saved. However, what this speech highlights is not so much how Jesus saves us, but where that act of saving takes us. It takes us to God's Spirit and a restored relationship with God rooted in enablement to respond to God. This parallels what is said about the new covenant in Jeremiah, where forgiveness and the Law of God on the heart are the benefits God promises will come to his people one day. In this way, gospel and covenantal promise come together. God's having exalted Jesus makes all of this possible. That is the message of Acts 2.

ACTS 3–5: CONNECT TO THE PROMISED AND RETURNING MESSIAH TO FIND BLESSING

This chapter involves Peter's explanation for a healing that presents the promise through the backdrop of the Torah. The starting point for the speech is God's vindication of Jesus through resurrection and the scriptural promise, stated in summary, not with specific texts, that the Christ would suffer (vv. 12-18). Next comes the opportunity to have sins wiped away through repentance. The offer in association with this forgiveness is the coming of times of refreshing and the sending of the Messiah to his people in what could be described as a return to reclaim God's people in vindication (vv. 19-20). Where Acts 2 highlighted the immediate hope of life coming through the Spirit, Acts 3 focuses on the future hope of life and restoration that comes in the culmination of the program tied to the work of God through the Christ. In the meantime, Peter says, heaven holds Jesus until that coming time of restoration, a restoration that is also described in the prophets (v. 21). Jesus is a leader-delivering prophet like Moses as Deut 18:15 taught (vv. 22-23). It is the linked combination of leading and delivering that makes Jesus like Moses. The call is to obey that prophet. In this context it means that Jesus is to be embraced as the sent Messiah for all he does to bring restoration to life. Once again, the stress is not only on forgiveness of sin but on what comes out of it, life with God through Messiah. This is what the prophets since Samuel have taught (v. 24). This is the promise tied to the covenant God made with Abraham's seed. Through that seed, the world can be blessed. In effect Peter says this promise is especially suited to his Jewish audience (v. 25). God has raised up his servant and sent him first to the Jewish people, so that blessing can come if they turn from sins (v. 26).

Putting Acts 2 and 3 together we get a comprehensive offer of what Jesus provides. In the short term, there is the gift of life in the Spirit. In the long term, there is the restoration of life on earth. One can be experienced now; the other is yet to come. The mirroring of the already–not yet hope of the kingdom is found here. The observation is important in order to avoid the linguistic fallacy that one must have the term "kingdom" in order to talk about kingdom hope and promise. God's covenant program was about his kingdom program. The covenants serve as the administrative or dispensational backdrop to God's program of promise to restore the creation to wholeness. Where Acts 2 looks to the new covenant, Acts 3 sees the future realization of hope as the culmination of what was originally promised to Abraham. In a sense these two chapters present the alpha–omega of covenant promise, by invoking the first and last covenants of the promise. In the middle of it all stands the work of the promised Christ, which invokes the middle of the three covenants, the Davidic messianic hope of an anointed deliverer. This regal context shows up in the summarizing appeal of Acts 4:11, where Ps 118 and its regal backdrop is appealed to as the one rejected becomes the chief stone. This source of salvation is found in Jesus Christ the Nazarene (4:10).

Yet another short summary of all of this comes in 5:30-32 which reads, "The God of our forefathers raised up Jesus, whom you seized and killed by hanging him on a tree. God exalted him to his right hand as Leader and Savior, to give repentance to Israel and forgiveness of sins. And we are witnesses of these events, and so is the Holy Spirit whom God has given to those who obey him" (NET). The good news here is the exaltation of Jesus to offer forgiveness through repentance to Israel. The events described are true, as the witnesses to it attest. The offer is of the Spirit who is given to those who obey Him, which in this context surely means responding to the call to repent. The mention of the forefathers is a way of evoking the God of promise, the God of Abraham, Isaac and Jacob, as Acts 3:13 did. The stress in the evangelistic message is not so much how Jesus accomplishes this as much as who offers it, what is offered, and how God stands behind the attestation of these claims through the vindication and exaltation of Jesus to share in God's very presence.

ACTS 10: ATTESTATION THROUGH THE BESTOWAL OF THE SPIRIT

Acts 10 presents Luke's introduction of hope for Gentiles. Peter speaks to the house of the centurion, Cornelius. In 10:36, Jesus' message to Israel is characterized as a gospel of peace, a way of picturing reconciliation between God and his people as Jesus is described as ministering in Galilee with a ministry of healing and exorcism in vv. 36-38. An aside in the speech should not be overlooked. It is the parenthetical remark that Jesus is Lord of all in v. 36. This is the introduction of the vindicated exalted Jesus we saw in the earlier speeches. Vindication becomes the topic again when Peter mentions the resurrection as having made Jesus manifest to those chosen to be his witnesses (vv. 39-41). So Jesus is the one marked out by God to be the judge of the living and the dead (v. 42). He is the one the prophets testified to as the one who bestows forgiveness of sins through his name to those who believe in him (v. 43). At this point, before Peter finishes what he is saying the Spirit falls on the crowd of Gentiles in the room, leading to their being baptized (vv. 44-48). So the same combination we saw in Acts 2, forgiveness and the promise of the Spirit, shows up in Acts 10 as the gospel goes to Gentiles for the first time.

This scene receives elaboration in Acts 11:15-18. Peter relates that as he was speaking the "Spirit fell on them just as on us at the beginning" (Acts 11:5 NET). This caused Peter to recall the word Jesus taught (as had John as noted in Luke 3:16) that "John baptized with water, but you shall be baptized by the Spirit" (Acts 11:16 NET). Acts 1:4-5 also alluded to the teaching of Jesus. The theme is one that literally stitches Luke-Acts together. Peter calls the Spirit "the same gift as he [God] also gave to us" upon belief (Acts 11:17 NET). This description of the act of God ends the debate over whether Gentiles can be saved and whether they must be circumcised. God is said to have granted the repentance unto life by the evidence shown in the bestowal of the Spirit. In a Jewish context, the picture is of an unclean vessel now made clean through forgiveness so that now the forgiven can house the presence of God. Such cleanliness came while Gentiles were uncircumcised. Spirit baptism pictures the cleansing, acceptance, and restoration involved.

Once again the gospel is seen to focus on who brings salvation and what is brought: forgiveness and life in the Spirit. How this works is not explained. The allegiance called for by faith emphasizes who stands at the hub of the relationship, the exalted Jesus Christ, the Lord.

ACTS 13: THE LEAP OF HISTORY—FROM DAVID TO MESSIAH

The final evangelistic speech to a Jewish audience appears in Acts 13. Paul speaks to a synagogue in Pisidia Antioch. This speech traces the history of Israel very carefully for a time. It moves from the fathers to the Exodus, to the wilderness experience, followed by the conquest and period of the judges (vv. 17-20). From there the speech notes Saul and David (vv. 21-22). One would expect Solomon to be next, but when David is reached a note is made about God's promise of a Savior from David's seed, an allusion to Davidic hope (v. 23). Paul identifies this savior as Jesus and promptly leaps over a millennium of Israel's history straight to John the Baptist. Here Paul cites the remarks of the prophet John the Baptist as not being worthy to untie the sandals of the feet of this one to come (vv. 24-25). This is an allusion back to the crucial verse of hope given in Luke 3:16, where following this remark about being unworthy John notes how the one to come will baptize with the Spirit, the indication that the new era and Messiah have come (see Luke 3:15 with its unique introduction to these remarks). After reviewing the events that led to Jesus' death in vv. 26-29, Paul declares God's vindication of Jesus through resurrection followed by appearances to his witnesses, so that the promise may be preached to God's people (vv. 30-32). In language that alludes to the hope of Davidic promise coming to the people from Isa 55:3, Paul goes on to identify Jesus as the promised Son of Ps 2 and the one promised to be raised from Ps 16 (vv. 33-35). Through this raised, exalted and vindicated one comes the offer of forgiveness and the opportunity through faith to be freed of all the law of Moses could not accomplish (vv. 36-39). The speech ends with a warning not to scoff at the opportunity (vv. 40-41).

In this text we get Davidic hope and New Covenant expectation as serving to make possible what the old covenant could not accomplish. These speeches are consistently setting forth the gospel in the context of the covenant promise narrative of God to his people. This is a story line our modern presentation of the gospel often lacks. When one realizes that the promise of Gen 12:1-3 to Abraham began God's effort to reclaim a straying creation (just read the story of Babel), it is clear that gospel, kingdom and covenant go together. Forgiveness paves the way for restored relationship with God among a called people who have responded in faith to what God has done through a now exalted Jesus. Forgiveness leads to life in the Spirit, sent by the greater one to come who is God's Son.

But this narrative makes sense in a context where people understand the scriptural hope of promise. What about when the attention turns to a purely Gentile audience with no exposure to this story?

ACTS 17—FINDING GOD THROUGH JESUS

This is the final evangelistic speech in Acts. It is not completed as the mention of resurrection interrupts Paul's message in its tracks. Nonetheless, the outlines of Paul's trajectory are clear. Paul seeks to make known the unknown god that the Athenians give homage to without knowing about him (vv. 22-23). Paul speaks of the Creator God, who made everything and cannot dwell in a temple nor can he be represented by an idol (vv. 24-25). Humanity was created by this God to seek him out, as we appreciate we are his children and his presence surrounds us (vv. 26-28). God has called on all people to repent and holds them all accountable by one man who is judge (vv. 29-31a). This role is testified to by God's having raised this one from the dead (v. 31b). Paul never gets to name Jesus, but it is clear that is who is meant. At this point the crowd starts to discuss resurrection. Paul's speech never resumes. Even though this speech is never completed, it is God's role as Creator and the human responsibility to be accountable to him that is the starting point for this effort to make Jesus known. Where the other speeches work with Jesus as salvation bringer and appeal to well known promises, this speech appeals simply to the relationship creation makes between God and creature. Where the rest of this speech would have gone, one can only speculate, but once again the stress in the presentation was on who it was through whom hope comes, the exalted Jesus who one day will judge. One gets to God only through repenting and coming through Jesus.

SUMMARY OF SPEECHES IN ACTS

What is remarkable in our overview of these speeches is how little is said about how Jesus brings the forgiveness he offers. In fact, nothing is said about that at all. In these speeches there is no description of atonement, even though the scene of the Last Supper and the speech by Paul to the elders at Miletus indicates that that is precisely how this was accomplished. What is pursued is a personal link between the exalted one and the person who responds to his offer. More than that what is also presented is the opportunity for life that comes from that forgiveness, often summarized in the promise of the gift of life that comes with the Spirit Jesus bestows to his own. How is this like what we see elsewhere in the NT? We have already noted how the hope of life in a work of the Spirit coming from the one God sends is a theme in Luke-Acts. What about elsewhere in the NT?

A LOOK AT OTHER NEW TESTAMENT BOOKS

John's gospel has this emphasis as well, as that is indicated by the Upper Room Discourse, where Jesus must go and be lifted up (crucified) in order that Jesus might send the Paraclete who will guide the disciples into all the truth and they will be his witnesses, much as Acts has also described them (John 14:26;

16:26-27). John even concludes his gospel with a scene where the raised Jesus breathes the Spirit upon the disciples enabling them for mission (John 20:19-23).

Paul's book of Romans outlines the gospel Paul presents. It starts with men in need of being reconnected to the Creator, a theme like Acts 17 (Rom 1:18-32). Jesus secures this connection by his work through his blood (Rom 3:21-26). Here is how the gospel can be offered, a theme Paul loved to highlight. But Paul goes on in Rom 4 to use Abraham and how he received the promise by faith and before circumcision to make the point that Abraham is the father of all who believe and the example of faith that leads to justification. The story and relationship of covenant promise is still in play with Paul. What is it that Abraham believed God for? God could bring life out of death (4:17-19). He believed God for new life. The faith that reckons to righteousness is the faith that God can bring life to that which is dead. Just as God raised Jesus from the dead, so we can have hope of life, peace and grace, through the love God pours out in the Holy Spirit God has given to us (5:1-5). Here the chapter break may cause us to miss the connection between forgiveness and the gift of the Spirit, leading into our reconciliation that comes through the life the Savior now leads (5:9-11). The rest of this epistle underscores the work of the Spirit in generating a life of honor for God, by enabling us to live in ways that honor God and in ways the law could not achieve (Rom 6–8). These themes echo Acts 13, as well as Acts 2.

Peter calls this hope being born anew and being sanctified by the Spirit for obedience to Jesus Christ and for sprinkling with his blood (1 Pet 1:2-3; see also this juxtaposition in 1:22-23). Peter has all the elements. Who makes it possible (Jesus), how the way is cleared (through his death) and what comes as a result (new life in a Spirit who sanctifies).

CONCLUSION

So we have completed our trip through the evangelistic speeches of Acts, looking at the gospel as it was preached in the earliest era. What we find is the presentation of the vindicated and exalted Jesus as the relational key to restoring our relationship with God. Our attachment is not to an idea, but to a person who gave himself and cleared the way for us. Interestingly, there is not so much detail about how Jesus accomplished this in the speeches. Rather what is offered is highlighted: forgiveness and new life in God's Spirit. The narrative of God's covenant promises is prominent as well. Through the exalted and vindicated Jesus, God has done what he had long promised he would do in various pronouncements made through the prophets. In other words, the narrative of salvation is rooted in the covenant narrative of promise and hope. The good news is not only that our sins can be forgiven, but that the result is a relationship with God sealed by his Spirit, made possible by his Son. Forgiveness into eternal new life is the core of the gospel preached before the gospels were penned.

6

MATTHEW 5:17–20 AND "A TALE OF TWO MISSIONS"?

Esther Yue L. Ng

As those familiar with NT scholarship will undoubtedly notice, the title of this paper alludes to the monograph by Michael Goulder entitled *St. Paul versus St. Peter: A Tale of Two Missions*.[1] In this work, Goulder asserts that there were two competing missions in the early church: one overseen by Peter and James in Jerusalem, and the other run by Paul from centers elsewhere. According to Goulder, among conflicting views on various issues, the two parties had bitter controversies over the place of the Mosaic law in the life of a Christian, and in Matt 5:17-20 the Petrine author (Matthew) implied that the disciples of Paul like Mark who taught that food-laws have been abrogated can hardly expect to go to heaven, while people like Peter and James who have stood up for the validity of God's law will be honored there.[2] Goulder is of course not the first person to make such assertions: F. C. Baur in the nineteenth century already argued for the antithesis between Pauline Christianity and Jewish Christianity. Nor is Goulder the last proponent of such views: David Sim and others have been writing in more recent years on Matthew's Jewish orientation against Paul's law-free gospel.[3] Faced with the vast literature already written on Matthean and Pauline views of the Mosaic law and on the exegesis of Matt 5:17-20, the present paper is limited to a narrow focus: to see whether reading the unit narratologically in its immediate context and in Matthew as a whole would shed some light on the identity of the antagonists opposed by the evangelist, to make some preliminary observations on whether readers of Matthew in the first centuries saw anti-Paulinism in this Gospel or used Matthew this way, and finally to point out briefly the difficulties of seeing two opposing missions in the apostolic church.

READING MATTHEW 5:17–20 IN ITS LITERARY CONTEXT

To understand Matt 5:17-20 and the intended impact on its first readers, we will firstly trace the flow of thought in these verses, secondly draw some possible

---

[1] This is the title of the first American version (Louisville: Westminster/John Knox, 1995). The original British version was simply titled *A Tale of Two Missions* (London: SCM, 1994).
[2] Goulder, *A Tale of Two Missions*, 31-32.
[3] See, for example, David C. Sim, *The Gospel of Matthew and Christian Judaism: The History and Social Setting of the Matthean Community* (Edinburgh: T&T Clark, 1998).

implications previously neglected by scholars, and thirdly check the plausibility of such implications in view of what has been mentioned in the book so far and what subsequent chapters will reveal.

THE FLOW OF THOUGHT OF MATTHEW 5:17–20

These verses have been seen as one of the most difficult passages in this gospel owing to the difficulty in unraveling what is the evangelist's redaction from the tradition inherited and modified by him. Indeed scholars differ in their answers to this question.[4] However, even if the four verses of this periscope (or parts of them) did come initially from different contexts, it is good to remember with Donald A. Hagner that "the verses did cohere in the evangelist's mind, and every attempt should be made to consider them as a unified whole."[5] In this connection, it is noteworthy that beginning from v. 18, there is a connective particle in each verse (γάρ, οὖν, γάρ respectively). In view of such syntactical markers, there is much merit in David L. Turner's presentation of the flow of thought of these verses as follows:

1. Prohibition: Do not think that Jesus has come to abolish the law (5:17a).

2. Antithetical clarification: Jesus has come not to abolish but to fulfill (5:17b).

3. Explanation 1: Even the smallest parts of the law are permanently valid (5:18).

4. Implication: Spiritual status is measured by conformity to the law (5:19).

5. Explanation 2: Righteousness greater than that of the religious leaders [scribes and Pharisees] is required to enter the kingdom (5:20).[6]

However, apart from some reservation about Turner's use of the term "law" in line 1 as too restrictive—"Scripture" may be a better term to include both the "law" and the "prophets"[7]— syntactically it seems better to read 5:20 as an explanation or instantiation of v. 19 that precedes it immediately, rather than as another explanation in support of 5:17 and in parallel with 5:18. A decision on how 5:20 connects to previous verses would affect our view of the identity of the opponent envisaged in the pericope.

While there is no connective particle linking 5:21 with the previous

---

[4]Robert A. Guelich, *The Sermon on the Mount: A Foundation for Understanding* (Waco: Word Books, 1982), 135, 161. Likewise, Ulrich Luz, *Matthew 1-7: A Commentary* (trans. Wilhelm C. Linss; Minneapolis: Augsburg Fortress, 1989), 259.

[5] Donald Hagner, *Matthew* (2 vols.; WBC 33A-33B; Dallas: Word Books, 1993), 1:104.

[6]David L. Turner, *Matthew* (BECNT; Grand Rapids: Baker Academic, 2008), 161-62.

[7]So Turner himself (*Matthew*, n. 8) and most commentators, e.g. Guelich, *Sermon*, 134-38; D. A. Carson, "Matthew," in *Matthew, Mark, Luke* (vol. 8 of *Expositor's Bible Commentary*; ed. Frank E. Gaebelein; Grand Rapids: Zondervan, 1984), 1-599 [142].

pericope, many scholars rightly see v. 20 as a hinge exemplifying and connecting with vv. 17-19 backwards as well as introducing and providing the setting for the following Six Antitheses in vv. 21-48.[8] The role of v. 20 in introducing the Antitheses is practically stressed by all scholars whether they see this verse as a dominical saying, or as mostly or even entirely redactional.[9]

IMPLICATIONS OF THE FLOW OF ARGUMENT IN 5:17–20

If the above syntactical analysis is correct, then it is very unlikely that "the least in the kingdom of heaven" is the evangelist's derogatory depiction of Paul or Pauline Christianity for his/their allegedly "law-free" teaching as some scholars have maintained.[10] This is so for the following reasons.

Firstly, the logical connection between v. 19 and v. 20 would suggest that one reason why the righteousness of the scribes and Pharisees cannot qualify them for the kingdom of heaven (v. 20) is that they fail to do and teach "the least of these commandments" (v. 19).[11] This inference is valid no matter how "these commandments" is to be interpreted: whether a) referring back to the law seen as inviolable even regarding its "iota" (ἰῶτα) and "dot" (κεραία) in v. 18, and regarded as fulfilled by Jesus in v. 17 (whether by confirming it, drawing out its real meaning, or serving as its goal; whether by his deed or by teaching, or both),[12] or b) referring forwards to the following Antitheses or Jesus' entire teaching in the rest of the Gospel of Matthew.[13]

---

[8] Guelich, *Sermon*, 156-57, 170-71; Hagner, *Matthew*, 1:104.

[9] Thus Luz says, "Verse 20 is redactional according to almost universal judgment"; see Luz, *Matthew 1-7*, 259. However, speaking of the whole pericope, Carson notes that "Matthew presents these sayings as the teaching of the historical Jesus, not the creation of the church; and we detect no implausibility in his claim." (Carson, "Matthew," 141)

[10] For a list of scholars, see Ulrich Luz, *Matthew 1-7* (trans. James E. Crouch; Hermenia; Minneapolis: Fortress, 2007 [hereafter cited as *Matthew 1-7* Hermeneia]), 220, n. 85. For seeing Matt 5:19 as a polemic against the general Pauline position, see W. D. Davies and Dale C. Allison, Jr., *The Gospel according to St. Matthew* (ICC; Edinburgh: T&T Clark, 1988), 1:497; Goulder, *St. Paul*, 32. For seeing both included, see Luz, *loc. cit.*; and Sim, *Christian Judaism*, 208.

[11] While noting the presence of the γάρ at the beginning of v. 20, Luz sees the connection as very loose: "here there is certainly no substantiation of the preceding statements"; see his *Matthew 1-7* Hermeneia, 211. However, the repetition of the motif of being in the "kingdom of heaven" in v. 20 would suggest a close connection between v. 20 with v. 19, and γάρ should be taken seriously.

[12] Most scholars see a backward reference here. For various interpretations of how Jesus fulfils the Law and Prophets, see Davies and Allison, *Matthew*, 1:485-86 ; Guelich, *Sermon*, 140-42; Luz, *Matthew 1-7*, 260-61.

[13] For seeing "these commandments" as referring to Jesus' teaching, see Robert Banks, *Jesus and the Law in the Synoptic Tradition* (SNTSMS 28; Cambridge: University Press, 1975), 223; H. D. Betz, *The Sermon on the Mount* (Hermeneia; Minneapolis:

Secondly, the logical connection between v. 19 and v. 20 may also suggest that someone called "the least (ἐλάχιστος) in the kingdom of heaven" (v. 19) is one who never actually enters the kingdom (v. 20). If so, this expression is probably to be construed as a rhetorical device to balance "the least" of these commandments.[14] Conversely, to be called "great" (μέγας) in the kingdom of heaven is to be able to enter the kingdom. But if the "least" is to be taken in an exclusive sense in Matt 5:19, then it is unlikely to be an allusion to Paul's self-designation as "the least of the apostles" (1 Cor 15: 9), since Paul certainly considered himself an apostle. Moreover, "the least in the kingdom of heaven" (ἐλάχιστος ἐν τῇ βασιλείᾳ τῶν οὐρανῶν) in 5:19 has a different grammatical construction from the "the least of the apostles" (ὁ ἐλάχιστος τῶν ἀποστόλων).

Thirdly, if 5:20 introduces the following Six Antitheses which are directed against Pharisaic interpretations of the law, it would be strange if the evangelist first alludes to Paul and/or his disciples so indirectly in 5:19 and then names explicitly a different group of people for comparison followed by a sustained exposition of the latter group's inadequate treatment of the law.[15]

In view of such considerations, it does not seem likely that the evangelist is attacking Paul and/or Pauline Christianity in 5:17-19. Rather, like 5:20, we have in vv. 17-19 a polemic primarily directed against Pharisaic interpreters of the law. What remains to be seen is whether such an interpretation coheres with what the evangelist has said prior to, and subsequent to, this pericope.

PREPARATION IN MATTHEW PRIOR TO 5:17

Scholars have correctly noted that nothing in Matthew so far has prepared us for the statement in 5:17a: up to this point in the book we have not been told of people accusing Jesus of abrogating or annulling the Law and the Prophets. However, there is good reason to believe that the accent of 5:17 is not on Jesus' abrogating Scripture (17a), whether mentioned by opponents or not, but on its fulfillment by him (17b).[16] And the evangelist has certainly stressed already that Jesus' life events fulfilled prophecy. In the infancy narratives alone, the note of fulfillment was sounded five times (1:23; 2:6, 15, 17, 23). It is noteworthy also that the first quotation is preceded by "all this took place"

Fortress, 1995), 186-87, where he suggests that "the least" is to be taken ironically as a polemic against Pharisaic emphasis on "heavy" commandments.

[14] Luz (*Matthew 1-7* Hermeneia, 220, n. 88) notes that this interpretation was widespread in the ancient church. A comparison with Matt 18:3-4 also favors this interpretation.

[15] Thus Goulder, *St. Paul*, 32. But his logic is not convincing. Others (e.g., Sim, *Christian Judaism*, 123-31) who argue for v. 19 being directed against Pauline Christianity likewise fail to clarify the logical connection with v. 20.

[16] The parallel with 10:34 is instructive: there it is unlikely that opponents of Jesus claim that he came to bring peace to the earth; see also Carson, "Matthew," 141-42.

[ὅλον γέγονεν], an expression similar to πάντα γένηται ("all is accomplished") in 5:18d and making it likely that the latter refers to events happening with regard to Jesus (though not necessarily exhausted within his earthly life).[17] Later, Jesus' move from Nazareth to Capernaum is said to be in fulfillment of Isaiah's prophecy (4:13-16). As for the fulfillment of the Law, in the account of his temptation, Jesus is said to have quoted Scripture (all from the book of Deuteronomy, thus from the Law) to refute Satan three times, each time prefaced with "it is written" (4:4, 7, 10). Whereas the quotation of Scripture in the temptation is also found in Luke (thus already found in Q according to the Four-Source Hypothesis), the other quotations are unique to Matthew. Moreover, we have been told in 3:15 (in a conversation unique to Matthew) that Jesus submits to John's baptism because it is fitting for them "to fulfill all righteousness" (πληρῶσαι πᾶσαν δικαιοσύνην). Thus Jesus' answer in 3:15 prepares the way for the subsequent sayings in 5:17-20 by linking together Jesus, "righteousness," and "fulfillment".

While there is nothing before 5:17-20 that mentions the inadequacy of the righteousness of the scribes or Pharisees, we do have hints from the evangelist that prepares for the statement in 5:20. First, we understand from 2:4-6 that the "scribes of the people" (γραμματεῖς τοῦ λαοῦ) knew the Scriptures well and that they were ready to provide an answer to Herod on the birth-place of the Messiah. In light of v. 3, it is possible that the scribes in question were among those who were disturbed and troubled by the visit of the Magi in search of the new-born Jewish king.

As for the Pharisees, it is noteworthy that Matt 3:7 has John the Baptist address the Pharisees and Sadducees as a "brood of vipers" and warn them that "every tree that does not produce good fruit will be cut down and thrown into the fire"[18] (3:10), whereas the parallel passage in Luke tells us that John applied the epithet and the tree-imagery to the multitudes (ὄχλοι) (Luke 3:7, 9). Also interestingly, whereas Luke makes it clear that such harsh sayings were addressed to the multitudes who came to be baptized (3:7), Matthew's Greek expression (πολλοὺς τῶν Φαρισαίων καὶ Σαδδουκαίων ἐρχομένους ἐπὶ τὸ βάπτισμα αὐτοῦ) allows a different rendering: "many of the Pharisees and Sadducees coming to where he was baptizing" (so NIV), thus leaving it ambiguous whether they came merely to watch or to be baptized.[19]

---

[17] Thus many scholars have rightly taken the second ἕως clause in a Christological and salvation-historical sense, rather than seeing it as being basically synonymous to the first clause in v. 18a. If so, it seems preferable to see v. 18a as indicating extreme difficulty or meaning "never"; for the former interpretation, see Banks, *Jesus*, 215. For a list of proponents of the latter position, see Hagner, *Matthew*, 1:107().

[18] Unless specified, scriptural quotations are from RSV.

[19] In Matt 3:11, John goes on to say "I baptize you with water for repentance"; however, this may refer back to the truly penitent mentioned in vv. 5-6. For the view underlying the NIV translation, see Carson, "Matthew," 103, 106 n. 7.

It is also clear from the Beatitudes that righteousness is something to be hungered for and satisfied by God, thus not attainable by human effort.[20] Likewise, the clarification of the last Beatitude (5:11) shows that to be persecuted for righteousness is closely tied up with being insulted, persecuted and maligned on account of Jesus. This not only anticipates the opposition to Jesus and his followers that comes later in the book, but also once again draws the connection between righteousness and Jesus as we found in 3:15.

OPPOSITION TO PHARISAIC PRACTICE OF THE LAW IN THE REST OF MATTHEW

Further along in the Sermon on the Mount, Jesus prefaced his teaching on almsgiving, prayer and fasting by saying, "Beware of practicing your righteousness before men to be noticed by them" (6:1, NASB), recalling the greater righteousness required (5:20), thus hinting that the "hypocrites" with ostentatious, pious behavior (6:2, 5, 16) criticized by Jesus were Pharisees. If so, the hypocrite who sees the speck of sawdust in someone else's eye but ignores the plank in his own eye (7:5) is probably also a Pharisee. Whereas the identity of the hypocrite is only hinted at here, the Matthean Jesus openly calls the scribes and Pharisees "hypocrites" in six of the seven "woes" addressed to them later (23:13, 15, 23, 25, 27, 29). In 23:5-7, it is explicitly said of the scribes and Pharisees that "they do all their deeds to be seen by men," including broadening their phylacteries, lengthening the tassels on their garments, and craving for recognition of various kinds.

Similarly, while the identity of the "false prophets" to be guarded against is not disclosed in 7:15-20, certain descriptions occur elsewhere in the book and are explicitly used of scribes and Pharisees. Thus the contrast between the outward goodness ("sheep's clothing") with inward wickedness ("ravenous wolves") is similar to the imagery of outwardly clean cups/dishes and whitewashed tombs in Jesus' later excoriation of the scribes and Pharisees (23:25-32). As for Jesus' statement in 7: 19 ("Every tree that does not bear good fruit is cut down and thrown into the fire"), it is an exact repetition of what John the Baptist said earlier of the Pharisees and Sadducees (3:10).

It can be inferred from 5:20 that Jesus considers the scribes and Pharisees unfit for the kingdom of heaven. While Jesus' estimation of their destiny is stated obliquely here, the Matthean Jesus makes it very clear subsequently that

---

[20] The passive in 5:6 certainly has God as the implied subject, i.e., "filled by God." 6:33 also implies that righteousness is to be sought in prayer and will be given by God together with material blessings. But righteousness according to Matthew entails proper conduct as well, as the rest of the Sermon on the Mount makes clear. See Guelich, *Sermon*, 84-88; D. A. Hagner, "Righteousness in Matthew's Theology," in *Theology and Ministry in the Early Church* (ed. M. J. Wilkins and Terence Paige; Sheffield: JSOT Press, 1992), 101-20.

they don't enter the kingdom. Thus following the Parable of the Two Sons, Jesus said, "[T]he tax collectors and the harlots go into the kingdom of God[21] before you. For John came to you in the way of righteousness, and you did not believe him, but the tax collectors and the harlots believed him; and even when you saw it, you did not afterward repent and believe him" (21:31-32). It is noteworthy that this parable with its interpretation is unique to Matthew, and it precedes the Parable of the Vineyard and Tenants (vv. 33-44), following which it is said that "[w]hen the chief priests and the Pharisees heard his parables, they perceived that he was speaking about them" (v. 45). In their parallel accounts of the Parable of the Vineyard, however, neither Mark (11:27) nor Luke (20:19) explicitly mentions Pharisees among the listeners and targets of the parable. Thus Matthew uniquely makes it clear that the Pharisees were among those who did not follow the way of righteousness and thus were excluded from the kingdom of heaven.[22]

We have said so far that in the Sermon on the Mount subsequent to the Six Antitheses, much of the behavior clearly censured by Jesus can be attributed to scribes and Pharisees in the rest of Matthew. Thus the inadequacy of their personal righteousness mentioned in 5:20 is spelled out in the rest of the Sermon even though the evangelist does not name them as the doers of such deeds until later chapters. However, our discussion so far does not exhaust all the people explicitly or implicitly criticized by Jesus in the Sermon on the Mount. Thus apart from the tax collectors and Gentiles whom his disciples should not emulate in their treatment of others (5:46-47) or in prayer (6:7), there are those who call Jesus "Lord" and in his name prophesy, exorcise demons and perform miracles, but cannot enter the kingdom of heaven on the last day (7:21-23). Since these people overtly accept the lordship of Jesus and use his name in charismatic ministries, they are more likely nominal Christians rather than scribes and Pharisees. Thus if there is any anti-Pauline polemic in Matthew, this would be a good candidate. However, even here the case for anti-Paulinism cannot stand for the following reasons: 1) Such people are those "who practice lawlessness" (NASB) (οἱ ἐργαζόμενοι τὴν ἀνομίαν) and it is awkward to take the expression to mean those who practice a law-free faith.[23] Secondly, to be consistent with this understanding of ἀνομία, one would have to argue that the scribes and Pharisees are likewise without the law in 23:28, an

---

[21] With the majority of scholars, I take the expressions "kingdom of heaven" and "kingdom of God" as equivalent, at least in referring to the same entity, whether or not there are differences in connotation.

[22] While Luke does not include a saying about the Pharisees not entering the kingdom of God, we do have a saying similar in import in Luke 7:29-30: "all the people and the tax collectors justified God, having been baptized with the baptism of John, but the Pharisees and lawyers rejected the purpose of God for themselves, not having been baptized by him."

[23] Thus Sim, *Christian Judaism*, 204-205.

interpretation which surely is a case of special pleading. Thirdly, ἀπόστητε ἀπ' ἐμοῦ πάντες οἱ ἐργαζόμενοι τὴν ἀνομίαν in 7:23b is an exact quotation of Ps 6:8 in the LXX, and the word ἀνομία should be given the same and common meaning of "evil, iniquity." Fourthly, if the evangelist were really inveighing against Paul or his disciples in 5:19 and 7:23 on their stance regarding food laws, sacrifices, festivals and circumcision, it is inconceivable why the summation of the Law and Prophets in 7:12 is restricted to human relationships only (note the οἱ ἄνθρωποι in 12a).

OPPOSITION TO PHARISAIC INTERPRETATION OF THE LAW IN THE REST OF MATTHEW

In the last section, we have discussed how the rest of the Gospel subsequent to 5:17-20 shows that the scribes and Pharisees were those who broke the commandments by their *deeds*. In this section, we will see how their *teaching* too came short in Jesus' evaluation.

Firstly, as mentioned above, scholars generally regard the Six Antitheses in 5:21-48 as a presentation of Jesus' teaching in contrast to Pharisaic/Rabbinic interpretations of various commandments of the Law. This is surely correct, as the formula "you have heard . . ., but I say" approximates the pattern used by rabbis in their teaching.[24] Moreover, the subjects of divorce and of vows come up later in the book explicitly as issues of great interest to Pharisees wherein Jesus differed in interpretation precisely as in the third and fourth Antitheses (19:7; 23:16-20, with Jesus speaking against easy divorce and casuistic vows respectively).

Secondly, at the end of the Sermon on the Mount, a contrast is drawn between the teaching of the scribes and Jesus' teaching in that he taught with authority (7:28), indicating that the scribes were teachers of the people. This observation makes it plausible that the scribes and Pharisees are those who relax the commandments and teach men so in 5:19.

Thirdly, we see Jesus twice responding to the verbal attacks of the Pharisees (9:13; 12:7) by citing Hosea 6:6 ("I desire mercy, and not sacrifice"): on the occasion of his eating with tax collectors and sinners (9:10-13), and after his disciples plucked heads of grain to eat on a Sabbath (12:1-8). In the latter case, the disciples' action was seen as unlawful on account of the Pharisaic interpretation of work prohibited on the Sabbath according to their oral tradition, though this background is assumed and not mentioned.[25] In appealing

---

[24] For Jewish parallels to the antithesis formula, see D. Daube, *The New Testament and Rabbinic Judaism* (London: Athlone, 1956), 55-57; Luz, *Matthew 1-7* Hermeneia, 228. It is beyond our scope to decide whether the antitheses refer to the Jewish-Pharisaic interpretation of the OT or to the OT itself.

[25] The action may be considered reaping, grinding and preparing food among the thirty-nine activities later explicitly prohibited in the Mishnah (*m. Šabb.* 7:2).

to Hos 6:6, Jesus makes a distinction between moral and ceremonial aspects of the law (mercy versus sacrifice) in line with OT prophets and giving priority to the former.[26] In the second instance, his citation of Hos 6:6 also implies a distinction between written Scripture and human oral tradition and a criticism of the latter. In this connection, we may also examine Jesus' charge that the scribes and Pharisees "tithe mint and dill and cumin, and have neglected the weightier matters of the law, justice and mercy and faith; these you ought to have done, without neglecting the others. You blind guides, straining out a gnat and swallowing a camel" (23:23-24). Again, Jesus gives priority to moral values over ceremonial aspects of the law. However, this requirement of tithing has been seen as an endorsement of the latter and an indication that the Matthean community opposed the law-free gospel of Pauline Christianity.[27] Here we cannot fully examine the relevant issues and have to be content with one observation: the same saying is found in Luke 11:42, and it would be hard to argue that the third evangelist likewise reflects the concerns of a conservative Jewish Christian community.

Fourthly, if Jesus only implicitly disagreed with the oral tradition of the Pharisees in 12:7, he openly spoke against it after his disciples were accused for not washing their hands when they ate, thus transgressing "the tradition of the elders" (15:1-9). In his reply, Jesus mounted a counter-attack, accusing the Pharisees of transgressing the commandment of God (on honoring parents) for the sake of their tradition, when they taught that one could withhold something from his parents if he expressed his intention of treating the thing in question as an offering to God. In this pericope, we have a clear example of the Matthean Jesus accusing the Pharisees of making void a commandment (ἐντολή) of the law (as warned in 5:19) here seen as the commandment of God and the word of God, even though only the word for "commandment" is identical in the two passages, while the words for the annulling actions differ. Here again, the word "hypocrite" is used to address the Pharisees (v. 7).

Fifthly, whereas the pericope of 15:1-9 differs little from the parallel account in Mark 7:1-13, in the following story about the riddle of defilement there are interesting differences between the Matthean and Markan accounts (Matt 15:10-20; Mark 7:14-21). It has often been said that Matthew tones down the implication that Mark draws about all foods being clean (καθαρίζων πάντα τὰ βρώματα) and ends up with the lame conclusion that "to eat with unwashed hands does not defile a man." Moreover, it is said that this Matthean redaction is in line with his Jewish Christian perspective and his disagreement with Markan and Pauline abrogation of food laws. However, it is difficult not to

---

[26] The negative expression about sacrifice is certainly not to be taken literally. Rather the whole saying expresses a preference of the former over the latter, as in Mal 1:2; Luke 14:26.
[27] Thus Sim, *Christian Judaism*, 131-32.

draw the Markan implication even by reading the account in Matthew,[28] and it is probably fanciful thinking to imagine that the first readers of Matthew would compare with the Markan account meticulously and detect the four extra words in Mark. What is certainly noteworthy, rather, is the fact that Matthew (not Mark) mentions the disciples telling Jesus that the Pharisees were offended by the saying about defilement, and Jesus replied by saying that "every plant which my heavenly Father has not planted will be rooted up." He then went on to describe the Pharisees as blind guides. If the evangelist was engaged in polemics here, they were clearly aimed at Pharisaic teachers, not at Mark or Paul.

Sixthly, whereas Mark reports that Jesus told the disciples to beware of the leaven of the Pharisees and the leaven of Herod without explaining what it meant (Mark 8:14-21), in Matthew's parallel account the disciples eventually understood that the leaven of the Pharisees and Sadducees meant their teaching (16:5-12). Again, then, we find the evangelist Matthew showing his concern for the Pharisees as untrustworthy teachers.

Finally, we have in Matt 23 a sustained diatribe against the scribes and Pharisees, not only on account of their deeds (as discussed above) but also because of their teaching. Though their instruction is to be observed if in accordance with Moses' teaching (sitting on Moses' seat),[29] yet they lay heavy, unbearable, burdens on people's shoulders (v. 4). They are those who don't enter the kingdom of heaven and also shut it against people (vv. 13-15). They are blind guides whose teaching on vows was certainly oblivious of God and a distortion of priorities.

PART TWO: MATTHEAN RECEPTION AND EARLY CHURCH CONFLICTS

So far we have come to the conclusion that the evangelist Matthew has a sustained interest in showing the inadequacy of the scribes and Pharisees both in their deeds and in their teaching, and the necessity for followers of Jesus not to emulate them but to have a greater or higher righteousness. Space does not permit me to draw the implication of my findings here for the Matthean community or the circumstances under which the evangelist wrote this gospel. Suffice it to say that the evangelist must have viewed scribes and Pharisees or

---

[28] Thus I. Howard Marshall: "But it is rather more probable that Matthew is simply abbreviating Mark, and that his addition in Matthew 15:12-14 sufficiently indicates his rejection of the principle that foods can make people unclean." See his *New Testament Theology* (Downers Grove: InterVarsity, 2004), 104-5.

[29] It is obvious from the context that "to observe whatever they tell you" in v. 3 is not to be taken literally or without exception. So some commentators have taken this as sarcasm. However, it is better to find the command in v. 3 being qualified by the "sitting on Moses' seat" instead.

what they represent as a formidable influence in the lives of his readers.[30] Also, we have evidence that Jews later did attack Christians for disregarding God's commandments,[31] and that rabbis were probably aware of a version of Jesus' saying in Matt 5:17b.[32]

Rather than speculating on the Matthean community, what I propose to do in this second section of my paper is to see whether there are hints that early Christians saw the Gospel of Matthew as countering Pauline Christianity, and conversely whether there are indications that those who were anti-Paul used this gospel as their "ammunition." Following this, I will offer a few observations on certain NT passages that are germane to our discussion.

USE OF MATTHEW BY FOES AND FRIENDS OF PAUL IN THE EARLY CENTURIES

There is no disputing the fact that some Jewish Christian sects were specifically said to have used the Gospel of Matthew (in Hebrew and it may have been called the *Gospel According to the Hebrews*). Thus we know from early church fathers and more at length from Epiphanius that the Ebionites and the Nazarenes/Nazaraens did so. We also know that a number of Jewish Christian sects attacked Paul, including the Ebionites, and possibly those groups behind the Pseudo-Clementine writings (*Recognition* and *Homilies*) and the *Book of Elchasai*.[33]

However, it is not the case that those who used Matthew were necessarily anti-Paul. In Epiphanius' description of the Nazarenes, while it is said that they differed from most Christians in being still bound to the law, circumcision and Sabbath, there is no indication that they were anti-Paul. In addition, in his Commentary on Isaiah, Jerome mentioned that the Nazarenes accepted Paul as the apostle to Gentiles, and they regarded the scribes and Pharisees as engaged

---

[30] This could be true whether his readers stayed inside or outside Jewish synagogues. For various positions, see David Balch, ed., *Social History of the Matthean Community: Cross-Disciplinary Approaches* (Minneapolis: Fortress, 1991). In any case, Christians and Jews continued to have contact with each other well into the fifth century. See Robert L. Wilken, *Judaism and the Early Christian Mind* (New Haven: Yale University Press, 1971), 36-37. Such Jewish influence and the need of a Christian response can readily be seen in the *Epistle of Barnabas*; Ign. *Phld.* 6:1; 8:2; Ign. *Magn.* 8–12; and Justin Martyr's *Dialogue with Trypho*.

[31] See Trypho's charges against Christians in *Dialogue with Trypho* 8:3-4. According to Justin (17:1), selected Jewish men were sent out to speak against Christians.

[32] As reflected in *b. Šabb.* 116b. For comments on its ambiguity, see Luz, *Matthew 1-7* Hermeneia, 215-16.

[33] For the discussion on Jewish Christian sects mentioned here, see Oskar Skarsaune and Reidar Hvalvik, eds., *Jewish Believers in Jesus: The Early Centuries* (Peabody, Mass.: Hendrickson, 2007); Matt Jackson-McCabe, ed., *Jewish Christianity Reconsidered: Rethinking Ancient Groups and Texts* (Minneapolis: Fortress, 2007).

in idolatry in laying a heavy yoke of Jewish traditions on people. It is true that some scholars (F. C. Baur, Petri Luomanen, Gerd Lüdemann and Michael D. Goulder) regard such fourth-century descriptions of Nazarenes as representing a later phase of Jewish Christianity that had modified its strictly anti-Pauline stance (as evidenced in the Ebionites) to a more lenient attitude towards Paul.[34] However, it is more plausible (as argued by Albrecht Rischl and Ray Pritz, and as we shall see later) that anti-Paulinism was not a dominant current in first-century Christianity.[35] At least the fourth-century Nazarenes accepted the Gospel of Matthew and Paul's apostleship to Gentiles without seeing a contradiction between the two.

As for the Ebionites, we find both a use of the Gospel of Matthew and overt anti-Paulinism (*Panarion* 30.16.8-9). However, according to Epiphanius, the Ebionites rejected parts of the Pentateuch, the prophets, and animal flesh as food (the latter two practices probably based on *Circuits of Peter*) and used a modified version of Matthew (without the genealogy, and with changes in their account regarding John the Baptist's food and Jesus' baptism). Moreover, they taught that Christ came to abolish sacrifices and that James preached against the temple and sacrifices (basing on the *Ascent of James*). Thus while they inveighed against the allegedly pagan Paul for turning against Judaism (after failing to marry the daughter of a priest) by attacking circumcision, the Sabbath and the Law, they can hardly claim to be faithful to the teaching in Matt 5:17-19 as understood by scholars such as Goulder and Sim.

As for the Pseudo-Clementine writings, while some scholars have detected anti-Paulinism in the *Contestation* and in the *Epistle of Peter* introducing the *Homilies*, as well as within the *Homilies* (17.13-19),[36] it is to be noted that such attacks are at most indirect (Simon Magus being the *prima facie* opponent of Peter). To be sure, there is a version of Paul's persecution of Christians (as a Jew) and throwing James from the top of the stairs in the *Recognitions*. However, even here Paul is not named but alluded to as "the enemy" and nothing is said of his subsequent "law-free" teaching to Christians.

Another piece of Jewish Christian writing sometimes cited as indicative of anti-Paulinism influenced by Matthew is *The Didache*:[37] "But if the teacher

---

[34] See Petri Luomanen, "Ebionites and Nazarenes," in *Jewish Christianity Reconsidered*, 81-118.

[35] See Ray A. Pritz, *Nazarene Jewish Christianity from the End of the New Testament Period until Its Disappearance in the Fourth Century* (Leiden: Brill, 1988), especially 28, 82, 108-10.

[36] Thus Gerd Lüdemann, *Opposition to Paul in Jewish Christianity* (trans. M. E. Boring; Minneapolis: Fortress, 1989), 190-91; F. Stanley Jones, "The Pseudo-Clementines," in *Jewish Christianity Reconsidered*, 285-303; Graham Stanton, "Jewish Christian Elements in Pseudo-Clementine Writings," in *Jewish Believers in Jesus*, 305-24.

[37] See Magnus Zetterholm, "The Didache, Matthew, James—and Paul: Reconstructing Historical Developments in Antioch," in *Matthew, James, and Didache: Three Related*

himself goes astray and teaches a different teaching that undermines [καταλῦσαι] all this, do not listen to him. However, if his teaching contributes to righteousness and knowledge of the Lord, welcome him as you would the Lord" (11:2, trans. Michael W. Holmes). However, while the "undermining" and "righteousness" may recall Matt 5:19-20, there is no clear indication of anti-Paulinism here, as the teaching undermined is not said to be the Mosaic law. In fact the emphasis in the following is on practical tests regarding itinerant apostles and prophets. It is true that 4:13 admonishes readers not to "forsake the Lord's commandments, but must guard what you have received, neither adding or subtracting anything." While this may be taken in itself as strict legalism, we find the author quite accommodating later: "For if you are able to bear the whole yoke of the Lord, you will be perfect. But if you are not able, then do what you can. Now concerning food, bear what you are able, but in any case keep strictly away from meat sacrificed to idols, for it involves the worship of dead gods" (6:2-3). Rather than advocating a legalistic understanding of the Lord's commandments in opposition to Paul, *The Didache* pits the Christian way against the practice of hypocrites in prayer (8:2, quoting the Matthean version of the Lord's Prayer, and prefacing with "pray like this, just as the Lord commanded in his Gospel" [trans. Michael W. Holmes]). The "hypocrites" in question, as in the case of Matthew, most probably refer to Jewish leaders who are said in *Didache* 8:1 to fast on Monday and Thursday.

We next turn our attention to Ignatius as an early representative of pro-Pauline Christianity to examine whether he saw anti-Paulinism in Matthew. That Ignatius is a follower of Paul is not in doubt. Thus he refers to the Ephesians as fellow initiates of Paul (Παύλου συμμύσται) who mentions them in every letter (Ign. *Eph.* 12:2); he speaks of Peter and Paul as apostles while he himself is a convict (Ign. *Rom.* 4:3). What is disputed among scholars is the extent of his knowledge of the written Matthew, with some (e.g., Helmut Koester, Arthur Bellinzoni and William R. Schoedel) insisting that Ignatius only knew of oral traditions of a Matthean type, and others (Edouard Massaux, Martin Hengel, Raymond Brown, John P. Meier) convinced that Ignatius knew of the written Gospel of Matthew. With careful attention to methodology and after a close scrutiny of the parallels between Ignatius' letters and the First Gospel, Paul Turner's statement merits quoting in full as follows:

> A more balanced conclusion would be that Ignatius provides only one certain example, where it can be demonstrated that he knew and cited what is almost certainly Matthean redactional material. The most likely explanation is that he knew the version of the baptism story preserved in the first gospel, and probably knew this work directly and not by some circuitous route involving an unevidenced and no longer extant intermediary source. All other examples

---

Documents in Their Jewish and Christian Settings (ed. Huub van de Sandt and Jürgen K. Zangenberg; Atlanta: SBL, 2008), 73-90.

suggested show far fewer points of contact, but they are of value for building a cumulative case for Ignatius' use of Matthew's gospel.[38]

The undisputable example mentioned is Ign. *Smyrn.* 1:1 where, in a quasi-creedal statement Ignatius includes the point that Christ was baptized by John in order that "all righteousness might be fulfilled" (πληρωθῇ πᾶσα δικαισύνη) by him, most likely quoting from Matt 3:15. As we have seen above, this verse in Matthew reflects the same concern as 5:20. If 5:17-20 is a coherent unit as we argued above, we have strong reasons to believe that Ignatius and his community saw nothing incongruous between their acceptance of the Gospel of Matthew (with its conservatism about Jewish Law) and their great esteem for Paul, just as they revered both Paul and Peter as apostles.

FURTHER OBSERVATIONS ON THE ALLEGED TWO MISSIONS IN THE NEW TESTAMENT

To demonstrate that the NT writings evidence the existence of two conflicting missions in the first century, scholars generally appeal to the Antioch incident (recorded in Gal 2:11-14) in which Paul openly opposed Cephas because the latter withdrew from meals with Gentiles in fear of the circumcision party. According to this interpretation, the open confrontation spelled the defeat of Paul in Antioch, and the ascendancy of the conservative faction there loyal to James, Peter and the Jerusalem church in the late 40s of the first century. Moreover, contrary to the portrayal in Acts, Paul's later effort of presenting a goodwill collection to church leaders in Jerusalem was not accepted, and none of these leaders came to his rescue when he was arrested in the temple. This is not the place to evaluate the above reconstruction of Paul's last visit to Jerusalem or defend the trustworthiness of Acts. But with regard to the historical reconstruction of the Antioch incident and its aftermath, a few observations are necessary in view of our discussion so far and also since many scholars regard Antioch as the most likely provenance of the Gospel of Matthew.

First, it does not seem plausible that Paul would narrate the Antioch incident in this manner (right after his portrayal in 2:6-10 of his full acceptance by James, Cephas and John in Jerusalem) had it ended in a complete fiasco for him. For his argument from personal experience (from 1:11 to 2:21) to be convincing to his readers, especially in the "shame" culture prevalent then, he

---

[38] Paul Turner, "The Epistles of Ignatius of Antioch and the Writings that Later Formed the New Testament," in *The Reception of the New Testament in the Apostolic Fathers* (ed. Andrew F. Gregory and Christopher M. Tuckett; Oxford: Oxford University Press, 2005), 159-86. For a good discussion on theoretical issues, see the article by Gregory and Tuckett, "Reflections on Method: What Constitutes the Use of the Writings that Later Formed the New Testament in the Apostolic Fathers?" in the same volume, 61-82.

must expect them to infer that he succeeded in persuading Peter after the open confrontation in Antioch just as he succeeded in Jerusalem. If in fact he failed in that incident, he could only hide the failure if the Galatians would never have the opportunity to find out the facts for themselves. However, no matter whether we adopt the North Galatia or South Galatia theory for the destination of the letter, it is implausible that news about the church in Antioch would not spread to churches in Galatia.

Secondly, at a first glance, the theory of Paul's fiasco in Antioch seems supported by the alleged anti-Paulinism of the Gospel of Matthew supposedly written from Antioch. However, one would then have to explain how Ignatius the bishop of Antioch was an admirer of Paul in the early second century and yet quoted from the Gospel of Matthew without any qualms, as we have shown above. It seems special pleading and too speculative to argue, as Sim does,[39] that the death of James and the events of the Jewish War reversed the fortunes of the law-free Christianity in Antioch so that in Ignatius' time both forms of Christianity existed there, with Ignatius leading the law-free version and the Matthean version of Christianity being represented by the Judaism opposed by him. It is historically far more likely that Christians in Antioch were all along heirs to Paul and Peter as Ignatius indicated.

Thirdly, to posit a rupture of the early church resulting in two separate and opposing missions, one would also have to ignore many indicators of unity among the leaders or view them as fabrications in the NT letters besides the evidence from Acts. To be sure, in Gal 2:9, 11, this unity is emphasized in an apologetic context: Paul is trying to demonstrate that the Jerusalem leaders endorsed his gospel and apostleship. However, in other passages, the unity of purpose and compatibility in theology are presupposed rather than argued for. Thus we find Paul referring to the missionary practice of the other apostles, the brothers of the Lord, and Cephas as perfectly legitimate, even though he and Barnabas did work for a living (1 Cor 9:5-6). We find in Col 4:10 an instruction to receive Mark, the cousin of Barnabas, and 2 Tim 4:11 has a warm commendation of Mark. 1 Peter 5:12 says that the letter was written with the help of the faithful brother Silvanus/Silas, and the next verse has Peter referring to Mark as his son. Finally 2 Pet 3:15-16 refers to Paul as "our beloved brother" and sees his letters as similarly teaching the forbearance of the Lord conducive to salvation, even to the extent of treating them on a level with other scriptures. Even if one disputes the Pauline or Petrine authorship of some of the letters

---

[39] Sim, *Christian Judaism*, 165-72, 299-302. It should be remembered that the "Judaism" opposed by Ignatius at most existed in the cities he wrote to (Magnesia, Philadelphia), and may not reflect the situation in Antioch. Moreover, after writing to the Magnesians against Judaism (8–10), he said that he was merely forewarning them (11). As for the Philadelphians, Ignatius did not seem bothered if Christians heard about Christianity from a man who was circumcised so long as he spoke about Jesus Christ (6:1).

mentioned above, the amount of evidence of unity of purpose mutually perceived by the Pauline and Petrine circles is too great to dismiss.

Conversely, as one scholar has observed well,[40] if the Gospel of Matthew elevated Peter and denigrated Paul, it is strange that the primacy of Peter was never restored after his denial of Jesus in the account of post-Easter events, while the supposedly pro-Paul Gospel of Mark has the angels specifically mention Peter as among the recipients of their message (16:7) and Luke records Jesus appearing to Simon Peter alone (24:34; cf. 1 Cor 15:5). One may add that, while pitting the Beloved Disciple against Peter to a certain extent, the Gospel of John still has the resurrected Jesus re-installing Peter's leadership role by the Sea of Tiberias.

CONCLUSION

We have tried to show that Matt 5:17-20 is a coherent whole and that any polemic in the pericope is directed against scribes and Pharisees and not against Paul or Pauline Christianity. Moreover, we have demonstrated that this reading makes sense of the whole book which consistently depicts the scribes and Pharisees as people whose deeds and teaching fell short of the righteousness expected of those who enter the kingdom of heaven. In particular, they are said to have made void the commandment of God for the sake of their tradition, and that they fail to enter the kingdom of heaven.

With regard to the reception of Matthew, it seems clear that some early Jewish Christian sects that used the Gospel of Matthew were not anti-Paul, while those manifestly against Paul did not adhere to a strict interpretation of Matthew advocating the inviolability of all the Mosaic commandments. As for Jewish Christian writings like *The Didache*, again the use of the Gospel of Matthew did not apparently lead to anti-Pauline sentiments or require complete compliance regarding food laws. As for the manifestly Gentile Ignatius, his letters both showed him as a follower of Paul and Peter, and as one comfortable with the teaching of the Gospel of Matthew yet clearly against Judaizers.

Finally we pointed out difficulties for those who allege the existence of two conflicting missionary movements in the first century: the Antioch incident mentioned in Gal 2:10-15 cannot support such an edifice built on it; the view ignores the numerous indications of unity of early Christian leaders; and Matthew the allegedly pro-Peter evangelist strangely has nothing to say on the restoration of Peter after Jesus' resurrection.

All of the above arguments are insufficient to prove irrefutably that the various NT writers do not contradict one another in their teaching or that the practices of Paul were no different from Peter or James historically. A

---

[40] Arlo J. Nau, review of David C. Sim, *The Gospel of Matthew and Christian Judaism: The History and Social Setting of the Matthean Community*, *RBL* July 2003, point 4. Online: http://www.bookreviews.org/pdf/3532_3741.pdf.

definitive position on the former can only come about by examining each document and each corpus individually. Thus we are all indebted to Professor Howard Marshall for doing precisely this in his magisterial *New Testament Theology* and concluding that "there is a common, basic, theology that can be traced in all our witnesses."[41] May works of this caliber and nature continue to come from him and from those who regard him as a mentor, an example, and a friend.

---

[41] I. Howard Marshall, *New Testament Theology*, 726.

7

REVISITING THE JOHANNINE WATER MOTIF: JESUS, RITUAL CLEANSING, AND TWO PURIFICATION POOLS IN JERUSALEM

Gary M. Burge

The recent discovery of the Second Temple Siloam Pool in Jerusalem has drawn marked interest from the archaeology community, but it also bears important implications for our work in the Fourth Gospel. The connection between John and Siloam is well-known.[1] In John 9 Jesus heals a blind man, places a mud plaster on his eyes, and then tells him to "go wash in the Pool of Siloam." For John—as every commentary will report—this is another example of Johannine irony. In fact, John hands it to us: Siloam means "sent" and Jesus is the sent one from God. Therefore the pool is a not-so-veiled symbol of Jesus in whom true sight can be gained.

So far so good. But the discussion about Siloam has raised new implications not only for how we view John 9, but perhaps how we think about the gospel as a whole. And even about the historicity of the Johannine Jesus.

This is a fitting topic for a Festschrift devoted to Professor I. Howard Marshall. When I began PhD research on the Fourth Gospel in 1978 under his supervision, his interest in and concern for gospel historicity was clear not simply from his many publications both technical[2] and popular,[3] but in his regular counsel to his many, many students. Our ongoing concern for these same issues is a part of the legacy of his remarkable career.

---

[1] Urban von Wahlde, "The Pool of Siloam: The Importance of the New Discoveries for our Understanding of Ritual Immersion in Late Second Temple Judaism and the Gospel of John," in P. Anderson, F. Just, and T. Thatcher, eds., *Aspects of Historicity in the Fourth Gospel* (vol. 2 of *Jesus John and History*; Atlanta: SBL, 2009), 155-74. An earlier form of this essay was presented at the annual SBL meeting, "John, Jesus and History Section," November 2009. Important help with this paper came from my research assistant, Ms. Laura Gerlicher.

[2] Examples include *New Testament Interpretation: Essays on Principles and Methods* (Grand Rapids: Eerdmans, 1978); *The Gospel of Luke: A Commentary on the Greek Text* (Grand Rapids: Eerdmans, 1978) and more recently, *Luke: Historian and Theologian* (3d ed.; Downer's Grove: InterVarsity, 1998). However many (if not most) of Professor Marshall's publications demonstrate some interest in historicity as a theological concern.

[3] Examples include *I Believe in the Historical Jesus* (Grand Rapids: Eerdmans, 1979), *Mark* (Valley Forge, Pa.: Scripture Union, 1978) and his work on the *New Bible Dictionary* project now in its third edition (Downer's Grove: InterVarsity, 1996).

SILOAM AND BETHESDA

For centuries the Siloam Pool had always been identified with the narrow pool that stands at the outlet of Jerusalem's Hezekiah's tunnel. We can trace its origins to the fifth century when the Empress Eudocia built a church at the pool and refurbished it. Even pilgrim diaries mention it as an important destination for the pious. But all of that has now changed.

Let me review what has happened.[4] In the summer of 2004, repair work on a drain pipe at the lower end of the City of David—just above the "King's Garden"—yielded an unexpected find. Stone steps were discovered that at first glance looked Herodian. Ronny Reich and Eli Shukron were working near the Gihon Spring, they came over to inspect the find, and immediately Reich concluded that they were looking at the stairway that descended from the walled city and into the Siloam Pool. Reich and Shukron continued to excavate and as the steps descended, soon they widened and beneath the end of the rock scarp, the steps extended over 225 feet in width. Two corners were now exposed, their angles measured, and projections made. It was a massive pool, trapezoidal in shape, with every fifth step providing a wide landing. Three such sets of steps were found. Incidentally a few of these steps were discovered as early as 1898, but they were abandoned because the wider context of the southern city was not understood.

The Siloam site soon yielded a secure dating field: The earliest phase of the pool had plastered steps and in these were found coins from Alexander Jannaeus (102–76 B.C.). A second phase found the pool steps covered with limestone reminiscent of the Herodian steps at the temple's south entrance, below the Huldeh Gates. And along with these as well in the nearby terrace, they found late Second Temple pottery and coins from the first Jewish revolt. The earliest date for the pool was sometime in the Hasmonean era. Its *terminus ad quem* was likely A.D. 70 when Jerusalem was destroyed.

After the city was razed, water runoff from the south of the city brought centuries of mud that covered the pool, its access steps, and its drainage system. This made the Byzantine failure to find it understandable. And it explains why the pools were sitting under three meters of dirt when Reich and Shukron began working there. Today the pool has not been excavated completely. A small orchard just south of it belongs to the Greek Orthodox Church and no one wants it destroyed.

The discovery of the pool has raised a host of questions. For our purposes only one of these demands some attention. In their first published report on the pool, Reich and Shukron announced that this was not simply a water source for

---

[4] H. Shanks, "The Siloam Pool: Where Jesus Cured the Blind Man," *BAR* 31, no. 5 (2005): 16-23; see also the summary in von Wahlde, "The Pool of Siloam," 155-161. (Both articles include photos.)

Jerusalem, but a ritual bath or *miqveh*.[5] Its step design was reminiscent of other baths elsewhere in Jerusalem where about 150 have been found. But most important, the pool was fed by water that qualified for ritual bathing needs specified in the Mishnah (*m. Miqwa'ot*). Since this pool was fed by a spring it held *living water* and thus was ritually pure. They also pointed to a well-known *miqveh* in Jerusalem's southern excavations near the Huldeh Gate and one in the Jewish quarter. The steps, the plaster, and the design all fit the same pattern as they were uncovering at Siloam. This seemed to be a Herodian *miqveh*, a large public *miqveh*, serving the thousands of pilgrims who made their way to Jerusalem for the various festivals.

In 2008 Yoel Elitzur contested this result. In an extensive article in *Palestine Exploration Quarterly*, he argued that Siloam was not a *miqveh* but instead was a public swimming pool. Elitzur objected that since ritual bathing required nudity we can see why most were housed in private residences. And we can see how impractical such a *public miqveh* would be here in Jerusalem. Reich and Shukron have suggested that curtains or dividers could have been supplied. Elitzur rejected this as impractical and lacking physical evidence. Today this suggestion of required *miqveh* nudity is vigorously debated.[6] Josephus, for example, describes *miqveh* use among the Essenes saying that men wore a loin cloth (*J.W.* 2.8.5 §129) and it is likely that the Qumran sectarians were stricter than most.[7] Even *m. Miqw.* 9:1 implies that ritual bathing in wool or flax garments was taking place. Rabbi Judah is recorded as saying that wool does not invalidate a bath since it, like hair, can be penetrated by water.

But the interest of Herod in swimming pools is easily demonstrated at the Herodian near Bethlehem or Herod's palace at Jericho. And Herod's attempt to make Judea into a Roman province would fit here too: recreational swimming pools were common to the Romans, and Herod may have brought them along with his theaters and gymnasia. Elitzur thinks we have evidence of seven or eight such pools in Israel alone. Some, such as the one in Jericho, was even sufficient for sailing (180 x 250m).

Alongside Siloam another important site now has entered the discussion. Shimon Gibson at Jerusalem's Albright Institute argued in 2005 that the Pool of

---

[5] R. Reich and E. Shukron, "The Siloam Pool from the Second Temple Period in Jerusalem," *Qadmoniot* [Hebrew] 130 (2005): 91-96 [ET: private translation by G. Rivkin; supplied courtesy of U. von Wahlde].

[6] This objection is vigorously disputed by many. There is some evidence that garments which could be penetrated by water were occasionally worn (*m. Miqw.* 9:1). S. Gibson believes this was a practice among the Essenes (private correspondence, 14 Oct 2009). See the thorough arguments by von Wahlde, "The Pool of Siloam," 167-70.

[7] Von Wahlde, "The Pool of Siloam," 168.

Bethesda (or the Beit-Hisdah Pool or even Beth-zatha Pool)[8] near St. Anne's north of the temple was also a first-century *miqveh*, and he extended his argument in a recent publication in 2009.[9] Later this year he will publish a fascicule on Bethesda showing many new evidences pointing to its identity as a huge public *miqveh*. At the same time, in 2009 Urban von Wahlde offered an extensive article summarizing the results of the work at Bethesda and here he argued the same point independently.[10]

Gibson and von Wahlde believe Bethesda was a rainwater-fed *miqveh* system that qualified under the rules of *m. Miqw.* 1:1-8 as a purification pool. It held two basins: an upper reservoir for feeding the *miqveh* with water, called an *otzer* (53 x 40m) and a lower purification pool, the *miqveh* proper (47 x 52m).[11] These were divided by a barrier wall separating the two, and here he found a connecting sluice-gate that could replenish the lower pool as needed.[12] It was a very large complex and had five porticoes (one atop the barrier wall). But in addition Gibson points to the western side of the southern pool and how it had a long line of graduated plastered steps that facilitated entry into the pool. The similarities with the new Siloam pool immediately became obvious. And the connection to John 5 was clear too: not simply the pool's five porches, but the superstition that the waters were stirred by angels. This might well have stemmed from the deep sluice-gate opening at the *miqveh*'s bottom (John 5:4, 7). Mingled water fully qualified as ritual water if done correctly (*m. Miqw.* 6:1, 8) though there seems to be evidence that it the practice was controversial (*m. Yad.* 4:7).

This is the state of the discussion: we now have two massive pools on the north and south side of Herodian Jerusalem, each offering evidence of use as

---

[8] Manuscripts disagree on the name of the pool. Greek texts offer Bethzatha, Bethsaida, Belzetha, and Bethesda. Qumran refers to a location called "Beth'esda" which means "house of flowing."

[9] S. Gibson, "The Pool of Bethesda in Jerusalem and Jewish Purification Practices of the Second Temple Period," *Proche-Orient Chreten* 55 (2005): 270-93; idem, *The Final Days of Jesus: The Archaeological Evidence* (New York: HarperOne, 2009), 59-80.

[10] U. von Wahlde, "The Pool(s) of Bethesda and the Healing in John 5: A Reappraisal of Research and of the Johannine Text," *RB* 116 (2009): 111-36.

[11] According to von Wahlde, Siloam also held two pools, an upper pool (likely the traditional pool near the mouth of Hezekiah's tunnel) and the newly found lower pool ("The Pool of Siloam," 166-67). He has also demonstrated that the two pools at Bethesda followed the same pattern: the upper pool, originally built to supply the temple became an *otzer* when the lower pool was built as a *miqveh*. See von Wahlde, "The Pool(s) of Bethesda."

[12] In 2010 I was permitted (by St. Anne's *White Fathers*) to climb through the sluice gate/channel and examine the vertical shaft that once held the mechanism controlling the passage of water from the *otzer* to the *miqveh* itself. Gibson and von Wahlde's proposal is completely convincing. The *otzer* channel continues north into the now unexcavated upper pool showing its connection between the two pools.

miqva'ot.

TWO IMPORTANT CLUES

The Fourth Gospel intersects these discoveries in an unexpected way. And while Reich, Shukrun and Gibson each point to John's references to these pools in chs. 5 and 9, none of them have noted that John may lend weight to their argument that Siloam and Bethesda were indeed *miqva'ot*.[13] But in order to establish this link, two clues must be teased out.

First, it is no secret that John's gospel has an interest in water. The term ὕδωρ occurs twenty-one times in and by all accounts has become a symbolic motif throughout the Gospel. Water is what fills the wedding jars of Cana (2:7). Water is a feature of Nicodemus' rebirth (3:5). Water is what the Samaritan woman seeks (4:7). Water features in the healing of the crippled and the blind men in chs. 5 and 9 (5:7; 9:7 "*a pool*"). Water is Jesus' gift at Succoth (7:37). Jesus washes the disciples with water (13:5) and water is what flows from Jesus' side at the cross (19:34).

Many have recently probed the underlying meaning of these symbols. Two recent PhD dissertations have thoroughly dissected every aspect of this theme and underscored that John finds in water a vital symbol for the person and work of Christ.[14] And yet in most of these studies, water is viewed simply as a narrative device without regard for what may be its most obvious and interesting historical application. It may refer to personal renewal, the Holy Spirit, eternal life or for some it may refer symbolically to the cross.[15] But surprisingly a simple historical, contextual meaning is generally bypassed.

The most important development of this imagery in John is his use of the phrase *living water*.[16] This concept occurs in only three NT texts: the Samaritan woman story and the climax of Jesus' appearance at Tabernacles (4:10-11; 7:38). It also makes an appearance in the Book of Revelation (7:17) where the

---

[13] Discussion about the role of these pools has been going on in the pages of *Biblical Archaeology Review*. Urban von Wahlde of Loyola University has joined the debate (see his "The 'Upper Pool,' Its 'Conduit,' and 'the Road of the Fuller's Field' in Eighth Century BC Jerusalem and their Significance for the Pools of Bethesda and Siloam," *RB* 113 [2006]: 242-62). And he has been gently chided by Jewish bloggers that every NT scholar should see the link between a healed blind man and a *miqveh*. See http://frumheretic.blogspot.com/2008/09/great-mikvah-coverup.html. See also his "The pool of Siloam."

[14] L. P. Jones, *The Symbol of Water in the Gospel of John* (JSNTSup 145; Sheffield: Sheffield Academic Press, 1997); W. Ng, *Water Symbolism in John: An Eschatological Interpretation* (New York: Lang, 2001).

[15] B. Grigsby, "Washing in the Pool of Siloam—A Thematic Description of the Johannine Cross," *NovT* 27 (1985): 227-35.

[16] F. J. McCool, "Living Water in John," in *The Bible in Current Catholic Thought* (ed. J. L. McKenzie and M. Gruenthaner; New York: Herder & Herder, 1962), 226-33.

glorified lamb will guide his sheep to springs of living water (ἐπὶ ζωῆς πηγὰς ὑδάτων). The Fourth Gospel's use of this term is hardly innocent. Its use would evoke an immediate and unmistakable response in any Jewish reader acquainted with first-century ceremonial religious practices. And yet most commentary writers have viewed living water as metaphor for the Holy Spirit, the Torah, or even Wisdom much as it is suggested at Qumran.[17] Craig Keener's 2003 commentary may be the first to suggest that John is in a serious conversation over ritual purity.[18]

But now a second clue. There is ample evidence that, as Shimon Gibson says, "an explosion of purity took place within Judaism in the first century CE."[19] Gibson cites *t. Šabb.* 1:14 which says this explicitly.[20] Even though both the Mishnah and Tosefta likely idealize the practices of the Second Temple period, still, most scholars believe that significant trends had emerged. In a thorough study in 2006, Jonathan Lawrence amassed all of the relevant literary data demonstrating this development.[21] Ritual washing had become a common preoccupation and Lev 11–15 provided a guideline for impurities to which many things were added.[22] Josephus mentions the practice (*Ant.* 3:261-265, 269) as does Philo (*Spec.* 1:261-262) and both try to explain their people's ritual habits to a wider public. Ritual purity and the cultic washings to maintain it became a concern from the Hasmonean period until the war of 70 C.E. After this period, the evidence is limited.

But archaeological evidence demonstrates the flourishing of these practices as well. Ritual baths (*miqva'ot*) have been located in private homes from the

---

[17] For the traditional interpretative options see C. K. Barrett, *The Gospel According to St. John* (2d ed.; London: SPCK; Philadelphia: Westminster, 1978), 233; R. Schnackenburg, *The Gospel According to St. John* (trans. K. Smith et al. [vols. 1–2] and D. Smith and G. Kon [vol. 3]; 3 vols.; New York: Seabury, 1980 [vols. 1–2]; New York: Crossroad, 1982 [vol. 3]), 1:427.

[18] C. Keener, *The Gospel of John: A Commentary* (2 vols.; Peabody, Mass.: Hendrickson, 2003), 1:509-10, 601-605.

[19] S. Gibson, *The Final Days of Jesus*, 79.

[20] "Said R Simeon b. Eleazar, 'Come and see how far the keeping of cultic cleanness has spread, for the ancients did not decree making a rule that a ritually clean man should not eat a meal with a menstruating woman.' For the ancients did not eat with menstruating women [and therefore did not need to make such a rule]. But the ancients did rule: 'A Zab should not eat a meal with a woman-Zab, because it leads to transgression.'" (*t. Šabb.* 1:14 commenting on *m. Šabb.* 1:3. See also *t. Šabb.*1:15-18.

[21] J. D. Lawrence, *Washing in Water: Trajectories of Ritual Bathing in the Hebrew Bible and Second Temple Literature* (Atlanta: SBL, 2006).

[22] Lawrence outlines three general rubrics for washing: (1) General Washing—ritual purification for all people such as unclean animals, childbirth, skin diseases and mildew, and bodily discharges [Lev. 11-15]; (2) Priestly Washing—ritual purification before temple service; (3) Theophany Washing—preparation for a public ritual event (*Washing in Water*, 26-34).

first century, at Qumran, as well as near agricultural installations where the purity of grape and olive harvesters was necessary. But oddly few *miqva'ot* have been found near cemeteries.[23] The majority of these immersion pools are small and personal and have been uncovered from Hebron to Sepphoris with a remarkable concentration in Jerusalem. They each have characteristic features such as a plastered surface of burned lime or quicklime with crushed charcoal, steps (sometimes divided for entry and exit), and water sources that qualified under the law as having purifying capacity (in particular, *not* drawn by hand).[24] Recently R. Reich has shown that all of the proven first-century synagogues we have found had *miqva'ot* as a part of their building. This is true at Gamla, Herodium and the Zealot rebuilding on Masada.[25] Combined with this evidence is the development of a Galilee stoneware industry making vessels used for purification particularly in the five decades before the war with Rome.[26]

But in addition Judaism understood the need for *public* ritual washings and here too archaeological evidence comes in service. Two large *miqva'ot* may be present on the Temple Mount or Haram al-Sharif beneath the main fountain there and another is at the entrance of the Al-Aqsa Mosque beneath the paving stones.[27] But since these pools were within the temple enclosure they surely were not for the masses. One *miqveh* remains among the public buildings south of the city in the Ophel region, but this would hardly suffice for large public

---

[23] Y. Adler, "Second Temple Ritual Baths Adjacent to Agricultural Installations: The Archaeological Evidence in Light of Halakhic Sources," *JJS* 59 (2008): 62-72. For extensive references to archaeological evidences, see S. Gibson, "The Pool of Bethesda," 275 n. 6. A basin for ritual washing has been found in Jerusalem's *Tomb of the Kings* but this is exceptional. For a summary of the use of immersion pools or *miqva'ot* see E. P. Sanders, *Jewish Law from Jesus to the Mishnah* (Philadelphia: Trinity; London: SCM, 1990): 214-27.

[24] m. *Miqw.* 1:1-8 outlines the six grades of ritual water available: (1) rain ponds following rain; (2) ponds fed by ongoing rain; (3) immersion pools holding 40 seah of water [1 seah = 7.3 liters; hence, 40 seah = 293 liters or 77.4 U.S. gallons]; (4) wells with natural groundwater; (5) salty water from the sea or springs; (6) natural flowing *living water* from springs or rivers.

[25] R. Reich, "The Synagogue and the Miqweh in Eretz-Israel in the Second-Temple, Mishnaic, and Talmudic Periods," in *Ancient Synagogues: Historical Analysis and Archaeological Discovery* (ed. D. Urman and P. Flesher; Leiden: Brill, 1995), 289-97.

[26] Y. Magen, *The Stone Vessel Industry in the Second Temple Period: Excavations at Hizma and the Jerusalem Temple Mount* (Jerusalem: Israel Exploration Society, 2002); S. Gibson, "Stone Vessels of the Early Roman Period from Jerusalem and Palestine: A Reassessment," in *One Land—Many Cultures: Archaeological Studies in Honour of S. Loffreda* (ed. G. C. Bottini, L. Segni, and L. D. Chrupcala; Jerusalem: Franciscan Printing Press, 2003), 287-308.

[27] S. Gibson and D. M. Jacobson, *Below the Temple Mount in Jerusalem: A Sourcebook on the Cisterns, Subterranean Chambers and Conduits of the Haram al-Sharif* (Oxford: Tempus Reparatum, 1996).

crowds.[28] In 2009 another *miqveh* was found in the so-called Rabbinic tunnels west of the temple enclosure.

The dilemma is this: in a religious climate seriously preoccupied with ritual cleansing and the need to preserve the purity of the temple, how did the city manage the many arriving pilgrims for the various festivals? According to Reich and Gibson the answer is simple: both Bethesda and Siloam were enormous public *miqva'ot* in Jerusalem.

Is John aware of this climate? Does John put the theme of ritual purity in service? Is John aware of these pools as locations for ritual washing? I believe he is.

RITUAL PURITY, THE JOHANNINE CHRISTOLOGY, AND JESUS

One of the primary christological motifs in John's theology is the way in which the arrival of Christ is juxtaposed with traditional institutions of Jewish piety. Some scholars have referred to this as a Johannine *replacement motif* and it may be so. But at least we can say that John is aware of traditional forms of Jewish practice and celebration, he is willing to name them, and he is willing to describe Jesus operating in some manner in contrast to them. To select two: Jesus can appear at the temple in ch. 2, cleanse it, and then in a bit of Johannine irony, we learn that Jesus is the new temple that will be raised up (2:21-22; 1:14). Similarly Jesus can appear at Passover in ch. 6, exploit many of the ritual images associated with that festival, and then in another bit of irony, we learn that the manna so central to the festival's story is now supplanted in Christ who is the Bread of Life.

If this theological pattern is true, it follows that other pronounced Jewish ritual symbols would follow this same motif. In particular, John is likely aware of the remarkable interest in ritual purification within the first century. And he may be weaving this theme into his narrative explicitly. This is all the more significant concerning John 5 and 9. Here archaeology has identified these two locations as likely *miqva'ot*, and John has given each store a premier place in his gospel. John 5 and 9 have always been noted as having much in common and they serve as the two premier healing miracles in the Johannine Book of Signs when Jesus is revealed in public.[29]

This possibility of integrating *miqveh* practice with John's gospel serves in

---

[28] R. Reich, "Jewish Ritual Baths in the Second Temple Period and the Period of the Mishnah and Talmud," (PhD diss., Hebrew University, Jerusalem, 1991 [Hebrew]), cited by S. Gibson, "The Pool of Bethesda," 275 n. 6.

[29] These are the only two public healing miracles in John's gospel. In 4:46-54 the healing of the Capernaum official's son is private as is the raising of Lazarus in 11:1-44. In John 5 and 9 Jesus chooses a public locale in Jerusalem to display his identity vis-à-vis a Jewish festival (Shabbat, Succoth). Moreover he names the two locations specifically.

three directions. First, it contributes to the Gibson/Reich theory that Siloam and Bethesda were indeed *miqva'ot*. John's technical interest in water implies that he has a technical interest in the pools as serving his larger christological agenda. In other words, John may well be viewing the pools as sites of ritual purification because they serve his interest in Jewish ritual, purification and fulfillment. The public purification pools were well-known in Jerusalem as prominent landmarks. And they now join the list of established Jewish religious institutions Jesus' arrival has now made obsolete.

Second, if John does have this interest in *miqva'ot* and it has influenced the Johannine water motif, a variety of exegetical issues would need to be revisited. In a word, *we need to consider that wherever the Johannine water motif appears, we should wonder if ritual purification is its most natural referent.* Four texts provide this suggestion:

• The Cana episode is perhaps the most obvious immediate application. Here Galilee stoneware used for ritual washing is miraculously filled with wine. That is, Jesus works his first miracle on instruments of purification and shows that in his coming, a new purity will be available *in the hour* of his glorification. Water of ritual purity will now find a new form. Note that purification (καθαρισμός) is explicitly mentioned in 2:6. This opening scene immediately alerts the reader that the work of Jesus now has implications for ritual instruments of Judaism.

• In the Nicodemus episode Nicodemus learns that his rebirth must come through water and the spirit. And while the exegetical options for water here are many, a strong possibility is that we should look to ritual purity as Jesus' first prerequisite for entry to the kingdom. Rebirth cannot be facilitated by water alone but by water and the Spirit. This is likely a distilled summary of the Johannine theology: cleansing must be joined to the purifying work of the messianic Spirit present in Jesus (1:34). Note again in 3:25 John tells us explicitly that discussions concerning purification (καθαρισμός) continued to surround Jesus' work.

• At Samaria, Jesus meets with a woman in search of water; he deflects her quest and, in a conversation that highlights her isolation and impurity, offers her *living water*—the water of Jewish ritual cleansing. This is the one gift that can bring restoration to her community and to God. Her thirst will be quenched not through drinking from a well, but through immersion in Christ who will restore her.[30] It is interesting that in John 2 Jesus works his miracle on purification jars (ὑδρία) and in John 4 it is also a jar (ὑδρία) that the woman leaves behind. In John's metaphoric world, these are two jars whose original purpose is now lost.

---

[30] Commentaries written before 1975 did not have access to the wealth of information we have about *miqva'ot* in Jerusalem. But even modern commentaries fail to refer to this possibility.

- At the festival of Tabernacles, Jesus comes to the temple on the final great day and announces that he can offer *living water* to those who are in need. This overture follows the replacement motif seen everywhere at Succoth. Living water—the water used in a *miqveh* is here supplied by Jesus.

When we wed the Johannine water motif to the Jewish preoccupation with ritual cleansing and *miqva'ot*, a reexamination of these four texts is inevitable. More difficult are other water texts where the connection to ritual purity seems less obvious. Two come to mind. In ch. 13 Jesus *washes* his disciples in *water* and thereby makes them clean (13:10 καθαρός). Is this another Johannine allusion to *miqveh?* This is far less obvious. Then in John 19:35 we learn that blood and *water* flow from Jesus' side on the cross. This water is likely a fulfillment of the Succoth water promised in 7:37-38, water that springs from Christ's κοιλία. In John's thinking the hour of glorification does not simply record the return of the Son to the Father, but it is the anticipated hour when the promises offered throughout the gospel are realized. For John, true purity, ritual purity, now may be found at the cross. As Jesus says during his final meal, a part of his work has been to make his followers clean (καθαρός, 15:3).

If these suggestions are successful, then it should come as no surprise that John has anchored two major healing stories—chs. 5 and 9—in the midst of a discussion about ritual purity. Or taken differently: if the Johannine water motif is interested in ritual purity and *miqveh* practice, then John is looking at the stories of chs. 5 and 9 in the same manner. After Jesus applies mud to the blind man's eyes in ch. 9, he tells him to go and wash. Indeed any water would do. *But when tells the man to wash in Siloam, the natural understanding of the text is that Jesus is directing him to immerse himself in a public miqveh following his healing.* A blind man would have been presumed to be in a perpetual state of uncleanness because he could not avoid touching or contacting things that were impure. Now his ritual washing would complete the restoration begun by Jesus.[31]

We know that lepers and the infirm were given access to these ritual pools not unlike the way Elisha told the cured leper Naaman to "go wash" in the Jordan River (2 Kgs 5:1-14). He was reclaiming ritual purity. And yet—and here is the Johannine Christology at work—the Siloam pool actually echoes Jesus' own name, implicitly telling us that Jesus is the true *miqveh* in whom genuine purity can be found. This is the Johannine replacement motif expressed in its clearest form.

Bethesda in ch. 5 illustrates the exercise of futility. Here an infirm man is hoping to find in these waters the healing he seeks. And yet as the woman of Samaria needed to be deflected from her water quest, here too the invalid learns that the genuine healing waters he seeks are not in the pool. Christ alone can provide water that brings about healing.

---

[31] Von Wahlde, "Pool of Siloam," 173.

But there is a third (and final) result. This new view of Bethesda and Siloam—together with the Johannine water motif—tells us about the historical character of the Johannine Jesus as well. It at least confirms that these locations are not fictional and that John is confidently and accurately using topographical references. But these discoveries have also placed a Second Temple Jewish ritual practice at the center of Jesus' ministry. A practice that was flourishing before 70 C.E. is the focus of Jesus' work and it anchors him in what was perhaps the most characteristic practice of the early first century. Jesus' use of "water" does not need to be found in Hellenistic religious symbols nor is it merely a literary device of the Gospel's author. It is a primitive echo of Jesus traditions taking us back to the earliest moments of Christian memory. Even the Synoptic Gospels suggest this in the many echoes to the καθαρίζω word group there (used thirty-one times).[32]

Shimon Gibson is intrigued as well by the historical implications of this result.[33] He wonders if Jesus used these two pools strategically during the last week of his ministry. The dangers of the temple area were well-known to Jesus and his disciples. Talk about Jesus' arrest and death were already public among the disciples. Here at Bethesda and Siloam Jesus could find large groups of pilgrims where he could gain an audience, continue with his ministry of healing, and teach beyond the reach of the temple authorities. Unlike the temple courts, these were public sites, large public sites, that collected crowds and were free of temple oversight. Their prominence was well-known which explains in part why the gospel narrative names them.

The discovery of the true Pool of Siloam and the renewal of interest in Bethesda should alert every Johannine scholar that something significant is at work in the two major healing miracles in the public narratives of the gospel. Water is one of John's chief symbols, but only now perhaps we are seeing clearly what it meant for John as well as Jesus.

---

[32] See recently, Y. Furstenberg, "Defilement Penetrating the Body: A New Understanding of Contamination in Mark 7.15," *NTS* 54 (2008): 176-200.

[33] *The Final Days of Jesus*, 79-80.

8

THE PURPOSE OF LUKE–ACTS: REACHING A CONSENSUS

Mark L. Strauss

Few scholars have made a greater impact on the study of Luke-Acts, and more specifically the role of Luke as both historian and theologian, than I. Howard Marshall. Throughout his long and illustrious career, Professor Marshall has been a model of scholarly excellence, lucidity, and balance. I consider it a privilege to call him a mentor and a friend, and to offer this small contribution on Lukan purpose in his honor.

PROPOSALS FOR THE PURPOSE OF LUKE-ACTS

When Robert Maddox published his 1982 volume, *The Purpose of Luke-Acts*, the question of Luke's purpose in his two-volume work was a hotly-debated topic. Maddox identified seven proposals for the purpose of Luke-Acts. These included, (1) an attempt to resolve the crisis of the delay of the Parousia (Hans Conzelmann); (2) a defense of Paul at his Roman trial (A. J. Matill); (3) a defense of Christians in general in the eyes of the Roman government (B. S. Easton); (4) a defense of Paul's memory in the face of attacks by Jewish Christians (Jacob Jervell et al.[1]); (5) a defense of the church against Gnosticism (C. H. Talbert); (6) evangelism, to bring unbelievers to Christ (J. C. O'Neill); and (7) the confirmation of the gospel for believers in the church (W. C. van Unnik).[2]

The years since Maddox have seen the demise of most of these views, either through systematic refutation or scholarly disinterest. By far the most impactful theory of the early twentieth century was Hans Conzelmann's "delay-of-the-Parousia." In his landmark volume, *Die Mitte der Zeit,* Conzelmann claimed that Luke wrote to resolve the crisis in the early church created by the failure of Christ to return as expected.[3] Luke solved this crisis by re-writing church history, presenting the church not as the end-time, Spirit-led messianic community, but as one phase in God's purpose and plan. The OT period was

---

[1] M. Schneckenburger and F. C. Bauer are noted by Maddox as older advocates of this view.
[2] Robert Maddox, *The Purpose of Luke-Acts* (Edinburgh: T&T Clark, 1982), 20-23; cf. the summary of proposals in Joel Green, "Acts of the Apostles," *DLNT* 7-24.
[3] Hans Conzelmann, *Die Mitte der Zeit* (Tübingen: Mohr [Siebeck], 1954); ET: *The Theology of St Luke* (trans. Geoffrey Buswell; London: Faber & Faber, 1961).

the period of promise, the time of Jesus was the "middle of time" (*die Mitte der Zeit*) and the church age was the new era of salvation. With this new schema, the return of Christ was pushed into the distant future and the church was transformed from a Spirit-led eschatological community into an institutional religion equipped to last for an indefinite period of time.

Conzelmann's most important contribution to Lukan studies has been his groundbreaking assertion that Luke wrote as a purposeful theologian—a foundational starting point for all Lukan interpreters today. Conzelmann's delay-of-the-Parousia theory has not fared so well, and has been well answered by his critics.[4] Indeed, Charles Talbert, in surveying the state of Lukan studies in 1976, claimed that one of the few things upon which Lukan scholars agree is the *inadequacy* of Conzelmann's synthesis.[5] Against Conzelmann is the lack of clear evidence for a significant crisis over the delay of the Parousia in the early church. Nor can it be said that all of pre-Lukan Christianity was characterized by intense eschatological expectation. Nolland sums up well when he says, "Those who posit a radical difference in the realm of eschatology between Mark and Luke seem to me to have both over-eschatologized Mark and to have under-eschatologized Luke."[6] Indeed Luke's Markan source itself provides evidence that a significant period of time might pass before the return of Christ: "And the Gospel must first be preached to all nations" (Mark 13:10 NIV). Although Luke places a greater emphasis on the present reign of Christ than his predecessors, he affirms the same already–not yet eschatology that appears throughout the NT.

The greatest weakness of Conzelmann's view was his failure to take into account so much of Luke's material. For example, Conzelmann dismissed Luke's birth narrative as irrelevant to his view of salvation-history, and so failed to account for Luke's intense interest in the Jewish foundations of Christianity and the continuity between Israel and the church. Today Luke's birth narrative is viewed almost universally as introductory and programmatic for the whole of Luke-Acts.

Other theories of Lukan purpose suffer from a similar problem, that is (assuming the unity of Luke-Acts), a failure to account for so much of the evidence. This is true, for example, of the claim that Luke wrote to defend Paul at his Roman trial, a perspective defended by A. J. Mattill[7] and others. C. K.

---

[4] See especially I. H. Marshall, *Luke: Historian and Theologian* (3d ed.; Grand Rapids: Zondervan, 1998).

[5] Charles Talbert, "Shifting Sands: The Recent Study of the Gospel of Luke," *Int* 30 (1976): 381-95 [395]; reprinted in James Luther Mays, ed., *Interpreting the Gospels* (Philadelphia: Fortress Press, 1981), 197-213.

[6] John Nolland, *Luke* (3 vols.; WBC 35A-35C; Dallas: Word Books, 1989), 1:xxxviii.

[7] See, for example, A. J. Mattill, "Naherwartung, Fernerwartung and the Purpose of Luke-Acts: Weymouth Reconsidered," *CBQ* 34 (1972): 276-93; idem, "The Jesus-Paul Parallels and the Purpose of Luke-Acts: H. H. Evans Reconsidered," *NovT* 17 (1975):

Barrett's oft-quoted remark sums up this view's inadequacy: "No Roman official would ever have filtered out so much of what to him would be theological and ecclesiastical rubbish in order to reach so tiny a grain of relevant apology."[8] A statement of Lukan purpose must take into account the unity of Luke-Acts and its many inter-related themes. The same problem plagues the view that Luke-Acts was written to defend Christianity in the eyes of the Roman government. B. S. Easton asserted that Luke's purpose was to establish Christianity as a *religio licita,* worthy of the same protection under Roman law that was given to Judaism.[9] The problem, again, is that while this works well for portions of Acts, it fails to account for so much of the Gospel material.

It is similarly unlikely that Luke's primary purpose was to defend the memory of Paul in the face of attacks by Jewish Christians—the view of Jacob Jervell.[10] While this might work for portions of Acts, where Paul is presented as a faithful Jew who does not abandon his Jewish heritage, it does not account for the multiplicity of themes in the Gospel. Most notably, Luke takes great pains both in the Gospel and in Acts to defend Jesus' messianic identity and the scriptural necessity of his death. The repeated refrain that the Christ had to suffer (Luke 24:26, 46; Acts 3:18; 17:3; 26:23) suggests an apologetic concern related to *Christology.* Yet such an apology would be unnecessary for Jewish Christians, who certainly accepted that Jesus was the Messiah, now vindicated through his resurrection.

We can dismiss on the same paucity of evidence C. H. Talbert's claim that Luke wrote to oppose the growing heresy of Gnosticism.[11] While passages like Luke 24:39 ("Touch me and see; a ghost does not have flesh and bones, as you see I have" NIV) indicate Luke's interest in the physicality of Jesus' resurrection body—perhaps in opposition to Docetic claims—this cannot be the overarching or central purpose of Luke-Acts, since it factors into so little of Luke's writing. Like these other views, it is based on potentially valid, but very limited, insights from the Lukan corpus. In later works, Talbert himself backed away from his earlier claims and adopted a broader approach to Lukan

---

15-46; idem, "The Date and Purpose of Luke-Acts: Rackham reconsidered," *CBQ* 40 (1978): 335-50.

[8] C. K. Barrett, *Luke the Historian in Recent Study* (London: Epworth, 1961), 63.

[9] B. S. Easton, *The Purpose of Acts* (London: SPCK, 1936); reprinted as *Early Christianity: The Purpose of Acts and Other Papers* (ed. F. C. Grant, London: SPCK, 1955), 33-57.

[10] Jacob Jervell, *Luke and the People of God: A New Look at Luke-Acts* (Minneapolis: Augsburg, 1972).

[11] Charles Talbert, *Luke and the Gnostics: An Examination of Lucan Purpose* (Nashville: Abingdon, 1966).

purpose.¹²

This leaves two main views—that Luke-Acts was written for the purpose of evangelism, that is, to convince unbelievers of the truth of Christianity or for the purpose of legitimation, to assure and confirm Christians of the truth of their message. J. C. O'Neill argued for the former, claiming that Luke's purpose was to lead educated pagans to faith in Christ.¹³ John Nolland agrees that Luke's audience was not-yet-Christian, but sees them as God-fearers rather than pagans. He writes

> that Luke made considerable use in his argumentation of reader-assumptions which could only be true for people whose religious values had been considerably shaped by first-century Judaism, and that he was vigorously engaged apologetically in responding to Jewish polemic against the Christian movement, polemic of a kind which, once again, would be effective only for those whose value structure was coming essentially from Judaism.¹⁴

Nolland concludes that the ideal first-century reader for much of Luke and Acts would be a God-fearer, one whose birth is not Jewish and whose background is Hellenistic, but who had been attracted to Judaism, drawn to the God of Israel and the worship of the synagogue. He concludes that Theophilus was likely a God-fearer considering the claims of Christianity.

In a recent article on "The Purpose of Luke-Acts," David Wenham reaches similar conclusions.¹⁵ The trouble between Jews and Christians would have raised all sorts of questions for the people in Rome. Noting key Lukan themes, such as the strong Jewish roots of the gospel, the defense of the Gentile mission and the assertion of Christian innocence in the context of Roman law, Wenham suggests a plausible historical context and purpose in the growing conflict between Jews and Christians evident in the expulsion of Jews from Rome by Claudius (A.D. 49) and continuing into the 60s of the first century.

While rightly stressing important Lukan themes, Wenham's essay probably moves too quickly to a specific precipitating event. In response to Wenham's article, F. Scott Spencer cautions—appropriately in my opinion—against the tendency to propose a specific historical context and then interpret the text accordingly. Too often this results in a circular reading:

---

[12] Charles Talbert, "Reading Chance, Moessner, and Parsons," in *Cadbury, Knox and Talbert: American Contributions to the Study of Acts* (ed. Mikeal C. Parsons and Joseph B. Tyson; SBLBSNA 18; Atlanta: Scholars Press, 1992), 229-40 [229-30].

[13] J. C. O'Neill, *The Theology of Acts in Its Historical Setting* (London: SPCK, 1961), 172-85.

[14] Nolland, *Luke*, 1:xxxii.

[15] David Wenham, "The Purpose of Luke-Acts: Israel's Story in the Context of the Roman Empire," in *Reading Luke: Interpretation, Reflection, Formation* (ed. C. G. Bartholomew, J. B. Green, and A. C. Thiselton; Grand Rapids: Zondervan, 2005), 79-103.

By locking too early in the interpretive process on an event or other piece of evidence outside a narrative that happen to correspond with some feature(s) within the story, and then hypothesizing that external matter as a *primary, precipitant cause* for writing the story, the reader's vision may become skewed in one direction, to the neglect of other dynamic vectors in the story. [16]

William J. Larkin also favors an evangelistic purpose over a legitimizing one.[17] He points out that while κατηχέω in Luke 1:4 may refer to a kind of catechism for new believers, it could also refer to general information about the Christian faith through evangelistic contacts. Various details in Acts point to this evangelistic purpose and a Roman reading public. For example, "no matter the numbers or ethnicity involved, each conversion account focuses on the desired response to the gospel and in that way fulfills an evangelistic purpose." The conversion accounts of Paul (22:14-16; 26:16-18; 26:22-23) and Cornelius (10:1–11:18) progressively bring out more aspects of the gospel's content, "including the values and responses worth emulating" (10:4-8, 22, 32; 11:14). What is highlighted in these and other conversion accounts, Larkin argues, "is not the example of the witness but its reception."[18]

There is no doubt that Luke holds up those who respond to the gospel as models to be emulated. Furthermore, it seems likely that Luke would consider his work to be an effective evangelistic tool for bringing others to Christ. But a closer examination of these accounts in the larger context of Luke-Acts indicates a purpose greater than models for evangelism. The stress throughout the Cornelius account and the reason for its repetition is to demonstrate that it was not Peter's initiative, but the promptings of the Holy Spirit that brought the gospel to Cornelius (Acts 10:15, 20, 28, 31, 34-35, 44-47; 11:4-10, 15-17, 18). The Gentile mission was not launched through human initiative, but because it was part of God's purpose and plan (cf. Acts 13:2; 15:14-18). Peter's report to the Jerusalem church (11:4-17) and his speech to the Jerusalem council (15:7-11) serve as apologetics for the Gentile mission. Similarly, in the accounts of Saul's conversion and his various defenses, the emphasis is on God's intervention to transform the persecutor into the apostle to the Gentiles (22:2-5, 21; 23:6; 24:14-16; 26:1-18) and his innocence of the false charges leveled against him (24:12-16, 18; 25:8, 10-11, 18; 26:31-32; 28:17-18). Paul is not a renegade Jew or lawbreaker in opposition to his people and his God, but a faithful Jew called from his misguided zeal to the salvation-historical purpose

---

[16] F. Scott Spencer, "Preparing the Way of the Lord Introducing and Interpreting Luke's Narrative: A Response to David Wenham," in *Reading Luke: Interpretation, Reflection, Formation* (ed. C. G. Bartholomew, J. B. Green, and A. C. Thiselton; Grand Rapids: Zondervan, 2005), 104-24 [122].

[17] William J. Larkin, "Acts" in *The Gospel of Luke, Acts* (vol. 12 of *Cornerstone Biblical Commentary*; ed. P. W. Comfort; Carol Stream, Ill.: Tyndale House Publishers, 2006), 349-668 [353-57].

[18] Larkin, "Acts," 356.

of God for the world. The conversion accounts in Acts, while certainly models for unbelievers to follow, are, more importantly, evidence for the unrelenting progress of the gospel, proof that Jesus is the Messiah, and confirmation that the church made up of Jews and Gentiles represents the true people of God. This theme fits a legitimizing purpose better than an evangelistic one.[19]

A LEGITIMIZING PURPOSE

Over against these other proposals, Maddox concluded that Luke-Acts was written for a Christian audience to legitimize and vindicate their faith. Drawing on the work of W. C. van Unnik, he claimed that Luke wrote to "confirm the Gospel" or to reassure the faith of his readers. Luke's purpose was not primarily Christological, soteriological, or pneumatological, but rather eschatological and ecclesiological. In terms of eschatology, his purpose was not to explain the delay of the Parousia, as Conzelmann had supposed, but "to appreciate the great extent to which God's salvation *has already been fulfilled* in what has happened in the mission of Jesus and its sequel in the gift of the Holy Spirit."[20] In terms of ecclesiology, Maddox asserts that, "Luke-Acts is in every way a book devoted to clarifying the Christian self-understanding."[21] Luke writes to Christians suffering doubts caused by the Jewish rejection of the Gospel and Jewish propaganda leveled against them, "to reassure the Christians of his day that their faith in Jesus is not an aberration, but the authentic goal towards which God's ancient dealings with Israel were driving."[22]

In a 1983 article on Lukan purpose, I. Howard Marshall suggested a similar purpose related to Christian self-identity. He begins by noting various Lukan themes that must be taken into account when seeking Luke's main aim in writing: (1) Most basically, Luke's theme is Jesus himself—what he did and taught and subsequently what his followers taught concerning him. (2) From this Luke writes to show how these words and deeds of Jesus led to the experience of salvation and the community of the saved. (3) Luke seeks to show the truth of the Gospel by the correspondence between prophecy and fulfillment. (4) Finally, within this framework special importance is given to the theme of the conversion of individuals and the *creation of the church* that functions both as the community of believers and as the instrument of mission:

Luke . . . writes to tell the members of the church in his day "how we got here"

---

[19] Another argument against an evangelistic purpose was suggested to me by Jeff Hubing, who noted the exorbitant cost of producing books in the ancient world. The length, scope and grandeur of the narrative of Luke-Acts suggests it is meant to be a foundational narrative for the fledgling Christian movement, not an evangelistic tract.
[20] Maddox, *Purpose*, 183.
[21] Maddox, *Purpose*, 181.
[22] Maddox, *Purpose*, 187.

both in terms of individual faith and of corporate union in the people of God. He is particularly concerned with showing *how the church has come together as a company of believing Jews and Gentiles and how it is related to the Jewish roots from which it sprang* (emphasis mine).[23]

Marshall concludes that this last theme probably sums up most comprehensively what Luke is trying to do. Luke's particular interest in the Jewish origin of the church, questions of promise and fulfillment, the reasons for Jewish rejection of the Gospel, and the legitimacy of the Gentile mission all point to the issue of the *church's self-identity*—the questions of "who we are and how we got here."[24]

In my 1992 dissertation and subsequent 1995 monograph, *The Davidic Messiah in Luke-Acts*,[25] I reached similar conclusions. Though my main topic was Christological, I concluded that Luke's *primary* purpose was not Christological, but ecclesiological, relating to Christian self-identity. Luke writes to a Christian community—probably made up of both Jews and Gentiles[26]—struggling to assert itself as the legitimate heirs of the promises made to Israel. There appears to be an ongoing debate with unbelieving Jews that is threatening to undermine the faith of this community. Three key Lukan themes point in this direction: the legitimacy of Gentile mission, the widespread rejection of the message by the Jews, and the validity of Jesus' messianic identity. Luke writes to reassure his readers that they are the eschatological people of God, the legitimate heirs to the promises made to Israel. Ecclesiologically, Luke seeks to show that God's plan from the beginning was to bring salvation to the Gentiles, and that Jewish rejection was predicted in scripture and was part of Israel's long history of stubborn resistance to God's purposes. Christologically, Luke seeks to show that Jesus is the messianic deliverer promised in scripture, the Messiah spoken about by Moses and all the prophets. The theme that holds these threads together is promise and fulfillment. The church is the true eschatological community of

---

[23] I. H. Marshall, "Luke and His 'Gospel,'" in *Das Evangelium und die Evangelien* (ed. Peter Stuhlmacher; WUNT 28; Tübingen: Mohr [Siebeck], 1983), 289-308 [302]; cf. idem, "The Present State of Lucan Studies," *Them* 14 (1989): 52-56.

[24] As far as a concrete situation is concerned, Marshall suggests a catechetical motivation. Luke seeks to fill out the story of Jesus and the growth of the church left incomplete by the general catechetical instruction in the kerygma that Theophilus and other Christians had received. This would assure them of the reliability of the Christian message.

[25] *The Davidic Messiah in Luke-Acts: The Promise and Its Fulfillment in Lukan Christology* (Sheffield: Sheffield Academic Press, 1995).

[26] For evidence of a mixed community see P. F. Esler, *Community and Gospel in Luke-Acts: The Social and Political Motivations of Lucan Theology* (Cambridge: Cambridge University Press, 1987), 30-45; M. A. Moscato, "Current Theories regarding the Audience of Luke-Acts," *CTM* 3 (1976): 355-61.

faith because it is for her and through her God's promises are being fulfilled.

In his commentary on the Gospel of Luke, Joel Green comes to similar conclusions, based especially on his identification of the genre of Luke-Acts as historiography. He claims that Luke's goals center on legitimation and apologetic:

> We propose that the purpose of Luke-Acts would have been to strengthen the Christian movement in the face of opposition by (1) ensuring them in their interpretation and experience of the redemptive purpose and faithfulness of God and by (2) calling them to continued faithfulness and witness in God's salvific project. The purpose of Luke-Acts, then, would be primarily ecclesiological—concerned with the practices that define and the criteria for legitimating the community of God's people, and centered on the invitation to participate in God's project.[27]

Dozens of scholars could be cited who, utilizing a variety of methods and focusing on various Lukan themes, have reached similar conclusions concerning the purpose of Luke-Acts, including Robert Brawley,[28] Philip Esler,[29] Robert O'Toole,[30] C. H. Talbert,[31] John T. Carroll,[32] Darrell Bock,[33] and

---

[27] Joel B. Green, *The Gospel of Luke* (NICNT; Grand Rapids: Eerdmans, 1997), 21-22.

[28] R. L. Brawley, *Luke-Acts and the Jews: Conflict, Apology, and Conciliation* (SBLMS 33; Atlanta: Scholars Press, 1987).

[29] P. F. Esler, *Community and Gospel in Luke-Acts: The Social and Political Motivations of Lucan Theology* (Cambridge: Cambridge University Press, 1987).

[30] R. F. O'Toole, *The Unity of Luke's Theology: An Analysis of Luke-Acts* (GNS 9; Wilmington, Del.: Glazier, 1984): "Luke's main theological theme is that God who brought salvation to his people in the OT continues to do this, especially through Jesus Christ" (17).

[31] C. H. Talbert, *Reading Luke: A Literary and Theological Commentary on the Third Gospel* (Macon, Ga.: Smyth and Helwys, 2002). Talbert rejects the traditional argument that Luke-Acts is an "occasional" document like the epistles of Paul, written to address some specific issue or crisis in the church. Instead, it is a legitimizing work, a narrative theology that "tells the story of the community's founder (and in Acts, of the early church) in a way that expresses the values of the group in a balanced way" (Talbert, *Reading Luke*, 3). He continues, "Attempts at legitimation by religious groups were the norm in antiquity. According to Berger and Luckman, legitimation is a process that is carried out often in the second and third generations after a social institution's origins. Legitimation is the collection of ways in which an institution is justified to its members. Techniques include showing that the movement is the manifestation of something that has existed already for a very long time. . . . Certainly both the Third Gospel and Acts attempt to show how the Jesus movement is linked to and is derivative of ancient Israel and its scriptures. . . . The Third Gospel, then, is a biography written to provide certainty (to insiders and/or outsiders) by telling the story using numerous legitimation techniques" (Talbert, *Reading Luke*, 4; citing Peter L. Berger and T. Luckman, *The Social Construction of Reality* [London: Faber & Faber, 1969]).

David Pao. In *Acts and the Isaianic New Exodus*, Pao argues "that one of the main functions of Isaiah in the Lukan writings is to establish the identity of the early Christian movement in the midst of competitive claims."[34] He concludes that Luke's purpose is fundamentally ecclesiological, confirming and legitimizing the church as the authentic people of God, and that the Isaianic new exodus is the central theme through which this purpose is worked out. Pao writes, "Through such evocation of the Isaianic traditions, Luke is able to emphasize both the continuity of his community with the ancient Israelite traditions and the distinctive identity of the community as the people of God."[35]

My thesis in this paper is that the basic contours of this approach have been confirmed by the last quarter century of research, so that we can speak of a general consensus concerning the purpose of Luke-Acts. Of course mentioning the word *consensus* is a dangerous thing in the scholarly world. The very nature of scholarship demands a constant probing, testing and challenging of the status quo. My claim, however, is that those pursuing studies in Luke-Acts will be on firm footing by starting with the broad premise that Luke's purpose in his two-volume work centers around legitimation and apologetic. In the face of growing attack, especially from unbelieving Jews (but also from a skeptical Roman public), Luke seeks to prove and confirm that God's great plan of salvation, inaugurated through Israel in the OT, has come to its climax in the life, death, resurrection and exaltation of Jesus the Messiah and continues to unfold in the growth and expansion of the early church. Luke seeks to assure his readers that the church, made up of Jews and Gentiles, represents the eschatological people of God. This purpose, of course, has a strong missional focus (the theme of the present Festschrift). The legitimation of the church serves to legitimize its mission, which is to take the message of salvation to the ends of the earth (Acts 1:8).

SUPPORT FOR THE CONSENSUS

The question of Luke's purpose is closely related to three key factors: (1) Luke's stated purpose in his prologue; (2) the genre utilized by the author; and most importantly, (3) the convergence of central themes around a unifying purpose. We will briefly examine these three.

---

[32] J. T. Carroll, *Response to the End of History: Eschatology and Situation in Luke-Acts* (SBLDS 92; Atlanta: Scholars Press, 1989), 165.
[33] Darrell L. Bock, *Luke* (2 vols.; BECNT; Grand Rapids: Baker, 1994), 1:14-15.
[34] David W. Pao, *Acts and the Isaianic New Exodus* (Grand Rapids: Baker, 2000), 37.
[35] Pao, *Isaianic New Exodus*, 109-10.

THE PROLOGUE OF THE GOSPEL

Though Luke's prologue would fit comfortably under a variety of suggested purposes, none fits better than the apologetic and legitimizing function described above.[36] Having followed all things from the beginning, Luke writes so that Theophilus might know with certainty (ἀσφάλεια) the things that he has been taught. While it is disputed whether Theophilus is a Christian or an interested unbeliever, it is clear that (a) he has already been instructed in the gospel message, and (b) he needs further confirmation of its truth.

THE GENRE OF LUKE-ACTS

The purpose of Luke-Acts is closely related to its genre. While there is a growing consensus that the closest antecedent to the NT Gospels lies in the Greco-Roman genre known as *bioi*, or biography, this does not quite work for Luke-Acts, since the second volume moves the Lukan enterprise beyond the category of biography, per se.[37] David Aune, in *The New Testament in Its Literary Environment*, claimed instead that Luke-Acts should be classified as general history,[38] with a purpose of self-definition and legitimation. Aune writes that

> Luke-Acts provided historical definition and identity as well as theological legitimation for the author's conception of normative Christianity. Luke defines Christianity not only in terms of a particular conception of Jesus but also in terms of the role of the twelve apostles as an official group guaranteeing the tradition. . . . More than half of Acts centers on Paul, not biographically or personally, but as a representative of the kind of apostolic Gentile Christianity that Luke himself represented.[39]

There is much to commend in this identification. Indeed, Daryl Schmidt refers to the identification of Luke-Acts as Hellenistic historiography as an "emerging consensus . . . that can now form the basis for further probing

---

[36] See W. C. van Unnik, "The 'Book of Acts' the Confirmation of the Gospel," in *Sparsa Collecta: The Collected Essays of W. C. van Unnik* (Leiden: Brill, 1973), 340-73; idem, "Once More St. Luke's Prologue," *Neot* 7 (1973): 7-26.

[37] Assuming, of course, the narrative and theological unity of Luke-Acts. For a challenge to this unity, see Mikeal C. Parsons and Richard I. Pervo, *Rethinking the Unity of Luke and Acts* (Minneapolis: Fortress, 1993). They challenge the unity of Luke-Acts in part on the basis of this difference in genre between the Gospel and Acts.

[38] David E. Aune, *The New Testament in Its Literary Environment* (Philadelphia: Westminster, 1987), 77.

[39] Aune, *Literary Environment*, 137-38.

insights into the narrative of Luke-Acts."[40]

Others, however, say, "Not so fast." Two of the most recent alternatives for Luke's genre come from Loveday Alexander[41] and Marianne Palmer Bonz.[42] In a monograph and a series of articles, Alexander compares the Lukan prologue to a variety of ancient prefaces and suggests that its closest parallel is to be found in the so-called "scientific tradition," the professional and technical writings on medicine, mathematics, engineering, and the like. Bonz goes in a different direction, claiming that Luke-Acts may best be compared to the heroic epics of the ancient world, such as Homer's *Iliad*, the *Odyssey*, and especially Virgil's first century B.C., *Aeneid*. According to Bonz, the *Aeneid* was written "to define Rome's moral and religious values and to inspire its people with a patriotic vision of a world whose eschatological fulfillment was embodied in the Augustan identification with the return of the Golden Age."[43] Though the *Aeneid* is poetic, it was repeatedly translated into Greek prose, most notably by Polybius during the reign of Claudius. Luke and his audience would have known these prose adaptations and would view them as *the* literary model for a great founding epic. Bonz seeks to show parallels between such epics and Luke-Acts in terms of structure and themes. For example, just as the *Aeneid* linked the founding of Rome to noble roots and the city of Troy, so Luke connects the founding of Christianity to Israel and its sacred scriptural tradition. Both epics also center on journey motifs.

Though both these proposals are interesting and original, neither is fully convincing. Apart from similarities in the prologues, Luke's writings show little affinity with the scientific and technical writings of his day. Furthermore, though Luke is certainly theologically and apologetically motivated, Luke-Acts shows closer parallels to Greco-Roman historiography than to the ancient epics, even in their prose forms. Nevertheless, it is significant that Bonz, like so many others, sees Luke-Acts as an apologetic and legitimizing document, meant to confirm the ancient roots and divine validation of Christianity.

It seems to me one of the problems with all such genre identifications is that they demand too much congruence in features and parameters. The individual works within each of these categories exhibit significant variation. Ancient

---

[40] Darryl D. Schmidt, "Luke's Preface and the Rhetoric of Hellenistic Historiography," in *Jesus and the Heritage of Israel: Luke's Narrative Claim upon Israel's Legacy* (ed. David P. Moessner; Harrisburg, Pa.: Trinity Press International, 1999), 27-60 [60].

[41] L. C. A. Alexander, "Which Greco-Roman Prologues Most Closely Parallel the Lukan Prologues?," in *Jesus and the Heritage of Israel* (Harrisburg, Pa.: Trinity Press International, 1999), 9-26; idem, *The Preface of Luke's Gospel: Literary Convention and Social Context in Luke 1.1-4 and Acts 1.1* (SNTSMS 78; Cambridge: Cambridge University Press, 1993); idem, "Luke's Preface in the Context of Greek Preface-Writing," *NovT* 28 (1986): 4-74.

[42] Marianne Palmer Bonz, *The Past As Legacy: Luke-Acts and Ancient Epic* (Minneapolis: Fortress, 2000).

[43] Bonz, *The Past As Legacy*, 38.

biographies differ significantly from one other and there are almost as many types of histories as there are ancient historians. It is not surprising that in Luke-Acts we find both parallels and differences with biography, historiography, and yes, even epic. My sense is that Luke did not consciously imitate any single genre, but instead wrote an apologetic and legitimizing account (i.e., a narrative) about the origins of the Christian movement, adopting various literary conventions of his day. These he drew from biblical narratives, biography, historiography, and foundational epic. Instead of seeking a precise or specific identification of genre, we should speak in general of a literary landscape and literary predecessors.[44]

We turn finally to the main themes of Luke-Acts as indicators of the larger Lukan purpose.

THE MAIN THEMES OF LUKE-ACTS

If Luke-Acts has a primary or central purpose, we would expect to find that all of its major themes revolve around this center. This is certainly true for the legitimizing purpose, from which the following themes can be seen to have arisen.

(1) *The Jewish roots of Christianity and the continuity between the Hebrew Scriptures, the righteous remnant within Israel, the coming of Jesus and the establishment of the early church.* This first theme is central to the Lukan birth narrative, but continues throughout Luke-Acts. The most likely connection of this theme to Lukan purpose is that Luke is responding to claims from the synagogue that they, not the messianic community of Jesus' followers, are the true people of God. Luke seeks to show that God's purpose and plan as presented in the Hebrew Scriptures finds its fulfillment and continuation not in apostate Israel, but in the messianic community of Christ-followers.

(2) A second theme is christological: *Jesus as promised Messiah, Son of God, and prophet/herald of eschatological salvation.* Against claims from the Jewish community that Jesus did not have messianic credentials, Luke seeks to confirm that Jesus is the savior promised in the Hebrew Scriptures. He does this through angelic annunciations (Luke 1:32-35; 2:10-12), Spirit-inspired prophecy of narrative characters (1:69; 2:26-32), divine acclamation from heaven (3:22; 9:35), genealogical verification (3:31, 38), and the authority Jesus demonstrates through teaching and performing the miracles associated with Isaianic eschatological salvation (Luke 4:36; 7:22 [Isa 26:19; 35:5-6; 61:1]; Acts 2:22; 9:22).

(3) A third theme is pneumatological: *for Luke the eschatological renewal of the Spirit represents the fulfillment of prophecy and the dawn of the age of*

---

[44] This would negate the argument of Parsons and Pervo against the unity of Luke-Acts based on the difference in genre between Luke and Acts. Luke has created a hybrid genre by combining features of biography, historiography and other literary forms.

salvation. There was a strong prophetic tradition in Judaism that God's end-time salvation would be marked by the outpouring of God's Spirit on all humanity (Isa 32:15; 44:3; 59:21; Ezek 37:14; 39:29; Joel 2:28). In Luke's birth narrative, Gabriel prophesies that John will be filled with the Holy Spirit from his mother's womb (1:15; cf. 1:41-44), and Elizabeth and Zechariah are filled with the Spirit when they break into prophetic utterance (1:41, 67). The Spirit rests upon the aged Simeon, granting guidance and revelation (2:25-27). The renewal of the prophetic gift confirms that God's salvation is about to arrive. When Jesus comes on the scene, he is "anointed" by the Spirit at his baptism, fulfilling Isaiah's prophecies and confirming his messianic identity (Isa 11:1-16; 42:1; 61:1-2; Luke 3:22; 4:1, 14, 18; 10:21). Following his ascension, Jesus pours out the Spirit, empowering his followers to take the message of salvation to the ends of the earth (Joel 2:28; Acts 2:17-41). The presence of the Spirit and the renewal of prophecy in the community of Christ-followers serve as confirmation that they are the eschatological people of God.

(4) A fourth theme is soteriological: *the necessity of Christ's death on the cross*. Though wicked people conspired to killed Jesus, Luke affirms that this was foretold in Scripture and part of God's purpose and plan to bring salvation to all people (Luke 9:22; 18:31-33; Acts 2:22-24; 3:13-26; 4:8-12; 10:39-40). Against claims that Jesus' humiliating death as a criminal nullified his messianic claims, Luke shows that Scripture predicted that the Christ had to suffer, and this refrain is repeated in the last part of the Gospel and throughout Acts (Luke 24:26, 46; Acts 3:18; 17:3; 26:23). Furthermore, Luke repeatedly stresses that Jesus suffered innocently. He was the Righteous (or, "innocent") One (ὁ δίκαιος; Acts 3:14). Pilate four times declares Jesus innocent (Luke 23:4, 14, 15, 22; cf. Acts 13:28) and Herod confirms this (23:15). The repentant criminal says Jesus has done nothing wrong (23:41), and the centurion, rather than declaring Jesus the "son of God," as in Mark, identifies him as "righteous" or "innocent" (δίκαιος; 23:47; cf. 23:25, 48; Acts 3:14-15).

This apologetic emphasis on the Scriptural necessity of the death of Christ also helps to explain the absence of a developed theology of the atonement in Luke-Acts. It is sometimes claimed that Luke sees no soteriological significance in the death of Christ and has transformed Paul's *theologia crucis* into a *theologia gloria*.[45] A better explanation is that Luke's purpose is primarily ecclesiological rather than soteriological. He is more interested in the *that* of salvation than its *how*. Luke is not writing an essay on the atonement,

---

[45] See W. Kümmel, "Current Theological Accusations against Luke," *ANQ* 16 (1975): 131-45; E. Käsemann, "Ministry and Community in the New Testament," in *Essays on New Testament Themes* (SBT 41; London: SCM, 1964), 63-94 [92]; H. J. Cadbury, *Making of Luke-Acts* (London: Macmillan, 1927), 280-82; Conzelmann, *Theology*, 201; E. Haenchen, *Acts* (Oxford: Blackwell, 1971), 92; P. Vielhauer, "On the 'Paulinism' of Acts," in *Studies in Luke-Acts* (ed. L. E. Keck and J. L. Martyn; London: SPCK, 1966), 33-50 [41-42]; Talbert, *Luke and the Gnostics*, 71-82.

but narrating the story of how salvation came to Israel through Jesus the Messiah, how it was made available to Gentiles, and how it is now being experienced in and through the church. Because of this narrative presentation, the emphasis falls on the *arrival* of salvation through the life, death and resurrection of Jesus, rather than on the theological means by which Jesus saves.[46]

(5) A fifth theme is eschatological: While not rejecting a future eschatology, Luke places greater stress than the other Synoptics on *the present reign of Christ at the right hand of God*. This is unlikely to be a response to the delay of the Parousia, as Conzelmann claimed. More likely, against accusations that the messianic kingdom has not arrived physically on earth, Luke seeks to show that Jesus is indeed the Messiah, vindicated at his resurrection and reigning at the right hand of God (Ps 110:1-2; Acts 2:34-36). The pouring out of the Spirit at Pentecost and the continuing work of the Spirit in Acts is confirmation that the end times have begun and that the church made up of Jews and Gentiles are heirs to Israel's eschatological promises.

(6) This last sentence leads us to the sixth and seventh themes, which are ecclesiological and related to the make-up of the church of Luke's day. The first is *the rejection of the gospel by so many Jews*. Against accusations that the church cannot be the true people of God since so many in Israel have rejected the message, Luke affirms that, (a) the rejection of the Messiah is simply a continuation of Israel's rebellious history (Acts 7:51), (b) that it was predicted in Scripture (Acts 28:25) and (c) that, nevertheless, a remnant of Israel has been saved. This last point is confirmed by statements in Acts about the extraordinary growth of church among Jews in Jerusalem (Acts 2:41; 4:4; 6:7; 21:20). Though the majority of Jews have rejected the gospel, the righteous remnant has responded, and it is from them that salvation is now going forth.

(7) A second ecclesiological theme is *the defense of the Gentile mission and its greatest advocate, the apostle Paul*. Against claims that the church cannot be the true people of God because it is increasingly becoming a Gentile entity, Luke responds, (a) that the acceptance of the gospel by Gentiles was predicted in Scripture and was part of God's purpose and plan (Luke 2:32; Acts 10:34-35; 13:47; 15:16-18); (b) that the Gentile mission was provoked by the Holy Spirit, not by any human being (Acts 10–11; 15); and (c) that Paul, the apostle to the Gentiles, is not a renegade Jew, but is faithful to the God of his ancestors (Acts 22:3-21; 28:17).

(8) The one pervasive Lukan theme that may not find ready explanation within this larger purpose of legitimation is Luke's emphasis on God's love for

---

[46] See Strauss, *Davidic Messiah*, 351-53. This is another argument against a primarily evangelistic purpose of Luke-Acts. If evangelism were Luke's primary purpose, one would expect a greater emphasis on the means by which Jesus saves.

the poor, sinners, the outsider, and the marginalized.[47] This theme is so central to Luke's Gospel that it would be impossible to propose a central purpose of Luke-Acts without accounting for it. I would suggest two likely connections to our legitimizing purpose.

(a) First, Luke stresses God's love for the outcast because the church of Luke's day is made up especially of marginalized people. It is clear from the NT that the churches in Syria, Greece and Asia Minor had members from diverse social and ethnic backgrounds, including rich and the poor, slave and free, male and female, and, of course, Jew and Gentile (Gal 3:28; Acts 13:1; 1 Cor 1:26; 11:21-22). Both in the Gospel and Acts, Luke seeks to show that these are the very people that God has seen fit to bring into the eschatological community of faith. The church is legitimized, rather than invalidated, by virtue of its diverse ethnic, social and economic membership—because God loves the lost (Luke 19:10).

(b) Second, the grace offered to the poor, the sick, the demonized, sinners, Samaritans and outcasts in the Gospel serves as a preview and foreshadowing of the Gentile mission in Acts. This is not an inappropriate stretch, since Luke's programmatic Nazareth sermon makes a direct connection between the two (Luke 4:14-30). In Nazareth, Jesus announces that the eschatological Jubilee predicted in Isa 61 has come to fulfillment in his ministry, and that the recipients are the poor, the oppressed and prisoners (4:18–19). Yet when he illustrates this truth he speaks about God's grace offered to *Gentiles* through the prophets Elijah and Elisha (4:25-27), thus provoking the wrath of the Nazareth townspeople (4:28-30). Jesus' ministry to the poor and outcast in the Gospel is a preview of the Gentile mission in Acts.

CONCLUSION

In summary, a general consensus has emerged that Luke's purpose in Luke-Acts is to offer the church a foundational narrative that serves to legitimize its status as the people of God and the recipients of God's eschatological salvation now accomplished through the life, death, resurrection and ascension of Jesus the Messiah. This purpose, in turn, legitimizes the church's *mission*, which is to take this message of salvation to the ends of the earth (Acts 1:8). This legitimizing and apologetic purpose fits well with all of Luke's major theological and narrative themes.

To be sure, within this broad consensus, many details remain unresolved, including (1) the author's background and the provenance of the work, (2) the

---

[47] In the Gospel Luke demonstrates a special interest in the poor and oppressed (1:53; 4:16-22; 6:20-21, 24-25; 12:13-21; 14:12, 13; 16:19-31), sinners and tax-collectors (7:36-50; 15:11-32; 18:9-14; 19:1-10; 23:39-43), Samaritans (9:51-56; 10:29-37; 17:11-19; cf. Acts 1:8; 8:4-25), and women (7:12-15, 36-50; 8:1-3, 43-48; 10:38-42; 13:10-17; 21:1-4; 23:27-31, 49; 23:55–24:11).

destination and specific *Sitz im Leben* of its recipients,[48] (3) the ethnic make-up of the audience, whether pagan Gentile, God-fearing Gentile, Jewish or some combination of these, (4) the date, especially whether pre- or post-A.D. 70,[49] (5) the author's stance toward Judaism, whether pro-Jewish, viewing the righteous remnant of Israel as responding favorably to the gospel despite the rejection of the majority, or anti-Jewish, viewing the Jewish people as a whole as apostate and unresponsive to the gospel.[50] With these and many more open questions, the Lukan corpus will no doubt continue to be a fertile field for scholarly investigation.

---

[48] Ancient and modern suggestions vary widely, including Achaia, Rome, Asia Minor, Caesarea, Decapolis (i.e., almost anywhere in the Greco-Roman world!). Fitzmyer sums up the conclusion of many when he writes that the provenance "is really anyone's guess" (J. A. Fitzmyer, *The Gospel According to Luke: A New Translation with Introduction and Commentary* [AB 28; New York: Doubleday, 1981], 57).

[49] While the majority of scholars favor a post-A.D. 70 date, a significant minority hold to an earlier date, including J. A. T. Robinson, I. H. Marshall, F. F. Bruce, E. E. Ellis, David Moessner, Colin Hemer, William Larkin and others.

[50] For surveys see *Luke-Acts and the Jewish People: Eight Critical Perspectives* (ed. J. B. Tyson; Minneapolis: Augsburg, 1988), 76-82; J. B. Tyson, *Luke, Judaism, and the Scholars: Critical Approaches to Luke-Acts* (Columbia: University of South Carolina Press, 1999).

9

NEGLECTING WIDOWS AND SERVING THE WORD?
ACTS 6:1–7 AS A TEST CASE FOR A MISSIONAL
HERMENEUTIC

Joel B. Green

Luke's account of the choosing of the Seven in Acts 6:1-7 is an interesting candidate for a missiological reading of a biblical text for two reasons.[1] First, missiological readings generally concern themselves less with reconstructions of historical events and historical narratives, a mainstay of classical historical criticism, and more with the "final form" of the text(s) under study. Such an approach stands in tension with readings that assume, for example, that because the Seven were chosen "to wait on tables" then this is surely what they did—a claim out of sync with the narrative Luke actually relates. It also stands in tension with readings that assume that Luke has somehow misrepresented "what actually happened" with the result that his account must be rewritten to reflect greater historical veracity.[2] Instead, a missiological approach asks how the text as it presently stands might shape ecclesial identity and mission. This interest in the final form should not be confused with those literary (or "new critical") interests that sunder the biblical texts from the sociohistorical worlds that gave rise to those texts. Rather, a missional hermeneutic is less interested in that sort of historical analysis concerned with construing scriptural texts as windows to a past that must either be verified or reconstructed, but remains very much open to socio-historical analysis more generally.

Second, missiological readings typically concern themselves with the location of texts within the arc of God's mission as this is articulated in Scripture. Consequently, they are suspicious of readings more likely to serve the institutional and maintenance needs of an established church structure. This would be especially true of a missiological reading of Acts, given both its transparently outward-oriented witness (Acts 1:8) and its emphasis on Christian life and mission in the service of God's agenda as a divinely directed "journey"

---

[1] On the emerging identification of a "missional hermeneutic," see, e.g., David J. Bosch, "Towards a Hermeneutic for 'Biblical Studies and Mission,'" *Mission Studies* 3, no. 2 (1986): 65-79; Michael Barram, "The Bible, Mission, and Social Location: Toward a Missional Hermeneutic," *Int* 61 (2007): 42-58.

[2] E.g., Michael Livingston, "The Seven: Hebrews, Hellenists, and Heptines," *JHC* 6 (1999): 32-63. Livingston does not question the basic historicity of the account, but does think he can reconstruct a better picture of "what truly lies behind Luke's work" (33).

rather than a static location.³ For example, as is well know, Acts 6:1-7 has in fact been read (and continues to be read) in support of the institution of an ecclesial office, sometimes referred to as "deacons"⁴—a reading, then, that a missiological reading might want to test.

In this essay, I will focus our attention on some neglected features of this well-known text in order to urge that we understand that, in Acts 6:1-7, Luke recounts how a profoundly theological problem related to the nature of the gospel and the church's mission was resolved in favor of a transfer of missional leadership from the Twelve to the Seven. In order to do so, I will first interact with two recent attempts at historical reconstruction of the Lukan narrative. This will allow me opportunity to bring to the surface what has troubled biblical scholars about this textual unit, before moving on to suggest the coherence of the account as it presently stands within the larger Lukan narrative.

ACTS 6:1-7: TWO HISTORICAL RECONSTRUCTIONS

A survey of both older and several more recent commentaries reveals little interest in questioning the basic historical outline of Luke's account of the resolution of the problem that surfaced as a consequence of the Jerusalem community's neglect of its Hellenist widows.⁵ The question of the identity of

---

³ Statistically, this is marked by the prominent use of such terms as πορεύομαι (88 of 153 uses in the NT) and ὁδός (40 of 101 uses in the NT) in Luke-Acts. As Robert Maddox rightly observed, "the story of Jesus and of the church is a story full of purposeful movement" (*The Purpose of Luke-Acts* [SNTW; Edinburgh: T&T Clark, 1982], 11). Note the thematic use of ὁδός in Luke 3:4 (cf. 7:27) to identify obedience as a "going" and God's will as a "path"; the identification of God's purpose as "the way" (Luke 20:21; Acts 18:25, 26; cf. Acts 16:17: "the way of salvation"); the language of traveling with reference to Jesus' journey to Jerusalem in the service of God's redemptive agenda (Luke 9:52; 10:38; 13:22, 33; 17:11; 19:4; cf. Acts 20:22), including Jesus' assessment of his journey through rejection and death to his exaltation as an ἔξοδος (Luke 9:31); and, especially, the use of ὁδός in Luke's identification of the community of Jesus' followers—together with their characteristic patterns of belief and practice—as "The Way" (Acts 9:2; 19:9, 23; 22:4; 24:14, 22). Indeed, the coming of a powerful savior is to this end: "to guide our feet into the way of peace" (Luke 1:79).
⁴ See the brief discussion in Albert Collver, "Deacons: Order of Service or Office of the Word," *Logia* 16, no. 2 (2007): 31-35 [33-34]; Armin J. Panning, "Acts 6: The 'Ministry' of the Seven," *Wisconsin Lutheran Quarterly* 93 (1996): 11-17.
⁵ Cf., e.g., Richard Belward Rackham, *The Acts of the Apostles: An Exposition* (London: Methuen, 1906), 81-87; F. J. Foakes-Jackson, *The Acts of the Apostles* (MNTC; London: Hodder & Stoughton, 1931); Hans Conzelmann, *Acts of the Apostles* (Hermeneia; Philadelphia: Fortress, 1987), 44-46; F. F. Bruce, *The Book of Acts* (rev. ed.; NICNT; Grand Rapids: Eerdmans, 1988); C. K. Barrett, *A Critical and Exegetical Commentary on the Acts of the Apostles* (2 vols.; ICC; Edinburgh: T&T Clark, 1994), 1:302-17. See,

the Hellenists and Hebrews has spawned a longstanding scholarly discussion,[6] and scholars have also wondered whether Luke has not downplayed the nature and extent of the division he reports. Moreover, some readers have worried over the nature of the "poor relief" envisioned here.[7] The account as a whole, however, was often taken more or less at face value as students of Acts quickly moved on to the many questions raised by the Stephen-material beginning in 6:8. Two recent studies have focused their historical concerns more narrowly, however, offering different assessments of certain key aspects of the story behind Luke's narrative.

Among the historical issues on which he focuses, Richard Pervo notices that the resolution offered in this account immediately deconstructs itself, since the Seven chosen for "serving tables" appear rather as missionaries. As Henry Cadbury had recognized long before, "It is not clear . . . why men chosen to allow the Twelve to preach rather than to 'serve tables' appear later only as preachers and evangelists."[8] The problem, Pervo asserts, is one of Luke's own making since he would have been the one to introduce the business of food distribution into the tradition of the Seven. What is more, Luke's scene is anachronistic; assuming an identifiable body of widows and a group of subordinate ministers, it is reminiscent not so much of the early church but of the organizational structures of the Pastoral Epistles and Polycarp. For Pervo, then, Acts portrays the widows functioning as a group that complains about the treatment they have received.[9]

In her book *Of Widows and Meals*, Reta Halteman Finger attempts a different sort of reconstruction of the situation behind Acts 6:1-7. Reading Luke's account against the background of the earlier summary in 2:42-47, she postulates that shared faith in Jesus had generated a community of believers who shared daily meals. Accordingly, the daily διακονία in Acts 6:1-6 is nothing other than the daily table service for which widows had essential roles in the work of food preparation and distribution. The disruption Luke envisions may have occurred because the Hebraic widows received more honor than the Hellenist widows in the organization, preparation, and serving of the daily

---

though, Joseph T. Lienhard, "Acts 6:1-6: A Redactional View," *CBQ* 37 (1975): 228-36; his reconstruction of the core-Lukan tradition retains only a minimal historical account.

[6] The literature is voluminous; see the monograph-length treatment by Craig C. Hill, *Hellenists and Hebrews: Reappraising Division within the Earliest Church* (Minneapolis: Fortress, 1992).

[7] On the question of "poor relief," cf., e.g., Ernst Haenchen, *The Acts of the Apostles* (Oxford: Basil Blackwell, 1971), 261-62.

[8] Henry J. Cadbury, "Note VII: The Hellenists," in *Additional Notes to the Commentary* (vol. 5 of *Beginnings of Christianity*, Part One: *The Acts of the Apostles*; ed. Kirsopp Lake and Henry J. Cadbury; Grand Rapids: Baker, 1933), 59-74 [62].

[9] Richard I. Pervo, *Dating Acts: Between the Evangelists and the Apologists* (Santa Rosa, Calif.: Polebridge, 2006), 219; idem, *Acts: A Commentary* (Hermeneia; Minneapolis: Fortress, 2009), 151-63.

meal. The decision to appoint a group of men to oversee the daily meals could have been either to quell the quarreling widows or to extend Jesus' directive to male leaders that they serve others at table.[10]

Unfortunately, in both of these instances, we find interests in historical reconstruction rushing ahead at the expense of the narrative Luke has given us. For example, Pervo assumes what is not in evidence—namely, that the widows comprise a group sufficiently organized to lodge a complaint. Instead, Acts portrays a complaint registered on behalf of certain widows—not by the widows themselves and not by widows functioning implicitly as a kind of pressure group. Finger envisions widows preparing food rather than receiving it (or not), and focuses on widows quarreling with one another rather than on the situation of Hellenist widows against whom a disservice was being perpetrated.[11] Her approach to the social history behind the Acts account seems less indebted to the narrative of Acts than to practices among Anabaptists like herself. Of course, this would not be the first time that an interpreter had looked to 6:1-7 through the lens of later ecclesial practices, as the traditional tendency to find in this text either a general model for leaders to delegate their responsibilities or a specific grounding for the ordination of sub-leaders known as "deacons" demonstrates.[12]

ACTS 6:1–7: THEOLOGICAL DILEMMA AND THEOLOGICAL RESPONSE

Historical questions concerning Acts 6:1-7, and the reconstructions they spawn, are typically grounded in the perception of an incongruence between Luke's account and the missional activity in which Stephen and Philip are subsequently involved. I will argue that this incongruence is more perceived than real, with the result that, as a narrative representation of historical events, Luke's account is internally coherent.

Most importantly, we must recognize that, contra a number of interpreters, the problem Luke presents cannot be understood reductively as a "practical" one.[13] Of course, it is true that this textual unit is boundaried by dual references to the growth of the church (πληθύνω, vv. 1, 7) so that the dilemma recounted might be understood as having been precipitated by the expanding numbers of disciples. Five considerations tell against this view, however.

---

[10] Reta Halteman Finger, *Of Widows and Meals: Communal Meals in the Book of Acts* (Grand Rapids: Eerdmans, 2007), esp. 246-75.

[11] Key to this reading is the use of παραθεωρέω—that is, the act of failing to account for someone or something worth acknowledging, typically with a bad result, so that this failure puts the person guilty of overlooking in a bad light (e.g., Diodorus Siculus, *Bibliotheca historica* 40.5; Dionysius, *Is.* 18; cf. MM, s.v.; BDAG, s.v.).

[12] Cf. Jarolsav Pelikan, *Acts* (Brazos Theological Commentary on the Bible; Grand Rapids: Brazos, 2005), 91-93.

[13] Contra, e.g., Bruce, *Acts*, 120: "It was over a practical issue, and not over a matter of theological importance, that disagreement became acute."

First, just as Luke's repeated emphasis on the unity of the believers is theologically grounded, so we should anticipate that the introduction of any dissension would be theological grounded. The term with which the narrator captures the situation of the disciples is ὁμοθυμαδόν—found thus far in the narrative in 1:14, where the disciples are defined by their tenacious orientation toward a common aim, single-minded in their solidarity, giving themselves to prayer; 2:46, where the disciples are "persisting in their unity in the temple"; in 4:24, where Luke declares their solidarity over against their detractors and, again, associates their unity with a community-defining practice: prayer; and finally in 5:12, where the betrayal of community dispositions by Ananias and Sapphira is set in opposition to the disciples' oneness. We may add to this the phrase ἐπὶ τὸ αὐτό in 1:15; 2:1, 44, 47, which Luke uses to underscore the oneness of this company of believers both as a consequence of their obedience to Jesus and as an expression of the Spirit's generative work. The introduction of dissension within the community in 6:1, then, is startling not only because it disrupts the portrait of the believers' extraordinary solidarity but also because it raises questions theologically about what has gone amiss.

Second, just as Luke has demonstrated that the economic *koinonia* characteristic of the Jerusalem believers is the Spirit's work and an expression of the unity of those who together call on the name of the Lord Jesus, so this failure of that same economic *koinonia* must be read as a disruption of the Spirit's work. Both of the summaries whereby Luke pictures the economic *koinonia* of the community of believers follow immediately, sequentially and generatively, from the outpouring of the Holy Spirit (2:1-41 → 2:42-47; 4:31 → 4:32-35), the consequence of which is that there was "no needy person among them" (4:34). Although it makes good sense to characterize the community of goods Luke reports in terms borrowed from economic anthropology, as "generalized reciprocity,"[14] it cannot be overlooked that this is the sort of economic exchange expressive among close kin—and that the "family" of believers Luke presents are "kin" in theological and not merely sociological (and certainly not biological) terms. Had not Jesus redefined family when he said, "My mother and my brothers are those who hear the word of God and do it" (Luke 8:21; cf. Luke 3:7-14)? How can it be that need has arisen within the community apart from a failure of the community in terms of its appropriation of the Spirit's generative work in their midst?

Third, it should not escape our notice that, rather than reporting that some widows from among the Hellenists and some from the Hebrews had been overlooked, Luke has it only that the Hellenist widows were slighted. Were this merely a practical problem arising from too many people and too little food, from the law of averages we would have anticipated the neglect of both Hebrew and Hellenist widows.

Fourth, from within the biblical tradition that Luke has both inherited and

---

[14] See Marshall Sahlins, *Stone Age Economics* (London: Routledge, 1972), 193-94.

embraced, to neglect widows *at all* is offensive theologically. Together with the alien and orphan, the widow symbolizes in Israel's Scriptures the plight of the vulnerable and dispossessed who come in for explicit protection under the law (e.g., Exod 22:22; Deut 10:18), for God is the "father of the fatherless and protector of widows" (Ps 68:5; cf. Ps 146:9). For Luke-Acts, widows are models of faithfulness to God on the one hand, poverty and vulnerability on the other, as well as those to whom the good news is directed (e.g., Luke 2:36-38; 4:25-26; 7:11-17; 20:45–21:4). Thus, as Joseph Tyson summarizes:

> In Luke-Acts, widowhood means grief, poverty, vulnerability, and piety. The exclusion of widows from the common meal would, therefore, appear as an act of extreme cruelty and impiety, but also as a condition that underlined the urgent need for a solution. The reader should recognize immediately that here is an intolerable situation, one which can have only one solution: the widows must not be excluded.[15]

Fifth, irrespective of scholarly speculation regarding the identity of the Hellenists and Hebrews more generally, for Luke they obviously represent different sides in a dispute.[16] In Acts, ‛Εβραῖος refers to Aramaic-speaking Jews.[17] Luke uses ‛Ελληνιστής in 6:1 and 9:29, in both instances to refer to Greek-speaking Jews within Jerusalem. That is, he uses the term where such a distinction would make sense, as outside of a city or region where the majority population would speak Aramaic it would make little sense to qualify Jews as Greek-speaking.[18] Given the focus of the present textual unit on "disciples" (v. 1), we should think of two different sets of Christ-followers, Greek-speaking Jews and Aramaic-speaking Jews. Of course, even this is a misnomer since it is hard to imagine Aramaic-speaking Jews in Jerusalem who were not also able to traffic in Greek—an observation that presses for greater clarity in our

---

[15] Joseph B. Tyson, "Acts 6:1-7 and Dietary Regulations in Early Christianity," *PRSt* 10 (1983): 145-61 [158]; cf. F. Scott Spencer, "Neglected Widows in Acts 6:1-7," *CBQ* 56 (1994): 715-33.

[16] Indeed, Lienhard urges that the actual identity of the Hellenists and Hebrews is less important to Luke's presentation than the mere fact that there is dissension ("Acts 6:1-6," 231). The larger question concerns the basis on which one might accord privilege to reconstructions of the Hellenists based on minimal textual evidence outside of Acts, over against the portrait one finds in Luke's narrative. He is theologically motivated, but other sources are not?

[17] See the pattern in 21:40; 22:2; 26:14; cf. Martin Hengel, "Between Jesus and Paul: The 'Hellenists', the 'Seven' and Stephen," in *Between Jesus and Paul: Studies in the Earliest History of Christianity* (Philadelphia: Fortress, 1983), 1-29 [9-10].

[18] Luke may use the term in 11:20, but the text is disputed. ῞Ηληνας is read by 𝔓74 ℵ2 A D*. BDAG, s.v. "‛Ελληνιστής": "a Greek-speaking Israelite in contrast to one speaking a Semitic [language]."

understanding of what Luke has portrayed.[19] On the one hand, we should think of these two groups as characterized by their dominant language, Greek and Aramaic, respectively, leaving open the probability of additional language competencies. On the other hand, we cannot think merely in terms of linguistic choice since identification of dominant language necessarily involves long-term formation and affiliations with respect to cultural (and, therefore, religious) identification. Indeed, in 2 Macc 7:8, 21; 12:37; 15:29, speaking in the ancestral language was integral to boundary maintenance when Jewish identity was threatened. Speech assumes but also builds community, with language and language choices both a product of and involved in the further production of social relations. In other words, however else one might decide to parse the boundaries between Hellenists and Hebrews in 6:1, we cannot reduce the controversy to differences of language. Whatever would have been common among Jesus' Jewish disciples, differences marked by dominant language would have introduced potential distinctions too at the level of religious structures: myth, ritual, the divine, and systems of purity.[20] Even if we cannot determine from Acts with much specificity or certainty the nature of those differences, such differences are nonetheless implicatures of Luke's reference to the primary languages of the two groups he has identified.

If, from the perspective of Luke's narrative, the problem introduced in 6:1 must be understood in theological terms, it can hardly be that the solution would be something other than theological. The often-repeated view that the apostles hit upon delegation as a key ingredient of effective leadership is thus problematic for its failure to work theologically with what Luke has given us.[21] Actually, it is problematic in two other ways as well. First, it assumes without warrant that Luke presents the apostles as authorized representatives of the narrator's perspective (and, thus, of the divine perspective, which the narrator represents and mediates in Luke-Acts). Accordingly, when the apostles deny the appropriateness of abandoning the word of God in favor of waiting on tables, their words are typically taken as a reasonable assessment of things. Rather than presuming that the apostles are above reproach we ought to wonder about the opposite. After all, was it not under their watch that the disciples had digressed from their idyllic state of unity and violated the character of their own community as one in which there was no needy person? Second, the solution the apostles propose ought to strike a sharp note of discord in our hearing. Can one serve the word *and not care for widows*? Can one serve the word *and not*

---

[19] For what follows, I am dependent on the theory of linguistic pragmatics sketched in Alessandro Duranti, *Linguistic Anthropology* (Cambridge Textbooks in Linguistics; Cambridge: Cambridge University Press, 1997).

[20] For this pattern of religious structures, see William E. Paden, *Religious Worlds: The Comparative Study of Religion* (Boston: Beacon, 1994).

[21] Among recent commentators, this view is supported, e.g., by Mikeal Parsons, *Acts* (Paideia; Grand Rapids: Baker, 2008), 83-84.

serve at table? These may appear to be practical issues, but for Luke they are profoundly theological. This is because Luke has already developed the language of διακονία in terms that belie the possibility that these phrases—serving the word and serving at table—might refer to segregated responsibilities. Is not Jesus himself one who serves at table (Luke 22:24-27; cf. 12:37)—with διακονέω understood not in its sense of attending to someone at a meal but metaphorically with regard to providing leadership in carrying out a mission that puts into practice the good news of God? That is, even if, in principle, we might allow for differentiation of kinds of "service," support for this sort of distinction finds little traction in the Lukan narrative itself. After all, the apostolic task is simply διακονία (Acts 1:17, 25) and the same is true of Paul's commission (20:45; 21:19).[22]

In other words, the apostles are implicated in a failure that can be grasped only in theological terms. Evidence for this failure rests, first, in the neglect of Hellenist widows and, then, in the apostles' attempt to fracture the singular ministry (διακονία) modeled for them by Jesus. This failure is not simply the practical one that might lead to a new organizational structure capable of allowing poor relief to be carried out in a more efficient way. Rather, their failure surfaces in their allowing a wedge to be driven between the Hellenists and Hebrews such that the most vulnerable of their community—doubly marginal, first as Hellenists among an Aramaic-speaking majority and then as widows among the minority group—suffer need at this most basic level of daily sustenance. This is not "good news to the poor" (Luke 4:18).

This line of interpretation is furthered by the choice of the Seven to engage in διακονία. First, given their Greek (and Latin) names, their movement into positions of service signifies the decentralizing of the Aramaic-speaking apostles and, then, an affirmation of the Greek-speaking Jewish followers of Jesus. Second, as is widely recognized, their διακονία within Luke's narrative is manifestly not waiting on tables, but the διακονία of preaching and evangelism. Rather than dismissing Luke's narration as incoherent, then, it makes more sense to assume coherence by allowing the actual nature of their διακονία to clarify the nature of the διακονία suffering neglect in 6:1-7. This would be putting into play a gospel that did not allow differences between Hellenist and Hebrew followers of Jesus to resolve themselves into disunity and conflict at the table. Accordingly, it is no surprise that, from among the Seven, Stephen goes on to provide the theological bridge that moves the mission outside of Jerusalem and Philip is the first missionary Luke names who takes

---

[22] For διακονία in Luke, see the helpful perspective in Turid Karlsen Seim, *The Double Message: Patterns of Gender in Luke and Acts* (Nashville: Abingdon, 1994), 81-87 (though Seim reads Acts 6:1-7 differently—see 108-12). On the term more generally, see John N. Collins, *Diakonia: Reinterpreting the Ancient Sources* (New York: Oxford University Press, 1990).

the gospel to Samaria and, indeed, to the end of the earth.[23] The new missionary leadership, drawn from among the Hellenists, receives its authorization from this: they are witnesses, as Jesus had directed, "in Jerusalem, in all Judea and Samaria, and to the end of the earth" (1:8).

CONCLUSION: ACTS 6:1–7 AND LUKE'S AIM

Having cleared the ground, so to speak, it now remains to ask how best to make sense of Luke's aim in this narrative account. The *inclusio* marked by the repetition of πληθύνω in vv. 1, 7 makes clear the pericope's interest in "growth" and allows us to follow its progression in three steps: from growth to impediment to growth, and from impediment to growth to (renewed) growth.[24]

Our exploration of Luke's account has clarified the nature of the problem and its resolution. This scene is an indictment against the apostles for their failure to practice the διακονία modeled for them by Jesus (Luke 22:24-27); for their failure to be the Spirit-generated community of the baptized—which held all things in common so as to care for those in need (Acts 2:42-47); for their failure to embody the message of the resurrection of the Lord Jesus—that is, to be a community among whom could be found no needy person (4:32-35). The result of this theological failure is a fracture in the community, setting Hellenist against Hebrew, which surfaces in the neglect of the widows who now qualify as needy persons among them. By way of resolution, Luke portrays the authorization of fresh leadership for the mission, with this leadership drawn from among the minority of the Jerusalem community. The subsequent narrative turns its spotlight on two of their number and the apostles *qua* "the Twelve" disappear into the shadows, returning to center stage only sparingly in subsequent chapters.

If every narrative representation of historical events is partial—i.e., incomplete and oriented toward an aim—then we can hardly fault Luke if we think he has not "told it like it really was." This is because no such narrative representation could ever do so. Choices are forever being made, and those choices are tied to the objectives of the historiographer. As Albert Cook has observed, then, a key test for any historical narrative is its internal coherence.[25]

---

[23] Although for Acts, "end of the earth" probably refers more generally to "Gentiles" (see 13:47, with its citation of Isa 49:6; see further Isa 8:9; 45:22; 48:20; 62:10-11), Strabo repeats the view of Homer that Ethiopians live at "the end of the earth" (Strabo, *Geogr.* 1.1.6).

[24] In the background of this brief account, we might hear the Aristotelian analysis of a "narrative" as possessing a beginning, middle, and end—a perspective on narrative that includes but transcends the passing of time in order to claim some sort of meaningful, even necessary, set of relationships among the events that, in narrative, order time (*Poet.* 1450b).

[25] Albert Cook, *History/Writing: The Theory and Practice of History in Antiquity and in Modern Times* (Cambridge: Cambridge University Press, 1988).

Reading Acts 6:1-7 within its cotext, and particularly in relation to Acts 1–5, we have observed that the disruption Luke has recounted takes its significance from the preceding theological focus on unity and provision for those in need. So too does the resolution to the problem, as Luke recounts it. Historical reconstructions are therefore unnecessary to make good sense of the story as Luke has written it. His account is congruent with a narrative aim oriented to a missiological agenda in which the crossing of sociocultural boundaries, including even those boundaries at work within one's own community, is prioritized. Luke's theological history has thus characterized people and structured the cycle of events in relation to the missionary mandate Jesus had set forth in 1:8: "to the end of the earth."

10

LUKE: HISTORIAN, RHETOR, AND THEOLOGIAN. HISTORIOGRAPHY AND THE THEOLOGY OF THE SPEECHES IN ACTS

Gene L. Green

Some years ago now, Howard Marshall offered us an able account of Luke's work as both a historian and theologian. In his volume *Luke: Historian & Theologian*, he argued that because the author of Luke-Acts "was a theologian he had to be a historian."[1] At no point is this historical claim put to the test more than in the speeches of Acts which are at the service of both the theology and the history of this second of Luke's two volume work. Howard posed the problem this way: "The question is, therefore, largely one of determining the theological outlook present in the speeches; is it Lukan theology or is it a distinguishable theology (or theologies) which can be attributed to his sources?"[2] He echoed the question in his *New Testament Theology*: "What is the nature of Luke's theology, and how does it relate to the actual theologies of the characters in the story?"[3] Howard holds a "high view" of the historical reliability of Acts but argues that "this does not mean that the theology of the author of Acts is to be simply identified with that of any of the characters in the narrative, nor does it deny that Luke's reconstruction of their positions may be open to question in detail."[4] Luke has engaged theological, indeed rhetorical, "doctoring" of his sources, a practice which is in line with the canons of historiography which he inherited and utilized. Luke's history is marked both by his careful use of sources and his rhetorical and theological concerns as a communicator to Theophilus and his circle. We would expect no less of him.

SPEECHES IN WRITING HISTORY

A considerable portion of the Acts of the Apostles consists of speeches and these serve as a vehicle in the unfolding missional history and theology of the

---

[1] I. Howard Marshall, *Luke: Historian and Theologian* (Downers Grove: InterVarsity, 1988), 52.
[2] Marshall, *Luke: Historian and Theologian*, 72.
[3] I. Howard Marshall, *New Testament Theology: Many Witnesses, One Gospel* (Downers Grove: InterVarsity, 2004), 157.
[4] Marshall, *New Testament Theology*, 157.

early church.⁵ Acts contains twenty-four or more speeches, depending on what forms of direct address we classify as a speech.⁶ These occupy close to 300 of the 1000 verses in this book. The history of the early church's mission as recorded by Luke, whom the Fathers named as the author of Luke/Acts, is distinct from modern histories which tend not to include speeches as part of the historical narrative. Luke embraced the historiographic conventions of his day. Ancient historians commonly inserted lengthy speeches into their histories since these served to explicate the events which were selected and arranged in the history. Indeed, as Gempf notes, "conventional Greek historiography regarded history as a matter of both πράξεις καὶ λόγοι [deeds and words]."⁷ Polybius comments that the public speeches and discourses "sum up events and hold the whole history together" (*Histories* 12.25a.3 [Paton, LCL]). The speeches were part of the history and one of the means by which history itself moved forward. But in Acts are the points of view reflected in the speeches those of the author or the protagonists in the narrative?

Writers of history sought not only to display the facts but also the causes of events and the reasons for either the failure or success of the recorded acts and words. Polybius regards interpretation as an essential function of the historian—the one who writes history but does not move on to interpret is someone who betrays the craft. In his extended assault on the practices of the historian Timaeus, Polybius advocates for interpretation:

> The peculiar function of history is to discover, in the first place, the words actually spoken, whatever they were, and next to ascertain the reason why what was done or spoken led to failure or success. For the mere statement of a fact may interest us but is of no benefit to us: but when we add the cause of it, study of history becomes fruitful. . . . But a writer who passes over in silence the speeches made and the causes of events and in their place introduces false rhetorical exercises and discursive speeches, destroys the peculiar virtue of history. (*Histories* 12.25b.1-4 [Paton, LCL])

---

⁵ Luke/Acts, as the rest of the New Testament literature, are "the documents of a mission," with Acts providing the structured history of "the mission of his [Christ's] followers called to continue his work by proclaiming his as Lord and Savior" (Marshall, *Theology of the New Testament*, 34-35). This history provides both the deeds and words of that mission.

⁶ Scholars are not fully agreed regarding what should count as a speech and, consequently, how many speeches appear in Acts (Marion L. Soards, *The Speeches in Acts: Their Content, Context, and Concerns* [Louisville: Westminster/John Knox, 1994], 18-22).

⁷ Conrad Gempf, "Public Speaking and Published Accounts," in *The Book of Acts in Its Ancient Literary Setting* (ed. Bruce W. Winter and Andrew D. Clarke; vol. 1 of *The Book of Acts in Its First Century Setting*, ed. Bruce W. Winter; Grand Rapids: Eerdmans; Carlisle: Paternoster, 1993), 259-304 [264].

The speeches are a principal vehicle within the text for interpreting the historical narrative and, therefore, become particularly important for studying the theology of Acts.[8]

While the speeches are replete with theology, the question is whether the theology reflected in them is that of Peter, Paul, and others or that of the author of Acts. Are these addresses free inventions of the author or do they, in some way, reflect what was actually spoken by the apostles on these or perhaps other occasions? What principles of ancient historiography guided the author in his use of sources (if indeed he used any) and the presentation of the content of speeches? Martin Dibelius's well-known 1949 essay on "The Speeches in Acts and Ancient Historiography"[9] argues the case that "in the last analysis, however, he [the author of Acts] is not an historian but a preacher; we must not allow our attempts to prove the authenticity of the speeches to cloud our perception of their kerygmatic nature."[10] The content of the speeches, according to Dibelius, is testimony to the creative artifice of the book's author and we should not seek the treasure of a historical core which served as their foundation. The vigorous debate which ensued over whether the speeches are in any way historically authentic has led some, like Soards, to avoid the historical question altogether.[11] There is no way to know whether Luke is summarizing speeches or simply inventing them *ex nihilo*.[12]

The reasons for the skepticism of some and the agnosticism of others regarding the historicity of the speeches in Acts are rooted in the arguments forwarded by Dibelius and elaborated by others. The first question is whether ancient historians sought to discover and record what was actually spoken or whether their own rhetorical concerns guided their composition of the speeches. Dibelius's position is that ancient historians felt no compunction to reproduce speeches as they had been delivered. We may compare, for example, the versions of a speech Claudius delivered before the Roman Senate regarding the Gauls. One edition comes down to us in an inscription while another was

---

[8] Henry J. Cadbury, "The Speeches in Acts," in *The Acts of the Apostles: Additional Notes to the Commentary* (vol. 5 of *The Beginnings of Christianity*; ed. F. J. Foakes-Jackson and Kirsopp Lake; Grand Rapids: Baker, 1979), 402-27 [402]. Mark Cogan (*The Human Thing: The Speeches and Principles of Thucydides' History* [Chicago: University of Chicago Press, 1981], 3) remarks that "Thucydides believed that an understanding of the Peloponnesian War required the exhibition of the public statements of policy or of the rationales for policy" and "that political addresses can provide for the perception of motivations behind and meanings attributed to the events as they occurred."

[9] Martin Dibelius, *Studies in the Acts of the Apostles* (trans. Mary Ling; ed. Heinrich Greeven; London: SCM, 1956), 138-91.

[10] Dibelius, *Studies in the Acts of the Apostles*, 183.

[11] Marion L. Soards, *The Speeches in Acts: Their Content, Context, and Concerns* (Louisville: Westminster/John Knox, 1994), 16 n. 53.

[12] Cadbury, "The Speeches in Acts," 405.

recorded by Tacitus.[13] Tacitus' rendition of the speech was highly modified due to stylistic considerations. Also, when Josephus reports speeches found in the Bible, he sees no need to follow the text which is before him. Moreover, speeches inserted more than once take on a different character with each telling, such as the address by Herod regarding war against the Arabs (cf. *J.W.* 1.373-379 and *Ant.* 15.127-146). Dibelius concludes that "this shows how little he feels bound by respect for the text."[14] The author's aims, and not those of the speaker, dominate in the historian's rendition of the speeches.

Thucydides provides another well-known talking point in this discussion. In his *History of the Peloponnesian War*, he remarks on the methodology employed in recording speeches: "Therefore the speeches are given in the language in which, as it seemed to me, the several speakers would express, on the subjects under consideration, the sentiments most befitting the occasion, though at the same time I have adhered as closely as possible to the general sense of what was actually said" (1.22.1 [Smith, LCL]). According to Dibelius, Thucydides was the historian who "raised the speech to an artistic device of the highest order."[15] Dibelius takes note of Thucydides' admission that it was difficult "to recall with strict accuracy" (ἀκρίβεια) what was actually spoken and therefore Thucydides "allowed the speakers to express themselves in the way he thought individuals would have found it necessary to speak on the subject to be discussed."[16] At the same time, Thucydides claimed to have adhered to the "general sense" (ξύμπασα γνώμη) of what had been said, thus generating questions in his interpreters "concerning the relationship of subjective judgment and objective reproduction in the speeches."[17] Dibelius admits to some "objective basis" for Thucydides' speeches[18] but concludes that Thucydides' "chief concern is what is characteristic of the situation, rather than what is characteristic of the persons."[19]

While admitting that Thucydides' speeches may reflect some historical core, Dibelius also notes that subsequent historians departed from his expressed concern for the sources and placed more emphasis upon the "rhetorical arts." He remarks on the way Dionysius of Halicarnassus (*Pomp.* 3.20) critiques Thucydides and how Sallust interprets the events of his history through the speeches he inserts. For these, the crudeness of Thucydides' style was the trouble. In the end, Dibelius concludes, an ancient historian did not hold that

---

[13] See William Stearns Davis, ed., *Rome and the West* (vol. 2 of *Readings in Ancient History: Illustrative Extracts from the Sources*; Boston: Allyn and Bacon, 1912-13), 186-88 and Tacitus, *Annals* 10.24.
[14] Dibelius, *Studies in the Acts of the Apostles*, 139.
[15] Dibelius, *Studies in the Acts of the Apostles*, 140.
[16] Dibelius, *Studies in the Acts of the Apostles*, 141.
[17] Dibelius, *Studies in the Acts of the Apostles*, 141.
[18] Dibelius, *Studies in the Acts of the Apostles*, 142.
[19] Dibelius, *Studies in the Acts of the Apostles*, 142.

his chief obligation was "that of establishing what speech was actually made; to him, it is rather that of introducing speeches into the structure in a way which will be relevant to his purpose."[20] Even if the content of a speech lay at hand, the historian was not obliged to use it since such historical scraps "will serve as an artistic device to help to achieve the author's aims."[21]

According to Dibelius, the speeches Luke records are not intended to present the various sides of a debate—the author has a point of view which he wishes to promote. "The author does not wish to be impartial," Dibelius remarks, "indeed he wants to plead his cause."[22] Luke is preaching and does not allow each side to present its position, unlike the way Sallust presented Caesar and Cato. In speeches such as that in Athens (Acts 17), Luke

> is not concerned with portraying an event which happened once in history . . .; he is concerned with a typical exposition, which is in that sense historical, and perhaps was more real in his own day than in the apostle's time. He follows the great tradition of historical writing in antiquity in that he freely fixes the occasion of the speech and fashions its content himself.[23]

Given the author's interest in interpreting the events of the history, we should not expect the speeches to be "authentic" in a contemporary sense. The main theme of the speeches is that of the book as a whole and not that of a particular historical situation portrayed in the narrative.[24] Therefore, we are not surprised to find common elements appearing in speeches of different actors on Luke's stage[25] as well as a common style throughout.[26] Indeed, given the overarching concern of the author, some of the speeches simply do not fit with the historical narrative where they are located. Dibelius argues his point to the very end: the author of Acts "is not an historian but a preacher; we must not allow our attempts to prove the authenticity of the speeches to cloud our perception of their kerygmatic nature."[27]

---

[20] Dibelius, *Studies in the Acts of the Apostles*, 144.
[21] Dibelius, *Studies in the Acts of the Apostles*, 145.
[22] Dibelius, *Studies in the Acts of the Apostles*, 151.
[23] Dibelius, *Studies in the Acts of the Apostles*, 155.
[24] Dibelius, *Studies in the Acts of the Apostles*, 174-75.
[25] Eduard Schweizer ("Concerning the Speeches in Acts," in *Studies in Luke-Acts* [ed. Leander E. Keck and J. Louis Martyn; Nashville: Abingdon, 1966], 208-16 [210-12]) speaks of "a *far-reaching identity of structure*" in the speeches. He concludes that "*one and the same author* is decisively involved in the composition of all the speeches here investigated" and so "basically the Paul of Acts speaks exactly like Peter."
[26] Hans Conzelmann (*Acts of the Apostles* [trans. James Limburg, et al.; Philadelphia: Fortress, 1987], xliii) states, "Nevertheless, the speeches do not attempt to reflect the individual style of the speaker, but rather the substantial unity of early Christian (i.e. normative) preaching."
[27] Dibelius, *Studies in the Acts of the Apostles*, 184.

Dibelius moves a step further by disassociating Luke's practice in Acts from that in the Gospel. In the Gospel he needed to fit into an extant tradition and therefore did not take a creative hand to his sources. Like Dibelius, Cadbury notes that Luke may have used a different method in the Gospel than in Acts since he was "dealing with different kinds of material" which goes back to the early tradition.[28] Therefore Luke did not have the same creative freedom which he had in writing Acts. In Acts he is a historian writing literature and, since he was the first to attempt a Christian history, he was free to play the evangelist.[29]

Not everyone, however, would agree that ancient historians played loose with their sources for history because their own rhetorical concerns dominated. Witherington, for example, emphatically states that "there was no *convention* that ancient historians were free to create speeches."[30] Some, however, did precisely this and the practice was widespread enough to invite comment by those who chose to avoid this approach to writing history. Polybius, for example, rails on Timaeus and others whose creative powers eclipsed the historian's task: "But a writer who passes over in silence the speeches made and the causes of events and in their place introduces false rhetorical exercises and discursive speeches, destroys the peculiar virtue of history. And of this Timaeus especially is guilty, and we know that his work is full of blemishes of the kind" (*Histories* 12.25b.4 [Paton, LCL]). The audacity of Timaeus is that he "gives no report of what was actually spoken" (*Histories* 12.25a.5 [Paton, LCL]). Yet Timaeus was well-known and approved by many who put confidence in him (*Histories* 12.25c.1 [Paton, LCL]). Josephus likewise invented speeches—this no one doubts since his rhetorical compositions placed in patriarchal mouths are not rooted in the soil of their supposed scriptural source. Rhetorical concerns eclipsed the attention to historical fact in the speeches recorded by Dionysius of Halicarnassus. Hemer observes, "In Dionysius literary and rhetorical criteria are elevated above the historical conscience."[31] A number of ancient historians did indeed create speeches. So even if it were not a *conventional* or common practice, it was a practice. There can be no doubt that historians at times invented speeches. The questions are what kind of historical reporting was deemed appropriate and what model did Luke follow when he penned the speeches in Acts.

As noted previously, history writing in the ancient world was a matter of recording both πράξεις καὶ λόγοι (deeds and words).[32] Speeches were a part

---

[28] Cadbury, "The Speeches in Acts," 416.

[29] Dibelius, *Studies in the Acts of the Apostles*, 185.

[30] Ben Witherington, *The Acts of the Apostles: A Socio-Rhetorical Commentary* (Grand Rapids: Eerdmans; Carlisle: Paternoster, 1998), 40.

[31] Colin J. Hemer, *The Book of Acts in the Setting of Hellenistic History* (ed. Conrad H. Gempf; Winona Lake, Ind.: Eisenbrauns, 1990), 77.

[32] Gempf, "Public Speaking and Published Accounts," 264.

of the history and so discussion about the use of sources for speeches often parallels the reflection on how the historian recorded the events of history. All the utterances in a history, as Polybius noted, "sum up events and hold the whole history together" (*Histories* 12.25a.3 [Paton, LCL]). While the reflections on ancient historiography singled out the peculiar issues surrounding recording deeds and words, common principles applied to both. For example, Lucian (*How to Write History* [Kilburn, LCL]) will not abide those who cannot get the geographical details correct (26) or who have no knowledge of their subject matter (29). Such people "invent and manufacture whatever 'comes to the tip of an unlucky tongue'" (32). A true historian, however, will maintain a single loyalty: "This, as I have said, is the one thing peculiar to history, and only to Truth must sacrifice be made. When a man is going to write history, everything else he must ignore" (40). The historian should pay critical attention to sources as he ferrets out the reliable ones: "He should for preference be an eyewitness, but, if not, listen to those who tell the more impartial story, those whom one would suppose least likely to subtract from the facts or add to them out of favour or malice" (47). Involvement in the history, credible sources, and judicious evaluation of testimony are the bedrock of historiography for Lucian.

The historian should also attend to questions of arrangement and style, a consideration which Lucian places alongside his concern for faithful reporting of events (48) which will hand down "a true account of what happened" to posterity (42). In the same way, the historian should pay due attention to style in recording speeches while, at the same time, remaining faithful to the historical setting and persons: "If a person has to be introduced to make a speech, above all let his language suit his person and his subject [ἐοικότα τῷ προσώπῳ καὶ τῷ πράγματι], and next let these also be as clear [σαφέστατα] as possible. It is then, however, that you can play the orator and show your eloquence" (58). The requisite that speeches be "clear" [σαφέστατα] is not a statement about the need for eloquence or clarity of expression but rather that speeches should be certain or true.[33] Lucian's concern for truth in reporting the deeds of history here attaches to the speeches as well. He is also concerned for suitability (ἐοικότα) to the "person" and "subject," but what is suitable or likely for a speaker to say is not detached from what was spoken. Lucian's final note regarding speeches embraces rhetoric ("then, however, you can play the orator and show your eloquence"), a concern for historians when chronicling the deeds of history as well (47). According to Lucian, the historian should let the speech image the speaker—both in language and subject matter—and there should be historical certainty. But the historian should exhibit a rhetorical concern, letting his own eloquence come through. These two emphases are not antithetical for Lucian any more than his concern for accurate recording of deeds, on the one hand, and arrangement and style, on the other, are in conflict. Quintilian likewise applauded the use of fine rhetoric

---

[33] See Homer, *Od.* 2.31; *Il.* 4.440; LSJ, s.v. "σαφής."

in his comments on Livy's method while, at the same time, underscoring his faithfulness to both the setting of the speeches and their speakers (*Inst.* 10.1.101).

The double foci of historical faithfulness and rhetorical adaptation evolved from the well-discussed statement Thucydides made about speeches. He muses on the difficulty of accrediting every piece of testimony yet his concern for faithfulness is the bedrock of his history: "Now the state of affairs in early times I have found to have been such as I have described, although it is difficult in such matters to credit any and every piece of testimony [τεκμηρίῳ]" (*History of the Peloponnesian War* 1.20.1 [Smith, LCL]). He reiterates this affirmation (1.21.1), elaborating that he has not given "greater credence to the accounts, on the one hand, which the poets have put into song, adorning and amplifying their theme, and, on the other, which the chroniclers have composed with a view rather of pleasing the ear than of telling the truth." His concern for the truth leads him to avoid those accounts in which rhetorical concerns overtake the history, whether the sources are poets or chroniclers occupied with the effect of their public recitations. Thucydides values accuracy and evidence (1.21.1).

Thucydides' reflection on recording speeches parallels his norms for recording the deeds of history. His declaration merits a second look:

> As to the speeches that were made by different men, either when they were about to begin the war or when they were already engaged therein, it has been difficult to recall with strict accuracy the words actually spoken, both for me as regards that which I myself heard, and for those who from various other sources have brought me reports. Therefore the speeches are given in the language in which, as it seemed to me, the several speakers would express, on the subjects under consideration, the sentiments most befitting the occasion, though at the same time I have adhered as closely as possible to the general sense [τὰ δέοντα][34] of what was actually said [τῶν ἀληθῶς λεχθέντων]. (1.22.1)

While impediments keep him from recording the *ipsissima verba*, he seeks to preserve the *ipsissima vox*. Immediately following his statement about the speeches, he lays out his approach to the deeds which he records:

> But as to the facts [ἔργα] of the occurrences of the war, I have thought it my duty to give them, not as ascertained from any chance informant nor as seemed to me probable, but only after investigating with the greatest possible accuracy each detail, in the case both of the events in which I myself participated and of those regarding which I got my information from others. And the endeavour to ascertain

---

[34] Simon Hornblower (*A Commentary on Thucydides* [3 vols.; Oxford: Clarendon, 1991], 1:60) rejects the notion that τὰ δέοντα means simply that which seems appropriate. Rather Thucydides is trying to be accurate in reporting and not merely to present what was probably the case (see Thucydides 1.22.2).

these facts was a laborious task, because those who were eye-witnesses of the several events did not give the same reports about the same things, but reports varying according to their championship of one side or the other, or according to their recollection. And it may well be that the absence of the fabulous [μυθῶδες] from my narrative will seem less pleasing to the ear but whoever shall wish to have a clear view both of the events which have happened and of those which will some day, in all human probability, happen again in the same or a similar way— for these to adjudge my history profitable will be enough for me. And, indeed, it has been composed, not as a prize-essay to be heard for the moment, but as a possession for all time. (1.22.2-4)

As with the speeches, Thucydides claims to take care with his sources which report the deeds of history. He notes that he was able to witness some events, as he had heard some speeches, yet other events were reported to him, as was the case with the speeches. He knows there was inaccurate reporting so he avoids recording the fabulous and will not allow the pleasure of hearing the narrative overshadow his historical concern. He is writing for posterity and not just for the moment. His critical capacity is fully engaged and he will not allow either the rhetorical concerns of his sources or his audience to override his reporting.

So in reporting deeds (1.22.2-4) and in recording speeches (1.22.1) Thucydides demonstrates a deep commitment to what actually happened ("only after investigating with the greatest possible accuracy each detail") and what was actually spoken ("I have adhered as closely as possible to the general sense of what was actually said [τῶν ἀληθῶς λεχθέντων]"). This was a difficult task given the problems of evaluating the sources, on the one hand, and of recording and memory, on the other. Yet he claims faithfulness to the deeds of the history just as he affirms his faithfulness to the speakers, the subject, and the occasion of the speeches as he adheres to the "general sense" (τὰ δέοντα) of what was "actually said." What he says of the deeds he says of the speeches. With the speeches, however, he must admit his creative hand ("Therefore the speeches are given in the language in which, as it seemed to me, the several speakers would express, on the subjects under consideration, the sentiments most befitting the occasion"), but even here he admits to faithfulness both to the person and the setting of the speech (as Lucian after him who said, "above all let his language suit his person and his subject"). He has testimony from his own memory and the reports of others regarding what was "actually said" and he is unwilling to betray this in order to give full vent to his own rhetorical artistry. He refused to make it up as he was going along.

As noted above, Polybius follows a similar track. His standards for recording the deeds of history correspond to those applied in reporting speeches. He presents these two together within the same frame stating,

A historical author should not try to thrill his readers by such exaggerated pictures, nor should he, like a tragic poet, try to imagine the probable utterances of his characters or reckon up all the consequences probably incidental to the occurrences with which he deals, but simply record what really happened and what really was said [τῶν δὲ πραχθέντων καὶ ῥηθέντων κατ' ἀλήθειαν], however commonplace. For the object of tragedy is not the same as that of history but quite the opposite. The tragic poet should thrill and charm his audience for the moment by the verisimilitude of the words he puts into his characters' mouths, but it is the task of the historian to instruct and convince for all time serious students by the truth of the facts and the speeches he narrates [διὰ τῶν ἀληθινῶν ἔργων καὶ λόγων], since in the one case it is the probable that takes precedence, even if it be untrue, the purpose being to create illusion in spectators, in the other it is the truth, the purpose being to confer benefit on learners. (*Histories* 2.56.10-12 [Paton, LCL])

The same norms apply for recording both the deeds and the speeches of the history since both are essential to the historian's purpose of conferring "benefit on learners." Rhetorical concerns should not overtake the historian's task nor should mere imagination be his tool. Polybius appears to keep Thucydides' words in mind, and is cautious about allowing probability to rule. Thucydides admitted to using "the language in which, as it seemed to me, the several speakers would express . . . the sentiments most befitting the occasion" (1.22.1), but Polybius throws in the cautionary note which will not permit the historian to run with the point without Thucydides' strong tether to "the general sense of what was actually said [τῶν ἀληθῶς λεχθέντων]."[35] We hear another loud echo from Thucydides later in Polybius' history: ". . . nor is it the proper part of a historian to practice on his readers and make a display of his ability to them, but rather to find out by the most diligent inquiry and report to them what was actually said (<τὰ> κατ' ἀλήθειαν ῥηθέντα), and even of this only what was most vital and effectual" (36.1.7).

Polybius expresses special caution regarding the way the historian should not let his own rhetoric carry him away from the historical event. He critiques Timaeus for not writing "the words spoken nor the sense of what was really said" (12.25a.5). In this critique he allows for recording either the *ipsissima verba* or the *ipsissima vox*, but will give no place to mere rhetorical flourish. Timaeus has "made up his mind as to what ought to have been said, he recounts all these speeches and all else that follows upon events like a man in school of rhetoric attempting to speak on a given subject, and shows off his oratorical power, but gives no report of what was actually spoken [τῶν κατ' ἀλήθειαν

---

[35] F. W. Walbank (*Speeches in the Greek Historians* [Oxford: Blackwell, 1965], 8) interprets Polybius as saying that "in reporting a speech a historian must restrict himself to what was actually said, and indeed the most important part of that, but he may cast it in his own words, which may in fact be identical for different occasions. In short τὰ κατ' ἀλήθειαν ῥηθέντα does not mean 'the actual words spoken'; it means 'the sense of what was said', indeed something very close to Thucydides' ἡ ξυμπᾶσα γνώμη τῶν ἀληθῶς λεχθέντων."

εἰρημένους]" (12.25a.5). Whether the historian records events or speeches which interpret them, diligent inquiry is required. This, Polybius details, includes "the industrious study of memoirs and other documents and a comparison of their contents" (12.25e.1). He is diligent in working with sources and critical as he compares their content. Polybius remarks that the historian must take account of "political events" (12.25e.1). This is not enough, however, since one must obtain an understanding of the meaning of events and movements of history (12.25e.2–12.25g.4). The speeches, in particular, are part of the historian's arsenal to describe the movements and meaning within the history (12.25b.4). Polybius also makes a strong case for the historian's personal involvement in the history.

In his *On Thucydides*, Dionysius of Halicarnassus reflects on Thucydides' speeches, judging them from the standpoint of their rhetorical effect and suitability (for example: 42, 44-46, 49, 51 [Usher, LCL]). While he quotes and acknowledges Thucydides' claim to adhere "as closely as possible to the general sense of what was actually said" (41), he questions whether Thucydides accomplished his mission. On the other hand, Dionysius observes his technique: "Thucydides assigns to both sides speeches such as each might naturally have made. They are suited to the characters of the speakers and relevant to the situation, and neither inadequate nor overdone" (36). Dionysius regards Thucydides' speeches as appropriate yet as creative compositions, representing what the various speakers "might naturally have made." While Dionysius does not discuss the question of the sources Thucydides employed, he makes critical historical judgments in his extensive evaluation of the speeches in the history.

In summary, the discussion regarding writing speeches in histories parallels ancient reflection on recording deeds. Sources should be consulted and used critically and, indeed, it is preferable for the historian to have been an eyewitness and earwitness of some aspects of the history he is writing. The historian must always keep in mind that he is writing for posterity and should not attempt to flatter those of his own time. The concern for posterity will also keep him from sacrificing truth upon the altar of rhetorical flourish. What the various speakers said in the history cannot be reported exactly according to Thucydides, although Polybius raises this as a possibility more so than his predecessor. In any case, the historian should adhere "as closely as possible to the general sense of what was actually said" (Thucydides, *History of the Peloponnesian War* 1.22.1 [Smith, LCL]). Historians remembered and echoed Thucydides' interest in being faithful to the speaker's sense. Even Dionysius of Halicarnassus took careful note of his concern (*On Thucydides* 41). Polybius makes the strongest case against those, such as Timaeus, who would invent speeches. Such practice was out of line with the very nature of historical writing. On the other hand, the sources replay the note from Thucydides that the speech should be suitable to the person making it and the setting in which it was given. The speech had to "fit" well given all the historian knew about the times and persons, preserving also the *ipsissima vox*. But we also hear caution even at this point: suitability to both the person and setting are not adequate. As in the case of deeds, there must be some tether to what actually occurred, whether the event was spoken or acted out on the stage of history.

But at the same time, rhetorical concerns were very much in play. The historian must also take into account his own audience and hence he must keep in mind the form of his expression. Given these concerns, we are not surprised to find a common voice throughout the various speeches. Indeed, this is precisely what we would expect of authors who are holding in tension historical faithfulness and the need for their history to speak to those of their day. The historian must not only present facts but must interpret. The speeches are the vehicle which most particularly offers perspective and interpretation of the deeds. The recognition that speeches had an essential place in the interpretation of history assists us in getting to the heart of the apparent tension between historical and rhetorical concerns. Walsh's comments on Livy and other historians are instructive:

> Further, the insertion of composed speeches, a convention as old as Herodotus, is ingrained in Roman history-writing. . . . But the purpose of these composed speeches is not an empty demonstration of rhetorical virtuosity; Livy attempts to 'get inside' the speaker, and to present, through the words attributed to him, a psychological portrait of his qualities.[36]

In other words, instead of taking us *away* from a historical speaker and his concerns, the rhetorical art of the historian is intended to bring the reader *toward* the speaker by getting inside his perspectives. There is more to recording any aspect of history than chronicling events and citing words. The historian's task is one of interpretation and hence the rhetorical art is to bring the reader into the history. While a historian may take unwarranted liberties with this, as did Timaeus, we should not assume that evidences of the author's rhetorical craft constitute proof of his unfaithfulness to the deeds or speeches of history. All history is interpreted and thus embraces the subjective interpretive element.

THE SPEECHES IN ACTS

The history Luke presents in Acts of the Apostles includes, as did all ancient histories, both πράξεις καὶ λόγοι (deeds and words). The question which occupies us here is whether Luke adhered to the conventions laid down by Thucydides, Polybius, and Lucian who would not allow the rhetorical interests

---

[36] Patrick G. Walsh, *Livy: His Historical Aims and Methods* (Cambridge: Cambridge University Press, 1961), 219-20. See Cogan, *The Human Thing*, 3-4, 121, 233-34; Colin W. Macleod, *Collected Essays* (Oxford: Clarendon, 1983), 68.

of the historian to eclipse the concern for what was "actually spoken." Or was Luke like Timaeus who invented his speeches with little concern for investigation and sources and therefore provided "no report of what was actually spoken"? As noted above, ancient historians tended to treat the question of πράξεις καὶ λόγοι (deeds and words) in similar ways. Speeches presented particular problems for the historian since there were no transcripts of what was actually said. Moreover, the peculiar function of the speeches was to interpret the events of history. Nonetheless, reflection on the historian's task regarding recording speeches paralleled that of recording the deeds. Sources were sought and the historian evaluated the testimony handed down regarding both deeds and words before including it in the history. We may, therefore, rightly ask how Luke dealt with the πράξεις of this history as a key to understanding his approach to the λόγοι.

Luke's own declarations in the prologues to Luke and Acts provide the first keys to his approach to historical writing. Luke summarizes the content of his first volume in his prologue to Acts: "In the first book, Theophilus, I wrote about all that Jesus did and taught [ποιεῖν τε καὶ διδάσκειν]" (1:1). In focusing upon the deeds and words of Jesus, the author recognized that historical writing must include both events and speeches. As his βίος of Jesus, Luke's second volume brought together both the events and speeches of early Christian history.[37] Luke also locates himself squarely within ancient historiographic traditions in his prologue to the first volume (Luke 1:1-4). As was common among ancient historians, he acknowledges that others have gone about the task of writing a similar history to the "historical account" (διήγησιν)[38] he is about to pen ("many have undertaken to set down an orderly account [διήγησιν] of the events [πραγμάτων] that have been fulfilled among us"). By mentioning these other histories, Luke may imply that he referenced or used them as sources when constructing his own history. As Luke, Dionysius of Halicarnassus (*Ant. rom.* 1.7.1-3) reveals the historical narratives he used, juxtaposing them with the oral testimony he also received (cf. Luke 1:2). Dionysius carefully acknowledges his sources to make sure that no one can accuse him of inventing the events he records. By noting that there were others who wrote historical accounts regarding the same subject, Luke is not critiquing them but only pointing to their role with respect to his own

---

[37] The declaration that the first volume was about what "Jesus began [ἤρξατο] to do and to teach" (TNIV) may imply that the second volume contains the continuing deeds and speeches of Jesus. But while Jesus remains an active figure in Acts (as Acts 9), he is not the principal actor or speaker in the narrative. Luke's expression may only mean that the narrative in these two volumes starts from the very beginning (*NRSV*, "all that Jesus did and taught from the beginning").

[38] Lucian, *How to Write History* 55; Polybius, *Histories* 3.4.1; 3.38.4; 3.39.1; Diodorus Siculus, *Library of History* 11.20.1; Dionysius of Halicarnassus, *Ant. rom.*1.7.4; 2 Macc. 2:32; 6:17.

composition and affirming thereby the credibility of his history.[39] Indeed, by referencing the other writings he elevates their status as works worthy of imitation (μιμήσις/*imitatio*). Dionysius of Halicarnassus even names those authors whom he considers worthy of *imitatio* when writing history (*Pomp.* 3). The author of Acts also attends to "the events" (πραγμάτων) of the history. While Alexander correctly observes that ancient historians most commonly spoke of the πράξεις (deeds) of history,[40] ancient historians also referred to the subject or the events of history using the cognate πραγμάτα (Dionysius of Halicarnassus, *Ant. rom.* 1.7.4; Josephus, *Life* 40). The "events" or subject of the history may include not only the deeds but also the words spoken in the history (Lucian, *How to Write History* 58).

Luke also places himself within ancient historiographic traditions by mentioning what the eyewitnesses of these events had handed down (1:2, "just as [καθώς] they were handed on to us by those who from the beginning were eyewitnesses [αὐτόπται] and servants of the word"). The meaning of Luke's affirmation in 1:2 is not entirely clear. The clause which begins with καθώς may refer to the way the previous historical accounts (1:1, διήγησιν) of the events (πραγμάτων) which occurred were based upon eyewitness testimony. In that case, Luke would be making a statement regarding the credibility of his sources referred to in 1:1. On the other hand, Nolland observes that "the καθώς clause can be located either before or after the clause with which it is compared."[41] Nolland argues that the clause parallels the previous affirmation about Luke's written sources (1:1) and looks forward to v. 3. In other words, this reading understands that Luke claims to have used two types of sources: those written and the testimony of those who were "eyewitnesses." This reading is preferable since Luke's point in v. 2 is about what was handed on "to us" (ἡμῖν) rather than what the "eyewitnesses" handed on to "many" (v. 1, πολλοί) who previously drew up historical accounts. The content of what the "eyewitnesses and servants of the word" had "handed on" (παρέδοσαν) must be supplied from the preceding context. In this case the content would be "the events" (v. 1, πράγματα).[42] Luke, therefore, notes that he has two sources—the historical accounts and the eyewitness testimony—both of which had to do with the πράγματα of the life of Jesus. As other authors of his day, Luke affirms that he used both written sources and eyewitness testimony (most likely oral) in composing his history (cf. Lucian, *How to Write History* 47). His reference to the eyewitnesses was, as van Unnik notes, "a safeguard against

---

[39] Contra Francois Bovon, *Luke 1: A Commentary on The Gospel of Luke 1:1–9:50* (Hermeneia; Minneapolis: Fortress, 2002), 19.

[40] Loveday Alexander, *The Preface to Luke's Gospel: Literary Convention and Social Context in Luke 1.1-4 and Acts 1.1* (SNTSMS 78; Cambridge: Cambridge University Press, 1993), 112.

[41] John Nolland, *Luke* (3 vols.; WBC 35A-35C; Dallas: Word Books, 1989), 1:8.

[42] So Josephus, *Ag. Ap.* 1.50, 53; Polybius 9.2.2; Diodorus Siculus 1.3.6; 2.1.4.

fallacies and opened the way to the truth."[43] Such testimony was a hedge against "mere hearsay evidence" (Polybius, *Histories* 4.2.3 [Paton, LCL]). Luke once again displays a knowledge of the best historiographic practices which have come down to him and claims to have adhered to them.

Luke's methodological assertions in the prologues to Luke and Acts place him squarely within the discussion regarding history writing which can be traced through Thucydides, Polybius, and Lucian. We expect him to avoid the specious practices of Timaeus which Polybius critiqued so severely. The question is whether he adhered to these "best practices" or took a maverick approach to writing history, allowing rhetorical concerns to eclipse the record of the events or seeking to flatter rather than write for posterity. It is most likely that, as Thucydides, Polybius, and Lucian, the principles which guided how Luke chronicled events were also in play when he recorded speeches, with due consideration to the particular challenges facing historians when recording the spoken word.

Colin Hemer's work on *The Book of Acts in the Setting of Hellenistic History*[44] offers us the most detailed and documented study of Luke's historiographic practices in Acts. In this underutilized study, Hemer looks at the text of Acts "as we have it to see how it stands up historically."[45] In opening the question, Hemer states, "I am merely asking whether Acts is essentially unreliable in what it narrates of Paul and the primitive church and insisting that we should not make the judgment based on easy extrapolation from the corroborations or difficulties of a few debated passages, unless they are shown to be central to the veracity of the book."[46] Hemer nuances the definition of "historicity," asking whether Luke is "in general a trustworthy source by the standards of his day, whether he exhibits accuracy or inaccuracy of mind, a general conscience for, or a general disregard of, historical fact."[47] He discusses at some length the canons of ancient historiography (ch. 3)[48] before launching into a detailed analysis of the narrative in Acts in light of ancient literature and archaeology. Hemer sifts through Acts in light of the independent historical record which has come down to us (chs. 4–5), including discussion on the relationship of Acts to the Epistles and the sources the author utilized (chs. 6–8)

---

[43] W. C. van Unnik, "Once More St. Luke's Prologue," *Neot* 7 (1973): 7-26 [14]. See Polybius 4.2.2-3; Dionysius of Halicarnassus, *Ant. rom.* 1.6.1.

[44] Colin Hemer, *The Book of Acts in the Setting of Hellenistic History* (Winona Lake: Eisenbrauns, 1990). See also Colin J. Hemer, "Luke the Historian," *BJRL* 60 (1977–1978): 28-51.

[45] I. Howard Marshall, foreword to *The Book of Acts in the Setting of Hellenistic History*, by Colin Hemer, viii.

[46] Hemer, *The Book of Acts in the Setting of Hellenistic History*, 29.

[47] Hemer, *The Book of Acts in the Setting of Hellenistic History*, 47, and the discussion on 49.

[48] Hemer, *The Book of Acts in the Setting of Hellenistic History*, 63-100.

as well as his own participation in that history.[49] His conclusion begins with a comment on the "pronounced lack of discussion about the relation of the Acts of the Apostles . . . to the world and history around it," especially in light of the "wealth of new data from inscriptions and papyri from the Graeco-Roman world."[50] Hemer rises to this task and, after careful examination of the extant evidence, concludes, "By and large, these perspectives all converged to support the general reliability of the narrative, through the details so intricately yet often unintentionally woven into the narrative."[51] Luke was no Timaeus.

Hemer affirms the credibility of the narrative, given the extant data, yet acknowledges the historical difficulty presented by the reference to Theudas (Acts 5:36-37). The Acts account in the recorded speech of Gamaliel locates him chronologically before Judas, although his revolt occurred some forty years later than Judas during the time when Fadus was procurator, at least according to Josephus (*Ant.* 20.5.1.97-98).[52] This may constitute a historical inaccuracy, although we cannot assume *a priori* that Luke was wrong and not Josephus. On the other hand, even if this is "a genuine historical error," Hemer remarks, it "would not be of sufficient magnitude to call into question the basic credibility of the author."[53] The reliability of the historical record in Acts is in harmony with the author's own claims in the prologues about having used best practices in the composition of his narrative. Given Luke's reliability as a historian where we have the opportunity to verify his references against the historical record, we should assume that he exercised the same type of care with the speeches as he did with the deeds of the history. It is highly unlikely that he, as Timaeus, departed from his sources in order to invent speeches. To put the matter another way, Luke roots his history in written and eyewitness testimony connected to the events and words reported. His account demonstrates a high degree of reliability which inclines us to accept this testimony. Moreover, we do not have adequate knock-down arguments to discredit the testimony provided. It is not irrational to accept the testimony he presents.[54]

Luke Timothy Johnson admits that the author of Acts

---

[49] Hemer argues that the "we" sections of Acts are evidence of the author's own involvement in the history, this interpretation giving "the most reasonable explanation" (*The Book of Acts in the Setting of Hellenistic History*, 312-34).

[50] Hemer, *The Book of Acts in the Setting of Hellenistic History*, 411.

51 Hemer, *The Book of Acts in the Setting of Hellenistic History*, 412. In addition to Hemer's study, see also Martin Hengel, *Acts and the History of Earliest Christianity* (trans. John Bowden; Philadelphia: Fortress, 1979), 1-68; Joseph A. Fitzmyer, *The Acts of the Apostles* (AB; New York: Doubleday, 1998), 126-27.

[52] Hemer, *The Book of Acts in the Setting of Hellenistic History*, 162–63.

[53] Hemer, *The Book of Acts in the Setting of Hellenistic History*, 412 n. 5.

[54] Jennifer Lackey, "It Takes Two to Tango: Beyond Reductionism and Non-Reductionism in the Epistemology of Testimony," in *The Epistemology of Testimony* (ed. Jennifer Lackey and Ernest Sosa; Oxford: Clarendon, 2006), 160-89 [169, 172].

is impressively precise in matters of local color and detail. Places are where he says they are; things seemed to have worked pretty much the way he describes them; he accurately records the titles, functions, and time of tenure of various local officials. He captures the peculiarities of different regions. All of these suggest an author close to the scene.[55]

Johnson even admits that even when we compare Acts with Paul's letters, it appears that Acts "provides a reliable if partial framework for reconstructing that portion of Paul's career."[56] His conclusion accords with Hemer's findings: "Where we can check him on details, Luke's factual accuracy in the latter part of Acts is impressive."[57] However, Johnson urges caution since such careful attention to detail "is also characteristic of good fiction!" While the author may have faithfully portrayed the world of the early church, this does not mean that we can have full confidence "that he got exactly right the sequence or meaning or character of events that form the substance of his narrative."[58] Luke's presentation appears to appropriate "Hellenistic literary and social tropes" and his treatment of Paul places his hero "in settings and scenes evocative of Hellenistic models."[59] We may say that Luke has interpreted Christian history in light of extant narratives within his social world. After pointing up the tensions between Paul's letters and Acts, he concludes that we should avoid extreme positions: "It is true that we cannot, because of Luke's artistry, determine the extent or even the existence of written sources. But this does not imply that Luke did not make use of tradition or that he made up events solely from his imagination. Likewise, because Luke selected and shaped his story does not mean that it is simply fiction."[60]

Johnson's caution is well taken since we cannot verify every event of the history nor can every historical problem be resolved. Yet Luke makes a claim to participate in a particular genre, that of history-writing, and he also points the reader to his methodology which accords with the best practices during the era. These included the use of written as well as eyewitness sources, in addition to his own participation in some aspects of the history about which he writes.[61] Such practices included the avoidance of hearsay and myth.[62] Polybius' critique of Timaeus shows that simply fabricating history was not an accepted practice although it was an approach employed by Timaeus and others. In other words,

---

[55] Luke Timothy Johnson, *The Acts of the Apostles* (SP; Collegeville, Minn.: Liturgical, 1992), 5.
[56] Johnson, *The Acts of the Apostles*, 5.
[57] Johnson, *The Acts of the Apostles*, 5.
[58] Johnson, *The Acts of the Apostles*, 5.
[59] Johnson, *The Acts of the Apostles*, 5.
[60] Johnson, *The Acts of the Apostles*, 7.
[61] See the discussion on the "we" sections in Acts in Hemer, *The Book of Acts in the Setting of Hellenistic History*, 312-34.
[62] Hengel, *Acts and the History of Earliest Christianity*, 60.

while some invented events in their history, Luke's prologues and his practices, as far as we can verify them, show that he did not embrace that approach to history. He demonstrated the type of rhetorical concern which was part of ancient historiography, but he did not submerge historical concerns under these rhetorical interests. His history is interpreted, or theological, as we would expect from a work based on testimony.

We possess compelling evidence of the way that the author of Acts used his sources when we compare the Gospel of Luke with Mark and Q.[63] Luke's handling of these sources in composing his gospel offers a vivid illustration of his method for appropriating the material, especially the speeches, which were part of those documents he refers to in the prologue of the gospel ("Since many have undertaken to set down an orderly account of the events that have been fulfilled among us," Luke 1:1).[64] Over and again we are impressed with Luke's close reading and careful handling of Mark and Q, as a reading of a gospel synopsis illustrates.[65] We have no reason to suspect that his method was any different in writing Acts. Since he adhered closely to his source material in composing the gospel, we should expect that he did the same in Acts. Luke and Acts are one book in two volumes, the two being unified on various levels. They are stitched together as one continuous narrative both by the prologues, the theological themes, and the structure of the books.[66] Compositionally it becomes quite difficult to distinguish between Luke and Acts. Cadbury's assertion that in the gospel and Acts we are "dealing with different kinds of material" cannot be sustained.[67] We are therefore inclined to expect a consistency in method in the use of sources in both volumes, even with regard to recording speeches. These two volumes were composed as a single unit, and we should not think that the author changed his method for including source material in this second volume. Put simply, we hear a faithful reporting of the testimony handed down to him regarding the speeches of Peter, Paul, and others. Luke carefully handled his sources whether they reported the events or the speeches which he wrote down in his history.

---

[63] I assume the four source theory of B. H. Streeter (*The Four Gospels: A Study of the Origins, Treating of the Manuscript Tradition, Sources, Authorship, and Dates* [London: Macmillan, 1924]) and many others.

[64] As Hengel (*Acts and the History of Earliest Christianity*, 61) says, "Going by ancient standards, the relative reliability of his account can be tested in the gospels by a synoptic comparison with Matthew and Mark. We have no reason to assume that he acted completely differently in Acts from the way in which he composed his first work, and that he made up his narrative largely out of his head."

[65] Compare Jesus' last day discourse in Mark 13:1-3 and Luke 21:5-33, or the way Luke handles Q (Matt 11:7-19 and Luke 7:24-35; Matt 11:20-42 and Luke 10:13-15; Matt 12:43-45 and Luke 11:24-26).

[66] Joel B. Green, *The Gospel of Luke* (NICNT; Grand Rapids: Eerdmans, 1997), 6-10. The debate regarding the unity of Luke-Acts is larger than can be discussed here.

[67] Cadbury, "The Speeches in Acts," 416.

Luke's assertions about his historical method and the evidence we have as we compare him with his known sources lead us to believe that he, like Thucydides, held a deep commitment to what actually happened ("only after investigating with the greatest possible accuracy each detail," *History of the Peloponnesian War* 1.22.1 [Smith, LCL]) and what was actually spoken ("I have adhered as closely as possible to the general sense of what was actually said," 1.22.1). Like Thucydides, and unlike Livy or even Josephus, Luke writes of the events happening during his own time.[68] He carefully investigated (Luke 1:3; cf. Lucian, *How to Write History* 47) and used reliable sources, both written and oral, but at the same time paid particular attention to rhetorical concerns. While he was the preacher, his theological concerns did not supplant his interest in the deeds and words of history as handed down to him. To do that would, in the words of Polybius, destroy "the peculiar virtue of history" (*Histories* 12.25b.4 [Paton, LCL]). While Polybius critiqued Timaeus since he "shows off his oratorical power, but gives no report of what was actually spoken" (12.25a.5), he prescribed to the idea that historians should interpret events (12.25b.1-4). Moreover, the historian was expected to attend to rhetorical style after historical considerations were satisfied. The space given to rhetoric included more than assuring that the speeches suited the "person and his subject." Once grounded in his sources, the person and circumstances, "It is then, however, that you can play the orator and show your eloquence" according to Lucian (*How to Write History* 58 [Kilburn, LCL]). Interpretation of the sources was encouraged and eloquence was not shunned in writing speeches.

At this intersection we begin to understand how Luke has been viewed as no more than the "preacher." While Dibelius and others have identified common themes and a consistent rhetorical style laced through the speeches in Acts as evidence that the author paid scant attention to his sources, this weave of history and rhetoric is exactly what we would expect from an ancient historian.[69] In historical writing, speeches had both a historical and rhetorical function, whether their author was Thucydides or Luke. Luke's theological art in the speeches of Acts is evidence of his concern for rhetoric in writing history.

CONCLUSION

The speeches in Acts, therefore, should not be dismissed as mere Lukan inventions which evidence no higher concern on the author's part than the display of his own rhetorical skill and the preservation of his own perspective. He holds to his sources which provided testimony, yet he shapes that which

---

[68] T. Francis Glasson, "The Speeches in Acts and Thucydides," *ExpTim* 76 (1964–1965): 165.

[69] See Gempf, "Public Speaking and Published Accounts," 264.

was handed down to him in order to present his theological understanding of the events and speeches which have transpired. The speeches are colored with the author's viewpoint and are accented with his rhetorical voice. We should not expect to hear the *ipsissima verba* of any of the actors on this stage. But if Luke is indeed a credible historian of his age, as his own methodological reflections and evidence which we can verify confirm, then we may indeed hope to hear within these pages the *ipsissima vox* of the ones who speak as he, too, "adhered as closely as possible to the general sense of what was actually said" (Thucydides, *History of the Peloponnesian War* 1.22.1 [Smith LCL]). Luke is not like Timaeus who "shows off his oratorical power, but gives no report of what was actually spoken" (Polybius, *Histories* 12.25a.5 [Paton, LCL]). We may not be able to fully tease out what interpretive elements Luke wove with the Petrine and Pauline speeches in Acts. Every speech, on the one hand, summarizes apostles' words. Yet we may expect that Luke remained faithful to the "gist" of the apostles' ideas, staying faithful to both the persons and the settings to which he bears witness. We should also not forget that the author of Acts wrote one missional history with one approach to his sources. Indeed, Luke's record of the πράξεις καὶ λόγοι [deeds and words] of this history is integral to the mission itself. His careful handling of his sources when composing the Gospel was most likely his method when composing the second volume of his work. With these qualifications in mind, we may affirm that we hear the particular theological perspectives of Peter and Paul in the speeches recorded in Acts. Luke is indeed a historian and rhetor and, as such, a theologian. Howard was right all along.

11

THE MISSIONARY CHARACTER OF 1 CORINTHIANS

Brian S. Rosner

INTRODUCTION

In Howard Marshall's *New Testament Theology* he argues that the NT writings should be recognized as "the documents of a mission." He also asserts that "New Testament theology is essentially missionary theology."[1] Taking mission to be primary is pitted against "the mistake of seeing the theology of the New Testament as ecclesiastical or ecclesiological, that is, of seeing the central interest as being the church and its life and structures."[2] Both "mission documents" and "missionary theology" are broad and flexible terms in Marshall's account, and different texts support the thesis more readily than others. In the end, the hypothesis of the missionary focus for New Testament theology can only be tested on a case-by-case basis and the sense in which various documents evince missionary theology will differ.[3] This essay considers one Pauline epistle, 1 Corinthians, a text whose "missionary character"[4] is not obvious.

At first blush the letter appears to contradict Marshall's position. Commentators routinely praise the teaching of 1 Corinthians on the church and barely mention the subject of mission. In Hans Conzelmann's view, "[t]heology here [in 1 Corinthians] is translated into an illumination of the existence of the church and of the individual Christian in it."[5] According to Victor Paul Furnish, 1 Corinthians is about "the church's struggle to be the church."[6] And James D.

---

[1] I. Howard Marshall, *New Testament Theology: Many Witnesses, One Gospel* (Downers Grove: InterVarsity, 2004), 34. Howard was my colleague and head of department for eight years in the 1990s at the University of Aberdeen, my first academic post. This essay is offered in gratitude for his fine example of, as he once put it, being a Christian who happens to be a scholar.

[2] Marshall, *New Testament Theology*, 36. Cf. David Wenham, "Appendix: Unity and Diversity in the New Testament," in George Eldon Ladd, *A Theology of the New Testament* (Grand Rapids: Eerdmans, 1993), 684-720 [712-13]: "New Testament theology is all about the divine mission to the world."

[3] Cf. Marshall, *New Testament Theology*, 37.

[4] Marshall's terminology, *New Testament Theology*, 35.

[5] Hans Conzelmann, *A Commentary on the First Epistle to the Corinthians* (trans. James W. Leitch; Hermeneia; Philadelphia: Fortress, 1975), 9.

[6] Victor Paul Furnish, *The Theology of the First Letter to the Corinthians* (NTT; Cambridge: Cambridge University Press, 1999), 16. In terms of the distinctive

G. Dunn believes that in terms of its theology 1 Corinthians "repays careful study" not least because of its "ecclesiological value."[7] Even Marshall himself lists "divisions in the congregation" and "the life of the congregation" as two of the letter's seven main theological themes.[8]

Correspondingly, most studies of mission in the NT do not do much with 1 Corinthians. In their biblical theology of mission, Andreas K. Kostenberger and Peter T. O'Brien include only a few pages on a few texts from 1 Corinthians in an extensive chapter on Paul. 1 Corinthians 9:19-23 is the main interest, appearing in sections entitled, "Fulfilling the aims of his missionary apostleship: the content of Paul's ministry" and "Paul as a model [of partnership in the gospel] for believers."[9] In his study of Paul the missionary Eckhard Schnabel notes the same passage in the letter and adds a second. In his words, in 1 Cor 9:19-23 Paul "describes his behavior as a missionary" and in 1 Cor 3:5-15 Paul expounds "his understanding of missionary work."[10] We might add a third, namely 2:1-5, where Paul recalls the manner of his coming to Corinth to preach the gospel. However, as valuable as these passages may be for our understanding of Paul's view of mission, in all three cases his reflections on aspects of mission serve a larger purpose and are auxiliary to the main argument.

1 Corinthians 2:1-5 is part of Paul's argument in 1:8ff that the gospel is the antithesis of human wisdom and power. To prove his point Paul cites the (supposed) wisdom of those who reject the message (1:18-25), the low social standing of those who accept it (1:26-31) and the unimpressive conduct of the messenger (2:1-5). 1 Corinthians 3:5-15 establishes the accusation in 3:4 that the Corinthian Christians are behaving like "mere human beings" (TNIV), by showing that the ministers of the gospel, whether beloved or belittled, are in reality mere servants of Christ. And 1 Cor 9:19-23 is part of Paul's exposition in 9:1-23 of his own practice of waiving rights for the sake of the gospel, a custom he advocates in relation to the issue of eating food sacrificed to idols in the larger unit of 8:1–10:31. The three passages in question do address mission, but in context they can hardly be said to point to mission as a central concern of the letter.

---

contribution of 1 Corinthians to a NT theology of the church Furnish, 130-31, notes the "one body" image, spiritual gifts and the eucharistic institution.

[7] James D. G. Dunn, *1 Corinthians: New Testament Guides* (Sheffield: Sheffield Academic Press, 1995), 10.

[8] Marshall, *New Testament Theology*, 265-79.

[9] Andreas K. Kostenberger and Peter T. O'Brien, *Salvation to the Ends of the Earth: A Biblical Theology of Mission* (NSBT 11; Downers Grove: InterVarsity, 2001), 179-81 and 194-95. 1 Corinthians also does not figure prominently in Christopher J. H. Wright, *The Mission of God: Unlocking the Bible's Grand Narrative* (Downers Grove: InterVarsity, 2006).

[10] Eckhard J. Schnabel, *Paul the Missionary: Realities, Strategies and Methods* (Downers Grove: InterVarsity, 2008), 135 and 130 respectively.

To what extent, then, and in what sense is 1 Corinthians a mission document, with missionary theology? Answering this question is the task of the rest of this essay.

1 CORINTHIANS AS A MISSION DOCUMENT

1 Corinthians is not evangelistic, written to persuade outsiders, nor does it enlist the Corinthian believers to active participation in mission as evangelists. In the most general sense the letter reflects a chapter in Paul's missionary career. It is part of his own story as one "sent to preach the gospel" (1 Cor 1:17), in that he founded the church (cf. 1 Cor 4:15; "I became your father"), spent some eighteen months there, and engaged in a correspondence involving at least four letters to and fro.[11] In this formal sense the letter is a mission document, primary evidence of Paul carrying out his calling as an apostle/missionary to plant and establish churches.

However, more can be said in recognition of 1 Corinthians as a mission document: first, 1 Corinthians gives a number of indications that Paul expects the Corinthians to embrace a mission-commitment themselves; and secondly, the argument and structure of the letter as a whole itself bears witness to Paul's missionary preaching.

PAUL EXPECTS THE CHURCH OF GOD IN CORINTH TO BE COMMITTED TO MISSION

Eckhard J. Schnabel's comments about the Pauline corpus apply well to 1 Corinthians:

> Paul does not direct the churches to initiate missionary projects in other regions of their province or the Roman Empire: this is primarily the task of the apostles and of other missionaries whom the churches have commissioned. But Paul commends and praises the missionary commitment of individual churches.[12]

What evidence is there that in 1 Corinthians Paul expects the Corinthian believers to be committed to mission? What does this commitment look like? Although he does not call them to preach the gospel, Paul expects the Corinthian Christians to express mission-commitment in at least four ways: by way of financial assistance, social integration, ethical apologetic and public

---

[11] The four include a "previous letter" (1 Cor 5:9) of Paul to the Corinthians, a letter from the Corinthians to Paul (cf. 1 Cor 7:1), 1 and 2 Corinthians.

[12] Eckhard J. Schnabel, *Paul and the Early Church* (vol. 2 of *Early Christian Mission*; Downers Grove: InterVarsity, 2004), 1485.

worship.[13] In each case the casual, almost incidental nature of Paul's remarks suggests that Paul took involvement in mission to be the ordinary and expected responsibility of the churches.

MISSION-COMMITMENT AS FINANCIAL ASSISTANCE

In 1 Cor 9:3-14 Paul argues that missionaries have the right (ἐξουσία) to material support: "those who preach the gospel should receive their living from the gospel" (v. 14b TNIV). In context, to "live from the gospel" entails the provision of the basic necessities of life, such as food and drink (v. 3) and lodgings with the intention of being free from the necessity to "work for a living" (v. 6). The issue is hospitality and maintenance and not payments. Such support of missionaries is also taught in 1 Thess 2:1-9 (v. 7 NRSV: "we might have made demands as apostles of Christ") and 2 Thess 3:8, where in both cases Paul reports his willingness to forgo such entitlements.

Even if Paul waived this right for himself during his visit to Corinth, he does not completely excuse the Corinthians from the obligation to support missionaries. In the closing chapter of the letter Paul issues two instructions for the Corinthian believers to help certain people on their journey (16:6, 11). Both use the verb, προπέμπω, which BDAG understands as "to assist someone in making a journey . . . with food, money, by arranging for companions, means of travel, etc."[14] In the first it is Paul himself who looks to benefit from their assistance after his next visit to Corinth. As Dickson notes, "[t]he casual way Paul states his expectations in v. 6 probably suggests that the obligation of churches to 'send off' missionaries in this way was a shared assumption among Pauline communities": "Perhaps I will stay with you for a while, or even spend the winter, so that you can *help me on my journey*, wherever I go" (TNIV, emphasis added).

In the second, 1 Cor 16:10-11, Paul gives instructions concerning Timothy's next visit to Corinth: "When Timothy comes, see to it that he has nothing to fear while he is with you, for he is carrying on the work of the Lord, just as I am. . . . *Send him on his way* in peace so that he may return to me" (TNIV, emphasis added). To "send Timothy on his way in peace" entails more than maintaining a cordial relationship with him at the time of his departure. The verb, as noted above, in a context like this, means "to assist someone [materially] in making a journey."[15] Timothy would need the Corinthians to provide him with a variety of things to make his return to Paul possible. Paul

---

[13] I am indebted throughout this section to John P. Dickson, *Mission-Commitment in Ancient Judaism and in the Pauline Communities* (WUNT 2/159; Tubingen: Mohr [Siebeck], 2003), whose work I summarize and build upon.

[14] This meaning is confirmed by broader usage in Titus 3:13; 3 John 6; Acts 15:3; 2 Cor 1:16; Rom 15:24.

[15] BDAG, s.v. "προπέμπω."

considers it nothing out of the ordinary for the Corinthians to assist him on his way.

MISSION-COMMITMENT AS SOCIAL INTEGRATION

In 1 Cor 9:19-22 Paul describes his extraordinary determination to connect culturally with a wide range of people with an overt missionary aim: "I have become all things to all people so that by all possible means I might save some" (v. 22b TNIV). Did Paul expect the Corinthians to do likewise? Three texts in 1 Corinthians suggest that he did want the Corinthians to follow his example, at least in regard to paying attention to the mission implications and possibilities of their social intercourse. If the first insists on a high level of social integration for believers with unbelievers, the second and third are explicit in regarding this as including the aim of the salvation of outsiders.

In 1 Cor 5:9-10 Paul seeks to clear up a misunderstanding arising from a misreading of his first letter to the Corinthians: "I wrote to you in my letter not to associate with sexually immoral people—not at all meaning the people of this world who are immoral, or the greedy and swindlers, or idolaters. In that case you would have to leave this world" (TNIV). Paul states clearly that his instruction in his previous letter was not concerned with prohibiting associations with outsiders. There are of course some forms of social intercourse with unbelievers that Paul would not allow, such as dining with them in an idolatrous temple (see 10:14-22), but that is not his point here. Paul lists four examples of people with whom social contact in the world is not to be avoided: the immoral, greedy, swindlers and idolaters. He then states what he takes to be obvious: it would be wrong for the Corinthian Christians "to leave the world," that is, to be cut off from contact with non-Christians. Paul takes it for granted that believers take a full part in the community and society in which they live.

In 1 Cor 10:31–11:1 Paul concludes his discussion of idol food in chapters 8–10 in general, and of eating at pagan banquets in particular:

> So whether you eat or drink or whatever you do, do it all for the glory of God. Do not cause anyone to stumble, whether Jews, Greeks or the church of God—even as I try to please everyone in every way. For I am not seeking my own good but the good of many, so that they may be saved. Follow my example, as I follow the example of Christ. (TNIV)

Paul makes clear the high degree of social contact he expects believers to maintain with outsiders. As John Dickson puts it, "Paul's exhortation in v. 32 calls on the Corinthians so to modify their social intercourse that the salvation of insiders and outsiders would in no way be put at jeopardy."[16] Not only must

---

[16] Dickson, *Mission-Commitment*, 252.

they "not leave the world," they must "try to please everyone in every way." Paul evokes his own example of accommodating others for the sake of the gospel in 1 Cor 9:19-23, and also that of Christ the suffering servant, who is described in Isa 53:11-12 LXX as one who gave himself for the good of "many." His instructions also recall the biblical motif of maintaining a good reputation before outsiders for the dual (negative and positive) motives of protecting the honor of God's name and winning over the heathen.

The three-part description of those who are not to be offended, "whether Jews, Greeks or the church of God," casts the net as widely as possible. In Jewish and Christian writings the dualism reflected in "Jews and Greeks/Gentiles" is usually sufficient to refer to all peoples. Paul's addition of "the church of God" reflects the transformation effected by Christ in the lives of Jews and Greeks/Gentiles that makes them something different from what they were previously. That Paul intends to include all people under the categories of "Jews, Greeks and church of God" is confirmed in the following verse where Paul speaks of his attempt to please "everyone."

The dangers of stumbling differ for the three groups. Dickson suggests that "[t]he reference [in 10:31] to Jews [stumbling] probably reflects an awareness on the part of Paul of a large Jewish community in Corinth which could easily have taken offence at the 'liberal' social habits of the 'knowledgeable' in the Corinthian church."[17] The stumbling of the "Greeks" could easily come about if some Corinthians were to eat food in such a way that could be interpreted as "a tacit affirmation of idolatrous beliefs thereby strengthening the 'Greeks' in a form of 'piety' destined for destruction."[18] With reference to causing "the church of God" to stumble, as Dickson points out, the scenario is "analogous to that described in 8:7-13 . . . . A weaker brother who 'up until now had been accustomed to idols' could be led back into idolatry, which would be a stumbling block and result in their destruction since idolatry stands under the eschatological judgement of God."[19]

How far does the missionary import of 10:31–11:1 extend? Is Paul's exhortation to imitate him, as O'Brien argues, "an admonition to engage in evangelistic outreach,"[20] deliberately recalling Paul's full example in 9:19-23 ("that I might save some" by preaching the gospel)? In context, 10:31–11:1 concerns the Corinthian Christians' behavior at pagan banquets and the imitation of Paul should not be taken too broadly. O'Brien acknowledges that Paul "expects a changed attitude and right behaviour in relation to these cultic meals."[21] And the phrase, "whatever you do" (10:31 NRSV), as Dickson

---

[17] Dickson, *Mission-Commitment*, 255.
[18] Dickson, *Mission-Commitment*, 255.
[19] Dickson, *Mission-Commitment*, 255.
[20] Peter O'Brien, *Gospel and Mission*, 128. For his full argument see 83-107. See Dickson' persuasive refutation, *Mission-Commitment*, 256-59.
[21] O'Brien, *Gospel and Mission*, 103.

argues, "does not indicate a move away from the discussion of food. It is parenthetical and refers to any other activity not explicitly mentioned that relates to the discussion of chapters 8–10."[22] Likewise, the adjective, "all," in the command to do "all for the glory of God" (10:31) stands in apposition to "whether you eat or drink." The evidence that Paul wants the Corinthian Christians to imitate him in preaching the gospel is lacking. Still, the missionary import of these verses is profound: Paul expects the Corinthians to modify their dining practices with the explicit goal of "the good of many, so that they may be saved."

1 Corinthians 7:16 closes off Paul's advice (in 7:12-16) to those Corinthian Christians married to unbelievers to stay married. Paul's final words to Christians in mixed marriages have been taken as striking a pessimistic (e.g., TNIV below) or optimistic note (e.g., NRSV):

"How do you know, wife, whether you will save your husband? Or, how do you know, husband, whether you will save your wife?" (TNIV)

"Wife, for all you know, you might save your husband. Husband, for all you know, you might save your wife." (NRSV)

The context favors an optimistic thrust.[23] Paul's main stress is on reasons why such marriages should be preserved rather than abandoned. He is not being sarcastic with the use of the verb "to save" (σώζω); it can be a missionary term meaning "to convert" (e.g., 1 Cor 9:22: "that I might *save* some"). In context, v. 16 provides both Christian husbands and wives one more reason for staying in their mixed marriages. Paul's point that the unbelieving spouse has been sanctified by the marriage to a believer (v. 14) with the result that they have been brought into an unusually powerful position from which to receive Christian influence and witness in the midst of God's temple, the "sphere in which God's holiness and transforming power operate,"[24] would certainly raise one's hopes for the potential conversion of the unbelieving spouse. Also, the idiom "how do you know" is used positively in a range of Greek sources.[25] What Paul is advising is the sacrificing of the supposed ease of divorce from a difficult partner for the possible attainment of what is a great, though uncertain gain, the conversion of your spouse. Remarkably, integration of the most

---

[22] Dickson, *Mission-Commitment*, 259.
[23] The majority of commentators take the verse optimistically. For the pessimistic interpretation see, e.g., A. Robertson and A. Plummer, *A Critical and Exegetical Commentary on the First Epistle of St. Paul to the Corinthians* (ICC; Edinburgh: T&T Clark, 1911).
[24] Richard B. Hays, *First Corinthians* (Interpretation; Louisville: Westminster/John Knox, 1997), 122.
[25] David E. Garland, *1 Corinthians* (BECNT; Grand Rapids: Baker Academic, 2003), 294.

intimate social sort, that of the union of marriage, is thus viewed by Paul as being of possible missionary significance.

MISSION-COMMITMENT AS ETHICAL APOLOGETIC

In the ethical exhortations of a number of Pauline letters there is a discernable missionary orientation. Right conduct is seen as adorning the gospel.[26] While such intimations of ethical apologetics do not break the surface in 1 Corinthians, the sentiment that Christians ought to be aware of the fact that they live in full view of an unbelieving society and should strive to make a good impression is clearly present. Two texts stand out.

In 1 Cor 5 Paul chastises the Corinthians for condoning a form of sexual immorality (πορνεία) "that does not occur even among pagans" (NIV). The unfavorable comparison of the Corinthians to the Gentiles is designed to amplify Corinthian guilt. It was a ploy sometimes used by the OT prophets.[27] The implication is that God's people are to be a light to the nations, not the other way around, for the sake of God's reputation and to facilitate evangelism.

In 1 Cor 6:1-6 Paul opposes believers taking their civil lawsuits to secular courts. Roman courts could not be trusted to administer justice impartially since they were open to bribes and were partial to the status and power of the prosecutor or defendant or both. As Garnsey observes, the Roman judicial system was damaged by "improper influences" that "made equality before the law unattainable."[28] But the injustice of secular courts was not Paul's only reason for opposing their use to settle disputes between Christians.

Paul is also concerned about unity and concord within the body, and of interest for our purposes, the reputation of the church before outsiders is probably also at stake. The rebuke in v. 5a is suggestive: "I say this to your shame (ἐντροπή)." Louw and Nida's lexicon lists more than a dozen terms and idioms for the concept of "shame, disgrace and humiliation"[29] in the NT. While those before whom one should be embarrassed, other believers or unbelievers or God, is not entirely clear with ἐντροπή, several others are used in the NT to denote public humiliation. In a culture obsessed with status, honor and shame, such concerns are never far from the surface. It is likely that in 1 Cor 6:1-6 Paul writes to shame the Corinthians at least partly because of the disrepute they

---

[26] Cf. 1 Thess 4:11-12; Phil 2:14-15; Col 4:5; 1 Tim 3:7; 6:1; Titus 2:10: "so that in every way they will make the teaching about God our Savior attractive" (TNIV; cf. Titus 2:5, 8). See Dickson, *Mission-Commitment*, ch. 9 and pp. 51-60 on ethical apologetics in Paul's letters and its Jewish background respectively.

[27] Cf. 2 Kgs 21:9,11. In Deut 12:29-31 and 1 Kgs 14:24 the nations are used as a negative model for Israelite behavior.

[28] Peter Garnsey, *Social Status and Legal Privilege in the Roman Empire* (Oxford: Clarendon Press, 1970), 207.

[29] Louw and Nida, 25.189–25.202.

have brought upon themselves by airing their dissensions in public before "unbelievers" (6:6) and the collateral damage this inevitably brings on the reputation of God and the gospel.

MISSION-COMMITMENT AS PUBLIC WORSHIP

In 1 Cor 14:24-25, in his lengthy discussion of the superiority of prophetic ministry over speaking in tongues in church meetings, Paul argues that prophecy can actually lead to unbelievers being saved: "But if an unbeliever or an inquirer comes in while everyone is prophesying, they are convicted of sin and are brought under judgment by all, as the secrets of their hearts are laid bare. So they will fall down and worship God, exclaiming, 'God is really among you!'" (TNIV).

Paul's expectation that the prophetic ministry of the gathered community will lead to the conversion of visiting outsiders echoes Isa 45:14 and Zech 8:23. Isaiah prophesies the conversion of Gentile nations in the time of the post-exilic restoration of God's people. At that time he says the various peoples will become Israel's servants and will bow down to them and make supplication to them—"since God is among you!"—and they will say, "there is no god besides you, for you are God and we did not know it, the God of Israel, the Savior" (Isa 45:14-15). Paul expects Isaiah's eschatological vision to be realized in the midst of the Christian gathered community as it exercises its prophetic ministry, with Gentiles turning to God from idols.

SUMMARY

Thus there is ample evidence in 1 Corinthians that Paul expects the church of God in Corinth to be committed to promoting the gospel. For Paul the eschatological announcement of the gospel (the εὐαγγελ– word group) was the duty of authorized heralds.[30] Nonetheless, a careful look at the letter reveals that Paul envisaged a comprehensive partnership of the churches and individual Christians with the evangelists for the active support of this activity. Simply put, when writing to churches like the one in Corinth, the apostle inculcated not only certain behaviors for the sake of brothers and sisters in Christ, but also other actions for the sake of outsiders. The latter may justifiably be called mission-commitment.

In 1 Corinthians mission-commitment finds expression in financial assistance (providing missionaries with material support for their journeys), social integration (not withdrawing from the world, and looking for mission opportunities at banquets and in the home), ethical apologetic (behaving well rather than shamefully) and public worship (conducting meetings with outsiders in mind).

---

[30] See Dickson, *Mission-Commitment*, chs. 3–5 and Appendix B.

THE STRUCTURE AND ARGUMENT OF 1 CORINTHIANS REFLECTS PAUL'S MISSIONARY PREACHING

Compared with Paul's letter to the Romans, 1 Corinthians has occasioned much less debate as to its purpose.[31] When the reasons for 1 Corinthians are canvassed, scholars routinely refer to difficulties in the church, a previous letter, and oral and written reports being received by Paul. In terms of Paul's response, the goal of church unity is sometimes given prominence.[32] Apart from that the letter is thought to have at best only a loose coherence and reflects little of Paul's own agenda beyond this general aim. As to its structure, Murphy-O'Connor expresses the consensus view when he writes: "[t]he salient feature of I Corinthians is the absence of any detectable logic in the arrangement of its contents."[33]

However, when compared with some of Paul's reflections on key aspects of his missionary preaching to Gentiles in other letters, connections and patterns emerge and the argument and structure of 1 Corinthians can be detected. What follows is a summary of the position that I have expounded, with Roy Ciampa, at length elsewhere.[34] The element I wish to underscore here is the simple observation that the patterns in question specifically reflect Paul's missionary preaching. We shall note three passages that figure prominently in discussions of Paul the missionary. If the first encapsulates Paul's conception of the nature of Gentile conversion, the second and third summarize his understanding of the dynamics of pagan sin and his missionary agenda respectively.

In 1 Thess 1:9-10 Paul describes the paradigmatic experience of the Thessalonian Christians in response to his evangelistic preaching: they "turned to God from idols to serve the living and true God and to wait for his Son from heaven, whom he raised from the dead." Here Gentile conversion is understood to entail the rejection of idolatry in favor of the service of the true and living God and his resurrected Son. Likewise, in 1 Corinthians Paul expects his converts to eschew idolatry (1 Cor 8:1–11:1), to worship the one, true God (1 Cor 11:2–14:40) and to live in the light of the reward and vindication guaranteed by the resurrection of Christ (1 Cor 15).

According to Romans 1:21-28 the Gentile vices of idolatry and sexual

---

[31] Cf., e.g., A. J. M. Wedderburn, *The Reasons for Romans* (Edinburgh: T&T Clark, 1991).

[32] See especially Margaret M. Mitchell, *Paul and the Rhetoric of Reconciliation: An Exegetical Investigation of the Language and Composition of 1 Corinthians* (Louisville: Westminster/John Knox, 1992).

[33] J. Murphy-O'Connor, *Paul: A Critical Life* (Oxford: Oxford University Press, 1996), 253.

[34] See Roy E. Ciampa and Brian S. Rosner, "The Structure and Argument of 1 Corinthians: A Biblical/Jewish Approach," *NTS* 52 (2006): 205-18; and Roy E. Ciampa and Brian S. Rosner, *The First Letter to the Corinthians* (Pillar New Testament Commentary; Grand Rapids: Eerdmans, forthcoming).

immorality are rooted in the futility of Gentile thinking and the senselessness of Gentile hearts (v. 21): "Claiming to be wise, they became fools" (v. 22 NRSV). It was their lack of true wisdom (despite their claim to possess it) that led them to "exchange the glory of the immortal God for images" of human or other creatures (v. 23) and as a result "God gave them over in the lusts of their hearts to impurity" (NRSV) which is most characteristically seen in sexual immorality, especially homosexual behavior (vv. 24-28). Thus it is the lack of true wisdom that ultimately led to idolatry and sexual immorality. Presumably, true wisdom (1:22) would have led Gentiles to avoid idolatry and sexual immorality (1:23-28). With respect to 1 Corinthians, a pattern emerges that helps explain the sequence of material in chs. 1–14: True wisdom (1 Cor 1-4; cf. Rom 1:22) will keep the Corinthians from sexual immorality (1 Cor 4:18–7:40; cf. Rom 1:24) and idolatry (1 Cor 8–14; cf. Rom 1:23).[35]

In Rom 15:5-16 Paul explains his missionary strategy and priorities using temple imagery: as "a minister of Christ Jesus to the Gentiles," Paul is to discharge his "priestly duty of proclaiming the gospel of God, so that the Gentiles might become an offering acceptable to God, sanctified by the Holy Spirit" (15:16 NIV). Stated differently, Paul's purpose is that "the Gentiles might glorify God" (15:9 NRSV; cf. 15:6, 7). Romans 15:7 makes it clear that this will be achieved by sorting out certain ethical problems: "Accept one another . . . in order to bring glory to God." Four OT quotations reiterate the goal of Gentiles praising God along "with his people." The final quotation introduces the notion of hope, which Paul expands in a prayer in 15:13.

Paul's stated agenda in Rom 15 also clarifies the order in which he tackles the problems he confronts in 1 Corinthians. Both texts emphasize Christian unity, glorifying God and include a focus on a temple motif. In fact, the main sections of 1 Corinthians correspond to the main movements in Rom 15: (1) Rom 15:5 = 1 Cor 1:10–4:17—Paul calls for unity; (2) Rom 15:6, 7, 9 = 1 Cor 4:18–14:40 (cf. esp. the two commands to glorify God in 6:20 and 10:31 which summarize the two main subsections of 7:1-40 and 12:1–14:40)—unity is to be established in order that ethical problems can be resolved and the Gentiles will "glorify" God; and (3) Rom 15:12-13 = 1 Cor 15 (cf. esp. v. 19)—believers are to put their hope in God's Son.

Seeing the structure and argument of 1 Corinthians as reflecting Paul's missionary preaching adds conviction to the description of 1 Corinthians as a mission document. Not only does Paul in 1 Corinthians call the Corinthians to a

---

[35] Significantly, in Rom 1:21-28 this is all tied to the glory of God. The foolishness of the Gentiles is related to the fact that they "neither glorified [God] as God nor gave thanks to him" (v. 21) and their idolatry is described as an act of exchanging "the glory of the immortal God for images" (v. 23). The proper glorification of God was replaced by idolatry and sexual immorality. Correspondingly, in 1 Corinthians, Paul's imperatives to glorify God in concluding the sections on sexual immorality (chs. 5–6) and idolatry (chs. 8–10) in 6:18 and 10:14 reflect a similar pattern of thought.

mission-commitment, several of the letter's main themes and the sequence in which he treats them testify to the consistency of the apostle to the Gentiles' work as a missionary. While not everyone may agree with the proposed argument and structure for the letter, Furnish points in the same direction when he describes 1 Corinthians as a letter where it is "especially evident" that Paul's thinking "about the gospel took shape within the crucible of his missionary and pastoral labors."[36]

1 CORINTHIANS AND MISSIONARY THEOLOGY

Doctrinal delineation for a document as diverse as 1 Corinthians is never straightforward. And even if the goal in biblical theology is to allow the categories of enquiry and major themes to arise organically from the text, configurations can differ radically from one interpreter to the next. In assessing the missionary dimension of the theology of 1 Corinthians it is not sufficient to notice gospel summaries and evangelistic intentions. The mission of God is bigger than the means of its manifestation. Nor does a section-by-section investigation of the letter suffice, even if careful exegesis is essential. If 1 Corinthians has an argument and structure, the theological contribution of the letter as a whole is worth pursuing.

With this in mind, as a modest beginning, the main features of the biblical-theological framework of the letter's argument may be mined for missionary veins. As a second step, the letter's famous doctrine of the church will be examined for missionary connections.

MAJOR THEOLOGICAL THEMES HAVE A MISSIONARY DIMENSION

This section examines two theological themes that traverse sections of the letter. The first appears in every unit as a prime motivation for the actions Paul proposes. The second is the goal towards which the letter and its instructions move. Both are of keen interest to any theology of mission.

THE LORDSHIP OF CHRIST

If Corinthian problems can be attributed to their cultural background, Paul's various responses may be ascribed to his understanding of Christ and the significance of his lordship; in almost every case Paul pits Christ against the prevailing culture. He appeals for unity in the name of Christ (1:10), who is the power and wisdom of God (2:23-24) and the foundation of the church (3:11). The church must be cleansed of the incestuous man because of Christ's sacrifice (5:7). To have relations with a prostitute is to violate Christ (6:15). Eating food sacrificed to idols must be avoided for the sake of one for whom

---

[36] Furnish, *The Theology of the First Letter to the Corinthians*, 123.

Christ died (8:11) and in imitation of Christ (11:1). With respect to head coverings, he notes that Christ is the head of every man (11:3). The Lord's Supper must be celebrated by discerning "the body" of Christ (11:29). Spiritual gifts are to be exercised in order to build up the body of Christ (12:27). Finally, the resurrection of believers is grounded in the resurrection of Christ (15:3-23). Throughout the letter "Christ" appears sixty-four times, "Lord" sixty-six times and "Jesus" twenty-six times.[37]

In terms of missionary theology, the expectation that universal glory and worship would be given to God is at the heart of the significance of the lordship of Jesus Christ, whose post-crucifixion exaltation is understood by Paul to inaugurate the long-awaited time of the universal and eternal kingdom of God which would result in every knee bowing and every tongue confessing that "Jesus Christ is Lord, to the glory of God the Father" (Phil 2:11 NRSV; cf. Rev 15:3-4). The Lord of the church is the Lord of all. 1 Corinthians comes to a climax in ch. 15 with Paul's discussion of the resurrection as it relates to the ultimate triumph of Christ over all adversaries.

THE GLORY OF GOD

In large measure 1 Corinthians is Paul's response to a congregation plagued by the residual Gentile vices of sexual immorality and idolatry. Paul tells the church to "flee" both, in 6:18 and 10:14 respectively, and instead to "glorify God" in sexual purity and proper worship, in 6:20 (δοξάζω) and 10:31 (δόξα). The theme of bringing glory to God actually pervades the whole letter, using a range of synonyms. Along with these two pivotal commands, the Corinthians are to boast (or glory) in the Lord (1:31; καυχάομαι), not human leaders (3:21; καυχάομαι); worship in a fashion that brings glory and not dishonor to God in 11:2-16; and, in ch. 15, to await their resurrection and glorification, which leads to "the glory of God, even the Father, who freely gives to this mortal immortality, and to this corruptible incorruption."[38] Rather than the glory of God serving other doctrines (whether the purity of believers, church leadership, worship or the resurrection of the dead), such subjects serve to explicate the ultimate aim of all of creation rendering an appropriate response to the God of glory. As the goal of Christian existence both now and in the age to come, the glory of God, "that God may be all in all" (15:28 NRSV), is essentially an eschatological and missiological theme. It is the end to which the mission of God is leading.

---

[37] R. B. Terry, "Patterns of Discourse Structure in I Corinthians," *JOTT* 7, no. 4 (1996): 1-32, also draws attention to the centrality of Christ in 1 Corinthians.
[38] Irenaeus, *Against Heresies* 5.2 (*ANF* 1:528).

THE DOCTRINE OF THE CHURCH IS SUBSIDIARY TO THE MISSION OF GOD

Having noted considerable evidence for the mission character of 1 Corinthians on a number of levels, the question of the place of the doctrine of the church in the letter must still be answered. Does the celebrated ecclesiology of 1 Corinthians displace the primacy of mission? Since this is the subject of an essay in itself, space allows only a brief and suggestive response. Three soundings in the ecclesiology of 1 Corinthians suggest that it is best considered as subordinate to the mission of God. The church and its activities have an eschatological character and as such serve mission, rather than vice versa.

First, Paul addresses the believers in Corinth in 1:2 as "the church of God." The term "church" (ἐκκλησία) referred to Israel as the gathered people of God in the LXX and to the public political assembly in a Greek city. Paul uses it to mean the local community of believers. The addition "of God" to "the church" is unique to 1 and 2 Corinthians among the epistolary prescripts of Paul's letters. In apocalyptic Judaism, the equivalent Hebrew expression for "church of God" is used to refer to God's eschatological people. Roloff suggests that the term was used by Paul "because it corresponded with the eschatological self-understanding of the Church, which understood itself to be the company elect by God and determined by him to be the center and crystallization-point of the eschatological Israel now being called into existence by him."[39] Thus, when Paul designates the Corinthians "the church of God" he is not comparing them to any other club or society in town but evokes their place in God's cosmic plan.

Secondly, in 1 Corinthians, preeminently, the church is the temple of God. Twice in the opening chapters this is made explicit (3:16; 6:19). Other elements reinforce the identification, such as the accent on edification in ch. 14, introduced in 8:1 ("love edifies"), which Michel takes as a reference to the building up of the church as the eschatological temple.[40] Since the temple was a central pillar of Judaism, to identify the church with the temple is a critical move. It required a re-conceptualizing of the nature and role of the temple, one

---

[39] J. Roloff, "ἐκκλησία," *EDNT* 1:410-15 [412]; cf. Roy E. Ciampa, *The Presence and Function of Scripture in Galatians 1 and 2* (WUNT 2/102; Tübingen: Mohr [Siebeck], 1998), 47.

[40] The term in question (οἰκοδομέω) refers literally to construction of a building. While a figurative sense is obviously intended, Paul's usage must be understood in the light of his broader development of the motif of "building/edifying" and its background in OT prophetic promises regarding God's future plans for the redemption and restoration of Israel. In Jeremiah it is normally God who does the planting and building, but in Jer 1:10 these activities are ascribed to Jeremiah's own prophetic activity. This background may be important for understanding Paul's language of "building up" the church. As O. Michel points out, "οἶκος, . . . , οἰκοδομέω," *TDNT* 5:119-59 [139], in the NT building "is primarily an apocalyptic and Messianic concept. . . . The Messiah will build the future temple and the new community."

which was already developing in Second Temple Judaism[41] and which is reflected in the rest of the NT as well.[42] As the temple of God, Paul finds it imperative that the Corinthians glorify God. After all, "[t]he purpose of the Old Testament temple . . . was to house and show forth God's glory"[43] and all four OT "temples" are filled with God's glory.[44] That both Ezekiel and Revelation utilize a reconstituted temple as a motif of the age of consummation points to its significance in biblical eschatology.

A third aspect of the doctrine of the church in 1 Corinthians is the subject of worship. This is present especially in chs. 11–14, a unit which is juxtaposed with a call to reject pagan worship in chs. 8–10 (note how 12:2 recalls the idolatrous past of many of the church members). Tobit 14:5-7 demonstrates how the mass conversion of Gentiles accompanied by a clear rejection of idolatry was a feature of Jewish eschatological expectation in some quarters: "All the nations of the world shall be converted and shall offer God true worship; all shall abandon their idols." According to a broad range of OT texts this would be the time when the Lord's name would be glorified in all the earth (Ps 57:11; 86:9; Isa 24:15; 42:10, 12; 66:18-19; Ezek 39:21; 43:2-5; Mic 5:4; Hab 2:14).

That Paul subscribed to the missiological and eschatological significance of Corinthian worship is suggested by an echo of Mal 1:11 in 1 Cor 1:2. Paul's statement there that the Corinthians are united with all those who call on the name of the Lord "in every place" evokes a significant scriptural tradition going back to a key theme in Deuteronomy, namely, the Lord's selection of one particular place where people would call on his name (understood to refer to Jerusalem). Repeated reference is made to "the place which the Lord your God will choose to have people call upon his name" (cf. LXX Deut 12:11, 21, 26; 14:23-24; 16:2, 6, 11; 17:8, 10; 26:2). Rather than refer to that place, however, Paul says the Corinthians join those who call on the name of our Lord "in every place [ἐν παντὶ τόπῳ]." The expression is only found in the Pauline corpus (1 Cor 1:2; 2 Cor 2:14; 1 Thess 1:8; 1 Tim 2:8) and he uses it to refer to the worship of God that is spreading around the world through his ministry to the Gentiles.[45]

---

[41] Cf. 1QS 8:5-10; 9:4-6.
[42] Matt 26:61; 27:40; Mark 14:58; 15:29; John 2:19, 21; 1 Pet 2:5.
[43] G. K. Beale, *The Temple and the Church's Mission: A Biblical Theology of the Dwelling Place of God* (NSBT 17, Downers Grove: InterVarsity, 2004), 252.
[44] Cf. the tabernacle (Exod 40:34-35; Num 14:10; 16:42; cf. Exod 20:24; 1 Sam 4:21-22), Solomon's temple (2 Chron 7:1-3 [3x]), the rebuilt temple (Ezra 7:27; 8:36; cf. 1 Macc 15:9; 2 Macc 3:2; 1 Esd 8:25), the eschatological temple in Ezekiel (43:4-5). Likewise, the consummated temple in Revelation is associated with glory (Rev 15:8; 21:11, 23, 26).
[45] Significantly, in context all four texts evince one or more of the following temple motifs: offerings, worship, the Spirit, holiness and prayer.

The expression echoes Mal 1:11 LXX,[46] which (in a context of frustration over the way the Lord is being worshipped in Jerusalem) prophesies a future time when God would be worshiped by Gentiles "in every place": "From the rising of the sun until its setting my name will be glorified [τὸ ὄνομά μου δεδόξασται] among the Gentiles and in every place [ἐν παντὶ τόπῳ] incense is offered to my name and a pure offering, for my name is great among the Gentiles, says the Lord Almighty."[47] Similarly, Hag 2:7 anticipates a time when the Gentiles will glorify God in his temple: "all nations will come in, and I will fill this house with glory, says the LORD of hosts." The echo of Mal 1:11 in 1 Cor 1:2 suggests the worshipping Corinthians are part of the fulfillment of God's plan to be worshipped among all the Gentiles, and it is Paul's ultimate purpose in writing to them to see them play their part in fulfilling this world-wide eschatological vision by glorifying God (see 6:20b and 10:31b).

CONCLUSION

What is the mission character of 1 Corinthians? My answer to this question is in two parts: first, 1 Corinthians is a mission document in that Paul expects the church of God in Corinth to be committed to mission, and the structure and argument of the letter reflects Paul's missionary preaching; and secondly, 1 Corinthians has missionary theology in that its major theological themes have a missionary dimension, and the doctrine of the church it espouses is subsidiary to Paul's understanding of the fulfillment of the mission of God.

What is at stake in describing 1 Corinthians as a mission document containing missionary theology? To say that 1 Corinthians is primarily about the church, with no reference to its eschatological significance, can lead to a focus on the church as an insular institution. Noticing the mission character of the whole letter raises ours eyes to the consummation of all things and places the church into the ennobling narrative of the mission of God.

---

[46] The influence of the text on the NT is suggested by the UBS4 references to it in 2 Thess 1:12 and Rev 15:4 (note "all nations") as also alluding to Mal 1:11, picking up "the glorifying of God's name" language. That Paul knew and appreciated Malachi is clear from his description of the fiery judgment of God's temple in 1 Cor 3 which alludes to Mal 3.

[47] P. Towner, "The Pastoral Epistles," *NDBT* 330-36 [333]. As A. E. Hill notes (*Malachi: A New Translation with Introduction and Commentary* [AB; New York: Doubleday, 1998], 188) this perspective of Malachi is not an isolated thought: "Like his earlier contemporaries Haggai (2:7) and Zechariah (8:22), Malachi calls upon his audience to recognize that the worship of Yahweh extends universally to the nations."

12

CHURCH MEMBERSHIP AND THE ἰδιώτης IN THE EARLY CORINTHIAN COMMUNITY

Andrew D. Clarke

STUDYING ANCIENT CONTEXTS FROM THE PERSPECTIVE OF A CONTEMPORARY CONTEXT

Since the turn of the present millennium, there has been a notable resurgence in focus on mission as a primary articulation of the church's task. This has motivated and energized reflection within many churches about the form and structure of a twenty-first century church that is focused on its call to local mission; and it has consequently spawned a considerable number of popular Christian publications.[1] Perhaps more remarkably, mission has also become a significant, recent focus among biblical scholars, who have turned to exploring the topic both theologically and historically.[2]

Although in large measure prompted by the grass-roots interest, this scholarly focus on mission is also an obvious and welcome development from an earlier, but still vibrant, explosion of interest in other characteristics of the first-century churches. Over the last twenty-five years, social studies of the NT have focused successively on description and analysis of a number of fundamental aspects of those earliest Christian communities, including: social rank and status,[3] economic levels and diversity,[4] community formation and

---

[1] The adjective "missional" has only become a commonplace in churches during the present century. A review of the two largest online library catalogues (the Library of Congress Online Catalog [USA] containing thirty-two million catalogued books and print materials; and the Copac National, Academic, & Specialist Library Catalogue [UK and Ireland] containing thirty-two million records) shows that, together, they contain only two holdings published prior to 1998 which contain the word "missional" in their title.

[2] Cf. e.g., the following large volumes: I. Howard Marshall, *New Testament Theology: Many Witnesses, One Gospel* (Downers Grove: InterVarsity, 2004); Eckhard J. Schnabel, *Jesus and the Twelve* (vol. 1 of *Early Christian Mission*; Leicester: InterVarsity, 2004); Eckhard J. Schnabel, *Paul and the Early Church* (vol. 2 of *Early Christian Mission*; Leicester: InterVarsity, 2004); Christopher J. H. Wright, *The Mission of God: Unlocking the Bible's Grand Narrative* (Nottingham: InterVarsity, 2006).

[3] E.g., Edwin A. Judge, *The Social Pattern of the Christian Groups in the First Century: Some Prolegomena to the Study of New Testament Ideas of Social Obligation* (London: Tyndale, 1960); Gerd Theissen, *The Social Setting of Pauline Christianity: Essays on*

organization,[5] leadership models and dynamics (including the role of women),[6] group dynamics (especially issues of conflict),[7] ethnic and cultural identity,[8]

Corinth (Edinburgh: T&T Clark, 1982); Wayne A. Meeks, *The First Urban Christians: The Social World of the Apostle Paul* (New Haven: Yale University Press, 2003).

[4] E.g., Justin J. Meggitt, *Paul, Poverty and Survival* (Edinburgh: T&T Clark, 1998); John M. G. Barclay, "Poverty in Pauline Studies: A Response to Steven Friesen," *JSNT* 26 (2004): 363-66; Steven J. Friesen, "Poverty in Pauline Studies: Beyond the So-Called New Consensus," *JSNT* 26 (2004): 323-61; Peter Oakes, "Constructing Poverty Scales for Graeco-Roman Society: A Response to Steven Friesen's 'Poverty in Pauline Studies,'" *JSNT* 26 (2004): 367-71; Bruce W. Longenecker, "Exposing the Economic Middle: A Revised Economy Scale for the Study of Early Urban Christianity," *JSNT* 31 (2009): 243-78; Bruce W. Longenecker and Kelly D. Liebengood, eds., *Engaging Economics: New Testament Scenarios and Early Christian Reception* (Grand Rapids: Eerdmans, 2009).

[5] E.g., Andrew D. Clarke, ed., *Serve the Community of the Church: Christians as Leaders and Ministers* (Grand Rapids: Eerdmans, 2000); Richard N. Longenecker, ed., *Community Formation in the Early Church and the Church Today* (Peabody: Hendrickson, 2002).

[6] E.g., John K. Chow, *Patronage and Power: A Study of Social Networks in Corinth* (Sheffield: JSOT Press, 1992); Andrew D. Clarke, *Secular and Christian Leadership in Corinth: A Socio-Historical and Exegetical Study of 1 Corinthians 1–6* (Leiden: Brill, 1993); Ritva H. Williams, *Stewards, Prophets, Keepers of the Word: Leadership in the Early Church* (Peabody: Hendrickson, 2006); Andrew D. Clarke, *A Pauline Theology of Church Leadership* (London: T&T Clark, 2008).

[7] E.g., Jeffrey A. Crafton, *The Agency of the Apostle: A Dramatic Analysis of Paul's Responses to Conflict in 2 Corinthians* (Sheffield: JSOT Press, 1991); Todd D. Still, *Conflict at Thessalonica: A Pauline Church and Its Neighbours* (Sheffield: Sheffield Academic Press, 1999); Demetrius K. Williams, *Enemies of the Cross of Christ: The Terminology of the Cross and Conflict in Philippians* (Sheffield: Sheffield Academic Press, 2002); Trevor J. Burke and J. K. Elliott, eds., *Paul and the Corinthians: Studies on a Community in Conflict: Essays in Honour of Margaret Thrall* (NovTSup 109; Leiden: Brill, 2003); Michelle Slee, *The Church in Antioch in the First Century CE: Communion and Conflict* (Sheffield: Sheffield Academic Press, 2003); Robert S. Dutch, *The Educated Elite in 1 Corinthians: Education and Community Conflict in Graeco-Roman Context* (New York: T&T Clark, 2005); Robinson Butarbutar, *Paul and Conflict Resolution: An Exegetical Study of Paul's Apostolic Paradigm in 1 Corinthians 9* (Milton Keynes: Paternoster, 2007); Carl N. Toney, *Paul's Inclusive Ethic: Resolving Community Conflicts and Promoting Mission in Romans 14–15* (Tübingen: Mohr [Siebeck], 2008).

[8] E.g., Atsuhiro Asano, *Community–Identity Construction in Galatians: Exegetical, Social-Anthropological, and Socio-Historical Studies* (London: T&T Clark, 2005); Torrey Seland, *Strangers in the Light: Philonic Perspectives on Christian Identity in 1 Peter* (Leiden: Brill, 2005); William S. Campbell, *Paul and the Creation of Christian Identity* (London: T&T Clark, 2006); Bengt Holmberg, ed., *Exploring Early Christian Identity* (WUNT 226; Tübingen: Mohr [Siebeck], 2008); V. Henry T. Nguyen, *Christian Identity in Corinth: A Comparative Study of 2 Corinthians, Epictetus and Valerius*

and, most recently, the physical settings of congregational meetings.[9]

However, for a number of years, one of the most intransigent problems in the growing field of NT social studies concerned debates over method; and, especially, whether scholars ought to restrict their research to investigation of the hard, tangible data of ancient sources, including not only literary texts, but also non-literary and other archaeological sources, ideally from the first century. In contrast, there was growing interest in the application of more theoretical methods, especially from a number of the social sciences. Models constructed in the light of more accessible, contemporary communities could be adapted, if necessary, before being applied as interpretive lenses through which to view the frustratingly partial social data available from the NT. In many instances, these investigations brought to the text innovative questions and generated pioneering insights and ground-breaking conclusions.

The difficulty perceived by some was not simply that NT scholars were bringing to their task new, inter-disciplinary methods, but rather that there was polarized disagreement in regard to whether some of these new approaches were even appropriate to the study of ancient communities in which a scholar's findings were corroborated by fieldwork pursued within societies and communities that were neither contemporaneous with, nor unequivocally similar to those described in the NT. The frequent accusation was that theoretical assumptions were being brought to the NT texts that were alien to their ancient context. The social historians, on the other hand, were at least restricting themselves to exploring evidence that was contemporaneous with the ancient context—or so they argued.[10]

By the turn of the present century, this stand-off between the social

---

Maximus (Tübingen: Mohr [Siebeck], 2008); Philip A Harland, *Dynamics of Identity in the World of the Early Christians: Associations, Judeans and Cultural Minorities* (New York: T&T Clark, 2009); Mikael Tellbe, *Christ-Believers in Ephesus: A Textual Analysis of Early Christian Identity Formation in a Local Perspective* (Tübingen: Mohr [Siebeck], 2009).

[9] E.g., David L. Balch, "Rich Pompeiian Houses, Shops for Rent, and the Huge Apartment Building in Herculaneum as Typical Spaces for Pauline House Churches," *JSNT* 27 (2004): 27-46; Roger W. Gehring, *House Church and Mission: The Importance of Household Structures in Early Christianity* (Peabody: Hendrickson, 2004); Michele George, "Domestic Architecture and Household Relations: Pompeii and Roman Ephesos," *JSNT* 27 (2004): 7-25; David G. Horrell, "Domestic Space and Christian Meetings at Corinth: Imagining New Contexts and the Buildings East of the Theatre," *NTS* 50 (2004): 349-69; Jorunn Økland, *Women in Their Place: Paul and the Corinthian Discourse of Gender and Sanctuary Space* (London: T&T Clark, 2004); David L. Balch, *Roman Domestic Art and Early House Churches* (Tübingen: Mohr [Siebeck], 2008).

[10] Cf. the public debate between Philip Francis Esler, "Models in New Testament Interpretation: A Reply to David Horrell," *JSNT* 78 (2000): 107-13; David G. Horrell, "Models and Methods in Social-Scientific Interpretation: A Response to Philip Esler," *JSNT* 78 (2000): 83-105.

historians and the social theorists had, in large measure, become dissipated by the increasing awareness in postmodern debates that elements of an original author's context are always inaccessible, in some measure, to a subsequent reader, and therefore the intended message of that text cannot be as objectively reconstructed as had widely been assumed. Instead, *all* scholars bring to *any* text (but especially historical texts) a set of questions and theoretical assumptions that are alien to the contexts of both the original author(s) and original reader(s), and are, therefore, influenced in some ways by the contemporary perspectives of the subsequent interpreter.[11] The debate is then no longer over whether or not a social theorist is applying an appropriate hermeneutical model, but whether each scholar is aware of, and explicit about, the particular set of assumptions or theoretical models being applied, and recognizes that both the questions brought to the text and the conclusions drawn from the text are in some measure filtered through the lens of the interpreter, and are influenced by contemporary agenda. As a consequence, throughout the last decade of the millennium, this broader field of the social description and analysis of the earliest Christian communities has remained both energetic and constructively diverse; and, it is clear that there are presently far greater sensitivities to issues of social dynamic and, consequently, a far more nuanced portrait of the early Christian communities.

One important consequence of this present context for study of the social questions of the NT, however, is that scholars should remain cautious about declaring their detailed conclusions about the social context of the earliest Christians as "assured results." As contemporary social, ethical and philosophical debates change, new questions and different aspects of the broader social setting of the earliest Christian communities will be identified and pursued. However, each new area of investigation is so closely integrated with other aspects of the social context that new findings in regard to one aspect of that context require scholars to reconsider conclusions previously reached about other aspects of social setting, as part of a process in which ever more detailed, refined and historically plausible portraits are painted. These new findings are, on the one hand, inevitably vulnerable to the charge of being prompted by contemporary agenda; and, on the other hand, they may not only raise challenges to some of the previously assured results, but may also shed fresh light on some of the more intransigent areas of earlier debate.

One particular debate, which has been especially vibrant in social and political circles from the start of the twenty-first century, has concerned categories of social inclusion/exclusion and group boundaries. As similar questions are being brought to the study of the NT, it becomes clear that this

---

[11] Edward Adams and David G. Horrell, "The Scholarly Quest for Paul's Church at Corinth: A Critical Survey," in *Christianity at Corinth: The Quest for the Pauline Church* (ed. Edward Adams and David G. Horrell; Louisville: Westminster/John Knox, 2004), 1-43 [40-43].

issue is closely related to all of the different social aspects of the early church mentioned at the outset: the mission of the church, its social class, organizational models, leadership dynamics, group dynamics, ethnic or cultural identity, economic levels and diversity, and the physical setting of congregational meetings.

GROUP BOUNDARIES IN THE CORINTHIAN COMMUNITY

An essential feature of social groups is the existence of boundaries or categories of membership, whether or not these are formally defined.[12] The recent growth in scholarly interest in aspects of "mission" in the NT impinges on the defining of boundaries to a significant extent. In this sense, "mission" motivates an attitude or activity of one group in regard to those who are not group members. In the Judeo-Christian tradition, the roots of mission are most clearly expressed in the covenant between God and Abraham, that this patriarch would father a community, which would be a blessing to all families on earth— that is, this one group receives a divinely ordained mission in regard to others outside the group ("in you all the families of the earth shall be blessed," Gen 12:3 ESV).[13] Group boundaries are at the heart of this, and NT scholars have long identified that boundary markers, together with the grounds on which Gentiles may be included within the people of God, were critical issues from the earliest days of the Christian mission.[14]

While group boundaries in regard to the church have normally been framed in theological categories, they are not always expressed in obviously theological terms, such as circumcision or baptism. Indeed, the early Christians were also familiar with much less technical language, which distinguished believers from unbelievers. The book of Acts records, at a number of points and in what appears to be language that is typical of Acts within the NT, that significant numbers of people were being "added to" (προστίθημι; Acts 2:41, 47; 5:14; 11:24), or attempting to "join," or fearing to "join" (κολλάω; Acts 5:13; 9:26; 17:34), the believers; or, the disciples were multiplying (πληθύνω; Acts 6:1, 7; 9:31). The transfer of individuals into group membership and the consequent growth in numbers are presented as regular and measurable features in the account—the consequences of mission.

In four different letters within the Pauline corpus, we find stark language to distinguish those who are clearly in the church from those who are not.

---

[12] Mary B. McRae and Ellen L. Short, *Racial and Cultural Dynamics in Group and Organizational Life: Crossing Boundaries* (London: Sage, 2010), 39-40.
[13] Cf. the extensive discussion of this in Wright, *Mission of God*, 189-264.
[14] Cf. these questions explored in regard to Paul, in Ellen Juhl Christiansen, *The Covenant in Judaism and Paul: A Study of Ritual Boundaries as Identity Markers* (Leiden: Brill, 1995).

... so that you may walk properly *before outsiders* (πρὸς τοὺς ἔξω) and be dependent on no one. (1 Thess 4:12 ESV)

For what have I to do with judging *outsiders* (τοὺς ἔξω)? Is it not *those inside* (τοὺς ἔσω) the church whom you are to judge? God judges *those outside* (τοὺς δὲ ἔξω). "Purge the evil person from among you." (1 Cor 5:12-13 ESV)

Walk in wisdom *toward outsiders* (πρὸς τοὺς ἔξω), making the best use of the time. (Col 4:5 ESV)

Moreover, [the ἐπίσκοπος] must be well thought of by *outsiders* (ἀπὸ τῶν ἔξωθεν), so that he may not fall into disgrace, into a snare of the devil. (1 Tim 3:7 ESV)

This binary "us-and-them" language is categorical, and regarded by many as insensitive in contemporary contexts, where accommodation and the embrace of both diversity and reasonable pluralism are regarded as more appropriate, rather than the kind of discrimination, which appears to be exclusivist, and even imperialist.[15] A more accommodating stance would be one that is inclusivist or universalist,[16] or the language of "journeying" in search of God (in contrast to a stark boundary marked by conversion). These contemporary, political sensitivities are clearly influential on the hermeneutical task, and may direct interpreters to focus on certain texts, while marginalizing the relevance of others, or alternatively suggesting that contemporary approaches should distance themselves from those of our forebears.

Avoiding such language is problematic given that the Bible is unequivocally concerned with defining, or even constructing, "the other," and this lies at the heart of the mission of proselytizing religions.[17] In this overwhelmingly black-

---

[15] Cf. similar usage in Mark's rendition of the parable of the sower: "To you has been given the secret of the kingdom of God, but for those outside (δὲ τοῖς ἔξω) everything is in parables," Mark 4:11 (ESV) (and, τοῖς δὲ λοιποῖς in Luke 8:10). Also, 2 *Clem.* 13:1 (Holmes), "But let us not desire to please only ourselves with our righteousness, but also those who are outsiders (καὶ τοῖς ἔξω ἀνθρώποις), that the Name may not be blasphemed on our account." Cf. also 2 *Clem.* 12:2, 4; Rev 22:15; and, Josephus, *J.W.* 4.179 (Whiston), "However, although I must say that submission to foreigners (τοῖς ἔξωθεν) may be borne because fortune hath already doomed us to it, while submission to wicked people of our own nation (τοῖς οἰκείοις) is too unmanly, and brought upon us by our own consent"; *Ant.* 15.316 (Whiston), "it also procured him great fame among foreigners (παρὰ τῶν ἔξωθεν)."

[16] Richard A. Burridge, *Imitating Jesus: An Inclusive Approach to New Testament Ethics* (Grand Rapids: Eerdmans, 2007).

[17] Note works like Lawrence M. Wills, *Not God's People: Insiders and Outsiders in the Biblical World* (Lanham: Roman & Littlefield, 2008) which, looking especially at Ezra–Nehemiah, 1 and 2 Maccabees, Matthew, John, the Pauline corpus and Acts, explores how the people of God have sought to define their identity; also, F. C. Synge, "A Plea

and-white biblical context, the contemporary interpreter may nonetheless search in the NT for evidence of a spectrum of positive associations a first-century individual might have with a Christian group—degrees of association other than the stark insider/outsider language—and whether any such flexibility of association received apostolic endorsement.

In this chapter, I suggest the presence not only of unequivocal boundary markers within the Pauline epistles, but also a number of features specifically in 1 Corinthians that appear to suggest areas that are rather more grey—that is an apparent blurring of boundaries, and, at times even a mandate to accommodate those who do not fulfill all the standard requirements of full association. In so doing, I recognize that such an exploration is in response to particularly contemporary aspects of social and political awareness.

THE IMMORAL BROTHER

Paul understands that an individual's allegiance to Christ was normally marked by confession of faith (Rom 10:9-10) that Jesus is Lord (1 Cor 12:3), and belief in his resurrection (1 Cor 15:13-14),[18] followed by baptism (1 Cor 1:13-17); and together, these marked incorporation into the body of Christ—a single body, not limited by geographical boundaries (1 Cor 12:13),[19] consisting of "all those who in every place call on the name of our Lord Jesus Christ, both their Lord and ours" (1 Cor 1:2). We have no extant instructions from the apostle about a local community exercising jurisdiction over the process of admitting an individual into the distinct category of membership of a *local* church.

However, Paul does lay down explicit instructions to the Corinthians about removing an immoral brother from their community, in order that his spirit

---

for the Outsiders: Commentary on Mark 4:10-12," *JTSA* 30 (1980): 53-58; Louis Stulman, "Insiders and Outsiders in the Book of Jeremiah: Shifts in Symbolic Arrangements," *JSOT* 66 (1995): 65-85; F. A. Spina, *The Faith of the Outsider: Exclusion and Inclusion in the Biblical Story* (Grand Rapids: Eerdmans, 2005). Cf. the depiction of "the Jews" and the Samaritans in John's Gospel. Although, note also the many OT instances of praise of the outsider: Pharaoh, who appoints Joseph; Pharaoh's daughter, who saves Moses' life; Rahab the Canaanite prostitute, who saves the spies and testifies to the greatness of Israel's God; Jethro the Midianite, Moses' father-in-law, who helps institute legal reforms in Israel; and Naaman the Aramean general who worships the God of Israel.

[18] James D. G. Dunn, *Romans* (2 vols.; WBC 38A-B; Dallas: Word Books, 1988), 2:616.

[19] The debate as to whether or not ἐν ἑνὶ πνεύματι is instrumental or locative (Anthony C. Thiselton, *The First Epistle to the Corinthians: A Commentary on the Greek Text* [eds. I. Howard Marshall and Donald A. Hagner; Carlisle: Paternoster; Grand Rapids: Eerdmans, 2000], 997) does not impinge on the relevant point in the present discussion, namely that it is a single body.

might be saved (1 Cor 5:1-5, 13); and, not to mix indiscriminately,[20] or eat, with "anyone who *bears the name of brother* if he is guilty of sexual immorality," or other specific sins (1 Cor 5:9-11). Here, such individuals are explicitly distinguished from those who are "outsiders" (1 Cor 5:12-13), and yet they are, in very specific ways, to be treated neither as insiders nor outsiders. While believers should positively associate with fellow believers (so long as they are not sexually immoral), and should not fail to associate with unbelievers (even though they may be sexually immoral), nonetheless, Paul's instruction is that believers should not associate with a *brother* who is sexually immoral—and they should adopt this stance in order to secure the salvation of the soul of the immoral brother. To this extent, boundaries of inclusion and exclusion are clear, although believers should not distance themselves from unbelievers; but, a distinct category of neither insider nor outsider seems to exist in regard to treatment of the *immoral* brother.

MEMBERSHIP OF A HOUSEHOLD

The descriptive term "Voluntary Association" is widely applied to the Graeco-Roman *collegiae,* throughout the Roman empire, suggesting an element of membership by choice, often maintained by subscription and adherence to established rules.[21] For some, however, membership of a given Voluntary Association was not only expected, but even required (e.g., incorporation into a household or trade-oriented association).[22] Similarly, while cult associations were often voluntary, there may also have been elements of automatic incorporation, especially where the head of a household expected or required all those under his *patria potestas* to have the same cultic allegiance.[23] As with some of these Private (and, not always "voluntary") Clubs or Guilds, for some people, their association with one of the first-century Christian communities is likely to have been a direct, and inevitable, consequence of their identification with a particular family, whether as a spouse, an infant, a resident member of the extended family, or a slave or associated freedman/woman.

---

[20] Cf. the discussion of Paul's unusual vocabulary, by Thiselton, *First Epistle to the Corinthians*, 409.

[21] Stephen G. Wilson, "Voluntary Associations: An Overview," in *Voluntary Associations in the Graeco-Roman World* (ed. John S. Kloppenborg and Stephen G. Wilson; London: Routledge, 1996), 1-15 [1]; Stephen J. Chester, *Conversion at Corinth: An Exploration of the Understandings of Conversion Held by the Apostle Paul and the Corinthian Christians* (Edinburgh: T&T Clark, 2003), 227.

[22] Where a trade was inherited from a parent, the son's membership in the associated professional guild may have been automatic. In the Byzantine period, however, the state started to use compulsory membership in a professional guild as a mechanism of taxation; cf. Brian Muhs, "Membership in Private Associations in Ptolemaic Tebtunis," *JESHO* 44 (2001): 1-21 [1-3].

[23] The term "Private Association" may thus be considered a better term.

In Corinth, the household of Stephanas was regarded by Paul to have been the first fruits in Achaia (1 Cor 16:15). That household, as well as two other named individuals, Crispus and Gaius, had unusually been baptized by the apostle himself—a role he appears to have resisted conducting (1 Cor 1:16). At the end of the letter, Stephanas is again mentioned, along with two other names, Fortunatus and Achaicus (1 Cor 16:17). The nomenclature of these additional individuals suggests the reasonable possibility that they may both have been either slaves or freedmen within Stephanas' household.[24] As such, it would be unremarkable if it were on grounds of loyalty and cultural expectation that they first identified with the cultic allegiance of Stephanas, the head of the household.[25]

As many of these communities met in a domestic location (cf. the phrase, "Aquila and Prisca, together with the church in their house," 1 Cor 16:19), and gathered for a cultic meal, all those associated with that household may well have been, in some sense, also engaged in the meal. Indeed, it is to be understood that Paul's injunctions to the Corinthians about the cultic meal (1 Cor 11:20-22, 33-34) incorporate his objection that some members of the Corinthian community were eating to the exclusion of, or without regard for, others, specifically the disadvantaged.[26] To the extent that this meal had become exclusive among some of the Christians in Corinth, it was considered by Paul to be inappropriate.[27] The domestic context of some church meetings allows for the possibility in the first century that there were some present at such meals (perhaps as infants or by virtue of being involved in preparing and serving the meals), who were not, in terms of their own faith, recognized to be members of the body of Christ. In later ecclesiastical contexts, those who prepared and served the Lord's Supper were the senior members of the religious community, but in the more primitive setting, where breaking of bread was tantamount to eating a meal, the regular presence of people additional to the strict faith community might not be considered unusual.

In this context, Paul's enigmatic explanation that an unbelieving spouse or children are in some sense made holy (ἡγίασται) by virtue of the believing

---

[24] Andrew D. Clarke, "'Refresh the Hearts of the Saints': A Unique Pauline Context?," *TynBul* 47 (1996): 277-300.

[25] Of course, there is also the suggestion of evidence that some slaves, in becoming Christians, did not continue with the pagan allegiances of their master or mistress. The references to "Chloe's people" (ὑπὸ τῶν Χλόης, 1 Cor 1:11), or "those in the Lord who belong to the family of Narcissus (τοὺς ἐκ τῶν Ναρκίσσου)" (Rom 16:11) may suggest that members of these households were known by the name of their master/mistress, but, contrary to their master/mistress, were Christian believers.

[26] This interpretation is contrary to the view that Paul is urging believers to distinguish between social eating and the celebration of the Lord's Supper; cf. Thiselton, *First Epistle to the Corinthians*, 864-65.

[27] Cf. David E. Garland, *1 Corinthians* (eds. Robert W. Yarbrough and Robert H. Stein; Grand Rapids: Baker Academic, 2003), 542-44.

spouse or parent is especially interesting (1 Cor 7:12-16).[28] Indeed, it is recognized by Paul that, without this continuing association, the unbelieving family member might not become saved (future tense, σώσεις). Such family members are not considered to be brothers or sisters (1 Cor 7:15), but neither are they regarded as outsiders—for "they are made holy." Again, there is the suggestion of a category of association other than that of a fully identified brother/sister.

THE ἰδιώτης

Ancient Greek usage has a number of very different meanings for the enigmatic term ἰδιώτης, depending on context. In its most frequent sense, it refers to a private individual (one who is concerned with his own affairs, τὰ ἴδια), that is a common or ordinary person, as opposed to a public official.[29] In this sense, there are similarities with the military rank of "private." The term also may refer to an untrained, unskilled, uneducated or inexperienced person (e.g., a layman), as opposed to an expert. Thirdly, it may be applied to an outsider, in contrast to a member.[30]

The second of these meanings is clearly reflected when the words of Peter before the High Priest, the rulers and elders are met with astonishment, because he and John had been perceived as "uneducated" (ἀγράμματοί), "common/ordinary" (ἰδιῶται) men (Acts 4:13).[31] Justin, in 1 *Apol.* 39.3, similarly describes the twelve disciples as uneducated men (ἰδιῶται), characterized by being unable to speak eloquently (λαλεῖν μὴ δυνάμενοι).[32] Indeed, Paul also suggests that he may have been considered an ἰδιώτης τῷ λόγῳ by his Corinthian detractors, presumably because he came across as comparatively "unskilled in speaking" (2 Cor 11:6)—although he himself

---

[28] Thiselton translates the phrase in such a way that possibilities of meaning are left open, but nonetheless suggests that "[t]he lifestyle of the Christian partner cannot but affect the ethos and to some extent the values and lifestyle of the home, whether this be the husband or the wife. The spouse's example, witness, prayer, and living out of the gospel make the spouse (and the children) *in this sense holy*"; Thiselton, *First Epistle to the Corinthians*, 530.

[29] Cf. the majority of the sixty-five references to the term in the Philo corpus.

[30] Cf. Heinrich Schlier, "ἰδιώτης," *TDNT* 3:215-17.

[31] Acts 4:13, "Now when they saw the boldness of Peter and John, and perceived that they were uneducated (ἀγράμματοί), common (ἰδιῶται) men, they were astonished. And they recognized that they had been with Jesus."

[32] Cf. Justin, *1 Apol.* 60.11, further describes those from whom can be learned the deep truths of God as ignorant of the shapes of letters, uneducated, and barbarous in speech (οὐδὲ τοὺς χαρακτῆρας τῶν στοιχείων ἐπισταμένων, ἰδιωτῶν μὲν καὶ βαρβάρων τὸ φθέγμα).

defended that he was both a clear speaker and not lacking in knowledge.³³ In these instances, the general meaning of ἰδιώτης can be grasped as one who is either uneducated or, comparatively speaking, untrained.

However, in two further instances, both in 1 Corinthians, the meaning is less obvious. "... if you give thanks in the spirit, how can anyone occupying the position of an ἰδιώτης (ὁ ἀναπληρῶν τὸν τόπον τοῦ ἰδιώτου) say 'Amen' to your thanksgiving, since he does not know what you are saying?" (1 Cor 14:16 ESV). Here, the REB and Worldwide English New Testament translate the term as "an ordinary person"; the ESV, NRSV and RSV as "outsider"; the Today's NIV as "the inquirer"; the NJB as "the uninitiated"; the ASV, KJV, and the Wycliffe New Testament as "unlearned"; the NIV as "those who do not understand"; the NKJV and Holman Christian Standard Bible as "uninformed"; the NASB and Phillips as "the ungifted"; and similarly, the RV margin as "without gifts." This range of competing interpretations is extensive, focusing variously on degrees of belonging, or on knowledge, or on gifting.

The uncertainty underlines the question as to whether Paul's Corinthian readers would have regarded such an ἰδιώτης—a fiction of the author—to have been an unbeliever, and therefore unable to comprehend the tongues and echo, with others, an affirming "amen"—and, would therefore be embarrassed.³⁴ Alternatively, would this person have been regarded by the Corinthians as a believer, and normally therefore able to say "Amen" to Christian thanksgiving, if articulated in a known language, but not fully initiated in the ways or gifts prevalent in the Corinthian community, whether through being on the fringes of the community, although perhaps a regular attender, or by virtue of being a visitor?³⁵ In other words, does ἰδιώτης signify being beyond the boundaries of the community, or somebody merely on the fringes of the community – perhaps one who is not fully initiated, but is nonetheless well-disposed? Clearly, Paul is envisaging somebody who is voluntarily present in what is a private, rather than public, gathering, and presumably is therefore not negatively disposed. The description, however, that this fictitious person is "occupying the *place/position* of an ἰδιώτης" (ὁ ἀναπληρῶν τὸν τόπον τοῦ ἰδιώτου) seems to carry a technical connotation—a recognized *position* within, or stance in regard to, the community, perhaps that of somebody who is in the process of gaining fuller incorporation. This would suggest that the ἰδιώτης would not be regarded an insider (clearly not being proficient in tongues),³⁶ but neither is such a person categorized as an outsider—and, furthermore, there appears to be a recognized

---

³³ 2 Cor 11:6, "Even if I am unskilled in speaking (ἰδιώτης τῷ λόγῳ), I am not so in knowledge; indeed, in every way we have made this plain to you in all things."
³⁴ Thiselton, *First Epistle to the Corinthians*, 1114.
³⁵ This latter suggestion is one put forward by I. Howard Marshall in seminar discussion of this passage at the University of Aberdeen.
³⁶ Schlier, *TDNT* 3:217.

place for such people. Such a scenario within an early Christian community, it would appear, at least in Paul's view, is not unremarkable, but the community needs to moderate its behavior and practices in such an eventuality.

A few verses later, the term is used again, but in conjunction with another, clearer term—that of the unbeliever. "If, therefore, the whole church comes together and all speak in tongues, and ἰδιῶται or unbelievers (ἄπιστοι) enter, will they not say that you are out of your minds? But if all prophesy, and an unbeliever (τις ἄπιστος) or ἰδιώτης enters, he is convicted by all, he is called to account by all" (1 Cor 14:23-24 ESV). In this hypothetical scenario, either unbelievers or ἰδιῶται are deemed to have entered the meeting place, and are presumably regarded as welcome, rather than hostile, visitors in what we may reasonably assume to be a private setting—probably the home of a believer—and, again, this is not considered by the apostle to be a remote possibility. The obvious question raised here is whether there is an intended distinction or identification between the ἰδιῶται and the unbelievers (ἄπιστοι).

At this point, Schlier categorically affirms that the context demands there be no distinction: "the ἰδιῶται are not a middle group between ἄπιστοι and πιστοί."[37] BDAG, on the other hand, considers the two adjacent terms ἰδιώτης and ἄπιστος not to be identical; rather the ἰδιώτης is a relative outsider, equivalent to a non-member of a religious group, who may nonetheless participate in sacrifices, whereas the ἄπιστος is a clear outsider—albeit that it is considered conceivable that either of these may be present in the church gathering.[38] It is clear that the eventual and desired reaction of both categories of people is that they fall on their face and worship God, declaring the divine presence in their midst (1 Cor 14:25)—and, to this end, prophecy is to be preferred to tongues when either an ἰδιώτης or ἄπιστος is present.

As it stands, the context in 1 Corinthians is not sufficiently clear for the interpreter to make a categorical decision here about the nature of one who is an ἰδιώτης. Irenaeus, in *Against Heresies* 1.6.4, outlining what he understands to be the views of the later Gnostics, notes that they consider there to be three categories of people: there are those who are spiritual, perfect and elect; then, there are those of the church, among whom Irenaeus is numbered, and these are considered to be "animal persons," without understanding (ὡς ἰδιωτῶν, καὶ μηδὲν ἐπισταμένων);[39] and lastly, there are those who are "material," that is unconverted. The second grouping consists in those described as ἰδιῶται. Here, the term is clearly not used to denote those who merely lack education, but those who are not elect (but nonetheless in the church). Irenaeus' concern for his own readers is that his opponents will, by their deceit, lead astray those who are "simple-minded" (ἄπειρος, Irenaeus, *Against Heresies* 1.Pref.1). He

---

[37] Schlier, *TDNT* 3:217.

[38] BDAG, s.v.

[39] Cf. the phrase μηδὲν ἐπιστάμενος in 1 Tim 6:4.

later argues that it is better to be classed among the unlearned (ἰδιώτας καὶ ὀλιγομαθεῖς), than consider oneself to be learned (πολυμαθεῖς καὶ ἐμπείρους), but, in fact be blasphemous (*Against Heresies* 2.26.1). In these passages, it is evident that both Irenaeus and his opponents consider that there are those who are "unlearned," but nonetheless of the church—but, they disagree over the nature of the salvation of these ἰδιῶται. For Irenaeus, the salvation of the ἰδιῶται is to be protected.

Earlier, in 1 Cor 6:1, 6, Paul has linked the terms "unbelievers" and "unrighteous"—and clearly both are referring to those who engage in judicial processes, and are contrasted with the terms "brother" and "saints." Paul makes a clear distinction between insiders and outsiders. We have now seen that the term "unbeliever" also occurs alongside ἰδιώτης in 1 Cor 14:23-24, but that it is not only a term that Luke can use of Peter and John, and Paul can use, at least hypothetically, in regard to himself, but it also seems that the ἰδιώτης might have a recognized "place" within the community (1 Cor 14:16), perhaps as a visitor from another community, or a regularly attending, non-believing member of the household of a brother or sister. If so, the apostle is saying that when the church gathers and is either praying in tongues or prophesying, one may expect the presence of three categories of people: the believer, the ἰδιώτης, and the unbeliever. Although perhaps distinct categories, the believers should consider the potential reactions of *both* the unbeliever *and* the ἰδιώτης on entering and in some measure modify their traditional worship in order to accommodate whichever of these is present. To this extent, behavior is moderated in one and the same way in order to accommodate both categories of people. The suggestion here is that the ἰδιώτης has a foot in both camps—he has a recognized place but does not fully comprehend the Corinthian cultic practices; accordingly, the Corinthians should modify their behavior for this person in much the same way that their behavior should accommodate the presence of an unbeliever.

FURTHER DISTINCTIONS WITHIN THE CORINTHIAN COMMUNITY

Other instances in 1 Corinthians further suggest that distinctions are recognized by Paul in regard to the Corinthian congregation. Paul is aware of some among them who lack knowledge and whose consciences are weak (1 Cor 8:7-12), but should nonetheless, or all the more, be shown love and built up. There are some who are considered πνευματικοί (1 Cor 2:13, 15) where others are σαρκικοί (1 Cor 3:3). Also, there are some who possess insufficient maturity (contrasted with those who are numbered ἐν τοῖς τελείοις [1 Cor 2:6]). These are chastised by the apostle for acting like mere infants (1 Cor 3:1-2).

Each of these categories constitutes a measure of distinction between different members, in the eyes of the apostle. In addition, Paul is also critical of some in Corinth who were observing distinctions, or degrees of inclusion, where there should be none. For example, some brothers were pursuing their fellow believers in the lawcourts before the unrighteous and unbelievers (1 Cor 6:1-11)—but they failed to recognize that even those who might be considered the least in the church (τοὺς ἐξουθενημένους, 1 Cor 6:4) are better able to adjudicate minor civil disagreements than those outside. Finally, there were some who might be regarded by certain Corinthians as "more presentable," while others might have been considered unpresentable, weaker and less honorable (1 Cor 12:22-24). Paul's corrective message is that the same regard should be held for all, and the weaker parts are actually indispensable.

Thus, both Paul and the Corinthians, on a number of issues and not always in agreement, were recognizing differences among those who belonged—and from some perspectives this amounted to degrees of belonging. Counter to this, and apparently at odds with it, is Paul's extensive use in 1 Corinthians, and elsewhere, of language that clearly reinforces black-and-white categories of belonging. For the apostle, there is an absolute distinction between those who do and those who do not inherit the Kingdom of God (1 Cor 6:9-11)—and among the latter are numbered the greedy and the drunk (cf. also 1 Cor 5:9-11). A favorite category of his are those who are described as being "in Christ" or "in Christ Jesus" (1 Cor 1:2, 4, 30; 4:10, 15; 15:18). This mystical language of being a unity "in Christ" is extended by a number of other Corinthian metaphors of community: a single body into which all are initiated by the boundary marker of baptism (1 Cor 12, 14);[40] a single temple (1 Cor 3:16-17; 6:19); a single building or field (1 Cor 3:9); and a single loaf (1 Cor 10:17). Significantly, in 1 Corinthians Paul also makes wide use of kinship language as a category that distinguishes those who belong from those who do not.[41] Furthermore, "insiders" were together expected to have an exclusive relation with God, reflected in 1 Corinthians by means of sacred "temple of the Holy Spirit/God" language (1 Cor 3:16-17; 6:19). Similarly, no one who belongs to Christ can drink both the cup of the Lord and the cup of demons (1 Cor 10:20-21). There is, after all, only one God, the father, and one Lord, Jesus Christ (1 Cor 8:6).

So, in a letter in which Paul clearly and categorically distinguishes between "insiders" and "outsiders," language expressing the unity of the body is juxtaposed alongside language about accommodating difference. In the same letter, Paul criticizes some Corinthians for the ways in which they had developed degrees of segregation and inclusion. Yet, on the one hand he himself criticizes the less mature in the church, and on the other hand he urges the more mature to engender a greater sense of inclusion of those who are less

---

[40] In the metaphor of the body, of course, Paul underlines the significance of diversity and many parts.

[41] Mary Katherine Birge, *The Language of Belonging: A Rhetorical Analysis of Kinship Language in First Corinthians* (Leuven: Peeters, 2002); Philip A. Harland, "Familial Dimensions of Group Identity: 'Brothers' (ἀδελφοί) in Associations of the Greek East," *JBL* 124 (2005): 491-513.

mature, whether in their theology or their actions. Furthermore, there appear to be aspects of black and white alongside large areas of grey—a recognition that some who attend may be in a different "place" in regard to their grasp of tongues; others, although not yet saved, are nonetheless made holy by their spouse or parent; and still others may remain brothers, but, on account of their immorality, should be kept at a distance, in order that their souls may nonetheless be saved. A consistent feature, however, is that behavior within the Christian community should, in particular ways, accommodate those who are on the fringes of that community.

13

OLD TESTAMENT PARADOXES IN GALATIANS: RETHINKING THE THEOLOGY OF GALATIANS

Maureen W. Yeung

INTRODUCTION

It is no exaggeration that Professor I. Howard Marshall's works represent British biblical scholarship at its finest. My journey as a student of the New Testament benefited greatly from his friendship and mentorship not only during my stay in Aberdeen, but also during his subsequent visits to Evangel Seminary. I learned from his inspiring example what true biblical scholarship means: rigorous pursuit of the meaning of the Word of God done in a spirit of openness and humility. It is my honor to dedicate the following article to my good friend and mentor in recognition of his enduring contribution to biblical scholarship.

The significance of Professor Marshall's *New Testament Theology* (2004) lies in his methodology of doing NT theology.[1] His four main concerns reflect his convictions about NT theology. First, NT theology should be seen as part of biblical theology, thus due attention must be given to the substructure provided by the OT. Second, NT theology was articulated in the context of missions. "New Testament theology is essentially missionary theology."[2] Third and fourth, the theology of each document must be examined individually first, followed by attempts to detect the theological unity that permeates them. New Testament theology is found to be one unified theology with complementary voices. In each NT text a strong voice is heard, which should not be drowned by the other voices. Together they constitute multiple and complementary witnesses to the one gospel.[3]

This article is an attempt to rethink the theology of the Letter to the Galatians in the spirit of Professor Marshall's *New Testament Theology*. According to Professor Marshall, the contribution of Galatians to the message of the gospel is "an understanding of Jesus as the son of God sent into the world to redeem people from the curse of the law, and of God's Spirit sent into

---

[1] I. Howard Marshall, *New Testament Theology* (Downers Grove: InterVarsity, 2004), 17-48.
[2] Marshall, *New Testament Theology*, 34.
[3] Marshall, *New Testament Theology*, 707-708.

the hearts of believers to make them children of God."⁴ He rightly recognizes the enormous impact of the Jewish Scriptures on Paul's thought: "Characteristic of this letter is the way in which the use of Scripture dominates much of the discussion, almost providing the structure of the argument as well as the basis for it."⁵ We want to take up this characteristic and examine the extent to which the Jewish Scriptures provide seminal ideas or grids for the gospel preached by Paul as expressed in the Letter to the Galatians. Our specific questions are: How significant is the OT background at the back of the mind of one of the greatest missionaries of the early Church as he reiterates the gospel to the Galatians? If the OT background dominates Paul's thought in the Letter to the Galatians, can it help us to unlock key expressions in the letter which are hitherto controversial in meaning?

THREE PARADOXES IN GALATIANS

In the following we shall focus our attention on three expressions in Galatians pertaining to the gospel and study how the OT background serves as a crucial aid to unlock their meanings. Interestingly, they all constitute *surprises* to the readers, albeit in different ways:

1."The Seed of Abraham" (Gal 3:16, 29)

After emphasizing that "the seed (σπέρμα) of Abraham" refers to one person and not many (3:16), Paul surprises his readers later when he says that all believers are also "the seed (σπέρμα) of Abraham" (3:29). Although Paul has prepared his readers for the concept of plurality in 3:7: "it is those of faith that are sons [υἱοί] of Abraham," the word used there is "sons" and not "seed."

2."The Law of Christ" (Gal 6:2)

After denigrating the Mosaic law throughout his letter, Paul surprises the reader when he suddenly injects the expression "the law of Christ" at the final section of the letter (6:2). Paul appears to hold a negative view of the law, using expressions such as "works of the law" (2:16 [twice]; 3:2, 5, 10) and "under law" (4:5, 21) to describe people under the slavery of the law. It baffles the mind of the readers to see Paul associating the law with Christ in his conclusion.

3."The Israel of God" (Gal 6:16)

Throughout his letter Paul erases the ethnic differences between Jewish and Gentile believers (e.g., 3:28). What matters is not whether one is circumcised, but whether one is God's new creation (6:15). It comes as a surprise when Paul in what immediately follows pronounces that "for all who walk by this rule, peace and mercy be upon them, and

---

⁴ Marshall, *New Testament Theology*, 234.
⁵ Marshall, *New Testament Theology*, 216.

upon the Israel of God." Why does he bring in the ethnic category "Israel" if ethnic distinctions are erased?

What is Paul doing here? While the first surprise is easier to explain, the second and the third are *cruces interpretum*. Many scholars, in an attempt to eliminate these uncomfortable or contradictory strands in the letter, interpret Paul's difficult expressions metaphorically or loosely. Thus, "the law of Christ" refers either to Christ's teachings or the love command of Jesus Christ. "The Israel of God" is understood to be an umbrella term for all believers, Gentile as well as Jewish. Obviously any difficult passage in a book should be interpreted against the context of the whole book, but the issue at stake is whether such readings aiming at harmonization actually do justice to the context of the book. The efforts at harmonization may well be in danger of stressing the dominant voice at the expense of drowning a counterpoint. The questions that need to be asked are thus: does the context of the letter allow for room for such tensions or contradictions? Does the plain meaning of the difficult expressions make better sense of the text and does it do greater justice to the message of the letter? Does the acceptance of tensions and contradictions in the Apostle's thought actually yield a more comprehensive understanding of the gospel presented by Paul?

Our answers to the above questions are affirmative. If we allow Paul to express himself in contradictory terms, then we are in a position to appreciate these three surprises as genuine *paradoxes*. These paradoxes encapsulate the tensions in the letter:

1."The Seed of Abraham" refers at the same time to one person (i.e., Christ, 3:16) and to many people (i.e., believers, 3:29).

2."The law of Christ" probably means that Christ is the Lord of the Mosaic law. Only in Christ who frees the believer from keeping the law (2:19) can the believer truly fulfill the law (5:14, 22-23; 6:2).

3."The Israel of God" refers to the faithful remnant in the nation of Israel (6:16). Seen in this light, the gospel both eliminates and retains ethnic distinctions. On the one hand, God justifies all people on the basis of faith irrespective of his/her ethnicity (5:15). Thus, in Christ all believers gain the same identity as children of God (3:28). On the other hand, parallel missions undertaken to evangelize the Jews and the Gentiles result in the formation of God's people comprising two entities, Jewish and Gentile Christians (2:7-9). The fellowship between these two groups within God's community testifies to the unity achieved in Christ (2:10). The benefits of the gospel are evident when God's peace and mercy rests upon his people: the restored Israel together with all the believing Gentiles (6:16).

RESEARCH QUESTIONS

If we accept the paradoxes in Galatians at face value, the next question is: Are the paradoxes more likely Paul's invention or Paul's development of the biblical traditions? To answer this question we may ask further: Can we find precedents in the Hebrew Scriptures or in the Jewish biblical traditions? If so, in what way has Paul used Scripture and/or the traditions? Do the Hebrew Scriptures and/or the Jewish biblical traditions provide the background for the interpretation of Paul's difficult expressions?

In the following discussion we will see that there are indeed precedents in the Hebrew Scriptures. We shall see that they function as keys to unlocking the difficult expressions in Galatians.

"THE SEED OF ABRAHAM"

C. John Collins, building on the work of Jack Collins and Desmond Alexander, demonstrates that Paul's interpretation of "the seed of Abraham" as a single individual (Gal 3:16) is legitimate.[6] He proposes that the text in Paul's thought is Gen 22:18, where the term "seed", by virtue of its syntactical usage, must refer to a single individual. His arguments need not be rehearsed here. Suffice to point out the ramifications of his arguments for our study.

C. John Collins's conclusion has immense implication for the understanding of the paradox of "the seed of Abraham" in Galatians. If "the seed of Abraham" in the account of Abraham can refer to a single individual (the Messiah as Paul understands it) and/or all of Abraham's descendants, the paradox of "the seed of Abraham" in Galatians as referring at the same time to Christ (Gal 3:16) and to all believers in Christ (Gal 3:29) is not Paul's invention. Paul is merely putting to the fore the paradox already implicit in the Genesis narrative. Indeed, Gen 22:17-18 may well be one of the key passages in Paul's mind when he expounds the meaning of "the seed of Abraham". When he says that all nations will be blessed by the one "seed" (Gal 3:16), he may well be referring to that special descendant of Abraham that "will possess the gate of his enemies" and in whom all nations will be blessed in Gen 22:17b-18. When Paul says all Christians are the "seed" of Abraham (Gal 3:29), he may have in mind Gen 22:17a and all the related passages, which promise that Abraham's seed will be as numerous as the stars in the sky and as the sand on the seashore. Paul presents this paradox skillfully using the Greek word σπέρμα which, similar to the Hebrew word זרע, can have singular or collective references. This is parallel but not equivalent to the concept of υἱός/υἱοί, which is another key theme in Galatians. Whereas the word play does not work in the case of υἱός/υἱοί, it works in the case of σπέρμα.

In actual fact the Son Christology is important in Galatians.[7] Jesus Christ, as

---

[6] Jack Collins, "A Syntactical Note (Genesis 3:15): Is the Woman's Seed Singular or Plural?" *TynBul* 48 (1997): 139-48; T. D. Alexander, "Further Observations on the Term 'Seed' in Genesis," *TynBul* 48 (1997): 363-67; C. John Collins, "Galatians 3:16: What Kind of Exegete was Paul?" *TynBul* 54 (2003): 75-86.

[7] Gordon Fee, *Pauline Christology: An Exegetical-Theological Study* (Peabody, Mass.: Hendrickson Publishers, 2007), 208-209.

the Son of God (1:16), completes his work on the cross. In accepting the Son of God, believers become sons of God. Believers do not become sons of God ontologically, but they are bestowed the spirit of Christ, which means they inherit the life of Christ, thereby making them truly sons of God. In using the son imagery, Paul draws an important parallel between Christ and the believers, thereby highlighting the theme of grace.

The σπέρμα paradox serves a slightly different purpose. It is used in conjunction with the theme of promise. In the days of yore, God had promised the blessing through Christ. Christ is the seed of Abraham, which emphasizes his human nature when he came to abolish the hold of the law through becoming a man under the law. When Christian believers accept Christ's work on the cross by faith, they die to the law. In following Abraham's example of justification by faith, Christian believers express the same kind of faith as their ancestor did and thereby prove that they are truly the seed of Abraham.

Whereas the paradox of "the seed of Abraham" is implicit in the Hebrew Scriptures, Paul's discussion of the plural reference of "the seed of Abraham" is to a great extent his own reflection on the Scriptures. His explicit application of "the seed of Abraham" to Gentile as well as Jewish believers is unusual in the Jewish biblical tradition, if not unique. His use of Isa 54:1 (Gal 4:27) to support such reference of "the seed of Abraham" is fresh, if not unprecedented.

When we compare Paul's thought with contemporary Jewish literature, Paul's uniqueness stands out. The Septuagint does not show any remarkable difference from the MT.[8] Josephus states that God promised Abraham that his race would swell "into many nations" (εἰς ἔθνη πολλά) and would subdue Canaan (*Ant.* 1.235, my translation). Philo briefly mentions the proliferation of Abraham's seed (*Alleg. Interp.* 3.203) but does not develop the theme further. When we compare Paul with the Isaiah Targum, however, there are some interesting findings.

"Abraham" is one of the characteristic terms of the Isaiah Targum.[9] Unlike Paul, the Targum consistently describes Abraham as the father of the ethnic nation of Israel (5:1; 41:2; 43:12a; 46:11; 48:15-16), so much so that Abraham is separated from the Gentiles:

I, *by my Memra decreed a covenant with Abraham your father* and *exalted* him, I brought him *to the land of my Shekhinah's house* and *I*

---

[8] The Septuagint is less clear than the MT on the singular reference of the seed in Gen 22:17b: "and your seed shall possess the cities of the enemies [καὶ κληρονομήσει τὸ σπέρμα σου τὰς πόλεις τῶν ὑπεναντίων]."

[9] Bruce D. Chilton, *The Glory of Israel: The Theology and Provenience of the Isaiah Targum* (JSOTSup 23; Sheffield: JSOT Press, 1983), 46-48.

prosper*ed his way.*[10] (*Tg. Isa.* 43:15)

> Draw near to *my Memra,* hear this: from *the* beginning I have not spoken in secret, from the time *the Gentiles separated from my fear, from* there I *brought Abraham near to my service."* The prophet said, and now the LORD God has sent me and his *Memra.* (*Tg. Isa.* 43:16)

Accordingly, there is "no stranger" when God gave the law to Israel, Abraham's descendants:

> I declared *to Abraham your father what was about to come,* I saved *you from Egypt, just as I swore to him between the pieces,* I proclaimed *to you the teaching of my law from Sinai,* when *you were present and* there was no stranger among you; and you are witnesses *before* me," says the LORD, "and I am God." (*Tg. Isa.* 43:12)

Note especially that the Targum has converted "no foreign god" in the Hebrew text to "no foreigner/stranger."

This is not to say that the Isaiah Targum does not envisage the inclusion of Gentiles into God's people, because there are obvious references. For instance:

> Let not a son of *Gentiles* who has *been added* to *the people of* the LORD say, "The LORD will surely separate me from his people" .... (*Tg. Isa.* 56:3)

> And the sons of the *Gentiles* who *have been added* to *the people of* the LORD, to minister to him .... (*Tg. Isa.* 56:6)

Indeed, immediately following 43:12, the Targum speaks favorably of a river in Gentile land and interestingly mixes the numerous descendants of Abraham with the river language. Nonetheless, these descendants are still clearly "Israel":

> If you had hearkened to my commandments, *then* your peace would have been like *the overflowing of the Euphrates* river, and your *innocence* like the waves of the sea; (*Tg. Isa.* 48:18)

> *then* your *sons* would have been *numerous* as the sand *of the sea,* and your *sons' sons* as its pebbles; the name *of Israel* would not *cease* or be destroyed before me *for ever.* (*Tg. Isa.* 48:19)

---

[10] Translations from the Targum of Isaiah are quoted from Bruce D. Chilton, *The Isaiah Targum* (The Aramaic Bible 11; Collegeville: Liturgical Press, 1987). The additions and deviations from the MT are represented in italics.

The understanding of the collective seed of Abraham as including not just Israel, but also the Gentiles, is Paul's fresh interpretation of the Isaianic oracles. Paul probably interprets Isa 54:1 against the immediate context, which in the following verses describes the expansion of God's people into the lands of the nations (54:3). More importantly, "the Holy One of Israel" is seen to be "the God of all the earth" (54:5). Paul probably sees it as describing the inclusion of the Gentiles into God's people, the heavenly Jerusalem, which is the barren woman, and also the seed of Abraham and Sarah.

Whereas the Isaiah Targum also identifies the barren woman with Jerusalem, it strangely contrasts it with Rome:

> Sing, O *Jerusalem who was as a* barren *woman* who did not bear; shout in singing and exult, *[you who were]* as a woman who did not become pregnant! For the children of desolate *Jerusalem will be* more than the children of *inhabited Rome*, says the LORD. (*Tg. Isa.* 54:1)

It is Paul who reinterprets the Isaianic oracles and draws out the implicit references to the inclusion of Gentiles into the people of God.

The above discussion shows that Paul's understanding of "the seed of Abraham" is influenced by multiple Jewish texts. He brings the implicit double reference of "the seed of Abraham" in the Genesis narrative to the fore, demonstrating that "the seed of Abraham" refers at the same time to Christ and the spiritual heirs of Abraham. He departs from the Jewish traditions in extending the reference of the descendants of Abraham to incorporate Gentile believers into the community of Jewish believers. He does this partly on the basis of the Isaianic oracles. In other words, Paul traces the gospel to the OT and establishes the continuity of justification by faith throughout all generations. Paul's understanding of the gospel is therefore very much a gospel based on the Hebrew Scriptures.

"THE LAW OF CHRIST"

"The law of Christ" is more difficult. There is an increasing tendency among scholars to take the law as a reference to the Mosaic law.[11] This is required by the text, as we can see for the following three reasons.

First, there are altogether twenty-nine uses of the word νόμος in the Letter to the Galatians, and all refer to the Mosaic Law. The burden of proof is therefore for scholars to prove that the νόμος in 6:2 refers to something other than the Mosaic law.

Second, the understanding of the νόμος in 6:2 is heralded by 5:14, which

---

[11] See the trend portrayed by Todd A. Wilson in "The Law of Christ and the Law of Moses: Reflections on a Recent Trend in Interpretation," *Currents in Biblical Research* 5 (2006): 123-44.

announces that the whole law is fulfilled by "love." Leviticus 19:18 is cited, which suggests that Paul still upholds the standards of the Mosaic law. Galatians 6:2 continues to enumerate the practical outworkings of love.

If the νόμος of 6:2 refers to Mosaic law, what does "the law of Christ" mean? Grammatically, the expression can mean something like "Christ is the lord of the law," "the law which belongs to Christ," "Christ is the author or originator of the law." Does such understanding fit well into the letter?

A close examination of Paul's stance toward the law shows that his attitude toward it is not altogether negative. He is surely negative about "the works of the law," which is another way of saying "keeping the law," but nowhere does he disparage the law itself. As a matter of fact, he cites at least two positive values of the law: curtailing sin (3:19) and leading people to Christ (3:24).

If Paul's attitude towards the law is not that negative, what could the expression "the law of Christ" mean? Can any OT reference point be at the back of Paul's mind? Can any OT passage help to unlock Paul's expression?

I suggest that Isa 40–66 could well have influenced Paul. In the next section, we shall cite evidence showing that Paul, besides quoting Isa 54:1 in Gal 4:27, actually uses the immediate context of Isa 54 in his argument. In this section, we suggest that not only Isa 54, but also the larger context of Isa 40–66, forms the background of Paul's theology.

What is worthy of note is that the key theological concepts in the Letter to the Galatians are also present in Isa 40–66, namely: the gospel (Gal 1:6, 7, 8; cf. Isa 40:9; 52:7; 61:1); faith in the message (Gal 2:20; 3:7-14; cf. Isa 53:1; 55:1); redemption (Gal 3:13; 4:5; 5:1; cf. Isa 42:7; 43:4; 61:1); the Son/Servant of God (Gal 1:16; 2:20; cf. LXX Isa 42:1 παῖς = servant/child/son); the law of loving one's neighbor (Gal 5:14; 6:2; cf. Isa 58:6-7); and finally the Spirit (Gal 3:14; 5:16; cf. Isa 42:1; 59:21; 61:1). The thesis that Paul defends in this letter is that the gospel emancipates us from sin when by faith we trust the Son of God who then sends his Spirit into our hearts to enable us to live out the law. This message corresponds to the Isaianic oracles, especially the paradigm relating to the Spirit and the law.

In Isa 40–66, we see how God promises to save his people through his servant (which can also be translated as "son" according to LXX Isa 42:1). This servant/son is anointed by God's Spirit (Isa 61:1), who is also the Spirit God places in his covenant people (Isa 59:21). With the power of God's Spirit, God's covenant people are able to shine (Isa 60:1) and live out God's commandments like loving one's neighbor, which the people hitherto had failed to do (Isa 58).

Isaiah 59:21 is particularly telling. God's promise to place his Spirit in his covenant people is accompanied by his promise to place his words in their mouths forever. God's words are nothing other than his law and commandments. In other words, when God places his Spirit in his people, he places his law in them as well.

Such association between the law and the Spirit is strengthened in the Isaiah

Targum which adds "to the law" to 59:20 and specifies the Spirit in 59:21 as the "holy" Spirit:

> And he will come to Zion as Redeemer, to *return the rebels of the house of* Jacob *to the law,* says the LORD. And as for me, this is my covenant with them, says the LORD, my *holy* spirit which is upon you, and *the* words *of* my *prophecy* which I have put in your mouth, shall not *pass* out of your mouth, or out of the mouth of your *sons,* or out of the mouth of your *sons' sons,* says the Lord, from this time forth and for evermore. (*Tg. Isa.* 58:20-21)

This relationship between God's bestowal of his Spirit and his law on his people may shed light on Paul's phrase of "the law of Christ." As Gordon Fee points out, "the Christological dimension of this phrase is considerable indeed and is related in concept to Christ's being 'formed' in them (4:19)."[12] Christ the Son is the perfect image of God the Father. He defines the law and lives out the law. To have Christ is to have the law. To have his Spirit is to have the law. When a person believes in the gospel message, this Son of God begins to live in him/her (2:20) as God sends his Spirit (= Spirit of his Son, 4:6), which he had promised in the OT, into that person's heart (3:14). When that believer walks in step with the Spirit, that is, follows the promptings of the Son of God who lives in him/her, that person will naturally be able to fulfill the desires of Christ, which is equivalent to fulfilling the ultimate purpose of the Mosaic law.

Seen in this light, Paul's expression "the law of Christ" is a genuine paradox. No one can keep the law by his/her own efforts because of one's own sinful human nature (5:17). Paradoxically, only in Christ, who frees the believer from the impossible task of keeping the Mosaic law, can the believer fulfill the law. Christ is the lord of the law. Christ defines the law and imparts the ability to fulfill the law. The believer fulfills the law of Christ by following the lead of the Spirit of Christ, who now dwells inside him/her.

If our interpretation is correct, then we should not pitch the gospel against the law. Inasmuch as the gospel is "the gospel of Christ" (1:7), so also the law is "the law of Christ" (6:2). The dichotomy between the gospel and the law concerns the way one attains to the standards of God, not the origin of the gospel and the law, for both come from God. After all, the gospel is attested by the law (cf. Rom 3:21)!

"THE ISRAEL OF GOD"

There is also good evidence that the difficult expression "the Israel of God" (Gal 6:16) may be better understood using the OT background.

---

[12] Fee, *Pauline Christology*, 231.

We are indebted to the works of Roy Ciampa,[13] G. Beale,[14] Ross Wagner,[15] and others for the possible allusions to Scripture in Galatians, specifically the use of the concept of servanthood in Gal 1 and 2, and the use of Isa 54 in Gal 6:15-16. The cumulative effect is that Isaiah is seen to be an important background in Galatians.

Beale draws attention to several features which suggest the use of Isa 54 in Gal 6:15-16, the more important ones being: Isa 54:1 as quoted in Gal 4:27; the occurrence of "peace" and "mercy" in close proximity; and the mentioning of "a new creation" in Gal 6:15, which alludes to Isaiah.[16]

In our view, however, Beale has not fully capitalized on his important finding. While Beale is right in suggesting Isa 54 as the probable background to the idea of peace and mercy resting on the Israel of God, his interpretation of the Isaianic background falls short of presenting the import of the prophecy.

Paul's paradox on the relationship between the Jews and the Gentiles is implicit in the Isaianic oracles. The picture in Isaiah, however, is a fairly complex one.

Attention should be drawn to the fact that there are already tensions of thought concerning the eschatological people of God in Isa 40–66. The relationship between Israel the elect of God and the Gentiles (regularly denoted by terms such as "nations" and "islands," as well as by phrases such as "all flesh" and "the ends of the earth") is particularly intricate for at least three reasons.

First, the nations are both enemies of and fellow-worshippers with Israel. The contrasting tones are set from the outset in Isa 40. The Lord promises to vindicate Israel (or Jerusalem) against the nations, which He uses to discipline his people (40:2, 10). The nations cannot stand before the Lord who comes to rescue Israel (40:15-17, 23). At the same time, when the Lord acts in a mighty way, the nations are astounded and come to see the glory of God. The term "all" in "all flesh" (40:5) and "all the nations" (40:17) is significant in introducing the theme of the nations coming to the knowledge of God. In the subsequent passages, these two contrasting themes form the counterpoints in the Isaianic symphony. Thus, while God will subdue the nations (e.g., 63:6), nations will come to join Israel in worshipping the Lord (e.g., 66:19-21).

Second, there is a certain fluidity in the identity of Israel. Israel is both the ethnic Israel and the spiritual Israel at the same time. The term "Israel" appears forty-eight times in Isa 40–66. Apart from that reference in 63:16, which refers to Jacob the patriarch, and the exceptional use in 49:3, which probably refers to

---

[13] Roy E. Ciampa, *The Presence and Function of Scripture in Galatians 1 and 2* (Tübingen: Mohr [Siebeck], 1998).

[14] G. K. Beale, "Peace and Mercy upon the Israel of God," *Bib* 80 (1999): 204-23.

[15] J. Ross Wagner, *Heralds of the Good News: Isaiah and Paul <in Concert> in the Letter to the Romans* (NovTSup 101; Leiden: Brill, 2002).

[16] Beale, "Peace and Mercy," 208-11.

the Messiah (cf. 49:6), most occurrences refer to the ethnic people of Israel. This usage is obvious in cases such as 40:27; 42:24; 43:14, 28; 45:3, 4, 15; 48:1, 2; and 49:6. Israel is God's people whom God had chosen from ancient days. They had the law but rebelled against God. God in his faithfulness to his covenant with Abraham had promised to redeem the exiled from among the nations. This usage places "Israel" in contradistinction, and sometimes even in opposition, to the nations.

On the other hand, there are also a few instances where the preceding contexts suggest that the term "Israel" must include the nations, so especially in 45:25 and 56:8. In the former case, God appeals to "all you ends of the earth," that is, all the peoples, to turn to him (45:22). The "descendants of Israel" in 45:25 must include all the people, Gentiles as well as Israelites, who bend their knees before God (45:23), and they will certainly be found righteous (45:25). In the latter case, God promises he will not exclude the foreigner who joins himself to God (56:3), but will grant him joy and the privilege of serving him (56:6-7). Seen in this context, "the exiles of Israel" (56:8a) whom God will gather probably comprise the Gentiles ("others," 56:8b) as well as the ethnic Israelites ("those already gathered," 56:8c). This more metaphorical or spiritual usage of the term "Israel" enlarges Israel to include the nations. The two entities form the true Israel, which obeys and adheres to the Lord.

Third, at times in Isa 40–66, the nations are seen to be a parallel member of Israel. This is particularly the case in the process of forming a spiritual Israel from the two entities. In 49:6, the mission of the Servant of the Lord to "restore the tribes of Jacob and bring back . . . Israel" is paralleled with the mission to "be a light for the Gentiles . . . and bring . . . salvation to the ends of the earth." In 66:20, the brothers brought from among the nations are accepted by God just as are the grain offerings offered by the sons of Israel. In other words, the Gentiles are accepted as clean and holy by God just as are the obedient Israelites.

Spectacularly, in 54:5b God is called the God of these two communities: "the Holy One of Israel is your Redeemer; he is called the God of all the earth." Here, "the Holy One of Israel" parallels "the God of all the earth." This equal footing and juxtaposing relationship between Israel and the nations is missed by the Septuagint, which translates the clause as "and the one who delivered you is the very God of Israel; he shall be called thus in all the earth" (καὶ ὁ ῥυσάμενός σε αὐτὸς θεὸς Ἰσραηλ πάσῃ τῇ γῇ κληθήσεται).

The coexistence of the above three strands sheds light on the complex relationship between Israel and the Gentiles in the Isaianic oracles. Paradoxically the ethnic boundaries are both preserved and eradicated in Isaiah's eschatological vision. Isaiah envisions an eschatological people of God, which includes not only the repentant ethnic Israel, but also the Gentiles. Ethnicity is no longer a barrier to drawing close to God. In the process of the formation of this people of God, however, ethnicity plays a historical role. Nations come to worship the Lord through contact with Israel. They see the mighty acts of "the Holy One of Israel" for the sake of his people, and they come to worship him who is also "the God of all the earth."

The paradoxical relationship between Israel and the Gentiles is kept in later Jewish biblical traditions. The Isaianic Targum sharpens the paradox by its additions and deviations. On the one hand, Israel is opposed to the Gentiles:

> For you shall not go out in haste *from among the peoples,* and you shall not *be brought* in flight *to your land.* (*Tg. Isa.* 52:12)

Similar usages are found in *Tg. Isa.* 53:8, 11; 55:12. Moreover, the Israelites are the special people of God by virtue of their possession of the law:

> *Behold,* we are *your people who are* from of old. You *did* not *give your law to the Gentiles,* your name is not called upon them. (*Tg. Isa.* 63:19)

However, amidst this negative assessment of the Gentiles, a clear and astounding note is sounded concerning the acceptance of Gentiles into the people of God:

> Let not a son of *Gentiles* who has *been added* to *the people of* the LORD say, "The LORD will surely separate me from his people" . . . . (*Tg. Isa.* 56:3)

> And the sons of the *Gentiles* who *have been added* to *the people of* the LORD, to minister to him . . . . (*Tg. Isa.* 56:6)

Furthermore, the Gentiles are not just absorbed into Israel as if they were mere recipients of the benefits of Israel. They are equal partners of Israel as they also bring blessings to Israel:

> For thus saith the LORD: "Behold, I *bring* peace to her like *the overflowing of the Euphrates* river, and the glory of the *Gentiles* like a swelling stream; and you shall *be indulged,* you shall be carried upon hips, and *exalted* upon knees. (*Tg. Isa.* 66:12)

The Isaianic oracles and the subsequent biblical tradition may well have provided the background to Paul's thought. Seen against this backdrop, the expression "the Israel of God" becomes comprehensible. It is not out of place in Galatians. It provides an apt conclusion to Paul's argument. As a conclusion, when Paul speaks of the rich benefits of the gospel, in contrast to the curse brought about by preaching a false gospel, it is most appropriate to pronounce the blessings upon the two equal entities, which constitute the one people of God.

A close examination of the preceding context of Galatians confirms this suggestion. Many who object to understanding "the Israel of God" as referring to Jewish Christians claim that to interpret it in this way is to introduce a new idea to the letter, especially in its conclusion of all places. However, the existence of the entity of Jewish Christians is by no means a new idea in the letter. An earlier paragraph had already prepared the readers for the introduction of ethnic Israel. In 2:7-9, Paul parallels his ministry to the Gentiles with Peter's ministry to the Jews. His mission to the Gentiles is seen to be just as God-commissioned and powerful as Peter's mission to the Jews. The fact that Paul fights to maintain the distinctiveness of his Gentile mission does not mean that he regards his mission to the Gentiles as taking over the mission to the Jews. In fact, Paul assumes the priority of Peter's mission to the Jews while asserting the comparable importance of his mission to the Gentiles. The proliferation of the *seed* of Abraham requires two parallel missions to the Jews and Gentiles.

Paul assumes the importance of the mission to God's elect. He in no way denigrates Peter's mission to the Jews. As a matter of fact, although Paul insists that the Galatian Christians should not succumb to the temptation of receiving circumcision, and although he denounces Peter as hypocritical in withdrawing from table-fellowship with the uncircumcised Galatian believers, and although Paul urges the Galatians to follow his example in not keeping the law (by table-fellowshipping with the uncircumcised believers), there is no hint that Paul would object to Jewish Christians still practicing the law if they treat it as daily habits and not as grounds of justification. Paul says that the believer has died to the law, but this does not necessarily mean that he would not perform some aspects of what the law requires in order to save people. Even though Paul does not air this sentiment in his Letter to the Galatians (cf. 1 Cor. 9:20), there is no hint in this letter that he requires Jews to relinquish their Jewish habits other than their previous refusal to accept Gentile believers. All this is to say that Paul values the mission to the Jews just as much as he values that to the Gentiles.

Seen in this light, Paul's statement that there is no difference between Jew and Gentile in 3:28 must be understood exclusively in the context of the benefits of the gospel and not in the context of evangelism. The gospel places all peoples on the same footing in Christ, but the process of preaching the gospel and making converts still takes place within different cultural contexts. In other words, Paul, in line with the Isaianic oracles, envisages the new creation of God's people as comprising Jews and Gentiles. His concluding benediction on those who follow "this rule" (the rule of boasting of Christ only and not of the law) and on "the Israel of God" is a blessing on the two entities of the one people of God, that is, the Gentiles represented by the Galatian converts who resist circumcision and the Jewish believers who are truly the Israel of God. God's salvific purpose is accomplished when these two groups share as equal partners in God's redemptive plan.

In sum, Paul's paradox already exists in Isaiah. An ethnic distinction both is and is not maintained in the new creation. On the one hand, it is maintained because it witnesses to God's plan of using the restored Zion to bless the nations. On the other hand, it is abolished because all peoples are equally blessed. Such a prominent theme in Isaiah is not likely to be missed by Paul. We suggest that it is this that prompts Paul to interject "the Israel of God" at the end of his letter, to remind the Gentiles that their blessings are to be enjoyed jointly with their Jewish counterparts. For the Apostle to pronounce blessings first to the Gentile believers, and then to the Israel of God (= Jewish believers) is most appropriate.

Conclusion

We started the discussion by asking whether we should take Paul's apparent paradoxes at face value. We wanted to know if the plain meaning of the difficult expressions makes better sense of the text and does greater justice to the message of the letter. We further wanted to know whether the OT background can help to unlock the meaning of these paradoxes.

After a detailed comparison between Paul and the Jewish biblical traditions, we finally conclude that there is good evidence indicating that the three paradoxes are genuine ones. They are not Paul's inventions, but paradoxes already implicit in the Hebrew Scriptures. What Paul has done is to develop the implicit paradoxes in the context of missionary theology. He has done so for the following three reasons.

First, in order to convince the Galatian believers that they are truly Abraham's seed solely by virtue of the redemptive work of *the* seed of Abraham, Paul follows the Genesis account to develop the twin ideas of a singular and plural seed of Abraham. Paul shows that Abraham's seed is one and many at the same time. On the sole basis of the work on the cross by Christ *the seed* of Abraham, which has nothing to do with works of the law, the Galatian believers are reckoned as Abraham's descendants.

Second, in order to dissuade the Galatian believers from being circumcised, Paul maintains that only when one dies to the law in Christ can he/she fulfill the law by the power of Christ in him/her. It is only through the paradoxical release from the Mosaic law that one can truly fulfill the law. The Spirit of Christ sent by God into the heart of the believer is the key to fulfilling the law.

Third, in order to encourage the Galatian believers to remain in the gospel and not to resort to keeping the law, Paul expounds the paradoxical relationship between Israel and the nations inherent in the Isaianic oracles. He seeks to eliminate and maintain ethnic differences at the same time. On the one hand, in Christ there is neither Jew nor Greek because all believers are children of God. The Galatian believers need not keep the law in order to be sons of God. On the other hand, the making of the one people of God comprises the two parallel missions to the Jews and the Gentiles. The Galatian believers need to bear in mind that, as Gentiles, they are fellow partakers with the Jews in the gospel.

Our study has demonstrated that the recognition of the paradoxical nature of the three difficult expressions does greater justice to the text than the effort to explain away exegetical difficulties by way of harmonization. The paradoxes are comprehensible if interpreted in the light of the OT. The acceptance of tensions in Paul's thought can actually help us to appreciate the complexities of the Apostle's theology in his Letter to the Galatians. Paul's gospel is seen to be very much a gospel foretold and promised in the Hebrew Scriptures (cf. Rom 1:2)!

14

MISSIO DEI AND *IMITATIO DEI* IN EPHESIANS

Roy E. Ciampa

I. Howard Marshall has suggested that the writings of the NT may most helpfully be described as "the documents of a mission" and that "New Testament theology is essentially missionary theology."[1]

The theology springs out of this movement and is shaped by it, and in turn the theology shapes the continuing mission of the church. The primary function of the documents is thus to testify to the gospel that is proclaimed by Jesus and his followers. Their teaching can be seen as the fuller exposition of that gospel. They are also concerned with the spiritual growth of those who are converted to the Christian faith. They show how the church should be shaped for its mission, and they deal with those problems that form obstacles to the advancement of the mission.[2]

This essay seeks to demonstrate the appropriateness of this way of understanding the letter to the Ephesians, particularly through a consideration of the *missio Dei* and *imitatio Dei* themes within the letter and the relationship between the two. It will give special attention to the missionary implications of the theological vision of a benevolent Christocentric empire promoted by some of the scriptural material evoked in the letter. It will also give attention to the nature of the rule depicted and the manner in which people enter into the blessings of the gracious reign of God in Christ.

MISSIO DEI IN EPHESIANS

The question of *missio Dei* has been articulated by numerous theologians and missiologists. The expression *missio Dei* has come to be used "to point to the fact that all mission is God's mission and thus the church is called by God to be an instrument in making the Kingdom of God known."[3] It reminds us that mission "is God's mission" and that it "derives from God's nature and God's

---

[1] I. Howard Marshall, *New Testament Theology: Many Witnesses, One Gospel* (Downers Grove: InterVarsity, 2004), 34.
[2] Marshall, *New Testament Theology*, 35.
[3] David Claydon, "Holistic Mission," in *Global Dictionary of Theology: A Resource for the Worldwide Church* (ed. William A. Dyrness and Veli-Matti Kärkkäinen; Downers Grove: IVP Academic, 2008), 402-404 [403].

intention."[4] David Bosch explains it as follows:

> Our mission has no life of its own: only in the hands of the sending God can it truly be called mission. Not least since the missionary initiative comes from God alone.... [M]ission is not primarily an activity of the church, but an attribute of God. God is a missionary God.[5] "It is not the church that has a mission of salvation to fulfill in the world; it is the mission of the Son and the Spirit through the Father that includes the church."[6] Mission is thereby seen as a movement from God to the world; the church is viewed as an instrument for that mission.[7] There is church because there is mission, not vice versa.[8] To participate in mission is to participate in the movement of God's love toward people, since God is a fountain of sending love.[9]

As we consider the letter to the Ephesians, the first question we need to address is how that letter presents its particular understanding of God's own mission to the world. The letter describes a situation in which all people, including both Jews and Gentiles, have died through their practice of trespasses and sins, following the lead or customs of this fallen world, its satanic ruler and their corrupt desires (2:1-3, 5a). The idea that sin leads to death goes back, of course, to Gen 2:17 and is found elsewhere throughout Scripture (cf. Rom 5:12). Gentiles in particular were living "in the futility of their minds" (4:17), "darkened in their understanding, alienated from the life of God because of their ignorance and hardness of heart" (4:18). We are told they "have lost all sensitivity and have abandoned themselves to licentiousness, greedy to practice every kind of impurity" (Eph 4:17-19 NRSV). According to the argument in 2:1-3, however, all human beings find themselves in the same basic situation. Gentiles were also alienated from the covenant people of God, separated by a dividing wall of hostility that kept them far from the promises and covenants that gave Jews hope, and from the one true God who was behind the covenants, promises and the hope (Eph 2:11-12, 14, 19).

We are to understand that God would be completely within his rights to destroy such rebellious people (2:3), but because God is an incredibly loving and merciful God he acted differently (2:4). He treats us as people who had

---

[4] Charles Van Engen, "Mission, Theology of," in *Global Dictionary of Theology: A Resource for the Worldwide Church* (ed. William A. Dyrness and Veli-Matti Kärkkäinen; Downers Grove: IVP Academic, 2008), 550- 62 [557].

[5] Bosch references Anna Marie Aagaard, "Trends in Missiological Thinking During the Sixties," *International Review of Mission* 62 (1973): 8-25 [11-15], and, idem, "Missio Dei in katholischer Sicht," *Evangelische Theologie* 34 (1974): 420-33 [421].

[6] Citing Jürgen Moltmann, *The Church in the Power of the Spirit: A Contribution to Messianic Ecclesiology* (New York: Harper & Row, 1977), 64.

[7] Aagaard, "Trends in Missiological Thinking During the Sixties," 13.

[8] Aagaard, "Missio Dei in katholischer Sicht," 423.

[9] David J. Bosch, *Transforming Mission: Paradigm Shifts in Theology of Mission* (American Society of Missiology Series 16; Maryknoll, N.Y.: Orbis, 1991), 390.

been forcibly enslaved by a tyrant and takes action not against us but against the rulers who had recruited us to their cause. He chose the readers from eternity so that they would be holy and blameless in his presence and determined to adopt them as his children (1:4-5). He provided them with forgiveness for their sins, redeeming them by the blood of the Messiah and is in the process of working out his plan to unite all of creation in the Messiah (1:7-10), whom he raised from the dead and seated at his right hand far above all other powers and authorities (1:20-21). Having an "inheritance in the kingdom of Christ and of God" (5:5), the readers have already been raised and seated with Christ in principle and are presumably destined to be physically raised up and to reign with Christ in the future (2:6), and the work that God is doing in them is such that they will advance the praise of God's glory (1:6, 12, 14).

CHRIST'S REIGN AND OURS

Ephesians 1:20-22 reveals how Christ's resurrection and ascension relate to God's strategy and plan for our redemption. There Paul alludes to both Ps 110:1 and Ps 8:5-6. He prays that the readers may know God's "incomparably great power for us who believe" (NIV).

> That power is like the working of his mighty strength,[20] which he exerted in Christ when he raised him from the dead and seated him at his right hand in the heavenly realms,[21] far above all rule and authority, power and dominion, and every title that can be given, not only in the present age but also in the one to come.[22] And God placed all things under his feet and appointed him to be head over everything for the church . . . . (Eph 1:19-22 NIV)

Here Christ's resurrection and exaltation are fused together and are implicitly, at least, related to God's plans for the church. We notice that the power to which Paul refers is not just a world-transforming demonstration of power, but the world-transforming demonstration of power "for us who believe." Ephesians 1:20-22 combines allusions to Ps 110:1 and Ps 8:5-6,[10] two psalms that share in developing the motif of the reign of the human vice-regent

---

[10] Thorsten Moritz points out that "Eph. 1:22 is only marginally closer to Psalm 8 than to Psalm 110" and that it "is possible that Paul only thought of Psalm 110 at this point, but that his choice of wording was subconsciously influenced by the wording of Psalm 8. However, the fact that Paul in 1 Cor. 15:25, 27 appears to have combined fragments from the same two psalms—using the same wording in the case of Psalm 8(!)—may favor the assumption that in Ephesians we also have a combination of elements taken from both psalms" (Thorsten Moritz, "The Psalms in Ephesians and Colossians," in *The Psalms in the New Testament* [ed. Steve Moyise and Maarten J. J. Menken; London: T&T Clark, 2004], 181-95 [184]).

found in Gen 1:26, 28.[11]

Ephesians 1:20 refers to Christ being seated at God's right hand, alluding to Ps 110:1: "The LORD says to my Lord: 'Sit at my right hand until I make your enemies a footstool for your feet'" (NIV). Despite a lack of disagreement about the original context of Ps 110, most would agree that it describes the Davidic king as a vice-regent,[12] anticipating the use of Ps 8, where the same motif is found. Here the Davidic king (who is much greater than David himself) is invited to sit at the place of honor beside God as he brings all his enemies into submission. Psalm 110 looks forward to the restoration of the pattern described in Gen 1 and Ps 8 through the Davidic king. Paul informs us that this has begun to find its fulfillment through the resurrection and exaltation of our Lord Jesus Christ.

The statement that God "placed all things under his feet" (v. 22) is an allusion to the second half of Ps 8:6. Psalm 8 is a meditation on God's creation of humanity to serve as his vice-regents as reflected in Gen 1 (see, for example, the references to having dominion over the realms of the beasts, birds and fish in Ps 8:7-8 and compare with Gen 1:20-25 and note the dominion language in how it relates to the material in Gen 1:26, 28). The psalm describes God's commissioning of the human race with their dominion as over all creatures in terms of having all things placed under their feet, that is, under their reign and authority. This is applied to Christ, who, as Messiah, represents Israel[13] and the whole human race[14] and fulfills our destiny in his own person.

As Moritz helpfully puts it, Ephesians

> reflects the same clear appreciation of the relationship between protology (Gen. 1!) and eschatological potential in Psalm 8 as evidenced in 1 Cor. 15:25-27 . . . . By singularly combining these psalms in this fashion, Ephesians and 1 Corinthians 15 highlight the role of the messianic death-resurrection-enthronement cluster as a hinge between protology and eschatology. Christ is centrally engaged in the restoration of humanity, a point picked up more explicitly in 2:15 with reference to the role of the cross in the creation (!) of this renewed humanity. The application of Ps. 110:1, with its reference to enthronement to the subjection of the powers, is intensified in v. 22 precisely by appealing to the

---

[11] Both psalms also make reference to the enemies of the king and their subjection (τῶν ἐχθρῶν σου in both Ps 8:3 LXX and 109:2 LXX).

[12] Leslie C. Allen, *Psalms 101-150* (rev. ed.; WBC 21; Dallas: Word Books, 2002), 115.

[13] Frank Thielman points out that "Jewish interpreters in the Second Temple period believed that Adam's right to rule the world had been transferred to Israel" and that "Paul's use of Ps. 8:6 in 1:22 probably fits within this conceptual framework" (Frank S. Thielman, "Ephesians," in *Commentary on the New Testament Use of the Old Testament* [ed. G. K. Beale and D. A. Carson; Grand Rapids: Baker Academic, 2007], 813-33 [816]).

[14] See N. T. Wright, *The Climax of the Covenant: Christ and the Law in Pauline Theology* (Minneapolis: Fortress, 1992), 18-40.

eschatological overcoming of evil longed for in Psalm 8. In so doing, Psalm 8 is accorded a role in the eschatological interpretation of the present which outpaces the explicit claims of the psalm itself. But this role is entirely compatible with the psalm's conceptual gap between protology and eschatology and the eschatological potential opened up thereby.[15]

The resurrection of Jesus Christ establishes his triumph over all his enemies, including sin and death, and provides the foundation for our confidence that in him we find not only the forgiveness of our sins and new life in Christ by the Spirit, but also the promise of the ultimate redemption and restoration of creation, including our restoration to the role God originally had intended for us.

Moritz argues that the motifs from Ps 8 and Ps 110 are brought together here not because they were commonly conjoined in early Christianity, "but because Paul saw fit to make the connection between the two psalms and his own 'subjection of the evil powers' theme." His otherwise helpful presentation seems to assume that Paul has his own "subjection of the evil powers theme," independent of the scriptural sources he alludes to in the passage. That may be so, but it seems at least as likely that whatever "subjection of the evil powers theme" Paul has he discerned in his reading of these very texts. This part of his theology may not have any source independent of the text. That the Messiah's enemies include (or even consist primarily of) spiritual powers does not come from these psalms, but reflects an apocalyptic understanding reflected in the various references to spiritual powers throughout this letter, and would be a natural conclusion to draw from the fact that the Davidic king sits at God's right hand.[16]

---

[15] Moritz, "The Psalms in Ephesians and Colossians," 188. Moritz goes on to argue that "[c]rucially, and in fulfilment of the implied expectation of Psalm 8, the 'son of man'(=humanity) is no longer 'a little lower'. Insofar as people are found 'in Christ', they are now enthroned with him (Eph. 2:6)" (188). It should be pointed out that the meaning of that part of the psalm is contested. Although the LXX has humanity "diminished . . . a little in comparison with angels" (NETS; ἠλάττωσας αὐτὸν βραχύ τι παρ' ἀγγέλους), the Hebrew text reads ותחסרהו מאלהים מעט, where אלהים could be taken as a reference to God in keeping with the suggestion from Gen 1 that humanity (rather than the angels) was created to serve as God's vice-regents. It is not clear if Paul's understanding was the same as that reflected in the LXX. It may be that in light of Ps 110 he understood Ps 8 to refer to dominion a little lower than God's. Moritz's point about being enthroned with Christ still stands. It may still be that the idea is one in which we occupy a slightly subordinate place on the same throne (a little lower/less).

[16] Note Mortiz's suggestion that "[t]he conviction expressed in Ephesians 1 that all powers will be subjected implies that no-one other than God himself will be directly involved in the subjection. Psalm 110 proved eminently suitable for this purpose, given that it speaks in uncharacteristically high terms of Israel's king, even to the point of him being invited by God to share his throne" ("The Psalms in Ephesians and Colossians,"

The combination of allusions and their background in the Genesis creation material suggest that God's redeeming work in Christ is destined to restore humanity to the original role that God had intended for us through Christ.[17] Through and with Christ we should reign as God's vice-regents over a creation that has been renewed in the wake of Christ's own resurrection from the dead. That Christ's enthronement is part and parcel of God's intention to reestablish the rest of God's redeemed people to their originally intended role as vice-regents as well is confirmed in Eph 2:6 where we learn that death, resurrection and reigning are not merely the contours of Christ's personal story, but the contours of our story as well, due to our union with him.[18]

But the kind of reign God has in store for us is also suggested by the pattern established by Christ and held out to us in Ephesians. It is not an authoritarian or self-indulgent reign in which we grasp at power for the sake of our own agendas. Rather, it is a reign in which whatever power we might ever have is always power for the sake of others, as God's own power was demonstrated through Christ as "power for us who believe" (1:19). Christ did not conquer us to make us his slaves but to make us one with him, following the pattern expressed in Gen 2:24 (the two becoming one). Similarly, Gentiles who bow the knee to Christ do not become the slaves of his Jewish compatriots, but are made one with them just as the church becomes one with Christ (compare Eph 2:14-16 with Eph 5:31-32).

The reign Christ has in mind for us is patterned on the one he himself has exemplified. It is a cruciform reign, not one marked by imperial conquests of human enemies, but by doing battle against spiritual powers that would undermine the righteousness, peace, truth, and salvation-extending ministry of the gospel that are to mark the church of Christ. It is to be a reign marked by manifestations of his love, grace, and mercy to those around us.

---

186). The suggestion that Paul came up with his convictions elsewhere and then looked for "eminently suitable" passages to support his own ideas is gratuitous. Here and in 1 Cor 15 when Paul expresses these ideas he does so in the language of the texts themselves and there is little reason to conclude that the ideas did not originate from his knowledge of the texts to begin with. What he actually points to in the king's invitation to share God's throne suggests that may be the very thing that led Paul to conclude that even spiritual powers would be brought in subjection to him.

[17] As Thielman puts it, "the hegemony that God intended for humanity to have over all creation is in the process of coming to pass through the Messiah's kingly rule over 'all things'" (Thielman, "Ephesians," 816).

[18] Paul's use of the Psalms "suggests that the Messiah (the Christ of v. 20) is the one whose dominion over all things fulfills what it is to be truly human in the world" and in conjunction with Eph 2:6 suggests that "[t]he end of this story is like the beginning: humanity too, is called back to their original rule and calling" (Sylvia C. Keesmaat, "In the Face of the Empire: Paul's Use of Scripture in the Shorter Epistles," in *Hearing the Old Testament in the New Testament* [ed. Stanley E. Porter; Grand Rapids: Eerdmans, 2006], 182-212 [188]). Cf. Col 3:1.

CHRIST'S TRIUMPH AND OUR PEACE

The triumph scene in Eph 4:8-10, with its quotation from Ps 68:18 (HB 68:19; LXX 67:19) expands upon the material found in 1:20-22.[19] In 1:20-22 we are told that Christ was seated "far above all rule and authority and power and dominion, and above every name that is named" (v. 21) while in 4:10 we are told that he "ascended far above all the heavens." In both texts Christ is exalted above all else except God the Father to bring blessings to his people. The preposition ὑπεράνω ("high/far above") appears only in these two verses in all the Pauline literature. The description of Christ's triumph found in 4:8-10 is remarkable. Although the readers were God's enemies, aligned with the force(s) opposing him and his agenda (2:1-3), when God took captivity captive he did not humiliate them, confiscate their belongings or exact tribute from them. Rather, he gave them gifts.[20] As Keesmaat argues, Paul's subsequent material describing the effect of God's gifts on the church in terms of attaining unity supports the conclusion that "this ruler, this Messiah, is one whose gifts work for unity, for upbuilding, for peace."[21] She suggests Paul's use of the psalm "results in a subversion of any authority and rule that violently deal in death rather than in building up a new body rooted in peace."[22] It turns out that when God put on his battle armor (see below) he went to battle not to destroy people but to bring them salvation, to bring peace to those who had no reason to expect that it would be granted them. This is, as Sylvia Keesmaat points out, a remarkable turn of events.

In Ps 110 such disobedient Gentiles, alienated from Israel and strangers to the covenant, would have been the recipients of God's judgment. Not so here. In Ephesians, these former enemies are precisely those with whom God has made peace. In this Messiah, what is put to death is not the enemies, but the

---

[19] See Timothy G. Gombis, "Cosmic Lordship and Divine Gift-Giving: Psalm 68 in Ephesians 4:8," *NovT* 47 (2005): 367-80, for key issues in the use of the psalm in this passage.

[20] According to Keesmaat ("In the Face of the Empire," 191), Paul "describes a different Lord and Messiah who made *captivity* a captive (Eph 4:8). That is, no more is captivity the way that enemies are to be treated; no more is servile subjection the order of the day. This Messiah overturns captivity, and instead of receiving tribute as gifts he *gives* gifts (4:8)" (Keesmaat, 191 [her emphases]). Her interpretation of "taking captivity captive" is unfounded, overlooking the facts that Paul's language is drawn straight from Ps 67:19 LXX (rather than introducing his own subversive meaning) and that, as BDAG (s.v. "αἰχμαλωσία") demonstrates, although the term translated "captivity" (αἰχμαλωσία) was an abstract term for a "state of captivity," the usage of the abstract term for the concrete idea of "a captured military force" is common enough (listing Diodorus Siculus 17, 70, 6; Num 31:12; Jdt 2:9; 1 Esd 6:5, 8; 1 Macc 9:70, 72; 2 Macc 8:10; Josephus, *Ant.* 11, 1). So the commonly understood meaning of the expression as reported in the LXX would simply be that he "captured prisoners of war."

[21] Keesmaat, "In the Face of the Empire," 191.

[22] Keesmaat, "In the Face of the Empire," 192.

hostility between those far off and those near (Eph 2:13-16), culminating in the peace of v. 17: "So he came and proclaimed peace to you who were far off and peace to those who were near" (NRSV). We find in this verse an allusion to Isa 57:19. In the context of attacking the unfaithful idolatry of the people, the prophet turns from condemnation to hope: "Build up, build up, prepare the way, remove every obstruction from my people's way" (Isa 57:14 NRSV). Prepare the way for what? "Peace, peace, to the far and the near, says the Lord; and I will heal them" (Isa 57:19 NRSV).[23]

Furthermore, "whereas Rome severely judged those who were unfaithful to its *politeias*—and did so by subjecting them to death on a cross—Paul describes a Messiah who makes peace with those who are alien, and who does so by offering himself on such a cross."[24] Christ's proclamation of peace is based upon his work of establishing peace through his death on the cross, depicted as the ultimate act of self-sacrificing love for others. God's purposes are accomplished through Christ's blood (1:7; 2:13), that is, through the cross of Christ (2:16) and his resurrection (1:20) which also becomes ours (2:6) by which we participate in the new creation (2:10).

RECONCILIATION, THE MYSTERY AND GENESIS 2:24

Part and parcel of God's mission of redeeming and restoring creation is the reconciliation and harmonization of the fragmented world in which we find ourselves. God is bringing peace where there has been alienation and enmity. It is a commonplace in studies of Ephesians that it treats of cosmic reconciliation. The part of this motif which usually receives the greatest stress is that of the reconciliation of Jews and Gentiles to each other and to God, as expounded in Eph 2:11-19. It is also reflected in much of the material in Ephesians that discusses the "mystery" that God has revealed to Paul (3:3), as well as to other apostles and prophets (3:4-5) and now, through them, to the church as a whole (1:9).

In 1:9-10 the mystery is summarized as being God's intention "to bring all things in heaven and on earth together under one head, even Christ." According to BDAG, the key word here, ἀνακεφαλαιόω, when "used of literary or rhetorical summation" means to "sum up" or "recapitulate" with the proposed meaning of this particular verse being "to bring everything together in Christ."[25] Hoehner argues that the word means "to bring all the parts into a coherent whole."[26] Best proposes that the idea of "summing up" suggests that

---

[23] Keesmaat, "In the Face of the Empire," 189.
[24] Keesmaat, "In the Face of the Empire," 190.
[25] BDAG, s.v. "ἀνακεφαλαιόω."
[26] Harold W. Hoehner, *Ephesians: An Exegetical Commentary* (Grand Rapids: Baker Academic, 2002), 220. Other parts of Hoehner's presentation go a bit too far (including following Chrysostom's motivated inclusion of the idea of bringing under a "head" and

"everything comes together in him; what is divided is unified in him."[27] Lincoln suggests the thought here is of "the summing up and bringing together of the diverse elements of the cosmos in Christ as the focal point." It has to do with "a restoration of harmony with Christ as the point of reintegration."[28] Chrysostom felt the need to explain the meaning to his congregation and suggested it meant "to knit [or join] together" (συνάψαι): "So also here He hath brought all under one and the same Head. For thus will an union be effected, thus will a close bond be effected . . . ."[29]

Taken together the evidence suggests that the mystery has to do with the uniting or joining together of the disparate parts of creation into one harmonious whole in or under Christ. In 3:6 we are told that the mystery is that "the Gentiles have become fellow heirs, members of the same body, and sharers in the promise in Christ Jesus through the gospel" (NRSV). In 5:31-32 we are told that Gen 2:24 reflects a "profound mystery" that has to do with "Christ and the church." That is, the union of which Gen 2:24 speaks applies not only to the union of husbands and wives but also (and above all) to the union of Christ and the church. As husband and wife become one flesh, Christ and the church also become one.

Why does Paul apply Gen 2:24 to Christ and the church? In the context he has already suggested that the church is the bride of Christ (5:25-27). But does Gen 2:24 only illuminate Paul's understanding of the profound mystery of Christ and the church, or might is also be a key to some of the other references to the "mystery" in Ephesians? In Ephesians 3:6 we are told that Gentiles are members of the same body (σύσσωμος) with the Jews. Does the concept of the "same body" flow from the idea of the "one flesh" in Gen 2:24? In Eph 2:14-16 we are told that Christ "has made us both one" (ὁ ποιήσας τὰ ἀμφότερα ἕν), creating "one new man/person in place of the two," reconciling "both in one body" (ἀμφοτέρους ἐν ἑνὶ σώματι). Here again we have the idea of the

---

the idea that since the word refers to "main points" "it has the idea of 'the main point' to which others are subordinate" (citing Heb 8:1). But an *anakephalaion* refers to a summary or bringing together of the main points and does not entail a reference to one "main point" to which the others are subordinate. The discussion of headship belongs in other texts and this one must be understood in light of those other texts without importing any explicit headship idea into the key word used here. Arguments that go beyond the idea of summing up or bringing parts together into a whole are moving beyond lexical meaning and following the Fathers in exploiting this verse.

[27] Ernest Best, *A Critical and Exegetical Commentary on Ephesians* (Edinburgh: T&T Clark, 1998), 142. He also argues (142-43) that this is not a reference to a yet-to-be realized future reality, but reflects other elements in the letter on the "future as already present": "In 1:20–3 Christ already holds the powers in subjection; in 2:6 believers already sit with him in the heavenlies. It is not out of keeping with these passages if then we say that the universe is . . ., and not will be, summed up in Christ."

[28] Andrew T. Lincoln, *Ephesians* (WBC 42; Dallas: Word Books, 1990), 33.

[29] Chrysostom, *Hom. Eph.* 1 (*NPNF*1 13:54-55).

creation of one new person out of two. And this takes place "in one body." It is difficult to imagine any other place from where the idea of two people being joined together as one might originate.

One cannot do more than speculate, but perhaps Paul saw in the early narrative of Genesis a telegraphing of God's plan for the universe. God creates humankind as a single entity which gets divided, at its most basic partition, into two genders. But no sooner has humanity been divided into two when, in Gen 2:24, God indicates the two should come together again to form one flesh, one unified being. If Gen 2:24 applies not only to husbands and wives, but also to Christ and the church,[30] perhaps it is also the key to how Jews and Gentiles, described as two persons, are brought together to be made one new person where there were two. It would only be a matter of extending that perception further to conclude that God's plan for all of creation is to unite together all the disparate parts of the broken universe into one harmonious whole in and under Christ. It may have been that Paul found the clue to God's intentions for his creation, the mystery that explains what God is up to in Christ, in the narrative sequence that goes from the creation of a singular humanity to its division into two genders and then the uniting of those two again as one flesh or as one body.[31]

It is proposed, then, that the perception of the mystery found in Ephesians grows out of reflection on Gen 2:24 in its narrative context and consists of the idea that all of creation (including, but not limited to humanity as constituted of Jews and Gentiles) is to be summed up, woven or united together as one in Christ, just as God takes a man and a woman and makes them one flesh, one body, one new person, in Christ. In 2:14-17 we can see that this motif is intimately tied to the theme of peace. Christ is our peace (2:14), he made peace (2:15) and he came and preached peace (2:17). The making of one out of two (or many) is about the bringing of peace where there was alienation.

IMITATIO DEI IN EPHESIANS AND ITS RELATIONSHIP TO *MISSIO DEI*

In Eph 5:1 the readers are told to be "imitators of God as beloved children" (μιμηταὶ ὡς τέκνα ἀγαπητά). The motif of the imitation of God is reflected throughout the second half of that letter, and shows up indirectly in the first three chapters as well. Most of the references to the theme in the second half of

---

[30] Of course we have already been told that Christ is the head over all things for his body, the church (1:22-23). It may not be possible to discern if the head-body metaphor occurred to Paul before and/or separately from his application of Gen 2:24 to Christ and the church, or if the head-body metaphor originated as one way of unpacking the "one flesh/body" understanding of Christ and the church based on Gen 2:24.

[31] The alternation between "flesh" and "body" in Pauline interpretations of Gen 2:24 is found in 1 Cor 6:16 ("one body" . . . "one flesh") and in Eph 5:28-31 ("bodies . . . flesh . . . body . . . one flesh").

Ephesians may be traced by paying attention to the motif of "walking" and how it develops. The second half of the letter begins (4:1) with a call to "walk in a way that is worthy of the calling with which you were called (ἀξίως περιπατῆσαι τῆς κλήσεως ἧς ἐκλήθητε). The next verse indicates that such a walk would be marked by humility, gentleness, patience, and bearing with one another in love (4:2). It does not take much reflection to realize that the first half of the letter had made it clear that those same qualities had marked God's own treatment of the readers. Although God would have been within his rights to destroy the readers, out of his great love, mercy and grace he had seen fit to give them life and numerous other blessings instead. Ephesians 4:3-16 emphasizes the theme of unity (and its establishment through love), and along the way, in support of that theme, mentions that there is "one Lord" and "one God and Father of all" (vv. 5-6; cf. 1 Cor 8:6). This would not in itself be sufficient to tip off the readers that the theme of the imitation of God is about to be expounded, but after reading the rest of the letter one may be excused from suggesting that this unit on unity already reflects that theme. Just as God is one, the readers are also to be one, guarding and protecting the unity that God worked to create in their midst.

The theme of "walking" shows up again in 4:17, only in vv. 17-32 the main theme is that the readers (despite being Gentiles) are not to imitate the Gentiles in walking (that is, living) in a way that manifests the vices for which they were known. They "must no longer walk as the Gentiles do" (μηκέτι ὑμᾶς περιπατεῖν, καθὼς καὶ τὰ ἔθνη περιπατεῖ). This negative foil seems to set up the explicit development of the theme of the proper object of their imitative lifestyles.

As Paul[32] prepares to transition to the next major section of his argument he evokes the motif of the *imitatio Dei* in the practice of forgiveness: they are to forgive each other just as God has also forgiven them in Christ (χαριζόμενοι ἑαυτοῖς, καθὼς καὶ ὁ θεὸς ἐν Χριστῷ ἐχαρίσατο ὑμῖν). It is the very next verse that introduces the explicit language of imitation (5:1). And the focal point for the intended imitation is already subtly implied in the final words of 5:1—they are to imitate God *as dearly loved children* (ὡς τέκνα ἀγαπητά). This implies at least two things. First, it is natural and expected that children will imitate their parents (especially in their best qualities). Second, what God has modeled for them is his loving nature.

The next reference to "walking," then, follows immediately after this reference to being dearly loved children as Paul calls on the readers to "*walk in love*, just as Christ loved us and gave himself up for us, a fragrant offering and sacrifice to God" (5:2 ESV). Here the nature of the love modeled and expected is unambiguous. The reference to Christ's loving example is repeated again

---

[32] Although I take the author to be the apostle Paul (employing an unusually elaborate style for the sake of rhetorical effect), the question of authorship is not essential for the argument of this essay.

later in 5:25, where husbands are exhorted to love their wives "just as Christ loved the church and gave himself up for her" (NRSV).

Much of the material in Eph 5:23-33 seems to reflect a combining of ideas from Gen 2:24 (the two become one flesh) and Lev 19:18 (love your neighbor as yourself). Genesis 2:24 is quoted in 5:31 (as noted above). Once it is quoted it is instantly apparent that the verse's influence is felt throughout vv. 28-33. It clarifies Paul's meaning in 5:28 when he says husbands should love their wives "as their own bodies": they have become one flesh/body with their wives and therefore they should treat them as their own body. That is also why, in the same verse, Paul can say that the husband who loves his wife "loves himself." That also explains the reference to "his own flesh" in 5:29 and why a husband should love his wife "as he loves himself" in 5:33.

Although Lev 19:18 is not quoted, it is the most likely source of the idea of "loving [another] as oneself" (see 5:28, 33).[33] There is no closer neighbor than the person who has become one with me! I don't just love them as I love myself, I love them because they are in fact now part of myself! God's approach to us is less like that of a conquering warrior, and more like that of a man wooing a woman, giving up everything to win her love and loyalty.

While in 5:25-33 the self-sacrificing love Christ modeled for the church is held out as the model for the love that husbands are to show their wives, in 5:1-2 Christ's example of self-sacrificing love is held out as a more universally applicable example of how Christians are to treat each other. That motif of love penetrates every part of this letter (1:4, 6, 15; 2:4; 3:17, 19; 4:2, 15-16; 5:1-2, 25, 28, 33; 6:21, 23-24).

The final two references to how the readers are to walk refer to walking "as children of light" (ὡς τέκνα φωτὸς περιπατεῖτε; 5:8) and being careful to walk as wise people (Βλέπετε οὖν ἀκριβῶς πῶς περιπατεῖτε μὴ ὡς ἄσοφοι ἀλλ' ὡς σοφοί; 5:15).

When we step back to ponder the sections on walking in love, light and wisdom and how they may relate to the exhortation to imitate God, we are struck by the fact that love, light and wisdom were all well-known divine attributes. 1 John explicitly identifies God with the first two attributes: God is light (1 John 1:5); God is love (1 John 4:8, 16). Wisdom, of course, was an even better-known divine attribute.[34] Ephesians 5:14 identifies Christ with light by way of the quotation that refers to him as shining on believers (ἐπιφαύσει σοι ὁ Χριστός). Ephesians 5:9 identifies the fruit of light as "all goodness, and righteousness and truthfulness" (πάσῃ ἀγαθωσύνῃ καὶ δικαιοσύνῃ καὶ

---

[33] See J. Paul Sampley, *"And the Two Shall Become One Flesh": A Study of Traditions in Ephesians 5:21-33* (SNTSMS 16; Cambridge: Cambridge University Press, 2004), 30-34.

[34] In the Pauline corpus, see 1 Cor 1:21, 24; Rom 11:33; Eph 3:10.

ἀληθείᾳ), qualities which are also associated with God himself.[35] The references to walking in Eph 4:17; 5:2, 8, 15, may be taken as headings over their respective sections with the result being that the readers are not to imitate the vices of the Gentiles (4:17-34), but are to imitate God (5:1), particularly his attributes of love (5:2), light (5:3-14) and wisdom (5:15-6:9). The divine attribute of oneness had already been highlighted in 4:3-16. In 6:10-20 the metaphor of walking is left behind, but the motif of the imitation of God continues. This becomes clear when it is recognized that the "armor of God" that the readers are to put on is not merely armor from God or given by God but the allusions make it clear that we are dealing with God's own armor, which he puts on as the divine warrior. In putting on the "breastplate of righteousness" and the "helmet of salvation" (among other things), and thus in putting on the armor in general, the readers are following in God's own footsteps.

THE ARMOR OF GOD AND THE PREACHING AND LIVING OF THE GOSPEL

In 6:10-20, the passage about donning God's armor, Paul revisits several of the motifs of the letter. Paul presents a virtue list by associating various virtues with the different elements of a soldier's armor or equipment. The belt of truth (6:14a) reminds the reader of the various ways in which the importance of truth has been highlighted throughout the letter (1:13; 4:15, 21, 25; 6:14). The breastplate of righteousness (6:14b) reminds the reader of 4:24 and 5:9, where righteousness (δικαιοσύνη) was previously discussed. The gospel of peace reminds the reader of previous references to the gospel in 1:13 and 3:6-7 and of previous references to peace in 1:2; 2:14-15, 17; 4:3. The shield of faith recalls the many previous references to faith throughout the letter (1:13, 15; 2:8; 3:12, 17; 4:5, 13). The same goes for the helmet of salvation (1:13), the sword of the Spirit (1:13, 17; 2:2, 18, 22; 3:5, 16; 4:3-4, 23, 30; 5:18). Several of the themes highlighted in this passage are found concentrated together in the place where they were all first introduced, namely, in 1:13. There we read, "In him you also, when you had heard the word of truth, the gospel of your salvation, and had believed in him, were marked with the seal of the promised Holy Spirit" (NRSV). There we find, combined in one verse, references to the word, to truth, the gospel, salvation, faith (believing), and the Spirit (λόγος, ἀλήθεια, εὐαγγέλιον, σωτηρία, πιστ–, πνεῦμα). The verse that introduces so many of the themes of the final pericope of the body of the letter is focused on the readers' entrance into the blessings provided in Christ through the preaching of the gospel. God had reached them with his blessings, with the new life in Christ

---

[35] On God's goodness (ἀγαθωσύνη), see Neh 9:25, 35; 13:31; *Pr. Man.* 14; Gal 5:22. For his truthfulness or faithfulness (ἀλήθεια) cf. LXX Gen 24:27; Ps 24:5; 30:6; 56:4; 68:14; 70:22; 88:9; 97:3. The theme of God's righteousness (δικαιοσύνη) is, of course, ubiquitous in the Old and New Testaments (see, e.g., Gen 24:27; Ps 7:18; 21:32; 49:6; 96:6; 97:2; 102:17; 110:3; 111:3,9; Isa 63:7; Rom 3:21, 25-26).

and all that comes with it, through the communication of the gospel message. Had they never heard the gospel they would still be in darkness, still without God or hope, still children of wrath. Through the preaching of the gospel they have begun to experience God's great redeeming and reconciling work.

In Isa 59:17, the "helmet of salvation" is worn by the Lord as part of the armor he dons as the divine warrior. There it obviously does not refer to any salvation that he has received, but to the salvation that he brings to those in need by going to battle on their behalf. In that context, many of the themes found in Ephesians, and especially the themes highlighted in the material on the armor of God, are clearly present:

> [14] Justice is turned back, and righteousness stands at a distance; for truth stumbles in the public square, and uprightness cannot enter. [15] Truth is lacking, and whoever turns from evil is despoiled. The LORD saw it, and it displeased him that there was no justice. [16] He saw that there was no one, and was appalled that there was no one to intervene; so his own arm brought him victory, and his righteousness upheld him. [17] He put on righteousness like a breastplate, and a helmet of salvation on his head; he put on garments of vengeance for clothing, and wrapped himself in fury as in a mantle. (Isa 59:14-17 NRSV)

It was due to a lack of justice, righteousness and truth in the land and the fact that no one else was about to intervene to correct the situation that the Lord acted to bring victory over the oppressive reality from which his people needed deliverance. Here to put on a helmet of salvation is to go to battle to bring salvation to those in need. God's presence in the world is reflected in the love, light, wisdom, righteousness, justice, truth, faith, salvation and Spirit that are to mark the community of believers. According to Eph 1:13 it was through hearing "the word of truth, the gospel of your salvation" that the readers were brought into these realities, into the light and blessings of Christ and out of the power of darkness. It is undoubtedly that strategic function of the gospel that leads Paul to call on the readers to "put on whatever will make you ready to proclaim the gospel of peace" (6:15 NRSV).

CONCLUSION

In Ephesians, God's mission, as a manifestation of his own nature and intention, is reflected in a variety of ways. It is seen above all in the love and mercy demonstrated in sending Christ to bring light out of darkness, to bring redemption and renewal to all creation and the establishment of a harmonious peace where there was division and alienation. God accomplishes his mission through the death and resurrection of Christ and through the preaching and living out of the gospel message. Ephesians also stresses the imitation of God in a variety of ways, especially through living lives marked by the divine attributes of love, light, wisdom and power (as demonstrated in spiritual battle).

God has demonstrated for us what it means to love one's enemies. His royal-military feats have been dedicated not to our destruction, but to freeing us from the oppressive powers to which we had previously given our allegiance. Obedience to the call to imitate God in the reign to which he has called us in Christ must take into consideration God's own radically sacrificial commitment to bringing salvation to those who are currently his enemies and the key role that is given to the communication of the gospel in bringing people into the experience of salvation for which God has offered his son. The way people enter into the blessings Christ offers is through hearing and believing the gospel (Eph 1:13, 19). Through the preaching of the gospel hearers are brought from death to life and from being outsiders to citizens who reign with their gracious sovereign. A community marked by the presence and power of God's love, light, wisdom and power provides the crucial context for the powerful advancement of the gospel message as the church participates in *missio Dei* by way of *imitatio Dei*.

How does the letter to the Ephesians portray God as carrying out his mission of redeeming love for and in the church? God's approach to the world is most essentially reflected in the self-sacrificing love reflected in Christ's love for the church (5:2, 25), and in God's own mercy and love that led him to forgive the readers (4:32) and give them life rather than destroying them (2:4-5). It would seem that the most fundamental way in which the church may participate in *missio Dei* is via *imitatio Dei* especially by loving others as Christ has loved us and by committing itself to the communication of the gospel of peace, the gospel of our salvation, as an expression of God's love for those whose hearts have yet to be captured by that love.

Given the emphasis on how the readers are to treat "one-another" or "each other" in 4:32 it may be argued that the exhortation to "walk in love just as Christ loved us" amounts to no more than an exhortation to "love one another." That is undoubtedly the idea being stressed, but this immediately follows the exhortation to "be imitators of God," and readers may well be expected to remember that God loved them/us "even when we were dead in transgressions" (2:5). That God's love extends beyond the community of believers at any given moment has been made clear in a variety of ways. That God's love extended even to the readers only became clear when they heard the gospel message, believed and were sealed with the Spirit (1:13). They had been far off but had been brought near by Christ's blood (2:13). Christ had come and preached peace not only to those who were near, but also to the readers, despite the fact that they were "far off" (2:17). A proper understanding of *missio Dei* and *imitatio Dei* as reflected in Ephesians will compel the church to also commit itself to proclaiming Christ's peace to both those who are near and those who are far.

15

AN IDEAL MISSIONARY PRAYER LETTER: REFLECTIONS ON PAUL'S MISSION THEOLOGY AS EXPRESSED IN PHILIPPIANS

Alistair I. Wilson

INTRODUCTION

"New Testament theology is essentially missionary theology."[1] Howard Marshall highlights mission as both the context and the content of the documents of the NT and he has gone to considerable lengths to emphasize the importance of this issue for the contemporary church.[2] In this paper I intend to highlight some theological themes and pastoral counsel in Paul's letter to the Philippians which, I believe, reveal Paul's understanding of "mission." In doing so, I want to suggest that this letter may usefully be considered as an ideal ancient "missionary prayer letter." This suggestion is not intended to challenge the consensus that the genre of Philippians may be identified as a letter of friendship.[3] Rather it is to suggest that what binds Paul and his Christian brothers and sisters in Philippi together is their sharing in a common mission and to highlight how Paul's remarkable letter may provide a relevant and valuable model to help those who share in the missionary task today to rethink their priorities and practices as they engage in the task of mission.

---

[1] I. Howard Marshall, *New Testament Theology* (Nottingham: Apollos, 2004), 34.

[2] It is a great honor to be invited to contribute this essay to a volume in honor of my mentor and friend, Howard Marshall. Howard's commitment to the life of the church and to the central theme of mission has recently been highlighted for me by his willingness to visit the small theological institution where I currently serve in the Eastern Cape of South Africa and to give a series of lectures here during March 2010, including one on Paul's Theology of Mission in Romans. It was a challenge to ensure that I said nothing about this project during his visit! Howard's commitment to listening carefully to the individual biblical documents on their own terms and in the light of significant interpreters, explaining their contents in clear language and applying their contents to the church of today has provided the model which I will seek to work out in this essay. It is dedicated to Howard with gratitude for his friendship and support.

[3] See the discussions in Gordon D. Fee, *Paul's Letter to the Philippians* (NICNT; Grand Rapids: Eerdmans, 1995), 2-7 but note the discussion and cautionary remarks of Markus Bockmuehl, *The Epistle to the Philippians* (BNTC; London: A&C Black, 1997), 34-38, about relying too heavily on one classical model. See also the extended theological reflections on "friendship' in Stephen E. Fowl, *Philippians* (THNTC; Grand Rapids: Eerdmans, 2005), 205-35.

Philippians has not received much attention in discussion of Paul's theology of mission. The only full scale study of which I am aware appeared in 2005.[4] In fact, it is rare for any single Pauline letter to be examined in its own right with reference to its missionary theology. Several of the standard studies of mission in the NT (for very understandable reasons of effective presentation within limited space) consider Paul's thought as a whole, drawing on all his letters, rather than listening to each Pauline document in turn.[5] In fact, Bockmuehl goes so far as to suggest that there is little value in attempting to find the "theology" of one short letter and that any attempt to do so "cannot fail to exaggerate situational aspects, to over-interpret silences, and to distend supposed theological differences which to the writer may hardly have merited a second thought."[6] While Bockmuehl is correct to note that Paul's theology is so rich that it cannot be confined or fully encompassed by a single situational letter, it is nonetheless the case that such letters are the only primary sources we possess from which to grasp something of Paul's overarching theology.[7] We agree with James Dunn that even once we have gathered all the information found in Paul's letters, we may still not have access to the full extent of Paul's theological thinking; only that which he chose to express in writing in the context of specific communication with churches and individuals.[8] But it may still be useful to see how a particular letter *contributes* to Paul's overall

---

[4] James P. Ware, *The Mission of the Church in Paul's Letter to the Philippians in the Context of Ancient Judaism* (NovTSup 120; Leiden: Brill, 2005). Ware comments (163), "The letter has received very little attention in treatments of early Christian mission, and interpreters have not traditionally identified mission as a major concern of the epistle."

[5] See, for example, Andreas J. Köstenberger and Peter T. O'Brien, *Salvation to the Ends of the Earth* (Leicester: Apollos, 2001), 161-201 and *Mission in the New Testament: An Evangelical Approach* (eds William J. Larkin Jr. and Joel F. Williams; Maryknoll: Orbis, 1998), 63-116. See also David J. Bosch, *Transforming Mission* (Maryknoll: Orbis, 1991), 123-78, and Donald P. Senior and Carroll Stuhlmueller, *The Biblical Foundations for Mission* (Maryknoll: Orbis, 1983). Senior and Stuhlmueller have a similar chapter on "The Mission Theology of Paul" (161-90) and then a separate chapter on "the Cosmic Scope of the Church's Mission in Colossians and Ephesians" (191-210) due to their understanding that "a significant development in the mission theology of the New Testament" is reflected in these letters (191). E. J. Schnabel includes a chapter on "The Missionary Task According to Paul's Letters" in his significant recent book, *Paul the Missionary* (Downers Grove: InterVarsity, 2008), in which he does consider relevant material in individual letters or small groups of letters. Within this chapter, there is a section on "The Letters to the Christians in Macedonia: Thessalonians and Philippians" (126-30), but all the discussion relates to passages in 1 Thessalonians.

[6] Bockmuehl, *Philippians*, 42.

[7] I regard Acts as an extremely valuable source of information regarding Paul's life and thought, but it is nonetheless a secondary source by another author.

[8] James D. G. Dunn, *The Theology of Paul the Apostle* (Edinburgh: T&T Clark, 1998), 13-19. See also Thomas R. Schreiner, *Paul, Apostle of God's Glory in Christ* (Leicester: Apollos, 2001), 39.

theological thinking and so we proceed while noting the helpful cautions to avoid misrepresenting the text. One recent exception to the lack of studies of specific letters with respect to Paul's missionary theology is Howard Marshall's treatment of Romans,[9] which has provided significant stimulus to my own thinking about how this approach could be applied to Philippians. In fact, Marshall comments towards the end of his chapter on Philippians in his *New Testament Theology* that "possibly no other Pauline letter brings out so clearly the ongoing work of mission by the local church."[10]

The concept of a missionary prayer letter is well enough known in the modern missionary context. Missionaries who are carrying out Christian service in some (frequently foreign) context will write with greater or lesser regularity to supporters to inform them of encouragements and problems in their work and to provide news of their own personal circumstances. The purposes of the prayer letter are normally several: to raise awareness and interest in the work; to request thanksgiving and prayer for the more and less positive aspects of the work; and to request practical and/or financial support for the work which is being carried out. Although this is a modern literary category, it may be helpful as a means of highlighting the importance of mission themes in this letter and also for recognizing how theological themes and ethical instructions relate to Paul's concern for mission. Thinking of Philippians in these terms may also help those who write modern missionary prayer letters to follow Paul's pattern more closely.

DEFINITIONS

"MISSION"

Before we proceed any further, it is important to define the key term "mission." This is not, of course, a term found within the vocabulary of the Greek NT. Rather it is derived from the Latin term, *mittere*, meaning "to send."[11] This does not mean that we should not use the word; only that we should be careful to define it properly. This is particularly so when "mission" (or sometimes "missions") is used in various ways. Scott Moreau et al. assert that "missions" is used to describe "the specific work of the church and agencies in the task of reaching people for Christ by crossing cultural boundaries."[12] One also finds

---

[9] I. Howard Marshall, "Paul's Mission According to Romans," in *Bible and Mission: A Conversation Between Biblical Studies and Missiology* (ed. R. G. Grams et al.; Schwarzenfeld: Neufeld Verlag, 2008), 96-130.
[10] Marshall, *New Testament Theology*, 359.
11 Eckhard J. Schnabel, *Jesus and the Twelve* (vol. 1 of *Early Christian Mission*; Downers Grove: InterVarsity, 2004), 10.
12 A. Scott Moreau, Gary B. Corwin and Gary B. McGee, *Introducing World Missions* (Grand Rapids: Baker Academic, 2004), 17.

frequent reference in literature to the Latin phrase *missio Dei*, which may be translated as "mission of God"[13] Although use of this phrase was popularized in the ecumenical circles of the World Council of Churches during the mid-twentieth century, it has its roots in the writings of Augustine where it was used to refer to the sending of the Son by the Father (particularly as found in John's Gospel).[14] In its more recent, missiological use, this term is intended to emphasize the biblical truth that the initiator and primary actor in mission is God. It is evident, then, that definition of "mission" is not a simple matter. Recently, Eckhard Schnabel has provided a full definition which he applies to both "mission" and "missions":

> the activity of a community of faith that distinguishes itself from its environment in terms of both religious belief (theology) and social behavior (ethics), that is convinced of the truth claims of its faith, and that actively works to win other people to the content of faith and to the way of life of whose truth and necessity the members of that faith community are convinced.[15]

One significant benefit of Schnabel's definition over that suggested by Moreau et al. is that it does not limit mission or missions to evangelism across cultural boundaries but instead regards the primary boundary as that between those who are within the community of faith and those who are not, regardless of their particular cultural context. A broader definition, which helpfully relates "mission" to the notion of the *missio Dei*, is provided by Chris Wright:

> Mission, then, in biblical terms, while it inescapably involves us in planning and action, is not *primarily* a matter of our activity or our initiative. Mission, from the point of view of human endeavor, means the committed *participation* of God's people in the purposes of God for the redemption of the whole creation. The mission is God's. The marvel is that God invites us to join in.[16]

David Bosch prefers not to restrict the term "mission" to the activity of "evangelism,"[17] and Wright's definition also allows a broad meaning. I acknowledge that participation in God's plan of redemption may involve many activities besides evangelism, but I believe that Paul's priority in Philippians is the declaration of the message of Jesus and so, for the purposes of this paper, I

---

13 Moreau, Corwin and McGee, *Introducing World Missions*, 17. See especially D. J. Bosch, *Transforming Mission* (Maryknoll: Orbis, 1991).
14 John A. McIntosh, "Missio Dei," in *Evangelical Dictionary of World Missions* (ed. A. Scott Moreau et al; Grand Rapids: Baker), 631.
15 Schnabel, *Jesus and the Twelve*, 11. See also *Paul the Missionary*, 22.
16 Chris Wright, *The Mission of God* (Leicester: IVP Academic, 2006), 67. I am grateful to my friend, Dr. Harold Le Roux, for drawing this quotation to my attention and also for his careful reading of, and helpful comments on, the whole manuscript.
17 Bosch, *Transforming Mission*, 409-20.

will assume that the *primary* connotation of "mission" is the proclamation of the gospel of Jesus Christ with a view to the conversion of non-Christians (while living in a way which is consistent with that message). I believe that the ethical element within Schnabel's definition should be sufficient to take account of most of Bosch's concerns.

"MISSION THEOLOGY"

We might define "mission theology" as theology which explicitly discusses the missionary activity of the church, that is, the teaching contained in passages where Paul directs a church to evangelize. But it is generally recognized that there would be very little material to use, not only in Philippians but in Paul's other letters.[18] As Bosch comments, "one cannot really study our theme by looking for and analyzing 'mission texts' in Paul's letters."[19] I wish to suggest that when we ask about Paul's "mission theology" in Philippians, we will rather look more inclusively for the theological themes which compel mission or provide the foundation for mission or discuss the hope of mission. In this way, we may find that Philippians has more mission theology in it than we first thought. So let us see the results by engaging directly with the text.

PAUL'S GOSPEL

Paul's priority, as expressed in Philippians, is "to advance the gospel" (1:12 NIV).[20] The term "gospel" (εὐαγγέλιον) is used several times in the letter, especially in the first chapter (1:5, 7, 12, 16, 27 [twice]; 2:22; 4:3, 15). In fact, James Ware notes that this term is used more frequently in this brief letter than in any other Pauline letter.[21] Although the term is not explicitly defined, information from other Pauline letters, particularly 1 Cor 15:3-5, gives us a good indication of the core elements of Paul's message of good news: in particular, the death of Jesus Christ for his people and his resurrection from the dead.[22] In fact, the so-called "Hymn of Christ" in Phil 2:6-11, which might be regarded as a dramatic summary of the gospel, includes the following elements:

---

[18] See I. Howard Marshall, "Who were the evangelists?," in *The Mission of the Early Church to Jews and Gentiles* (ed. Jostein Ådna and Hans Kvalbein; WUNT 127; Tübingen: Mohr [Siebeck] 2000), 251-63 [251]. In this article, Marshall later (253) notes that Paul Bowers "argued powerfully that Paul did not expect the churches in his mission area to assume responsibility for missionary outreach," referring to Bowers's article, "Church and Mission in Paul," *JSNT* 44 (1991): 89-111.
[19] Bosch, *Transforming Mission*, 124.
[20] All quotations of biblical texts are taken from the New International Version, unless otherwise indicated..
[21] Ware, *The Mission of the Church*, 165-66.
[22] See I. Howard Marshall, *Aspects of the Atonement* (Milton Keynes: Authentic, 2007), 69.

Christology (in that there is reference both to the status of the Son as "being in very nature God" and the incarnation); the cross (although there is no particular explanation of its place in the atonement); and the resurrection/the ascension (although there is no clear distinction made between the two events). It seems likely that Paul intends this term to designate not only the theological content of the message but also the active proclamation of that message with the call to respond.[23] Thus, when Paul writes of the Philippians' "partnership in the gospel," it is likely that he means that they share in some way in the task of making the theological message of the gospel known to those who are then urged to respond.

Howard Marshall comments, "In identifying this whole complex of motifs as the heart of Paul's theology we are recognizing that he was essentially a missionary and that therefore a theological statement of the gospel that he preached takes us to the central theme of his Christian thinking."[24]

It is possible to see Paul's emphasis on the theological content of the gospel come through in various parts of the letter. We will note just a few of the significant themes here.

THE CENTRALITY OF GOD IN MISSION

Paul's mission theology as expressed in Philippians is *theology* in the strict sense of the word because it lays a heavy emphasis on the person and work of God (even where the term θεός may not be explicitly used). The term θεός is used some twenty-four times throughout the letter. All but one of these references (the exception is 3:19, which refers to a false god) refer to the God of the Scriptures of Israel whom Paul has now come to know in Christ. It is important to recognize that Paul's theology was not created out of nothing on the road to Damascus, but that "it is clear that the Old Testament has decisively helped to shape Paul's thought."[25] God is "God our Father" (1:2) from whom grace and peace flow; the one Paul thanks in prayer (1:3); Paul's witness to the affection he feels for the Philippians (1:8); the one who is to receive glory and praise from the transformed lives of Christians (1:11); the one who accomplishes final salvation (1:28); the greatest being (2:6); the one who exalted the crucified Christ (2:9); the one who will receive glory from the confession that Jesus Christ is Lord (2:11); the one who works in believers according to his will (2:13); the Father whose character his children must display (2:15); the one who mercifully heals (2:27); the one whose Spirit enables Christians to worship (3:3); the one who makes righteousness available

---

[23] Peter T. O'Brien, "The Gospel in Philippians," in *God Who is Rich in Mercy* (ed. P. T. O'Brien and D. G. Peterson; Homebush West: Lancer, 1986) 213-33 [216], and Köstenberger and O'Brien, *Salvation*, 173-74, 192.
[24] Marshall, *New Testament Theology*, 423.
[25] Marshall, *New Testament Theology*, 421.

(3:9); the one who has called Paul heavenwards (3:14); the revealer of truth to Christians (3:15); the one to whom Christians must make known their requests (4:6); the provider of peace (4:7); characterized by peace (4:9); the one who accepts the offering of the Philippians (4:18); the one who satisfies the needs of believers (4:19); the recipient of glory in the benediction (4:20). All of these references fit into Paul's overall understanding of who God is. This understanding of God is drawn largely from the Scriptures of the OT which are now put in fresh perspective by Paul's encounter with the risen Jesus of Nazareth.[26] It should be clear simply from this brief summary that God's character and gracious activity lie at the heart of Paul's gospel. Regarding the significance of these references for Paul's understanding of mission, we may note the presentation of God as the one, firstly, who initiates the event of someone becoming a Christian and, secondly, who will receive praise for the ultimate completion of this event. That God initiates the event of Christian conversion is seen in Paul's comment in Philippians 3:14 where he writes, "I press on towards the goal to win the prize for which God has called me heavenwards in Christ Jesus." Although Paul can use κλῆσις and cognate terms to speak of his calling to the role of apostle (Rom 1:1), it "frequently refers to God's initial and effective call to salvation through the gospel,"[27] and this appears to be its sense here. This is confirmed by the addition of ἄνω, "upwards," which reflects the common biblical understanding that the place where God dwells is "above." Thus God's calling is a calling into his own presence. And this is a calling which God alone can make, whether to Paul or to anyone other person. Thus we see that Paul regards God as the initiator of Christian life. Mission is truly *missio Dei*, the mission of God.

We may also note verses which indicate that God's glory is the ultimate goal of the completion of the task of mission—not simply initial conversion, but believers brought to fullness of Christ-like character (1:9-11). Turning then to the so-called Hymn of Christ in Phil 2:6-11, we find that God's purpose (ἵνα, 2:10) in exalting Christ[28] is that all should confess that Jesus Christ is Lord. This act of confession will surely include many who do so willingly as they have been brought into the Christian church through the proclamation of the gospel, even if it also includes others who will do so because they have no

---

[26] David B. Capes, Rodney Reeves and E. Randolph Richards, *Rediscovering Paul: An Introduction to His World, Letters and Theology* (Leicester: Apollos, 2007), 257-58.

[27] O'Brien, *Philippians*, 432-33. So also Bockmuehl, *Philippians*, 222-23.

[28] Although Fee, *Philippians*, 223 n. 27, recognizes that ἵνα frequently expresses purpose, he prefers to read this instance as indicating result. I do not disagree that the exaltation of Jesus results in the confession of Jesus Christ as Lord; I would simply argue that the logic of 2:9-11 suggests God's deliberate intent. See Gerald F. Hawthorne, *Philippians* (WBC 43; Waco: Word Books, 1983), 92, where Hawthorne discusses "God's purpose in thus exalting Christ."

choice.²⁹ But a further purpose in this confession is that it is "to the glory of God the Father" (2:11).

Thus, although God is not described as commanding mission in these texts, Paul's understanding of God's fundamental role in the process of bringing others to faith in Christ and in enabling them to follow the course is of vital importance to the message that Paul declares.

Along with these explicit references to God, there are some important references which do not employ the term θεός. Of particular importance is Phil 1:6 where Paul states, as part of the thanksgiving section of his letter, that he is "confident of this, that he who began a good work in you will carry it on to completion until the day of Christ Jesus". It is clear that the one who began the good work is God. There is some discussion among commentators, however, regarding the nature of the "good work" which Paul has in mind here. Is it the act of providing support for Paul's mission or is it the creation of new life in the believer at the point of conversion? Hawthorne is convinced it is the former.³⁰ Howard Marshall comments briefly in his short study of the theology of Philippians, "As they share in Paul's mission, so too they share in God's grace."³¹ Likewise, in his recent study of NT theology, he comments on the sense of partnership between Paul and the Christians at Philippi, "that arose from their common experience of God's grace in their work for him."³² Neither of these statements makes it entirely clear which position Marshall favors; perhaps they are intended to be deliberately ambiguous so as to allow both possibilities to remain. In either case, we can see Paul responds to the encouraging activity of the Philippian Christians by thanking God rather than

---

[29] Fee, *Philippians*, 224, comments, "there is in this language no hint that those who bow are acknowledging his salvation," but he acknowledges a few lines later with regard to the parallel statement concerning confession of Christ as Lord that "this confession arose in the early Jewish Christian community" (225). It would seem unreasonable then, either to restrict the confession to those who have previously rejected Christ, or to deny that the group who will bow and the group who will testify are identical. O'Brien, *Philippians*, 250, sums up the intent of the passage well: "For those who, in the here and now, have already bowed the knee to Jesus and confessed him as Lord, as clearly the Philippian Christians had done, the acclamation at his parousia would spring from the heart. Others, however, such as the principalities and powers of Col 2:15, are not depicted as gladly surrendering to God's grace, but as submitting against their wills to a power they cannot resist." Hawthorne, *Philippians*, 94, resists this conclusion, however, suggesting that this passage speaks of "the hope of God" that "every intelligent being in his universe might proclaim openly and gladly . . . that Jesus Christ alone has the right to reign" but "it is also conceivable that these beings will never be forced to do so against their will."

[30] Hawthorne, *Philippians*, 21.

[31] Karl P. Donfried and I. Howard Marshall, *The Theology of the Shorter Pauline Letters* (Cambridge: Cambridge University Press, 1993), 158.

[32] Marshall, *New Testament Theology*, 345.

by thanking his friends directly for their efforts. This provides clear evidence that Paul regards the missionary activity of the church (in the sense of either the conversion of individuals or active commitment to the missionary task of the church) to be initiated and empowered by God. But we can take a step further because there is reason to think that when Paul refers to the "good work" which God has begun in the Philippian Christians he is referring to their salvation. This is particularly likely since Paul regards the ultimate conclusion of God's activity in their lives not as the completion of a missionary task but as the "day of Christ Jesus." This term is an adaptation of the OT phrase "the Day of the Lord," which was understood as the final eschatological act of God bringing all things fully into line with his purpose. This event is understood by Paul to be the Parousia, or glorious return of Jesus. Fee writes, "[H]aving reminded them of *his* own joy over their good past and present, he turns now to assure them of *their* own certain future."[33] Thus God is the one who is ultimately responsible for the new life which begins in a person and so the mission of the church must be viewed as participation in the mission of God. The *missio Dei*, then, includes much more (though no less) than God drawing a person into relationship with himself; it involves his commitment to bring his purposes for his people and for his world to their completion.

CHRISTOLOGY

Although a distinction can usefully be drawn between theology and Christology for the sake of our discussion, there can be no real separation of Paul's understanding of God from his understanding of Christ. This is seen particularly clearly in the opening salutation where Paul understands that grace and peace flow jointly from God (understood as the Father) and the Lord Jesus Christ (1:2).

There is so much rich christological material in this letter that we cannot survey it in detail, but we can note several themes which receive particularly effective presentation in the "exalted prose" of Phil 2:6-11:[34] Christ's preexistence (2:6); his selfless attitude (2:6); his incarnation and humble human existence (2:7); his crucifixion (2:8); his resurrection/ascension/glorification (2:9).

Christology lies at the heart of Paul's missionary proclamation, particularly with respect to Jesus' becoming fully human, his death on the cross and his resurrection.[35] This is summarized concisely in the phrase "Christ is preached"

---

[33] Fee, *Philippians*, 86 (emphasis original).
[34] The terminology is that of Gordon Fee, whose view I follow. See "Philippians 2:5-11: Hymn or Exalted Pauline Prose," *BBR* 2 (1992): 29-46 and also *Philippians*, 40-43.
[35] George W. Peters, *A Biblical Theology of Missions* (Chicago: Moody, 1974), 310, writes, "The deity-humanity mystery and the cross-resurrection event are inseparably

or "Christ is proclaimed" in 1:15, 17, 18. This short phrase serves synonymously for "the gospel is preached" and it can be understood to mean that the dominant theme in the proclamation is the person and work of Jesus Christ.[36]

That gospel, which is encapsulated so well in 2:6-11, also demonstrates vividly the self-giving character of the missionary God, as Jesus Christ consistently humbles himself for the sake of others, entering their experience and submitting to humiliation and suffering on their behalf. This pattern is the model for Paul, for his co-workers and for the Philippians. It remains the model for all who would share in the missionary task.

ESCHATOLOGY

Eschatology is a vital aspect of Paul's theology and it has a significant impact on his understanding of his mission.[37] Paul's eschatology can be seen in Philippians particularly in his focus on the events surrounding the glorious return of Jesus, or the "Parousia" and so eschatology is very closely related to Christology. We have already noted above Paul's reference to the day of Christ in Phil 1:6. A similar emphasis is found in 1:10. When Paul calls the Philippians to demonstrate Christian character in their witness (2:12-18, see further discussion below), he looks forward to the "day of Christ" as the moment when he may "boast" of fruit of his ministry. Likewise, when he comments on the rejection of the gospel by many, he reminds the Philippians that they "eagerly await a Savior" from heaven (3:20), a reference to the Parousia. So we can see that Paul's interest in Jesus' return and eschatology in general is not a matter of idle theological speculation but an incentive to faithful mission.

PAUL'S GOSPEL PROCLAIMED

Finally, having considered several of the key elements of Paul's gospel, it only remains to note that this gospel is a message to be proclaimed. Ware draws attention to numerous verbs which indicate the proclamation of a message (notably λαλεῖν, κηρύσσω, καταγγέλλω, in 1:12-18) and concludes, "Philippians reveals an extraordinary level of interest in the preaching of the

---

linked in the foundational message of the New Testament, the gospel of God and the gospel of our salvation."

[36] O'Brien, *Philippians*, 98-99.

[37] See I. Howard Marshall, "A New Understanding of the Present and the Future: Paul and Eschatology," in *The Road from Damascus: The Impact of Paul's Conversion on His Life, Thought, and Ministry* (ed. Richard N. Longenecker; MNTS; Grand Rapids: Eerdmans, 1997), 43-61.

gospel."[38]

PAUL'S PRIORITY OF PRAYER

Although there is a measure of formality in the prayer report section of a Pauline letter,[39] this should not be taken to mean that Paul does not treat prayer as a matter of utmost importance. Prayer plays an important role in the letter to the Philippians since it not only figures in Paul's introductory report of his prayers for the Philippians but also receives emphasis towards the end of the letter in Paul's exhortation to the Philippians to pray in turn. Thus Paul, in this "missionary prayer letter," provides his readers not only with matters which require prayer but also with a model of prayer in action. This letter is truly a "prayer letter," which describes, seeks and commands prayer.

We note just one text briefly. In Phil 1:19, Paul comments regarding his expectations concerning his imprisonment, "I know that through your prayers and the help given by the Spirit of Jesus Christ, what has happened to me will turn out for my deliverance." Paul clearly identifies two factors which he believes will be instrumental in the future outcome: the prayers of his Christian brothers and sisters and the help of the Holy Spirit. Fee notes that the use of a single article with the two nouns "assumes the closest kind of relationship between their prayer and the supply of the Spirit."[40] While this belief in the significance of both the prayers of God's people and the work of God's Spirit in his life relates to his personal future, this is to be understood within the broader context of Paul's understanding of what will be for the greatest benefit for the Philippians and thus for the mission of the church.

PAUL AND HIS COLLEAGUES

Philippians provides a considerable amount of information regarding Paul and his colleagues. In fact, it compares well with the lengthy chapter of Rom 16 with regard to the number of individuals who are identified but, more particularly, to the level of detailed information which is provided to enable us to appreciate their roles. In addition to the named colleagues, however, there are several significant passages where unnamed believers are also mentioned. In this section, we will consider Paul's reflections on his own role and on the role of some named fellow-workers, the Christians in Philippi, some local Roman Christians and some local people who seem to have been against Paul in some way.

---

[38] Ware, *Mission of the Church*, 166.
[39] Paul includes a report of his prayer for Christian brothers and sisters in the following letters: Romans, 1 Corinthians, Ephesians, Philippians, Colossians, 1 and 2 Thessalonians, 2 Timothy.
[40] Fee, *Philippians*, 132.

PAUL AND HIS CO-WORKERS

"If we want to get a clear angle of vision as to how Paul conceived of his relationship to the churches, then we need to consider Paul as missionary."[41] In the introduction to the letter, Paul does not employ the term ἀπόστολος, which he regularly uses elsewhere and which is clearly an important term for understanding Paul's concept of mission since it indicates that he has been commissioned to carry the gospel (see particularly Rom 1:1). The absence of this term in Philippians need not, however, be regarded as a sign of less interest in the missionary task.

Paul names several colleagues in the missionary task in this letter. As in several other letters, Paul includes a co-worker, in this case Timothy, in the opening salutation.[42] While it is generally agreed that Timothy has no significant role in the writing of the letter,[43] the inclusion of his name at the head of the letter is more than a mere formality. It indicates that Paul truly regards his mission as an activity carried out in partnership. This is not to say that Paul is not conscious of partnership when he only uses his own name at the beginning of a letter (e.g., Romans). Clearly this notion would make no sense in the light of his comments in Rom 16. What I am suggesting is that when there is a natural opportunity to express cooperation in the missionary task, it appears that Paul takes it willingly.

What is more, Paul chooses an unexpected self-designation for himself and Timothy—that of δοῦλοι, which is most appropriately rendered in English as "slaves."[44] While commentators note that there may be some association with the "Servant of the Lord" in the OT, it is much more natural to read this reference in the light of the use of the term in Philippians 2:7 where the term signifies humble service of others, since Paul regards himself and Timothy and Epaphroditus as those who follow the pattern of Christ and calls the Philippians to do likewise.

We also find very distinctive reference to fellow-workers in the extended discussion of the circumstances of Timothy and Epaphroditus.[45] In this section,

---

[41] Thomas R. Schreiner, *Paul, Apostle of God's Glory in Christ* (Leicester: Apollos, 2001), 38.

[42] Fee, *Philippians*, 60, notes that "Even though the practice is extremely rare among the extant Greco-Roman letters, Paul frequently includes his present companions with himself in his salutations." Apart from this case in Philippians, Paul includes one or more of his companions in the salutation of 1 and 2 Thessalonians, 1 and 2 Corinthians, Philemon and Colossians.

[43] Fee, *Philippians*, 60-61.

[44] So Fee, *Philippians*, 62-64 and Fowl, *Philippians*, 16-17. See especially Murray J. Harris, *Slave of Christ* (NSBT 8; Leicester: Apollos, 1999).

[45] See especially Peter T. O'Brien, "The Gospel and Godly Models in Philippians," in *Worship, Theology and Ministry in the Early Church: Essays in Honor of Ralph P. Martin* (ed. Michael J. Wilkins and Terence Paige; JSNTSup 87; Sheffield: JSOT Press, 1992), 273-84.

there is less specific reference to the evangelistic mission of the church, but the statements that Timothy "has served with me in the work of the gospel" (2:22) and that Epaphroditus "almost died for the work of Christ" certainly suggest that these men have contributed to the mission of the church, even if that is by providing support to Paul as opposed to being engaged in direct evangelism.[46]

The next workers to be identified by name are Euodia and Syntyche (4:2). Although they have the dubious privilege of being remembered for being addressed personally by Paul with the plea that they resolve whatever tension had developed between them, this should not distract us from Paul's remarkable statement about their contribution to the mission of the church: "these women who have contended at my side in the cause of the gospel, along with Clement and the rest of my fellow-workers, whose names are in the book of life" (4:3). The dominant note in Paul's comments is that these women had played a significant role in the mission of the church and that they will continue to make an indispensable contribution if they deal with whatever problem has been distracting them.

These various references to named colleagues indicate that Paul is committed to servant ministry along with a team of colleagues who are commended for their contributions to the mission of the church, even as they are challenged and guided regarding how they may share more effectively in the work.

EVANGELISM IN PHILIPPI

Paul also makes several references to the involvement of the Philippian church as a whole in the task of evangelism. He identifies one particular reason for his joyful thanksgiving and prayers for them: "because of your partnership in the gospel from the first day until now" (1:5). It is clear that Paul is writing in part to thank the Philippians for the gifts they sent to him in prison (4:18). While Paul would certainly require assistance from friends while in prison and it may be that the particular gifts he has in mind in the final chapter were those intended to sustain him during this difficult period, we should not restrict his comments about their partnership to the period of his imprisonment alone. Paul's reference to "the first day" is unlikely to mean "the first day of my imprisonment."[47] It is much more likely to mean "the first day we were brought together as members of God's family," that is, from the point at which the church in Philippi came into being through Paul's own missionary activity (Acts 16). The nature of the "partnership" of the Philippians is not stated here, but while the financial support they have given is bound to be in the forefront

---

[46] The reference in Acts 16:3 to Paul having Timothy circumcised "because of the Jews" certainly suggests that this was a matter of expediency to aid the acceptance of Timothy as a messenger of the gospel.

[47] So, correctly, Fowl, *Philippians*, 25.

of Paul's mind, there is no reason to think that he would exclude other forms of participation, such as direct involvement in evangelism, which are apparently in mind at other points in this letter and to which we now turn.

Firstly, we may note Paul's urgent concern in 1:12: "Now I want you to know, brothers, that what has happened to me has really served to advance the gospel." These are the first words with which Paul moves to address one of the main subjects of the letter and their significance is emphasized by the use of the "disclosure form" (Γινώσκειν δὲ ὑμᾶς βούλομαι) and the direct address in the vocative case (ἀδελφοί).[48] While Paul will go on to speak of the events which are taking place where he is (which I take to be Rome), the strongly worded desire to inform the Philippians (Γινώσκειν δὲ ὑμᾶς βούλομαι, ἀδελφοί, ὅτι τὰ κατ' ἐμὲ μᾶλλον εἰς προκοπὴν τοῦ εὐαγγελίου ἐλήλυθεν·) suggests that he anticipates that the Philippians will be distressed not simply because of Paul's own personal hardships but also because of the supposed harm to the cause of the gospel.[49] That is, he assumes that the Philippians are as committed to the task of making the gospel known as he is. Now he assures them that "[t]hey are to understand that [the effect of his imprisonment] has been quite the reverse of what they might have expected."[50]

Secondly, in his exhortation to the Philippians to maintain a harmonious spirit (2:14-18), Paul indicates that the need for a blameless character is not simply for the Philippians' own sake, but because they live "in a crooked and depraved generation, in which you shine like stars in the universe as you hold out the word of life" (2:15-16 NIV). Here Paul assumes that the Christians in Philippi will be actively engaged in making the word, which alone can bring life, known to non-Christians and indicates that the holiness of their lives must be the confirmation of the truth of the transformation which the gospel offers (from darkness to shining light).[51] Howard Marshall comments, "Part of the purpose of his description of the situation surrounding his imprisonment with the gospel being preached by people from a variety of motives, but nevertheless being a means of making Christ known, is to stimulate the readers to their own witness by living blameless lives in the community and by their testimony to Christ."[52] Christian morality is not seen here as an end in itself but as a means of demonstrating the transforming power of the gospel to those to whom the gospel is also preached.

---

[48] O'Brien, *Philippians*, 86. See also Ware, *Mission of the Church*, 173, 183.

[49] See the list of possible concerns suggested by O'Brien, *Philippians*, 85-86, which includes concerns both about Paul personally and the progress of the gospel.

[50] Fee, *Philippians*, 110.

[51] Fee, *Philippians*, 246, notes the strong intertextuality between 2:15 and the Greek of Dan 12:3, and suggests that the wider context of the Daniel reference which reads, "Those who are wise will shine like the brightness of the heavens, and those who lead many to righteousness, like the stars for ever and ever," confirms the evangelistic intent of the passage.

[52] Marshall, *New Testament Theology*, 360.

Paul may not, however, restrict the missionary activity of the Philippians to what we might call "passive" witness. He continues in Phil 2:16, "as you hold out [so NIV] /hold on to the word of life" (λόγον ζωῆς ἐπέχοντες). Bockmuehl notes that there are no direct parallels to the phrase "word of life" in Paul's writings but that "it is clearly a reference to God's word in the life-giving gospel."[53] There is some uncertainty among commentators regarding how best to translate ἐπέχοντες. O'Brien favors translating it as "hold fast" on the grounds that the context in Philippians has to do with steadfastness. Bockmuehl recognizes how finely balanced the argument is but favors "hold fast" because the text is not used to justify evangelistic activity in early Christian writings. Fee, on the other hand, notes that the preceding verses suggest evangelistic activity, and I follow him in believing that even if Paul is urging the Philippians to hold firmly to the gospel, its very character as "word of life" (or "life-giving word") demands that it be shared. We might also note that the pattern of Jesus which is presented in Philippians 2:6 is not to use his privilege for his own advantage but to make it a benefit to others, which is surely what the Philippians are urged to do here also. Howard Marshall also thinks "that there is a reasonable case for seeing outward witness to the gospel as the reference in this passage."[54]

Similarly, when Paul addresses Euodia and Syntyche in Phil 4:2-3, he does so in the context of comments on those who reject Christ (3:18, comments which he makes with evident distress) and also comments on those (including these two women) who have labored with Paul in the work of the gospel and who share the high privilege of having their names written in the book of life. The clear implication is that the urgency in resolving the tension between these two women (whatever it may have been) lies not simply in bringing peace to the Christian congregation in Philippi but in ridding the congregation of distractions from the primary task of proclaiming the gospel so that others may come to know the same privilege. Fee helpfully comments that Christians and "especially those in leadership, must learn to subordinate personal agendas to the larger agenda of the gospel."[55]

Finally, under this heading, we may note Paul's comments in 1:27-30 which include the key phrase "contending as one man for the faith of the gospel" (1:27). The same term is used here as is used of Euodia and Syntyche, suggesting vigorous partnership in a common struggle. In the context of Philippians, it is likely that an aspect of "contending" would involve defense of the gospel against the opponents identified in Phil 3, but from what we have seen of the use of "gospel" in Philippians, this would also seem to be a specific call to unity in the struggle to make the gospel known to an unbelieving world.

---

[53] Bockmuehl, *Philippians*, 158-59.
[54] Marshall, "Who were the evangelists?," 260.
[55] Fee, *Philippians*, 398.

EVANGELISM IN ROME

When Paul acknowledges that the circumstances he presently faces do not appear to have been beneficial for the mission of the church, he seeks to encourage his friends in Philippi by noting two significant outcomes which have in fact advanced the gospel. The first is that the whole imperial guard, along with many others, has come to recognize that Paul's imprisonment is on account of Christ. One can only assume that they are able to reach this conclusion because Paul makes it explicit for them in speech. O'Brien suggests that "throughout the whole palace guard and to everyone else" indicates "the sphere in which Paul's witness has been effective."[56] Thus Paul treats captivity not as a barrier to mission but as an evangelistic opportunity to speak to people who otherwise would be very difficult to reach with the gospel message.

The second outcome is that "most of the brothers in the Lord have been encouraged to speak the word of God more courageously and fearlessly" (1:14). This, Paul says, is "[b]ecause of my chains." We can highlight several implications of this passing reference. The first implication is that Paul takes it for granted that the Christians in Rome were already engaged in active evangelism since the term περισσοτέρως suggests an increase in degree. The second implication is that he regards this action as a positive characteristic which can be presented as a model. Although it is true that Paul does not issue a direct command to evangelize, we might regard the words of 4:17 as a call to follow every good pattern that has been brought before the Philippians, including that of the evangelizing Christians in Rome. The third implication is that there is an element of danger in the activity of evangelizing and that the Roman Christians have been encouraged by Paul's testimony in the heart of the Roman military machine not to allow the real risks to hold them back in presenting the gospel.

Paul's commitment to the spread of the gospel is demonstrated remarkably in his magnanimous attitude towards those who seek to do him harm through the preaching of the gospel (1:15-18). In stark contrast to his fierce reaction when a *false* gospel is preached (Gal 1:8-9), Paul rejoices (1:18) when Christ is preached, regardless of how suspect the motive may be.

PRACTICAL SUPPORT FOR MISSION

One of the most distinctive aspects of Philippians is that Paul expresses his thanks to the Christians in Philippi for their financial gift and for their support in other ways. We may identify the following ways in which Paul acknowledges or seeks practical support from the Philippians.

---

[56] O'Brien, *Philippians*, 92.

FINANCIAL SUPPORT

Although Paul is clearly grateful to the Philippians for their financial support, he is not slow to indicate that he believed that others have not offered support as they should have done (4:15). Yet he is explicitly grateful that this was not the first time that the Philippians had shown their support through financial gifts: "for even when I was in Thessalonica you sent me aid again and again when I was in need" (4:16). These gifts contribute to the mission of the church not necessarily by enabling some dramatic progress, but often by keeping the missionary alive and able to continue his or her daily witness to the gospel.

ENCOURAGEMENT

In 2:19, Paul indicates how significant Timothy is in providing a link between him and his Philippian friends. He hopes that "I also may be cheered when I receive news about you." The support of the wider Christian community is crucial to Paul's ministry.

Likewise, when Paul writes, "I rejoice greatly in the Lord that at last you have renewed your concern for me. Indeed you have been concerned but you had no opportunity to show it," he is indicating that his knowledge of the concern of the Philippians is of considerable importance to him. It is not simply a matter of money.

Thus we can see that practical support includes, but is not exhausted by, financial support. A sense of Christian support and communication are also of great importance.

PRACTICAL REFLECTIONS

Several comments can be made in the light of our discussion which may have relevance for missionary activity in the present day.

Firstly, missionary activity which looks to Paul for its character will be gospel-centered. Even where there is an appropriate emphasis on practical behavior, it will be founded on theological principles. These should certainly include an appropriate emphasis on the role of God the Father in initiating his plan of salvation and on the centrality of Jesus Christ as the one who has fully accomplished God's purposes. There should also be an appropriate eschatological note, not in a way that encourages wild and undisciplined speculation but with due recognition of both the challenge and incentive of the return of Jesus. The church must not allow itself to become driven by entirely pragmatic considerations.

Secondly, prayer is essential to the church's mission. If we share Paul's theological understanding, then prayer will not simply be a psychological encouragement for churches and workers, but will be true requests for the Lord's action in the circumstances to bring about events which are not within the power of the human beings involved. At the same time, it will be expressions of thanksgiving for the ways in which the Lord has already acted to bring about his purposes in the experience of the church and its mission. Prayer may also be regarded as a means of shaping one's mind in a Christ-like manner which may affect the way in which the church carries out its mission and the priorities it chooses regarding where and how and with whom to work. Clearly there is a direct relationship between good theology and appropriate prayer. Paul acknowledges God's sovereign action and thanks him for what he is accomplishing. He also prays for blessing in the future, but he never regards God's sovereignty as a reason for shirking responsibility or for fatalistic apathy. We may also note that he prays about a range of matters in this letter, from the spiritual health of his Christian brothers and sisters to his own welfare.

Thirdly, Philippians shows that opposition and even apparent catastrophes (such as a key missionary being imprisoned) must be regarded in the light of the sovereignty of God, who is the true Agent of the mission of the church and who directs all things. Philippians is surely intended to demonstrate, from the pattern of Jesus' life and also of Paul's, that the path to successful completion of one's mission may, in God's sovereign will, lie through suffering.

Fourthly, missionaries and missionary organizations can see from Philippians how important are the relationships which exist between co-workers and also between missionaries and their sending churches. These relationships are so absolutely crucial that they must be nurtured and protected. Communication and a sense of true collaboration are essential to all who are involved in the task. This will certainly involve financial support of missionaries and missionary work, but the members of the so-called "sending church" may not regard such support as the full extent of their responsibilities. In fact, there must be a greater realization that *all Christians* are in some sense "missionaries" and are to be engaged in the common task of sharing the gospel.

CONCLUSION

In his brief reflection on the significance of Philippians for today, Howard Marshall comments that "this letter is significant for the light it sheds on the work of other preachers and for the partnership of a congregation with Paul in evangelism."[57]

He also notes, "What is especially noteworthy here is the role of the congregations that he founded in this work in two ways. One is the support of Paul's work through a fellowship that involved tangible gifts of money and other resources, including the sending of colleagues to share with Paul in the work, but also the offering of prayers without which Paul believed that his

---

[57] I. Howard Marshall, Stephen Travis and Ian Paul, *The Letters and Revelation* (vol. 2 of *Exploring the New Testament*; London: SPCK, 2002), 140.

work could not continue fruitfully."[58]

We have seen that Philippians highlights Paul's commitment to making the message of the gospel known in the context both of his full confidence in the sovereign work of God in using all circumstances (even hardship and opposition) to bring about his purposes and of his commitment to working with a Christ-like servant attitude as part of a team of Christian brothers and sisters who all share in the task of making Christ known.

---

[58] Marshall, *New Testament Theology*, 360.

16

PAUL'S MISSIONARY PREACHING IN 1 THESSALONIANS 2:1–16, WITH AN APOCALYPTIC ADDITION FROM 2 THESSALONIANS

Anthony C. Thiselton

The main part of this paper concerns what is almost certainly the earliest account of missionary preaching in Paul, if not in the whole NT. Even if we take into account the "we" passages in Acts (from 16:11 onwards), allusions are more fragmentary than those in 1 Thessalonians. 1 Thessalonians 2:1-12 witnesses to Paul's memory of when he *declared* "to you the gospel of God, in spite of much opposition" (2:2). These verses also describe his behavior, mode of delivery, and motives. 1 Thessalonians 2:13-16 describes his memory of how the Thessalonians *received* this gospel: "You accepted it not as a human word, but as what it really is, God's word, which is also at work in you believers."

I

Debates about this passage take place at two distinct levels, or areas of discourse. A more technical discussion, for example, occurs in the volume published in 2000, *The Thessalonians Debate: Methodological Discord or Methodological Synthesis?*, in which Karl Donfried sees 1 Thess 2:1-12 not only as a dynamic speech-act, but also as part of "a friendship letter" rather than a piece of apologetic, designed to establish and strengthen Paul's personal relationship with the Thessalonian Church.[1] Traugott Holtz rejects arguments that 1 Thess 2:1-12 is not primarily apologetic in its aim. Holtz emphasizes the historical context of the letter in general and of 1 Thess 2:1-12 in particular, not least the fact of persecution and of "social discrimination." He considers historical, rhetorical, and epistolary factors.[2] In his response to Holtz, Johan Vos considers that Holtz's historical reconstruction of events is insufficiently

---

[1] Karl P. Donfried, "The Epistology and Rhetorical Context of 1 Thessalonians 2:1-12," in *The Thessalonians Debate: Methodological Discord or Methodological Synthesis?* (ed. Karl P. Donfried and Johannes Beutler; Grand Rapids: Eerdmans 2000), 31-60.

[2] Traugott Holtz, "On the Background of 1 Thessalonians 2:1-12," in *The Thessalonians Debate: Methodological Discord or Methodological Synthesis?*, 69-80; Traugott Holtz, *Der Erste Brief an die Thessalonicher* (Neukirchen: Neukirchener Verlag, 1986), 15-32; and T. Holtz, "Der Apostel der Christus: Die Paulnische 'Apologie', 1 Thess. 2:1-12," in *Als Boten des gekreuzigten Herrn: Festgabe für Werner Krusche* (ed. H. Falcke et al.; Berlin: Evangelische Verlagsanstalt, 1982), 101-16.

based on certain and precise evidence.³ Otto Merk underlines the earlier verdict of Friedrich Zimmer (in 1897) that this passage is "very far from being properly understood."⁴ He concludes that this passage is a "potential apologia" by a Christian missionary and congregation-founder, in which Paul's own behavior plays a positive role. The primary theme is the gospel. In 2:1-12 "gospel of God" is mentioned four times.

At this more specialist level, problems are numerous. Otto Merk relates the passage in question to Paul's abrupt enforced departure from Thessalonica. In response, Jeffrey Weima raises questions about a rhetorical approach, as Ben Witherington does in his commentary.⁵ Stephen Fowl debates the textual-critical and contextual grounds for reading νήπιοι (babes) or ἤπιοι (gentle) in 1 Thess 2:7.⁶ Charles Crawford discusses whether νήπιοι should be read as a vocative, not as a nominative, alongside ἤπιοι.⁷

II

All this may sound sometimes a little theoretical and remote from church life, although in the end it is not so. At a more popular level, however, there is a striking contrast between Paul's missionary presentation of the gospel and that followed by many evangelists today. (1) First, as Donfried notes, Paul has already established a *close relationship* with the Thessalonians, which deeply engages him. Furthermore, as Merk urges, he shows the deep concern of a *pastoral heart*. Both features stand in contrast with the remote preacher or even the televangelist who confronts an audience *from a distance*. (2) Second, Paul testifies that his speech and behavior were *gentle*. This stands in stark contrast to those preachers who rant against and berate or browbeat their congregations, perhaps in the hope that it will add *gravitas* to their personalities. But, as in 1 Cor 1–4, Paul rejects a *personality-centered* approach. J. A. Crafton argues that far from apostles drawing attention to themselves, they should be like

---

³ Johan S. Vos, "On the Background of 1 Thessalonians 2:1-12: A Response to Traugott Holtz," in *The Thessalonians Debate: Methodological Discord or Methodological Synthesis?*, 81-88.
⁴ Otto Merk, "1 Thessalonians 2:1-12: An Exegetical-and-Theological Study," in *The Thessalonians Debate: Methodological Discord or Methodological Synthesis?* (ed. Karl P. Donfried and Johannes Beutler; Grand Rapids: Eerdmans 2000), 89-113 [89].
⁵ Jeffrey A. D. Weima, "The Function of 1 Thessalonians 2:1-12 and the Use of Rhetorical Criticism: A Response to Otto Merk," in *The Thessalonians Debate: Methodological Discord or Methodological Synthesis?*, 114-31; and Ben Witherington III, *1 and 2 Thessalonians: A Socio-Rhetorical Commentary* (Grand Rapids: Eerdmans, 2006), esp. 76-86.
⁶ Stephen Fowl, "A Metaphor in Distress: A Reading of ΝΗΠΙΟΙ in 1 Thessalonians 2.7," *NTS* 36 (1990): 469-73.
⁷ Charles Crawford, "The 'Tiny' Problem of 1 Thessalonians 2,7: The Case of the Curious Vocative," *Bib* 54 (1973): 69-72.

transparent windows, through whom people see not the apostles, but only Christ.[8]

(3) There are many further contrasts. For example, third, Paul works closely in 1 Thessalonians with Silvanus and Timothy, who are his fellow-workers or *co-workers*.[9] Origen observes that the three made a harmony or symphony, yet were "found as one."[10] Nevertheless most evangelists today work as a single voice, often clamoring for recognition or status. (4) Fourth, Paul makes it clear that he is *no entertainer*, who aims first of all to please the crowd. He asserts, "[W]e speak not to please mortals, but to please God" (1 Thess 2:4), "We [plural] never came with words of flattery . . . nor did we seek praise from mortals" (1 Thess 2:6). Clement of Alexandria echoes Paul's words: "We sought no glory from man . . . as not pleasing men, but God."[11] In the Middle Ages Alain of Lille (d. 1202) argued, that "Preaching should not contain jesting words . . . or rhythms . . . better fitted to delight the ear than to edify the soul. Such preaching is theatrical and full of buffoonery"[12] (*The Art of Preaching*). Yet many "fresh expressions" of the Church in England and in America fall for doing precisely this: becoming an act of entertainment, in which the preacher becomes a celebrity.

(5) Paul and his co-workers would gladly have shared in *solidarity* with their converts the life of *hard work* and experience of *oppression* that befell them. They did not want to be socially "at arm's length" with them. Ronald F. Hock has devoted a book and a sequence of articles to elucidating how Paul was willing to lose high status and suffer a considerable loss of status in the eyes of the world by working at tent-making as an artisan.[13] L. L. Welborn follows Frederick Danker in understanding σκηνοποιός (Acts 18:3), not as a tentmaker, but as a "maker of stage properties."[14] Yet Welborn agrees that Paul describes himself and the apostles as "the meanest, the basest of people"; Paul

---

[8] J. A. Crafton, *The Agency of the Apostle* (JSNTSup 51; Sheffield: Sheffield Academic Press, 1991) 53-103.

[9] W. H. Ollrog, *Paulus und seiner Mitarbeiter* (Neukirchen: Neukirchener Verlag, 1979); F. F. Bruce, *The Pauline Circle* (Exeter: Paternoster, 1985); D. I. Harrington, "Paul and Collaborative Ministry," *New Theology Review* 3 (1990): 62-71.

[10] Origen, *Commentary on Matthew* 14.1 (*ANF* 10:495); *Commentary on Romans* 10.7.6 (FC 104, 270-71).

[11] *Stromata* 1.1 and 7.12 (*ANF* 2:300 and 543).

[12] *The Art of Preaching* (trans. Gillian R. Evans; Kalamazoo, Mich.: Cistercian Publications, 1981); for Latin, see J.-P. Migne, ed., *Patrologia Latina*, vol. 210.

[13] R. F. Hock, "Paul's Tentmaking and the Problem of his Social Class," *JBL* 97 (1978): 555-64; R. F. Hock, *The Social Context of Paul's Ministry: Tentmaking and Apostleship* (Philadelphia: Fortress, 1980); and R. F. Hock, "The Workshop as a Social Setting for Paul; Missionary Preaching," *CBQ* 41 (1979): 438-50.

[14] BDAG, s.v. "σκηνοποιός"; L. L. Welborn, *Paul, the Fool of Christ* (London: Continuum, 2005), 11; cf. 12-14.

"would have frequently suffered hunger," and was "poorly clothed."[15]

(6) Sixth, and possibly lastly, Andrew Clarke shows how different was the *style of "secular" leadership* from that of Paul and his fellow-workers.[16] Together with Stephen M. Pogoloff and Bruce Winter, he shows how far Paul was away from high status-claiming rhetoric. Pogoloff comments, "People would flock to the newest orator, just as they would to the newest actor or gladiator. According to Quintilian's disapproving comments, when fellow students declaimed, others would 'stand up or leap from their seats . . . . Every effusion is greeted with a storm of ready-made applause . . . . The result is vanity and empty self-sufficiency.'"[17] Quintilian attacks another artificial weapon in the amateur rhetorician's armory: they seek to acquire the reputation of speaking "with greater vigor than the trained orator" in their delivery.[18] How typical this is of many preachers, especially but not exclusively on television or in some parts of the Southern United States! Bruce Winter similarly shows how Paul renounced the ethics and conventions of sophistic orators.[19]

III

Paul's insistence that his appeal "does not spring from deceit or impure motives or trickery" corresponds with his later declarations in 2 Cor 4:2-5 and even 1 Cor 2:1-5. Howard Marshall comments, "There was no attempt to deceive the hearers . . . . They sought to please God, and not to claim anything for themselves, whether material gain or human prestige . . . . .They preferred to be gentle and to care for their hearers rather than make any demands on them."[20] Similarly in 2 Cor 3:1 Paul rejects any self-commendation except that of the effectiveness of the word of God. But this did not imply a total rejection of all contact with the language and certain values of Cynic philosophers. Abraham J. Malherbe has written several publications suggesting Paul's use of the language of Greek moral philosophers.[21] His most influential article refers to 1

---

[15] Welborn, *Paul, the Fool of Christ*, 54, 63, and 65.

[16] Andrew D. Clarke, *Secular and Christian Leadership in Corinth: A Socio-Historical and Exegetical Study of 1 Corinthians 1–6* (AGJU 18; Leiden: Brill, 1993), 41-134.

[17] Stephen M. Pogoloff, *Logos and Sophia: the Rhetorical Situation of 1 Corinthians* (SBLDS 134; Atlanta: Scholars Press, 1992), 176; cf. Quintilian, *Orations* 2.2.9-12.

[18] Pogoloff, *Logos and Sophia*, 188.

[19] Bruce W. Winter, "The Entries and Ethics of Orators and Paul (1 Thessalonians 2:1-12)," *TynBul* 44 (1993): 55-74. Cf. Bruce W. Winter, *Philo and Paul among the Sophists* (SNTSMS 961; Cambridge: Cambridge University Press, 1997), 116-244.

[20] I. Howard Marshall, *1 and 2 Thessalonians: A Commentary* (Vancouver: Regent College Publishing, 1983), 60.

[21] A. J. Malherbe, "Pastoral Care in the Thessalonian Church," *NTS* 36 (1990): 375-91; A. J. Malherbe, *The Letters to the Thessalonians* (AB 32B; New Haven: Yale University Press, 2000), 134-65, esp. 140-53.

Thessalonians.²² The article refers to 1 Thess 2:7, and concludes that this reflects the Cynic philosopher's stress on sincerity and integrity, as against a Sophistic emphasis on rhetoric and double-talk.²³

This, in turn, sheds much light on Elizabeth Castelli's attempt to argue that in 2:11 Paul invokes the image of fatherhood to exploit an authoritarian model of uniform and slavish imitation.²⁴ In this respect she follows Antoinette Wire's feminist reading of 1 Corinthians.²⁵ But the more we scrutinize Paul's claims about sincerity and integrity, the less convincing Castelli's claims become, unless Paul was an out-and-out ruthless liar and scoundrel, whose appeals to the witness of God were nothing but a bluff.

If Wire and Castelli were right, the Thessalonians would surely have exposed as false Paul's claims to be both gentle and sincere. To think of 1 Thessalonians as a "friendship letter" would then lose all credibility. It further becomes more difficult to explain Paul's undergoing suffering and persecution, and "struggle" (ἀγῶνι, v. 2). He explicitly dissociates himself from the "wandering charlatans," as F. F. Bruce calls them.²⁶ Bruce comments, "Every clause and phrase here expresses the sense of responsibility which Paul constantly felt with regard to his apostolic commission; cf. Rom. 1:14; 1 Cor. 1–4; 9:16-17 . . . 2 Cor. 2:17; 4:1-15; Gal. 1:15-17; 2:7-10 . . . ."²⁷ In fact, we are not forced to choose between seeing these verses as a "friendship letter," as Donfried does, or an apologia, as Holtz and most do. It can indeed be partly both.

George Lyons captures the purpose of this chapter better than most writers. He recognizes Paul's reluctance to speak autobiographically, as if he wanted above all to do this, like some evangelists who like to talk about themselves; his desire is, rather, to establish his ethos as an "incarnation" of the gospel of Jesus Christ. By imitating Christ and Paul, Paul longs that his converts may likewise incarnate the gospel. He does not want them to become the subject, as Castelli and Wire claim, of authoritarian manipulation.²⁸ Hence Paul moves on in vv. 9-14 to recall the behavior and conduct which went hand in hand with his preaching. Living a holy, blameless, hard-working life emerges as a major theme of 1 Thessalonians. Thus in a further related article Lyons shows that

---

²² A. J. Malherbe, "'Gentle as a Nurse': The Cynic Background to I Thess ii," *NovT* 12 (1970): 203-17.
²³ See also A. J. Malherbe, *Paul and Thessalonians: The Philosophical Tradition of Pastoral Care* (Philadelphia: Fortress Press, 1987), 9 and 18-23.
²⁴ E. A. Castelli, *Imitating Paul: A Discourse of Power* (Louisville: Westminster/John Knox, 1991), esp. 35-58 and 122-24.
²⁵ A. C. Wire, *The Corinthian Women Prophets: A Reconstruction through Paul's Rhetoric* (Minneapolis: Fortress Press, 1990).
²⁶ F. F. Bruce, *1 & 2 Thessalonians* (WBC 45; Waco: Word Books, 1982), 26.
²⁷ F. F. Bruce, *1 & 2 Thessalonians*, 27.
²⁸ George Leroy Lyons, *Pauline Autobiography: Toward a New Understanding* (SBLDS 73; Atlanta: Scholars Press, 1985).

especially in 1 Thess 2:1-12 Paul's autobiography becomes a model of living a holy and exemplary life.[29] Πλεονεξία (v. 5, "covetousness" or "greed") means strictly "the desire to get more," which stands in contrast to the *kenosis* of the incarnate Christ.

The reminiscence of conduct or behavior comes in 2:8-12. Paul, Timothy, and Silvanus showed "blameless behavior" (v. 10), and treated the community not only as a nurse (v. 7) but "like a father with his children" (v. 11). F. F. Bruce compares the missionaries' visit (2:1-4), the missionaries' behavior (2:5-8), and finally the missionaries' example (2:5-8).[30] John Chrysostom comments, "We exhibited nothing that was offensive or troublesome .... We would willingly have given our souls for you, because we were vehemently attached to you .... Nothing can be sweeter than such love."[31] In v. 9 Paul recalls that he and his co-workers "worked night and day, so that we might not be a burden to you." Howard Marshall observes that these verses bring out "the deep affection which the missionaries felt for their converts."[32] He adds, "This could mean that they were willing to lay down their lives in self-sacrifice," as J. B. Lightfoot also notes.[33] Paul's use of the two words κόπος and μόχθος, he continues, indicate that their hard work was tiring and painful.[34]

IV

The second section of 1 Thess 2:1-16 turns to review the readers' *reception* of the gospel and of Paul's preaching (vv. 13-16). The heart of the passage is, "When you received the word of God that you heard from us, you accepted it not as a human word, but as what it really is, God's word, which is also at work in you believers" (v. 13). As we might expect, Karl Barth highlights the difference between a merely or purely human word and the word of God. In the *Church Dogmatics*, he asserts, "The Word of God is itself the act of God."[35] He continues, "We can ... hear Holy Scripture simply ... [as] human words .... But if so, neither in proclamation nor in Holy Scripture has it been the Word of God that we have heard."[36] All the same, "God's own address becomes an event in the human word .... God by his activating, ratifying, and fulfilling the word of the Bible and preaching lets it become true."[37] Paul is no less interested

---

[29] George Leroy Lyons, "Modeling the Holiness Ethos: A Study Based on First Thessalonians," *Wesleyan Theological Journal* 30 (1995): 187-211.

[30] F. F. Bruce, *1 & 2 Thessalonians*, 3.

[31] John Chrysostom, "Homily 2" in *Homilies on Thessalonians* (*NPNF*1 13.331).

[32] Marshall, *1 and 2 Thessalonians*, 71.

[33] Marshall, *1 and 2 Thessalonians*, 71.

[34] Marshall, *1 and 2 Thessalonians*, 72.

[35] Karl Barth, *Church Dogmatics* (14 vols.; vol. 1.1-2, ed. G. W. Bromiley and T. F. Torrance; trans. G. W. Bromiley; Edinburgh: T&T Clark, 1975 and 1956), 1.1.143.

[36] Barth, *Church Dogmatics*, 1.1.143.

[37] Barth, *Church Dogmatics*, 1:1:109 and 120.

in "human religious aspiration" than Barth is.

This brings us back to Donfried's argument that 1 Thess 2:1-12 functions as a *speech-act*. Although Donfried criticizes and attacks much "loose talk" about seeing this passage as an apologia, such looseness is as nothing compared with biblical specialist talk about supposed speech-acts.[38] Donfried is sympathetic with F. W. Hughes's rhetorical analysis of epideictic rhetoric.[39] But even more strongly, he cites Paul's use of παράκλησις and the verb παρακαλέω (eight times in this brief letter), to mean *encouragement*.[40] He discusses Paul's practical behavior as moral in content, including being hardworking (2:9), suffering "personal hardship and social humiliation," and being an example to the Thessalonians. "Through these means he is 'appealing, encouraging, and testifying' (παρακαλοῦντες ὑμᾶς [*sic*] καὶ παραμυθούμενοι καὶ μαρτυρόμενοι) . . . ."[41] As we have seen, especially in Barth, the "word" which Paul preaches, and which his converts accept, is an *active and effective* word, not least because, as Donfried calls it, it is "the Spirit-Filled Word", proclaimed in Thessalonica "not only in word, but in power" (1:5).[42] This is linked with προφητεία, which concerns not an abstract situation but is "the announcement of the eschatological moment of salvation in the form of human weakness and frailty, and thus as the embodiment of the suffering God, as incarnation of the present moment . . . the dynamic announcement of God for the up building, encouragement, and consolation of the desolate."[43]

Donfried is right to see "prophecy" primarily as the announcement of the gospel, with practical consequences. I have constantly urged in several publications this prophecy in Paul is not a private message, but applied pastoral preaching of the gospel.[44] This has general support today from Ulrich Müller, David Hill, and Thomas Gillespie.[45] No less to the point, Ambrosiaster and Chrysostom in all probability, and Augustine certainly, speak of "prophecy" in the context of expounding scripture.[46] Thomas Aquinas speaks of prophets as

---

[38] Donfried, "Epistolary and Rhetorical Context," 31-38.
[39] Donfried, "Epistolary and Rhetorical Context," 38-48; cf. Frank W. Hughes, "The Social Situations Implied by Rhetoric," in *The Thessalonians Debate: Methodological Discord or Methodological Synthesis?* (ed. Karl P. Donfried and Johannes Beutler; Grand Rapids: Eerdmans 2000), 241-54.
[40] Donfried, "Epistolary and Rhetorical Context," 48-52.
[41] Donfried, "Epistolary and Rhetorical Context," 53-54.
[42] Donfried, "Epistolary and Rhetorical Context," 55; cf. 56-58.
[43] Donfried, "Epistolary and Rhetorical Context," 59.
[44] Anthony C. Thiselton, *First Corinthians: A Commentary on the Greek Text* (NIGTC; Grand Rapids: Eerdmans, 2000), 1087-98; cf. 956-64.
[45] U. B. Müller, *Prophetie und Predigt im Neuen Testament* (SNT 10; Gütersloh: Mohn, 1975); David Hill, *New Testament Prophecy* (London: Marshall, Morgan & Scott, 1979), 110-40 and 193-213; and Thomas W. Gillespie, *The First Theologians: A Study in Early Christian Prophecy* (Grand Rapids: Eerdmans, 1994).
[46] Augustine, *On the Psalms*, Ps 77:4; (*NPNF*1 8:361).

"those who explain divine doctrine . . . preachers."[47] John Calvin believed that concerning prophets "none such now exist, or they are less manifest," and prophetic work concerns reconciliation with God.[48] Matthew Henry asserts "By prophesyings we have understood the preaching of the word, the interpreting and applying of the scriptures."[49] John Wesley comments, "Prophesying . . . that is preaching, for the apostle is not speaking of extraordinary gifts."[50]

Nevertheless much more is entailed in speech-acts than being dynamic, active, and effective. This can be seen from the very first in the pioneering work of J. L. Austin, when he speaks of the *conditions* and *conventions* for a happy functioning of an illocutionary or performative speech-act.[51] He explains: "There must exist an accepted conventional procedure having a certain conventional effect"; for example, "My seconds will call on you" is operative in a society which accepts the conventions of dueling, but not if this is regarded as a relic of a by-gone age.[52] It is no good saying, "I take you to be my wedded wife," if I am already married. A given context is always presupposed. Actions such as rhetorical persuasions, Austin urges, are not illocutionary (performing an act *in* saying something) but elocutionary (performing an act *by* saying something).[53]

One year after the publication of Austin's lectures, Donald D. Evans attempted to apply Austin's speech-act theory to the biblical doctrine of creation.[54] In particular he distinguished between *"brute"* efficient cause (e.g., by persuasion or rhetoric) and *"institutional"* performative causal force. He rightly asserts, "The performative force is usually independent of the causal power."[55] He argued on the basis of performative language that God as Creator effectively ascribed a status, a role, and a value to Israel by virtue of the word-in-action. But Donfried does not sufficiently consider work such as that of

---

[47] Thomas Aquinas, *Commentary on the First Letter to Thessalonians* (New York: Magi Books, 1969), 52.

[48] John Calvin, *The Institutes of the Christian Religion* (2 vols.; London: James Clarke, 1957), 4:3:4 (Beveridge translation [John Calvin, *Institutes of the Christian Religion* (2 vols.; trans. Henry Beveridge; Grand Rapids: Eerdmans, 1957)], 2:319) and 1:6:2 (Beveridge translation, 1:66).

[49] Matthew Henry, *Concise Commentary on the Bible*, c. 1710, on disc by the Bible Truth Forum; no date, on 1 Thess 5:19; see his *Exposition of the Old and New Testament* (6 vols.; London: Bohn, 1851) 6.533.

[50] John Wesley, *Notes on the New Testament* (London: Boyer, 1755), 694.

[51] John L. Austin, *How to Do Things with Words* (Oxford: Clarendon Press, 1962), 8-11, 14-38, 44-45, and throughout.

[52] Austin, *How to Do Things with Words*, 26-27.

[53] Austin, *How to Do Things with Words*, 99-104.

[54] Donald D. Evans, *The Logic of Self-Involvement: A Philosophical Study of Everyday Language with Special Reference to the Christian Use of Language about God as Creator* (London: SCM, 1963).

[55] Evans, *The Logic of Self-Involvement*, 70.

Austin and Evans.

The notion of speech-act theory has become increasingly refined. John Searle produced works in 1969, 1979, and 1985 among others.[56] His work seriously modifies Austin's. We could enumerate many more. One of the latest is that of my doctoral graduate, Richard Briggs, who applies speech-act theory to biblical confessions and to testimony.[57] Recently a number of my own essays appeared in a single volume.[58] Again, Donfried does not show how the "facts" of Paul's behavior and conduct lend currency to the speech act. But this is vital. Many assume to explore speech-acts is to abandon propositional language about states of affairs. But performative or illocutionary speech acts can function effectively only if they have the appropriate "factual" language about their context to render this effective. This is why Paul's conduct in 2:9-16 is so important for rendering 2:1-8 a genuine speech act, rather than a piece of rhetorical persuasion. Only because God is witness to Paul's apostolic conduct can he transform Paul's preaching into an effective or "happy" speech act.

V

We must now seek to add a final piece of the jigsaw. Many dispute the authenticity of 2 Thessalonians. We cannot mount a full-scale debate on this, as it would distract us from our main subject, which is Paul's missionary preaching in 1 Thessalonians. We may note, however, that up to perhaps Grotius (1583-1645), and certainly to Johann Schmidt (1801), the traditional ascription of authorship to Paul was universally accepted. Chrysostom, Ambrosiaster, Theodoret, Peter Lombard, Thomas Aquinas, Nicholas of Lyra, John Calvin and Estius are among those who accepted it. Those who attacked it were Johann Schmidt, F. H. Kern, F. C. Baur and William Wrede in the nineteenth century. But in the same century, Benjamin Jowett and Gottlieb Lünemann, among others, defended the Pauline authorship. They examine every objection in detail.

Baur's argument was virtually circular. He assumed that the "true" Paul would always articulate his opposition to "works of the law," or the substance of the four major epistles. It never seemed to occur to him that the absence of Judaizing opponents provided Paul with a different agenda. Beda Rigaux rightly comments that Baur was dominated by a picture of Paul as found *only* in

---

[56] John R. Searle, *Speech Acts: An Essay in the Philosophy of Language* (Cambridge: Cambridge University Press, 1969); idem, *Expression and Meaning: Studies in the Theory of Speech Acts* (Cambridge: Cambridge University Press, 1979); and idem, *The Construction of Social Reality* (London: Allen Lane, 1985).

[57] Richard E. Briggs, *Words in Action: Speech Act Theory and Biblical Interpretation* (Edinburgh: T&T Clark, 2001).

[58] Anthony C. Thiselton, *Thiselton on Hermeneutics: Collected Works and New Essays* (Grand Rapids: Eerdmans; Aldershot: Ashgate, 2006): 51-150.

the major epistles.[59] W. Wrede claimed that 2 Thessalonians is a fiction. But Jowett and Lünemann painstakingly answer others' "objections" one by one.[60] Lünemann addresses the objections of Kern, Baur, and Hilgenfeld in particular. For example, similarities with the language of 1 Thessalonians arise, not through imitation, but because 2 Thessalonians was composed shortly afterwards. As Howard Marshall explains, today the major argument concerns the eschatological teaching of 2 Thessalonians, especially after the work of W. Trilling.[61] Further, there is less warmth in 2 Thessalonians than in the First Epistle, and it seems more formal and "objective." Marshall addresses these and other arguments in detail, and therefore we do not need to repeat them.[62]

Marshall himself provides a positive and convincing view of the date and purpose of 2 Thessalonians. It was written "shortly after 1 Thessalonians, and it may well date from later in Paul's first visit to Corinth."[63] This would account for many similarities also with 1 Corinthians and the Corinthian situation. Already in 1 Thessalonians we find "hints of afflictions" (1 Thess 2:14-16), and the Christians face persecution and opposition. Marshall writes, "The belief that the day of the Lord had already come would not be a surprising development in a church where an intense expectation of the parousia existed."[64] The addressees of 2 Thessalonians had been unsettled by false teachers, and many sponged on the Church in utter idleness. We may add that in the case of a growing church, and this time Jews as well as Gentiles, the audience would be larger, less intimate, and not quite the same. In the case of 1 Thessalonians, Paul and his readers knew each other; in 2 Thessalonians this was no longer the case. We should expect a more formal, less intimate, letter.

How far did corrections and additions extend? The readers of 1 Thessalonians had heard Paul's declaration of "the whole purpose of God" (Acts 20:27). Therefore if 1 Thess 2:1-16 seemed autobiographical and "subjective," something more "objective" is called for in 2 Thessalonians. 2 Thessalonians 2:1-12 is often called apocalyptic. This passage not only corrects the impression that the Parousia has occurred, but also paints on a large canvas concerning God's acts in world-history. Like other apocalyptists, Paul also speaks of the readers' participation in a cosmic battle against evil forces. Evil

---

[59] Beda Rigaux, *Saint Paul: Les Épitres aux Thessaloniciens* (Paris: Gabulda, 1956), 125.

[60] B. Jowett, *Thessalonians, Galatians and Romans* (London: Murray, 1859) and Gottlieb Lünemann, "The Epistles to the Thessalonians," in *Critical and Exegetical Commentary on the New Testament* (ed. H. A. W. Meyer; 3d ed.; Edinburgh: T&T Clark, 1867), 1-254 [169-82].

[61] Marshall, *1 and 2 Thessalonians*, 29; cf. W. Trilling, *Der zweite Brief an die Thessalonicher* (EKKNT; Neukirchen: Neukirchener Verlag, 1980), and W. Trilling, *Untersuchung zum 2 Thessalonicherbrief* (Leipzig: St. Benno-Verlag 1972).

[62] Marshall, *1 and 2 Thessalonians*, 30-45.

[63] Marshall, *1 and 2 Thessalonians*, 25.

[64] Marshall, *1 and 2 Thessalonians*, 24.

can transcend any single individual or institution, and becomes arrogant and incorrigible (2 Thess 2:4-10). As Klaus Koch, J. Christiaan Beker, and Alexandra Brown have convincingly argued, without apocalyptic the Christian gospel lacks something.[65] 1 Thessalonians 2:1-16 remains our principle paradigm of Christian missionary preaching. But the readers knew already *what else* Paul had said. For readers who had not heard Paul, eschatology complements the original message, especially in Paul's physical absence, and this can be found in 2 Thessalonians.

It may well be the case that in the strictest sense this does not have the same undisputed status as "missionary" preaching as 1 Thess 2:1-16. But among those who accept the Pauline authorship of 2 Thessalonians, Paul is both writing for the first time to new or additional members of the church, and adding, complementing, or correcting, previous right and wrong beliefs. We should not be over-hasty in neglecting certain apocalyptic supplements: the forces of evil, the future Parousia, world-history, revelation, resurrection, judgment, new creation and the triumph of God. All of these form part of the proclamation of the whole gospel in a missionary situation.

---

[65] Klaus Koch, *The Re-discovery of Apocalyptic: A Polemical Work on a Neglected Area of Biblical Studies and its Damaging Effects on Theology and Philosophy* (London: SCM, 1972); J. Christiaan Beker, *Paul's Apocalyptic Gospel: The Coming Triumph of God* (Philadelphia: Fortress, 1982); and Alexandra R. Brown, *The Cross and Human Transformation: Paul's Apocalyptic Word in 1 Corinthians* (Minneapolis: Fortress, 1995), 1-63 and 149-70; cf. also J. L. Martyn, "Epistemology at the Turn of the Ages," in *Christian History and Interpretation: Studies Presented to John Knox* (ed. W. R. Farmer et al.; Cambridge: Cambridge University Press, 1967), 269-87.

17

"PRAYER" AND THE PUBLIC SQUARE: 1 TIMOTHY 2:1–7 AND CHRISTIAN POLITICAL ENGAGEMENT

Greg A. Couser

1 Timothy 2:1-7 sets some manner of Christian political engagement firmly within God's redemptive work. The type of engagement urged here is that of "prayer" for those in authority, or so it seems. Exactly what did Paul want the Ephesians to "pray" for? In particular what is the "tranquil and quiet life"? Is this life something granted by the authorities or something taken up by the believers at their own initiative? In other words, if it is something granted, does this amount to asking God to intercede in the secular, civil arena in order that they, as the community of God's people, might live without oppression? Are they just trying to "get along" in the world and be left alone? Or, similarly, maybe they are asking to be left alone as an end in itself. Given the heavy emphasis on God's saving will in vv. 4-7, it could be that they are asking for the optimum civil conditions to carry out their evangelistic mission.[1] Or, might there be some other goal in mind altogether here? Could it be that the "prayers" are more about changing them than moving God?

As is so often the case, a text that seems straightforward enough at first read offers a number of exegetical challenges. First, how does the surrounding context inform this passage, given the explicit grammatical tie in the οὖν of 2:1 and the overall structure of the letter? Second, what is it that is being commanded, exactly? Is the focus on the types of prayers that should be made for all people? Or, on the other hand, is the emphasis more on the universal scope and priority of the prayers with the various types functioning pleonastically to further a sense of the urgency and priority of the command? Third, what is the content of the prayers? Fourth, what is the relationship of the ἵνα clause in v. 2b to that which precedes? Does it give the purpose of vv. 1-2a and, thus, define the salvation of vv. 3-7 in terms of v. 2b? Or does it only give the purpose of v. 2a such that it forms somewhat of a digression within 2:1-7 as

---

[1] Professor Marshall has addressed the civil implications of this passage along these very lines in "Biblical Patterns for Public Theology," *EuroJTh* 14 (2005): 73-86, esp. 79-83. As always, his work is full of penetrating and helpful insights. It also reflects his vision of biblical studies as something that ultimately serves to further God's saving purposes in Christ in and through his people, the church. Though the viewpoint in the following study may differ at some significant points, it is offered with a real appreciation for the life and work of a gracious *Doktorvater* and with a hope that it might offer some insights that will further our common passion to promote God's saving work in Christ.

a whole? And, finally, what is the type of relational orientation and associated behavior envisioned in a "peaceful and quiet" life lived out "in all godliness and holiness" (NIV)?

A PARALLEL, INTERWOVEN, PARADIGMATIC SECTION

Recent scholarship has continued to chip away at a fragmentary, "bag of marbles" understanding of the structure of 1 Timothy and the Pastoral Epistles generally, both on theological and structural grounds. In a previous study of the *theo*logy[2] of 1Timothy, this author proposed an ABABA structure (one recently supported in its essential substance by R. Van Neste).[3] This structure recapitulates and develops particular emphases as Paul transitions back and forth between sections directly and indirectly related to Timothy's assignment, "command" (1:3). The "A" sections (1:3-20; 3:14-4:16; 6:2b-21) are more concerned with Timothy as a person. Within these sections Paul addresses Timothy regarding his task at Ephesus in light of the nature of his opponents' teaching and his and Paul's common understanding of God's saving work in Christ. In the "B" sections (2:1–3:13; 5:1–6:2a), on the other hand, Paul speaks indirectly to Timothy and more directly to the congregation, in that he expresses the content and mode of the corrective teaching Timothy is to convey to the various segments of the community.[4] The importance of this observation can be seen along a number of lines, but two, in particular, are important for our present study. First, the concepts in the parallel sections may need to be explored in light of their development across those sections. Second, however, the parallelism that exists between the "A" sections differs from that between the "B" sections. With the former, there is a parallelism in terms of structure *and* content such that these sections constantly return to the same ideas and extend them. With the latter, the parallelism manifests itself in that both sections deal with identifiable groups which make up the "household of God" (3:15; cf. 1:4), but there is little parallelism in terms of structure and content. Thus, the way in which the parallel sections inform each other may need to be approached differently.

This opens up some intriguing possibilities for 2:1-7. To begin it is important to note the differences in this sub-section (2:1-7) from the other sub-

---

[2] "*Theo*logy" will be used as a designation for "theology in the strictest sense" (theology proper).

[3] G. Couser, "God and Christian Existence in the Pastoral Epistles: Toward *Theo*logical Method and Meaning," *NovT* 42:3 (2000): 262-83. Cf. R. Van Neste, *Cohesion and Structure in the Pastoral Epistles* (JSNTSup 280; T&T Clark: New York, 2004).

[4] F. Thielman suggests that this interplay fits the literary *modus operandi* of a "letter of official mandate." As such, the letter served both as a "reminder to the subordinate of his duties and as a public commission for this subordinate" (*Theology of the New Testament* [Grand Rapids: Zondervan, 2005], 414).

sections of the household material.[5] First, this is the only place where the "B" sections are grammatically linked to the "A" sections. In particular, this contrasts sharply with the anacolutha found at 5:1. There Paul resumes addressing Timothy's ministry to particular segments of the household of God following a section which focuses, in a manner structurally and conceptually parallel to ch. 1, on Timothy's personal activity and demeanor over against the antagonists and their teaching. At 2:1 the nature of the connection seems to be one of inference. This is to say that the οὖν of 2:1 suggests that Paul understands the "counsel" he is about to pass on to Timothy follows from the nature of Timothy's task at Ephesus.[6] Second, this is the only subsection within the household material that is given explicit theological grounding. Or, better yet, this is the only place where Paul explicitly links the theology of the Savior God's helping intervention in the Christ-event with the "B," or household, sections. This theology, with the added emphasis on its mediation to the present through the proclamation of the gospel (cf. 1:11, 15, 17; 3:16 and 4:10; and 6:12-16), is the theology developed in the "A" sections over against the teaching of the antagonists. Third, the πρῶτον πάντων of 2:1 suggests that this is the first in a series as well as first in importance.[7] 2:1-7 thus sits at the beginning of the counsel regarding the "how and what" of Timothy's engagement with the various segments of the household. As such, one could argue, by virtue of its connection to what precedes and its own recapitulation of the theological substructure woven throughout the "A" sections as the explicit theological grounding of the behavior encouraged in 2:1-7, that it suggests a

---

[5] On "household codes" see P. Towner, "Households and Household Codes," *DPL* 417-19, along with the corrective insights of R. Milliman, "Paul's Theology of the Parent-Child Relationship" (PhD diss., Trinity Evangelical Divinity School, 1997). Milliman convincingly argues that it is "unlikely that a *Haustafel* form existed in the first century which Paul then borrowed" (29). Similarities between Paul's household material and other works only suggest a shared interest in the subject matter at hand, and this resemblance does not "necessitate Paul's compromise with or dependence on general societal mores" (ibid.; cf. R. Kidd, *Wealth and Beneficence in the Pastoral Epistles: A "Bourgeois" Form of Early Christianity* [SBLDS 122; Atlanta: Scholars Press, 1990], 157-58).

[6] Contra J. Heckert who argues for a continuative οὖν here *(Dicourse Function of Conjoiners in the Pastoral Epistles* [Dallas: SIL, 1996], 98-99). Heckert's conclusion is hampered by his failure to see ch. 1 as an integrated whole bound tightly together by an *inclusio* (note, e.g., the reference to Timothy's charge in vv. 3, παραγγείλῃς, and 18, παραγγελίαν). There is no need to see Paul resuming a topic that he had earlier left since, in fact, he never left it (so also, G. Fee, *1 and 2 Timothy, Titus* [Peabody, Mass.: Hendrickson, 1988], 61).

[7] Marshall says this well: "In many cases it is difficult to judge whether priority of degree or time is stressed (e.g., Mt 6.33; Rom 1.16; 2.9f.; Acts 2.36), but where the latter is meant the former may be implied. Thus, although this is the first command in the letter intended for the church, the priority given to it probably also implies its importance for church life" *(The Pastoral Epistles* [ICC; T&T Clark: New York, 1999], 418-19).

link between all of the "B" material and the theological substructure informing Paul's more personal advice to Timothy. That 2:1-7 stands in a foundational role to 2:8-15 is clear from the οὖν linking v. 8 to what precedes and the ὡσαύτως that links vv. 9-15 to v. 8. Moreover, the ταῦτα of 3:14 at least refers backward to the whole of 2:1–3:13[8] and thereby anchors all of Paul's advice in this chapter to that which is proper for God's household/church (3:15), a people whose central confession is to God's saving acts in Christ as summarized in the early Christian hymn of 3:16. This could explain the center "A" section (3:14–4:16) as Paul breaking into his counsel regarding the household for the purpose of structurally and conceptually (in addition to 1:1-20 and 6:2b-21) furthering his emphasis on Timothy's pivotal role as the antitype to the antagonists plaguing the church. He serves as the antitype by virtue of the true doctrine he proclaims and his manner of life consistent with that doctrine. When one sees the direct way in which Paul brings the theological substructure of the first "A" section into relationship with the household material in 2:1-7, both through inference and through example, together with the way he frames the whole of 2:1–3:13[9] with the ταῦτα of 3:14, this sets up a literary pattern which would encourage the reader to see all of the household material as grounded in the theology standing behind Timothy's directive from Paul regarding his ministry at Ephesus. Likewise, given that the material in 5:1–6:2a is also household material, this also sets the pattern for understanding the ταῦτα of 6:2b as backward-looking such that there is a constant linkage between the theological substructure driving Timothy's life and ministry in the "A" sections and the directions for the household in the "B" sections. This would also allow for the variety and anacoloutha that are characteristic of the household material (3:1; 5:1, 3, 17; 6:1). Its continuity is found in its overarching framework which provides the interpretive matrix for the household material and gives it theological footing.

In the end, what this suggests for 2:1-7 is that it stands in a paradigmatic relationship to the household code material found in the "B" sections of the epistle. The theological substructure developed in the "A" sections is not only driving Paul's advice to Timothy with regard to his understanding of and interaction with the antagonists, but the nature of God's saving intervention in

---

[8] George W. Knight III argues that a reference to what precedes is the normal force of ταῦτα in the Pastoral Epistles, citing in 1 Timothy, 4:6, 11, 15; 5:7, 21; 6:2, 11. Moreover, "since chapters 2 and 3 both relate to conduct in God's house, the reference probably includes chapter 2 as well as chapter 3 (*Commentary on the Pastoral Epistles* [NIGTC; Grand Rapids: Eerdmans, 1992], 178)." Cf. also Marshall, *Pastoral*, 498.

[9] Through his use of οὖν in 2:1, Paul connects what is to follow with what precedes as an inference of the latter. Then, through grounding (in vv. 3-7) his exhortation in 2:1-2 in (what amounts to) a recapitulation and extension of the theological substructure driving Timothy's ministry at Ephesus laid out in 1:3-20 (esp. 1:4, 11-17; cf. Couser, "Christian Existence," 278-79), Paul exemplifies the type of theological reflection that lies behind his household code material altogether.

Christ also drives all of Paul's counsel regarding how God's household should operate. Theology drives ethics. In particular, as it will be seen in 2:1-7 below, soteriology, the nature of God's saving acts in Christ, is seen by Paul to be the central issue. As such, 1 Timothy is, in part, his re-articulation of the nature of God's saving acts in Christ in a manner necessary to counteract the antagonists and to restore focus and direction to the various segments of the household of God. Moreover, understanding that the theological substructure is developed throughout the "A" sections suggests that the explicit theological substructure in 2:1-7 (i.e., vv. 3-7) and even the nature of the topic there needs to be informed by the broader theology developed in those sections. In particular, the household imagery of 3:15 (cf. also 1:4), conditioned as it is by the characteristically Pauline church of God/temple imagery,[10] may provide insight into Paul's call for the household of God to be, essentially, a house of prayer.

THE NATURE OF THE COMMAND

Knight argues that the terms for prayer are primarily intended to communicate "distinguishable nuances that Paul wanted to specify" and points to the distinctiveness of εὐχαριστίας in support.[11] Though it could be argued that the three initial terms for prayer (δεήσεις, προσευχάς, and ἐντεύξεις) are largely synonymous, εὐχαριστίας, Knight argues, "is certainly different from the others."[12] One cannot deny that there are "distinguishable nuances" to the terms, as slight as they may be between some of them, but to stress these seems to put the emphasis on the wrong point. The emphasis running through the passage is the universality of the scope of these prayers and, as we will see below, their soteriological focus.

Not only are the prayers to be made "on behalf of *all* people" and "*all* those in authority" but the theological rationale provided in vv. 3-7 is primarily focused on substantiating this scope.[13] In vv. 3-4 Paul begins by asserting the inference that he has drawn from his reflection on the nature of God and the

---

[10] On the combination of household/temple imagery here see William D. Mounce, *Pastoral Epistles* (WBC 46; Nashville: Thomas Nelson, 2000), 220-21; Marshall, *Pastoral*, 508; Towner, "Households," *DPL*, 417-19. Elsewhere in Paul see 1 Cor 3:9; 4:1; 9:17; Gal 6:10 for household imagery; 1 Cor 3:16-17 and 6:19 for temple imagery; and Eph 2:19 for a combination of both in the same passage (cf. B. Gärtner, *The Temple and the Community in Qumran and the New Testament* [SNTSMS 1; Cambridge: Cambridge University Press, 1965], 60-66).
[11] Knight, *Pastoral*, 114.
[12] Knight, *Pastoral*, 114.
[13] The τοῦτο beginning v. 3 most likely envisions the whole of vv. 1-2. The use of the near demonstrative to refer to a previous statement as a whole is relatively common in 1 Timothy (cf. 1:9; 4:16; and 5:3). Each of these occurrences make it highly unlikely that the τοῦτο in 2:3 has v. 2 only, or even primarily, in view (contra R. Collins, *1 & II Timothy and Titus* [Louisville: Westminster/John Knox, 2002], 59).

nature of the ministries of Christ and his own ministry in vv. 5-7. Paul's conclusion concerning God's will is first a corollary of the fact that "God is one." Paul appears to be drawing here on the sense developed more explicitly in his earlier writings. In Rom 3:29-30 (cf. Gal 3:20; Eph 4:4-6) Paul argues from the singularity of God to the conclusion that salvation was open to the Jew *and* the Gentile.[14] This holds true even though the Jew-Gentile discussion that forms the original setting of its development is not the immediate backdrop here. This is made clear by the next plank in Paul's argument where he reflects on the saving work of Christ in a way which directly connects to and informs the εἷς θεός formula. First, with the repetition of "one" in conjunction with the mediatorial role of Christ, Paul makes explicit what is implicit in the εἷς θεός formula. Not only are God and Christ united in their "oneness," with decided overtones of deity with regard to Christ,[15] but that "oneness" is explicated in terms of Christ giving himself "as a ransom for *all* people." Lest the reader still be tempted to sever the sense of "oneness" seen in Christ from that of God, Paul further connects the work of Christ with God by specifying that this "testimony" of Christ, this self-giving ransom for *all*,[16] occurred at "God's own right time" (καιροῖς ἰδίοις). This is a phrase used elsewhere (1 Tim 6:15 and Titus 1:3) to designate the event to which it refers as divinely determined and, as such, as proceeding from God's salvation plan.[17] Moreover, two of the three uses serve to link the past and future epiphanies of Christ directly to the saving plan of God.[18] Thus, the character and, especially, the nature and the timing of

---

[14] Cf. P. Towner, *The Goal of Our Instruction: The Structure of Theology and Ethics in the Pastoral Epistles* (JSNTSup 34; Sheffield: JSOT Press, 1989), 50-51.

15 See Fee, *Timothy & Titus*, 68 and I. H. Marshall, "The Development of the Concept of Redemption in the New Testament" in *Jesus the Saviour: Studies in New Testament Theology* (Downers Grove: InterVarsity, 1990), 239-57 [256 n. 70].

[16] That the referent of τὸν μαρτύριον is the phrase, "the one who gave himself as a ransom for all" (v. 6a), see Couser, "'The Testimony about the Lord', 'Borne by the Lord', or Both?: An Insight into Paul and Jesus in the Pastoral Epistles," *TynBul* 55.2 [2004]: 301-304; J. N. D. Kelly, *The Pastoral Epistles* (BNTC; Peabody, Mass.: Hendrickson, 1988; repr., London: A&C Black, 1963), 64; and N. Brox, *Die Pastoralbriefe* (RNT; Regensburg: Verlag Friedrich Pustet, 1969), 129.

[17] See Roloff, *Erste Briefe an Timotheus* (EKKNT 15; Zürich/Neukirchen-Vluyn: Benziger/Neukirchener, 1988), 123-24; Fee, *Timothy & Titus*, 66; Kelly, *Pastoral*, 64; E. F. Scott, *The Pastoral Epistles* (London: Hodder & Stoughton, 1948), 22; M. Dibelius and Hans Conzelmann, *The Pastoral Epistles* (Hermeneia; Philadelphia: Fortress, 1972), 43, 131; O. Cullmann, *Christ and Time: The Primitive Christian Conception of Time and History* (trans. F. V. Filson; London: SCM, 1951), 39-43; A. J. Malherbe, "'In Season and Out of Season': 2 Timothy 4:2," *JBL* 103 (1984): 235-43 [243]; G. Delling, "καιρός," *TDNT* 3:455-64 [460-61].

[18] Its link to the epiphany/appearance of Christ is indisputable in the case of 1Tim 6:15. Titus 1:3 is the exception (cf. Roloff, *Erste Briefe*, 107, 112, and 123-24). Yet it is not unlikely that the Christ-event is implicit even here in that "Christ and the message concerning him are seen as one, unified event" (Marshall, *Pastoral*, 127).

the work of Christ add additional support to the universal scope of God's saving will. Paul's final plank in his argument for the universal scope of God's saving will lies in the depiction of his own call which rounds out this passage.[19] The relative, ὅ (v. 7a), which has the testimony (τὸ μαρτύριον) as its referent, specifies that "for which" (εἰς ὅ) Paul has been appointed by God (noting the divine passive, ἐτέθην). It is this "testimony," the self-giving of Christ as a ransom for *all* people that Paul is to proclaim as a preacher, apostle, and teacher, with the former two emphasizing what is implied in the passive ἐτέθην. Moreover, not only is his message universal in scope but the very subjects of his work as a preacher, apostle and teacher are "the Gentiles" (ἐθνῶν; cf. 2 Tim 4:17). Undoubtedly Paul is referring to his unique call as the "apostle to the Gentiles" (Gal 2:8; Rom 15:15-16) in order to emphasize that his very own calling, i.e., a Jewish believer called to take the message of God's saving acts in Christ to the Gentiles, verifies the universal scope of God's saving will. In fact, he makes this point with emphasis in that it is likely that his oath, "I am speaking the truth; I am not lying," falls where it does in the sentence because it is the nature of the subjects of his ministry that establishes his overall emphasis on the universal scope of God's saving work.

To return to our initial question, this survey of the passage tracing, as it does, the prominent thread of the universal scope of God's saving acts in Christ, puts the emphasis on the scope of the praying and not on the types of prayers offered. Thus, as many commentators have noted, the thrust of 2:1 calls for a sense along the lines of "make all kinds of prayers for all people." "The four terms which describe prayer characterise [*sic*] it in its totality and emphasise [*sic*] the scope of the responsibility which has 'all people' in view."[20]

This understanding of the thrust of 2:1 also has implications for the upcoming enquiry into the content of the prayers. The Marcan account of Jesus' cleansing of the temple may be instructive here. Similar to Jesus in Mark, Paul is likewise essentially reminding the Ephesians that God's household is to be a "house of prayer for every nation" (ὁ οἶκός μου οἶκος προσευχῆς κληθήσεται πᾶσιν τοῖς ἔθνεσιν [Mark 11:17 quoting Isa 56:7]). What Jesus is saying here is that temple practices are to be informed by and in service of the purposes of God for his "house" (temple)—a concern woefully absent in the activity of the money-changers.[21] Prayer, that activity prominently associated with a proper demeanor and attitude toward God, stands in for the priorities of God in general. The pleonastic figure of speech in 1 Tim 2:1 likewise focuses

---

[19] For a convincing and concise description of the function of 2:7 see Fee, *1 & 2 Timothy*, 67 (contra Towner, *Goal*, 205).

[20] Marshall, *Pastoral*, 419.

[21] Thus, R. T. France (*Mark* [NIGTC; Grand Rapids: Eerdmans, 2002], 446) states that Jesus protested "because the commercial activities had crowded out worship as the main purpose of the temple".

on adjusting the priorities governing the public meetings of the church. The focus on prayer here, as in the statement of Jesus in Mark, amounts to a call to be a community driven by the priorities of God in that it is an activity which signifies and proceeds from a humble dependence upon and submission to God.

Some may question whether or not Mark is an appropriate dialogue partner in this discussion. While the precise degree of the connection between the two cannot be definitely determined and this conception of the force of the command here in 1 Timothy is not completely dependent on such a link, there do seem to be a number of lines of evidence which support some real connection. This is initially probable given the prominence of the life and words of Jesus throughout 1 Timothy (cf. 1:12, 15, 16; 2:6; 5:18; 6:3, 13).[22] In fact, it is partially this factor that moves Knight to translate the disputed phrase, λόγοις τοῖς τοῦ κυρίου ἡμῶν Ἰησοῦ Χριστοῦ, in 6:3, as "the words that have come from our source of authority, 'our Lord Jesus Christ'."[23] In addition, this link to Jesus gains additional credibility in light of two additional factors. First, temple imagery is close at hand. In fact, it emerges in 3:15 (see n. 10 above) in association with the Pauline description of the church as "God's."[24] More precisely, the church is the community where God's presence is manifest, for it is the "church of the living God."[25] The temple thought suggested here is further confirmed by the temple imagery evident in the further description of the church as a "support and pillar of the truth." Moreover, as the passage is constructed, "the church of the living God, a support and pillar of the truth" likely stands as the controlling metaphor for Paul's use of the preceding οἴκῳ

---

[22] For a development of this general emphasis on the words and acts of Christ in 1 Timothy and the Pastorals generally, see Couser, "Paul and Jesus," 309-13. Marshall also notes how 1:15 and 2:6 very likely go back to synoptic material (Luke 19:10 and Mark 10:45 respectively) and both relate to presentations of Christ's self-understanding ("The Christology of the Pastoral Epistles," *SNTU-A* 13 [1988]: 157-77 [164-65]). P. Wolfe holds that the Pastoral Epistles "uphold the words, or teaching of Jesus as possessing inherent authority and representing a standard, that is, a canon, akin to γραφή" ("Scripture in the Pastoral Epistles: Premarcion Marcionism?," *PRSt* 16 [1989]: 5-16 [14]; cf. also his "The Sagacious Use of Scripture" in *Entrusted with the Gospel: Paul's Theology in the Pastoral Epistles* [ed. A. Köstenberger and T. Wilder; Nashville: Broadman and Holman, 2010], 199-218 [214]).

[23] *Pastoral*, 250; cf. also Roloff, *Erste Briefe*, 331.

[24] The designation of the ἐκκλησία as τοῦ θεοῦ occurs almost exclusively in Paul (e.g., Rom 16:16; 1 Cor 10:32; 11:16, 22; 12:28; Gal 1:13; 1 Thess 2:14), with Acts 20:28 being the only exception. Even there, Luke demonstrates a close affinity to Pauline conceptions (cf. K. Schmidt, "καλέω, κλῆσις, . . . , ἐκκλησία," *TDNT* 3:487-536 [506-507]).

[25] See Num 14:28 and Josh 3:10 for occasions where "living God" is used to emphasize God's presence with his people. For this sense here, cf. L. Oberlinner, *Die Pastoralbriefe. Erste Folge. Kommentar zum Ersten Timotheusbrief* (HTKNT 11/2; Freiburg: Herder, 1994), 1:157; M. J. Goodwin, "The Pauline Background of the Living God as Interpretive Context for 1 Timothy 4.10," *JSNT* 61 (1996): 65-85.

θεοῦ.²⁶ Thus, temple imagery is not only present but it may be intended by Paul to be the controlling metaphor governing their understanding of the church as God's household. Therefore, the behavior encouraged in 2:1-7 would be the type fitting to the temple, understood as God's people who live in his presence. In this light, it does not seem to be going too far to suggest that 2:1-7 is an instance of Paul extending the teaching of Jesus and bringing it to bear on the circumstances of the church at Ephesus. As the dwelling place of God which had now succeeded the temple in Jerusalem,²⁷ their life together must be driven and shaped by God's priorities. A second strong resonance with the teaching of Jesus on the temple, especially as presented in Mark (a gospel most likely already in the sights of Paul in 2:6), is the universal perspective on the "temple" here and in Mark. Mark is the only one of the Synoptics that brings forward the phrase from Isaiah that characterizes the temple as πᾶσιν τοῖς ἔθνεσιν. In Mark as in 1 Timothy the "temple" is a place open to and concerned about all people ("on behalf of all people," 1 Tim 2:1). Just as Jesus condemns the temple authorities for standing over against God's purposes for his temple (as initially articulated in Solomon's dedication, 1 Kgs 8:41-43; cf. Jer 7:6-11) and calls on them to live up to God's intention that the temple be "a house of prayer for all peoples,"²⁸ so here Paul exhorts the Ephesians to live up to God's purpose for them by being a people who welcome and invite "all people" through the proclamation of the gospel, in word and deed, into God's presence. Or, to use the words of the author of the *Psalms of Solomon*, Paul desires that the believers at Ephesus would desire that the nations would "come from the ends of the earth to see his glory" (the glory of the Davidic Messiah) and to "see the glory of the Lord" (*Pss. Sol.* 17:30-31; cf. "the gospel of the glory of the blessed God" in 1 Tim 1:11 and the doxology to the "honor and glory" of God in 1:17).²⁹

In conclusion, this understanding of the force of Paul's exhortation to pray compels us to look elsewhere within the passage for the makeup of these "prayers." The focus is neither on the types of prayers or on prayer and nothing else. As we have already seen, part of what is being emphasized is the all-

---

²⁶ The relative, ἥτις, is feminine by attraction to the predicate nominative in its clause, ἐκκλησία. According to D. Wallace attraction "occurs when the focus of the discourse is on the predicate nom.: the dominant gender reveals the dominant idea of the passage" (*Greek Grammar Beyond the Basics* [Grand Rapids: Zondervan, 1996], 338; cf. also Roloff, *Erste Briefe*, 199).

²⁷ On this general NT conception of the church as succeeding the Jerusalem temple see Marshall, *Pastoral*, 507-508.

²⁸ For a detailed development of this view see C. Evans, *Mark 8:27-16:20* (WBC 34B; Nashville: Thomas Nelson, 2001), 175-79.

²⁹ For this type of connection between the teaching of Jesus in Paul see S. Kim, "*Imitatio Christi* (1 Corinthians 11:1): How Paul Imitates Jesus Christ in Dealing with Idol Food (1 Corinthians 8–10)," *BBR* 13 (2003): 193-226. Kim argues that Paul discusses "things offered to idols" with the example and teaching of Jesus in view.

encompassing nature of God's priorities for his people in that they involve responsibilities toward all men and women, all peoples. Now we turn to delineate the nature of the responsibility that God's household has toward all people and, thus, to the "content" informing their devotion to God.

THE CONTENT OF THE "PRAYERS"

But what are these priorities that prayer stands as an emblem for? We have already seen that the passage strongly emphasizes that it is the universal scope of God's purpose that should be the driving force behind their corporate existence. Here we want to set out briefly the nature of the responsibility the members of God's household have toward all people, something already intimated in our discussion of their scope. The simplest way to get an idea of what this may be is to look at the structure of the passage.

1. οὖν
Παρακαλῶ ποιεῖσθαι δεήσεις προσευχὰς ἐντεύξεις εὐχαριστίας
   πρῶτον πάντων
   ὑπὲρ πάντων ἀνθρώπων
     2. ὑπὲρ βασιλέων καὶ πάντων τῶν ἐν ὑπεροχῇ ὄντων,
       ἵνα ἤρεμον καὶ ἡσύχιον βίον διάγωμεν
                 ἐν πάσῃ εὐσεβείᾳ καὶ σεμνότητι.
   3. τοῦτο καλὸν καὶ ἀπόδεκτον ἐνώπιον τοῦ σωτῆρος ἡμῶν θεοῦ,
     4. ὃς πάντας ἀνθρώπους θέλει σωθῆναι
   καὶ
   εἰς ἐπίγνωσιν ἀληθείας ἐλθεῖν.
     5. γὰρ
       εἷς..... θεός,
       εἷς καὶ μεσίτης = ἄνθρωπος Χριστὸς Ἰησοῦς,
         θεοῦ καὶ ἀνθρώπων
       6. ὁ δοὺς ἑαυτὸν ἀντίλυτρον ὑπὲρ πάντων = τὸ μαρτύριον
                                  καιροῖς ἰδίοις.
       7. εἰς ὃ [μαρτύριον] ἐτέθην ἐγὼ   κῆρυξ
                            καὶ
                            ἀπόστολος,
                           –ἀλήθειαν λέγω οὐ ψεύδομαι–
                            διδάσκαλος
                              ἐθνῶν
                              ἐν πίστει καὶ ἀληθείᾳ.

What becomes clear in a structural overview of this section is that the textual emphasis is given to the theological grounding (vv. 3-7) of the exhortation in vv. 1-2. That it is grounding the whole of vv. 1-2 is strongly suggested when the function of τοῦτο that begins v. 3 is seen in light of its similar uses throughout 1 Timothy (cf. 1:9; 4:16; and 5:3). As noted above (see n. 13), τοῦτο consistently refers to the whole statement immediately preceding it (vv. 1-2 constitute one sentence in the Greek), rendering a connection to v. 2 alone (or some part of it) very unlikely. Moreover, the universality in v. 1, "for all people," better corresponds to the universality found in the "all people" of v. 4, the sense of "one" in v. 5, Christ's self-giving death as a ransom "for all" in v. 6, and the emphasis on Paul's calling to the "Gentiles" (which indicates the universality of God's saving intentions).[30] Furthermore, the particular to general relationship between v. 2 ("kings . . .") and v. 1 ("all people"), makes it unlikely that Paul would build off of a sub-topic of (or digression in) his thought, especially in light of the universal thread running between v. 1 and vv.4-7 as developed above. Also, as noted previously, vv. 3-4 stand in a logical relationship to vv. 4-7 as deduction to premises. Thus the whole of vv. 3-7 are employed to theologically ground the exhortation of vv. 1-2.

Therefore, when we look carefully at the theological resources Paul draws upon to ground his exhortation we find that the universal scope is a dimension of his saving purposes. It is "God, the Savior," the one who desires "all to be saved and come to the knowledge of the truth," who finds the exhortation of vv. 1-2 "acceptable." "To be saved and come to the knowledge of the truth" is a phrase which gives the ultimate end of God's salvific work first and then provides the immediate end which leads to the former.[31] The cognitive side of conversion, the hearing and grasping of the "truth," the gospel message (1 Tim 2:7a; 4:3; 2 Tim 2:25), is most likely emphasized in light of the departure from the truth on the part of the antagonists (cf. 1 Tim 6:5).[32] This soteriological substructure is initially built upon the soteriological implications of God's "oneness." As noted above Paul argues from the singularity of God to the conclusion that salvation was open to all people. One could also argue that Paul's mention of the "one God" has strong undertones of singularity as well. God, as the "one God," can alone provide salvation. In this regard note that the interlocking doxologies of 1:17 and 6:15-16 both stress God's singularity (μόνος).[33] What is more, 6:16 explicitly links this singularity to God's

---

[30] Cf. Mounce, *Pastoral*, 85; Fee, *1 & 2 Timothy*, 62.

[31] Mounce (*Pastoral*, 86) citing C. J. Ellicott, *The Pastoral Epistles of St Paul* (3d ed.; London: Longman, 1864), 28.

[32] This stands contrary to G. Kretschmar's contention that the phrase, "to come to the knowledge of the truth," indicates that teaching has displaced faith such that salvation becomes a matter of attainment. Faith becomes something learned in the household ("Der paulinische Glaube in den Pastoralbriefe," in *Glaube im Neuen Testament* [ed. F. Hahn and H. Klein; Neukirchen: Neukirchener, 1982], 115-240). However, Kretschmar fails to note the polemical slant of this wording and neglects the place of faith throughout the Pastorals (cf. 1 Tim 1:16; 3:16; Titus 3:8), not to mention the strong emphasis on salvation by grace apart from works (2 Tim 1:9; Titus 3:5; cf. I. H. Marshall, "Salvation, Grace and Works in the Later Writings in the Pauline Corpus," *NTS* 42 [1996]: 339-58 [352-54]).

[33] Μόνος occurs once in 1:17 and twice in 6:15-16. The greater emphasis in the latter is in keeping with the more elaborated development in 6:15-16 of the epithets more briefly

"immortality," a quality in the Pastorals that is not so much an attribute of God as a gift God makes available through the Christ-event which is proclaimed in the gospel (a synonym of "life"[ζωή]; 2 Tim 1:10). With the mention that "the mediator" is "one also" and that his self-giving death occurred at "God's own right time" (καιροῖς ἰδίοις), Paul continues to strengthen the soteriological substructure both in terms of connecting Christ's saving work to God's will and by filling in the nature of that will in the description of the nature of Christ's mediation. As a "man" Christ effected the mediation of the New Covenant promises of God's salvation for the benefit of all people.[34] And it is this work of God in Christ, the testimony *par excellence* (τὸ μαρτύριον) to the universal saving will of God,[35] which Paul has been appointed to advance among the nations (v. 7).

Thus, Paul makes it clear that the nature of God and the nature of his saving acts in the work of Christ, primarily, and in Paul's call, secondarily, demand that the church make God's saving priority their "prayer" priority. "Prayer, therefore, is not the topic of this paragraph but rather the stage upon which Paul bases his teaching on the topic of salvation. Prayer is the context, salvation the content."[36] What this suggests is that the prayer for all people is so that they "might be saved and come to the knowledge of the truth." Or, to rephrase it in light of our understanding of prayer as an emblem for life in submission to God's will, the life of the community is to be focused around furthering God's saving desires for all people.

Moreover, as we have seen, there is nothing here (or elsewhere in the Pastorals)[37] to suggest that the type of salvation envisioned here is anything other than the fully Pauline conception of "the free offer of God's grace to sinners and the call to holiness."[38] Though the call to holiness is not explicit here, Paul's use of σῴζω in 2:15 and 4:16 suggests that the thought is very likely present (not to mention the many passages in the Pastorals which closely connect salvation and holiness, cf. Titus 2:11-14 in particular). In 2:15 women have the promise of realizing more of what their salvation entails for life by

---

mentioned in 1:17. For the relationship between the doxologies see Couser, "Christian Existence," 281.

[34] As such, this resonates with the conception of Christ's mediatorial work in Hebrews (8:6; 9:15; 12:24; cf. Towner, *Goal*, 53-56). Though interesting, Thielman's contention that Christ's mediatorial role has proto-gnostic concerns as its backdrop seems less convincing (*Theology*, 416-17). Thielman fails to account for Paul's emphasis on the self-giving death as a ransom for all (v. 6a), a thought closely associated with the role of Christ as mediator of the new covenant (cf. Heb 9:15).

[35] Cf. Kelly, *Pastoral*, 64.

[36] Mounce, *Pastoral*, 76.

[37] Cf. I. H. Marshall, "Faith and Works in the Pastoral Epistles," *SNTU-A* 9 (1984): 203-18.

[38] Mounce, *Pastoral*, cxxxiv.

embracing God's created design for them as women.[39] In 4:16, Timothy, by paying close attention to his life and teaching, "saves" himself and those who hear him—a passage apparently referring to the role of believers in working out their salvation (cf. Phil 2:12).[40] Therefore, "to be saved" includes God's intentions in conversion and sanctification, with the latter being a process that awaits the epiphany of Christ for its culmination (cf. esp. 1 Tim 6:14 and Titus 2:13). For the church to be gathered together to promote his saving priorities is to promote the extension of the gospel in the world and the extension of the gospel into the thinking and behavior of God's household in anticipation of the coming appearance of Christ. God's saving work in Christ constitutes his household to be a particular type of people in the world as well as mobilizes them to proclaim "the testimony" to the world.

THE CONTENT AND ROLE OF 1 TIMOTHY 2:2

Now we are ready to consider the content and role of 1 Tim 2:2. Given the fact that the theological substructure in vv. 3-7 is in support of the "prayer" for all people in v. 1, v. 2 clearly seems to be a digression. However we understand v. 2, the prayer for authorities with its intended result suggests that the end in view is not ultimate. The ἵνα clause specifies most directly the hoped-for result of the "prayers" with respect to authorities in particular.

At the same time there is no reason to think that the prayers for authorities differed in content from the prayers for "all people." Moreover, if "prayer" stands as the part for the whole, as a reference to that activity which is the prominent part of true worship (or a life dedicated to God's will), to "pray" for authorities is to be driven by God's saving priorities in their attitudes toward and interaction with those authorities. This would then parallel Titus 3:1-2 where the demeanor and attitude toward secular authorities, in particular (v. 1), and all people in general (v. 2), is grounded and commended in view of the believer's experience of God's "kindness and love" manifested in the Christ-event (v. 4). Because of their transformation through faith in God's saving work in Christ, they should no longer lead the same manner of life they used to lead (διάγοντες, v. 3; cf. διάγωμεν of 1 Tim 2:2). Thus, the ἵνα clause in 1 Tim 2:2 very likely expresses the effect of such an orientation *on the body of believers* as opposed to the effect upon the secular rulers. In other words, the ἵνα clause is not directed to the result of God's intervention in the civil arena such that the secular authorities leave the church alone. Indeed, this would clash with what Paul expects will be the lot of believers this side of the

---

[39] "In a somewhat awkward manner, Paul is saying that a woman's salvation and the practical outworking of that salvation . . . do not consist in altering her church role. Rather, she is to accept her God-given role, one of the specific functions being the bearing of children (synecdoche)" (Mounce, *Pastoral*, 146).

[40] Cf. Knight, *Pastoral*, 211-12.

eschaton. Paul himself had experienced persecution and he warns the Ephesians that "all who live godly in Christ Jesus will suffer persecution" (2 Tim 2:11-12). Rather, the ἵνα clause expresses the result of the "prayers" for those "praying." This is to say that a communal focus on God's saving purposes will result in the community, individually and corporately, leading the type of life that would positively reflect on the saving work of God and not negatively bring reproach on the church. In 1 Timothy and Titus Paul is frequently concerned with secular rulers and non-Christians,[41] "but it is not a concern for peace or a desire for the rulers to allow the church to grow unimpeded. Rather Paul is anxious that the church provide a good witness to nonbelievers."[42]

But what does this type of life look like? What is the "quiet and tranquil life in all godliness and moral earnestness"? The syntax of the ἵνα clause suggests that the phrase ἐν πάσῃ εὐσεβείᾳ καὶ σεμνότητι prescribes the boundaries within which the life of peace and tranquility are found. To put it another way, together they provide the "'state' of the Christian out of which (among other things) a proper regard for the world orders ought to proceed."[43] This is significant in that however we understand "peace and tranquility" it should be something consistent with Paul's conception of "godliness and moral earnestness." Thus, given the prominence and development of the latter terms (especially εὐσεβεία), we turn our attention to them first in order to observe Paul's own lexical parameters for our understanding of the rarer terms in the phrase, "quiet and tranquil life."

The Pastorals have the largest concentration of the εὐσεβεία word-group in the NT. This author's own examination of the use of the term in 1 Timothy aligns with an emerging consensus in the literature at large. Εὐσεβεία becomes "a shorthand expression for the quality of life demanded of the members of God's house."[44] It functions to describe the manner of life that is nothing less than "true Christianity."[45] Most likely through the mediation of Hellenistic Judaism,[46] the term brings together both a correct knowledge of God and the behavior that is consistent with that knowledge that has become possible through God's intervention in Christ.[47]

With regard to σεμνότητι (and σεμνός), though less frequent than the εὐσεβεία word-group, it does figure into Paul's description of the believer's life on several occasions (cf. 1 Tim 3:4, 8, 11; Titus 2:2, 7). Spicq copiously documents the sense of the term in common Hellenistic usage. When applied to people it "suggests grandeur, magnificence, solemnity, a quality that inspires

---

[41] Cf. Titus 3:1-2; 1:6; 2:5, 7, 10; 1 Tim 3:2, 8, 11; 5:14; 6:1.
[42] Mounce, *Pastoral*, 81; cf. Thielman, *Theology*, 417.
[43] Towner, *Goal*, 149.
[44] Couser, "Christian Existence," 274.
[45] Marshall, *Pastoral*, 142-43.
[46] J. D. Quinn, *The Letter to Titus* (AB 35; New York: Doubleday, 1990): 282-91.
[47] Towner, *Goal*, 150; cf. Mounce, *Pastoral*, 83; Knight, *Pastoral*, 117.

respect, fear, or reverence."⁴⁸ As such, its meaning is particularly context-dependent as the standard informing judgments of what constitutes σεμνότης would vary somewhat depending on the social context. Thus Spicq argues, in the context of 1 Timothy where the church is the "household or family of God" and "its members are a priestly congregation," σεμνότητι signifies a "mode of existence defined by piety and worship, marked by the seriousness, gravity, decency that are fitting in God's presence."⁴⁹ Again, similar to εὐσεβεία above, though this term had a wide currency in the secular culture, as used within the Pastorals it comes to embody the type of demeanor and bearing, with its consequent effects upon others, that is true of one who has grasped the grandeur and significance of God's saving acts in Christ.

From this look at the lexical elements making up the phrase delimiting the nature of the "quiet and tranquil life," it seems clear that the conceptions of the "quiet and tranquil life" are driven by theology and not by cultural norms. This, of course, does not mean that these will never coincide. E.g., for Paul government is appointed by God to reward the good and punish the evil (Rom 13:3-4). This is not to say that it always functions this way so as to be able to identify God's purposes or will with that of the secular rulers. However, it does assume that government can act in ways that are in accord with God's purposes and that, at times, to oppose the secular authorities is to oppose God. In the end, this only means that the shaping norm guiding Paul's conception of the "quiet and tranquil life" is not imposed from without, but arises from within Christian theological reflection (more particularly in the Pastorals, within Christian soteriological reflection). Thus, the observable dimension of these ways of being would likewise be shaped by theological norms. In this light, the regular concern of the Pastorals to live in a manner appropriate before outsiders is not to say, necessarily, that the outsiders themselves would see the Christian's manner of life as appropriate. As Paul states in 2 Tim 3:12 (cf. 2:12), Christians should expect persecution. Rather, it is to say that the Christian's manner of life, to use a phrase from Titus 2:10, would "adorn the teaching about God our Savior" by living in a manner consistent with that teaching.

So what does the "quiet and tranquil life" look like? The two terms are generally regarded as synonyms here, so we will not take time to try to distinguish particular nuances between them.⁵⁰ What seems more promising is to note the relationship of this concept, i.e. quietness, and of ἡσυχία, in particular, to what J. K. Brown calls the "topos of meddling in the Greco-

---

⁴⁸ C. Spicq, "σεμνός, σεμνότης," *TLNT* 3:244-48 [244].
⁴⁹ Spicq, *TLNT* 3:245.
⁵⁰ Ellicott's (*Pastoral*, 26) attempt to distinguish ἤρεμον and ἡσύχιον on the basis of the former indicating an absence of outer conflict and the latter an absence of inner, seems overly fine and hard to justify lexically.

Roman context."⁵¹ Brown points out that meddling, "overseeing the activities of others when one has no proper right to do so,"⁵² is "not only frowned upon by the ancients, but it is considered by some to be subversive to the fabric of society."⁵³ Concerning the use of ἡσυχία Brown writes: "The noun ἡσυχία is frequently used in association with (and as an opposite to) words for meddling."⁵⁴

These factors together suggest that 2:1-7, as the paradigmatic portion of the household code stretching through the end of ch. 2 and continuing in 5:1–6:2a, is the foundational move in Paul's attempt to re-structure God's household so that the various segments would fill their proper roles. His call to the "quiet and tranquil life" is a call for them to reorient themselves toward their proper roles and functions within God's household.

This conception is supported by the backdrop of the Pastorals, Timothy's commission and the household material itself, and Paul's approach in 2 Thessalonians. In the backdrop of the Pastorals, the false teachers have disrupted the community at Ephesus and Crete.⁵⁵ They are accused of "ruining whole households" (Titus 1:11) by "worm(ing) their way into homes" (cf. 2 Tim 3:6). Whether they can be accused of meddling or not from the perspective of the semantic range associated with the Greco-Roman topos is not certain, but what is certain is that their activities have resulted in some, the young widows in Ephesus, becoming "meddlers" (περίεργοι; 1 Tim 5:13). The disparagement of marriage by the false teachers (cf. 1 Tim 4:3), an act in itself that is arguably meddling, has apparently resulted in a number of young widows without family ties. Consequently, because they are not fulfilling their proper roles they are idle (ἀργός), a condition regularly associated with the meddling topos, and are using their free time to meddle in other people's affairs. The remedy that Paul urges upon them is to assume their proper roles by marrying, bearing children, and managing their household (1 Tim 5:14).

This also fits nicely alongside Timothy's "command" to silence the false teachers and to promote the οἰκονομίαν θεοῦ (1:4). The false teachers had, in essence, meddled in God's saving affairs and had misrepresented ("blasphemed," 1 Tim 1:20; cf. 6:1) him such that God's own household now functioned, in many ways, contrary to the furthering of God's saving plan, the οἰκονομίαν θεοῦ.⁵⁶ Thus, beginning with 2:1-7 Paul calls the church through

---

⁵¹ "Just a Busybody? A Look at the Greco-Roman Topos of Meddling for Defining ἀλλοτριεπίσκοπος in 1 Peter 4:15," *JBL* 125 (2006): 549-68 [552].
⁵² Brown, "Busybody," 554.
⁵³ Brown, "Busybody," 552.
⁵⁴ Brown, "Busybody," 553; cf. 564.
⁵⁵ That the antagonists active in Ephesus and on the horizon for Crete are essentially the same, see Couser, "Christian Existence," 267-71 and cf. Towner, *Goal*, 24-45.
⁵⁶ For this understanding of οἰκονομίαν θεοῦ see F. Young, *The Theology of the Pastoral Epistles* (Cambridge: Cambridge University Press, 1994), 55; L. Donelson,

Timothy back to the type of ordering consistent with God's saving purposes. There is also confirmatory evidence of this conception of the household material in how, as Brown mentions, the "quietness" motif emerges strongly in the ordering of the women in 2:11-12. Women are to learn "in quietness," i.e. "full submission," and they are not to exercise an improper social role by teaching or taking authority over a man. Rather, they are to have a demeanor of "quietness."[57]

Lastly, this approach is very similar to the meddling passage in 2 Thess 3:11-12. There as in 1 Timothy Paul censures some of the Thessalonians for their idleness (ἀτάκτως) that has led them to be "busybodies" (περιεργαζομένους; v. 11). Paul's prescription is for them to work "with quietness" (μετὰ ἡσυχίας; cf. 1 Thess 4:11), to fulfill their proper role—a thought very close to 1 Tim 2:2.

In sum "the quiet life in all godliness and dignity" is the type of life where individuals and the community as a whole are structured and ordered by God's saving work in Christ. This is a necessity so that God's οἰκονομίαν can be embodied and furthered. In 1 Tim 2:2, the implications of God's saving acts in Christ, if we are to take our cue from Titus 3:1-2 and elsewhere in Paul (e.g., Rom 13:1-2), likely means that believers are to be in proper submission to the civil authorities such that their ordering with respect to the government might not be a detriment to their evangelistic mission.[58] The believers are to assume their proper role of submission to and appreciation of the secular authorities insofar as they are able, given the constraints of "complete godliness and dignity." As 2 Tim 3:12 reminds them, persecution is a given. Therefore, this is not a call to conform to human expectations, but a call to conform to divine expectations and, thereby, to function effectively in the world as God's people.

CONCLUSION

The startling finding of this paper is that the type of political engagement envisioned in 1 Tim 2:1-7 has nothing to do with politics. This passage is Paul's call for the church to be the church. The church, as God's household, is to be structured and driven by his saving purposes (οἰκονομίαν θεοῦ, 1:4). The engagement with the civil authorities here has little to do with asking God to intervene in the civil arena in order to create optimal conditions for Christian life and witness. The focus here is on the family of God so as to encourage them to let God's saving priorities affect their interaction with the civil authorities. As such, they would respond to these authorities in a way that

---

Pseudepigraphy and Ethical Argument in the Pastoral Epistles (HUT 22; Tübingen: Mohr [Siebeck], 1986), 133; and Fee, *1 & 2 Timothy*, 42, 48, 92.

[57] Brown, "Busybody," 564-65.

[58] "Here ἡσυχία is linked to proper alignment with governing authorities (by praying and thanking God for them)" (Brown, "Busybody," 564).

acknowledges God's ordering of the civic sphere, respect and submission (cf. Titus 3:1-2; Rom 13:1-7). At the same time, because these responses are driven by theology and not by social convention, i.e., they arise from "godliness and dignity" (concepts informed by and rooted in God's saving acts in Christ), this engagement is redemptive in nature. Not only does the church clearly distinguish between the will of the state and God's will (recognizing that this does not mean that they are always distinct; cf. 1 Tim5:8), but the church is living to adorn the gospel as a people driven and shaped by it. When they are to be persecuted (an inevitability according to Paul, 2 Tim 3:12), Paul wants it to be a suffering "for Christ" (cf. Phil 1:13; 1 Pet 3:16-17), not because they are blameworthy by virtue of neglecting the personal and corporate demands of the gospel. To put it in different terms the church is to be a "workshop of Kingdom righteousness" where the work of God in Christ is made manifest in its life as a community of God's people and in its proclamation to the world, in word and deed, of God's blessing in Christ.[59] As D. Bock states,

> [T]he church is not an institution seeking to seize power on earth or exercise coercive sovereignty, but is to serve and love humankind, reflecting the love of God, his standards of righteousness, and the message of his forgiveness and love in Jesus Christ . . . . These elements make up the mission of the church as light in the world . . . .[60]

---

[59] C. Blaising and D. Bock, *Progressive Dispensationalism* (Wheaton, Ill.: Victor, 1993), 285-88.
[60] *Luke 9:51–24:53* (BECNT; Grand Rapids: Baker, 1996), 1222.

18

SCHLATTER ON THE PASTORALS: MISSION IN THE ACADEMY

Robert W. Yarbrough

The stereotype of a missionary as a pith-helmeted figure stalking steamy jungle trails is long since obsolete. Still fewer would associate missions with university or seminary classrooms. Yet for generations now, and particularly with the rise of Protestant missions in the nineteenth century, men and women engaged in ministry locally and all over the world have been trained by theology professors—"theology" here referring to the wide range of subjects in Bible, biblical languages, systematic and historical theology, church history, and related areas that are, or at least used to be, foundational for a typical professional ministry degree. In that sense, one of the most important players in the missionary enterprise has been the teacher and scholar preparing tomorrow's church and mission leaders for vocational service. The scholars who teach pastoral and missionary workers are, of necessity, at least missionary enablers.

Swiss-born Adolf Schlatter (1852–1938) taught for one hundred semesters in universities at Bern, Greifswald, Berlin, and Tübingen.[1] He went beyond being a missionary enabler to serve as a sort of practitioner, as an intent and effect of his scholarship was to uphold historic Christian understanding of the canonical Scriptures and their Christ-centered message. From the 1880s to the 1930s his influence on thousands of theology and ministry students was considerable as he lectured, primarily in NT, but also in systematics, history, ethics, and other areas. Through dozens of books still in print and ongoing scholarship on his ideas,[2] his voice still echoes. His influence has been significant in domestic and international ministries too numerous to count— there is, for example, a Schlatter study center in South Korea, and in recent

---

[1] For a concise biography of Schlatter in English see Werner Neuer, *Adolf Schlatter: A Biography of Germany's Premier Biblical Theologian* (trans. R. Yarbrough; Grand Rapids: Baker, 1995). For a comprehensive biography in German, see n. 4 below.

[2] See, e.g., Jochen Walldorf, *Realistische Philosophie: Der philosophische Entwurf Adolf Schlatters* (Göttingen: Vandenhoeck & Ruprecht, 1999); Hans-Martin Rieger, *Adolf Schlatters Rechtfertigungslehre und die Möglichkeit ökumenischer Verständigung* (Stuttgart: Calwer, 2000); Daniel Rüegg, *Der sich schenkende Christus. Adolf Schlatters Lehre von den Sakramenten* (Giessen: Brunnen, 2006); Clemens Hägele, *Die Schrift als Gnadenmittel: Adolf Schlatters Lehre von der Schrift in ihren Grundzügen* (Stuttgart: Calwer, 2007).

years a number of his works have been translated into English.

While an aim of many post-Enlightenment biblical scholars has been to disabuse students of historic Christian faith and a high view of Scripture's veracity, Schlatter stands out as a brilliant exegete who overall defended the Bible's accuracy.[3] This is typified in his work on the Pastoral Epistles (hereafter PE). This brief study will bring out prominent features of Schlatter's approach and findings. The goal will be recognition of Schlatter's distinctives not only as an exegete of the PE but as a missionary in and to the academic settings in which he largely lived out his calling. In upholding historic Christian understanding of the PE in an era and setting often not particularly amenable to this, Schlatter served a role in his times not unlike that so capably filled by the honoree of this volume, I. Howard Marshall. While Professor Marshall's service to scholarship at large is self-evident, it is fitting that I register gratitude here also for his informal assistance in the writing of my doctoral thesis (1982–1985) as well as for his service as internal examiner of that thesis. This is in addition to his example as a skillful and selfless exegetical leader at many levels internationally in the three decades that have passed since, a role which marks him as serving in his milieu a role not unlike that served by Schlatter in earlier generations.

SCHLATTER'S PE SCHOLARSHIP

By the late nineteenth century, when Schlatter wrote certifying exams prior to his first university appointment, the non-Pauline authorship of the PE was the dominant view in Germanic universities. This view, pioneered by F. D. E. Schleiermacher (1768–1834) and solidified by F. C. Baur (1792–1860), was voiced by Schlatter himself in 1880 in his examination essays: the PE contain authentic Pauline material but are deuteropauline,[4] stemming "perhaps from a man of the Pauline circle"[5] but not by Paul in the same sense as, say, Romans

---

[3] Without, however, endorsing a strict view of verbal inerrancy; see, e.g., his *Einleitung in die Bibel* (4th ed.; Stuttgart: Calwer, 1923), 483: "The Bible does not possess infallibility, either in its historical references or in its prophecy." On Schlatter's nevertheless high view of Scripture, note in his more mature scholarship the attribution of inerrancy (*Fehllosigkeit*) and infallibility (*Unfehlbarkeit*) to the Bible (Schlatter, *Das christliche Dogma* [2d ed.; Stuttgart: Calwer, 1923]). "Inerrancy" is however not something "that gives us unlimited knowledge; it rather places us in relationship with God, who is light without darkness, and it leads us upon the straight path to God's secure goal. The inerrancy of the Bible consists in this, that it summons us to God" (Schlatter, *Das christliche Dogma*, 376). Its "infallibility" consists in its "bringing us to the Infallible One, to God" (Schlatter, *Das christliche Dogma*, 378).

[4] Werner Neuer, *Adolf Schlatter: Ein Leben für Theologie und Kirche* (Stuttgart, Calwer, 1996), 156.

[5] Neuer (previous note) cites this as Schlatter's view expressed in the first edition (1888) of his *Einleitung* (n. 3 above). By the fourth edition of this work, however, it is clear that

or 1 and 2 Corinthians. Reviewers note that in Schlatter's first, lay-level PE commentary, Schlatter "does not hide ... even from this [conservative] readership that he long wavered in wondering whether the PE could stem from Paul or not."[6]

The PE were not a central component in Schlatter's pedagogy over the years—by the end of his life only two of his 133 NT courses (*Vorlesungen*) had been on the PE.[7] Yet he had written on them fairly extensively even prior to the major PE commentary published near the end of his career, a volume he started writing at the age of eighty-three and completed in ten months.[8]

For example, his NT introduction (we cite the 4th edition) numbers the PE among Paul's letters,[9] gives a brief exposition of the PE section by section,[10] and discusses their historical setting, teaching, and authorship.[11]

In 1904 Schlatter published a popular-level commentary on the PE in the series *Erläuterungen zum Neuen Testament*,[12] an exposition that eventually covered every book in the NT. Schlatter began the series with Romans in 1887 and completed it in 1910. Neuer points out no other German scholar of the twentieth century managed the feat of completing an exposition of every book in the NT. Neuer also notes: "With his *Erläuterungen* Schlatter certainly had the widest impact over the decades. They were (and are) used with profit by countless pastors, preachers, church workers, and Bible readers to the present day."[13] In the edition consulted for this essay, commentary on the PE consists of 164 pages in a 272-page book.[14]

References to the PE are scattered throughout the portion of Schlatter's NT theology devoted to Paul: *The Theology of the Apostles* (187-321).[15] Schlatter pays particular attention to "The Office in the Pastoral Epistles" (312-17) and "The Boundary between Authentic and Gnostic Christianity according to the Pastoral Epistles" (317-21). It was Schlatter's conviction that as Galatians

---

Schlatter no longer holds to this himself; it is a position he attributes to others (Neuer, *Adolf Schlatter*, 425-26).

[6] H. Holtzmann, R. Knopf, and J. Weiss, review of Schlatter *Die Briefe an die Thessalonicher, Philipper, Timotheus und Titus* (see n. 14 below), *Theologischer Jahresbericht* 24 (1904): 176. So also R. Knopf in his comment on the same book: *Theologische Rundschau* 9 (1906): 65.

[7] Neuer, *Adolf Schlatter*, 796.

[8] Neuer, *Adolf Schlatter*, 795-98.

[9] *Einleitung in die Bibel*, 357.

[10] *Einleitung in die Bibel*, 414-19.

[11] *Einleitung in die Bibel*, 419-26.

[12] Neuer, *Adolf Schlatter*, 407.

[13] Neuer, *Adolf Schlatter*, 510.

[14] *Die Briefe an die Thessalonicher, Philipper, Timotheus und Titus* (Erläuterungen zum Neuen Testament 8; Stuttgart: Calwer, 1964), 109-272.

[15] Schlatter, *The Theology of the Apostles* (trans. Andreas Köstenberger; Grand Rapids: Baker, 1999).

battled Jewish ethical incursions into church understanding of the gospel, the PE battled Greek malformations of gospel apprehension, many of them rooted in Gnostic belief.[16] Today the view is much less widespread that Gnosticism flourished so early in the first century and that NT writings interact with it. But it was common coin for many European NT scholars in Schlatter's era, although even in Schlatter's time J. Jeremias noted lack of documentary evidence for this view.[17]

Schlatter's most extensive analysis of the PE is found in his academic commentary *Die Kirche der Griechen im Urteil des Paulus*.[18] This was one of five substantial commentaries he completed after he reached his eightieth birthday, a literary output exceeding 2,000 published pages.[19] Joachim Jeremias remarked on this astonishing output at the time.[20] His PE commentary runs to some 283 pages. "In it not only does the content of the PE receive careful assessment and responsible discussion: the same is true of the critical questions associated with the PE."[21] Salient features of this commentary in relation to the theme of this essay, as well as of his PE exposition in *Erläuterungen* (above), will emerge in discussion below.

A CONTEMPORARY GERMAN UNIVERSITY READING OF THE PE: ULRICH WILCKENS[22]

In order to appreciate Schlatter's reading of the PE, it will be instructive to survey a current German treatment of the PE at three salient points: 1) the

---

[16] Noted also, e.g., by B. Brinkmann, review of Schlatter, *Die Kirche der Griechen im Urteil des Paulus*, *Schol* 12 (1937): 291.

[17] Jeremias, review of Schlatter, *Die Kirche der Griechen im Urteil des Paulus*, *TLZ* 62 (1937): 415-17.

[18] Schlatter, *Die Kirche der Griechen im Urteil des Paulus* (Stuttgart: Calwer, 1936).

[19] Neuer, *Adolf Schlatter*, 781. Other commentaries completed after he reached the age of 80 were on 1–2 Corinthians, Romans, Mark, and 1 Peter. He also wrote the substantial *Kennen wir Jesus? Ein Gang durch ein Jahr im Gespräch mit ihm* (Stuttgart: Calwer, 1937) during this time.

[20] Jeremias, review of Schlatter, 415.

[21] K. H. Rengstorf, review of Schlatter, *Die Kirche der Griechen im Urteil des Paulus*, *Pastoralblätter für Predigt, Seelsorge und kirchliche Unterweisung* 79 (1936/1937): 636-37 [637].

[22] *Die Briefe des Urchristentums: Paulus und seine Schüler, Theologen aus dem Bereich judenchristlicher Heindenmission* (Teilband 3 of *Geschichte der urchristlichen Theologie* [vol. 1 of *Theologie des Neuen Testaments*; Neukirchen-Vluyn: Neukirchener Verlag, 2005]). A prolific New Testament scholar (b. 1928), Wilckens taught at Marburg 1958–1960, Berlin 1960–1968, and in Hamburg 1968–1981. He has also served in German Protestant church leadership. He has authored numerous commentaries, including works on Romans and John, in addition to monographs on various NT topics.

origin and nature of the PE, 2) the theology of the PE, and 3) the significance of the PE in church-historical perspective. We will note points of contact and contrast with Schlatter in the next section.

ORIGIN AND NATURE OF THE PE

Wilckens groups 1–2 Timothy and Titus as part of a foursome, with Ephesians rounding out the group. Ephesians and the PE originated after Paul's death. Wilckens holds that Paul is displayed prominently as the writer because "he remains *the* central apostolic authority for the congregations that he founded or that grew up under his influence" (267).[23] Despite appearances (e.g., 1 Tim 1:4: "stay there in Ephesus"; Titus 1:5: "the reason I left you there in Crete"), none of these letters pertains to a particular local setting. Wilckens cites 1 Tim 3:15, which speaks of the church as "God's household," as the basis for this claim. It is not clear why this must connote only a general and not any particular setting. But because he thinks the PE lack local rootage, Wilckens groups them (and Ephesians) with other writings in the NT that are called "catholic letters."

The PE are concerned above all to ensure continuity in the churches with the faith and practice of the apostolic tradition (although Wilckens finds many contradictions between the PE and Paul; see below). The PE stem from the same author, judging from their style, but this author cannot be Paul (285). Yet biographical and other real-life details of the PE are not all literary creations, as N. Brox and J. Roloff have argued. Wilckens opts rather for the "assumption" (*Annahme*) that the unknown author or compiler used bits of actual correspondence between Paul and Timothy "for this very purpose: to make the epistles he created look to the readers like they are from Paul, in order to emphasize their apostolic legitimacy" (286 n. 29). Apparently Wilckens does not feel the ethical problem inherent in this view—how can writings whose author bases their persuasive force on deception be taken seriously as apostolic mandates communicating the truth of a God who does not lie (cf. Titus 1:2)?

Historically speaking, the setting of even the earliest PE, which Wilckens takes to be 2 Timothy, is the time of transition to the second century, when he asserts other pseudepigraphic letters arose (1–2 Peter, Jude, James) and the canonical Gospels were likewise distributed with (contrived) apostolic associations in order to give them authority (286-87).

THEOLOGY OF THE PE

Wilckens sees the PE's theology as centered in the "faithful sayings": 2 Tim 2:11; Titus 3:8; 1 Tim 3:1; 1:15; cf. 4:4 (*sic*; apparently 4:9 is meant). Wilckens suggests that this was a formula used in worship services. The PE author adapts it "to strengthen the impression of apostolic truth" (288). The PE focus on

---

[23] Parenthetical page numbers in this section refer to the work in the previous note.

"church office as defense against false teachers" (294-95) as well as on the false teachers themselves (295-97). In both discussions Wilckens finds the PE in fairly substantial contradiction with Paul in his known letters.

The biggest contradiction he posits is that on the one hand the PE want apostolic doctrine to be upheld in purity, but on the other that that same lived-out doctrine be acknowledged by the pagan world around the church as exemplary and beyond reproach (297). Here Wilckens seems to conflate the doctrine of the PE and the social ideals to which church leaders should conform—they should be ethical and godly in their behavior along the lines of established pagan cultural norms. But this seriously downplays the theological and christological bases for, and substance of, all that the PE state. To take just one example: the PE are steadfastly monotheistic and (like the OT) relate ethics closely to religion conceived as covenantal relationship with the one true creator and redeemer God who has become incarnate in Jesus, who died for sin and rose from the grave. Nothing in that sentence comports with the beliefs and practices of late first-century religion and culture in the Roman Empire, which was polytheistic, did not relate ethics and religion closely, and was not enamored of the notion of a cosmic savior in the form of a crucified Jewish king whose mortal body had been raised immortal.[24] Far from being mandates for cultural conformity, the PE are calls to defy convention, in precept and in deed, out of loyalty to the God revealed in Jesus, the gospel message, and its implications.

Wilckens sees in Timothy a contrast to the charismatic-based Christian authority of every believer as affirmed, e.g., in 1 Corinthians (see 97). The PE showcase rather an "official charisma" (*Amtscharisma*; 297). "Timothy" is a third-generation person (a follower of some follower of Paul?); his qualifications are grounded in the heritage of his Christian home (2 Tim 1:5; 3:15). Such a pedigree became one requirement for church office, on which in turn all truth in the church now rests. There was a second requirement: "a multi-year course of study of apostolic doctrine is conditio sine qua non for an apostolically ordained teacher" like him (298). This seems 1) to posit a course of formal study that is not explicit anywhere in the NT, 2) to ignore the fact that such a course of study is absent from the requirements for overseers given in 1 Timothy and Titus, and 3) to minimize the high level of doctrinal responsibility vested in apostles and appointed church leaders from the beginning of the founding of NT churches, not just beginning with a "third generation."

---

[24] Udo Schnelle, *Theology of the New Testament* (trans. M. Eugene Boring; Grand Rapids: Baker Academic, 2009), 581, ignores such elements in claiming that "God" in the PE is an adaptation of "Greco-Roman imagery" that is in full compliance with first-century pagan notions.

SIGNIFICANCE OF THE PE IN CHURCH-HISTORICAL PERSPECTIVE

Charges that the PE fall away from many Pauline ideals are justified, Wilckens thinks. But the third-generation setting left no choice. Doctrinal oversight had to be centralized, in Paul's name even if not very faithfully in his actual teaching. "The mediation [of Pauline authority] occurs through a liturgical act of transference of apostolic authority, which now is actually in the hands of 'bishops'" (299). Wilckens chooses, then, to view the continuity in formal and ecclesial terms rather than material[25] and doctrinal[26] ones as the PE themselves argue.

The PE author is probably one of these "bishops," who realizes that he needs Paul's name and weight to authorize his oversight. But although the words of the PE are often Pauline, the PE frequently fail to pass along Paul's theological concerns. E.g., the PE stress on works is foreign to Paul, for Wilckens, who sees freedom from the curse of the Mosaic law (and from that law itself) as essential to Paul's gospel but absent from the PE. Also he sees the "the salvation-historical horizon of *one* church of God composed of Gentiles and Jews," so prominent in Ephesians, to be lost from view in the PE (300). This raises the question of why Ephesians is grouped with the PE in the first place.

But this mistaking of Paul's teaching is actually good and instructive, Wilckens concludes. It shows that there is within the Pauline canon as traditionally conceived substantial material contradiction, which each generation must correct. The PE made a (failed) attempt faithfully to rearticulate Paul. We are and must not be bound to the reception of Paul found in the PE; we must rather transcend it (301), as "great theologians in the history of the church" have consistently attempted.

Wilckens also commends the PE's accommodation to its environment. The church today, and its leaders, must work hard not to be perceived as out of step with non-Christian cultural expectations and demands. He concedes that individual Christians must still reckon with the possibility of their own martyrdom. But it is hard to see why, if the PE are used as a model, when "the congregations of the PE were obviously able to live without incompatibilities, conflicts, or even persecutions in their surroundings" (301). Yet the PE do in fact repeatedly call on Timothy to live ready for persecution, which not just he but "all who desire to live godly in Christ Jesus" will face at some point and in one form or another (2 Tim 3:12), so radical is the Christian message if faithfully lived out. Titus does not speak of persecution but calls repeatedly for "good works" that defy and transcend prevailing cultural norms.

In the end, despite the grace and clear organization of Wilckens's treatment,

---

[25] E.g., 1 Tim 3:4-6 calls for an established, observed track record of exemplary character and behavior.

[26] Few stresses in the PE are more prominent than that both Timothy and Titus, and leaders they appoint, be grounded in and committed to true apostolic teaching.

his picture of the PE is at times markedly divergent from the sources as they stand, beginning from the very first word of each of the three documents, i.e., Παῦλος.

FEATURES OF SCHLATTER'S READING OF THE PE

ORIGIN AND NATURE OF THE PE

Whereas Wilckens groups the PE with Ephesians and terms them all catholic letters, in that sense divorcing them materially and temporally from the canonical Pauline witness, Schlatter is persuaded rather by the Pauline fabric of the PE.[27] One basis for this is linguistic, as the following chart indicates. It is adapted from Schlatter's academic PE commentary;[28] we reproduce below only the 1 Timothy portion of Schlatter's chart. Schlatter notes, by my count, thirty-four parallels in the ten-letter Pauline corpus with 1 Timothy, thirty-one parallels with 2 Timothy, and nine with Titus. That Schlatter is being selective, not exhaustive, is suggested by a recent study that finds eighty such parallels.[29] Below we supply Greek (not in Schlatter's chart) along with underlining to highlight linguistic or conceptual points of contact. Asterisks indicate that this parallel is *not* noted in the NA[27] cross-references

1 Tim 1:1 Παῦλος ἀπόστολος Χριστοῦ Ἰησοῦ <u>κατ' ἐπιταγὴν</u> <u>θεοῦ σωτῆρος ἡμῶν</u> καὶ Χριστοῦ Ἰησοῦ τῆς ἐλπίδος ἡμῶν	*Rom 16:26 φανερωθέντος δὲ νῦν διά τε γραφῶν προφητικῶν <u>κατ' ἐπιταγὴν τοῦ αἰωνίου θεοῦ</u> εἰς ὑπακοὴν πίστεως εἰς πάντα τὰ ἔθνη γνωρισθέντος,
1 Tim 1:3 Καθὼς παρεκάλεσά σε προσμεῖναι ἐν Ἐφέσῳ <u>πορευόμενος εἰς Μακεδονίαν</u>, ἵνα παραγγείλῃς τισὶν μὴ ἑτεροδιδασκαλεῖν	*Rom 15:24-25 ὡς ἂν <u>πορεύωμαι εἰς τὴν Σπανίαν</u> . . . *25 Νυνὶ δὲ <u>πορεύομαι εἰς</u> <u>Ἰερουσαλὴμ</u> διακονῶν τοῖς ἁγίοις.
1 Tim 1:8 <u>Οἴδαμεν δὲ ὅτι</u> <u>καλὸς ὁ νόμος</u>, ἐάν τις αὐτῷ νομίμως χρῆται,	Rom 7:14, 16 <u>Οἴδαμεν γὰρ ὅτι</u> <u>ὁ νόμος πνευματικός ἐστιν</u>, ἐγὼ δὲ σάρκινός εἰμι πεπραμένος ὑπὸ

---

[27] Schlatter's shift from affirming non-Pauline authorship of the PE at the time he began university teaching (cf. Neuer, *Adolf Schlatter*, 156) to his acceptance of Pauline authorship in his later scholarship has to my knowledge not been explained in detail in Schlatter biographical studies.

[28] *Die Kirche der Griechen im Urteil des Paulus*, 15.

[29] See Walter T. Wilson, *Pauline Parallels: A Comprehensive Guide* (Louisville: Westminster/John Knox, 2009), 403-32. A comprehensive study of the footnotes in Schlatter's *Die Kirche der Griechen im Urteil des Paulus* might uncover quite a few more.

	τὴν ἁμαρτίαν. 16 εἰ δὲ ὃ οὐ θέλω τοῦτο ποιῶ, σύμφημι τῷ νόμῳ ὅτι καλός.
1 Tim 1:11 <u>κατὰ τὸ εὐαγγέλιον τῆς δόξης τοῦ μακαρίου θεοῦ, ὃ ἐπιστεύθην ἐγώ</u>.	*Rom 2:16 ἐν ἡμέρᾳ ὅτε κρίνει ὁ θεὸς τὰ κρυπτὰ τῶν ἀνθρώπων <u>κατὰ τὸ εὐαγγέλιόν μου</u> διὰ Χριστοῦ Ἰησοῦ. 1 Thess 2:4 ἀλλὰ καθὼς <u>δεδοκιμάσμεθα ὑπὸ τοῦ θεοῦ πιστευθῆναι τὸ εὐαγγέλιον</u> . . .
1 Tim 1:12 Χάριν ἔχω <u>τῷ ἐνδυναμώσαντί με</u> Χριστῷ Ἰησοῦ τῷ κυρίῳ ἡμῶν, ὅτι <u>πιστόν με ἡγήσατο θέμενος εἰς διακονίαν</u>	1 Cor 7:25 Περὶ δὲ τῶν παρθένων ἐπιταγὴν κυρίου οὐκ ἔχω, γνώμην δὲ δίδωμι ὡς <u>ἠλεημένος ὑπὸ κυρίου πιστὸς εἶναι</u>. Phil 4:13 πάντα ἰσχύω <u>ἐν τῷ ἐνδυναμοῦντί με</u>.
1 Tim 1:14 <u>ὑπερεπλεόνασεν δὲ ἡ χάρις</u> τοῦ κυρίου ἡμῶν μετὰ πίστεως καὶ ἀγάπης τῆς ἐν Χριστῷ Ἰησοῦ.	Rom 5:20 νόμος δὲ παρεισῆλθεν, ἵνα πλεονάσῃ τὸ παράπτωμα· οὗ δὲ ἐπλεόνασεν ἡ ἁμαρτία, <u>ὑπερεπερίσσευσεν ἡ χάρις</u>,
1 Tim 1:16 ἀλλὰ διὰ τοῦτο ἠλεήθην, <u>ἵνα ἐν ἐμοὶ πρώτῳ ἐνδείξηται Χριστὸς Ἰησοῦς τὴν ἅπασαν μακροθυμίαν πρὸς ὑποτύπωσιν τῶν μελλόντων πιστεύειν ἐπ' αὐτῷ εἰς ζωὴν αἰώνιον</u>.	*Eph 2:7 <u>ἵνα ἐνδείξηται ἐν τοῖς αἰῶσιν τοῖς ἐπερχομένοις τὸ ὑπερβάλλον πλοῦτος τῆς χάριτος αὐτοῦ ἐν χρηστότητι ἐφ' ἡμᾶς ἐν Χριστῷ Ἰησοῦ</u>.
1 Tim 1:20 ὧν ἐστιν Ὑμέναιος καὶ Ἀλέξανδρος, οὓς <u>παρέδωκα τῷ σατανᾷ, ἵνα παιδευθῶσιν μὴ βλασφημεῖν</u>.	1 Cor 5:5 <u>παραδοῦναι τὸν τοιοῦτον τῷ σατανᾷ</u> εἰς ὄλεθρον τῆς σαρκός, <u>ἵνα τὸ πνεῦμα σωθῇ ἐν τῇ ἡμέρᾳ τοῦ κυρίου</u>. *1 Cor 11:32 <u>κρινόμενοι δὲ ὑπὸ [τοῦ] κυρίου παιδευόμεθα, ἵνα μὴ σὺν τῷ κόσμῳ κατακριθῶμεν</u>.
1 Tim 2:1 <u>Παρακαλῶ οὖν</u> πρῶτον πάντων <u>ποιεῖσθαι δεήσεις</u> προσευχὰς ἐντεύξεις εὐχαριστίας ὑπὲρ πάντων ἀνθρώπων,	*Eph 4:1 <u>Παρακαλῶ οὖν ὑμᾶς</u> ἐγὼ ὁ δέσμιος ἐν κυρίῳ ἀξίως περιπατῆσαι τῆς κλήσεως ἧς ἐκλήθητε, *Phil 1:4 <u>πάντοτε ἐν πάσῃ</u>

	δεήσει μου ὑπὲρ πάντων ὑμῶν, μετὰ χαρᾶς <u>τὴν δέησιν ποιούμενος</u>, Phil. 4:6 μηδὲν μεριμνᾶτε, ἀλλ' <u>ἐν παντὶ τῇ προσευχῇ καὶ τῇ δεήσει μετὰ εὐχαριστίας τὰ αἰτήματα ὑμῶν γνωριζέσθω πρὸς τὸν θεόν</u>.
1 Tim 2:2 <u>ὑπὲρ βασιλέων καὶ πάντων τῶν ἐν ὑπεροχῇ ὄντων</u>...	*Rom 13:1 Πᾶσα ψυχὴ <u>ἐξουσίαις ὑπερεχούσαις ὑποτασσέσθω</u>. οὐ γὰρ ἔστιν ἐξουσία εἰ μὴ ὑπὸ θεοῦ, αἱ δὲ οὖσαι ὑπὸ θεοῦ τεταγμέναι εἰσίν.
1 Tim 2:5 <u>Εἷς γὰρ θεός</u>, εἷς καὶ μεσίτης θεοῦ καὶ ἀνθρώπων, ἄνθρωπος Χριστὸς Ἰησοῦς,	Rom 3:30 εἴπερ <u>εἷς ὁ θεὸς ὃς δικαιώσει περιτομὴν ἐκ πίστεως καὶ ἀκροβυστίαν διὰ τῆς πίστεως</u>.
1 Tim 2:7 <u>εἰς ὃ ἐτέθην ἐγὼ κῆρυξ καὶ ἀπόστολος, ἀλήθειαν λέγω οὐ ψεύδομαι, διδάσκαλος ἐθνῶν ἐν πίστει καὶ ἀληθείᾳ</u>.	Rom 9:1 Ἀλήθειαν λέγω ἐν Χριστῷ, οὐ ψεύδομαι, συμμαρτυρούσης μοι τῆς συνειδήσεώς μου ἐν πνεύματι ἁγίῳ, *2 Thess 2:13 Ἡμεῖς δὲ ὀφείλομεν εὐχαριστεῖν τῷ θεῷ πάντοτε περὶ ὑμῶν, ἀδελφοὶ ἠγαπημένοι ὑπὸ κυρίου, <u>ὅτι εἵλατο ὑμᾶς ὁ θεὸς ἀπαρχὴν εἰς σωτηρίαν ἐν ἁγιασμῷ πνεύματος καὶ πίστει ἀληθείας</u>,
1 Tim 2:8 Βούλομαι οὖν προσεύχεσθαι τοὺς ἄνδρας ἐν παντὶ τόπῳ ἐπαίροντας ὁσίους χεῖρας <u>χωρὶς ὀργῆς καὶ διαλογισμοῦ</u>.	Phil 2:14 Πάντα ποιεῖτε <u>χωρὶς γογγυσμῶν καὶ διαλογισμῶν</u>,
1 Tim 2:11 <u>Γυνὴ ἐν ἡσυχίᾳ μανθανέτω ἐν πάσῃ ὑποταγῇ</u>· 1 Tim 2:12 <u>διδάσκειν δὲ γυναικὶ οὐκ ἐπιτρέπω οὐδὲ αὐθεντεῖν ἀνδρός, ἀλλ' εἶναι ἐν ἡσυχίᾳ</u>.	1 Cor 14:34 <u>αἱ γυναῖκες ἐν ταῖς ἐκκλησίαις σιγάτωσαν· οὐ γὰρ ἐπιτρέπεται αὐταῖς λαλεῖν, ἀλλὰ ὑποτασσέσθωσαν, καθὼς καὶ ὁ νόμος λέγει</u>. 1 Cor 14:35 εἰ δέ τι μαθεῖν θέλουσιν, ἐν οἴκῳ τοὺς ἰδίους

	ἄνδρας ἐπερωτάτωσαν· αἰσχρὸν γάρ ἐστιν γυναικὶ λαλεῖν ἐν ἐκκλησίᾳ.
1 Tim 3:13 οἱ γὰρ καλῶς διακονήσαντες βαθμὸν ἑαυτοῖς καλὸν περιποιοῦνται καὶ <u>πολλὴν παρρησίαν ἐν πίστει τῇ ἐν Χριστῷ Ἰησοῦ</u>.	*Phlm 8 Διὸ <u>πολλὴν ἐν Χριστῷ παρρησίαν ἔχων</u> ἐπιτάσσειν σοι τὸ ἀνῆκον
1 Tim 4:10 <u>εἰς τοῦτο γὰρ κοπιῶμεν καὶ ἀγωνιζόμεθα, ὅτι ἠλπίκαμεν ἐπὶ θεῷ ζῶντι</u>, ὅς ἐστιν σωτὴρ πάντων ἀνθρώπων μάλιστα πιστῶν.	*Gal 6:10 Ἄρα οὖν ὡς καιρὸν ἔχομεν, ἐργαζώμεθα τὸ ἀγαθὸν <u>πρὸς πάντας, μάλιστα δὲ πρὸς τοὺς οἰκείους τῆς πίστεως</u>.
	*Col 1:29 <u>εἰς ὃ καὶ κοπιῶ ἀγωνιζόμενος</u> κατὰ τὴν ἐνέργειαν αὐτοῦ τὴν ἐνεργουμένην ἐν ἐμοὶ ἐν δυνάμει.
1 Tim 4:12 Μηδείς σου τῆς νεότητος καταφρονείτω, ἀλλὰ <u>τύπος γίνου τῶν πιστῶν</u> ἐν λόγῳ, ἐν ἀναστροφῇ, ἐν ἀγάπῃ, ἐν πίστει, ἐν ἁγνείᾳ.	1 Thess 1:7 <u>ὥστε γενέσθαι ὑμᾶς τύπον πᾶσιν τοῖς πιστεύουσιν</u> ἐν τῇ Μακεδονίᾳ καὶ ἐν τῇ Ἀχαΐᾳ.
1 Tim 4:16 <u>ἔπεχε σεαυτῷ καὶ τῇ διδασκαλίᾳ, ἐπίμενε αὐτοῖς· τοῦτο γὰρ ποιῶν καὶ σεαυτὸν σώσεις καὶ τοὺς ἀκούοντάς σου</u>.	1 Cor 9:22 <u>ἐγενόμην τοῖς ἀσθενέσιν ἀσθενής, ἵνα τοὺς ἀσθενεῖς κερδήσω· τοῖς πᾶσιν γέγονα πάντα, ἵνα πάντως τινὰς σώσω</u>.
1 Tim 5:18 <u>λέγει γὰρ ἡ γραφή· βοῦν ἀλοῶντα οὐ φιμώσεις, καί· ἄξιος ὁ ἐργάτης τοῦ μισθοῦ αὐτοῦ</u>.	1 Cor 9:9 <u>ἐν γὰρ τῷ Μωϋσέως νόμῳ γέγραπται· οὐ κημώσεις βοῦν ἀλοῶντα</u>. μὴ τῶν βοῶν μέλει τῷ θεῷ
	*1Cor. 9:14 <u>οὕτως καὶ ὁ κύριος διέταξεν τοῖς τὸ εὐαγγέλιον καταγγέλλουσιν ἐκ τοῦ εὐαγγελίου ζῆν</u>.
1 Tim 5:19 <u>κατὰ πρεσβυτέρου κατηγορίαν μὴ παραδέχου, ἐκτὸς εἰ μὴ ἐπὶ δύο ἢ τριῶν μαρτύρων</u>.	2 Cor 13:1 Τρίτον τοῦτο ἔρχομαι πρὸς ὑμᾶς· <u>ἐπὶ στόματος δύο μαρτύρων καὶ τριῶν σταθήσεται πᾶν ῥῆμα</u>.
1 Tim 5:20 <u>Τοὺς ἁμαρτάνοντας ἐνώπιον πάντων ἔλεγχε</u>, ἵνα καὶ οἱ λοιποὶ φόβον ἔχωσιν.	Eph 5:11 καὶ <u>μὴ συγκοινωνεῖτε τοῖς ἔργοις τοῖς ἀκάρποις τοῦ σκότους, μᾶλλον δὲ καὶ ἐλέγχετε</u>.
1 Tim 6:1 Ὅσοι εἰσὶν ὑπὸ ζυγὸν δοῦλοι, τοὺς ἰδίους	*Rom 2:24 <u>τὸ γὰρ ὄνομα τοῦ θεοῦ δι' ὑμᾶς βλασφημεῖται ἐν</u>

δεσπότας πάσης τιμῆς ἀξίους ἡγείσθωσαν, ἵνα μὴ τὸ ὄνομα τοῦ θεοῦ καὶ ἡ διδασκαλία βλασφημῆται.	τοῖς ἔθνεσιν, καθὼς γέγραπται.
1 Tim 6:2 οἱ δὲ πιστοὺς ἔχοντες δεσπότας μὴ καταφρονείτωσαν, ὅτι ἀδελφοί εἰσιν, ἀλλὰ μᾶλλον δουλευέτωσαν, ὅτι πιστοί εἰσιν καὶ ἀγαπητοὶ οἱ τῆς εὐεργεσίας ἀντιλαμβανόμενοι. Ταῦτα δίδασκε καὶ παρακάλει.	*Col 4:9 σὺν Ὀνησίμῳ τῷ πιστῷ καὶ ἀγαπητῷ ἀδελφῷ, ὅς ἐστιν ἐξ ὑμῶν· πάντα ὑμῖν γνωρίσουσιν τὰ ὧδε.
1 Tim 6:3 εἴ τις ἑτεροδιδασκαλεῖ καὶ μὴ προσέρχεται ὑγιαίνουσιν λόγοις τοῖς τοῦ κυρίου ἡμῶν Ἰησοῦ Χριστοῦ καὶ τῇ κατ' εὐσέβειαν διδασκαλίᾳ,	*Rom 12:7 εἴτε διακονίαν ἐν τῇ διακονίᾳ, εἴτε ὁ διδάσκων ἐν τῇ διδασκαλίᾳ, *Rom 12:8 εἴτε ὁ παρακαλῶν ἐν τῇ παρακλήσει· ὁ μεταδιδοὺς ἐν ἁπλότητι, ὁ προϊστάμενος ἐν σπουδῇ, ὁ ἐλεῶν ἐν ἱλαρότητι.
1 Tim 6:12 ἀγωνίζου τὸν καλὸν ἀγῶνα τῆς πίστεως, ἐπιλαβοῦ τῆς αἰωνίου ζωῆς, εἰς ἣν ἐκλήθης καὶ ὡμολόγησας τὴν καλὴν ὁμολογίαν ἐνώπιον πολλῶν μαρτύρων.	*Col 3:15 καὶ ἡ εἰρήνη τοῦ Χριστοῦ βραβευέτω ἐν ταῖς καρδίαις ὑμῶν, εἰς ἣν καὶ ἐκλήθητε ἐν ἑνὶ σώματι· καὶ εὐχάριστοι γίνεσθε.

Such a chart does not of course "prove" Pauline authorship, as impressive lists of non-Pauline usage in the PE can easily be generated.[30] On the other hand, Schlatter points out that lists of non-Pauline words are also not "the last word" disproving Pauline origin: "the decisive weight falls on the exposition; if separation of the letters from Paul makes them into a riddle for which there is no explanation, the linguistic distinctiveness of the PE cannot separate them from Paul."[31] Schlatter wishes to show merely that the case for Pauline authorship is not utterly groundless even from a linguistic viewpoint. There are numerous instances of Pauline turns of phrase and diction, "over 70 literal points of contact with other Pauline letters in fact (most of all Romans and 1–2 Corinthians)."[32] These are not of the contrived and stilted sort one finds in, say, the apocryphal *Epistle to the Laodiceans*, much of which was manifestly

---

[30] As a reviewer of even Schlatter's popular-level PE commentary observes, Schlatter "indicates that doubts about Pauline authorship are not foreign to him" (R. Knopf, review of Schlatter, *Die Briefe an die Thessalonicher, Philipper, Timotheus und Titus* (n. 14 above), *TRu* 9 (1906): 62.

[31] *Die Kirche der Griechen im Urteil des Paulus*, 17.

[32] As Neuer, *Adolf Schlatter*, 796, observes.

cribbed from the canonical Philippians. They are often divergent enough not to qualify as slavish imitation of Paul, yet similar enough to raise the seeming likelihood of a common mind and hand.

This in turn justifies a careful look at the historical setting, since vocabulary alone hardly settles the matter. Like most commentators, Schlatter concedes that the PE do not fit in the life and movements of Paul as described in Acts. And yet "regarded in themselves, their references fit together seamlessly."[33] The details of the PE are consistent with a time after Paul's release from his first imprisonment,[34] a release which he stated he expected (Phil 1:25). And the conditions Paul describes in the PE, along with the language he uses,[35] are different from those reflected in his earlier epistles, which also argues for a later time[36] of composition. Schlatter notes that the only direct contradiction between the PE and the other ten Pauline letters is at 1 Tim 2:5, where Jesus is the mediator, whereas in Gal 3:19, 20 it is Moses. Yet he dryly observes, "The points of contact are so numerous that those who reject Pauline authorship must ascribe to their author not only familiarity with Paul's typical ecclesial language but also an intimate knowledge of the Pauline epistolary corpus."[37] Historically speaking it is more likely that Paul is the author of all of this material than that he was not, but that unknown writers so skillfully and comprehensively mastered and mimicked his voice in often precise detail at such an early juncture, without leaving any evidence of their existence much less identity in the annals of extant early church history and literature.

The issue of different language is significant enough for us to show one of the ways Schlatter viewed things to be quoted at length. How does he explain the shift in vocabulary from Paul's earlier letters to the PE? This is not all of Schlatter's explanation, but it gives the flavor of his shrewd approach to the problem (recall that he wrote during the era of Hitler's consolidation of power):

> How a shift in verbal usage arises we are experiencing vividly through the changes that our language has recently undergone. Today a number of words have become somewhat common which earlier we used rarely, or only with other connotations: *Führer, Führung, Boden, Blut, Rasse, Rassenseele, Erbgang, Brauchtum.*[38] But also key terms in church language have received new

---

[33] Schlatter, *Einleitung in die Bibel*, 420.
[34] Cf. Schlatter, *Die Kirche der Griechen im Urteil des Paulus*, 21.
[35] Schlatter, *Einleitung in die Bibel*, 420.
[36] No one suggests, of course, that the PE might precede the undoubted Pauline letters.
[37] Schlatter, *Die Kirche der Griechen im Urteil des Paulus*, 16, a point noted also by Brinkmann, review of Schlatter, 291.
[38] Readers may recognize these as words connected to Nazi ideology. *Führer* as title for Hitler should be obvious, but to translate the rest: "leadership, soil, blood, race, soul of the [Aryan] race, inheritance, usage." On *Rassenseele* see Cornelia Schmitz-Berning, *Vokabular des Nationalsozialismus* (Berlin: de Gruyter, 1998), 524. On *Brauchtum* see ibid., 616.

application: "faith" in relation to government authority, "fellowship" in relation to the German people, "confession" as a problem in "fellowship" with the German people. In addition there is the virtual elimination of Latin-based words. This shift in language arises not because we have changed but because those to whom we speak have changed . . . . The question posed by the new words of the PE is: do they point to new situations and aspirations of the church? Much had taken place during the more than five years of Paul's imprisonment and separation from the churches; this may be glimpsed from his writings to the Corinthians and the Romans, as well as from the Prison Epistles. It is true that the Prison Epistles are not vastly separate from the PE temporally; but Paul's situation had substantially altered: now he is in touch with the churches not only through friends and messengers but by his physical presence. He himself interacts with those who contradict him. Of the words in the PE that point to controversy—ζήτησις, ἐκζήτησις, μῦθος, γενεαλογίαι, ψευδώνυμος γνῶσις, κενοφωνία, λογομαχία, ἀντιθέσεις, αἱρετικός, τετύφωται, ἐξέστραπται, πίστεως ἀστοχῆσαι, περὶ τὴν πίστιν [ἐ]ναυάγησαι, αὐτοκατάκριτος—it is certain that they are not new words coined by the writer but rather terms brought into play by those he must engage. Likewise, the new words making up the list of qualifications for overseers and policies for widows conform to the conditions that are now current in the congregations.[39]

It is not possible, or necessary, to document all of Schlatter's arguments for the linguistic plausibility of Paul's authorship of the PE. Just the brief excerpts above bear out Neuer's statement that Schlatter's case for Paul's authorship is not just "repetition and preference for arguments traditionally brought forth for 'genuineness';" it rather consists of "a plenitude of independent observations on the language and content of the letters."[40] It should also be noted once more that Schlatter's late-life affirmation of Pauline authorship of the PE represents a shift of conviction from the earliest viewpoint of his career. Evidently his studies over the decades convinced him of this, rather than Pauline authorship being no more than a traditionally-grounded conviction in his thinking.

The bulk of Schlatter's exposition in his NT introduction relates the themes of the PE to a plausible Pauline ministry following his first imprisonment, a ministry with many points of contact to Jesus and to Paul's earlier letters, yet also with many disconnects, appropriate to the new and altered states of affairs he has encountered in Ephesus, and evidently hears about in Crete as he writes to Titus. Schlatter's comments on 1 Tim 1 give a flavor of the historical rootedness of the PE overall, in his understanding. The PE are both personally and ecclesially directed:

> The first epistle to Timothy states that Timothy has been left behind in Ephesus, where his main concern must be repudiation of false doctrines (ch.1). The damaging nature of the doctrines moving through the local congregations is

---

[39] *Die Kirche der Griechen im Urteil des Paulus*, 16-17.
[40] Neuer, *Adolf Schlatter*, 796.

shown by how they are degenerating into vacuous chatter. As a result, the purpose of the divine law is being overlooked and twisted. On both points Timothy is reminded, concisely and graphically, of the leading truths that govern every word that is spoken in the worship gatherings of the congregation. All Christian admonition has love as its goal, love rooted in a pure heart, a good conscience, and unfeigned faith. Whatever does not serve this goal is chatter, even if it promotes itself with lofty claims of spirituality relating to God and his mysteries. The purpose of the law is to deal with evildoers and to judge their wicked works; it is not to be used to hinder the righteous and restrict the gospel. With its administration of the law and the fight against evil, the church, through what has happened to Paul, receives forever the rule because of which it remembers his apostolic calling, through which in a distinctive manner the grace of Jesus was manifest. In service to this grace Timothy is to conduct himself as a good soldier, unlike a few of Paul's earlier co-workers who suffered shipwreck in their faith.[41]

In sum, whereas for Wilckens the "historical" setting of the PE is a speculative, undetermined place and time (probably around the onset of the second century) related to no concrete congregations, location, or known author, Schlatter reads the PE as an artifact of Paul's finals years of apostolic ministry based on linguistic, literary, and concrete historical considerations.

THEOLOGY OF THE PE

For Schlatter, the PE are dominated by direct connecting lines not only to Paul but to Jesus: "the admonition of the PE is not separate from the person and work of Jesus."[42] "The church is a unity and encompasses all believers in Jesus."[43] While Wilckens explains the PE from a hypothetical scenario decades after Paul's death, Schlatter's reconstruction grows out of the life of Paul and Paul's convictions about Christ, the God who sent him, and the gospel message that by the Spirit makes him known savingly to sinners, foremost Paul himself (cf. 1 Tim 1:15). Or to put it another way, while the historical Paul is a shadowy background figure for Wilckens's PE exposition, which devotes much space to showing disconnects between Paul and the PE, for Schlatter not only Paul but even Jesus plays a significant role, perhaps not surprising since the PE are replete with references to Jesus—there is no chapter in the PE that lacks explicit mention of him. Even Schlatter's popular-level exposition of Titus (which contains only four explicit references to "Jesus Christ" [1:1; 2:13; 3:6] or "Christ Jesus" [1:4]) mentions Jesus frequently.[44] Schlatter's scholarly PE commentary overall mentions Jesus with respect to at least these topics: his

---

[41] Schlatter, *Einleitung in die Bibel*, 414-15.
[42] Schlatter, *Einleitung in die Bibel*, 424.
[43] *Die Kirche der Griechen im Urteil des Paulus*, 14.
[44] Cf. *Die Briefe an die Thessalonicher, Philipper, Timotheus und Titus*, 245, 252, 257, 259, 260, 261, 264, 265, 267, 268, 270.

resurrection, his message, his messianic office, his patience, his history, his grace, his coming, his mediatorial role, his sending, and his death.[45] Schlatter also notes ties between Jesus and the Spirit, the law, the church, and his word.[46]

This may help explain reviewer recognition that Schlatter's PE exposition is user-friendly from a pastoral-preaching perspective and theologically oriented. Neuer notes that the significance of Schlatter's major PE commentary lies in its "mature *theological* interpretation: Erlangen NT scholar Jürgen Roloff pointed out decades later" that in this work "there are valuable formulations of polished theological wisdom on almost every page."[47] We note just four passages in Schlatter's exposition of Titus where such wisdom is glimpsed.

1. In Titus (as in 1 Timothy), according to Schlatter, "faith arises from full apprehension of the truth" (244).[48] Schlatter here has in mind Paul's opening remark that parallels "the faith of God's elect" with "their knowledge of the truth" (Titus 1:1).[49] In Titus 1:2, as Paul speaks of "the hope of eternal life," Schlatter observes that "man cannot conjure up this hope with his own ideas or moods, for it requires secure basis in God's action. It can only arise from the facts [*Tatsachen*] associated with God's sovereign reign" (245). The pastoral wisdom on display here is that Christian faith requires basis in fact. This has been widely denied in Teutonic scholarship since Kant, for which facts and Christian faith are typically adjudged to be at least in tension and probably in antithesis. For Schlatter, however, the truth of the gospel message advanced in the PE is of a piece with the historical verities surrounding its earliest proclamation. This common-sense pastoral insight is of course quintessentially Pauline (cf., e.g., 1 Cor 15:14), as is Paul's position advanced in Titus that believers "are not chosen because they believe but believe because they are chosen, which is the same view voiced in Romans,"[50] in Schlatter's estimation.

2. When Paul speaks of those who "must be silenced since they are upsetting whole families by teaching for shameful gain what they ought not to teach" (Titus 1:11), Schlatter cautions that "the overseer is not to silence these people through dictatorial means." He should rather appeal to believers' conscience with "the word that calls to repentance with the suasive force of truth" (250). This is supported by Titus 1:9, 14. The theological wisdom here involves understanding of the importance of the inner life and how that life can be disturbed by "empty words divorced from the gospel" if these words gain subversive force in Christian households. The antidote is not sterile and formal

---

[45] See references collected in *Die Kirche der Griechen im Urteil des Paulus*, 274.

[46] *Die Kirche der Griechen im Urteil des Paulus*, 274.

[47] Neuer, *Adolf Schlatter*, 798.

[48] In this section, parenthetical page numbers refer to Schlatter's *Die Briefe an die Thessalonicher, Philipper, Timotheus und Titus*. For more on this "full apprehension of the truth," cf. *Die Kirche der Griechen im Urteil des Paulus*, 175-76.

[49] In this section, citations from Titus are from the ESV.

[50] *Die Kirche der Griechen im Urteil des Paulus*, 176.

contradiction but pastoral correction that enables true apostolic faith to make whole those in families whose initially sound gospel convictions have been maliciously upset.[51]

3. Different locales pose varying threats to faithful gospel appropriation (251). Strategies to offset these threats and to offer ongoing faithful representation of apostolic truth must be sensitive to local conditions. The situation on the island of Crete (Titus 1:12-16) indicated how challenging Titus' work there would be (251). Paul did not offer Titus facile formulas for quick success. "Weak handling" of harmful Cretan distinctives "would only exacerbate those evils" (251).[52] A patient, firm, and positive pastoral administration of true Christian teaching would be necessary, one that mediated "redemption from evil" and thereby the experience of "how Christ is given to bring about righteousness and sanctification" (252). "Whether the congregations there would come to affirm teaching that was healthy or sick would depend on how thorough and earnest their repentance turned out to be" (252; cf. Titus 1:15-16). The pastoral wisdom here is wide-ranging but involves understanding of contextualization and the nuances of real-world ministry of the Christian message in complex, often hostile social settings.

4. Schlatter's grasp and explanation of the religious psychology at work in Titus 1:15 ("To the pure, all things are pure, but to the defiled and unbelieving, nothing is pure; but both their minds and their consciences are defiled") are clear and distinct. On the one hand, the way to purity is found when a person "is cleansed in his inner living core [*Lebensgestalt*], a cleansing attained by the one who has been made whole through his faith" (252). On the other, Schlatter unpacks carefully why those who reject the full cleansing of the gospel message necessarily defile all they regard (253):

> Impurity is inherent in them, specifically in the two inner functions that dominate the human condition [*Lebensstand*], thinking and making judgments. These functions are defiled, as people deploy them in connection with other people and life generally; they are directed downward into darkness. Likewise people's conscience is robbed of peace and condemns them . . . . The inner condemnation that ensues prevents peace with God and blocks faith that is certain of his grace.

Here is a principled and sensitive dissection of the human condition, both as to its healthy existence through faith in Christ and as to its pathological status when Christ's restorative work through reception of the apostolic message has been hampered.

Elsewhere Schlatter plausibly relates this to the teaching of Jesus, "who said that the contrast between clean and unclean was not through external things but

---

[51] Cf. *Die Kirche der Griechen im Urteil des Paulus*, 186.
[52] In *Die Kirche der Griechen im Urteil des Paulus*, 186 n. 2, Schlatter notes the parallel with "reprove them severely" in 2 Cor 13:10.

in the heart of man through the desires that arise in him."⁵³ Aspects of Titus 1:15-16 are also shown to relate directly to Pauline convictions in known Pauline writings.⁵⁴ Here is but a portion of how Schlatter unpacks the inner working of the soul among the "defiled and unbelieving" described in Titus 1:15-16:

> Every religious undertaking presupposes a knowledge of God. Those whose methods of salvation stand in opposition to the message of Jesus object that they know God.⁵⁵ But their confession of God occurs only through words, while their actions are not formed by their knowledge of God; their actions do not arise either out of the fear of God or out of that faith that submits to him. They thereby deny God. They cannot behave any differently, for what they are internally is despicable.⁵⁶ They do not obey the instruction offered to them, and when something good needs to be done, they are completely useless.⁵⁷ Through these [negative] results the new methods of salvation [advanced by the Cretan teachers] prove the exclusive saving force of the Christ and the saving power of his word. It is evident that only he is able to lead us out of the denial of God to establish us in faith in God. Separated from him, yes, there can be a knowledge of God. However, it is nullified by sinful desire, and the distinguishing mark of guilt attaches to its striving against God.⁵⁸

Passages like the four singled out above, in which both exegetical-historical acumen and theological-pastoral awareness are intertwined, are easily multiplied in Schlatter's exposition of Titus. Here are a few examples briefly summarized: 1) In Paul's age-specific counsel in Titus 2, Schlatter highlights what holy living looks like and calls for, namely, showing that believers live constantly in the conviction that "they stand continually in the presence of God" (254).⁵⁹ 2) With respect to the high and holy calling of the older women (Titus 2:3-5), Schlatter comments on the necessity of Titus and other pastoral leaders not working extensively with women in their personal family affairs; that is something women attend to most effectively among themselves (255). 3) The reception of the gospel is dramatically influenced, for good or ill, by its effects on women in congregations. "The pagan populace had low regard for the daily tasks of women and observed closely how believing Christian women

---

⁵³ *Die Kirche der Griechen im Urteil des Paulus*, 187.
⁵⁴ *Die Kirche der Griechen im Urteil des Paulus*, 187-89.
⁵⁵ Schlatter here references parallel Greek phrases in Gal 4:8; 1 Thess 4:5; Rom 1:21; cf. *Die Kirche der Griechen im Urteil des Paulus*, 188 n. 1.
⁵⁶ Schlatter relates the Greek word βδελυκτοί to its cognate in Rom 2:22; cf. *Die Kirche der Griechen im Urteil des Paulus*, 188 n. 2.
⁵⁷ Schlatter relates the Greek word ἀδόκιμοι to parallels in 1 Cor 9:27; 13:5-7; cf. *Die Kirche der Griechen im Urteil des Paulus*, 189 n. 3.
⁵⁸ *Die Kirche der Griechen im Urteil des Paulus*, 188-89.
⁵⁹ In each of these examples, more thorough explication will be found in *Die Kirche der Griechen im Urteil des Paulus* at the respective verses.

conducted themselves" (256). For that reason, "the comportment of the women will determine the impression about the divine Word that is formed in the city" (255). 4) Frequently repeated in all of Schlatter's PE exposition is the conviction that the task of being a Christian is not about some special knowledge or the effecting of peculiar experiences of divine grace; it lies rather in the daily actions and relationships that fill everyday life—a direct point of contact between Paul and Jesus (257).

A fifth and final example is perhaps most illustrative of Schlatter's theologically rich and pastorally suggestive PE exposition. With respect to how "the grace of God . . . [trains] us to renounce ungodliness and worldly passions, and to live self-controlled, upright, and godly lives in the present age" (Titus 2:11-12), Schlatter calls attention to how grace mediates divine defeat of such passions and replacement with God and desire for him:

> Grace frees us from these desires, and although the whole world furtively embraces them and is driven by them, we acquire through grace the power to condemn these desires and close ourselves off against them. Because God pulls us away from our godlessness and does not hand us over helplessly to our appetites, but gives us mastery over them, he acts upon us as the Grace-Bestowing One [*der Gnädige*]. This brings about a way of life, free from deluded passion and grounded in sensibleness and sobriety, that grants people what we owe them and God his honor. And all this is precisely God's benevolent, fatherly intention for us. Yes, the present world order is not the abiding one; it stands in profound opposition to the divine will. Nevertheless, through the illumination, stimulation, and training of God's grace, we are set free from this form of the world and given a desire that far transcends this world. (258-59)

SIGNIFICANCE OF THE PE IN CHURCH-HISTORICAL PERSPECTIVE

We saw above that for Wilckens, the church today rightly grasps the PE to the extent that it separates them from Paul's authentic writings and distances itself from much core PE counsel. For Schlatter the opposite is the case. Since he does not view the authentic writings and views of the historical Paul as in tension with and often antithesis to the PE, Schlatter's exegesis encourages a maximalist appropriation of the theology and ethics propounded in the PE for the present time.

Of course "present time" and its attendant circumstances vary for each generation of readers and their local settings. But one of Schlatter's most avid students and distinguished intellectual descendants, K. H. Rengstorf (1903–1992),[60] aptly characterized the significance of Schlatter's view of the PE in the volatile, Nazi-dominated atmosphere in which his scholarly PE commentary[61]

---

[60] For biographical information see http://www.bautz.de/bbkl/r/rengstorf_k_h.shtml, accessed June 14, 2010.

[61] I.e., *Die Kirche der Griechen im Urteil des Paulus*.

was first published. In Schlatter's reading "the [Pastoral] Epistles discuss matters that are highly pertinent precisely for our generation."[62] Among currently pressing issues which Rengstorf finds addressed in Schlatter's treatment are the questions of 1) "how the congregation of Jesus should conduct its own internal affairs," 2) "what legitimate church discipline looks like," and 3) "what constitutes an informed and responsible relation between the church and the state."[63] The point at which Rengstorf notes the relevance of Schlatter's exposition most fully "at precisely this time of painful disruption within the German Protestant church and its theology" lies in Schlatter's "indefatigable summons to the sources of Christian knowledge and Christian life."[64] Rengstorf elaborates:

> Regarding the PE and their contemporary significance, we refer simply to this: the PE battle against the burgeoning intellectualization of the Christian proclamation which was becoming visible in the Hellenistic congregations. Closer investigation, meanwhile, indicates that the author of PE did not share our sense of the meaning of the term "doctrine." Wherever *didaskalia* ["teaching"] and related terms are used (cf. 1 Tim 1:3 and elsewhere), abstract dogma is not in view but rather instruction for the ordering of everyday life (ethics). This [ethics] too is an extension of Jesus' teaching (1 Tim 6:3), so includes within itself "gospel" (in contrast to "myth") and "doctrine" (in contrast to heterodoxy). The goal of the PE, accordingly—and this is in keeping with saving work of God (1 Tim 1:1, 15)—is not merely a religious community having "a doctrine" in common but a compliant religious community that is willing and ready to perform good works.[65]

In addition, Rengstorf points out that Schlatter in full awareness of the critical questions[66] succeeds at situating the PE within the internal and external history of the growing early church and not only within the life of Paul.[67] The commentary accounts for both the history and the theology of the PE in their original setting in a way that makes their message pertinent for the present day. In the same vein J. Jeremias noted the contemporary aptness of the commentaries Schlatter published in his closing years, including this PE commentary; they all hold "significance for New Testament scholarship as well as for the preaching of the church."[68]

---

[62] Rengstorf, review of Schlatter, 637.
[63] Rengstorf, review of Schlatter, 637.
[64] Rengstorf, review of Schlatter, 636-37.
[65] Rengstorf, review of Schlatter, 637.
[66] Cf. also Brinkmann, review of Schlatter, 291: the commentary is "in general objective, though lacking proper scholarly apparatus. Yet the exhaustive knowledge of the author [i.e., Schlatter] is evident everywhere."
[67] Rengstorf, review of Schlatter, 637.
[68] Jeremias, review of Schlatter, 415.

SCHLATTER AND CONTEMPORARY READING OF THE PE

De rigueur in much scholarly PE interpretation is the view that the PE substantially postdate Paul and can therefore not be Pauline; the PE author is merely one voice among many competing for a hearing along a generations-long development toward what became (wrongly, in the view of the hegemony) a normative view in the great Church. This outlook is long since traditional in the academy. L. T. Johnson has noted, with respect to scholarship on 1 and 2 Timothy, that "those who hold the opposite view are considered odd or not truly critical in their thinking."[69]

Schlatter held a nuanced and skillfully articulated contrarian position in an era at least as inimical to it as the more recent setting Johnson describes (and critiques). He did not convince many in his surrounding university guild. But that guild is rapidly shrinking in influence: one source notes that the number of Protestant theology majors in German universities fell from 17,000 in 1985 to fewer than 4,700 in 2007.[70] Church attendance in German (and other European) churches continues to dwindle. This is understandable in the sense that "church" has historically been associated with the notion that the Bible in its testimony to Jesus and his saving work is God's Word, to be reverenced and lived out, not regarded as a largely deceptive historical artifact unsuited for appropriation today in any authoritative sense. To the extent the Bible is as error-ridden, and its message in urgent need of retooling, as guild interpreters seem to argue, church decoupling from the Bible is an understandable priority. So is abandonment of any church that still clings to the Bible, for intellectual honesty's sake.

But in the larger world church setting where the Bible is receiving fresh attention and respect,[71] and groups affirming a more historic high regard for the Bible are seeing meteoric growth,[72] there is reason to rethink traditional academic animus toward close association between Jesus seen as Savior in fulfillment of OT promises,[73] a Paul who actually encountered him in a life- and world-transforming way, and the PE seen as authentic Pauline writings.

---

[69] *The First and Second Letters to Timothy* (AB 35A; New York: Doubleday, 2001), 53-54.

[70] Freie Theologische Hochschule Giessen Freundesbrief, February 2010 (letter to supporters of the Giessen School of Theology, Germany).

[71] Cf., e.g., Philip Jenkins, *The New Faces of Christianity: Believing the Bible in the Global South* (Oxford: Oxford University Press, 2006).

[72] "The greatest surge in the history of Christianity occurred in Africa over the past one hundred years, and indeed continues its breathtaking trajectory into the twenty-first century" (Jonathan J. Bonk, "Ecclesiastical Cartography and the Invisible Continent," *International Bulletin of Missionary Research* 28, no. 4 [October 2004]: 153-58 [154]).

[73] Schnelle, *Theology of the New Testament*, 579, 582, notes the centrality of "savior" to the PE. But he separates the PE from Paul and the God of the PE from the God of salvation history. The distance between the PE and Jesus himself in Schnelle's schema would seem to be vast.

Globally many would affirm Mark Noll's missiological observation that "Scripture comes alive with new force when it is read as the book of God for all believers everywhere, as well as the book of God that speaks most directly to me in my particular time and place."[74] In learned fashion Schlatter upheld a reading of the PE that did not wither beneath establishment animus but credibly offset it. His approach—having far more in common with Howard Marshall's interpretation overall than not—is one that may merit fresh attention given distinctives sketched above and the direction of world Christianity.

---

[74] Mark Noll, *The New Shape of World Christianity* (Downers Grove: InterVarsity, 2009), 198.

19

"NOBODY KNOWS DE TROUBLE I SEEN": HARDSHIP LISTS IN PAUL AND ELSEWHERE

Paul Ellingworth

Paul, like his Master, knew that his call to mission would involve hardship. His hardships proved varied, difficult, and distinctively personal. Yet he bore them with ὑπομονή, that word notoriously difficult to translate. It is a privilege to contribute to this volume, in honor of my old friend, former supervisor, and still mentor Howard Marshall, this short study of one aspect of Paul's mission.

In 1910 there appeared a slim (109-page) dissertation by a twenty-six-year-old junior member[1] of the staff of Marburg University which popularized the use of the term *Peristasenkataloge* or "peristasis catalogues," in the letters of Paul. The thesis, entitled *The Style of Pauline Preaching and the Cynic-Stoic Diatribe*, was remarkable in its time for its clarity and moderation. Its treatment of hardship lists formed only a small part of a wider comparison between the style of Paul's letters and that of the Cynic-Stoic[2] diatribe. It led to the general conclusion that the style of Paul's letters, and thus by implication that of his preaching, was dependent on that of the Stoic-Cynic diatribe, as practiced by Epictetus, Seneca and others. It argued that Paul's Corinthian hearers were more likely to respond to this approach than if he had chosen the style of the Synoptics or the Fourth Gospel. Of striking contemporary interest was the author's insistence on the originally *oral* character of the writings discussed. The author however believed that "[w]e find perhaps the greatest similarity [with Stoic writings] in the *peristasis* catalogues" (71); however, Paul naturally lists different sufferings from the Stoic preachers. The argument concluded, in an italicized sentence: "*Paul's preaching partly moved in similar forms of expression to the preaching of popular Cynic-Stoic philosophers, such as the diatribe.*"

---

[1] The German title was *Repetent*, which now denotes a student who has to repeat a year, but in 1910 referred to a coach who would now be called a *Repetitor*.

[2] J. T. Fitzgerald, *Cracks in an Earthen Vessel: An Examination of Catalogues of Hardships in the Corinthian Correspondence* (SBLDS 99; Atlanta: Scholars Press, 1988), 57 quotes A. J. Malherbe, "Cynics," *IDBSup* 202, as distinguishing the two schools as follows: "The Cynics held to the profound distinction between the wise and the foolish, and confidently assumed that the ideal could be realized as it had been by the ancients. The Stoics, on the other hand, defined the ideal in such a way that its attainability was only an abstract possibility." More generally, it was said that the Cynic despised hardship whereas the Stoic was unaware of it.

Altogether, one formed the impression that the author was a young man who might go far. The next sixty-six years of Rudolf Bultmann's long life tended to confirm this view. They perhaps also added to the influence of the dissertation itself (it was reprinted seventy-four years later, something that doesn't happen to many doctoral theses).

Bultmann did not claim too much. He conceded that the Cynic-Stoic diatribe was only one influence on Paul's style of writing. "Paul's style can certainly not be explained from Greek literature alone; it is formed at least as much by Old Testament or generally Semitic style."[3] Not enough work, however, had been done on the latter for firm conclusions to be drawn from it. "We do not want to hide from ourselves the fact that the impression of difference is greater than that of similarity. Yet we should not therefore underestimate the similarity."[4]

Before we summarize later study of *Peristasenkataloge*, a word may be said about the term itself. In English, a catalogue is defined as "a *systematic* list,"[5] but this feature is not always so prominent in the German *Katalog*.[6] In any case, a list seems to presuppose at least three items; Bultmann's treatment has been criticized[7] for including items that did not meet this criterion.

As for the term *Peristase*, it is clearly a transcription of the Greek περίστασις, a literal equivalent of the English "circum-stances" and the German *Um-stände*. Only the context of a particular occurrence can indicate whether the circumstances are good, neutral, or (as in the English "reduced circumstances") bad. Περίστασις is scarcely a biblical word at all. It occurs twice in the Septuagint: in Ezek 26:8 of "warlike works" (where Codex Alexandrinus has the synonym βελοστάσεις) and 2 Macc 4:16 in the sense of "calamity." It is used in classical and hellenistic Greek in a variety of senses[8] and was borrowed into Latin,[9] sometimes transliterated and sometimes not. Cicero (*Att.* 4.8a.2) speaks of περίστασις *nostra*, meaning "our circumstances" or "our affairs." The word occurs in patristic texts[10] in both neutral and negative senses. It does not, however, have any distinctive theological meaning, and it is not a New Testament word. Its use in connection with Paul tends therefore to bias discussion in the direction of extrabiblical parallels, so for this among other reasons we shall use the simpler expression "hardship lists."

---

[3] *Der Stil der paulinischen Predigt und die kynisch-stoische Diatribe* (FRLANT 13; Göttingen: Vandenhoeck & Ruprecht, 1910), 3.
[4] *Der Stil*, 107.
[5] Chambers English Dictionary, s.v. "Catalogue."
[6] *Duden*, s.v., gives as the fourth, apparently most relevant, meaning of *Katalog*: "lange Reihe, große Anzahl, zusammenfassende Aufzählung."
[7] Fitzgerald, *Earthen Vessel*, 11 n. 29.
[8] LSJ, s.v., including the 1968 Supplement.
[9] Oxford Latin Dictionary, s.v.
[10] *PGL*, s.v.

Study of these lists since Bultmann has followed an increasingly well-trodden[11] but not entirely straight path, along which we shall mention only a few significant milestones. Bultmann's thesis of Paul's dependence (*Abhängigkeit*) on Cynic-Stoic texts has been sustained by many commentators and other scholars. In 1952 J. Dupont claimed that Paul's stylistic relationship to Stoic texts was "unquestionable and universally recognized."[12] Martin Ebner, writing in 1991, finds in Paul a general influence of the diatribe, plus more specific echoes of retellings of the labors of Hercules, example lists, and Stoic teaching about *adiaphora*, indifference to circumstances whether favorable or unfavorable.

The first systematic questioning of Bultmann's thesis had however come in a 1974 article by Wolfgang Schrage, entitled "Suffering, Cross and Eschaton: The Peristasis Catalogues as Features of Pauline theologia crucis and Eschatology." Schrage noted similar themes and features in a wide range of Jewish apocalyptic writings, anticipating the eschatological dimension of Paul's thought, and cautiously concluding that Jewish apocalyptic was "*probably* [our emphasis] the primary traditional background of the *peristasis* catalogues."[13]

The net was cast still wider in 1983 by Robert Hodgson in an article which "aim[ed] at setting forth a history of religions background for Paul's tribulation lists that is broader than the one generally found . . . ."[14] He distinguished between "simple lists" (Rom 8:35; 2 Cor 6:4b-5; 11:23-29; 12:10) and "antithetical lists" (1 Cor 4:10-13a; 2 Cor 4:8-9; 6:8-10; Phil 4:12), and went on to find parallels in Josephus, the Nag Hammadi library, the Mishnah, Plutarch, and Arrian.

In the following year came a study by Karl Theodor Kleinknecht which placed Paul's hardship lists within the Old Testament, intertestamental, Qumran, and rabbinic tradition of the suffering of the righteous. His argument leads to the conclusion that "Pauline statements are not a direct adaptation of Stoic statements, but the extrapolation [*Fortschreibung*] of a line of statements growing out of his own traditional roots."[15]

---

[11] On the history of research to 1988, see Fitzgerald, *Earthen Vessel*, 7-31; further references in Wen H. Shi, "The Message of the Cross as 'Body Language' in Paul's Corinthian Polemics: An Inversion of the Greco-Roman Social Ethos" (PhD diss., Durham University, 2007), 272-81.

[12] J. Dupont, Syn Christo: *L'union avec le Christ suivant saint Paul* (Bruges: Nauwelaerts, 1952), 117, quoted with further references in Wolfgang Schrage, "Leid, Kreuz und Eschaton: Die Peristasenkataloge als Merkmale paulinischer theologia crucis und Eschatologie," *EvT* 34 (1974): 141-75 [142].

[13] Schrage, "Leid," 165.

[14] R. Hodgson, "Paul the Apostle and First Century Tribulation Lists," *ZNW* 74 (1983): 59-80 [59].

[15] K. T. Kleinknecht, *Der leidende Gerechtfertigte: Die alttestamentlich-jüdische Tradition vom "leidenden Gerechten" und ihre Rezeption bei Paulus* (WUNT 2/13; Tübingen: Mohr [Siebeck], 1984), 256-60, 287-97, here 260. Kleinknecht interestingly

In 1987, on a rather different track, came Karl A. Plank's *Paul and the Irony of Affliction*. As its title suggests, it is primarily concerned, not with parallels to or influences on Paul's lists, but with the relation between two types of irony, apparently contradictory but in fact complementary, defined as the irony of dissimulation and the irony of paradox. Plank draws on the work of Kierkegaard, Paul Ricoeur and others, and is particularly concerned with 1 Cor 4:9-13.

The area sketched out by Bultmann was fully explored by John T. Fitzgerald in his impressive 1988 book *Cracks in an Earthen Vessel: An Examination of the Catalogues of Hardships in the Corinthian Correspondence*. This presents exhaustive documentation from Cynic-Stoic and other ancient writings, convincingly establishing the existence of a firm tradition of hardship lists forming part of a standard description of a Stoic sage. Fitzgerald also refers to evidence, still to be explored, of such a tradition in Old Testament and later Jewish documents, but holds that its basic pattern is to be found in Stoic writings. He believes that Paul was familiar with these traditions, but that his "highly creative" use of them was "informed by OT traditions about the afflicted righteous man and suffering prophet, and . . . is transformed by his fixation on the cross of Christ. His *peristasis* catalogues thus represent the convergence of several traditions and reflect his own personal experiences of suffering and divine power. They take us to the center of Paul's understanding of God and his own self-understanding, yet anchor him in the culture and conventions of his time."[16]

Fitzgerald's study has been positively assessed in a 2007 doctoral thesis by Shi Wen Hwa. Shi notes that accounts of suffering, including hardship lists, work in two contrasting ways. On the one hand, as Fitzgerald and others have pointed out, they have the positive function of exalting the sage's indifference to misfortunes, and thus his masculine strength. On the other hand, however, they can function negatively as implying defeat and degradation. This aspect, "the other side of the coin," Shi maintains, is closer to Paul's view of both his own suffering and that of Christ.

Otherwise, a natural pause in this line of research seems to have been reached in 1991 with the publication of Markus Schiefer Ferrari's 500-page work *Die Sprache des Leids in den paulinischen Peristasenkatalogen*.[17] He sets his contribution within a wide discussion of different kinds of speaking about

---

cites Bultmann's posthumously published (1976) commentary on 2 Corinthians in support of his position.

[16] Fitzgerald, *Earthen Vessel*, 207. Cf. Michael E. Bird, "Reassessing a Rhetorical Approach to Paul's Letters," *ExpTim* 119 (2008): 374-79, which concludes that "it is necessary to integrate a study of rhetoric, in its various forms, into a comprehensive and holistic analysis of Paul's letters."

[17] M. S. Ferrari, *Die Sprache des Leids in den paulinischen Peristasenkatalogen* (BibB 23; Stuttgart: Verlag Katholisches Bibelwerk, 1991).

suffering. He offers an exhaustive catalogue (in the normal sense of the word) of echoes of Paul's hardship lists noted by previous scholars, including not only the works of Greek and Roman authors, the Old Testament pseudepigrapha, Qumran, Philo and Josephus, the New Testament, rabbinic writings, and Nag Hammadi, but also the Old Testament, the Apostolic Fathers, early Christian apologetics, church fathers, Shakespeare, and the German Catholic poet Annette von Droste-Hülshoff (1797–1848).[18] For good measure, Ferrari adds an epilogue comparing Paul's hardship lists with the lyrics of Paul Celan (1920–1970). He notes an inescapable tension between, on the one hand, the search for a distinct text form, and on the other hand recognition of the distinctive features of individual texts. He seeks a middle way by the use of the expression "peristasis catalogue-*like*" (*peristasenkatalogartig*) texts, which he believes will terminologically reflect "the great generality and fuzziness of description of the phenomenon."[19]

In the body of his work, Ferrari opts for specific description rather than the search for a comprehensive category. Taking the same option, though independently, we now turn to the relevant passages of Paul's letters themselves, with a view, not to detecting external influences on their style or content, but to identifying some of their distinctive features.

First, we note the astonishing range of Paul's vocabulary. Even counting as one related nouns and verbs, Paul refers to no less than thirty-eight hardships and closely linked lexical items, many of them only once.[20, 21] Even where he does repeat himself he sometimes varies between singular and plural: even

---

[18] Commemorated on the DM 20 banknote until the introduction of the euro.

[19] "Mit dem Begriff des peristasenkatalogartigen Textes sollte vielmehr versucht werden, auch terminologisch die große Allgemeinheit und Unschärfe der Beschreibung des Phänomens wiederzugeben" (Ferrari, *Die Sprache*, 147).

[20] Ἀγνοέω 2 Cor 6:9; ἀκαταστασία 2 Cor 6:5; ἀνάγκη 2 Cor 6:4; ἀποθνῃσκω 2 Cor 6:9; ἀπορέω 2 Cor 4:8 ἀσθενής 1 Cor 4:10; 2 Cor 11:29; ἀστατέω 1 Cor 4:11; ἀτιμία/ἄτιμος 1 Cor 4:10; 2 Cor 6:8; γυμνιτεύω/γυμνότης Rom 8:35; 1 Cor 4:11; 2 Cor 11:27; διψάω/δίψος 1 Cor 4:11; 2 Cor 11:27; διώκω/διωγμός Rom 8:35; 1 Cor 4:12; 2 Cor 4:9; δυσφημία/δυσφημέω 1 Cor 4:13; 2 Cor 6:8; θλῖψις Phil 4:14; καταβάλλω 2 Cor 4:9; κίνδυνος Rom 8:35; 2 Cor 11:26 (8 times); κολαφίζω 1 Cor 4:11; κοπιάω/κόπος 1 Cor 4:12; 2 Cor 6:5; 11:23,27; λιμός Rom 8:35; 2 Cor 11:27; λοιδορέω 1 Cor 4:12; λυπέω 2 Cor 6:10; μάχαιρα Rom 8:35; μηδὲν ἔχω 2 Cor 6:10; μόχθος 2 Cor 11:27; μῶρος 1 Cor 4:10; νηστεία 2 Cor 6:5; 11:23; παιδεύω 2 Cor 6:9; πεινάω 1 Cor 4:11; Phil 4:12; πλάνος 2 Cor 6:8; πληγή 2 Cor 6:5; 11:23; πτωχός 2 Cor 6:10; πυρόομαι 2 Cor 11:29; σκανδαλίζω 2 Cor 11:29; στενοχωρία Rom 8:35; 2 Cor 6:4; ταπεινόω Phil 4:12; ὑπομονή 2 Cor 6:4; ὑστερέω/ὑστέρησις Phil 4:11, 12; φυλακή 2 Cor 6:5; ψῦχος 2 Cor 11:27.

[21] Ferrari, *Die Sprache*, 142-43, notes thirteen words and eight stems used in Paul's hardship lists which also appear in "peristasis catalogue-like" texts of the Septuagint, and twenty-two words and nine stems which also appear in such texts of Epictetus. Note also Ferrari's tables (*Die Sprache*, 327) of the vocabulary of Paul's hardship lists, divided into negative, positive and indeterminate categories.

between "death" and "deaths." The greatest amount of repetition is between 2 Cor 4:8-12 and 6:4-10, which may or may not say anything about the integrity of that epistle. It may also be noted that Paul frequently uses hardship terms outside hardship lists: for example, θλίψις in 2 Cor 1:4ab, 8; 2:4 (with συνοχή, never used in a list); 4:17; 7:4; 8:2; κόπος in 1 Cor 3:8; 15:58; 2 Cor 10:15 and elsewhere). All this tends to suggest that, whether or not Paul is placing himself within an established rhetorical tradition, his references to hardships show strong marks of personal creativity.

This impression is strengthened when we move from the level of vocabulary to the higher linguistic levels of grammar and discourse structure. The great number of hardship lists and similar texts cited by Fitzgerald from non-biblical writers may serve as a sample for comparison. Two groups among these form together a large majority. The bigger of the two consists of third person (usually singular) descriptions of the sage, his ideal character, and his trials. The other large group consists of dialogues with imaginary interlocutors, sometimes reminiscent for example of Rom 2:1-5. Occasionally[22] the interlocutor is God. Quite often the authors quoted use "we" forms, whether as author or as representing a philosophical school. Only rarely is an "I" form used to refer to the writer's own experiences, and even then usually in a general way. The closest to a personal, as opposed to a rhetorical, "I" among Fitzgerald's numerous examples is what he describes as a "remarkable passage" from Seneca[23] containing such specific statements as: "The Emperor Gaius did not rob me of my loyalty in my friendship with Gaetulicus . . ."; but on examination it appears that Seneca is not speaking in his own name, but making a recommendation to his friend Lucilius.

All this is in striking contrast to Paul's usage, and this in two respects which may be considered together. On the one hand, his lists are those of personal hardships really undergone by himself, and usually by others as well. As Schrage puts it in his monumental commentary on 1 Corinthians, "In sharp contrast to Corinthian illusionism, the peristasis catalogue [of 1 Cor 4:11-13] illustrates above all the hard reality of apostolic existence."[24] On the other hand, Paul's lists show the kind of flexibility in construction that does not suggest derivation from an existing model.

At this point, as an introduction to discussion of the discourse structure of the lists, we may insert a brief excursus on Paul's use of verb forms and associated personal pronouns.

Apart from a few authorial asides, first person singular forms in these passages relate to personally experienced hardships, in a way unparalleled in any of the Cynic-Stoic lists cited by Fitzgerald and others. More often Paul uses

---

[22] Fitzgerald, *Earthen Vessel*, 83.
[23] *Quaestiones Naturales* 4A, Pref. 14-17, quoted in Fitzgerald, *Earthen Vessel*, 112-13.
[24] W. Schrage, *Der erste Brief an die Korinther* (4 vols.; Neukirchen-Vluyn: Neukirchener, 1991), 1:350.

first person plural forms, in typically flexible ways that call for careful definition. I have found no place where a "we" form undoubtedly refers to Paul alone: when he wishes to say "I," he says "I." "We" forms may be initially assigned to one of two broad categories: (1) inclusive "we's" that embrace both senders and receptors, and (2) exclusive "we's", namely those that refer only to the senders, to the exclusion of the receptors. (Many languages make this distinction at surface level.) Exclusive "we's", in the passages under discussion, normally refer to Paul and his fellow-evangelists. Exclusive "we's" are often clearly identified by the presence in the immediate context of a contrasting "you," for example "death is at work in us, but life in you" (2 Cor 4:12). Depending on the context, inclusive "we's" may include only the recipients, for example the Christian community in Corinth, or the entire body of Christians, or the whole of humanity.[25]

Romans 8:35-39 forms part of an extended "we" passage (vv. 15b-39) which almost certainly refers to Christians in general (apart from the rhetorical τί οὖν ἐροῦμεν; in v. 31). It includes a sequence of rhetorical (vv. 31b-32), real (vv. 33-34), and again rhetorical (v. 35) questions, the last including a list of hardships. It then intersperses a quotation from Ps 44:22 (v. 36), followed by a statement (v. 37), and finally a list of antitheses (vv. 38-39) which carries individual hardships into the realm of cosmic conflict. As if this flexibility were not enough, the passage is followed by Paul's moving statement about the "sorrow and unceasing anguish" in his own heart (9:2).

The hardship list in 1 Cor 4:11-12a forms part of an equally flexible, and heavily ironic, passage.[26] The reference to "myself and Apollos" in v. 6 occurs in an extremely difficult statement, most of the problems of which we can for our purposes fortunately bypass.[27] It is at least probable that the words "so that you may learn from us" later in the verse still refer to Paul and Apollos, though the implicit widening of the reference to include other evangelists is not impossible already here. This widening is more likely in v. 8, leading to the explicit "us apostles" in v. 9, continuing by implication to the end of v. 12. After the rhetorical questions of v. 7 and the ironic description of the Corinthians' (v. 8) and the apostles' (v. 9) situations, the two are contrasted in v. 10, leading to the relatively conventional hardship list in v. 11, the more personal, "We work hard with our own hands" (v. 12a), three antitheses in 12b-13a, and the climactic "scum of the earth, garbage of the world" statement in 13b. In the following "I" section (vv. 14-21) Paul obviously speaks for himself alone. Again, the personal note throughout the passage, with the just possible

---

[25] See E. Verhof, "The Senders of the Letters to the Corinthians and the Use of 'I' and 'We,'" in *The Corinthian Correspondence* (ed. R. Bieringer; Leuven: Leuven University Press, 1996), 417-25.
[26] See K. A. Plank, *Paul and the Irony of Affliction* (Atlanta: Scholars Press, 1987).
[27] See for example A. C. Thiselton, *The First Epistle to the Corinthians* (Grand Rapids: Eerdmans, 2000), 344-56.

exception of v. 11, is matched and reinforced by the flexibility of its construction. The account appears to owe little if anything, at least directly, to conventional models.

2 Corinthians 6:4-10 forms part of a long "we" section extending from 2:14 to 6:12 (excluding the exegetical passage 3:7-11, 13b-17). Most of the "we's" refer to the evangelists, as the plurals διακόνους (3:6), δούλους (4:5) indicate. Exceptionally ἡμεῖς . . . πάντες in 3:18 and πάντας ἡμᾶς in 5:10, explicitly widen the reference to include Christians in general. This long section is framed by "I" statements in 1:23–2:13, a parenthetical ὡς τέκνοις λέγω in 6:13, paraenetic rhetorical questions in 6:14b-16a, and a series of OT quotations (6:16b-18) introduced by an inclusive "we" (6:16a) taken up in 7:1. The hardship list proper in 6:4b-5 is thus seamlessly integrated into Paul's commendation of himself and his fellow-evangelists (v. 4a), itself supported by the positive counterparts of the hardships listed in vv. 6-7, and the typical antitheses of vv. 8-10. Verses 2b-10 form an enormous 118-word sentence. If *per impossibile* it did include material cited from or even echoing a Cynic-Stoic list, it would contrast with the explicit way in which, shortly afterwards, Paul introduces an OT catena: καθὼς εἶπεν ὁ θεὸς ὅτι (v.16, compare διὸ . . . λέγει κύριος v. 17, καί v. 18). Once again, the flexibility of the structure witnesses to Paul's creativity.

Among Paul's hardship lists, 2 Cor 11:23b-29 stands at the furthest distance from any traditional list, being marked by its explicitly personal content. From 11:16 to 12:17a Paul consistently uses "I" forms in speaking of his own sufferings, except in 11:21 where ἡμεῖς ἠσθενήκαμεν associates himself momentarily with the other evangelists, this usage resuming in 12:18b with περιεπατήσαμεν.[28] Verse 21 announces a "boasting" passage which continues into ch. 12, though without reference to hardships until the summary in v. 10. Verses 22-23a list four ways in which Paul's Hebrew qualifications equal those of his unidentified rivals, while v. 23b notes three ways in which his hardships exceed those of his opponents. Verses 24[29]-25 refer to specific occasions on which he has experienced five types of hardship, while v. 26 lists more generally the dangers he has incurred. Verse 27 comes closest to a traditional hardship list, but still Paul is speaking of personal experiences, at least two types of them frequent. Verse 28 loosely (χωρὶς τῶν παρεκτός) associates with his hardships the weight of his responsibilities for the churches, leading in v. 29 to two rhetorical questions that misleadingly sound like a conclusion. The boasting theme is however renewed in vv. 32-33 by a unique piece of autobiography. The variety of this passage, and even its apparently loose construction, reinforce its personal tone, taking it far away from generalized descriptions of the character of the sage.

2 Corinthians 12:7-9 is sometimes included among Paul's hardship lists, but

---

[28] "Our brother" in 12:18a (TNIV) is simply τὸν ἀδελφόν.
[29] TNIV "the Jews" is misleading: there is no article in the Greek.

it deals, albeit in detail, with only one hardship, the unidentified "thorn in the flesh." Verse 10, however, recapitulates reference to five types of hardship, now, as already in 11:30, defined as "weaknesses." The conclusion to the whole passage is that Paul "delight[s]" in them, because they are borne "for Christ's sake," and through them "Christ's power" rests on him.

Philippians 4:12 forms part of a personal statement in which "I" forms dominate throughout, except in v. 20 where "my God" (v. 19) gives place to the inclusive "our God." The contrasting statements of hardship and plenty are set within the wider theme of thanks for the Philippians' generosity to Paul in his "trouble" (θλίψις, v. 14). If his use in v. 11 of αὐτάρκης, a New Testament *hapax*, appears to strike a Stoic note, this is immediately neutralized in v. 13 by Paul's statement: "I can do all this through him who gives me strength."[30]

The cumulative effect of looking at Paul's hardship lists in their contexts is to emphasize their flexibility of construction, their originality, and their firm embedding in the wider discourse.

These linguistic features are reinforced by a feature of their content which in substance is more important than any we have considered, yet it requires only brief mention because one would not expect to find it outside Christian writings. This is precisely their christocentric orientation.[31] Where the Stoic sage would speak of his resistance to misfortune as a means of honorable self-defense (not excluding incidental reference to God), Paul's hardship lists are regularly related to what Fitzgerald[32] called his "fixation on the cross of Christ" and on his resurrection. The specific rhetorical questions of Rom 8:35 are introduced by and subsumed under the question "Who shall separate us from the love of Christ?" 1 Corinthians 4:11-12 is set in Paul's defense of the evangelists "as servants of Christ and as those entrusted with the mysteries God has revealed" (4:1), and of himself as the Corinthians' "father in the gospel" (4:15). 2 Corinthians 4:8-12 directly links the evangelists' life and death with the death and resurrection of Christ, and with future judgment and glory (4:17f.; 5:5, 10). This is quickly followed by 5:21 ("God made him who had no sin to be sin for us . . ."), and the further list in 2 Cor 6:4-10. The "boasting" of 2 Cor 11:23b-27 is set within a wider contrast between human weakness and Christ's power (12:10). Paul repeatedly lists his humiliating hardships in order to show how his own weakness throws divine power into relief. This is a long way from the picture of the Stoic sage whose philosophy is claimed to enable him to treat misfortunes with disdain. Philippians 4:12 similarly follows a defense of his readers against "enemies of the cross of Christ" (3:18), and, more distantly, Paul's own longing to know "the power of [Christ's] resurrection and

---

[30] Similarly in 2 Cor 9:8, where "in all things at all times, having all that you need" (ἐν παντὶ πάντοτε πᾶσαν αὐτάρκειαν ἔχοντες) is balanced by "God is able to bless you abundantly"; cf. 1 Tim 6:6.
[31] On which see particularly Schrage, "Leid."
[32] Fitzgerald, *Earthen Vessel*, 207, cf. Shi, Message of the Cross, passim.

participation in his sufferings, becoming like him in his death, and so, somehow, attaining to the resurrection from the dead" (3:10-11).

Our discussion, like that of scholars we have cited, has concentrated on *Pauline* hardship lists. It is surprising that none of them has paid comparable attention to Heb 11, where a long example list[33] accelerates to become in vv. 36-38 a third-person list of hardships borne by unnamed but generally identifiable figures from the OT and intertestamental writings.[34]

This leads one in conclusion to enquire whether the affinities of New Testament hardship lists do not lie in a more deeply rooted human tendency to refer to sufferings and misfortunes, whether one's own or others', in a cumulative manner. As Hodgson states: "The conventionality of the tribulation list form is indicated by appearances of lists in such diverse literatures and ages as those of Aristotle (*Ethics* III.6; IX.2), Shakespeare (*Macbeth* III.2.23-24[35]; *Lear* I.1.252[36]) and the Buddah [*sic*]."[37] (To the Shakespeare references one may add *Hamlet* III.1.70-74.[38]) To the extent that this is so, it may no longer be necessary to argue for the sole or predominant influence on Paul's lists of a single tradition, or to minimize their distinctiveness by pressing them into a particular form-critical straitjacket.

---

[33] See M. R. Cosby, *The Rhetorical Composition and Function of Hebrews 11 In Light of Example Lists in Antiquity* (Macon, Ga.: Mercer University Press, 1988), who emphasizes like Bultmann the oral dimension of the writing.

[34] Fitzgerald, *Earthen Vessel*, 24 n. 90 notes that Hartwig Thyen, *Der Stil der Jüdisch-Hellenistischen Homilie* (FRLANT 65; Göttingen: Vandenhoeck & Ruprecht, 1955), 47 mentions this passage together with *1 Clem.* 45:4.

[35] (Macbeth speaking)
Duncan is in his grave;
After life's fitful fever he sleeps well;
Treason has done his worst: nor steel, nor poison,
Malice domestic, foreign levy, nothing,
Can touch him further.

[36] There is a lot about hardship in *King Lear*, but this reference appears incorrect.

[37] Hodgson 62 n. 8, citing C. H. Hamilton, ed., *Buddhism: A Religion of Infinite Compassion* (New York: Liberal Arts Press 1952), 23 (Hodgson's reference corrected).

[38] (Hamlet speaking)
For who would bear the whips and scorns of time,
The oppressor's wrong, the proud man's contumely,
The pangs of despised love, the law's delay,
The insolence of office, and the spurns
That patient merit of the unworthy takes,
When he himself might his quietus make
With a bare bodkin? . . .

20

HEBREWS AND THE MISSION OF THE EARLIEST CHURCH

Jon C. Laansma

INTRODUCTION

"A recognition of the missionary character of the documents [of the New Testament] will help us to see them in true perspective and to interpret them in the light of their intention."[1] The following essay, written out of profound gratitude to and respect for the author of that thesis, will undertake to draw out some of the ways in which this is true of the book of Hebrews.[2]

On the face of it this would seem to be an exercise in reading against the grain. Little on the surface of Hebrews suggests that there is anything outward looking, anything missiological about it. The entire thrust of the letter appears to revolve around community maintenance, around holding onto salvation until "he who is coming, comes."

Thus, in his impressive sociological analysis of Hebrews, Iustione Salevao has argued that the overarching concern of the author of Hebrews was to create "a symbolic universe to legitimate the institutional order of the community of the readers.... Put more specifically, the letter may be seen as a carefully

---

[1] I. Howard Marshall, *New Testament Theology: Many Witnesses, One Gospel* (Downers Grove: InterVarsity, 2004), 35. For his own development of his thesis with respect to Hebrews I refer to that section of his work. He should of course not be held responsible for the argument that follows. In keeping with Marshall's thesis is the argument of J. Ross Wagner, "*Missio Dei:* Envisioning an Apostolic Reading of Scripture," *Missiology: An International Review* 37, no. 1 (2009), 19-32 [29], that, "the overarching narrative of the *missio Dei* provides the proper context for offering an account of the nature and function of Scripture in the church .... While redemption is from first to last the work of God in Jesus Christ through the power of the Holy Spirit, it is a work that nonetheless establishes reconciled human beings as active co-laborers with God. In union with Christ, we find our lives increasingly conformed to the pattern of Jesus' own self-giving love, as in the power of the Spirit and under the tutelage of the Scriptures we participate in the on-going mission of the triune God to the world." This comports nicely with the vision that we will draw from Hebrews in the following.

[2] I wish to acknowledge Andrew Burlingame (both for assistance in research and the wording of the text), Jeff Shamess, Karen Jobes and Doug Moo, who assisted with earlier drafts of this essay. They bear no responsibility for its faults.

designed attempt to maintain the symbolic universe of the readers."[3] It is not my purpose to engage Salevao directly, and it should be noted that his characterization of Hebrews' community as a "conversionist sect" entails a "missionary enterprise."[4] Nevertheless the latter is given almost no attention and could be missed altogether with the overriding emphasis on the need to reinforce community boundaries through the creation of a convincing symbolic universe. Indeed, one question that the present investigation will raise is whether a sociological analysis can properly assess a discourse apart from assumptions about its nature and orientation as a speech-act within a given setting. That is, can such an analysis give us what the author was "doing" (e.g., "creating a symbolic universe to legitimate . . .") without *prior* assumptions about what he was "doing"?

The present essay will operate from the view that to miss the missionary orientation and heart of the whole would be a mistake. If we were to overhear a coach of a football team exhorting his players to work together and in harmony with each other, we could draw the mistaken conclusion that this was a team focused solely on its internal dynamics and not on the objective of moving the ball down the field and scoring. Likewise, the letter to the church of Philadelphia in Rev 3:7-13 might suggest a non-missionary outlook, were it to be read without the context in which the Apocalypse embeds it.[5] Perhaps this is even truer of the letter to the believers in Antioch, Syria, and Cilicia (Acts 15:23-29). Indeed, the burden of proof should be placed on those who deny the missionary heart of Hebrews.[6]

---

[3] Iutisone Salevao, *Legitimation in the Letter to the Hebrews: The Construction and Maintenance of a Symbolic Universe* (JSNTSup 219; London: Sheffield Academic, 2002), 93.

[4] Salevao, *Legitimation*, 227, cf. 203-204, 205-206, 230-31.

[5] See the chapters by Osborne and Schnabel elsewhere in this volume.

[6] Situating our argument in a larger reconstruction of the earliest Christian mission is not possible but it is appropriate to indicate a few assumptions here. Firstly, with John P. Dickson, *Mission-Commitment in Ancient Judaism and in the Pauline Communities* (WUNT 2/159; Tübingen: Mohr [Siebeck], 2003), 10, we will define "mission" as "the range of activities by which members of a religious community desirous of the conversion of outsiders seek to promote their religion to non-adherents" (italicized in original); this includes activities that support that mission, such as prayer and financial support. Secondly, as argued by James LaGrand, *The Earliest Christian Mission to 'All Nations' in the Light of Matthew's Gospel* (Grand Rapids: Eerdmans, 1995), 205-206 *et passim*, the mission to all nations stems back to and out of Jesus' Jewish particularism as narrated by Matthew; cf. also P. Stuhlmacher, "Matt 28:16-20 and the Course of Mission in the Apostolic and Postapostolic Age," in *The Mission of the Early Church to Jews and Gentiles* (ed. Jostein Ådna and Hans Kvalbein; WUNT 127; Tübingen: Mohr [Siebeck], 2000), 17-43. The mission of the Hellenists (Acts 6–9), which we will note below, was accordingly not entirely a new departure. Thirdly, I. H. Marshall, "Who were the Evangelists?" in *The Mission of the Early Church to Jews and Gentiles* (ed. Jostein Ådna and Hans Kvalbein; WUNT 127; Tübingen: Mohr [Siebeck], 2000), 251-

Our task, then, will not be to deny the obvious in respect of the leading emphasis of this "epistolary homily"—that is, we are not going to deny its call to communal faithfulness—but to make explicit its missionary heart, by which we have in mind the worldwide expansion of the gospel (with its effects for society and creation), beyond Judaism to all nations.

Our argument will proceed in three movements. We may visualize ourselves moving in from the wider context of the church's mission, to the framing chapters 1:1–4:13 and 10:19–13:26,[7] and ending with the central exposition of 4:14–10:25 itself. The choice to survey several lines of evidence means that we will forego a detailed exegetical defense of any one of them. Points that are weaker on their own[8] naturally gain strength if the whole has been aligned on the right interpretive axis.

INDICATIONS OF MISSIONARY PRACTICE AND SETTING

We begin with a few very general observations and assertions. It is immediately

---

63, argues that the combined picture of Acts and Paul suggests that the very idea of missionary activity may have been original to the church, that the mission was carried out first of all by missionaries such as Paul, but that local congregations also engaged in evangelism. Fourthly, Stuhlmacher, op. cit., 42, makes a comment that speaks to the importance of missions in general in the earliest church. Noting that the "concept of missions present [in Matthew] is represented by *all* main witnesses of the New Testament, Günther Baumbach's observation should be recalled that missions according to Matthew 'do not constitute merely one of the many tasks of the Church, but they are an essential aspect of it'. With Martin Hengel one can add: 'History and theology of early Christianity are a "history of missions" and a "theology of missions". A church and theology which forgets or denies the missionary commission of the believers as messengers of salvation in a world threatened by destruction, gives up its foundation and, thereby, gives itself up too'" (italicized in original). Stuhlmacher is citing Günther Baumbach, "Die Mission im Matthäus-Evangelium," *TLZ* 92 (1967): 890-93 [892]; Martin Hengel, "Die Ursprünge der christlichen Mission," *NTS* 18 (1971/72): 15-28 [27 n. 42]. Hence our claim that the burden of proof should be placed on the argument that the author and recipients of Hebrews were exempt from the missionary heart of early Christianity. Fifthly, the history of the earliest mission has been chronicled in detail by Eckhard J. Schnabel, *Jesus and the Twelve* (vol. 1 of *Early Christian Mission*; Downers Grove: InterVarsity, 2004); idem, *Paul and the Early Church* (vol. 2 of *Early Christian Mission*; Downers Grove: InterVarsity, 2004).

[7] Throughout I will assume that while there is a structural break between chs. 12 and 13, nevertheless ch. 13 is an integral part of the original discourse as sent and received; cf. Harold W. Attridge, *The Epistle to the Hebrews* (ed. H. Koester; Hermeneia; Philadelphia: Fortress, 1989), 384-85; Craig R. Koester, *Hebrews* (AB 36; New York: Doubleday, 2001), 83-86, 554-56 (who prefers to outline as 12:28–13:21 and 13:22-25).

[8] For example, does παρρησία indicate a public witness in some of its uses (as I accept) or is it closer to the idea of boldness in living faithfully?

apparent that Hebrews' approach to the priesthood and sacrifice of Christ vis-à-vis the Mosaic covenant is *consistent* with a decentralized gospel that reaches beyond Jerusalem and Israel to all humanity—marking not centripetal but centrifugal forces. Indeed, we can observe that the world mission is the "elephant in the room" of Hebrews' discourse. One should not overlook the facts that the readers are themselves the product of the world mission— particularly if we are right in supposing that this is addressed to believers in Italy, if not Rome—and that if Pauline authorship can scarcely be defended, yet everything about the letter suggests deep-running consistency with and involvement in the theological outlook we encounter in Paul's writings, not to mention Luke's and Peter's.[9] One may then *presume* involvement in the missiological character of these traditions. In fact, as we will see, the vision of salvation in Hebrews is universalistic[10] in scope. Moreover, among the explicit warnings and exhortations in Hebrews the vision is forward-looking and the problems revolve around a weakened theology's inability to cope with the hardships of the way of faith, hardly a merely parochial Jewish problem.[11] Given this, and anticipating other aspects of our argument below, it will not be hard to picture a community of believers that has slackened not merely in their willingness to self-identify publicly as Christians, but in their positive witness, in their role as participants in the church's world mission. It would then be the

---

[9] For Hebrews' relation to these other NT strands, see L. D. Hurst, *The Epistle to the Hebrews: Its Background of Thought* (SNTSMS 65; Cambridge: Cambridge University Press, 1990), 89-130; Attridge, *Hebrews*, 30-31; Koester, *Hebrews*, 56-58. One may also note that the writer's argument presumes some familiarity with at least parts of the narrative of Jesus' life. Connections with John's Gospel have often been noted as well; cf. C. J. A. Hickling, "John and Hebrews: The Background of Hebrews 2.10-18," *NTS* 29 (1988): 112-15; C. Spicq, *L'épître aux Hébreux* (2 vols.; Paris: Gabalda, 1952–1953), 1:103-38; Oscar Cullmann, *The Johannine Circle* (Philadelphia: Westminster, 1976), 54-55. I. H. Marshall, "Soteriology in Hebrews," in *The Epistle to the Hebrews and Christian Theology* (ed. Richard Bauckham et al.; Grand Rapids: Eerdmans, 2009), 253-77 [253], comments, "The soteriological teaching in the letter to the Hebrews is broadly in agreement with what we find elsewhere in the New Testament." See further Barnabas Lindars, *The Theology of the Letter to the Hebrews* (NTT; Cambridge: Cambridge University Press, 1991), 26-42; F. F. Bruce, "The Kerygma of Hebrews," *Int* 23 (1969): 3-19; R. V. G. Tasker, *The Gospel in the Epistle to the Hebrews* (London: Tyndale Press, 1950); Morna D. Hooker, "Christ, the 'End' of the Cult," in *The Epistle to the Hebrews and Christian Theology*, 189-212 [204-207].

[10] Here and throughout, "universalistic" means simply that the mission extends beyond the boundaries of Judaism to all the nations, as we see developed in Acts.

[11] Hooker, "Christ," 197, is closer to the mark than the "relapse" theories when she writes, ". . . the author's message to his readers was not 'Do not *fall back* into Judaism,' but rather, 'It is time to *move on*, and to *leave behind* your former understanding of Judaism"; cf. op. cit., 207, 209-10; likewise Manson, *Hebrews*, 15-16; I. H. Marshall, *Kept by the Power of God: A Study of Perseverance and Falling Away* (Minneapolis: Bethany House Publishers, 1969), 137.

writer of Hebrews' task to weave out of the strains of theology that will resonate with these believers[12] a compelling summons to communal faithfulness in precisely *that* role. In other words, as will become clear, faithfulness is missionary in character.

That presumption of active involvement in the world mission comports with the details of life that peek through Hebrews: the importance of showing hospitality,[13] the past history and continuing reality of imprisonment and loss of property,[14] the apparent threat to their very lives,[15] and the encouragement towards παρρησία.[16] In any event we must probably assume a social setting in

---

[12] As to what might "resonate" with these readers: It is likely that if the readers are not ethnically Jewish Christians (it is arguably a mix of Jewish and Gentile believers), they are "Jewish" in outlook. The whole argument assumes a deep-running investment in the LXX and the religious outlook of Judaism and Jewish Christianity. Assuming some part in the Jewish-Christian "hellenist tradition" (see below), Dunn's tentative sketch of "a hellenist/Antiochene theology" (James D. G. Dunn, *Beginning from Jerusalem* [vol. 2 of *Christianity in the Making*; Grand Rapids: Eerdmans, 2009], 308-21), not least in respect of its attitudes to the temple, provides possible perspective on what the writer of Hebrews would have known himself to share with his readers. Dunn's comment, op. cit., 315, is certainly relevant: "*we should probably credit the Hellenists with turning the new sect within Second Temple Judaism into an evangelistic sect*, the first sustained evangelistic outreach in the history of Israel—a major development indeed" (italics in original). Dunn, however, overstates the degree to which this is a new development; see Joel Green's chapter elsewhere in the present volume and n. 6, above.

[13] 13:1-2; probably 6:10. By itself, φιλοξενία (hospitality) had no necessary relation to mission; it was very simply a cultural and now Christian virtue, and its inclusion here may say no more. It was in fact, however, an essential component of the church's mission, and its inclusion here may have that association in mind; cf. Attridge, *Hebrews*, 386; William L. Lane, *Hebrews* (2 vols.; WBC 47A-47B; Dallas: Word Books, 1991), 2:512-13; J. H. Elliot, *A Home for the Homeless: A Sociological Exegesis of 1 Peter* (Philadelphia: Fortress Press, 1981), 146; Gustav Stählin, "ξένος κτλ," *TDNT* 5:1-36 [20-23]; D. W. Riddle, "Early Christian Hospitality: A Factor in the Gospel Transmission," *JBL* 57 (1938): 141-54; Wayne A. Meeks, *The First Urban Christians: The Social World of the Apostle Paul* (New Haven: Yale University Press, 1983), 109.

[14] 10:32-34; 13:3; likely also 13:23.

[15] The presence of that threat permeates the discourse, beginning with 2:15; cf. 12:4 in the wake of 10:32–12:3.

[16] The noun παρρησία occurs in 3:6; 4:16; 10:19; and 10:35. Koester, *Hebrews*, 247, comments that the word "includes both the internal disposition of confidence . . . or courage . . . and the external expression of clear and public speaking"; Attridge, *Hebrews*, 112, states that it "is basically a confident self-assurance that issues in a bold 'freedom of speech.'" For the latter, in both 3:6 and 10:35 it "refers to a public demonstration of Christian commitment." On 10:35 Attridge, *Hebrews*, 300, comments (correctly, in my opinion), "the connotations of public boldness in proclaiming the gospel message are particularly clear." On παρρησία in 3:6, Paul Ellingworth, *The Epistle to the Hebrews: A Commentary on the Greek Text* (NIGTC; Grand Rapids: Eerdmans, 1993), 212, writes, "The section concludes as it began, by stressing the need

which the line between *intra-communal* confession and *public* confession is blurred or functionally non-existent, in contrast to the comfortable partitioning of them in many modern societies; we should probably also assume that their faithful endurance is defined not by self-preservation and a spirit of indifference to the fate of their persecutors. In particular, reading 10:32-39 with its summons to παρρησία together with 12:1-3—since they comprise a single thread of thought, with the long list of 11:1-40 linking them—impresses us with a call to a public, verbal witness in keeping with Jesus' own mission, making clear that the suffering has much to do with this activity of open witness.[17] In other words, it does not seem to be the case that these believers have merely been publicly marked and targeted and must now hold their ground. Rather it is that in their confession they have been openly witnessing to the gospel and precisely for that reason encountering persecution. In short, there is a problem past which these readers must get in the interest of this very witness. Close to the heart of that problem is the very suffering we just noted, suffering apparently effected by their public verbal witness. *Without the author's commenting in any direct way on that mission it is the* raison d'être *of the discourse.*

In the light of these observations, which by themselves would fit with a range of theories as to the letter's setting, we may then recall that it was one of the chief concerns of William Manson's 1949 Baird Lecture to argue that the key to Hebrews "is only to be found by examining the history of the world-mission of Christianity from its inception in the work of Stephen."[18] Thus, in its argument that the change of priesthood necessarily entails a change of law (7:12), Hebrews "supplements the Pauline argument [regarding the law] at a point which St. Paul had left untouched, but which was of very great importance and interest to the world mission. For who shall say that a less

---

for open witness to Christ." On the word παρρησία, see further Stanley B. Marrow, S.J., "*Parrhesia* and the New Testament," *CBQ* 44 (1982): 431-46; Alan C. Mitchell, S.J., "Holding on to the Confidence: PARRHSIA in Hebrews," in *Friendship, Flattery, and Frankness of Speech*, (ed. J. T. Fitzgerald; NovTSup 82; Leiden: Brill, 1996), 203-26.

[17] It is arguable that the same idea is in view in 13:7. Commenting on the "conduct" (ἀναστροφή) that the readers are to imitate in the latter passage, Attridge, *Hebrews*, 392, opines that it "could refer to the leaders' general moral probity, but it may relate specifically to their function as proclaimers of God's word. In such activity their fidelity (τὴν πίστιν) would have been particularly manifest and it may even have been responsible for the 'outcome' of death."

[18] W. Manson, *The Epistle to the Hebrews: An Historical and Theological Reconsideration. The Baird Lecture, 1949* (London: Hodder and Stoughton, 1951), 23. Likewise, op. cit., 159: ". . . the key to Hebrews, alike in its practical and theoretical aspects, was to be found only by bringing the Epistle into close integration with historical and doctrinal developments occurring within the sphere of the world-mission of Christianity as inaugurated by Stephen and his successors."

urgent practical necessity dictated the course of this writer's 'word of exhortation' to his Roman readers than dictated the letter of St. Paul to the Galatians?"[19] And again, in commenting on 13:13, Manson writes, "This going out—the putting into practice of the great watch-word of Stephen and of the world mission—is the true Christian approach to the altar; the sharing of the reproach of Christ is the true Christian communion of the altar; and it is in this going out and in this communion that the 'grace' is to be experienced, by which ... the spirit is to be fortified."[20]

In part, Manson's point is that the very warp and woof of Hebrews' theology—thus, e.g., its wisdom christology[21]—emerged precisely out of the context of the world mission of the church as we see that represented by the early Hellenists (esp. Acts 6-8). The mission constitutes the living matrix within which that theology evolved, whatever the use to which it is put in this discourse. *But in part,* as is evident from the above citations, *his argument is that this mission belongs to the very point of the "word of exhortation."*

It is tempting to repeat Manson's arguments for this thesis[22] and to bolster them with further support, but there is no space for that here. I allude to the cautiously sympathetic review of the argument as carried out by L. D. Hurst,[23] and note that, although not all are convinced, there is in fact continuing support.[24] It is by no means necessary to think in terms of literary dependence,

---

[19] Manson, *Hebrews*, 115.

[20] Manson, *Hebrews*, 151.

[21] Manson, *Hebrews*, 95-97.

[22] In fact Manson, *Hebrews*, 23-24, advances several, related theses. Where I refer in the present essay to his "thesis" I have in mind the specifics of the previous two paragraphs.

[23] Hurst, *Background*, 89-106, 131.

[24] E.g., C. K. Barrett, "The Christology of Hebrews," in *Who Do You Say That I Am? Essays on Christology* (ed. M. A. Powell and D. R. Bauer; Louisville: Westminster/John Knox, 1999), 110-27. My own work supported Manson's proposed association with Acts 7 and the "Hellenists" from a limited frame of reference: cf. *I Will Give You Rest: The Rest Motif in the New Testament with Special Reference to Mt 11 and Heb 3-4* (WUNT 2/98; Tübingen: Mohr [Siebeck], 1997), 335-38. Likewise, partial support, at least, is given by Hooker, "Christ," 197. Lane, *Hebrews*, 1:cxliv-cl, develops at some length the hypothesis that Hebrews stands in the "Hellenistic tradition" of the earliest church. Utilizing a sociological approach, Richard W. Johnson, *Going Outside the Camp: The Sociological Function of the Levitical Critique in the Epistle to the Hebrews* (JSNTSup 209; London: Sheffield Academic Press, 2001), 146, argues that "Manson's proposal is most in harmony with the analysis presented in this study"; Manson's "theory is more consistent with the implicit sociological data in the epistle than are the competing theories" (148). Johnson concludes: "In his implicit advocacy of an ideal society, the author of Hebrews promoted conditions conducive to the entry of outsiders into the community of believers.... Following the author's lead, his readers would be better equipped to carry out the world mission of the church. With the increased exposure to those 'outside the camp' (13.13) incumbent in the world mission, the believers would require courage to face the risk of persecution, but would find security

either of Hebrews on Acts or of Acts on Hebrews. Nor is it necessary or wise to gloss over the differences between Acts and Hebrews or to attempt any sort of harmonization. Plainly, if we imagine Hebrews to be addressed to a church in Italy, perhaps Rome, sometime in the mid-60s or 70s, then we are a long way from the situation of Stephen and the ensuing events narrated by Luke. Moreover, given the necessarily speculative nature of this historical reconstruction it would be unwise to rest everything on it. I find it reasonably convincing, and at the very least it serves to highlight in a compelling way the fact that Hebrews *can* be read as *the animating theology of churches reaching aggressively forward in their mission beyond the synagogue to the wider world.*[25]

But rather than seeming to base too much on a particular and necessarily tenuous historical reconstruction, it will be wiser to press forward and consider more fully the theology and argument of the discourse itself.

JESUS, ὁ τῆς πίστεως ἀρχηγὸς καὶ τελειωτής

Ultimately, support for the thesis that Hebrews represents a church vitally interested and involved in the world mission stems from the convergence of several lines of evidence: a defensible theory as to the writing's setting within the world mission (i.e., Manson's theory), the letter's overlap with other dominant strands of NT theology, specific indications of the behaviors and experiences of the community, the exhortations to faithfulness (the hortatory passages), and the theological vision of the book coupled with the deployment of that theology in the letter's argument. It is the last of these that concerns us in this section.

There will doubtless be several means by which to show that the theology of Hebrews is missiological in character. I will do so using the heuristic device of a narrative substructure, correlating that with the role of Jesus as a model of

---

in their faithful lives as citizens of the city of the living God" (153). The sociological analysis of Salevao, already cited, is generally accepting of Manson's thesis (Salevao, *Legitimation*, 107-108); quite apart from that theory Salevao assumes for the church of Hebrews a "missionary enterprise" (227, cf. 203-204, 205-206, 230-31), but does not develop this in any way. Very tentative support for Manson's general argument (the association of Hebrews with the "Hellenists" of Acts 7) is voiced by James D. G. Dunn, *The Partings of the Ways Between Christianity and Judaism and their Significance for the Character of Christianity* (London: SCM, 1991), 70.

[25] There is nothing overtly missionary about Stephen's speech in Acts 7. It is the trajectory of the Hellenists' outreach as evidenced especially through Acts narrative that reveals impulses at work in the speech of ch. 7, not least in its view of the temple. For a recent and detailed study of "The Hellenists and the First Outreach" within the larger context of the church's history from the resurrection of Jesus to the fall of Jerusalem, see Dunn, *Beginning*, 241-321. Unfortunately, Dunn's discussion of Hebrews is reserved for vol. 3.

faithfulness, and concentrating this lens on the framing passages of 1:1–4:13 and 10:26–13:25.

The identification of a narrative substructure behind NT letters is by now well accepted.[26] Indeed, making explicit the subnarrative behind Hebrews seems to me necessary towards accounting for the observation that motifs come and go, mix and constellate in its argument in ways that are at once rhetorically effective and logically elusive. Providing one brief account of that narrative is dangerous for so rich a discourse as Hebrews, but I might prefer to summarize it like this:[27] it is the story of the entrance of humanity (Jews *and* Gentiles) through God's Son into the ultimate sacred space[28] in fulfillment of God's *promise* to Abraham; the correlative of promise is the enduring *faith* of the υἱός; the means of entrance into sacred space is cultic *cleansing*,[29] and,

---

[26] See R. B. Hays, *The Faith of Jesus Christ: An Investigation of the Narrative Substructure of Galatians 3:1–4:11* (SBLDS 56; Chico, Calif.: Scholars Press, 1983). It has been utilized for the interpretation of Hebrews by Kenneth L. Schenck, *Understanding the Book of Hebrews: The Story Behind the Sermon* (Louisville: Westminster/John Knox, 2003); idem, *Cosmology and Eschatology in Hebrews: The Setting of the Sacrifice* (Cambridge: Cambridge University Press, 2007), 10-17 *et passim*; cf. also, with further references, James C. Miller, "Paul and Hebrews: A Comparison of Narrative Worlds," in *Hebrews: Contemporary Methods—New Insights* (ed. G. Gelardini; Leiden: Brill, 2005), 245-64. My proposal is independent of Schenck's.

[27] There are *many* threads in the rich theological tapestry that this writer weaves—e.g., the need to overcome the obstacle of death (cf. Marshall, "Soteriology," 257-61). And once we begin to think in terms of narrative, we must reckon on setting, subplots and so forth. As well, almost everything in this writer's thought can be mapped onto other parts of the NT, as we have already noted; imagery and emphasis will change but the basics are consistent. Even Hebrews most creative theology is finally traditional in substance. All this to say that I am not *reducing* the writer's theology to the following subnarrative, but merely looking for the coherence in the broadest patterns.

[28] This locale is variously designated: κληρονομία, κατάπαυσις (cf. Deut 12:9 through to 2 Sam 7; 1 Chr 22; 23; 28; for the importance of this thread for the OT itself, see Laansma, *Rest*, 17-76), δόξα (Ps 8 in Heb 2). It is of course the "city" of 11:10, 16; 12:22; 13:14.

[29] Especially καθαρίζω, ἁγιάζω, ῥαντίζω τῷ αἵματι; cf. Lane, *Hebrews*, 1:15; Marshall, "Soteriology," 254-55; William G. Johnsson, "Defilement and Purgation in the Book of Hebrews" (PhD diss., Vanderbilt University, 1973), 430-31. This point regarding "cleansing" as the leading soteriological category is one of emphasis in the employment of images, not exclusivity and certainly not incompatability (with, e.g., law court imagery). For the importance of sacred space to Hebrews, quite apart from the theory of historical location for the letter that Isaacs suggests, see Marie E. Isaacs, *Sacred Space: An Approach to the Theology of the Epistle to the Hebrews* (JSNTSup 73; Sheffield: JSOT Press, 1992). More generally, *inter alia*, see John H. Walton, *Ancient Near Eastern Thought and the Old Testament: Introducing the Conceptual World of the Hebrew Bible* (Grand Rapids: Baker, 2006), 118-19, 196-99; W. D. Davies, *The Territorial Dimension of Judaism* (Berkeley: University of California Press, 1982), 18-

ultimately, of *bringing "perfection."* The *Eternal* (New) Covenant is inaugurated by and mediates the consecrating sacrifice.

The subnarrative of Hebrews, therefore, finally locates the story of *humanity* (Ps 8!) in the norming story of *Israel*. This is a story that is fractured, incomplete, and disjointed in the OT form (1:1)—e.g., the diverse aspects of the Mosaic cultus, or the different aspects of kingship and priesthood—but it is brought to its intended unity, simplicity, coherence, and perfection in Christ; moreover, what is a geographically restricted and ethnocentric *type* is cosmically universalized in the antitype. As well, the writer conceives of salvation locally as sacred space—the throne room of God. The coming world (2:5) is *all* "the Most Holy Place," where believers stand directly in the presence of God. Unlike the type of Israel's land, there is no gradation of holiness working out in concentric circles from the Most Holy Place to the rest of the land, but it is all perfectly sanctified. In line with this model of salvation, the obstacle becomes that of cultic uncleanness, and therefore the need is of *cleansing*—of the entire community and of the cosmos itself as God's temple.

It would be possible to illustrate how this narrative informs both parts (1:1–4:13) and the whole of Hebrews, but doing so would prove a distraction in the present context. Observations apropos of our concern with mission are in order.

Firstly, we note that there is at the least an implied or potential missionary vision in all this. Ultimately, this narrative is indeed the story of *humanity/the cosmos*—it is *universalistic* in scope—and of humanity's/the cosmos' *salvation* through the promise made to Abraham, that is, through Israel.[30] Moreover, this is the same story that animated Paul's theology and that animated his worldwide *mission*. Here I have in mind the argument of N. T. Wright, who summarizes his essential point about Paul's theological vision in this way: "It is

---

21; Joachim Jeremias, *Jerusalem in the Time of Jesus* (Philadelphia: Fortress Press, 1969), 79, making reference to *m. Kelim* 1:6-9; Jacob Milgrom, *Leviticus* (3 vols.; AB 3–3B; New York: Doubleday, 1991), 47-51.

[29] E.g., Phil 2:5-11. George H. Guthrie, *The Structure of Hebrews: A Text-Linguistic Analysis* (NovTSup 73; Leiden: Brill, 1994), 122, uses this spatial imagery to explain the logic of all of Heb 1:5–10:18. Presently we are observing that the humiliation-exaltation pattern is played out within Heb 2:5-16 itself.

[30] For the cosmic elements, see my two earlier essays, "Hidden Stories in Hebrews: Cosmology and Theology," in *A Cloud of Witnesses: The Theology of Hebrews in its Ancient Contexts* (ed. Richard Bauckham et al.; LNTS 387; London: T&T Clark, 2008), 9-18; "Hebrews," in *Cosmology and New Testament Theology* (ed. Jonathan T. Pennington and Sean M. MacDonough; LNTS 355; London: T&T Clark, 2008), 125-43; see further below. As to the inclusion of Gentiles, beyond the universalistic scope of Ps 8 it is deserving of note that the history of the conquest as summarized in Heb 11 culminates not with Joshua but with the faith of a Gentile woman, Rahab; on this see, Carl Mosser, "Rahab Outside the Camp," in *The Epistle to the Hebrews and Christian Theology*, 383-404. Earlier interpreters emphasized the inclusion of the Gentiles in Ps 2:8; cf. John Chrysostom and Thomas Aquinas on Heb 1:2.

central to Paul, but almost entirely ignored in perspectives old, new and otherwise, that *God had a single plan all along through which to rescue the world and the human race, and that this single plan was centered upon the call of Israel, a call which Paul saw as coming to fruition in Israel's representative, the Messiah.*"[31] Again, "Abraham is not simply an 'example' of someone who is justified by faith . . . . [Paul] sees God's promise to Abraham as the foundation of the single-plan-through-Israel-for-the-world, in short, the covenant."[32] Hebrews of course adapts this common subnarrative to its vision of salvation as the ultimate destination of humanity *qua* sacred space, but the essence is the same. In a word, then, this is *missionary* theology of universalistic scope.

It may of course be argued that all of this theological potential for missions is only potential. Might it not be that the writer placed all this in the service of his own, *inward*-looking ends of community maintenance, of moving ahead with the gospel's implications for their ancestral practices and of holding onto salvation till the end? The answer, it will be observed, is contained within the subnarrative itself.

Secondly, then, Hebrews' own deployment of this gospel theology is consistent with an *active interest* in its missionary character. One quite pronounced strand of the writer's theology centers on the need to follow Christ's example, conceived either as being brought through the same process (e.g., 2:10-11)[33] or actively imitating Christ's faithfulness as God's Son (esp. 12:1-17; 13:12-14).[34] The importance of this theme for Hebrews was highlighted by its inclusion within the subnarrative as we outlined it, though its significance must be made explicit. Once stated it may seem to have been too obvious for words, but in our present context we must say this: In precisely what *way* was Christ faithful? For what *ends*? Precisely what was he about in this life that these readers are called to imitate? And the answer is: It was the offering of his body for the sanctification of the world (10:5-10). His faithfulness was specifically *salvific, missionary*. From the treatment of God's *redemptive* will (τὸ θέλημά σου) in 10:5-10 the logic proceeds organically to our own accomplishment of God's will (τὸ θέλημα τοῦ θεοῦ) in 10:36 upon which hangs the obtainment of the promise. From here we can proceed to 13:21 (the next use of the noun phrase) where the benediction prays that God will equip us for the doing of his will (τὸ θέλημα αὐτοῦ). Faithfulness, in other words, is not merely an abstract virtue, but is itself meaningful only within an

---

[31] N. T. Wright, *Justification: God's Plan and Paul's Vision* (Downers Grove: IVP Academic, 2009), 35 (italics in original).
[32] Wright, *Justification*, 216. He repeats this in different ways at numerous points; cf. 65, 94-95, *et passim*.
[33] When reading 12:4-11 regarding God's discipline of his "sons" we are to recall the perfecting of the Son in 2:10-17 and 5:7-10.
[34] Also 3:1-6 as followed by 3:7–4:11.

assumed story that revolves around God's reclamation and cleansing of his creation, his works. Faithfulness, therefore, is not about securing one's own (actually, for Hebrews, the *community's*) salvation by hanging on till the end, but about doing that precisely through adopting the same missiological aims that are at the heart of the gospel.[35]

Here, too, we can note a deep running parallel with Paul's idea of justification as outlined by Wright. Thus, "God made humans for a purpose: not simply for themselves, not simply so that they could be in relationship with him, but so that *through* them, as his image-bearers, he could bring his wise, glad, fruitful order to the world . . . . God is rescuing us from the shipwreck of the world, not so that we can sit back and put our feet up in his company, but so that we can be part of his plan to remake the world. *We* are in orbit around *God and his purposes*, not the other way around."[36] What Wright finds so explosive in all this, and precisely what he argues has been so completely overlooked in modern scholarship, is what we are stressing is the animating theology of Hebrews as well.

In short, if we pay attention to the framing passages of 1:1–4:13 and 10:26–13:25 we find not only hints of concrete missionary behaviors but a universalistic missionary theology[37] deployed for missionary ends.

TEMPLE AND PRIESTHOOD

Approaching 1:1–4:13 and 10:26–13:25 through the heuristic device of a narrative substructure draws out the missiological nature and deployment of Hebrews' theology. The dramatic action of that story slows down in 4:14–10:25, however, as the critical moment of how the approach and entrance are cultically effected is isolated. We will therefore alter our approach, leaving behind the notion of substructure and focusing the missiological aspects of

---

[35] Along similar lines Wagner, "*Missio Dei*," 27-29, argues that 1 John is a "'missional' letter"; it ultimately calls for a life "that conforms to the pattern of Jesus' self-giving love . . . ." He concludes, 29, "Guided by the example of Jesus and by the cruciform reasoning of the apostolic witness, Augustine finds the 'perfection of love' of which 1 John speaks (2:5) to consist in nothing less than 'to love our enemies, and to love them to this end; that they may be our brothers and sisters' (*ep. Jo.* 1.9)." This in response to those who would argue that 1 John limits the love commandment to those "within the boundaries of the community."

[36] Wright, *Justification*, 23-24 (italics in original).

[37] We have highlighted the presence of the gospel in Hebrews by noticing the epistle's subnarrative. More generally, note again Lindars, *Theology*, 26-42; Bruce, "Kerygma," 3-19; Tasker, *Gospel*. Yet another way of highlighting the presence of the gospel in Hebrews would be to plot echoes of or parallels to Hebrews right through the first five chapters of Athanasius' *The Incarnation of the Word of God*. The gospel is the mother of Hebrews and its very substance, and by its very nature the gospel impels to mission those who receive it in faith.

4:14–10:25 in three ways: Firstly, noting the way in which the cultic cleansing provides the needed παράκλησις for the difficulties the faithful face on this way; secondly, noting the way in which the cultic cosmology of the book correlates with the mission of the church; thirdly, noting how the priestly role of the readers involves them in bringing others to God.

Firstly, in his comment on the use of παρρησία in 10:35, which we have already cited in part, Harold Attridge avers,

> In this context, where behavior in the face of persecution is in view, the connotations of public boldness in proclaiming the gospel message are particularly clear. Yet this public boldness is rooted in the assurance of access to God through the sacrifice of Christ. The assurance of entrance to the transcendent realm which that sacrifice provides is ultimately the ground for "going forth" in Christ's footsteps to service in the world (13:13).[38]

This is a very helpful way of seeing the matter: The παρρησία—defined as a bold "freedom of speech"—that is won and required for the approach to the divine throne (4:16; 10:19), serves the παρρησία of their public witness (10:35 and likely 3:6). This relates to the whole way that the cultic argument of the discourse bears on the circumstances of the readers. The direct exhortations of Hebrews consistently revolve around faithful, communal endurance (*in their open witness!*) through suffering toward eschatological arrival at the place of salvation *qua* sacred space. We have already observed that the condition for entrance into that sacred space is cleansing (καθαρίζω, καθαρισμός). We may also observe that this cleansing, related as it is to the gains for the conscience (συνείδησις),[39] provides exactly the fortitude that is necessary if believers are to endure such a course as this, even perhaps μέχρις αἵματος. In short, the major emphasis of the discourse on cultic cleansing and the approach to the divine presence should not cause us to think that the point is either merely that of properly appropriating the gospel in relation to the temple sacrifices, nor merely a reinvigorated prayer life, nor even merely their own safe arrival at the future goal of salvation. Our argument has no need to exclude any of these, but our point is that *the cultic argument, precisely as a λόγος παρακλήσεως (13:22), serves the paraenetic concern with faithfulness in public witness, that is, in doing what Jesus did, even to death if need be, toward ultimate participation in his reward.*[40]

Secondly, in two discussions of the cosmology of Hebrews I have argued

---

[38] Attridge, *Hebrews*, 300. Likewise, Lane, *Hebrews*, 2:301-302: "Precisely because he [*sic*] enjoys free access to God through Christ's sacrificial death and heavenly intercessory ministry . . . , he can confidently acknowledge his faith before the world."
[39] 9:9, 14; 10:2, 22; 13:18.
[40] See also my *Rest*, 272, for the way in which the exhortation to faithfulness in 3:1–4:13 (future eschatology) is framed by assurances of Christ's priestly assistance along the way (realized eschatology).

that this discourse does not anticipate the annihilation of the universe but rather its "cleansing" and reclamation as God's temple, that is, his κατάπαυσις (*resting place*; see above).[41] Within this vision the Mosaic tabernacle is understood to be patterned after the preexistent heavenly world and thus to serve as a pattern for the world to come.[42]

Rather than repeat those arguments here I will simply register two implications for our present concerns. Just as we emphasized with the subnarrative above, the *cosmic* vision of this theological outlook, by its very logic, would naturally fuel the centrifugal forces of a worldwide mission. For those for whom it was a living gospel (4:2, 6) it is a fair guess that the world mission was both the originating matrix and the practical corollary of this vision. Once again, this comports with and so receives some confirmation from the rest of what we are arguing here. Further support stems from the canonical development of this theme by Greg Beale in his book, *The Temple and the Church's Mission*. Here Beale argues both that a unifying theme of Scripture, stretching from Genesis to Revelation, is that "God's tabernacling presence, formerly limited to the holy of holies, was to be extended throughout the whole earth,"[43] and that this theme carried the practical implication that believers "are to extend the boundaries of the new garden-temple until Christ returns, when, finally, they will be expanded worldwide."[44] If Beale is correct that elsewhere in the apostolic world this theological *vision* went hand in hand with missionary *practice*, then it is fair to assume the same would hold true for those invested in the theological outlook of Hebrews.[45]

The other implication to be drawn from this theme of "cleansed creation as temple" observes that, consistent with this vision within Hebrews, Golgotha is conceived as the new Most Holy Place, the divine throne room where heaven

---

[41] Laansma, "Hidden Stories"; Laansma, "Hebrews." The relationship of the κατάπαυσις-theme to creation-as-temple and the tabernacle/temple ideas more broadly had been explored earlier in my *Rest*, 41-45, 67-75, 94-101, 252-358. This general pattern likely explains the imagery of the house (οἶκος) in 3:1-6, where both the cosmos as a whole (v. 4) and the faithful (v. 6) are God's "house," over which is Christ the Son/High Priest (3:1, 6; 10:21; cf. *Rest*, 268-72).

[42] "Hidden Stories," 16-17.

[43] G. K. Beale, *The Temple and the Church's Mission: A Biblical Theology of the Dwelling Place of God* (NSBT 17; Downers Grove: InterVarsity, 2004), 25; cf. 392-93. Both broader in vision and fewer in words are Gerhard Von Rad, *The Theology of Israel's Historical Traditions* (vol. 1 of *Old Testament Theology*; trans. D. M. G. Stalker; New York: Harper & Row, 1962), 205, 207; and Wolfhart Pannenberg, *Systematic Theology* (3 vols.; trans. Geoffrey W. Bromiley; Grand Rapids: Eerdmans, 1988), 1:397-401.

[44] Beale, *Temple*, 395.

[45] For Beale's own treatment of Hebrews, see "The inauguration of a new temple in Hebrews," ch. 9 in *Temple*, 293-312, as well as 373-75.

and earth intersect.⁴⁶ In this light we read 13:12-13 as at once a universalization of the act of consecration (no longer just the Levitical priests in the Mosaic sanctuary but *all* of "the people") in which act we are called to participate, and as a summons—grounded in the epochal and covenantal shift that has been the subject matter of the preceding exposition—to the new way for God's people of *redemptive suffering*.⁴⁷ More specifically, the agonistic (12:1-3) way of salvation and the gracious provision are even more closely bound together than the preceding point relating to 10:35 suggested, for here the summons to suffering redemptively⁴⁸ with Christ (ἐξέρχομαι) and the earlier summons to approach the divine throne (προσέρχομαι)⁴⁹ constitute a *single* movement of worship. To put it bluntly, the sacred space of the divine throne—that which we are to "approach" for mercy and grace—is not a "safe enclave" in the midst of a violent and evil world but precisely the place of slaughter and sacrifice, of suffering redemptively with Christ. Even in the summons to "approach the divine throne" the concern is not merely with personal comfort (on the vertical) but at the same time with a life of faithful obedience (on the horizontal).

In short, the cultic imagery of Hebrews' argument finally serves a cosmically universal vision of salvation that has swept up the people of God and, in its exhortations, carries them forward as *active participants* in that great drama.

Thirdly, I merely mention another possible line of thought that is consistent with all of the above, but which is of necessity more speculative. One notices that while other NT writings refer to believers as priests⁵⁰ but never Christ, this is exactly reversed in Hebrews. And yet the priestly *identity* of believers is

---

⁴⁶ Laansma, "Hebrews," 130-33, 142-43; Laansma, "Hidden Stories," 17.

⁴⁷ Note also Attridge, *Hebrews*, 399: "In this equivalent of the call to take up the cross, Hebrews suggests where it is that true participation in the Christian altar is to be found—in accepting the 'reproach of Christ.'"

⁴⁸ Note well, the purpose clause of 13:12 (διὸ καὶ ᾽Ιησοῦς, ἵνα ἁγιάσῃ διὰ τοῦ ἰδίου αἵματος τὸν λαόν, ἔξω τῆς πύλης ἔπαθεν), which informs the meaning of τὸν ὀνειδισμὸν αὐτοῦ φέροντες. There are far deeper currents of theology beneath this, which I cannot develop here, but which pervade the NT writings. For a beginning I refer to Scott Hafemann, "The Role of Suffering in the Mission of Paul," in *The Mission of the Early Church to Jews and Gentiles* (ed. Jostein Ådna and Hans Kvalbein; WUNT 127; Tübingen: Mohr [Siebeck], 2000), 165-84; idem., "A Call to Pastoral Suffering: The Need for Recovering Paul's Model of Ministry in 2 Corinthians," *SBJT* 4 (2000): 22-36; idem., "'Because of Weakness' (Galatians 4:13): The role of suffering in the mission of Paul," in *The Gospel to the Nations, Perspectives on Paul's Mission, In Honor of Peter T. O'Brien* (ed. Peter Bolt and Mark Thompson; Leicester: InterVarsity, 2000), 131-46. Hafemann is dealing with Paul's theology, but I would argue that all this informs *Hebrews'* theological vision.

⁴⁹ 4:16; 7:25; 10:22; 11:6; 12:18, 22.

⁵⁰ Esp. 1 Pet 2:5, 9; Rev 1:6; 5:10; 20:6. The role is implied of course in Rom 15:16.

strongly implied in Hebrews by the very language that is used of them.[51] Considered broadly in the OT context, the priest, according to de Vaux, "is always an intermediary. What the Epistle to the Hebrews says of the high priest is true of every priest: 'Every high priest who is taken from among men is appointed to intervene on behalf of men with God' (He 5:1). . . . the priesthood is an institution for mediation."[52] There is in such a notion at least the potential for a missionary application when this is brought into the NT context. Thus, commenting on Rev 1:6, Greg Beale argues that the roles of priest and king are fulfilled by believers in the present age "especially by being faithful witnesses by mediating Christ's priestly and royal authority to the world. . . . The remainder of [Revelation] will explain exactly how they do this in the midst of the suffering brought on by life in a pagan society."[53] A missiological aspect of the priestly role is explicit in Rom 15:16; its presence in 1 Pet 2:5, 9—recalling Hebrews' many parallels with 1 Peter[54]—is contested,[55] though it seems likely to me.[56] And with a view to the NT generally, Beale contends, "When unbelievers accept the church's mediating witness, they not only come into God's presence, but they begin to participate themselves as mediating priests

---

[51] Cf. John M. Scholer, *Proleptic Priests: Priesthood in the Epistle to the Hebrews* (JSNTSup 49; Sheffield: JSOT, 1991), *passim*; Lindars, *Theology*, 138. From a theological angle, see Douglas Farrow, "Melchizedek and Modernity," in *The Epistle to the Hebrews and Christian Theology* (ed. Richard Bauckham et al.; Grand Rapids: Eerdmans, 2009), 281-301 [293].

[52] Roland de Vaux, *Religious Institutions* (vol. 2 of *Ancient Israel*; New York: McGraw-Hill, 1961), 357. For John H. Walton in *Ancient Near Eastern Thought and the Old Testament*, 130, and in personal communication, the priests served firstly to maintain sacred space, a role that included but was not restricted to that of mediation. Still, *Hebrews* stresses the mediatorial role (5:1). Perhaps I should make explicit as well that, in my view, within the OT narrative broadly (at least, as read through the NT), the Mosaic covenant is to be seen as embedded within and serving the ends of the Abrahamic covenant. Accordingly the priestly role is not restricted merely to mediating on behalf of God's chosen, the Israelites, but is ultimately with a view to God's purposes to bring all nations to himself (Isa 2:1-4; 66:1-24; cf. Gen 12:3; Gal 3:15-18).

[53] G. K. Beale, *The Book of Revelation: A Commentary on the Greek Text* (NIGTC; Grand Rapids: Eerdmans, 1999), 193. David E. Aune, *Revelation* (3 vols.; WBC 52A–52C; Dallas: Word Books, 1997), 1:47-49, differs.

[54] Attridge, *Hebrews*, 30-31; Hurst, *Background*, 125-30.

[55] J. Ramsey Michaels, *1 Peter* (WBC 49; Waco: Word Books, 1988), 106-13; David L. Balch, *Let Wives Be Submissive: The Domestic Code in 1 Peter* (SBLMS 26; Atlanta: Scholars Press, 1981), 132-36.

[56] With Paul J. Achtemeier, *1 Peter* (Hermeneia; Minneapolis: Fortress, 1996), 154-58, 163-67; E. G. Selwyn, *The First Epistle of St. Peter*, (2d ed.; London: Macmillan, 1947; repr., Grand Rapids: Baker, 1981), 291-98; John H. Elliott, *The Elect and the Holy: An Exegetical Examination of 1 Peter 2:4-10 and the Phrase* βασίλειον ἱεράτευμα (NovTSup 12; Leiden: Brill, 1966), 196-98, 219-26.

who witness."⁵⁷ But I will take it no further as we are drawing an implication from an implication: from the implied priesthood of believers to the entailment of a mediatorial role on behalf of the surrounding world. And yet it will be clear enough that such an idea falls in line with the whole tendency of Hebrews' theology as we have sketched it to this point. Indeed, I would suggest that it is through this filter that we might hear *paraenetic* strains even in Hebrews 5:1-2, and *missiological* strains in 13:15-16.⁵⁸

CONCLUSION

In focusing on the immediate need of endurance and faithfulness Hebrews deploys a missionary theology for missionary ends. It is not merely about securing their own salvation but doing so precisely through the faithfulness that carried forward Jesus' own mission. Support for this thesis stems from the convergence of several lines of evidence: a defensible theory as to the writing's setting within the world mission, its overlap with other dominant strands of NT theology, indications of the behaviors and experiences of the community, the theological vision of the book and the deployment of that theology, and the exhortations to faithfulness. And, admitting that little on the surface of Hebrews asserts this outlook, we note once again that whatever modern scholars might speculate about the "community" and *Sitz im Leben* of the letter of Acts 15:23-29 (distrusting Luke's narrative setting, that is), for Luke its genesis and point lay *precisely* in the world mission. For Luke, at least, to miss this would be fundamentally to misunderstand that letter as a speech-act.

In sum, then, when we ask why the readers of Hebrews had evidently slackened in their enthusiasm for their Christian identity, it is clear that there were both internal (psychological, intellectual) and external (social, material) causes. The latter causes feature prominently, both explicitly (e.g., in the recollection of their earlier suffering and endurance) and implicitly (e.g., in ch. 11), in the writer's argument. And whence the suffering?⁵⁹ Ultimately, we have

---

⁵⁷ Beale, *Temple*, 399.

⁵⁸ It should be clear that I am certainly not arguing that the missiological aspect is the only or even primary aspect of the priestly identity of believers in Hebrews, but only that it *is*, perhaps, an aspect and, as such, would be consistent with the theological vision of the discourse as a whole.

⁵⁹ There were possibly, perhaps even probably, a range of issues at play in the apostatizing trend that the author sensed: material persecution, direct and indirect social pressures, theological ignorance, struggles of conscience in the light of a lifetime of religious practice prior to conversion, and more. I am not reducing the problem to a theory of "diminished fervor for evangelization," as if this can be listed as just another option! It is rather the case that in this writer's view, as in Paul's, a robust πίστις in the gospel naturally and logically correlates with an enthusiasm for its advancement in the world—that is, with mission. Faithfulness is finally, irreducibly, and crucially missionary in character.

argued, one should envisage a community that had been bold in its open witness, moving forward with the world mission. Now, however, they have shied from the struggle. The writer understood that at the heart of the matter was a lack of understanding of and confidence in the nature and efficacy of the salvation wrought for them by Christ. Accordingly in terms with which they can identify—albeit quite likely in a fresh way as it relates to the exposition of Psalm 110:4—the writer of Hebrews is urging them not merely to stand their ground, but to resume their struggle in and for the gospel, following τὸν τῆς πίστεως ἀρχηγὸν καὶ τελειωτήν toward arrival at the ultimate goal of entrance into the sacred space of God's κατάπαυσις.[60]

---

[60] I began by characterizing this essay as an exercise in reading against the grain. If, however, we take all this for granted and read Hebrews in its light, it might be possible to hear positive, missionary applications in (firstly) Ps 110:1 (1:13; 10:13; cf. Isa 60:13-14). At the least, an author who finds a positive *promise* in a solemn *threat* (Ps 95 in Heb 3:7–4:11) might not protest at such a reading of his own argument. If in Ps 110 it is God's enemies who are made a footstool, in Isa 60:13 God glorifies the place of his feet through the homage of foreigners. J. Blenkinsopp, *Isaiah* (3 vols.; AB 19–19B; New York: Doubleday, 2000–2003), 3:211, comments on the poem of Isa 60:1-22, "We hear unmistakable echoes of our poem in an eschatological addendum to a late liturgical passage in the first major section of the book [citing 24:23] . . . . This in its turn links with the hymns celebrating the kingship of YHVH (Pss 93, 95-99) that take up old, familiar hymns of combat, the subduing of the chaotic waters, creation, and temple building (von Rad). These enthronement psalms speak of the coming of God in salvation and judgment . . . , they describe how he sets up his throne and, with it, his footstool in Jerusalem . . . , his 'holy mountian' . . . , and how this will be an occasion for Zion to rejoice . . . and for all people to see his glory . . . This is what the poem in ch. 60 is about, and it leads us to think of this first stanza as in essence proclaiming the inauguration of the kingship of YHVH in Jerusalem, specifically in the temple rebuilt or to be rebuilt." There are considerable contacts with Hebrews in general in all this (note the allusion to Ps 95, among other things), even if the direction of flow is toward Zion rather than a "going out." Secondly, e.g., it might be that the role of a "teacher" (διδάσκαλος) in 5:12 was not confined to intra-faith instruction; cf. David Peterson, *Hebrews and Perfection: An Examination of the Concept of Perfection in the 'Epistle to the Hebrews'* (SNTSMS 47; Cambridge: Cambridge University Press, 1982), 178: "The rebuke of 5:12 may be related to this tendency to withdraw from confrontation with the world and the loss of certainty that this presupposes. In this case, διδάσκαλοι may refer specifically to the idea of communicating the faith to outsiders." Thirdly, perhaps it is also along these lines that we should hear the exhortation to "pursue peace along with everyone, and the holiness without which no one will see the Lord" (for this translation see Lane, *Hebrews*, 2:437-38, 449-51). This pursuit is meant to be understood in keeping with the commission to extend the sanctifying effects of Christ's sacrifice to all people (13:12).

POSTSCRIPT

We have mounted a narrowly historical argument with respect to the author, recipients, and the earliest church's mission. If we may now speak in frankly theological terms, we would do well to situate the entire argument of Hebrews within the most basic movement of the *missio Dei*.

With its focus on entrance into the divine presence, into the Most Holy Place by means of cultic cleansing, God is encountered in Hebrews above all in his *holiness*. In this Hebrews moves within the deepest currents of the Old and New Testaments. From this perspective we recall the words of Wolfart Pannenberg in his *Systematic Theology*: ". . . the holy threatens the profane world because God does not remain a totally otherworldly God but manifests his deity in the human world. . . . The power of the holy, which is a threat to life in its destructive force, invades the human world in order to incorporate it into its own sphere."[61] Likewise Gerhard von Rad: the OT "regards the hitherto existing limitation of Jahweh's holiness to a special cultic sphere as something temporary, which will be followed by the ultimate universalizing." Finally, according to Zech 14, "the whole realm of the secular will be taken up into Jahweh's holiness. When that happens, Jahweh's holiness will have attained its utmost goal."[62] In this light, and thinking of the disregard paid Hebrews by those who consider it to be too narrowly taken up with parochial, antiquated problems of temple and sacrifice within Jewish Christianity of the first century, we may say that perhaps no book of Scripture is brought more directly to bear on what is properly basic to the existence of *all* humanity and *all* of creation in the presence of a holy God. Out of the mystery of God's infinity,[63] Hebrews sounds forth *gospel*.

---

[61] Wolfhart Pannenberg, *Systematic Theology*, 1:398.
[62] Gerhard von Rad, *The Theology of Israel's Historical Traditions* (vol. 1 of *Old Testament Theology*; trans. D. M. G. Stalker; New York: Harper & Row, 1962), 207.
[63] Pannenberg, *Theology*, 1:397: "The confession of God's holiness is also closely related to his infinity, so closely, indeed, that the thought of infinity as *God's* infinity needs the statement of his holiness for its elucidation . . ." (italics in original).

21

THE MISSION TO THE NATIONS IN THE BOOK OF REVELATION

Grant R. Osborne

At first glance it would seem that the theme of "mission" is incongruous in an apocalyptic work that centers on the judgment of God upon the nations.[1] Yet the argument of this article is that mission is not just present but is a key theme in the book and is intended to act as a counterpoint to the judgment motif. First, let me define mission as the proclamation of truth intended to bring about the conversion of people from one worldview to another. I. Howard Marshall says that the NT documents centered on this theme and resulted from

> a two-part mission, first, the mission of Jesus sent by God to inaugurate his kingdom with the blessings that it brings to people and to call people to respond to it, and then the mission of his followers called to continue his work by proclaiming him as Lord and Savior, and calling people to faith and ongoing commitment to him, as a result of which his church grows.[2]

Therefore, it is fitting that this article be dedicated to him, as it attempts to argue that Revelation is part of this NT theme.

I believe that there are three purposes in the book: to encourage the beleaguered Christians and challenge them to persevere and remain faithful; to warn weak Christians that they must stop following the lies of the false teachers or suffer the wrath of God; and to convince the non-Christians that they must turn to God or suffer eternal punishment. The latter two purposes contain within them God's continuing mission to redeem the lost. We will begin with the place of the nations in the book.

---

[1] Jon Paulien, "The Lion/Lamb King: Reading the Apocalypse from Current Culture," in *Reading the Book of Revelation: A Resource for Students* (ed. D. L. Barr; Atlanta: SBL, 2003), 151-63 [159], states that the value of apocalyptic is "not primarily in its predictive power, but in its diagnostic ability. Apocalyptic helps us to understand ourselves . . . (and) mirrors reality in a way that bypasses our psychological and emotional defense mechanisms, and strikes home with powerful force where we least expect it." This is the case with the mission theme; it is unexpected and especially striking in an apocalyptic environment.

[2] I. Howard Marshall, *New Testament Theology: Many Witnesses, One Gospel* (Downers Grove: InterVarsity, 2004), 34-35.

THE NATIONS IN THE BOOK OF REVELATION

The nations, contrary to what we would expect, are not just the subject of rebellion and the object of God's wrath. Τὰ ἔθνη occurs twenty-three times in the book, with three connotations—predominantly rebellion and judgment (fourteen occurrences), yet also the subject of God's grace and mercy (seven times), and twice with both connotations. In addition, "those who inhabit the earth" occurs ten times and primarily describes rebellious humanity (e.g., in 13:8 they worship the beast) which lives only for the things of this world. Seven times the full formula "every tribe and language and people and nation" (with differing order of the terms) occurs in the book, with three centering on mission and repentance (5:9; 7:9; 14:6), three on opposition and judgment (11:9; 13:7; 17:15), and one deliberately ambiguous (10:11).[3] Let us explore these themes, beginning with the negative passages.

THE NATIONS UNDER CONDEMNATION

There are four levels to this aspect of our study. First, the nations reject God, standing as enemies against his people. In 11:1-2 John uses the temple as a symbol for the Christian community (whether it is Solomon's, Ezekiel's, or Herod's temple is not important for our point), and the measuring of temple and worshippers (as in land surveying today) indicates God's ownership over his people and his protection of them, replicating the sealing of the saints in 7:4-8.[4] The exclusion of the "outer court" builds on the fact that in Herod's court the Gentiles were restricted to the "court of the Gentiles," so this "trampling" (alluding to Dan 8:11-14; Zech 12:3) parallels Luke 21:24, Jerusalem "trampled on by the Gentiles until the times of the Gentiles are fulfilled." Thus the nations join the false trinity (16:13, the dragon, beast, and false prophet) in persecuting and killing the saints.

This image continues in 11:9 where all the nations rejoice over the death of the two witnesses, who function as symbols of the witnessing church (more on this later).[5] Their ministry of prophecy continues unabated until the end of the

---

[3] See the extensive study of this fourfold formula in Richard Bauckham, *The Climax of Prophecy: Studies on the Book of Revelation* (Edinburgh: T&T Clark, 1993), 326-37. We will interact with his thesis on the conversion of the nations later.

[4] So the majority of commentators, e.g., David Aune, *Revelation* (3 vols.; WBC 52A–C; Nashville: Thomas Nelson, 1998), 2:593-98; Stephen S. Smalley, *The Revelation to John: A Commentary on the Greek Text of the Apocalypse* (Downers Grove: InterVarsity, 2005), 270-71. Measuring is a prophetic acted parable for God preserving his people, as in Ezek 40:1-6; 42:20.

[5] This is the interpretation of the majority of scholars. For other possibilities, see Grant R. Osborne, *Revelation* (BECNT; Grand Rapids: Baker, 2002), 417.

42 months/1260 days (11:2, 3), when the "beast"[6] arises and kills them. The "nations" have clearly joined the beast and refuse them burial (the ultimate indignity for both Jews and Romans), gloating over them and turning the scene into a virtual religious celebration, seen both in "rejoice" (εὐφραίνονται, used often in the LXX for cultic joy)[7] and in the exchange of gifts (as in the Jewish feast of Purim and the Roman feasts of Saturnalia and Kalends).[8] The primary term for the unbelieving nations is "earthdwellers" (lit. "those who inhabit the earth"), connoting the fact that they live only for the things of this world (3:10; 6:10; 8:13 et al.) and worship the earthly gods (9:20-21). They have joined the beast in pursuing and martyring the saints (6:9, 15), as seen in the quote in 11:18 from Ps 2:1, "The nations were angry," depicted in the psalm as rage "against the Lord and against his Anointed One" (Ps 2:2), here adding also their anger against the people of God.

Second, the nations follow the beast and are under his direct authority (13:7b), meaning they willingly participate in his evil. Thus they are personified as under the control of their sins. In 14:8 Babylon the Great (from Dan 4:30) is prophesied as "fallen" (from Isa 21:9) because she "made all the nations drink" the "wine of her passion for immorality" (also 18:3), with τοῦ θυμοῦ a play on words moving from the "passion" for sin on the part of the nations in v. 8 to 14:10, where as a result God will make them drink a new wine, "the wine of the wrath [τοῦ θυμοῦ] of God." It is debated whether "immorality" in Revelation is idolatry or spiritual immorality[9] or whether it refers to sexual sin as well,[10] but either way it connotes a deliberate turning from God to a life of self-centered living. In 17:15 the Great Prostitute "sits" or rules (is enthroned) over the nations, meaning they are completely under her control, embedded within the sphere of her sin.

This sinful lifestyle is also seen as economic in 18:23, where the merchants are condemned because "by your magic spell all the nations were led astray." Economic exploitation is a major emphasis in Rev 17–18, seen in the extravagant jewelry and clothes of the Great Prostitute in 17:4, the list of luxuries in 18:12-13, the condemnation of the "wealth and splendor" of Babylon the Great in 18:14-17, and the "riches" gained by the shipping industry in 18:19. Clearly, luxurious living is part of the "immorality" of the nations.

Third, the "nations" are central in the so-called "millennial" passage of

---

[6] The identity of τὸ θηρίον is not important to this paper. Whether the final Antichrist or a symbol of all the opponents to God (cf. Dan 7:7-22), this creature personifies the tendency of God's enemies to stand against all that he is and against all who constitute his people.

[7] So Bultmann, "εὐφραίνω, εὐφροσύνη," *TDNT* 2:772-75 [773-74].

[8] So Aune, *Revelation*, 2:623; Robert Mounce, *The Book of Revelation* (2d ed.; NICNT; Grand Rapids: Eerdmans, 1998), 227.

[9] Beale, *Revelation*, 756.

[10] Osborne, *Revelation*, 538-39.

20:1-10. The great debate between amillennial, premillennial, and postmillennial positions is not germane to this paper; I will center on its place in the narrative of the book, where it serves to sum up the themes of chs. 6–19. All can agree on the core themes of the sovereignty of God and futility of Satan (20:1-3), the vindication of the saints (20:4-6), and the guilt and judgment of the nations (20:7-9). Satan is bound in v. 3 "to keep him from deceiving the nations." Deception is the primary activity of Satan, as he "leads the whole world astray" (12:9). This sums up NT teaching on this point. Satan is the "prince" or "ruler" of this world (John 12:31; Eph 2:2), "the God of this world" who "blinds the minds" of unbelievers (2 Cor 4:4). He is a "roaring lion" trying to "devour" (1 Pet 5:8) and "trap" (1 Tim 3:7) those not trusting in God. Yet in v. 8 when Satan is released, he immediately "deceives the nations" and they flock after him to their doom.

The Book of Revelation has the strongest teaching on total depravity in the Bible. "There is a great deal of emphasis on the evil acts of the nations: their shameful deeds (17:4, 5; 21:27), murder (6:9; 9:21; 13:7, 10, 15; 20:4), celebrating evil (11:10), immorality (2:14, 20, 21), sorcery (8:21; 18:23; 22:15), idolatry and blasphemy (2:14, 20; 9:20), falsehood (2:2; 3:9; 14:20), and a summary in 21:8."[11] This theme is present also in the passages where God calls the sinners to repentance (see further below), and they refuse, preferring to worship their earthly gods and curse his name than come to him (9:20-21; 16:9, 11, 21). As in the plagues on Egypt (the trumpet and bowl judgments reproduce the plagues) the outpouring of judgment disproves the earthly gods and shows the impotence and foolishness of lives lived only for this world. Yet still they reject Christ and turn against his followers. God has been shown to be completely sovereign (the main theme of the book), yet the nations want nothing to do with "Lord God Almighty" (the primary title, occurring nine times). This theme culminates in 20:1-10 where in the narrative plot the nations who have experienced Satan for one lifetime live for fourteen lifetimes (= 1000 years) with Christ in charge and the saints "ruling" under him.[12] Then at the end of that time Satan is released and in an instant the nations flock after him. Their refusal of all things having to do with God and Christ is complete.

Fourth, the nations are subject to judgment. Yet the theme in the book is not so much judgment as the absolute justice of God's judgment, the *lex talionis* (law of retribution) motif, seen especially in 16:5-7, "You are just in these judgments . . . true and just are your judgments" (= 15:3; 19:2). All condemnation by God flows out of his δίκαιος, with a double meaning connoting his "justice" that results from his "righteous" being. In 16:19 the great earthquake of the seventh bowl causes "all the cities of the nations" to "collapse," in 19:15 the "sharp sword" that comes out of the mouth of Christ

---

[11] Osborne, *Revelation*, 39.

[12] This does not assume 1000 years is literal; I actually think it symbolic. Rather, this is the "story" of 20:1-10 as a narrative.

"strikes down the nations" at the battle of Armageddon, and in 20:9-10 the nations surround God's people and then are "devoured" by "fire from heaven." The absolute destruction of those who oppose God is clear. Two other passages use Ps 2:8—in 12:5 the "male child" (Christ) is destined to "rule all the nations with an iron scepter," and in 2:26-27 the victorious saints will be given by Christ "authority over the nations—he will rule them with an iron scepter; he will dash them to pieces like pottery." From the psalm itself this is not the "scepter" of kingly rule[13] but the shepherd's club (following the imagery of Ps 2) to "shatter" or destroy the nations. The idea of the saints joining Christ in destroying the nations is probably linked to the image of them as part of the army (with the angelic hosts) that accompany Christ at his Parousia in 17:14; 19:14. The final image of judgment is the most terrible of all, the "great white throne" judgment of 20:11-15 when those whose names are "not found written in the book of life" are "thrown into the lake of fire," joining the false trinity (19:20; 20:10) in eternal torment (cf. 14:10-11). Yet throughout this the emphasis is not just on God punishing his enemies, especially not on his getting even with them for their rebellion, but on the deserved nature of these judgments. God is just, and the earthdwellers have brought it on themselves. God is "destroying" the "destroyers of the earth" (11:18d).

There are many in modern times who are greatly offended by this litany of terrible abuse, as if God had anger issues and was taking out his frustration on all who had crossed him. Many today call this one of the terrible books of history because it depicts a judging God. Yet these themes would have offended no one in the ancient world. Keener states, "Jewish traditions often describe this day (of final judgment), the time for mercy and patience are [sic] over (4 Ezra 7:33), and the wicked will be ashamed (1 Enoch 97:6)" as "angels report human misdeeds before God's tribunal immediately after the earth's destruction and before the resurrection of the wicked (cf. *Sib. Or.* 2:215-16)."[14] Those who decry this book do not understand the holiness of God, the fact that sin is detestable to him and must be wiped away; this was the basis for the laws of clean and unclean and the sacrificial system in the OT. The Jewish people did not see how they could walk into God's temple and walk out alive. "What made the purity laws so critical in the Levitical system is the fact that in the tabernacle and temple Yahweh was actually present among his people. A holy

---

[13] See Colin J. Hemer, *The Letters to the Seven Churches of Asia in Their Local Setting* (JSNTSup 11; Sheffield: JSOT Press, 1986), 123-24, who says the rod of iron here parallels the sword at Thyatira and connotes "dominion" rather than "destruction."

[14] Craig Keener, *Revelation* (NIVAC; Grand Rapids: Zondervan, 2000), 469. See further Ronald Herms, *An Apocalypse for the Church and for the World: The Narrative Function of Universal Language in the Book of Revelation* (New York: Walter de Gruyter, 2006), 161-65, who discusses this from the standpoint of 17:1–21:8 and points out that the judgment centers entirely on the enemies of God in contrast to the faithful followers of the Lamb.

God must destroy all uncleanness from the land, so what is to keep him from destroying Israel?"[15] In Rev 4:8 God is worshipped as "holy, holy, holy," and the *trisagion* is not just the key for our worship; it is the key for understanding divine justice. David Barr says it well:

> Surely this story is built on the mythology of holy war (and that itself may be ethically problematic), but just as surely John consistently demythologizes the war—or perhaps more accurately, remythologizes the warrior with the image of the suffering savior so that the death of the warrior and not some later battle is the crucial event. At every juncture in this story where good triumphs over evil a close examination shows that the victory is finally attributed to the death of Jesus.[16]

THE NATIONS AS THE FOCUS OF DIVINE GRACE AND MERCY

This book does not focus only on the destruction of the evil nations; it centers also on the redemption of the nations and the mission by which this occurs. We must begin with the critical use of Dan 7:13 and Zech 12:10 in Rev 1:7 which forms the first of a two-part conclusion (vv. 7, 8) to the prologue of 1:1-8. The same conflation of OT texts occurs in reverse order in Matt 24:30 where it follows the prophecy from Joel 2:10 and heralds the coming of the Son of Man to "gather his elect" (24:31). This shows the two passages were likely familiar as part of a *testimonia* tradition.[17] The Danielic material details the destruction of the four "beasts" by the Ancient of Days (7:11-12) and the coming of "the one like the son of man" to receive "everlasting dominion" over the nations. The Zechariah text also follows a description of the destruction of the "nations of the earth" who have become Jerusalem's enemies (12:1-9). Yet in 12:10 the "mourning" takes place among "the inhabitants of Jerusalem" who are given "a spirit of grace and supplication" and thereby "mourn" in repentance when they look upon "the one they have pierced." As Beale points out, John alters the Zechariah text by adding both πᾶς ὀφθαλμός and αἱ φυλαὶ τῆς γῆς, thus universalizing the repentance from Israel to the nations. Thereby Beale sees this

---

[15] Grant R. Osborne, *The Hermeneutical Spiral: A Comprehensive Introduction to Biblical Interpretation* (2d ed.; Downers Grove: InterVarsity, 2006), cf. Richard Averbeck, "Clean and Unclean," *NIDOTTE* 4:477-86.

[16] David L. Barr, "Moral Issues in Reading John's Apocalypse," in *Reading the Book of Revelation*, 97-108 [101]. So also Edith M. Humphrey, *And I Turned to See the Voice: The Rhetoric of Vision in the New Testament* (Grand Rapids: Baker, 2007), 182-83, who says, "Though the book, in word and picture, is concerned with power, it does not concern itself in the first place with empowerment but with suffering and reliance on a mighty God."

[17] Bauckham, *Climax*, 318.

as a positive promise as the nations "assume the role of repentant Israel."[18] Marko Jauhiainen similarly sees this as repentance signifying that the nations join in the "deliverance and restoration of God's people."[19] However, many commentators believe that in Rev 1:7 the mourning is not in repentance but connotes a consternation in light of the divine judgment about to fall on them, as in the parallel Rev 18:9, when "the kings of the earth . . . weep and mourn over" Babylon's destruction.[20]

These two alternatives are not an either-or but a both-and. "Whether repentance will follow, John does not say; only that sorrow will be one outcome of the divine judgment which is arriving."[21] Most likely John intends a deliberate ambiguity here, as judgment can be connoted in terms of Christ as "ruler of the kings of the earth" in 1:5c and depicted with blazing eyes and bronze feet ablaze in 1:14b-15 (from Dan 10:6) while at the same time mission and repentance can be seen in Christ as faithful witness in 1:5b, as freeing people by his blood in 1:5e, and as standing among the seven lampstands (established by his mission) in 1:13-14. As such this establishes a pattern that inaugurates the two paths the nations take in the book (some to repentance, others to rejection and judgment), for this ambiguity continues. We have already traced the theme of judgment among the nations. Now let us consider the themes of mission and salvation among the nations in the book.

The throne room scene of Rev 4–5 is the turning point of the book as the focus moves from the troubled problems of earth to the majestic glory of the transcendent God in heaven (ch. 4) and the redemptive work of the Lamb on earth (ch. 5). The oneness motif is evident as the Lamb joins God at "the center of the throne" (v. 6) and in the worship by the elders and living creatures (vv. 8-12). In these two chapters God is worshipped twice as the one (unlike Caesar) who is "worthy" (4:6b-11), the Lamb is worshipped twice as "worthy" (5:8-12), and then God and the Lamb are worshipped together as deserving "praise and glory and honor and power forever and ever" (5:13-14). The two are one in worship! The important verse for our purposes is 5:9, where the emphasis of 1:5 is made more explicit, where Christ is shown "worthy" because of his sacrificial death (ἐσφάγης, depicting the "lamb to the slaughter" of Isa 53:7). The result is, "you have purchased men for God by your blood." In John ἠγόρασας utilizes a commercial metaphor with redemptive significance, as it was often used of freeing prisoners of war from bondage as well as of

---

[18] G. K. Beale, *The Book of Revelation* (NIGTC; Grand Rapids: Eerdmans, 1999), 196-97; see also Bauckham, *Climax*, 318-22.
[19] Marko Jauhiainen, *The Use of Zechariah in Revelation* (WUNT 199; Tübingen: Mohr [Siebeck], 2005), 144 (cf. 102-107, 142-44).
[20] E.g., Robert Mounce, *Revelation*, 51; Heinz Giesen, *Die Offenbarung des Johannes* (RNT; Regensburg: Friedrich Pustet, 1997), 79-80; Keener, *Revelation*, 73.
[21] Smalley, *Revelation*, 38.

emancipating people from bondage to sin.[22]

The "blood of the lamb" from 1:5d "freed us" (the church), but this is made more explicit in 5:9 where it is explained that this redemption has freed[23] people "from every tribe and language and people and nation." This four-fold formula (see above) stems from the threefold list of "peoples, languages, and nations" in Dan 3:4 (expanded to four in the LXX, cf. also Dan 3:7, 29; 5:19; 6:25; 7:14) and reflects also the fourfold formula for the table of nations in Gen 10:5, 20, 31.[24] We are at the heart of the mission theme—Jesus' sacrificial blood has brought God's redemption to all the nations and made it possible for them "to be a kingdom and priests to serve our God" (1:6 = 5:10). In Christ the nations, by responding to God's redemptive mission, will be elevated to royalty and priesthood, fulfilling Exod 19:5, 6.

In 5:9 we see how the nations are brought into the people of God, but in 7:9 we see the results of that salvific activity, as "a great multitude . . . from every nation, tribe, people, and language stand before the throne" to receive their reward. This is the first of four passages (7:9; 15:3, 4; 21:24, 26; 22:2) describing the believing nations in terms of their heavenly reward, and the first two occur in sections that are proleptic of the new heavens and new earth of 21:1–22:5 (which contains the last two passages). There is direct continuity between the saints who are sealed in 7:4-8 and the multitude that is before the throne in heaven in 7:9-17. "As 7:1-8 presents the church militant on earth, sealed and drawn up in battle formation before the coming struggle, 7:9-17 presents the church after the battle, triumphant in heaven."[25] The nations, though rebellious and in opposition, are nevertheless the focus of divine grace, and those who respond are redeemed, included among God's people, and recipients of eternal reward. Once again we have here the fourfold formula to highlight the extent of the divine mercy. "The Christian church is international in character and includes not only those from every race . . . picking up the listing in 7:4-8, but also those with every possible background: national, social, political, and cultural. They are now united with a common language."[26] In a later section we will discuss the implications of this for the extent of the

---

[22] See Elisabeth Schüssler Fiorenza, *The Book of Revelation: Justice and Judgment* (Philadelphia: Fortress, 1985), 73-74; George R. Beasley-Murray, *The Book of Revelation* (NCBC; London: Marshall, Morgan and Todd, 1978), 127.

[23] For this as connoting forgiveness of sin, see Mark Bredin, *Jesus, Revolutionary of Peace: A Nonviolent Christology in the Book of Revelation* (Milton Keynes, UK: Paternoster, 2005), 182.

[24] For this theme see Bauckham, *Climax*, 327-29; Aune, *Revelation*, 1:361-62; Beale, *Revelation*, 359-60.

[25] M. E. Boring, *Revelation* (Interpretation; Louisville: John Knox, 1989), 131. The 144,000 who are sealed is an ideal number (multiples of twelve and ten) for the "great multitude" here. The twelve tribes are in part pictured in battle formation according to many.

[26] Smalley, *Revelation*, 191.

success of the mission.

This image of the triumphant Gospel among the nations and their presence in heaven is continued in the song of the victorious saints in 15:2-4. The scene is reminiscent of the throne room scene of 4:6, with the saints standing on a "crystal sea," alluding to the firmament of the waters in Gen 1:7, itself symbolized in the bronze sea of Solomon's temple (1 Kgs 7:23-26) and the icy expanse above the living creatures in Ezek 1:22. Here though the crystal sea is not clear as in 4:6 but is "mixed with fire," connoting the fiery judgments about to descend in the seven bowls but also reminiscent of God's deliverance of his people through the Red Sea, depicting the "new exodus" of the triumphant saints[27] ("victorious over the beast"—note the image of the believers as conquerors in the "overcomer" passages of 2:7, 11, 17, 26; 3:5, 12, 21 as well as 5:5; 6:2; 11:7; 12:11; 13:7; 17:14; 21:7). These followers from among the nations are given "harps" (linking them with the celestial elders of 5:8) and join in the heavenly worship of the book by singing "the song of Moses" (reflecting both Exod 15:1-19 and Deut 31:30–32:43), again with the new exodus imagery of liberation and deliverance. In the appositional addition, "namely, the song of the Lamb," it is clear that the victory was wrought by the Lamb in the sacrificial offering of his blood (cf. 1:5; 5:9).

The hymn has an ABA pattern, with praise for the salvific deeds of God framing the central question/affirmation, "Who will not fear you, O Lord, and glorify your name?" In the next section we will discuss the importance of "fear/glorify" language in Revelation as the language of repentance. For our purposes here the two important parts are the title of God in 15:3b and the nations worshipping in 15:4b. The normal title for the omnipotent God in the book, "Lord God Almighty" (nine times, stressing that God shows himself to be cosmic Lord by exercising his all-powerful sovereignty), is further clarified by the title "King of the nations"[28] (related to Jesus as "ruler of the kings of the earth" in 1:5). Alluding to Jer 10:7 ("Who will not fear you, O King of the nations?") this introduces one of the main themes of the book, the absolute justice of God in judging the nations, for the acclamation "just and true are your ways" will be repeated twice more in 16:5 and 19:2 to celebrate God's righteous wrath against his enemies. Thus 15:3 sums up the first half of this essay, the nations as the subjects of God's just anger. But 15:4 introduces a startling new image—because of the just, righteous deeds of God "all the nations will come and worship before you." So this acts as a fitting summary of both the themes regarding the nations, who experience wrath due to rejection

---

[27] See George B. Caird, *A Commentary of the Revelation of St. John the Divine* (BNTC; New York: Harper & Row, 1966), 197; Beale, *Revelation*, 789; Smalley, *Revelation*, 384.

[28] See Herms, *Apocalypse for the Church*, 207-208, who notes the contrast with the frequent phrase "kings of the earth" (1:5; 6:15; 16:12-16; 17:14; 19:15-19; 21:24) to emphasize "the universal kingship of God and Christ."

but receive mercy when they repent. As said in Jas 2:13, "mercy triumphs over judgment," for God is first of all a gracious and merciful God. As will be stated below, this does not mean universal salvation, as the phrase "all the nations" is hyperbole for "many among" the nations who will rejoice in God's redemptive deeds.[29]

The third passage describing the nations in heaven is 21:24, 26, and it is part of the "new heavens and new earth" vision of 21:1–22:5. In that glorious description, the basic story is told in 21:1-6 (the descending of the New Jerusalem) and it is then expanded in two ways, describing heaven as the eternal Holy of Holies (21:9-27) and then as the final Eden (22:1-5). In v. 24 "the nations will walk by the light" of the glory of God and of the Lamb, meaning they will bask in the Shekinah glory of God that will infuse the heavenly realm. This statement completes the theme of the conversion of the nations in the book, and the rest of this passage confirms it. In v. 24b "the kings of the earth bring their splendor [δόξα] into" the Holy City, and in v. 26 "the glory [δόξα] and honor [τιμή] of the nations will be brought into it." The "glory" and "honor" of the nations reflects the gifts the nations will lay at the feet of their sovereign God. All the "fame and reputation"[30] that belonged to the nations on earth are now submitted to the glorious God of the heavens. This fulfills the Isaianic promise of the pilgrimage of the nations to Zion, especially Isa 60:3, 5, 11, "Nations will come to your light . . . to you the riches of the nations will come . . . the wealth of the nations—their kings led in triumphal procession" (cf. also Isa 2:2, 5; 9:2; 42:6; 49:6-8, 23; 51:4; 60:17).[31]

Finally, Rev 22:2 provides the conclusion to this theme. The heavenly throne is now occupied by "God and the Lamb," and the salvific highway of Isa 40:3 is at the heart of the New Eden, made out of "pure gold like transparent glass" according to 21:21. In the middle of this great thoroughfare is "the water of life," with "tree(s) of life" on both sides of the river in fulfillment of Ezek 47:12, with "fruit trees of all kinds" growing "on both banks of the river." In Jewish literature these trees root in "an immortal land" (*Odes Sol.* 11:16) with "unspoiled fruit" growing in Paradise (*4 Ezra* 7:123-24) and made available to the righteous (*1 En.* 25:4-5).[32] In this "the leaves of the tree are for the healing of the nations," with τῶν ἐθνῶν an objective genitive, "will heal the nations," another reference to Ezek 47:12 where the leaves produce healing.[33] The final Eden will be characterized by eternal healing. This does not mean that healing

---

[29] Beale, *Revelation*, 797-98; Smalley, *Revelation*, 388. Keener, *Revelation*, 386, speaks of "representatives of all peoples."
[30] Aune, *Revelation*, 1:17-22; 3:1173.
[31] See Aune, *Revelation*, 3:1171.
[32] Osborne, *Revelation*, 771.
[33] Simon Woodman, *The Book of Revelation* (London: SCM, 2008), 210-11, sees this "indicating that creation itself has a role in the restoration of the fractured human condition," culminating the theme in the book of a renewed and restored creation.

will still be needed, for we are told in 21:4, 27 that there will be no more death, mourning, pain or impurity in the eternal city. Rather, this symbolizes all the spiritual "healing" that the Lamb has brought to the nations.

THE MISSION TO THE NATIONS

THE MEANING AND EXTENT OF THE MISSION

If the average reader were to be asked if such a theme existed in the Apocalypse, they would doubt it strongly due to the predominant theme of judgment and the wrath of God in the book. Yet both themes exist side-by-side. Marshall states that the main purpose of the visions regarding God's work in the world "was to assure them that although there would be martyrdoms, nevertheless God would vindicate his people by judging their opponents both in such a way as to warn them to repent before it was too late and also as a final judgment upon their opposition to him."[34] In other words, mission and judgment are interdependent aspects of Revelation. In my commentary I propose seven theological themes that reverberate through the three great judgment septets, and one of them is that

> the outpouring of judgment has a redemptive purpose and is part of the final chance to repent (9:20; 14:6-7; 16:9, 11). God's judgments are an act of mercy, for he shows the powerlessness of the earthly gods (as in the Egyptian plagues . . .) and calls on sinful mankind to "fear God and give him glory, because the hour of his judgment has come (14:7)." In this way the judgments are part of God's mission to the world.[35]

Yet this is controversial, because some reject the viability of an offer of repentance and say judgment is the entire purpose of the book. Therefore we must examine the relevant material in some detail to ascertain which side of the issue best fits the relevant data.

The key passage for any such discussion is 14:6-7, opening that section of the final interlude (chs. 12–14) which details the message of the three angels (14:6-13).[36] There is a progressive emphasis in the three. The first angel calls upon the nations to fear God and give him glory, then the second prophesies the

---

[34] Marshall, *New Testament Theology*, 560-61.
[35] Osborne, *Revelation*, 271.
[36] David A. deSilva, *Seeing Things John's Way: The Rhetoric of the Book of Revelation* (Lousiville: Westminster/John Knox, 2009), in an interesting chapter entitled "Argumentation in John's Visions: Revelation 14:6-13 as Focal Summary of Main Points" (257-84), believes this passage is the epicenter of the book's deliberative argumentation (warnings regarding worshipping God rather than the beast) and epideictic discourse (praising the virtuous and condemning the sinner).

destruction of Babylon the Great, and the third details the eternal torment awaiting those who worship the beast. This is a special event, for the text details ἄλλον ἄγγελον, "another" of the mighty angels God has sent, recalling the sets of angels God sends to bring his judgments upon the world in chs. 6, 7–8, 16. The fact that he is "flying in mid-air" and "proclaiming loudly" his message to "every nation" replicates especially the "eagle" announcing the "three woes" of 8:13. This is a special message to the "earthdwellers" throughout the world.

The debate is whether the first angelic message (14:7) offers repentance to the nations. The angel is bearing εὐαγγέλιον αἰώνιον, the only place "gospel" occurs in the Apocalypse and the only place anarthrous εὐαγγέλιον appears in the NT (except for Rom 1:1, where the form is due to it being part of a salutation). This could mean it centers only on the wrath of God, not his gracious gift of salvation,[37] or perhaps on the proclamation of impending judgment in this context.[38] Yet at the same time too much can be read into this anarthrous form, for generally the absence of the article brings out the qualitative, abstract, or theological overtones of a term.[39] There is no question that impending judgment is a key aspect of the "eternal gospel" (which is eternal in terms of its ultimate effects), but should we see it here as wholly negative, announcing only the doom of the earthdwellers? This does not fit the language, "Fear God and give him glory." These imperatives might be "a compulsory edict for antagonistic humanity, signifying that they will be forced to acknowledge the reality of God's imminent judgment (as in Phil 2:9-11)."[40] But is this the more natural meaning of the language? Aune calls this message "purely eschatological; i.e. it announces the necessity of repentance and conversion in view of the imminent end of the world and the judgment of God."[41] Smalley concludes that while judgment is central, it is better "to take the command in verse 7 as an appeal to the nations for people to be converted, and come in their own time to faith in Christ; even if, as experience shows and the following verses (14:8-20) demonstrate, that call is not universally

---

[37] Mounce, *Revelation*, 273.

[38] Keener, *Revelation*, 372. Beale, *Revelation*, 748-49, sees two indicators of judgment here: 1) the build-up from 10:7 (with the verb form centering on salvation and judgment) to 11:1-13 (with judgment as a key stress) to ch. 14 contains a progressive emphasis on judgment. 2) This climaxes in the judgment scene of ch. 14, with the angelic proclamation of doom (14:8-13) and then the two judgment harvests (14:14-20).

[39] See Murray J. Harris, "The Definite Article in the Greek New Testament: Some General and Specific Principles," in *Jesus as God: The New Testament Use of Theos in Reference to Jesus* (Grand Rapids: Baker, 1992), 302-13 (cf. especially 303), where he states "the absence of the article" generally indicates "the quality or nature of that person or thing," namely "the distinctive content of a term."

[40] Beale, *Revelation*, 751.

[41] Aune, *Revelation*, 2:826.

heeded."[42] In Revelation God is glorified in 1:6 (John), 4:9 (the living creatures), 5:12-13 (the angels of heaven), 7:12 (the angels around the throne), 15:4 (the saints in heaven), 19:1, 7 (the multitude in heaven). The imagery could allude to Dan 4:34, where Nebuchadnezzar gives glory to God after experiencing divine judgment, but should it be restricted to reluctant homage? This is doubtful.

Let us see how this works out in the so-called "repentance" passages of the book. We must begin with 9:20, where after the fifth and sixth trumpet judgments (the first two "woes," in which demonic forces torture only their followers for five months and then kill one-third of mankind), all the survivors refuse to repent and prefer to worship the very demons who have killed many of them rather than turn to God. The question is whether an offer to repent is ever given in the context of ch. 9. Aune here states that οὐδὲ μετενόησαν does not comprise an actual offer of "repentance" because in the Exodus story of the Egyptian plagues that underlies this narrative "there is no doubt that a change of mind on the part of the pharaoh of Egypt was never considered a real possibility." Thus repentance, as in the seven letters, is restricted to the Christian world.[43] Beale concurs, stating that the plagues in chs. 8–9 were not meant to produce repentance (since the people "did not have it in them") but rather to demonstrate the sovereignty of God as he judges them.[44]

However, the use of repentance language throughout the NT refers simply to a change of heart, and there is never any distinction between Christian and non-Christian with respect to who repents. Several scholars bring out the fact that the limitation of the trumpet judgments (God restricts the destruction to one-third of mankind) inherently implies "an opportunity for a change of heart" so that they turn to God.[45] That is more likely the case here. Certainly the emphasis is upon the depravity of their minds and hearts, their absolute refusal to turn to God, and their preference to continue their lives of sin. Yet these are interdependent aspects of the developing themes of this book. God utilizes the judgment septets to both punish the nations for sin but at the same time to make them aware that they are following false gods and need to repent. Yet the nations refuse to acknowledge that message and demand to live by their own depraved standards.

That is also the case in the bowl judgments, where there are three places language of repentance and rejection are used (16:9, 11, 21). The language in v.

---

[42] Smalley, *Revelation*, 362-63. For a similar conclusion, see Ian Boxall, *The Revelation of St. John* (BNTC; Peabody, Mass.: Hendrickson, 2006), 206.
[43] Aune, *Revelation*, 2:541.
[44] Beale, *Revelation*, 517-18.
[45] Phillip E. Hughes, *The Book of Revelation* (Grand Rapids: Eerdmans, 1990), 114-15; cf. also George E. Ladd, *A Commentary on the Revelation of John* (Grand Rapids: Eerdmans, 1972), 138; Keener, *Revelation*, 272-73; Smalley, *Revelation*, 242; Boxall, *Revelation*, 149.

9, "they refused to repent and glorify him," replicates the "eternal gospel" of 14:7, "Fear God and give him glory" as well as the worship of 15:4, "Who will not fear you, O Lord, and glorify your name?" Both passages were discussed above. This is language of repentance and indicates that the bowl judgments included an offer of repentance. Throughout the Apocalypse, "giving God glory" is seen as reverence and worship (1:6; 4:9, 11; 5:12, 13; 7:12; 19:1, 7). That is the more likely meaning in ch. 16 as well. The bowl judgments are no longer partial and so constitute the absolutely final chance to repent.[46] The emphasis, as in 9:20-21, is certainly upon their total surrender to depravity and their complete refusal to repent, but this does not obviate the fact that God has given them a final opportunity to repent. After this all that remains is the destruction of evil (17:1–19:5) and the coming of Christ in judgment (19:11-21).

A critical segue into the next issue, the extent of the success of God's mission to the nations, involves consideration of the one place where the nations do seem to repent, 11:13. This concludes the section on the ministry of the two witnesses (11:3-13), which virtually everyone takes as symbolizing the witnessing church. After the two witnesses are taken up to heaven (11:11-12), a terrible earthquake destroys the city, killing one-tenth of the inhabitants (7000, a deliberate contrast with 1 Kgs 19:18, the faithful remnant spared in the days of Elijah). The rest, we are told, are "terrified and give glory to the God of heaven." This reaction has already been discussed above as language of repentance and worship (14:7; 15:4; 16:9; 19:7), and many commentators conclude that this pictures the success of the witnessing, martyred church in bringing the nations to God.[47] This is not quite correct, because in 11:13 the reaction is not to the witnessing church but to the judgment/great earthquake God has poured out on the city. Still, the conclusion that this is genuine repentance stands. However, several dispute this and argue the "fear and glory" refer to terror and amazement rather than homage.[48]

Does "fear and glory" in 11:13 connote repentance or terror, and if conversion, how extensive is the repentance? Here we will interact with the two main voices on this, Richard Bauckham and Eckhard Schnabel. For Bauckham John has chosen to replicate in the two witnesses the miracles of Elijah (the first two in 11:5-6a) and Moses (the last two in 11:6b) to symbolize the successful witness of the church through martyrdom and vindication. This

---

[46] Contra Beale, *Revelation*, 823, 826, 845.
[47] J. P. M. Sweet, *Revelation* (Westminster Pelican Commentaries; Philadelphia: Westminster, 1979), 189; Aune, *Revelation*, 2:628; Ben Witherington III, *Revelation* (New Cambridge Bible Commentary; Cambridge: Cambridge University Press, 2003), 160; Ladd, *Revelation*, 159; Caird, *Revelation*, 139-40; Keener, *Revelation*, 296-97; Smalley, *Revelation*, 286; Boxall, *Revelation*, 167.
[48] Mounce, *Revelation*, 229; Hughes, *Revelation*, 130; Giesen, *Offenbarung*, 259; Beale, *Revelation*, 605.

results in the true repentance of the nations. What the judgments could not produce (9:20) is achieved via witness; what Moses and Elijah failed to achieve in the OT (to effect true repentance) now takes place via martyrdom. The redemptive sacrifice of the Lamb and the suffering witness of the church bring about the conversion of the nations, and thereby the meaning of the scroll (chs. 5, 10) is unveiled—"this revelation of the role which the church's suffering witness is to play in the conversion of the nations is the content of the scroll which the Lamb's victory qualified him to open."[49]

Schnabel strongly demurs in this scenario. He concurs that the witnessing church proclaims the gospel and calls for repentance among the nations, and that this constitutes "a time of mission and evangelism in which the Christians, despite continued unbelief (9:20-21), seek to reach tribes, languages, peoples, and nations with God's message (11:3-13)."[50] However, he does not agree that 11:13 portrays a mass conversion in which the nations turn to God. He gives several reasons for this: 1) the commission of 10:11 is to "prophecy *against* many nations" as evidenced in its background from Ezek 2–3, where it is a prophecy of judgment. 2) The use of ἔμφοβοι in 11:13 means "terror" not reverence. 3) Giving "glory" to God here is "judgment doxology" rather than repentance and is part of the second woe connoting defeat rather than conversion. 4) The focus is not on the fate of the "great city" but on the vindication of the witnesses. Therefore 11:3-13 is not about the conversion of the nations but details the future victory of the saints in spite of the antagonism and martyrdom they experience at the hands of the nations.[51] Ronald Herms agrees, pointing out the weakness of Bauckham's attempt to reconcile the presence of both "universal salvation and judgment language" in the book, since it involves giving the former "theological priority" over the latter.[52] He believes that the "rest" in 11:13 must be understood on the basis of the "rest" in 9:20-21 who refused to repent and the "rest" in 19:21 who are destroyed, so that in all three cases these are "the inhabitants of the earth" who stand against Christ and his people.[53]

These are in a sense the poles of the debate, but there is a middle position that I believe better represents the data. The meaning of 11:13 is difficult, for on the one hand there is a negative atmosphere centering on the nations as enemies of God, yet on the other hand the book everywhere else has a positive presentation of "fear God and give him glory" as language of repentance (see above). Overall, I believe that 11:13 likely does represent conversion, but at the

---

[49] Bauckham, *Climax*, 283 (cf. 274-83).
[50] Eckhard Schnabel, "John and the Future of the Nations," *BBR* 12, no. 2 (2002): 243-71 [249-50].
[51] Schnabel, "John and the Nations," 250-57. See also David Mathewson, "The Destiny of the Nations in Revelation 21:1–22:5," *TynBul* 53 (2002): 121-42.
[52] Herms, *Apocalypse for the Church*, 142.
[53] Herms, *Apocalypse for the Church*, 194-96.

same time, there is no evidence whatsoever that this denotes the conversion of all the nations. The two images (noted above on Rev 1:7) of most among the nations standing against Christ while some repent should supplement one another. Those who argue for universal salvation also look to Rev 21:24-26 and 22:1-5. Rissi believes that the vision of the nations bringing their glory into the New Jerusalem replaces the lake of fire from 20:11-15, and that judgment leads to the conversion of all the nations,[54] and Caird says that the curse of Adam has now been "abrogated . . . for the whole creation has been renewed by the re-creating hand of God; and no flaming sword bars the way to the tree of life."[55] However, this view of universal salvation in Revelation does not fit the whole of the book. It is better to follow Herms and realize that "universal language does not necessarily presuppose universal salvation; rather, it serves to vindicate the faithful community, and validate their present circumstances in light of future reversal."[56] There is a mission to all the nations, but the nations must decide whether or not to respond and become part of the people of God. The majority who refuse to do so will face judgment and see the vindication of the saints. Those who respond with repentance will become part of God's people and inherit eternal life.

THE MEANS OF THE MISSION: FAITHFUL WITNESS

An important aspect of mission in the Apocalypse is the witness motif, itself an aspect of the perseverance theme in the book. As I have said, "While the vertical axis of the book is the sovereignty of God, the horizontal axis is the responsibility of the saints to persevere. . . . Five concepts carry this theme; endurance, faithfulness, witness, conquering, and obedience."[57] All relate to the required ethical and moral response of the saints to these final events portrayed in the book. As evil and opposition grow in the world and the earth-dwellers turn more and more against God and his people, the followers of Christ are to respond as in 1 Pet 2:12, "Live such good lives among the pagans that, though they accuse you of doing wrong, they may see your good deeds and glorify God on the day he visits us." Stephen Pattemore, in his excellent study of the "people of God" in the Apocalypse, denotes three methods by which John motivates ethical conduct: 1) Their identity is tied to the "slaughtered lamb" so that they become Christ-like in the "sacrificial offering of their lives." 2) The narrative challenges the readers to conduct themselves in ways that are desirable. 3) By "delineating boundaries" throughout the work, John warns readers to make certain they are "in" rather than "out." Negatively, God's

---

[54] Matthias Rissi, *The Future of the World: An Exegetical Study of Rev. 19:11–22:15* (SBT; London: SCM, 1972), 81.
[55] Caird, *Revelation*, 280.
[56] Herms, *Apocalypse for the Church*, 260.
[57] Osborne, *Revelation*, 42.

people must resist the seductive idolatry associated with the religious and power structures of the society within which they live. Positively, they must remain faithful in obedience to God's ways and bear witness in difficult times.[58]

There are three levels to the witness motif: 1) God conducts his mission/witness via judgment (which shows the earthly gods to be false and gives the nations a final opportunity to repent, 9:20; 16:9). 2) The Lamb witnesses by giving himself up to be slaughtered so as to purchase/redeem people from sin to God (1:2, 6; 3:14; 5:6, 9). 3) The people of God witness by proclaiming these truths to the world and being willing to suffer for them.[59] The theme begins with the archetypal witness, Jesus, who is "faithful witness" in 1:5 (cf. "witness of Jesus Christ" in 1:2, a subjective genitive referring to his witness) and "faithful and true witness" in 3:14. In places where the "testimony of Jesus" is connected to "the word of God" as in 1:2, it tends to be an objective genitive, the testimony of the saints "about" Jesus (1:6; 6:9; 12:17; 19:10; 20:4), but in 1:2 Jesus is portrayed as the revealer of the heavenly secrets, so the subjective sense is most likely.[60] In 1:5 and 3:14 Jesus becomes the model of the "faithful witness," and especially in 3:5 this is in contrast to the failure of the Laodicean church to do so. Both aspects lead into primary themes for the people of God, "faithful" in their conduct and obedience (2:10, 13; 13:10; 17:14) and witnesses in their reaction to the evil world around them. Sigve Tonstad's study of πίστις 'Ιησοῦ in 14:12 argues that it employs a subjective genitive and connotes "'the faithfulness of Jesus' in the unveiling of the character of evil and his faithful disclosure of God's character."[61] It is common to take this as an objective genitive, "remaining faithful to Jesus,"[62] but either way the Christian must respond to an evil world by echoing Jesus' own faithfulness in conduct and witness.

The witness of the church is its weapon in the holy war against evil.[63] As

---

[58] Stephen Pattemore, *The People of God in the Apocalypse: Discourse, Structure, and Exegesis* (SNTSMS 128; Cambridge: Cambridge University Press, 2004), 218.

[59] deSilva, *Rhetoric*, 71, sees two aspects of witness in the book: "prophetic witness to the One God and what that God values in human community, and witness *against* the abuses of that God and God's values in the practices of Roman imperialism" (italics his).

[60] So Giesen, *Offenbarung*, 59; Aune, *Revelation*, 1:19; Beale, *Revelation*, 184, and Smalley, *Revelation*, 30, see both subjective and objective aspects here.

[61] Sigve K. Tonstad, *Saving God's Reputation: The Theological Function of Pistis Iesou in the Cosmic Narratives of Revelation* (LNTS 337; New York: T&T Clark, 2006), 3 (cf. 190-94). So also Boxall, *Revelation*, 210.

[62] So Caird, *Revelation*, 188; Aune, *Revelation*, 2:838; Smalley, *Revelation*, 369. Beale, *Revelation*, 766-67, takes it as a general genitive, connoting both faith in Jesus and his faithfulness.

[63] On the concept of holy war, see Bauckham, "The Apocalypse as a Christian War Scroll," in *The Climax of Prophecy: Studies on the Book of Revelation* (Edinburgh: T&T Clark, 1993), 210-37.

Paul says in 2 Cor 10:4, "The weapons we fight with are not the weapons of the world" but instead contain "divine power to demolish strongholds." The saints fight with eternal truths and witness to eternal realities, and Satan has no response to that. Let us trace this theme briefly through the Apocalypse. As Bauckham states, "The word 'witness' (*martys*) does not yet, in Revelation, carry the technical Christian meaning of 'martyr' (one who bears witness by dying for the faith).... But to verbal witness to the truth of God ... along with living obedience to the commands of God."[64] In two places it comes close. In 2:13 we learn of the martyrdom of "Antipas, my faithful witness, who was put to death in my city"; and in 6:9 John sees "under the altar the souls of those who had been slain because of the word of God and the testimony [μαρτυρία] they had maintained." While the term did not take on the meaning of martyrdom until the second century, it is clear that Revelation was a primary reason it came to bear that connotation.

Martyrdom as witness and victory over the powers of evil is a frequent thrust. In 6:9-11 after the martyrs cry out for victory and vengeance, God gives them white robes (the symbol of victory as well as purity) and promises that he will vindicate them. Pattemore says that "seen from the perspective of 6:9-11, the rest of the book is an answer to the cry of the martyrs."[65] This begins right away, as in 6:15-17 the very ones who have killed the saints (the princes, generals, rich, mighty, slaves as well as free) are cowering under the mountains and calling in insane terror for an avalanche to cover them and hide them from God and the "wrath of the Lamb." Then in 8:2-5 these very prayers for vindication ascend to God and lead to the trumpet judgments. In other words, the trumpet and bowl judgments are in part God's response to the prayers of the saints for vengeance! In 12:11 the people of God become conquerors of Satan "by the blood of the Lamb, and by the word of their testimony; they did not love their lives so much as to shrink from death." There is an ironic contrast with 13:7. In the latter God gives the beast/Antichrist permission (ἐδόθη) "to make war against the saints and to conquer them." Yet in 12:11 the believers conquer the dragon by giving up their lives to him. Martyrdom is a participation in the Messianic Woes and as such replicates the death of Christ, when Satan participated in his own defeat by entering Judas and leading Christ to the cross. The martyrs are the victors. They "stand before the throne" (7:9, 14) and "reign with Christ a thousand years" (20:4).

In 16:5-7 the "true and just" judgments upon the earth-dwellers occur because "they have shed the blood of your saints and prophets," and in 19:1-2 the great multitude sings "hallelujah" because God "has avenged on [the great prostitute] the blood of his servants." Not all the saints are martyred, of course (contra Caird, Bauckham), but all suffer ignominy and opposition as they

---

[64] Richard Bauckham, *The Theology of the Book of Revelation* (Cambridge: Cambridge University Press, 1993), 72.

[65] Pattemore, *People of God*, 113.

witness to a fallen world. This can be shown by the three groups noted in 20:4—those on the thrones, those beheaded, and those who have resisted the beast. The latter two define those who sit on the thrones and reign a thousand years, referring to both the martyrs and those who did not lose their lives but still were victorious over the beast's demands.[66] All the saints will share the victory, both martyrs and those who were faithful in the midst of persecution.

The witness motif is especially prominent in 11:3-7. While I personally believe the "two witnesses" are two individual prophets who will appear at the end in the appearance and power of Moses and Elijah,[67] the important thing for our purpose here is that they symbolize the witnessing church (nearly all commentators). Schnabel says this well: "As the seven golden lampstands that stand in God's presence (1:12, 20; 2:1) represent 'the church as the true temple and the totality of the people of God' empowered primarily 'to witness as a light uncompromisingly to the world,' so 'the two lampstands that stand before the Lord of the earth' in 11:4 represent the church in its role as witness."[68] The witnesses "prophesy" and stand with John as commissioned witnesses (10:9-10) prophesying "against" the nations (10:11), warning them undoubtedly to "fear God and give him glory, for the hour of judgment has come" (14:7). This prophetic witness cannot be stopped, for in spite of the terrible price the people of God have to pay, God's hand of protection is upon them. The fire from their mouths and the plagues of 11:5-6 reproduce the judgment septets and imply a call to repentance as in 9:20-21; 16:9 (see above). Schnabel adds that "Christian witness, even though it may focus on the announcement of divine judgment, always includes the proclamation of the gospel, which promises immediate and eternal salvation for those who believe in Jesus Christ."[69] Therefore this passage summarizes the mission activity of the church in this period of conflagration and hatred. The people of God respond to the murderous intents of the nations with holy war, but that war is conducted via witness, as indeed it is today in places like China or the Sudan.

This theme continues in the several passages centering on the church's "witness for Jesus" (μαρτυρία Ἰησοῦ), and while some are general genitives (Jesus' witness to the world leads to the church's witness to Jesus), most are objective genitives and depict the verbal witness of the Christ-followers. In 1:9 John had been banished "on account of the word of God and his witness for

---

[66] Ladd, *Revelataion*, 263; Beale, *Revelation*, 1001; Pattemore, *People of God*, 110-11. Contra Bauckham, *Theology*, 106-107; Beasley-Murray, *Revelation*, 293-94; Smalley, *Revelation*, 506, who hold to this being a single group.

[67] See Osborne, *Revelation*, 417-18, on the grounds that the beast in 11:17 and 13:1-10 will certainly be an individual who will appear in history. On the basis of 2 Thess 2:3-12 and 1 John 2:18, 4:3, the early church expected such a figure to appear just before the Eschaton.

[68] Schnabel, "John and the Nations," 248, building upon Beale, *Revelation*, 207.

[69] Schnabel, "John and the Nations," 249.

Jesus," clearly his gospel ministry. In 6:9 the souls under the altar were martyred "on account of the Word of God and the witness they had maintained" (here τὴν μαρτυρίαν ἣν εἶχον, stressing the ongoing witness for Jesus). In 12:17 the dragon is enraged and goes to war against "those who obey the commandments of God and maintain their witness for Jesus," combining the ideas of faithful conduct and bold witness as the weapons by which the church engages in holy war with the dragon. In 19:10 the angel calls himself "a fellow slave" with "those who maintain witness for Jesus," clearly considering verbal witness the apex of the Christian task. Then the angel goes on to state, "[T]estimony about Jesus is Spirit-inspired prophecy," a very debated phrase which could mean that Jesus' own testimony provides the essence of prophecy.[70] However, it is better in light of the emphasis on the Spirit in Revelation inspiring prophecy to take this as an affirmation of the Spirit's role in prophetic witness to the world.[71] Finally, in 20:4 the souls on the thrones have been beheaded "because of their witness for Jesus," stressing once more their mission of active witness in an oppressive world that pursued them in order to kill them, echoing 17:6 where the great prostitute is drunk on "the blood of those who bore witness to Jesus."

Clearly three aspects of witness predominate—verbal witness that echoes Jesus' witness to himself, witness through a life of faithful conduct in a sinful world, and a witness of suffering for the faith even unto death. Death is the ultimate witness, for it is the final victory over the powers of evil and leads to God's final vindication. As Bauckham says, "The theme of witness is connected with Revelation's dominant concern with truth and falsehood. The world is a kind of courtroom in which the issue of who is the true God is being decided. In this judicial context Jesus and the followers bear witness to the truth."[72] Yet it is also more than this, for witness is the means by which God's mission of bringing repentance to an evil world is taking place. The world turns against God's people in hatred, rejection, and violence, but the saints turn to the world with gospel proclamation, bearing Christ's weapon, the sword that comes out of his mouth[73] proclaiming judgment and calling the nations to repentance (14:6-7).

---

[70] Sweet, *Revelation*, 280; Giesen, *Offenbarung*, 415-16; Beasley-Murray, *Revelation*, 276.
[71] So Caird, *Revelation*, 238; Aune, *Revelation*, 3:1038-39; Smalley, *Revelation*, 487. Beale, *Revelation*, 947, calls the witnessing church "prophetic people."
[72] Bauckham, *Theology*, 73.
[73] The "sharp sword coming out of his mouth" is found in 1:16; 2:12, 16; 19:15, 21 (echoing Isa 11:4; 49:2). This was the *ius gladii*, the symbol of Roman authority and power. It symbolizes Christ's proclamation of judgment.

CONCLUSION

Revelation, as the last book in the canon, both concludes and summarizes the metanarrative of the Bible as a whole. Mankind/the nations (Gen 12) have fallen into sin and marred God's image in them. As such they are under divine judgment and condemnation, but God acts throughout Scripture out of his grace and mercy to bring a remnant home to himself. The mission to the nations began the moment Adam and Eve sinned, and at first it was God himself who conducted it. He chose a people to be his own and in the Abrahamic covenant ("all the peoples of the earth will be blessed by you," Gen 12:3; 15:5; 18:18; 22:18; 26:4) involved his covenant people in his mission. They failed to embrace that aspect of the covenant responsibility, but the mission of God continued, as recognized in the procession of the nations to Zion in Isaiah (2:2-4; 9:2; 11:9; 27:13; 42:1-4, 6; 49:6; 52:7; 56:7; 57:13; 60:3-5; 65:25; 66:19-20). In the New Covenant of Christ, mission became a primary purpose of his followers, but still the majority among the nations refused to respond. Revelation finalizes those great themes of Scripture.

The primary theological theme of the book is the sovereignty of God who alone will destroy evil and vindicate the saints. He is Lord of history, and the powers of evil answer to him alone. Those who reject his grace and turn against him and his people will be destroyed. Yet herein lies the mission. As in the plagues of Egypt, the wilderness wanderings, and the exile, God's judgment has a redemptive side, showing the foolishness of following the earthly gods and calling the wicked to repentance. God's mission is highlighted in the Apocalypse, and it is interdependent with the judgment scenes. The nations are called to a choice, and that choice will determine their destiny. The sacrificial death of Christ made that faith-decision possible, and the people of God join this mission via verbal witness and a willingness to suffer as testimony to the nations of their enduring faithfulness to God. As Schnabel says, John "does not predict a universal success of the missionary proclamation of the church. John predicts the decisive victory that Jesus will finally win over the hostile powers and over the people who follow them when he returns (19:11-21)."[74] In the midst of this, the mission of God and his followers is to proclaim that future salvation and call the nations to it.

---

[74] Schnabel, "John and the Nations," 270.

22

EARLY CHRISTIAN MISSION AND CHRISTIAN IDENTITY IN THE CONTEXT OF THE ETHNIC, SOCIAL, AND POLITICAL AFFILIATIONS IN REVELATION

Eckhard J. Schnabel

John designates the nations of the world in a fourfold phrase—"every tribe and language and people and nation"—which occurs, with variations, in Rev 5:9; 7:9; 10:11; 11:9; 13:7; 14:6; 17:15. The fourfold phrase, repeated seven times, can be interpreted in the context of John's numerical symbolism in which four is the number of the world and seven the number of completeness and in the context of an allusion to and interpretation of several OT passages (Exod 19:5-6; Dan 3:4, 7, 31 [4:11]; 5:19; 6:25 [26]; 7:14;[1] Gen 10:20, 31): the phrase refers to all the nations of the world, and the phrase is used in connection with the prophetic conviction that the nations will be transferred from the rule of the beast to the rule of God.[2] While symbolic and intertextual readings are certainly important, interpreters need to keep in mind the reminder that John's symbols "do not create a purely self-contained aesthetic world with no reference outside itself, but intend to relate to the world in which the readers live in order to reform and to redirect the readers' response to that world."[3] This is true not only for symbols but for intertextual references as well. This essay seeks to establish the "outside reference" of the fourfold, seven times repeated phrase "every tribe and language and people and nation," a phrase that can and should be connected with the missionary work of the early church, a dimension that pervades the NT, as I. H. Marshall has emphasized when he described the

---

[1] Daniel speaks of "peoples, nations, and languages" (עממיא אמיא ולשניא), which the LXX translates as πάντα τὰ ἔθνη, φυλαὶ καὶ γλῶσσαι.
[2] Richard J. Bauckham, *The Climax of Prophecy: Studies on the Book of Revelation* (Edinburgh: T&T Clark, 1993), 34, 326-36. Bauckham posits a connection with John's symbolism when he asserts with regard to the seven times repeated fourfold phrase that "in the symbolic world of Revelation, there could hardly be a more emphatic indication of universalism" (ibid. 34). Bauckham is followed by David E. Aune, *Revelation* (3 vols.; WBC 52A–C; Dallas: Word, 1997–1998), 1:361-62; Gregory K. Beale, *The Book of Revelation: A Commentary on the Greek Text* (NIGTC; Grand Rapids: Eerdmans, 1999), 359-60; Grant R. Osborne, *Revelation* (BECNT; Grand Rapids: Baker Academic, 2002), 260.
[3] Richard J. Bauckham, *The Theology of the Book of Revelation* (NTT; Cambridge: Cambridge University Press, 1993), 20.

writings of the NT as "documents of a mission."[4] The missionary task of the church, to be carried out with courage and with the willingness to endure opposition, suffering, and even death, is portrayed in Revelation in the vision of the two witnesses of Rev 11:3, who are most plausibly interpreted as standing for the persevering witness of the followers of Jesus in the face of fierce opposition.[5]

Most readers of John's Revelation, which was sent as a letter to churches in the province of Asia,[6] presumably would not have been able to grasp the intertextual connections between the fourfold phrase and OT passages that speak of the nations of the world in a phrase that employs three or four synonyms for "nations." This is true particularly for Gentile believers for whom Greek terms connoted not automatically, and certainly not exclusively, passages in the LXX, but historical and contemporary "secular" meanings. Most scholars treat the fourfold phrase as a universalistic formula[7] without considering the range of meanings of the individual terms.[8] The following survey of the four Greek terms explores how readers of Revelation, whose vocabulary was informed not primarily by the Greek Bible but by contemporary Greek usage, might have understood John's reference to people(s), nations, languages, and tribes. And it explores how Christian believers may have understood these terms given the reality of the work of

---

[4] I. Howard Marshall, *New Testament Theology: Many Witnesses, One Gospel* (Downers Grove: InterVarsity, 2004), 34. This missionary theme is not developed in the section on the Revelation of John (ibid. 570-78).

[5] Cf. G. R. Beasley-Murray, *The Book of Revelation* (London: Oliphants: 1974; repr., NCBC; Grand Rapids: Eerdmans, 1981), 183-84; Robert H. Mounce, *The Book of Revelation* (rev. ed.; Grand Rapids: Eerdmans, 1997), 217-18; Beale, *Revelation*, 556, 573; Ben Witherington, *Revelation* (New Cambridge Bible Commentary; Cambridge: Cambridge University Press, 2003), 158-59; Osborne, *Revelation*, 418 (in addition to two historical figures whom John expects to appear); also Aune, *Revelation*, 603; see ibid. 598-602 for a survey of other interpretations.

[6] On the epistolary character of Revelation cf. Martin Karrer, *Die Johannesoffenbarung als Brief: Studien zu ihrem literarischen, historischen und theologischen Ort* (FRLANT 140; Göttingen: Vandenhoeck & Ruprecht, 1986).

[7] Cf. Beale, *Revelation*, 882, who speaks of a "formula of universality."

[8] Akira Satake, *Die Offenbarung des Johannes* (KEK 16; Göttingen: Vandenhoeck & Ruprecht, 2008), 212, goes so far as to claim that the individual terms do not matter much, asserting that the four terms designated together the entire human race ("Der Bedeutung der einzelnen Begriffe kommt keine große Bedeutung zu; vielmehr bezeichnen diese vier Worte in ihrer Gesamtheit die ganze Menschheit"). One exception is, not surprisingly, Theodor Zahn, *Die Offenbarung des Johannes* (Leipzig: Deichert, 1924–1926; repr., TVG; Nachdruck der 3. Auflage; Wuppertal: Brockhaus, 1986), 343-44, who relates φυλή to the twelve tribes of Israel, and then comments on the many languages that were represented in all the larger cities of the Roman empire; he suggests that λαός refers to the ruling people (the *Populus Romanus*), and ἔθνη to the provinces with their populations, which is not convincing.

missionaries who proclaimed the gospel in the cities and villages of Asia Minor and other regions, seeking to reach all ethnic, social, and political groups. The sequence in which we discuss the nouns of John's fourfold phrase follows the sequence of the four terms in the first occurrence of the phrase in the "new song" which celebrates the singular worthiness of the Lamb, i.e., of Jesus, who was slaughtered and who "ransomed for God" by his blood "saints from every tribe and language and people and nation" (ἐκ πάσης φυλῆς καὶ γλώσσης καὶ λαοῦ καὶ ἔθνους; Rev 5:9).

φυλή

A general definition of φυλή reads, "The Greeks described as *phylai* groups or categories of extremely various sizes of people (or animals), and therefore also the peoples and tribes into which they divided themselves and the 'ethnic groups' (*éthnē*) of barbarians."[9] The standard lexicon of NT Greek gives two meanings for φυλή:[10] 1. a "subgroup of a nation characterized by a distinctive blood line," translated as "tribe, clan," e.g., a tribe within a people (Agamemnon arranges the people κατὰ φῦλα, κατὰ φρήτρας, "by tribes and clans," Homer, *Il.* 2.362f); the four Ionic tribes (Herodotus); the twelve tribes of Israel (Isa 49:6; Matt 19:28; Luke 22:30; cf. Rev 21:12; cf. 7:4, 5-8), the Edomite tribes (Gen 36:40), the Egyptian and Arabian and Phoenician tribes who live north of Judea (Strabo, *Geogr.* 16.2.34). 2. A "relatively large people group that forms a sociopolitical subgroup of the human race" or "nation, people," e.g., in the phrase "all the tribes of the earth" (Gen 12:3 LXX: πᾶσαι αἱ φυλαὶ τῆς γῆς; cf. Gen 28:14; Ezek 20:32; Matt 24:30; Rev 1:7).

There is a third meaning which reflects the predominant use in Greek literature and documentary texts, unfortunately not mentioned by BDAG: 3. a subgroup "by local habitation,"[11] with φυλή used as a technical term for the largest subunit of a *polis* state; e.g., the ten local "tribes" of Athens formed by Cleisthenes (Herodotus 5.69; 6.131; IG I² 10.44), the "tribes" formed by Servius in Rome (Dionysius Halicarnassus 4.14; Plutarch, *Rom.* 20).[12] The term φυλαί was used in this sense originally only by the Ionians and the Dorians; it appears since the eighth century B.C. as the most widespread structural element of the city (*polis*) states; in northwestern Greece, φυλαί were introduced only in the Hellenistic period. Initially there was general agreement between the number and the names of φυλαί in the cities of the Ionians (Geleontes, Aegicoreis, Argadeis, Hopletes) and the cities of the Dorians (Hylleis, Dymanes, Pamphyli). In the course of colonization, the φυλή structure of the

---

[9] B. Smarczyk, "Phyle [1]," *BNP* 11:210-12.
[10] BDAG, s.v. φυλή 1-2. Cf. C. Maurer, "φυλή," *TDNT* 9:245-50.
[11] LSJ, s.v. φυλή, I.2; Maurer, *TDNT* 9:245.
[12] Cf. B. Smarczyk, "Phyle [1]," *BNP* 11:210; the following summary is adapted from ibid. 210-12.

"mother city" (μητρόπολις) was exported to the new foundation (ἀποικία), where it could be supplemented with further φυλαί.[13] The name of a φυλή was originally derived from the name of a hero or leader who was worshipped as ancestor, a fiction in which the citizens believed and which promoted the integration of the members of the local φυλή. In the Hellenistic and Roman periods, the number of φυλαί increased; they were often renamed, taking the names of monarchs and of emperors or their followers, as a demonstration of loyalty. Membership in the φυλή of a city was a prerequisite for full citizenship. The φυλή cooperated in the appointment of magistrates, of members of commissions, and of judges. In many cities in Asia Minor, honorary decrees displayed in the theater or in other public places of the city reminded the public of persons who were voted by the δῆμος to be registered as member of one of the φυλαί of the city. Examples from Miletus include an honorary decree for the grain merchant Thyssos from Mylasa who was granted citizenship and who was voted into a φυλή by the Prytanes (the stele was to be put into the temple of Apollo), and an honorary decree for a delegation from Miletus to Athens whose members were granted Athenian citizenship and inscription into one of the φυλαί of Athens (a stele was to be erected in Athens and another stele in Miletus).[14]

Most interpreters of John's fourfold phrase understand the reference to φυλή (φυλαί) as a synonym of λαός, ἔθνος, and γλῶσσα and thus, usually without discussion of the various meanings of the word, in terms of sense 2 as "nation." It is not impossible, however, to assume that many readers would

---

[13] Strabo relates that Tlepolemos came to Rhodes "where his people settled in three divisions by tribes" (καταφυλαδόν; *Geogr.* 14.2.6); cf. Strabo 14.2.10 (quoting Homer on the Rhodians).

[14] I. Milet III 1023, lines 12-13 (330-320 B.C.), and I. Milet III 1038, lines 12-13 (180-160 B.C.) (Peter Herrmann, Wolfgang Günther, and Norbert Ehrhardt, *Milet VI. iii. Inschriften von Milet III: Inschriften n. 1020–1580* [Ergebnisse der Ausgrabungen und Untersuchungen seit dem Jahr 1899; Berlin: De Gruyter, 2006], 4-5, 19-20). For the various formulae of the enrollment clauses see Nicholas F. Jones, "Enrollment Clauses in Greek Citizenship Decrees," *ZPE* 87 (1991): 79-112, who comments that among the honors and privileges conferred by the typical Greek citizenship decree is a formulaic clause calling for, or permitting, the enrollment of the honorand(s) in one or more segments of the honoring state's citizen population. Only with such enrollment might the grant of citizenship be utilized, since customarily many, if not all, of a state's public functions were conducted through the organizational apparatus that these segments provided. Barring enrollment, full, or even partial, participation in the public life of the honoring state was simply not possible. To take the best known example, at Athens the enrollment clause in its fully developed form enabled the honorand "to enroll himself in phyle, deme, and phratry, whichever he wishes, in accordance with the law." (79). Jones presents enrollment clauses from Athens and fifty-two additional city states, including in Asia Minor from Smyrna, Erythrai, Ephesus, Magnesia ad Maeandrum, Priene, Miletus, and Mylasa. A search in PHI #7 yields sixty-three examples of the expression εἰς φυλήν.

have heard a more narrow connotation as well: either in terms of "tribe," i.e., a subgroup of a larger population unit (sense 1), or in terms of the "tribes" or gentilic groups of the cities (sense 3). As regards sense 1, Strabo still speaks of the "tribes" (φῦλα, plural) of the Pelasgi at the beginning of the first century, emphasizing that they consisted not of one tribe (φῦλον, singular) but of many tribes (*Geogr.* 13.3.2) as they were a great nation (μέγα ἔθνος). He deplores the fact that the parts of Asia Minor in which the Phrygians, Carians, Lydians, and Mysians live are hard to distinguish, a confusion to which the Romans contributed because they "did not divide them according to tribes (μὴ κατὰ φῦλα), but in another way organized their jurisdictions" (*Geogr.* 13.4.12). The ethnic names of individuals, added after the patronymic and the ὄνομα, indicated the membership of a group—either of a "clan" (e.g., a γένος), a "brotherhood" (e.g., a φρατρία), a "tribe" (a φυλή), a municipality (e.g., a δῆμος), a state (e.g., a πόλις), or an entire region (ἔθνος).[15] Sub-ethnics designating a φυλή kept the awareness of "tribal" or regional identity alive, both for the family and for the public, at least for a few generations, after which they became political.

The visions of Rev 5:9 and 7:9 can be understood as prophecies that eventually members of every tribe or clan would come to faith in Jesus and worship the one true God, as prophecies of the eschatological, messianic fulfillment of God's promise to Abraham (Gen 12:3). Paul refers to a Scythian (Col 3:11), a term that implies tribal affiliation, and he asserts that his missionary responsibility extends not only to Greeks but also to barbarians (Rom 1:14), whom Greeks knew to be subdivided into φυλαί. Jesus' expectation that his witnesses would visit houses, i.e., families (Matt 10:13-14), told the apostles that they should not just preach to large crowds of people but also to smaller population units.

The political φυλαί of the cities (sense 3) are such smaller units as well. Citizens of Pergamum belonged to one of at least fifteen φυλαί (Apollonias, Attalis, Diodoris, Eumeneia, Philetairis, and others)[16] who played a highly visible role in the affairs of the city. A decree that welcomed Attalos III when he returned from a victorious campaign stipulates for the public celebration, "And the day on which he [i.e., Attalos] arrives in the city is to be sacred; and the citizens are to sacrifice in a mass κατὰ φυλάς with the phylarchs furnishing the victims; and there is to be given to each φυλή for the victims twenty drachmas from sacred and civic revenues" (IPergamon 246, lines 38-

---

[15] Mogens H. Hansen, "City-Ethnics as Evidence for *Polis* Identity," in *More Studies in the Ancient Greek Polis* (ed. M. H. Hansen and K. Raaflaub; Historia Einzelschriften 108; Stuttgart: Steiner, 1996), 169-96 [170]; for examples of φυλαί as ethnics see ibid. 178-81; for the following comment see ibid. 182.

[16] Cf. Nicholas F. Jones, *Public Organization in Ancient Greece: A Documentary Study* (Memoirs of the American Philosophical Society 176; Philadelphia: American Philosophical Society, 1987), 353-55.

42).¹⁷ Christians from Pergamum (Rev 1:11; 2:12) who held Pergamese citizenship and belonged to one of the φυλαί of the city would rather naturally think of their civic affiliation when they heard John's vision mention that people "from all φυλαί" (ἐκ πάσης φυλῆς) will one day stand before the throne and before the Lamb (Rev 7:9). They would have known in which φυλαί other Christians in the city had membership. And the evangelists of the church might well have regarded it as their duty to make sure that the gospel is proclaimed to members of all φυλαί of the city.

The term φυλή/φυλαί in Rev 5:9; 7:9; 14:6 could thus indeed remind John's readers that Jesus' missionary commission sends them to the members of all ethnic, regional, and civic subgroups of the city and of the area in which a congregation and its evangelists and missionaries are active. At the same time, the announcement of God's judgment against the ethnic, social, and political subgroups of cities and regions who are affiliated with God's enemies (Rev 10:11; 13:7) is plausible in this context as well: as God's judgment falls on nations and on individuals, it will fall on the subgroups of the social organization of a nation and of a city.

In Rev 10:11 the term φυλαί is replaced by βασιλεῖς ("kings"), which can be explained as "a good summary of one aspect of Daniel 7: the universal empires which are to be taken from their tyrannical, pagan rulers and transferred to the dominion of the 'one like a son of man' and the holy ones of the Most High."¹⁸ A specific historical and local meaning in the context of Asia Minor in the first century is also possible: βασιλεύς can refer, particularly in Ionia (the region to which Ephesus and Smyrna belonged), to the descendants of a royal house.¹⁹ Strabo relates that Androclus, the son of Codrus, the king of Athens, was the leader of the Ionian colonization that founded Ephesus, pointing out that "still now the descendants of his family are called kings [ἔτι νῦν οἱ ἐκ τοῦ γένους ὀνομάζονται βασιλεῖς]; and they have certain honors, I mean the privilege of front seats at the games and of wearing purple robes as insignia of royal descent [ἐπίστημον τοῦ βασιλικοῦ γένους], and staff instead of scepter, and of the superintendence of the sacrifices in honor of the Eleusinian Demeter" (*Geogr.* 14.1.3 [Jones, LCL]). The citizens of Ephesus in the first century were reminded of Androclus by the U-shaped monument built toward the end of the second century B.C. at the southwestern end of Curetes Street close to the Tetragonos Agora.²⁰ Ephesian coins minted during the

---

¹⁷ Cf. Max Fränkel, *Die Inschriften von Pergamon* (Altertümer von Pergamon VIII,1–2; Berlin: Spemann, 1890), no. 246.
¹⁸ Bauckham, *Climax of Prophecy*, 331.
¹⁹ LSJ, s.v. βασιλεύς I.2b, with reference to Aristotle, *Ath. pol.* 41.3.
²⁰ Cf. Hilke Thür, "The Processional Way in Ephesos as a Place of Cult and Burial," in *Ephesos, Metropolis of Asia: An Interdisciplinary Approach to its Archaeology, Religion, and Culture* (ed. H. Koester; HTS 41; Valley Forge: Trinity Press

imperial period show the image of Androclus,²¹ proof that his memory was kept alive. It is not impossible that John's use of the term βασιλεῖς in Rev 10:11 would have reminded at least the Ephesian readers of the members of the local family who claimed descent from Androclus and who enjoyed elite status in the city, perhaps playing a role in the opposition against the Christians. Even if the charge "you must prophesy again about many peoples and nations and languages and kings" concerns kings universally (including the emperor, who was called βασιλεύς), the local "royals" are certainly affected by John's prophecy as well.

In Rev 17:15 the term φυλαί is replaced by ὄχλοι ("multitudes") which is linked with λαοί (here used as the first noun) by καί in the phrase λαοὶ καὶ ὄχλοι, while the third and fourth nouns are also linked (ἔθνη καὶ γλῶσσαι). It can be argued that since John's vision of Babylon uses ἔθνος for the nations over which Babylon rules (18:3, 23; cf. 14:8; 16:19), whereas λαός and ὄχλος are used for the people of God (18:4; 19:1, 6; cf. 7:9), the unique inclusion of ὄχλος indicates that "John has highlighted, in this form of the fourfold phrase, the contrast between the nations who serve Babylon and the people of God who suffer at her hands (17:6; 18:20, 24)."²² If the term ὄχλοι refers to the "multitudes" controlled by Babylon,²³ the term can be understood to indicate that the "peoples" (λαοί) consist of crowds, particularly the people living in the cities—crowds who are under the control of Babylon and to whom John's prophecy applies, and who thus need to come to faith in Jesus if they want to escape God's judgment and find salvation.

γλῶσσα

In the context of John's fourfold phrase, the term γλῶσσα designates "a language viewed in terms of persons using it," particularly "as a distinctive feature of nations."²⁴ The term γλῶσσα occurs three times after φυλή (5:9; 11:9; 14:6): it is the tribes, the sub-units of nations of peoples, who speak different languages; the term occurs twice after λαός (7:9; 13:7), and twice after ἔθνη (10:11; 17:15). The term occurs four times as the third noun in the fourfold phrase: in 10:11 after ἔθνη, in 11:9 after φυλαί, in 13:7 after λαός, and in 14:6 after φυλή. While the term can be used as a synonym of φυλή, λαός, and ἔθνος,²⁵ it is possible, indeed likely, that John's readers would have

---

International, 1995), 157-99; Peter Scherrer, *Ephesus: The New Guide* (Istanbul: Ege Yayinlari, 2000), 126.
²¹ Cf. F. Graf, "Androclus," *BNP* 1:683.
²² Bauckham, *Climax of Prophecy*, 331-32, quotation ibid. 332.
²³ Cf. Osborne, *Revelation*, 625, who relates all four terms of the phrase in 17:5 to "the sinners."
²⁴ BDAG, s.v. γλῶσσα 2b, for the following comment see ibid.
²⁵ Cf. Isa 66:18; Dan 3:4, 7; Jdt 3:8; *Ascen. Isa.* 3:18.

thought of specific people groups with specific languages. Christians living in the major cities of western Asia Minor such as Ephesus, Pergamum, and Smyrna spoke Greek, they were aware of Latin, they may have heard Hebrew and Aramaic spoken by the earliest missionaries (perhaps in prayers), and they were aware of the existence of the old indigenous languages in the region.

Even though most Greeks did not speak another language,[26] they knew that other languages existed. Galen asserts that one could write in a language other than Greek if necessary, but insists that the use of Greek is preferable: it is used everywhere, it is sweet-voiced (εὔγλωττον) and human (ἀνθρωπική), while non-Greek languages can be compared with the sounds of pigs, frogs, ravens and jackdaws (*De differentia pulsuum* 8.586). While Greek had become the lingua franca in Asia Minor during the Hellenistic period, the people could see inscriptions written in Latin,[27] in Hebrew (in cities with a Jewish community),[28] in Aramaic and in Phoenician, as well as in Carian, Lycian, Lydian and in several Pamphylian dialects dating to the classical and the Hellenistic periods.[29] Most of the ethnic groups in Asia Minor continued to use their indigenous languages: the absence of inscriptions does not prove the opposite, since the epigraphic practice was the result of Hellenization: the means of communication among the local tribes was largely oral.[30] The Carian language continued to be spoken in the region around Kaunos, and in the region of Kibyra one could still hear the Lydian language (Strabo, *Geogr.* 14.2.3; 14.2.8). Mithradates VI Eupator (120–163 B.C.) was evidently able to communicate in all twenty-two languages that were used in Pontus. Educated Cappadocians

---

[26] Cf. Anika Strobach, *Plutarch und die Sprachen: Ein Beitrag zur Fremdsprachenproblematik in der Antike* (Palingenesia 64; Stuttgart: Steiner, 1997), 183, who thinks that there was "a lack of necessity and a lack of interest." Note Galen's observation that "there was formerly a bilingualist, this was a miracle: a person who understood and spoke two languages" (δίγλωττος γάρ τις ἐλέγετο πάλαι, καὶ θαῦμα τοῦτο ἦν; *De differentia pulsuum* 8.585).

[27] Cf. Rosalinde A. Kearsley, Greeks and Romans in Imperial Asia: Mixed Language Inscriptions and Linguistic Evidence for Cultural Interaction until the End of AD III (Inschriften greichischer Stadte aus Kleinasien 59; Bonn: Habelt, 2001), with 171 bilingual, Latin-Greek inscriptions from Asia Minor, among them stones from Ephesus, Miletus, Smyrna (Ionia), Pergamum (Mysia), Philadelphia, Sardis, Thyatira (Lydia), Hierapolis, Laodicea (Phrygia).

[28] Cf. Walter Ameling, *Inscriptiones Judaicae Orientis: Band II: Kleinasien* (TSAJ 99; Tübingen: Mohr [Siebeck], 2004).

[29] Cf. Stephen Mitchell, *Anatolia: Land, Men, and Gods in Asia Minor* (2 vols.; Oxford: Oxford University Press, 1995), 1:172 n. 66-67. On Lydian see Roberti Gusmani, "Zum Stand der Erforschung der lydischen Sprache," in *Forschungen in Lydien* (ed. E. Schwertheim; Asia Minor Studien 17; Bonn: Habelt, 1995), 9-19.

[30] On the territory controlled by Selge, two long texts have been found that have not yet been deciphered; they are probably written in Pisidian; Mitchell, *Anatolia*, 1:173 with n. 82.

spoke Greek with a strong accent, while the simple people spoke various Cappadocian languages (Philostratus, *Vit. soph.* 2.13), while Iranian was still spoken in the fourth century A.D. in some settlements in the region. In the border areas of the provinces of Asia and Lycia, four indigenous languages could be heard: Pisidian, Solymian, Greek and Lydian (Strabo, *Geogr.* 13.1.65). In rural Galatia, the Celtic language continued to be spoken for a long time; ethnic Galatians (Celts) who consulted the oracle of Glykon in Abonuteichos in Paphlagonia needed a translator.[31] In the towns of Lycaonia, the Lycaonian language was still used in the first century (Acts 14:11-12). The Phrygian language was still in use in the fourth century A.D.: Socrates (A.D. 380–440) reports that the Arian bishop Selinus from Cotiaeum, who was of mixed Gothic and Phrygian origin, used both of these languages in his sermons (Socrates, *Hist. eccl.* 5.23).

Geographers, naturally, were aware of the languages spoken by the peoples living in the regions which they described. Strabo asserts that the distribution and difference of races (τὰ ἔθνη) and languages (αἱ διάλεκτοι) is not the result of design (providence) but accidental (*Geogr.* 2.3.7). He knows that the name of the city of Pola, located on the tip of the peninsula of Histria, comes from the language (γλῶσσα) of the Colthians who founded the city (*Geogr.* 1.2.39; 5.1.9). He describes Crete as a place where, beside the indigenous Cretans, we find Achaeans, Cydonians, Dorians, and Pelasgians, all of whom continue to speak their own languages, with the result that in Crete "one language[32] with others is mixed" (ἄλλη δ' ἄλλων γλῶσσα μεμιγμένη; 5.2.4; also 10.4.6). Even though the Faliscan language disappeared in the second century B.C., Strabo records the fact that the "special and distinct tribe" (ἴδιον ἔθνος) of the Falisci, with their city of Faliscum (northeast of Rome), had "a special language all its own" (ἰδιόγλωσσον; 5.2.9). Faliscan is known from ca. 280 inscriptions.[33] Strabo criticizes Apollodoros for saying that the language of the Carians (ἡ γλῶττα τῶν Καρῶν) is harsh, "for it is not, but even has very many Greek words mixed up with it" (14.2.28). Apart from γλῶσσα (Ionic) and γλῶττα (Attic), Strabo uses the term διάλεκτος to describe the language of peoples and tribes. He is aware of the fact that the nation (ἔθνος) of the Armenians, the nation of the Syrians, and the nation of the Arabians "betray a close affinity, not only in their language [κατά τε τὴν διάλεκτον], but in their mode of life" (1.2.34 [Jones, LCL]). He knows that the language of the people who live on both sides of the Euphrates is the same (2.1.31). He relates that a certain Indian whose ship had become stranded in Egypt had to learn Greek before he could speak with the king; the people who found him could not

---

[31] Mitchell, *Anatolia*, 1:173.

[32] H. L. Jones translated "tongue," departing from his normal rendering of γλῶσσα as "language" (LCL).

[33] Cf. G. Meiser, "Faliscan," *BNP* 5:325-26. The Faliscan alphabet is derived from Etruscan, and the language is closely related to Latin.

understand his language (μὴ συνιέντας τὴν διάλεκτον; 2.3.4). Strabo insists that the Greeks have four dialects: Attic, Ionic, Doric, and Aeolic (8.12.2; 14.5.26).[34] He argues that since there is no difference in either the language or in other customs between the Cataonians and the Cappadocians, "it is remarkable how utterly all signs of their being a different tribe [τὰ σημεῖα τῆς ἀλλοεθνίας] have disappeared" (12.1.2 [Jones, LCL]). The Mariandyni and the Caucones are similar to the Bithynians because the people do not appear to be "characterized by any ethnic difference, either in dialect (language) or otherwise" (οὐδὲ διάλεκτος οὐδ' ἄλλη διαφορὰ ἐθνική; 12.3.4 [Jones, LCL]). He knows that "the whole of that part of Cappadocia near the Halys river which extends along Paphlagonia uses two languages [ταῖς δυσὶ χρῆται διαλέκτοις] which abound in Paphlagonian names" (12.3.25; examples follow). He records the fact that as a result of the reign of the Romans and their different partition of the country, "most of the people have already lost both their dialects and their names" (ἐφ' ὧν ἤδη καὶ τὰς διαλέκτους καὶ τὰ ὀνόματα ἀποβεβλήκασιν οἱ πλεῖστοι; 12.4.6 [Jones, LCL]), i.e., their indigenous languages and their traditional personal names. He knows that the language of the Mysians "is, in a way, a mixture of the Lydian and the Phrygian languages" (μαρτυρεῖν δὲ καὶ τὴν διάλεκτον· μιξολύδιον γάρ πως εἶναι καὶ μιξοφρύγιον; 12.8.3). He speaks of barbarians "who are only beginning to learn Greek and are unable to speak it accurately, as is also the case with us in speaking their languages" (14.2.28 [Jones, LCL]). Strabo occasionally uses words of other languages: in addition to Latin words, he uses words from Gallic (μάδαρις, "spear," 4.4.3), Samnite (ἵρπος, "wolf," 5.4.12), Mesapic (βρεντέσιον, "ram's head," 6.3.6), Thracian (βρία, "young donkey," 7.6.1), Molossian (πελίαι πελίοι, "old men and women," 7 fr. 1a), and Medic (τίγρις, "arrow," 11.14.8).[35]

The reference to γλῶσσαι in John's vision of the great multitude standing before God's throne and before the Lamb (Rev 7:9) had a specific meaning for John's audience. The Christians in the cities of Asia Minor would have been reminded of the various languages that they had witnessed being spoken, that they had heard about, and that they themselves were using. The vision of 7:9 speaks not about nations in a general universalistic sense, but about a "great multitude" (ὄχλος πολύς) whose members nobody could count but who were individuals nevertheless: they are "robed in white, with palm branches in their

---

[34] Cf. Anna Panayotou, "Ionic and Attic," in *A History of Ancient Greek: From the Beginnings to Late Antiquity* (ed. A.-F. Christidis; Cambridge: Cambridge University Press, 2007), 405-16; Julián Méndez Dosuna, "The Doric Dialects," in ibid., 444-59; Julián Méndez Dosuna, "The Aeolic Dialects," in ibid., 460-74.

[35] Daniela Dueck, *Strabo of Amasia: A Greek Man of Letters in Augustan Rome* (New York: Routledge, 2000), 92, points out that the evidence does not allow for the conclusion that Strabo had real knowledge of these languages; he probably found these terms "in written sources or in oral information acquired from local inhabitants."

hands"—and they are people who speak different languages. This vision, together with the words of the "new song" that celebrates the fact that people "from every tribe and language and people and nation" have been ransomed by Jesus' sacrificial death, implies the missionary program of John and his churches: people in all language groups need to be reached with the gospel of Jesus Christ.

λαός

The term λαός describes 1. "people" in a general sense, both in the sense of populace (distributive use; Matt 4:23; 27:64; Acts 6:8) and in terms of a close gathering of people, i.e., a crowd or multitude (Strabo, *Geogr.* 13.1.53: Aeneas collected "a host of followers (λαὸν ἀθροίσαντα), also the people living in a city (Gen 19:4 LXX). 2. The "mass of a community as distinguished from special interest groups," e.g., the people in contrast to their leaders (Matt 26:5; Acts 2:47), to the scribes and Pharisees (Luke 7:29), to the priests (Heb 2:17; 5:3; 7:5, 27). 3. A "body of people with common cultural bonds and ties to a specific territory," thus a people-group or "people as a nation"[36] (Gen 49:16 LXX for the people of Hamor and Shechem who intermarry "so that they may be one people" according to Gen 34:22 LXX; for the meaning "country" cf. 2 Kgs 16:15; Ezra 4:4; 10:2, 11; Neh 10:31). 4. The "people of God," both the people of Israel (e.g., Mark 7:6; Acts 3:23; 7:17; 28:17) and the followers of Jesus (Acts 15:14; Rom 9:25; Rev 18:4; 21:3).[37]

Apart from Rev 18:4; 21:3 where the term λαός refers to the followers of Jesus as the people of God, most interpreters assume sense 3 for λαός in 5:9; 13:7; 14:6 and for λαοί in 7:9; 10:11; 11:9; 17:15.[38] While this is both a possible and a plausible connotation, the third meaning is more complex than many NT scholars think, and the first and the second meanings need to be taken into account as well.

The first meaning ("people, crowd, multitude, people living in a city") is a possible connotation of the term λαός/λαοί, especially when it is the first element in John's fourfold phrase. Without the context of the three terms mentioned subsequently, λαοί in 10:11; 11:9; 17:15 readily denotes the populations of the cities of Asia Minor. Strabo describes the people who came from Greece to establish a colony in Ionia as λαός (*Geogr.* 14.1.3 with regard

---

[36] BDAG, s.v. λαός 3, with reference to Rev 5:9; 7:9; 10:11; 11:9; 13:7; 14:6; 17:15; Luke 2:31. Cf. Ceslas Spicq, "λαός," *TLNT* 2:371-74 [371].

[37] L&N give four meanings for λαός: crowd (entry 11.1), people of God (11.12), nation (11.55), common people (87.64). On λαός see H. Strathmann, "λαός," *TDNT* 4:29-57; H. Frankemölle, "λαός," *EDNT* 2:339-44; C. Spicq, *TLNT* 2:371-74.

[38] Typical are Bauckham, *Climax of Prophecy*, 328, who describes the four nouns in the fourfold phrase as nouns that describe "all the nations of the world", and Aune, *Revelation*, 361, who speaks of "four ethnic units."

to Priene).³⁹ The proclamation of the church and her witnesses is addressed to the people living in the cities in which the believers live, to the crowds of people who could be found in the Agora and in other public places (cf. Acts 17:17).

The second meaning ("the mass of a community as distinguished from special interest groups") is also a possible connotation of λαός/λαοί in John's fourfold phrase. Jesus, Peter, and Paul preached the good news to the mass of people living in a particular region (Galilee) or city (Jerusalem, or Corinth), whether the political or religious leaders approved of their activities or not, often in conscious contrast to the local leadership (e.g., Luke 13:31-33; Acts 5:27-42; 18:1-17).

The third meaning ("a body of people with common cultural bonds and ties to a specific territory")⁴⁰ is common in Hellenistic Greek, attested in the LXX,⁴¹ in literary and in documentary texts.⁴² Strabo refers to Herodotus for his assertion that "the Pamphylians are the descendants of the peoples (τῶν λαῶν) led by Amphilochus and Calchas, a miscellaneous throng who accompanied them from Troy," and he refers to Callinus for his assertion that Mopsus, the co-founding companion of Amphilochus and Calchas, led "peoples" (τοὺς λαούς) over the Taurus and that while some remained in Pamphylia, "the others were dispersed in Cilicia, and also in Syria as far even as Phoenicia" (*Geogr.* 14.4.3 [Jones, LCL]). Here the first reference to λαοί (the people from whom the Pamphylians descend) has what we would call an "ethnic" connotation, while the second reference to λαοί (people who settled in Cilicia and Syria), designating the same original "people group," does not describe ethnic cohesion, at least not in the first century A.D. when Strabo writes. While most NT scholars assume an ethnic meaning for λαός/λαοί in Revelation, in the ancient sources the social and political sense is primary. C. Spicq describes this meaning of λαός as "the legal and political sense in which 'the people' expresses the idea of an organism, tied together by legal structures directed toward the common good."⁴³ There are two specific uses of the term attested in inscriptions and papyri.

---

³⁹ H. L. Jones translates λαός in Strabo, *Geogr.* 14.1.3, as "colony" (LCL).

⁴⁰ Cf. L&N, entry 11.55: ἔθνος and λαός both describe (sometimes) "the largest unit into which the people of the world are divided on the basis of their constituting a sociopolitical community—'nation, people'."

⁴¹ Gen 41:40; Exod 1:22 (the Egyptians as Pharaoh's λαός); Neh 9:10 (the Pharaoh and his servants and the people of his land); Ezek 7:27 (the king mourns, the prince is in despair, the hands of the people of the land tremble).

⁴² Cf. Orsolina Montevecchi, "LAOS: Linee di una ricerca storico-linguistica [1979]," in *Scripta Selecta* (Biblioteca di Aevum antiquum; ed. S. Daris; Milano: Vita e pensiero, 1998), 401-19, 415. Cf. Theo A.W. van der Louw, *Transformations in the Septuagint: Towards an Interaction of Septuagint Studies and Translation Studies* (CBET 47; Leuven/Dudley, Mass.: Peters, 2007), 181.

⁴³ C. Spicq, *TLNT* 2:373.

(1) The meaning "common people, village peasants, serfs" of the plural λαοί is attested in inscriptions from western Asia Minor of the Hellenistic period,[44] designating the native population in the villages, i.e., indigenous peasants. Some have interpreted the epigraphic evidence from Asia Minor as indicating a change of the status of the common people (λαοί) during the Hellenistic period. P. Briant argued that the Seleucids, in their attempt to create a modern state, transformed the local serfs (slaves) into λαοί βασιλικοί who lived in the villages, owned houses, and had freedom of movement.[45] In the Laodike inscription from ca. 254/253 B.C. which records the sale of land by the Seleucid king Antiochos II to Laodike, his divorced queen, the relevant lines read: "Issue orders that the village and the mansion and the surrounding land be conveyed to Arrhidaios, the bailiff of Laodike, along with the *laoi* with all their households and all their belongings [τοὺς λαοὺς πανοικίους σὺν τοῖς ὑπάρχουσιν αὐτοῖς πᾶσιν], and record the sale in the royal registry at Sardeis and on five stone stelae" (IDidyma 492, lines 26-27). G. E. M. de St. Croix has disputed the view that all λαοί achieved freedom; he insists that the term λαοί βασιλικοί designates the native population who could be sold together with the village in which they lived, that the λαοί, "the native population of each area," consisted largely of serfs, and that the change during the Hellenistic period involved the transfer of the peasants from "king's land" (and the lordship of a local dynast) to a Greek city, with the result that sometimes the serfs became slaves while sometimes they became free leasehold tenants or, conceivably, freeholders.[46] In contemporary research,[47] the λαοί of Hellenistic Asia Minor

---

[44] Note the Aristodikides inscription Illion 33 (275 B.C.) = C. Bradford Welles, *Royal Correspondence in the Hellenistic Period: A Study in Greek Epigraphy* (New Haven: Kondakov Institute, 1934; repr., Chicago: Ares Publishers, 1974), No. 11-13; the Mnesimachos inscription ISardBR VII 1, 1 (ca. 200 B.C.) = William H. Buckler and David M. Robinson, *Sardis VII.i: Greek and Latin Inscriptions* (Leiden: Brill, 1932), No. 1; cf. Gerassimos G. Aperghis, *The Seleukid Royal Economy: The Finances and Financial Administration of the Seleukid Empire* (Cambridge: Cambridge University Press, 2004), 320-23; the Laodike inscription IDidyma 492 (254/253 B.C.) = Welles, *Royal Correspondence in the Hellenistic Period*, No. 18 (= OGI 225); Aperghis, *Seleukid Royal Economy*, 315-18. See also UPZ 110, 100-103; P.Stras. 93, 4. Note also Gen 41:40 LXX (the Egyptians are the λαός of Pharaoh); Luke 22:2; 23:13 (Pilate summons the chief priests, the elders, and the people); cf. Spicq, *TLNT* 2:373 with n. 7.
[45] Pierre Briant, "Remarques sur 'laoi' et esclavages ruraux en Asie Mineure hellénistique [1973]," in *Rois, tributs et paysans: Études sur les formations tributaires du Moyen-Orient ancien* (Annales littéraires de l'Université de Besançon 43; Paris: Les Belles lettres, 1982), 95-135; followed by Jean Georges Texier, "Nabis et les Hilotes," *Dialogues d'histoire ancienne* 1 (1974): 189-205 [195].
[46] Geoffrey E. M. de Ste. Croix, *The Class Struggle in the Ancient Greek World: From the Archaic Age to the Arab Conquests* (Ithaca: Cornell University Press, 1989), 151-52, 157-58; for a critique of Briant cf. ibid. 566 n. 26.
[47] Cf. J. Gerber, "Laoi," BNP 7:236; Pierre Debord, *Aspects sociaux et économiques de la vie religieuse dans l'anatolie gréco-romaine* (EPRO 88; Leiden: Brill, 1982), 250;

are regarded as village peasants who were not slaves in the classical sense of the term, but serfs.⁴⁸ As members of the community of the village, they lived in their own houses, had private property, could take legal action within a narrow framework, and had to pay dues to the king or their lord; they were evidently free to move to a different location, but they could be sold as a community to individuals or to a god (i.e., a temple). After the Hellenistic period, epigraphic references to the λαοί disappear. This fact, combined with the observation that this use of the term λαοί occurs only in inscriptions but not in literary sources, calls for caution in assuming the meaning "village peasants, serfs" as a connotation that the readers of John's Revelation would have assumed. However, since the inscriptions in question were still displayed in public places in the first century—the Laodike inscription notes that the text was to be recorded on five stone stelae, specifying, "of these one is to be set up at Ilion in the temple of Athene, another in the temple (of the Gods) in Samothrake, another at Ephesos in the temple of Artemis, the fourth at Didyma in the temple of Apollo and the fifth at Sardeis in the temple of Artemis" (IDidyma 492, lines 27-33)—both the citizens in the urban centers and the village people in rural areas would presumably have been aware of this (former) meaning of the term λαοί. It thus seems possible that the term λαοί reminded John's readers of the village people among whom missionaries preached the gospel, some of whom had responded by coming to faith in Jesus and who now belonged to the people (λαός) of God. Jesus had preached in the villages of Galilee (Matt 9:35; Mark 6:6, 56; 8:23, 27; Luke 8:1; 9:6; 10:38; 13:22; 17:12),⁴⁹ and Peter and John preached in Samaritan villages (Acts 8:25). While we have no specific reference to villages in Asia Minor being reached with the gospel, Luke's report that "all the residents of Asia [πάντας τοὺς κατοικοῦντας τὴν Ἀσίαν], both Jews and Greeks, heard the word of the Lord" (Acts 19:10) when

---

Fanoula Papazoglou, *Laoi et Paroikoi: Recherches sur la structure de la société hellénistique* (Études d'histoire ancienne 1; Beograd: Centre d'études épigraphiques et numismatiques, 1997), especially 113-40; Christof Schuler, *Ländliche Siedlungen und Gemeinden im hellenistischen und römischen Kleinasien* (Vestigia 50; München: Beck, 1998), 182-83; Aperghis, *Seleukid Royal Economy*, 111-12, who concludes that the term λαοί was a technical term "adopted by Hellenistic administrations to denote all the native inhabitants subject to them, as distinct from the Greeks" (ibid. 112); Mauro Corsaro, "Sovrani, cittadini, servi: aspetti sociali dell'Asia Minore ellenistica," Mediterraneo Antico 4 (2001): 17-40; Robartus J. van der Spek, "The Hellenistic Near East," in *The Cambridge Economic History of the Greco-Roman World* (ed. W. Scheidel, I. Morris, and R. Saller; Cambridge: Cambridge University Press, 2007), 409-33, 415, who describes the λαοὶ βασιλικοί as "serf-like peasants" or "king's people" who tilled the land on royal domains in the Hellenistic period.

⁴⁸ The Mnesimachus inscription mentions both λαοί (ISardBR VII 1, 1, line 11) and οἰκέται, i.e. slaves (col. 2, line 5). Cf. Schuler, *Siedlungen*, 182; Papazoglou, *Laoi et Paroikoi*, 46-47.

⁴⁹ In Mark 5:56 farms are mentioned besides villages and towns.

Paul was active in Ephesus suggests that besides people living in the cities, village people (who would have been called "Greeks" in the first century) would have been in view as well. When Paul asserts in his letter to the believers in Corinth that the church consists largely of the powerless, uneducated, and disenfranchised, whether freedmen or slaves (1 Cor 1:26-28), this would have been true for most other congregations as well, allowing for the presence of (former and/or present) village people in the church, among them possibly descendants of the serfs called λαοί of an earlier period.

(2) In Egyptian papyri, the term λαοί describes "noteworthies," the class of people who governed the villages, the officials above the common folk, distinct from the mass of farm laborers.[50] They announce the beginning of harvest time, they collect taxes, they carry out public works such as excavations and drainage projects.[51] They "enjoy not only a relative autonomy but also the confidence of the officials."[52] If this meaning is relevant not only for Egypt, if it would have been recognized in Asia Minor, it could denote, perhaps in the towns with little Roman influence, the local notables whom missionaries sought to reach with the gospel (cf. Acts 4:5-12; 13:6-12; 25:23–26:29), and who could make life difficult for Christians (and where thus included in the groups upon whom judgment is pronounced by John).

---

[50] Claude Vandersleyen, "Le mot λαός dans la langue des papyrus grecs," *Chronique d' Égypte* 48 (1973): 339-49, evaluating twenty-six papyri, e.g. UPZ 110, 101; SB 7179, 4; P.Tebt. 701, lines 74, 80. Cf. Montevecchi, "Laos," 407. Claude Orrieux, *Zénon de Caunos, parépidèmos, et le destin grec* (Centre de recherches d'histoire ancienne 64; Paris: Les Belles Lettres, 1985), 211, thinks that Vandersleyen is essentially correct, but disagrees with his designation of the λαοί as "notables," suggesting instead that their power derived from their active solidarity. Pierre Briant, "Villages et communautés villageoises d'Asie Achéménide et hellénistique [1975]," in *Rois, tributs et paysans: Études sur les formations tributaires du Moyen-Orient ancien* (Annales littéraires de l'Université de Besançon 43; Paris: Les Belles Lettres, 1982), 137-60 [143 n. 26], is critical, and insists that at least in Asia Minor the term λαοί designates without ambiguity "à toute le population rurale dépendante" (the entire dependent rural population). Note the term λαοκριταί which denotes a board of Egyptian judges "administering justice for the indigenous population" (S. R. Llewelyn, in *New Documents Illustrating Early Christianity* [ed. Greg H. R. Horsley and Stephen R. Llewelyn; 9 vols.; Macquarie University: North Ryde, New South Wales, Australia, 1981–2002], 9:53).
[51] PSI 577, 23; P.Petr. II, p. 52; 15, 1b; 13, 45, 3; SB 7179, 4; P.Petr. II, p. 14; 14, 11, 4; also P. Rev. 42, 11 ("let the *laoi* and the other farmers estimate their produce").
[52] Spicq, *TLNT* 2:373-74.

ἔθνος

In the NT, the term ἔθνος has two meanings:[53] 1. A "body of persons united by kinship, culture, and common traditions,"[54] translated as "nation, people," e.g., the Jewish people (τὸ ἔθνος τῶν Ἰουδαίων; Acts 10:22),[55] the Samaritan people (τὸ ἔθνος τῆς Σαμαρείας; Acts 8:9), the seven nations in Canaan (ἔθνη ἑπτὰ ἐν γῇ Χανάαν; Acts 13:19), all the nations of the world (πάντα τὰ ἔθνη τοῦ κόσμου; Luke 12:30), every nation of humankind (πᾶν ἔθνος ἀνθρώπων; Acts 17:26). In extra-biblical Greek texts, the plural term ἔθνη denotes also tribes, clans, nations, peoples, i.e., "ethnically homogeneous groups"[56] such as the Lycians (Λυκίων μέγα ἔθνος; Homer, *Il.* 12.330), the Achaian people (Ἀχαιῶν ἔθνος; Homer, *Il.* 17.552), the nations of the Greeks besides the Macedonians (IEph I 24B, lines 18-19), the Egyptian nations (μελαμπούδων ἐθνέων; ILaodikeia 95, line 6);[57] the term is also used to designate "swarms" of animals such as birds (Homer, *Il.* 2.84, 459, 469). 2. The plural term τὰ ἔθνη "people groups foreign to a specific people group." In the LXX this term corresponds to Hebr. גּוֹיִם, a nationalistic expression that designates foreigners, a meaning attested in Greek texts: barbarian nations (Aristotle, *Pol.* 1324b10), nomadic peoples (Νομάδων ἔθνος; Polybius, *Hist.* 1.31.2; Diodorus Siculus 26.23.1), at Athens for the athletic clubs of the non-Athenians (IG II 444), also for the governor of a Roman province (ὁ ἡγούμενος τοῦ ἔθνος, "the governor of the province," P.Oxy. VII 1020). In inscriptions, the cities are sometimes contrasted with the "people" or "tribes" living outside the cities.[58] In the LXX and the NT, the term designates in the context of this sense (a) non-Jews, Gentiles, polytheists (Matt 10:18; Acts 14:5; Rom 3:29), and (b) non-Jewish believers in Jesus, Gentile Christians (Gal 2:12;

---

[53] BDAG, s.v. ἔθνος 1-2. Cf. G. Bertram and K. L. Schmidt, "ἔθνος," *TDNT* 2:364-72; N. Walter, "ἔθνος," *EDNT* 1:381-83.

[54] LSJ, s.v. ἔθνος I.1 defines "number of people living together, company, body of men," e.g. ἔθνος ἑταίρων ("band of comrades"; Homer, *Il.* 3.32), ἔθνος λαῶν ("host of people"; Homer, *Il.* 13.495).

[55] Cf. Polybius, in Josephus, *Ant.* 12.135; Agatharchides, 86 Frag. 20b (Josephus, *Ant.* 12.6); Diodorus Siculus 34-35 Frag. 1, 2; Philo, *Decalogue* 96.

[56] Louw, *Transformations*, 182.

[57] Cf. Thomas Corsten, *Die Inschriften von Laodikeia am Lykos: Teil I: Die Inschriften* (Inschriften griechischer Städte aus Kleinasien 49.1; Bonn: Habelt, 1997), 94-97; the text dated ca. A.D. 250 is a poem inscribed on a triumphal arch, honoring a man who held various offices in Europe, Egypt, Asia, Spain, and "the blackfooted nations," i.e., in Egypt.

[58] In the decree that Miletus passed concerning the inauguration of the Didyma games as crowned statues *agones* (*SIG* III 590; I. Miletus III 1052; cf. Joseph E. Fontenrose, *Didyma: Apollo's Oracle, Cult, and Companions* [Berkeley: University of California Press, 1988], 185-87), the public is reminded of the oracles of Apollo of Didyma which benefited "not a few tribes, cities, and kings" (ἐξ ὧν ἔθνη τε οὐκ ὀλίγα καὶ πόλεις καὶ τῶν βασιλέων; lines 11-12).

Rom 16:4; Eph 3:1). A further meaning in extra-biblical texts is (c) "class of people" such as "orders" of priests (τὰ ἱερὰ ἔθνη; OGI 90.17), trade associations or guilds (ἔθνη καὶ ἐργαστήρια; P.Petr. 3; P.Köln 206.3).[59]

In Revelation, the term "the nations" (τὰ ἔθνη), used with meaning 1, occurs fifteen times outside of the fourfold formula, describing the nations that have aligned themselves with the powers of evil (Rev 11:2, 18; 12:5; 14:8; 18:3, 23; 19:15; 20:3; cf. 2:26). In view of 2:9 and 3:9 ("synagogue of Satan"), the "nations" include the Jewish people. Besides these negative statements, the "nations" are also said to one day worship God (15:4), a prophecy that is realized in the New Jerusalem (21:24, 26; 22:2). In John's fourfold phrase, the term ἔθνος in 5:9 and ἔθνη in 7:9 designates Christian believers who come from every people group united by kinship, culture, and common traditions, including the "others" who are despised by the general population and any associations or guilds that may be designated locally with the term ἔθνη. The term reminds the readers of Jesus' ministry in "the Galilee of the Gentiles" (Γαλιλαία τῶν ἐθνῶν), of Jesus' commission to proclaim the gospel to and make disciples of "all nations" (πάντα τὰ ἔθνη; Matt 28:19), "the whole human race" (πᾶν ἔθνος ἀνθρώπων) that God had created from one ancestor "to inhabit the whole earth" (κατοικεῖν ἐπὶ παντὸς προσώπου τῆς γῆς; Acts 17:26),[60] and of Paul's missionary work among the "nations" fulfilling the prophecy of Isaiah who announced that the Servant of the Lord would be "light to the Gentiles" (φῶς ἐθνῶν) bringing "salvation to the ends of the earth" (εἰς σωτηρίαν ἕως ἐσχάτου τῆς γῆς; Acts 13:47). At the same time, believers in John's audience would have heard the connotation of "foreigners" and "associations," while Jewish Christians would have heard the connotation "Gentiles" or "polytheists."

Conclusion

While the fourfold phrase certainly suggests universality—both of the existence of believers in Jesus in "every tribe and language and people and nation" and of God's judgment on "all peoples and tribes and languages and nations"—it also expresses ethnic, tribal, social, and political identity, both of the Christians and

---

[59] Cf. LSJ, s.v. ἔθνος I.3; cf. MM, s.v. ἔθνος. For the meaning "guild" or "association" see also P.Köln 260, discussed by S. R. Llewelyn in G. H. R. Horsley, *New Documents Illustrating Early Christianity* (Sydney: Ancient History Documentary Research Center, Macquarie University, 1981), 9:38-41 (for the evidence see ibid. 39 n. 2).

[60] In Revelation, the phrase "the inhabitants of the earth" (οἱ κατοικοῦντες ἐπὶ τῆς γῆς; 3:10; 6:10; 8:13; 11:10 [twice]; 13:8, 14 [twice]; 17:8; cf. 17:2) has a consistently negative overtone, describing "the universal worship of the beast and the universal corruption of the earth by Babylon" (Bauckham, *Climax of Prophecy*, 240). At the same time, the expression would have reminded the churches of Jesus' missionary commission to reach all people "to the ends of the earth" (ἕως ἐσχάτου τῆς γῆς; Acts 1:8).

of their oppressors. In Rev 5:9 and 7:9 John reminds the Christians who belong to churches in the cities of Asia Minor that they should look beyond their own congregations and realize that there are followers of Jesus in every tribe (φυλή), i.e., in every family clan and in each of the φυλαί of the cities; in every language group (γλῶσσα), i.e., in every tribe and nation who are distinguished by the languages that they speak; in every people (λαός), i.e., in every group connected through cultural bonds and ties to a specific territory, including the populace of the cities and the village people; in every nation (ἔθνος), i.e., in each group of people united by kinship, culture, and common traditions, including foreigners and members of associations. Individual people from all these ethnic, linguistic, tribal, civic, political, and social backgrounds have repented and now worship the one true and living God, having found salvation by faith in Jesus whose sacrificial death saves those who believe from God's judgment and integrates them into the messianic people of God. Since all people without exception, irrespective of heritage or status or affiliation will be judged by God, people from all ethnic, linguistic, tribal, civic, political, and social backgrounds need to hear the gospel of Jesus Christ. This is the task of the evangelists and missionaries of the congregations in the cities of Asia Minor: to proclaim the goods news of salvation by faith in Jesus Christ to all people—in every tribe and language and people and nation.

Index of Modern Authors

Aagaard, Marie 230.
Achtemeier, Paul J. 342.
Adams, Edward 200.
Adler, Y. 129.
Alexander, Loveday 145, 174.
Allen, G. 63.
Allen, Leslie C. 232.
Allison, Dale C. 107.
Ameling, Walter 376.
Aperghis, Gerassimos G. 381, 382.
Asano, Atsuhiro 198.
Attridge, H. W. 86, 329-32, 339, 341, 342.
Aune, David 144, 342, 348-49, 354, 356, 358-60, 363, 366, 369-70, 379.
Austen, Jane 83.
Austin, J. L. 272-73.
Averbeck, Richard 352.
Balibar, E. 59.
Balch, David 115, 199, 342.
Banks, R. J. 16, 33, 107, 109.
Barclay, John M. G. 198.
Barram, Michael 151.
Barrett, C. K. 17, 69, 77, 128, 137, 152, 333.
Barr, David 347, 352.
Barth, Karl 53, 270-71.
Barth, Markus 53.
Bauckham, R. 91, 330, 336, 342, 348, 352-54, 360-61, 364-66, 369, 374-75, 379, 385.
Baumbach, Gunther 329.
Baur, F. C. 105, 116, 274, 296.
Beale, G. K. 195, 222, 232, 340-43, 349, 352, 353, 354-56, 358-60, 363, 365, 366, 369-70.
Beasley-Murray, George R. 354, 365-66, 370.
Beker, J. Christiaan 275.
Bellinzoni, Arthur 117.

Berger, Peter L. 142.
Bertram, G. 384.
Best, Ernest 236-37.
Betz, H. D. 107.
Betz, O. 18.
Bhabha, H. K. 59.
Birge, Mary Katherine 210.
Blaising, C. 294.
Blenkinsopp, J. 344.
Blomberg, Craig 41, 46, 91.
Bock, Darrell 6, 24, 51, 55, 97, 143, 294.
Bockmuehl, Markus 245-46, 251, 259.
Bonk, Jonathan J. 315.
Bonz, Marianne Palmer 145.
Boring, M. E. 116, 300, 354.
Bosch, David J. 151, 230, 246, 248-49.
Bovon, Francois 174.
Boxall, Ian 359-60, 363.
Brawley, R. L. 142.
Bredin, Mark 354.
Briant, P. 381, 383.
Briggs, Richard 273.
Brinkmann, B. 298, 307, 314.
Brown, Alexandra 275.
Brown, J. K. 291-93.
Brown, Raymond 117.
Brox, N. 282, 299.
Bruce, F. F. 1-3, 15, 19, 88, 150, 152, 154, 267, 269-70, 330, 338.
Buckler, William H. 381.
Bultmann, Rudolf 318-20, 326, 349.
Burge, Gary M. 45, 123.
Burridge, Richard A. 202.
Butarbutar, Robinson 198.
Cadbury, H. J. 138, 147, 153, 163, 166, 178.

Caird, George B. 355, 360, 362-63, 365, 366.
Calvin, John 14, 272, 273.
Campbell, William S. 198.
Capes, David B. 251.
Carroll, J. T. 142-43.
Carson, D.A. 18, 45, 106-09, 232.
Castelli, Elizabeth 269.
Chester, Stephen J. 204.
Chilton, Bruce D. 217-18.
Chow, John K. 198.
Ciampa, Roy 190, 194, 222, 229.
Clarke, A. D. 19, 162, 197-98, 205, 268.
Claydon, David 229.
Collins, Adela Y. 47.
Collins, C. John 216.
Collins, Jack 216.
Collins, John N. 158.
Collver, Albert 152.
Conzelmann, Hanz 135-36, 140, 147-48, 152, 165, 181, 282.
Cook, Albert 159.
Corsaro, Mauro 382.
Corsten, Thomas 384.
Corwin, Gary B. 247-48.
Cosby, M. R. 326.
Couser, G. A. 277-78, 280, 282, 284, 288, 290, 292.
Crafton, J. A. 198, 267.
Cranfield, C. E. B. 56.
Crawford, Charles 266.
Cullmann, O. 282, 330.
Danker, Frederick 267.
Daube, D. 112.
Davies, W. D. 107, 336.
Davis, William Stearns 164.
Dawes, Gregory 50.
Delling, G. 282.
deSilva, David A. 357, 363.
Dibelius, Martin 163-66, 179, 282.
Dickens, Charles 83.
Dickson, John P. 184-89, 328.
Donelson, L. 292.

Donfried, Karl 13, 252, 265-66, 269, 271, 273.
Dodd, C. H. 35, 97.
Donaldson, Terence 56, 71.
Dosuna, Julian Mendez 378.
Dube, M. 60.
Dueck, Daniela 378.
Dunn, James D. G. 23, 25, 28, 30-33, 38-39, 182, 203, 246, 331, 334.
Dupont, J. 319.
Duranti, Alessandro 157.
Dutch, Robert S. 198.
Easton, B. S. 135, 137.
Ebner, Martin 319.
Ehrhardt, Norbert 372.
Elitzur, Yoel 125.
Ellicott, C. J. 287, 291.
Ellingworth, Paul 317, 331.
Elliot, J. H. 331, 342.
Ellis, E. E. 18, 150.
Esler, P. F. 141-42, 199.
Evans, Craig A. 45, 285.
Evans, Donald D. 272-73.
Evans, H. H. 136.
Even-zohar, I. 59.
Farrow, Douglas 342.
Fee, Gordon 21, 23, 49, 216, 221, 245, 251-53, 255-56, 258-59, 279, 282-83, 287, 293.
Ferrari, Markus Scheifer 320-21.
Finger, Reta H. 153-54.
Fischer, John 43, 47.
Fitzgerald, J. T. 317-20, 322, 325-26, 332.
Fitzmyer, J. A. 150, 176.
Foakes-Jackson, F. J. 152, 163.
Fontenrose, Joseph E. 384.
Fowl, Stephen E. 245, 256-57, 266.
France, R. T. 2, 4-5, 7, 81, 84, 283.
Frankel, Max 374.
Frankemolle, H. 379.
Friesen, Steven J. 198.

Index of Modern Authors

Fruchtenbaum, Arnold 43.
Furnish, V. P. 65, 73, 75, 181-82, 192.
Furstenberg, Y. 47, 133.
Garland, David E. 187, 205.
Garnsey, Peter 188.
Gehring, Roger W. 199.
Gempf, Conrad 162, 166, 179.
Gerber, J. 382.
Gibson, S. 125-31, 133.
Giesen, Heinz 353, 360, 363, 366.
Gilbert, Greg 97.
Gillespie, Thomas 272.
Glaser, Mitch 55.
Glasson, Francis T. 179.
Goldberg, Louis 47.
Gombis, Timothy 53, 235.
Goodwin, J. 284.
Gordon, R. P. 88, 91.
Goulder, Michael 20, 105, 107-08, 116.
Graf, F. 375.
Green, Gene L. 161.
Green, Joel 1, 6-7, 13, 135, 138-39, 142, 151, 178, 331.
Grigsby, B. 127.
Guelich, Robert A. 16, 106-07, 110.
Gunther, Wolfgang 372.
Gusmani, Roberti 376.
Guthrie, George H. 336.
Hacking, K. J. 27.
Haenchen, E. 147, 153.
Hagele, Clemens 295.
Hagner, Donald A. 3, 45, 106-07, 109-10, 203.
Hainz, J. 75.
Hall, Robert G. 50.
Hamilton, C. H. 326.
Hansen, M. H. 373.
Harland, Philip A. 198, 210.
Harris, Murray J. 256, 358.
Hawthorne, Gerald F. 18, 251-52.
Hays, Richard B. 187, 335.

Heckert, J. 279.
Hemer, Colin 150, 166, 175-77, 351.
Hengel, Martin 20, 117, 156, 176-78, 329.
Henry, Matthew 272.
Herrmann, Peter 372.
Hickling, C. J. A. 330.
Hill, A. E. 196.
Hill, Craig C. 153.
Hill, David 272.
Hock, R. F. 33, 267.
Hodgson, Robert 319, 326.
Hoehner, Harold W. 236.
Holmberg, Bengt 49, 198.
Holtz, Traugott 265-66, 269
Hooker, Morna D. 17, 330, 333.
Hornblower, Simon 168.
Horrell, D. G. 33, 199-200.
Horsley, H. R. 383, 385.
Hubbard, David 4.
Hughes, F. W. 271.
Hughes, Phillip E. 359-60.
Humphrey, Edith M. 352.
Hurst, L. D. 86, 330, 333, 342.
Hvalvik, Reidar 115.
Hwa, Shi Wen 320.
Isaacs, Marie E. 335.
Incigneri, B. J. 47.
Jackson-McCabe, Matt 115.
Jacobson, D. M. 129.
Jauhiainen, Marko 353.
Jenkins, Philip 315.
Jeremias, J. 298, 314, 336.
Jervell, Jacob 50, 135, 137.
Jewett, R. 33, 51.
Johnson, Luke Timothy 176-77, 315.
Johnson, Richard W. 333.
Jones, Nicholas F. 372-73.
Jones, F. Stanley 116.
Jones, L. P. 127.
Jowett, Benjamin 274.
Judge, Edwin A. 197.

Juster, Dan 43.
Karrer, Martin 370.
Kasemann, E. 147.
Kearsley, R. A. 376.
Keener, Craig 128, 351, 353, 356, 358-60.
Keesmaat, Sylvia C. 234-36.
Kelly, J. N. D. 282, 288.
Kern, F. H. 274.
Kidd, R. 279.
Kim, S. 285.
Kinzer, Mark 41-54.
Kleinknecht, K. T. 319.
Knight, George W. III 280-81, 284, 289-90.
Knopf, R. 297, 306.
Koch, Klaus 275.
Koester, Craig R. 329-31.
Koester, Helmut 117, 329, 375.
Kon, G. 128.
Kostenberger, Andreas 24, 53, 182, 246, 250, 284, 297.
Kraftchick, Steven 65.
Kretschmar, G. 287.
Kummel, W. 147.
Laansma, John C. 327, 335, 340-41.
Lachs, Samuel T. 45.
Lackey, Jennifer 176.
Ladd, George E. 16, 181, 359, 360, 365.
LaGrand, James 328.
Lane, William L. 331, 333, 335, 339, 344.
Larkin, William, J. 139, 150, 246.
Lawrence, Jonathan 128,
Lewis, Philip E. 71.
Lienhard, J. T. 153, 156.
Lightfoot, J. B. 270.
Lincoln, Andrew T. 53, 237.
Lindars, B. 18, 88, 330, 338, 342.
Livingston, Michael 151.
Llewelyn, S. R. 383, 385.
Longenecker, Bruce W. 23, 198.

Longenecker, Richard N. 16, 21-22, 198, 254.
Luckman, T. 142.
Ludemann, Gerd 116.
Lunemann, Gottlieb 274.
Luomanen, Petri 116.
Luther, Martin 88.
Luz, Ulrich 106-08, 112, 115.
Lyons, George 269-70.
Macleod, Colin W. 172.
Maddox, Robert 135, 140, 152.
Magen, Y. 129.
Malherbe, A. J. 268-69, 282, 317.
Manson, T. W. 87, 330, 332-34.
Marshall, Howard 1-8, 11-14, 16, 21, 24-25, 37, 46, 54, 56, 81-82, 97, 114, 121, 123, 135-36, 140-41, 150, 155, 161-62, 175, 181-82, 197, 203, 207, 213-14, 229, 245, 247, 249-50, 252, 254, 258-59, 262-63, 268, 270, 274, 277, 279-85, 287-88, 290, 296, 316-17, 327-28, 330, 335, 347, 354, 357, 369-70.
Martin, R. P. 15, 19, 69, 256.
Martyn, J. L. 147, 165, 275.
Massaux, Edouard 117.
Mathewson, Dave 56, 361.
Matill, A. J. 135.
McCool, F.J. 127.
McGee, Gary B. 247-48.
McIntosh, John A. 248.
McRae, Mary B. 201.
Meeks, Wayne A. 197, 331.
Meggitt, Justin J. 198.
Meier, John P. 117.
Meiser, G. 377.
Merk, Otto 266.
Michaels, J. Ramsey 342.
Milet III, I. 372.
Milne, A. A. 7.
Milne, Bruce 55.
Mitchell, Margaret M. 190.
Mitchell, Stephen 376-77.

Moessner, David 21, 138, 145, 150.
Moloney, F. J. 87.
Moltmann, Jurgen 230.
Montevecchi, Orsolina 380, 383.
Moo, Douglas J. 52, 327.
Moreau, A. Scott 247-48.
Moritz, Thorsten 231-33.
Moscato, M. A. 141.
Mosser, Carl 336.
Mounce, Robert 349, 353, 358, 360, 370.
Mounce, William 6, 281, 287-90.
Mouw, Richard 41-42.
Muller, U. 271-72.
Murphy-O'Connor, J. 190.
Nau, Arlo J. 120.
Neuer, Werner 295-98, 302, 306, 308, 310.
Noll, Mark 316.
Nguyen, V. Henry T. 198.
Nolland, John 136, 138, 174.
Oakes, Peter 198.
O'Brien, P. T. 21, 26, 182, 186, 246, 250-52, 254, 256, 258-60, 341.
Oberlinner, L. 284.
Økland, Jorunn 199.
Ollrog, W. H. 267.
O' Neill, J. C. 135, 138.
Osborne, Grant 6, 56, 328, 347-50, 352, 356-57, 362, 365, 369-70, 375.
O' Toole, Robert 142.
Paden, William E. 157.
Paige, Terrence 19, 110, 256.
Pannenberg, Wolfhart 340, 345.
Pao, David 143.
Parry, Robin 4, 22.
Parsons, Mikeal 138, 144, 146, 157.
Pattemore, Stephen 362-65.
Paulien, John 347.
Pelikan, Jarolsav 154.

Pervo, Richard 48, 144, 146, 153-54.
Peterson, Eugene 65, 76-77.
Peterson, David 13, 21, 46, 250, 344.
Peters, George W. 253.
Plank, Karl A. 320, 323.
Pogoloff, Stephen M. 268.
Pritz, Ray 116.
Quinn, J. D. 290.
Rackham, Richard B. 137, 152.
Rafael, V. L. 60.
Reeves, Rodney 251.
Reich, R. 124-25, 127, 129-31.
Rengstorf, K. H. 298, 313-14.
Richards, Randolph 251.
Riddle, D. W. 331.
Rieger, Hans-Martin 295.
Riesner, R. 71.
Rigaux, Beda 274.
Rischl, Albrecht 116.
Rissi, Matthias 362.
Robinson, David M. 381.
Robinson, J. A. T. 150.
Roloff, J. 194, 282, 284-85, 299, 310.
Rudolph, David J. 47.
Ruegg, Daniel 295.
Sahlins, Marshall 155.
Salevao, Iustione 327-28, 334.
Sampley, J. Paul 240.
Sanders, E. P. 129.
Saucy, Robert 51.
Scherrer, Peter 375.
Schleiermacher, F. D. E. 296.
Schiffman, Michael 43.
Schlatter, Adolf 295-99, 302, 306-16.
Schlier, Heinrich 206-08.
Schmidt, Daryl 144-45.
Schmidt, Johann 273-74.
Schmidt, K. L. 284, 384.
Schmitz-Berning, Cornelia 307.
Schmitz, O. 69.

Schnabel, Eckhard 182-83, 197, 246-49, 328-29, 360-61, 365, 367, 369.
Schnackenburg, R. 128.
Schnelle, Udo 300, 315.
Schoedel, William R. 117.
Scholer, John M. 342.
Schrage, Wolfgang 319, 322, 325.
Schreiner, Thomas R. 44, 51, 246, 256.
Schweizer, Eduard 165.
Scott, E. F. 282.
Searle, John R. 273.
Seim, Turid Karlsen 158.
Seland, Torrey 198.
Selwyn, E. G. 342.
Senior, Donald P. 246.
Shakespeare, William 83, 321, 326.
Shanks, H. 124.
Short, Ellen L. 201.
Shukron, E. 124-25.
Sim, David 105, 107-08, 111, 113, 116, 119-20.
Skarsaune, Oskar 115.
Slee, Michelle 198.
Smalley, Stephen S. 348, 353-56, 358-60, 363, 365-66.
Smarczyk, B. 371.
Smith, D. 128.
Snodgrass, K. R. 35.
Soards, Marion L. 162-63.
Spek, Robartus J. van der 382.
Spencer, F. Scott 138-39, 156.
Spicq, C. 290-91, 330, 379-81, 383.
Spina, F. A. 203.
Staehlin, G. 69.
Stalker, D. M. G. 340, 345.
Stanton, Graham 23, 116.
Staton, J. E. 53.
Ste Croix, G. E. M. de 381.
Steiner, George 59, 72.
Stern, David H. 43.

Still, John D. 198.
Stowers, S. K. 33.
Strathmann, H. 379.
Strauss, Mark L. 135, 148.
Streeter, B. H. 178.
Strobach, Anika 376.
Stuhlmacher, Peter 17, 141, 328-29.
Stuhlmueller, Carroll 246.
Sweet, J. P. M. 360, 366.
Synge, F. C. 202.
Talbert, C. H. 135-38, 142, 147.
Tasker, R. G. V. 330, 338.
Tellbe, Mikael 199.
Terry, R. B. 193.
Texier, Jean Georges 381.
Theissen, Gerd 197.
Thielman, Frank 232, 234, 278, 288, 290.
Thiselton, Anthony C. 138-39, 204-07, 265, 271, 273, 323.
Thrall, M. 69, 198.
Thur, Hilke 374.
Toney, Carl N. 198.
Tonstad, Sigve K. 363.
Towner, Philip H. 6, 57, 196, 279, 281-83, 288, 290, 292.
Trilling, W. 274.
Trueman, Carl 2-4, 7, 21.
Turner, David L. 106.
Turner, Max 1, 7.
Turner, Paul 117-18.
Tyson, J. B. 138, 150, 156.
van der Louw, Theo A. W. 380, 384.
Van Engen, Charles 230.
Vandersleyen, Claude 383.
Van Neste, Ray 1, 278.
Van Unnik, W. C. 135, 140, 144, 174-75.
Vaux, Roland de 342.
Venuti, L. 71.
Verhof, E. 323.
Vielhauer, P. 147.

Index of Modern Authors

Von Rad, Gerhard 340, 344-45.
Von Wahlde, Urban 123-27, 132.
Vos, Johan S. 266.
Wagner, Ross 222, 327, 338.
Wahlen, Clinton 48.
Walbank, F. W. 170.
Wallace, D. 285.
Walldorf, J. 295.
Walsh, Patrick G. 172.
Walter, N. 384.
Walton, John H. 335, 342.
Ware, James P. 246, 249, 254-55, 258.
Wasserman, Jeffrey 43.
Wedderburn, A J. M. 190.
Weima, Jeffrey 266.
Weiss, J. 297.
Welborn, L. L. 267-68.
Welles, C. Bradford 381.
Wenham, David 138-39, 181.
Wesley, John 8, 14, 272.
Wilckens, Ulrich 298-302, 309, 313.
Wilken, Robert L. 115.
Wilkins, M. J. 19, 110, 256.
Williams, Demetrius K. 198.
Williams, Ritva H. 198.
Wills, Lawrence M. 202.
Wilson, Alistair 245.
Wilson, Stephen G. 17, 204.
Wilson, Todd A. 219.
Wilson, Walter T. 302.
Winter, B. W. 19, 162, 268.
Wire, A. C. 269-70.
Witherington, Ben 24, 166, 266, 360, 370.
Wolfe, P. 284.
Woodman, Simon 356.
Wrede, William 274.
Wright, Christopher J. H. 182, 197, 201, 248.
Wright, D. F. 16, 20.
Wright, J. Stafford 11.
Wright, N. T. 21, 24, 232, 337-38.

Young, F. 292.
Zahn, Theodor 370.
Zetterholm, Magnus 116.
Zimmer, Friedrich 266.

Index of Ancient Sources

1 Apol. (*First Apology*) 206.
Aeneid 145.
Against Heresies 193, 208.
Ambrosiaster 272-73.
Anselm 87.
Ant. (*Jewish Antiquities* [Josephus]) 128, 164, 173-76, 202, 217, 235, 384.
Ant. Rom. (*Antiquitates romanae*) 173-75.
Aquila 85.
Aquinas, Thomas 272-73, 336.
Ascent of James 116.
Augustine 248, 272, 338.
Book of Elchasai 115.
b. Sabb (*Babylonian Talmud Sabbat*) 115.
Chaucer, Geoffrey 83.
Chrysostom 29, 236-37, 270, 272-73, 336.
Circuits of Peter 116.
Clement of Alexandria 267.
Contestation 116.
Decalogue (*On the Decalogue*) 384.
Dialogue with Trypho 115.
Didache 116-17, 120.
Diodorus Siculus 154, 173-74, 235, 384.
Dionysius (of) Halicarnassus 164, 166, 171, 173-75, 371.
Epistle of Barnabas 115.
Epistle of Peter 116.
Geogr. (*Geography*) 159, 371-74, 376-77, 379-80.
Hist. (*Histories*) 162, 166-67, 170, 173, 175, 179-80, 384.
Hist. Eccl. (*Historia Ecclesiastica*) 377.
Homer 145, 159, 167, 371-72, 384.
Homilies 115-16.

Homilies on Thessalonians 270.
Ignatius 29, 115, 117-20.
Iliad 145, 167, 371, 384.
Irenaeus 193, 208-09.
Is. (*De Isaeo*) 154.
Justin Martyr 115.
Josephus 28, 125, 128, 164, 166, 174, 176, 179, 202, 217, 235, 319, 321, 384.
Lucian 167, 169, 172-75, 179.
LXX (Septuagint) 28, 68, 70, 77, 85-92, 112, 186, 194-96, 217, 220, 223, 232-33, 235, 241, 318, 321, 331, 349, 354, 369-71, 379-81, 384.
m. Miqw. (*Mishnah Miqwa'ot*) 125-26, 129.
m. Sabb. (*Mishnah Sabbat*) 112, 128-30, 319.
Odyssey 145.
Origen 29, 267.
Panarion 116.
Pesiq. Rab Kah. (*Pesiqta de Rab Kahana*) 47.
Pol. (*Politics*) 384.
Polybius 145, 162, 166-67, 169-75, 177, 179-80, 384.
Polycarp 153.
Pomp. (*Epistula ad Pompeium Gemimum*) 164, 174.
Recognition 115-16.
Rom. (*Romulus*) 371.
Sib. Or. (*Sibylline Oracles*) 351.
Spec. (*De specialibus legibus*) (Philo) 128.
Strabo 159, 371-74, 376-80.
Stromata 267.
Symmachus 85.
Syriac 85.
Tacitus 164.
Targum 85, 217-19, 221, 224.

Theodotion 85.
Thucydides 163-64, 168-72, 175, 179-80.
Timaeus 162, 166, 170-73, 175-77, 179-80.
t. Sabb (*Tosefta Sabbat*) 128.
Virgil 145.
Vit. Soph. (*Vitae sophistarum*) 377.
Vulgate 85.

www.ingramcontent.com/pod-product-compliance
Lightning Source LLC
Chambersburg PA
CBHW021929290426
44108CB00012B/772